Pathways in theology: Ecumenical, African and Reformed
Beyers Naudé Centre Series on Public Theology

Published by SUN MeDIA Stellenbosch under the SUN PReSS imprint.
www.africansunmedia.co.za
www.sun-e-shop.co.za

All rights reserved.

Copyright © 2015 Stellenbosch University, Beyers Naudé Centre

No part of this book may be reproduced or transmitted in any form or by any electronic, photographic or mechanical means, including photocopying and recording on record, tape or laser disk, on microfilm, via the Internet, by e-mail, or by any other information storage and retrieval system, without prior written permission by the publisher.

First edition 2015

ISBN 978-1-920689-64-3
ISBN 978-1-920689-65-0 (e-book)

Set in 10/12 Palatino Linotype
Cover photograph Horia Varlan [www.flickr.com/photos/horiavarlan], modified and reproduced under the Creative Commons Attribution 2.0 Generic licence (CC BY 2.0)
Typesetting by SUN MeDIA Stellenbosch

SUN PReSS is an imprint of SUN MeDIA Stellenbosch. Academic, professional and reference works are published under this imprint in print and electronic format. This publication may be ordered directly from www.sun-e-shop.co.za

Printed and bound by SUN MeDIA Stellenbosch, Ryneveld Street, Stellenbosch, 7600.

Volume VIII in the Beyers Naudé Centre Series on Public Theology

PATHWAYS IN THEOLOGY:

ECUMENICAL, AFRICAN AND REFORMED

Piet Naudé

Editor
Henco van der Westhuizen

DEDICATION

For Jana, Jacques and Kari.
A small token for your huge sacrifices.
Thank you for your friendship and spiritual inspiration.

ACKNOWLEDGEMENTS

"Reception – ecumenical crisis or opportunity for South African churches? (with DJ Smit)" was first published in *Scriptura* 43 (2000), 175-188.

"Regaining our ritual coherence: The question of textuality and worship in ecumenical reception" was first published in *Journal of Ecumenical Studies* 35/2 (1998), 235-256.

"Doxology and praxis: The ecumenical significance of religious experience in a South Africa of the 1990's" was first published in Mouton J. (ed.): *The relevance of theology in South Africa in the 1990's*, (1994) 421-434. HSRC: Pretoria.

"Confessing Nicea today? Critical questions from a South African perspective" was first published in *Scriptura* 79 (2002), 47-54.

"Identity and Ecumenicity. How do we deal theologically with so-called non-theological factors?" was originally published in Wallace M Alston and Michael Welker (eds.): *Reformed theology. Identity and ecumenicity* (2003), 435-449. Eerdmans: New York.

"The Belhar Struggle in ecumenical perpsective" is an English translation of the article "Die Belharstryd in ekumeniese perspektief" first published in *Ned Geref Teologiese Tydskrif* xxxviii/3 (1997), 226-243.

"Belhar: For South Africa, North America and the Worldwide" was first published in *Perspectives. A Journal of Reformed Thought*. May, (2008), 17-21.

"Edmund Schlink (1903-1984): Telling his story from a South African perspective" was published as "On Edmund Schlink" in *Scriptura*, Volume 97 (2008), 122-136.

"Theology with a new voice? The case for an oral theology in South Africa" was first published in *Journal of Theology for Southern Africa* 94 (1996), 18-31.

"Toward a local Zionist theology? The role of the outsider theologian" was first published in *Scriptura* 45 (1993) 29-46.

"Jesus as *nanga*? Christological enrichment from a Zionist perspective" was first published in *Theologica Viatorum*, September (1992), 127-141.

"The 'pregnant' Christ: A Feminist reinterpretation. The role of the women in the 1990's" was first published in *Institute for Planning Research: University of Port Elizabeth* (1994), 3-14.

"Can our creeds speak a gendered truth? A feminist reading of the Nicene Creed and the Belhar Confession" was first published in *Scriptura* 86 (2004), 201-209.

"Liberation Theology as orthopractical theology: a methodological evaluation" is an English translation of "Bevrydingsteologie as ortopraktiese teologie: 'n Metodologiese evaluering". The essay was first published in *Ned. Geref. Teologiese Tydskrif* 19/2 (1988), 236-245.

"The poor as hermeneutical subjects in Liberation Theology" was first published in *Scriptura* 17 (1986), 15-34.

"Preaching from the Old Testament: A perspective from Liberation Theology" was first published in *Theologica Viatorum* 17 (1989), 63-73.

"Is there a future for scholarship? Reformed theological scholarship in a transforming higher education environment" was first published in *Journal of Theology for Southern Africa* 119 (2004), 32-45.

"The limitations of problem-solving as criterion for paradigms in theology" was first published in J. Mouton (ed.), *Paradigms and progress in theology* (1988), 142-151. HSRC: Pretoria.

"The two faces of Calvin in South Africa: In honour of the 500th commemoration of John Calvin's birth" was originally published in two parts in *Dutch Reformed Theological Journal,* 30 Numbers 3 & 4 (2009), 607-613 and 614-619.

"A letter from John Calvin to South African Christians – 500 years on" is a sermon that has not been published before.

"The reception of Karl Barth in South Africa 1960-1990 – Selected perspectives" was first published in *Reformed Churches in South Africa and the Struggle for Justice* (2013), 186-199. Sun Media: Stellenbosch.

"The marks of the church in South Africa today. In dialogue with Jürgen Moltmann on his 80th birthday" was first published in *Verbum et Ecclesia* 27/3 (2006), 944-963.

"'Public theology' from within the church? A theological portrait of WD Jonker" was first published in *Verbum et Ecclesia* 35(1) (2014), Art. #1136, 8 pages. *http://dx.doi.org/10.4102/ve.v35i1.1136.*

"The Dutch Reformed Church's role in the context of transition in South Africa" was first published in Wolfram Weisse & Carel Anthonissen (eds.) *Maintaining apartheid or promoting change? The role of the DRC in a phase of increasing conflict in South Africa* (2004), 31-52. Berlin: Waxmann.

"Constructing a coherent theological discourse: The main challenge facing the Dutch Reformed Church in South Africa today" was first published in *Scriptura* 83 (2003), 192-211.

"The *Belhar Confession* and *Church and Society*: A comparative reading in five statements" was first published in *Acta Theologica* 32 (2) (2012), 147-161.

CONTENTS

DEDICATION iv
ACKNOWLEDGEMENTS v
FOREWORD ix
INTRODUCTION 1

PART 1 – ESSAYS IN ECUMENICAL THEOLOGY

1.1 Accept one another 7
    An introduction to "reception" as ecumenical concept

1.2 Regaining our ritual coherence 23
    The question of textuality and worship in ecumenical reception

1.3 Doxology and praxis 45
    The ecumenical significance of religious experience in South Africa of the 1990s

1.4 Confessing Nicea today? 57
    Critical questions from a South African perspective

1.5 Identity and ecumenicity 67
    How do we deal theologically with so-called "non-theological" factors?

1.6 The Belhar struggle in ecumenical perspective 81

1.7 Belhar – For South Africa, North America and Worldwide 103

1.8 Edmund Schlink (1903-1984) 109
    Telling his story from a South African perspective

PART 2 – ESSAYS IN AFRICAN, LIBERATION AND FEMINIST THEOLOGIES

2.1 Theology with a new voice? 129
    The case for an Oral Theology in the South African context

2.2 Toward a local Zionist Theology 145
    The role of the outsider theologian

2.3 Jesus as *nanga*? 161
    Christological enrichment from a Zionist perspective

2.4	The 'pregnant' Christ: A feminist reinterpretation	171
	The role of women in the 1990s	
2.5	Can our creeds speak a gendered truth?...........................	177
	A feminist reading of the Nicene Creed and the Belhar Confession	
2.6	Liberation Theology as Orthopractical Theology...................	187
	A methodological evaluation	
2.7	The poor as hermeneutical subjects in Liberation Theology.........	199
2.8	Preaching from the Old Testament	211
	A perspective from Liberation Theology	

PART 3 – ESSAYS IN REFORMED THEOLOGY

3.1	Is there a future for scholarship?................................	223
	Reformed theological scholarship in a transforming higher education environment	
3.2	The limitations of problem solving as a criterion for paradigms in theology	237
	In dialogue with Wentzel van Huyssteen	
3.3	The two faces of Calvin in South Africa	247
	In honour of the 500th commemoration of John Calvin's birth	
3.4	A letter from John Calvin to South African Christians. 500 years on	261
3.5	The reception of Karl Barth in South Africa 1960-1990. Selected perspectives..	267
3.6	The marks of the church in South Africa today	279
	In dialogue with Jürgen Moltmann on his 80th birthday	
3.7	"Public theology" from within the church?........................	295
	A reflection on aspects of the theology of W.D. Jonker (1929-2006)	
3.8	The Belhar Confession (1982/1986) and Church and Society (1986)	311
	A comparative essay in five statements	
3.9	The Dutch Reformed Church's role in the context of transition in South Africa..	323
3.10	Constructing a coherent theological discourse	345
	The main challenge facing the Dutch Reformed Church in SA	

FOREWORD

Piet Naudé's theological work may *inter alia* be characterised as both ecumenical and as public. As theologian he has always been interested in the *diverse* contexts in which the church exists *today*, i.e. in the body of Christ in its *differentiated* configurations.

When writing about how Edmund Schlink's life and work shaped his and others' thinking in South Africa, Naudé makes a striking remark about being an *ecumenical* and also a *public* theologian: "An ecumenical theologian is rooted in a specific tradition, but she is able to relativise, critique and appreciate that tradition from the perspective of Christ, the apostolic faith, and the rich plurality of Christian beliefs and practices in other traditions. An ecumenical theologian actively addresses those theological questions pertaining to the visible unity of Christ's body and practical demands of the gospel in her specific context, but also on a catholic scale. Such a theologian is actively engaged in ecumenical bodies and practices, building networks of trust and love conducive to greater theological consensus" (p. 123).

This is indeed an accurate description of Piet Naudé himself.

As an *ecumenical* theologian he is rooted firmly in the Reformed tradition, often acknowledging his Dutch Reformed Church (DRC) affiliation where he served as an ordained minister.

This rootedness has through the years become evident through his interest in the God revealed in the biblical traditions – a theme he has often written on. For Naudé, the heart of this tradition is the centrality of the Word of God – the biblical traditions being the reference point and criterion against which all (what he likes to call) non-theological factors must be measured. For him this is also the ecumenical contribution of Reformed theology – resisting the temptation to disempower the Word by these differentiated factors. For Naudé, if the biblical traditions were to lose this role, the Reformed and also the Christian identity of the church would be at stake (p. 76).

His appreciation of this particular tradition has therefore persistently been accompanied by his ability to relativise and critique his own convictions from the perspective of the God of the biblical traditions.

For Naudé, writing in the South Africa of the 1980s and 1990s, it has been important to relativise and critique the tradition he is part of from the perspective of the rich plurality of Christian beliefs and practices in other traditions. This is especially clear in his intent listening to and learning from the so-called "illiterate" – for him, those whose oral voices have been marginalised by the power of a dominant, literate theological culture (p. 27, 137).

As ecumenical theologian he has also consistently questioned his own theology from the perspective of what he considers to be "the apostolic faith".

He has therefore been unequivocally interested in the creeds and confessions of the church of all ages, and has written extensively on the value of confession, as part of the heritage of witnesses to the apostolic faith, for theology and church today.

Foreword

He demonstrated a keen interest in what the church in South Africa considered to be a *status confessionis*. And he brings the Belhar confession that emanated from this conviction into the broader picture of the church of all ages, testing it against "the apostolic faith".

For him, however, writing from a South African perspective, the apostolicity of faith needs also to be carried forth by the enactment of confession, which he would most probably like to describe as the enactment of unity, reconciliation and justice (p. 62).

As a *public* theologian – for him, intrinsically part of being Reformed – Naudé has over the years actively addressed theological questions pertaining to the visible unity of Christ's body. This could be seen as one of Naudé's main concerns over the years – actively addressing what he believes to be the practical demands of the gospel in the South African context, especially the contexts of the DRC and the Uniting Reformed Church of Southern Africa (URCSA).

But this has also been his concern on a catholic scale. For Naudé there is absolutely no theological reason why visible church communion amongst the traditional faith communities cannot be realised – among other reasons – because the unity of the church is often being hindered by the non-theological factors mentioned above.

It is therefore apt that the 26 essays selected for this volume are divided into three sections. As already noted by Dirkie Smit in his foreword to the monograph, *Neither Calendar Nor Clock*,[1] Naudé, with his engaging and often challenging, even confrontational rhetoric, is always raising broader questions for theology and the contemporary church.

In the first section on *Ecumenical Theology*, the axle around which Naudé's theological thinking turns – doxology – is explored as constitutive of ecumenical dialogue. Already in these essays the significant value he places on so-called marginalised voices is emphasised.

Naudé asks how the concept of ecumenism might be interpreted today: What constitutes ecumenical theology? How could theology be done in ways constitutive of the body of Christ? What factors might be contributing to the schisms of the church?

The difficult question of identity and ecumenicity is raised, showing how the peculiarity of a specific tradition can enrich a movement towards the unity of the church, and how a disengagement and estrangement from an ecumenical way of thinking can lead to the proliferation of ideologies.

In the second section Naudé engages self-critically with *African, Feminist* and *Liberation Theology*.

Naudé here tries to make sense of the way in which doing theology in Africa, or rather by African theologians, might be conceived. He asks how the tradition he is part of can indeed learn to listen to these particular theological voices, clearly acknowledging the challenges posed by theologies that are not particularly interested in writing down their ways of thinking and doing. Here he often endeavours to create the necessary language for these theologies – in an attempt to help make these often neglected voices heard.

---

1   Smit, D.J. 2010. 'Foreword'. In Piet J. Naudé *Neither Calendar Nor Clock*. Grand Rapids: Eerdmans.

In this section Naudé's appreciation of feminist theology, and its remarkable sensitivity with regard to the reality-forming language employed to speak about God, becomes particularly clear. Here, again, he self-critically asks how his own tradition needs to be informed by these marginalised voices. Interested in their theological hermeneutic – in terms of methodology even calling himself a feminist theologian – he follows the road of what is known as reformist feminist theology. These theologians seek to critically, creatively and liberatively reinterpret the biblical traditions in order to include the womanist experience of reality (p. 172).

In conversation with Liberation Theology – an interest he has had since his early theological efforts – Naudé's appreciation of the public way in which theology is done, the *doing* of theology, is aptly underlined. Although the reasons for his particular appraisal of this theology's emphasis on liberation are outlined, it becomes comprehensible why he is critical of the methodological endeavour. Here the weight Naudé gives to the primacy of the Word of God is especially clear.

In the contributions selected for the final section on *Reformed Theology*, Naudé critically asks about the future of Reformed theology in South Africa.

Listening to a variety of different Reformed voices – those of Calvin, Barth, Moltmann and, closer to home, Jonker – he responds to the question that runs like a golden thread through this collection of essays: the visible unity of the church.

He does, however, help us think about much more.

Interested in methodology and hermeneutics he asks how a critical, interdisciplinary and creative Reformed theology could be ensured; how the public role of theology can be re-established in South Africa; and interestingly, what role the church might have in South African public theologies after the establishment of a modern constitutional state.

With the complex history and context of the DRC in mind, he also asks how his own tradition can remain Reformed, but in a non-authoritarian, pluralistic sense; how this tradition can re-join the ecumenical church and take its cue for a theological agenda from others, whilst making an own creative contribution.

He daringly asks the very important question: How can the tradition he is part of become a distinctly *African* Reformed church?

It is my hope that the important role Piet Naudé has played, and continues to play as ecumenical and as public theologian – as theologian interested in different *pathways in theology* – will inspire readers to actively engage in ecumenical bodies and practices, building networks of trust and love conducive to greater theological consensus – working towards the visible unity of the church.

Henco van der Westhuizen
Stellenbosch
January 2015

INTRODUCTION

The essays collected in this monograph represent an important part of my theological journey since the late 1980s. They hopefully serve as an example of reflections on the ground-breaking events in South Africa leading up to 1994 and beyond, including a theological understanding of our current situation in a constitutional democracy.

The essays were selected by the editor around three "pathways" in theology as expressed in the title: ecumenical, African/liberation, and Reformed.

My own spiritual roots lie in Pietism. For this I remain thankful to God. This childhood orientation was transformed via studies in philosophy and theology toward perspectives that one would find in the "Reformed" part of the Christian tradition.

The ecumenical orientation of this Reformed theology was in my case shaped by at least three sources: The critical and open approach to biblical sciences at the Stellenbosch theological faculty; the ecumenical spirit in which dogmatics was taught; and – for technical content – my sabbatical periods at Heidelberg University in Germany, where I encountered the work of Edmund Schlink and Dietrich Ritschl. Whilst there, I could read the vast collection of World Council of Churches documents in the library of the Ecumenical Institute (and had many enlightening coffee-break discussions with Dirk Smit in a café across the square).

Because ecumenical theology provides the wider framework in which other work finds its place, the first part of this volume contains a few essays on topics such as reception; the link between doxology, liturgy and dogmatics; the potential role of religious experience to bridge divides among people; how non-theological factors often dominate relations amongst Christian churches; and a short exposition of core ideas from Schlink's oeuvre interpreted for the South African situation.

Throughout these essays there is an attempt to apply the global insights regarding greater ecclesial unity to South Africa – in particular to the family of (Dutch) Reformed churches. In the last years of apartheid, and beyond, our context required us to serve societal cohesion via the way we reflect theologically.

It was my living and teaching for five years in the traditional rural Venda area (today part of the Northern Province) that radically challenged my education in Western, rationalist thinking, based on an assumed reading and writing culture. In Venda I found church communities functioning quite well without anyone being able to read. Here I encountered living theologies based on oral transmission akin to the early Jewish and Christian faith communities.

The first three essays of Part Two reflect some of my arguments for an "oral theology" in South Africa based on insights gained from actual field work in a Zion Christian Church congregation framed by a sizeable body of work in oral history, poetry and culture. The idea of "local theologies", especially influenced by Robert Schreiter, assisted me to see all theologies – even the assumed "universal" ones I was taught – as reflecting on faith in a specific context.

Introduction

The first cluster of "liberation" theologies derives from reading feminist writers both from a biblical exegesis and a systematic theological perspective. I found myself steeped in a patriarchal tradition where the very language in many cases oppressed and failed to express feminist or womanist experiences of God and our Christian tradition. The two middle essays in Part Two deal with the re-reading of biblical metaphors ("pregnancy" and "birth") and creeds (Nicea and Belhar) from a reformist-feminist viewpoint.

It was an interest in the relation between (theological) theory and (ethical) praxis that led me to read the works of Latin American liberation theologians in tandem with the political theologies of Johann Metz and Jürgen Moltmann. The last three essays in the second part of the volume are devoted to insights gained from a link between liberation theologies and biblical sciences. For a great part these insights were drawn from my doctoral thesis completed at the Stellenbosch Theological Faculty under Professor Willie Jonker.

African type "oral theologies" challenged my very understanding of theology and transmission of the gospel itself. And liberation theologies – in various forms – assisted me to develop a mind-set that was critical of ideologies that are so easily accepted as "normal".

The volume is concluded in Part Three with a number of essays in Reformed theology.

My role in university leadership since my early career is reflected in the first essay on scholarship in a challenging higher education context. It is furthermore no surprise to find two reflections on confessions – typical of the Reformed tradition – and the names of Calvin, Barth and Moltmann, who fundamentally shaped this tradition. The "letter from Calvin" is the (hitherto unpublished) text of a sermon held at Stellenbosch during the 500th anniversary celebrations of Calvin's birth and it therefore differs in genre from the more academically oriented essays in the rest of the volume.

Closer to home, there is one essay in philosophical theology (on problem solving) inspired by the work of Wentzel van Huyssteen, in whose chair I was appointed at the former University of Port Elizabeth. There is one essay attempting to take forward core ideas presented by my dogmatics teacher, Willie Jonker, supplementing my earlier work in Afrikaans on his relationship with Calvin and his pastoral approach to systematic theology. And there is a critical reflection on the role of my denomination, the Dutch Reformed Church, in the transition period after 1994, as well as a constructive essay on a theological framework required for the DRC's future.

The editor has excluded essays with a distinctly ethical orientation as there is the possibility of a second volume in which some of these could be collected. The essays in this volume were – except for translations from Afrikaans to English and minor editorial improvements – for the most part left unchanged. It is therefore left to today's readers to interpret and re-assess these dated essay in the context in which they were originally written – perhaps seeking better pathways for theology in the future?

I thank the former University of Port Elizabeth and the current Nelson Mandela Metropolitan University where I received good financial and sabbatical support.

The Alexander von Humboldt Foundation made several study visits to Germany possible where Michael Welker and Heinrich Bedford-Strohm acted as my hosts at different occasions.

I sincerely thank Dr Henco van der Westhuizen for his hard work in collecting and editing this volume, and writing a foreword for it. SUN Press was willing to take on this project and provided key guidance and support along the way.

I also thank the colleagues at the Stellenbosch University Faculty of Theology: Len Hansen, Mary-Anne Plaatjies-Van Huffel, Dirk Smit and Robert Vosloo, as well as the Dean, Nico Koopman, who provided kind support and encouragement over many years of cooperation. You provided me with an academic home for my theological work, honouring me with an extra-ordinary appointment from 2011 until my acceptance of a position as Director of the University of Stellenbosch Business School (USB) in 2014.

On a personal note, I honour my wife, Elize, for her years of support and taking on additional parental responsibilities. She, more than anyone else, always encourages me to test social, ecclesial, and intellectual boundaries. Anyone who is active in both research and in tough university leadership roles during transformation times will understand what it takes to continue reading, thinking and writing. Our three children are adults now. I also thank them for the joy and encouragement and for having to deal with a late-night father over many years.

I am humbled by the opportunity to publish this volume in the Beyers Naudé Centre Series on Public Theology.

Piet Naudé
Cape Town
January 2015

PART 1 –
ESSAYS IN
ECUMENICAL THEOLOGY

1.1 ACCEPT ONE ANOTHER ...

An introduction to "reception" as ecumenical concept[1]

"Reception" may be considered one of the most important challenges for the ecumenical process today. It may be especially urgent in South Africa as we – a divided nation, including ecclesial dis-unities – strive toward understanding and "receiving" one another in the post-apartheid era.

The aim of this essay is to provide a conceptual clarification of the ecumenical term "reception". This will be attempted by briefly discussing three related question: 1. What is the historical background of the notion? 2. How is the process of reception normally described? and 3. What complicating factors are involved in reception processes? This will hopefully provide a framework within which various forms and stages of "reception" amongst Christian churches may be interpreted.

1. THE HISTORICAL BACKGROUND OF THE NOTION: CANON, COUNCIL, ECUMENISM

Reception as theological term[2] within the Christian tradition stems from the recent history of ecumenical reflection. The first articles on this theme stem from about the 1970s with the appearance of studies by Alois Grillmeier (1970), Heinrich Bacht (1971) and Yves Congar (1972), with an official reference in the report of the German Bishop's Conference in its reply to Hans Küng's book *Unfehlbar?* (1971, see Bacht 1971:157 note 48). As a technical term, it did not appear in the *Lexikon für Theologie und Kirche*[3] (1962) and was still absent from the *Evangelisches Soziallexikon* (7th edition, 1980) and the *Evangelisches Staatslexikon* (3rd edition, 1983). It found its first official entry into the *Dictionary of the Ecumenical Movement* (edited by Lossky 1991) with an article on reception by Anton Houtepen.

This does not, however, mean that the matter to which reception refers is of recent origin. For the sake of clarification one could discern at least three distinctive stages in

---

1   This paper is an adapted version of a lecture delivered at the *Societät für Systematische Theologie* at the Ruprecht-Karl Universität, Heidelberg in Germany (12 February 1997). This essay, written in cooperation with DJ Smit, was later published in *Scriptura* 43 (2000), 175-188 with the title "'Reception' – ecumenical crisis or opportunity for South African churches?"
2   The concept found applications in other disciplines too. The most influential of these are from studies in legal history, specifically the reception of Roman law in the German legal system (see Wieacker 1967). It also found wide support in literary studies, primarily referring to a study of the "reception" of a literary work in specific communities (see Beinart 1991b:16; Loewe 1988:637-638). It is theologically noteworthy that especially New Testament hermeneutics developed reception as interpretative strategy by moving beyond historical and structuralist approaches to reader reception in describing the relation between text and reality. See e.g. Lategan and Vorster (1985) and the interpretation thereof in Naudé (1997b).
3   The revised edition of *LThK* is presently being published. The latest volume (Number 5), published in 1996, reaches the word "Kirchengemeinschaft" under the letter K. It is to be expected that reception will receive its due attention in the appropriate later volume.

the development of "reception" in the history of the church. These three stages may be described as canon, council, ecumenics. The purpose is not to give an exhaustive historical overview, but merely to orient us to our later discussion. The literature cited may be followed for detailed information on any given period.

The first is the *canonical* phase. In the New Testament itself words such as *lambanein/ apolambanein* (receive) and *dechestai/apodechestai* (accept) refer to the act of faith through which the word/Christian message (Mark 4:20, Acts 2:41) or Christ Himself (John 1:11-12) is accepted and the gospel (1 Corinthians 15:1) or Spirit (1 Corinthians 2:12) is received. Paul utilises technical rabbinical terms in 1 Corinthians 11:23 to describe the process of traditio/receptio (*paradidonai/ paralambanein*) whereby the institution of the Lord's Supper is recalled and carried forth.

This constitutes the church as fundamentally a "Rezeptionsgemeinschaft" (Beinart 1991c:36). The process through which she interpretatively serves as transmitter of tradition (*paradosis*, see Tillard 1986:414), is seen as profoundly pneumatological. The Spirit (according to the gospel of John) will teach the disciples and keep Christ's remembrance as guarantee of the truth (see Loewe 1988:639 and Vischer 1984:223). Whether the first reported "convention" of the apostles in Acts 15 may be seen as a form of "ecumenical" dialogue is as yet unexplored in the literature.

On the level of canon history one could designate the formation of both the Old and New Testaments as reception processes. Concerning the latter, the early Christian communities "received" the Scriptures, accepted their content as apostolic, and particular books "came to be confirmed and adopted as authoritative for the Church" (Kuhn 1983:166). This process of reception continued for more than three centuries until the first formal reception with the publication of Athanasius' canon in 367.

The second phase relates specifically to the *conciliar process* in the pre- and post-Constantinian periods. In the first three ages after Christ reception refers to the process whereby local or regional churches met under the leadership of the bishop to take decisions on matters of faith. They made their decisions known to other churches by means of synodal letters. The acceptance of these decisions confirmed the authenticity of the decision-making church and the retention of the community of believers. The basic assumption was that each local/regional church is the true church that can speak to and on behalf of other churches.[4]

In the post-Constantinian phase, reception is, apart from an ecclesial, also a political process.[5] In his excellent *Die Konzilidee der alte Kirche* (1979) HJ Sieben[6] shows that the concept of a universal, ecumenical council developed slowly via a long and varied historical-theological process. The shared conviction grew that "dass Konzilien

---

4   There are many examples of local synods held during this period. Two of these that assumed special position because of their wide influence and acceptance are the Synods of Athioch in 268 and Arles in 314. See Rusch (1988:29-31)

5   "Konzilentscheidungen wurden von jetzt an nicht mehr nur durch Synodalbriefe zur Anerkennung durch die Kirchen verbreitet, sondern durch den Kaiser direkt akzeptiert und zu einem Teil des Reichsrechts gemacht" (Rusch 1988:32).

6   Sieben wrote several authoritative volumes on the development of the council idea. See his *Die Konzilsidee des lateinsichen Mittelalters (847-1378)* (1984); *Die katholische Konzilsidee von der Reformation bis zur Aufklärung,* (1988); *Die katholische Konzilsidee im 19. und 20. Jahrhundert,* (1993) (all published by Ferdinand Schoening in Paderborn).

das Geheimnis der Christusglauben unverkürzt und unverfälscht *überliefert haben*" (Sieben 1979:512, his emphasis; see also Schatz 1991:96-107). A short-hand explanation of the councils is provided by the double consensus expressed (originally by Vincence of Lerin) as *consensio antiquitatis et universitatis*.

Vertical consensus refers to the traditionary process of being in congruence with the apostolic faith (*antiquitatis*), whereas horizontal consensus refers to the reception of a council by the universal church (*universitatis*). Sieben notes the "Wagnischarakter" of the councils, as there was no a priori guarantee that a council would be accepted as legitimate expression of tradition or received by all the churches[7] (1979:516; see Houtepen 1983:145). Seven of these Councils eventually emerged as truly ecumenical, i.e. as received in both the East and West. During the Middle Ages the church in the West grew more and more hierarchical, with reception being diminished to a juridical-institutional act, at a later stage reaching the declaration of the infallibility of the bishop of Rome (*pastor aeternus*) at Vaticanum I (1869-1870).

The position of the *Eastern Church* should be seen from its perspective of a more inclusive ecclesiology, where reception is primarily a dialectic process between laity and clerics and not so much a juridical and formal act as in the West.

The *Reformation* stood in continuity with the Ancient Church, accepting the creeds (such as Nicea) and the decisions of Councils (see e.g. articles 1 and 3 of the Confession of Augsburg and the acceptance of the Apostles' Creed by the Heidelberg Catechism), but radically reoriented the criterion for acceptance to the Scriptures alone. The authorisation process itself altered significantly as a result of a radically different conception of ministerial authority (see Fischer 1989:41; Beinart 1991c:44).

The third, and for our purposes the most significant phase,[8] was heralded by the modern *ecumenical movement* as represented specifically by the work of Faith and Order in the context of the World Council of Churches.[9] The very aim of the ecumenical movement attests to the reciprocal reception by churches of one another. Already at the First World Conference on Faith and Order[10] it was expressed as a

---

7   See his discussion of the decisions taken at the Nicene Council (325), which were only gradually accepted and formally ratified 56 years later at Constantinople (381)! See also Rusch (1988:32-33).

8   There are obviously links and differences between the "conciliar stage" and the modern ecumenical movement. Faith and Order, in its study on "The Importance of the Conciliar Process in the Ancient Church for the Ecumenical Movement" (requested by the WCC in New Delhi in 1961), makes the continuity explicit by stating that "in the ecumenical movement the churches find themselves in a process of continuing reception or re-reception of the councils" (Louvain 1971:29). It is clear from repeated references in ecumenical documents that only a truly Ecumenical Council (again requested at the recent Santiago meeting) or a kind of pan-Orthodox Synod will suffice to formalise church unity by serving as authoritative *determinatio fidei*. Contrasting notions of authority and ministries, however, make this more problematic than meets the eye.

9   Since its inception in 1948, the WCC grew from 147 to 320 member churches by 1991. The active participation of the Roman Catholic (no official member yet) and Orthodox Churches makes this the most significant form of inter-church dialogue in the history of the church since the split between East and West (1034) and between Rome and the Reformation (1521).

10 This original aim is retained in the present formulation of the aim of Faith and Order (Unit I), which follows the almost exact wording of the first purpose of the WCC referred

conviction "that it is the will of Christ that the one life of the one body should be manifest to the world" (quoted in Kelly 1996:226). The first purpose of the WCC expressed in its constitution is "to call the churches to the goal of visible unity in the one faith and in one eucharistic fellowship expressed in worship and in common life in Christ, and to advance towards that unity in order that the world may believe" (WCC:1996).

The effort to unite the churches is highlighted when reception is viewed in relation to two other important ecumenical terms which have acquired the status of technical terms. These are "consensus" and "recognition", and seen together these three terms describe the whole process of inter-church relations as consensus, recognition, reception.

2. THE PROCESS OF RECEPTION: CONSENSUS, RECOGNITION, RECEPTION

Without pursuing the many finer distinctions (see Burgess 1991; Meyer 1986), one may define *consensus* as the aim and desired result of inter-confessional doctrinal conversations. In ecumenical language the term "fundamental consensus" and "fundamental difference" are normally used as referring to church uniting or church dividing factors respectively. Following the essays edited by Burgess, one may distinguish between a hermeneutical and ecumenical definition of these terms.

The hermeneutical definition would emphasise that a specific fundamental consensus/difference serves as interpretative explanation for the nature of a comprehensive and systematic convergence/divergence between two traditions. As heuristic notion this type of consensus/difference does not necessarily influence the state of communion between two traditions. In other words, it is possible for churches to maintain a hermeneutical difference without necessarily affecting fellowship.

In the case of ecumenically defined fundamental consensus/difference, the opposite is true. The reference is to consensus or difference which has a direct, incompatible relation to church communion. In summary: "The differing senses of fundamental difference and fundamental consensus thus form two matched pairs: a hermeneutical pair defined by the presence or absence of a single difference that interprets and explains other differences and an ecumenical pair defined by the presence or absence of a difference incompatible with the full visible unity of the church" (Burgess 1991:14).

In terms of our discussion, it is important to note that fundamental consensus normally refers to the texts which are the outcome of inter-confessional doctrinal conversation. In some way this consensus (or for that matter, difference) must (officially) be accepted by the churches involved. And this is where a lot of frustration is created by the "widespread official inaction of proposals that have emerged from the dialogues" (Burgess 1991:11). This leads us directly to the next phase of inter-church relations, namely that of recognition.

That *recognition* is also a complex term emerges clearly from the careful analysis undertaken by Gerard Kelly in his doctoral thesis (1992) published as *Recognition:*

---

to above (WCC 1996:35). It should be noted that FO preceded the establishment of the WCC in 1948 and sees itself as continuing to call the churches to the goal of visible unity.

Advancing ecumenical thinking (1996). Apart from the historical complexities relating inter alia to the conciliar period, he argues for a distinct Catholic-Protestant difference on this issue.[11] Despite these complexities,[12] one may distinguish at least two contexts in which recognition functions.

It may, firstly, be understood in the context of the dialectic between consensus texts and an individual church. In this case a church would study such a text (such as *Baptism, Eucharist, Ministry* or *Confessing the one faith*, for example) and recognise the text as being in continuity with this church's understanding of Scripture and tradition, i.e. the apostolic faith as professed through the ages. Non-recognition may imply (partial) rejection of the consensus, or, where a church discovers neglected parts of the faith in her own tradition, a renewal of the church tradition.

Recognition may, secondly, be understood in the context of the mutual recognition of churches. In this case churches do not necessarily agree on all aspects of doctrinal formulation or church order, but recognise in each other a sufficient degree of communion in the faith to establish a relation of sister churches. Recognition normally occurs via the official decisions of churches[13] and – depending on the history of relations between the churches in question – develops in stages which (hopefully) act as a prelude to full intercommunion or reception.[14]

For the sake of some clarity, it seems therefore helpful to describe the relation among churches in terms of the process of fundamental consensus leading to official recognition and ultimately to full *reception*. It is clear that reception is at the same time the motivating force and ultimate goal of any ecumenical endeavour. It is only via reception that visible church unity will be reached. Let us look at this more closely.

Highly simplified, *reception refers to the process whereby churches accept one another in full communion as a result of ecumenical encounters.*[15] Rusch (1980:31) attempts a more elaborate definition that is worth quoting in full:

> Ecumenical reception includes all phases and aspects of an ongoing process by which a church under the guidance of God's Spirit makes the results of a bilateral or multilateral conversation a part of its faith and life, because the results are seen to be in conformity with the

---

11   See his comparison of Congar and Tillard (Catholic) with Harding Meyer (Lutheran) and the tension in the Roman Catholic-Lutheran Joint Commission's publication, *Facing unity* in 1985 (Kelly 1996:7-34).
12   See Meyer's illuminating analysis, which highlights seven dimensions of recognition (1980:34-38).
13   Meyer insists that the work of theologians alone is not sufficient. Genuine recognition ultimately requires an official act of the whole church in question (1980:36).
14   All the dialogues between the historical traditions are examples of this process. Perhaps the best example of a very advanced process is the relationship between the Orthodox and Roman Catholic Churches. They fully "recognise" one another, but have not yet crossed the threshold to "canonical reception" (Kelly 1996:218) which, in this discussion, would equal "reception" and full intercommunion.
15   Edward Kilmartin emphasises the reception as ecclesial reality. "It (reception) can be described as a process by which one ecclesiastical body adopts as its own a spiritual good which originates in another and acknowledges and appropriates it as applicable to its own life of faith" (Kilmartin 1984:36).

teachings of Christ and of the apostolic community, that is, the gospel as witnessed to in Scripture.

This definition correctly highlights the processual[16] character of reception in referring to the "fundamental consensus" aspect in the results of bilateral and multilateral encounters, as well as the "recognition" aspect (*"because the results are seen to be ..."*) on the basis of the apostolic faith. It perhaps overemphasises the results[17] of ecumenical encounters ("the results of a bilateral or multilateral conversation") as the object of reception instead of the reception by churches *of one another* as sister churches. Kilmartin correctly depicts "the number-one problem of the ecumenical movement" as "the reception of churches of one another" (1984:35). This is the real object of reception!

These definitions, and descriptions of specific reception processes,[18] give some hint of the complexity of the reception concept which may be highlighted by the following considerations.

3. COMPLICATING FACTORS: HISTORY, CONTEXT, THEOLOGY

Reception is *historically* complex, not merely because of its long prehistory and development as hinted at above, but also due to its employment in processual,[19] terms which leads to a certain diffusion of precision to include a wide range of derivatives. These vary from the processes of bi- and multilateral conversations themselves ("die Einsichten und Auswirkungen eines Dialogprozeses", Gassmann 1984:361), to re-reception in the life of the churches, which is an historically open-ended process (Gassmann 1974:322). Analyses of reception also include non-reception ("Ablehnung") as a form of "reception"! (See Evans 1996:212; Rusch 1980:59; Gassmann 1984:366; Kilmartin 1984:39-40.[20])

---

16   Gassmann, very early in the debate (1974:319-320), had already argued for an "erweiterte Rezeptionsverständnisse", which transcends the idea of reception as a single closed event of an official church decision. It includes a juridical dimension, but is fundamentally a spiritual (Spiritual!) *process*.

17   We are not underestimating these results in the process of consensus and recognition, but the results themselves (liturgy, canon law, doctrine, credal formulation, etc.) are serving the greater goal of visible church unity, i.e. where churches accept *one another*. See examples of instances of reception in Kilmartin (1984:40-51).

18   There are too many examples to list here. We refer to specific dialogues (e.g. the Anglican-Roman Catholic or Roman-Lutheran dialogues); how a specific consensus document was received in the churches (see volumes on Baptism, Eucharist, Ministry responses or case studies on BEM in Ford and Swan 1993); how a confession found its way into the church (see Mehlhausen 1985 for an excellent discussion of Barmen's reception in the Evangelical Landeskirchen since 1945); or how an inter-church agreement was received in specific congregations (see Brandt 1986:19ff on the "Leuenberger Konkordie"). All examples underline the complex processual character of reception.

19   The process character of ecumenical conversation is one of its most salient features. In the case of the project on Confessing the One Faith, it is structurally built into the method of the study project itself through recognition-explication-common confession, with the middle term as starting point (*Confessing the One Faith* 1991:3-7).

20   Kilmartin, on the basis of careful historical analysis of the conciliar period, states that "non-reception of spiritual goods is not a marginal aspect in the history of the church". He shows (1984:39-40) that not all instances of reception are beneficial (e.g. the

Reception is *contextually* complex – obviously on the level of inter-church relations, which took a dramatic turn when the Orthodox and Catholic Churches formally joined the ecumenical movement (in 1961 and 1968 respectively) and with the growing number of churches from the South enjoying full participation. To operate in the ecumenical field is to enter "in einer Konstellation von kirchlichen Beziehungen, der äussert komplex ist" (Gassmann 1974:315). The manifold bi- and multilateral conversations are evidence of this complexity, which in sheer scope and volume surpass all previous situations in the church's history and may justifiably be seen as a kairos moment for the ecumenical movement towards church unity.

But the contextual complexity also refers to the "Zeitgeist", where the church (at least in the West) is struggling between modernity's "flight from authority" (Stout 1981) and the Enlightenment prejudice against tradition (McGrath 1990:132-145 and 179-185), on the one hand, and strands in post-modernity, on the other hand, which opt for the rejection of metanarratives (Lyotard 1984) and for radical pluralism to the point of relativism.[21] In a time that the church is aiming for greater unity on the basis of a shared faith and Tradition, it has, in the words of Mark-Kline Taylor (1990:40), to struggle with the trilemma of acknowledging her tradition, but at the same time celebrating plurality whilst resisting domination.

The churches from the so-called Third World further increase the complexity of reception, because many of them operate in conditions of pre- or sub-modernity without the context of the Enlightenment tradition or supposition of secularism (see Naudé 1996:19). Nor do they share the cultural thought forms in which many of the Ancient Church's traditions are couched,[22] but which they are requested to accept.

Reception is also *theologically* complex. It calls into question, on a meta-theological level, the very presuppositions from which conversation partners operate. What will count as criterion for truth, and what relative weight is assigned to Scripture, the Tradition and variety of traditions?[23] It focuses on material doctrinal matters ranging from issues such as *Baptism, Eucharist and Ministry* (WCC:1982) to the specific creedal

---

Romanisation of the Eastern and German liturgies) and that non-reception "does not necessarily signal the end of the reception process. It may only indicate that the decision is not opportune, that it does not really touch the life of the church". Both Nicea and Chalcedon are examples of gradual reception processes which may take decades to run their course! For an analysis of the "non-reception" of the Belhar Confession in the DRC, see Naudé (1997a).

21 See the South African philosopher Van Niekerk (1992) for an extensive analysis and critique of, inter alia, the post-analytical pragmatism of Richard Rorty. See Michael Welker's incisive theological discussion (1994:21ff; 1995:1-57) in which he, drawing on insights from Luhmann, develops a coherent view on the structural dimension of pluralism whilst arguing for a "Ja zu einem konstruktiven, schöpferischen Pluralismus" (1995:117) in the church.

22 See Hood (1990:247-248) and the subsequent reaction by Stanley Harakas in Harakas (1991).

23 In 1963 (Montreal) the study on "Scripture, Tradition and traditions" clarified the concepts as follows in par 39: "We speak of *Tradition* (with a capital T), *tradition* (with a small t) and *traditions*. By the term *Tradition* is meant the Gospel itself, transmitted from generation to generation in and by the Church ... By *tradition* is meant the traditionary process. The term *traditions* is used in two senses, to indicate both the diversity of forms of expression and also what we call confessional traditions ... In the later part of our report the word appears in the further sense, when we speak of cultural traditions".

expression of the apostolic faith in *Confessing the One Faith* (WCC:1991). It forces into the open the question of theological authority in addressing the issues of conciliarity and how the church can teach with authority today, as well as what it means to be in a pre-conciliar stage of the ecumenical process.[24]

The most profound theological loci presupposed in the ecumenical movement are without doubt ecclesiology and pneumatology. Most questions arising from the struggle for church unity can in some way or another be linked to notions about the nature of the church and the work of the Spirit.

In the light of the discussion above, one may suggest that reception is the umbrella under which it is possible to house the whole ecumenical movement with its deepest intention of church unity as full reciprocal reception amidst the complexities of history, context and theology.

4. CONCLUSION

These complexities have led some to question the validity of the term "reception." Fischer (1989), for example, argues that the concept is too vague and wide-ranging to serve a useful purpose. Kelly, in discussing the responses to BEM, indicates that a precise definition of terms is crucial to make ecumenical progress (1996:226). Our suggestion of a three-phased description of ecumenical dialogue hopefully provides some clear direction which has to be clarified by dialogue partners in each specific case.

Although precision is sometimes lost, a wider connotation is simply truer to the real complexities of the ecumenical situation. This, and the fact that the term itself has found considerable reception(!) in ecumenical theology, are adequate grounds for its continued employment as heuristic framework in the ongoing search for (greater) Christian unity.

In particular we believe that, if we understand the term in a general sense, pointing to the diverse ways in which Christians, congregations and churches are called, and challenged, *to accept one another*, to learn to live with one another, then the ecumenical discussions concerning "reception" serve as a very useful reminder to South African churches of a serious challenge we face today. We have differed from one another for too long already, even about major moral and ethical issues, albeit for many reasons (see De Villiers and Smit 1994; 1995; 1996).

In a democratic, pluralistic, secular and multicultural society, we can no longer afford to ignore this challenge, and in the process ignore one another. We must learn to receive one another and to co-operate, for the sake of the gospel and for the sake of our public responsibilities (see Smit 1994, 1995a, 1995b, 1995c, 1996a, 1996b).

---

24 See extracts from Faith and Order papers on all these issues cited in Gassmann's useful guide, 1993, part IV.

BIBLIOGRAPHY

Altmann, W. 1978. "Theologischer Konsens und gelebte Gemeinschaft". In Hojen (Hg.) *Ökumenische Methodologie. Dokumentation und Bericht*. Genf: Lutherischer Weltbund, pp. 63-79.

Bacht, H. 1971. "Vom Lehramt der Kirche und in der Kirche". *Catholica* 25, pp. 144-167.

Beinert, W. 1984. "Die Rezeption der Dialoge". *ÖR* Vol. 33, pp. 357-368.

Beinert, W. 1987. "Konsens als Ziel des ökumenischen Dialoges". In H.J. Urban & H. Wagner (Hg.) *Handbuch der Ökumenik* III/1. Paderborn: Bonifatius, pp. 108-127.

Beinert, W. & Fischer, H. (Hrsg.) 1989. *Verständigung auf dem Prüfstand. Zum Problem von Rezeption und Verbindlichkeit ökumenischer Texte*. Berlin: Wichern Verlag.

Beinert, W. 1991a. "Zur mangelnden Effizienz ökumenischer Theologie. Soziologische Faktoren im Gesamtprozeß". *US* Vol. 46, pp. 279-291.

Beinart, W. 1991b. "Die Rezeption und ihre Bedeutung für Leben und Lehre der Kirche". In W. Beinart (Hrsg.) *Glaube als Zustimmung. Zur Interpretation kirchlicher Rezeptionsvorgänge*. Freiburg: Herder, pp. 7-34.

Best, T. & Gassmann, G. (eds). 1994. *On the way to fuller koinonia*. Geneva: WCC.

Birmelé, A. (Hg.). 1983. *Ökumene am Ort. Einheitsbemühungen in der Gemeinde*. Göttingen: Vandenhoeck & Ruprecht.

Bliss, F.M. 1991. *Understanding reception: A background to its ecumenical use*. Roma: Tipografia poliglotta delle Pontificia Universita Gregoriana.

Brandt, H. (Hg.) 1986. *Kirchliches Lehren in ökumenischer Verpflichtung. Eine Studie zur Rezeption ökumenischer Dokumente*. Stuttgart: Calwer Verlag.

Brinkman, M. 1996. *Progress in unity*. Grand Rapids: William B. Eerdmans.

Burgess, J.A. (ed.). 1991. *In search of Christian unity: Basic consensus/Basic difference*. Augsburg: Fortress Press.

Chandran, J.R. 1984. "Baptism, Eucharist, and Ministry: The Reception of the Text and Third World Concerns". In J. Gros (ed.), pp. 107-124.

Chandran, V. 1984. "BEM Reception and the Concerns of Women in the Third World". In J. Gros (ed.), pp. 125-128.

Coenen, L. (Hg.) 1990. *Unterwegs in Sachen Zukunft. Das Taschenbuch zum konziliaren Prozeß*. Stuttgart-München: Calwer.

Congar, Y.M. 1972. "La Reception comme realite ecclesiologique". *Rev. Sc. Phil. Theol.* Vol. 56, pp. 369-403. (Shorter German version: *Concilium* 8, 500-514).

Dahm, K.W. & De Bruin, H. 1971. *Ökumene in der Gemeinde. Eine Untersuchung zur evangelisch-katolischen Zusammenarbeit*. München: Claudius Verlag.

Dantine, J. 1990. "Hoffnung in Stagnation. Zur gegenwärtigen Situation der Ökumene". *ÖR* Vol. 39, pp. 46-57.

De Villiers, D.E. & Smit, D.J. 1994. "Hoe Christene in Suid-Afrika by mekaar verby praat ... Oor vier morele spreekwyses in die Suid-Afrikaanse kerklike konteks". *Skrif en Kerk* Vol. 15, No. 2, pp. 228-247.

De Villiers, D.E. & Smit, D.J. 1995. "'Met watter gesag sê u hierdie dinge?' Opmerkings oor kerklike dokumente oor die openbare lewe". *Skrif en Kerk* Vol. 16, No. 1, pp. 39-56.

De Villiers, D.E. & Smit, D.J. 1996. "'Waarom verskil ons so oor wat die wil van God is?' Opmerkings oor Christelike morele oordeelsvorming". *Skrif en Kerk* Vol 17, No. 1, pp. 31-47.

Döring, D. 1982. "Steine auf dem Weg zur Einheit. Überlegungen zur Rezeption ökumenischer Konsensdokumente. In P. Neuer & F. Wolfinger (Hg.), pp. 138-163.

Ehrenström, N. & Gassmann, G. (eds). 1975. *Confessions in Dialogue. A survey of Bilateral Conversations among World Confessional Families 1959-1974*. Geneva: WCC.

Evans, G.R. 1994. *The church and the churches. Toward an ecumenical ecclesiology*. Cambridge: Cambridge University Press.

Evans, G.R. 1996. *Method in ecumenical theology: The lessons so far*. Cambridge: Cambridge University Press.

Fischer, H. 1989. "Rezeption in ihre Bedeutung für Leben und Lehre der Kirche". In W. Beinart & H. Fischer (Hrsg.), pp. 35-57.

Ford, J.T. & Swan, D.J. (eds) 1993. *Twelve tales untold: A study guide for ecumenical reception*. Grand Rapids: Eerdmans.

Freyer, T. 1982. *Pneumatologie als Strukturprinzip der Dogmatik: Überlegungen im Anschluss an die Lehre von der "Geisttaufe" bei Karl Barth*. Paderborn: Schöningh.

Fries, H. 1991. "Der Beitrag der Gläuben für die Wahrheitsfindung in den Kirchen". *StZ* Vol. 209, pp. 3-16.

Fries, H. & Rahner, K. 1983. *Einigung der Kirchen – reale Möglichkeit*. Freiburg: Herder.

Garijo, M. 1981. "Der Begriff 'Rezeption' in sein Ort im Kernder katholoschen Ekklesiologie". In P. Lengfeld & H.G. Stobbe (Hrsg.), pp. 97-109.

Gassmann, G. 1977. "Rezeption im ökumenischen Kontext". *ÖR* Vol. 26, pp. 314-327.

Gassmann, G. 1984. "Die Rezeption der Dialoge". *ÖR* Vol. 33, pp. 357-368.

Gassmann, G. 1993. *Documentary history of Faith and Order 1963-1993*. Geneva: WCC.

Geldbach, E. 1987. *Ökumene in Gegensätzen*. Göttingen: Vandenhoeck & Ruprecht.

Geller, H. (Hg.). 1985. *Ökumene in Gemeinden. Struktur und Prozesse ökumenischer Beziehungen*. Frankfurt: Verlag der Action.

Grillmeier, A. 1970. "Konzil und Rezeption". *Theologie und Philosophie* Vol. 45, pp. 321-352.

Gros, J. (ed.). 1984. *The Search for Visible Unity: Baptism, Eucharist, Ministry*. New York: The Pilgrim Press.

Goßmann, K. (Hg.). 1988. *Ökumenisches Lernen in der Gemeinde*. Gütersloh: Gütersloher Verlagshaus.

Harakas, S. 1991. "Must God remain Greek?" *The Ecumenical Review* Vol. 43, pp. 194-199.

Hill, C. & Yarnold, E. (eds) 1994. *Anglicans and Roman Catholics: The search for unity*. London: Society for Promoting Christian Unity.

Hood, R. 1990. *Must God remain Greek? Afro-cultures and God-talk*. Minneapolis: Fortress Press.

Hojen, P. (Hg.). 1978. *Ökumenische Methodologie. Dokumentation und Bericht*. Genf: Lutherischer Weltbund.

Houtepen, A. 1983. "Reception, Tradition, Communion". In M. Thurian (ed.), pp. 140-160.

Houtepen, A. 1991. "Reception". In *Dictionary of the ecumenical movement*. Geneva: WCC, pp. 844-845.

Hryniewicz, W. 1981. "Ökumenische Rezeption und konfessionelle Identität". *US* Vol. 36, pp. 116-131.

Internationale Konsultation über ökumenische Methodologie. In P. Hojen (Hg.), pp. 212-230.

Kelly, G. 1992. *The significance and meaning of the idea of 'recognition' in the work of Faith and Order 1910-1991*. Ottawa: College dominicain de philosophie et de theologie, faculte de theologie.

Kelly, G. 1996. *Recognition. Advancing ecumenical thinking*. New York: Peter lang.

Kilmartin, E.J. 1984. "Reception in history: An ecclesiological phenomenon and its significance". In J. Gros (ed.), pp. 34-54.

Kindt-Siegwalt, I. 1989. "Die Antwort der Kirchen auf Lima und ihre Auswertung". *ÖR* Vol. 38, pp. 1-13.

Klein, A. 1991. "Rezeption der ökumenischen Dialogue". In K. Lüdicke, H. Messinghoff & H. Swendenwein (Hg.) *Iustus Iudex: Festgabe für Paul Wesemann zum 75. Geburtstag von seinen Freunden und Schülern*. Essen: Ludgerus-Verl.

Köllner, H. 1985. Ökumene gewinnt Profil (II). Zum Beispiel ökumenischer Gemeindezentren". *ÖR* Vol. 34, pp. 184-199.

Kreiner, A. 1985. "Aporien des Konsens-Rezeption Schemas". *Cath* Vol. 39, pp. 179-189.

Kretschmar, G. 1980. "Konvergenz- und Konsenstexte als Ergebnis bilateraler Dialoge über das hl. Abendmahl". *ÖR* Vol. 29, pp. 1-21.

Kuhn, U. 1983. "Reception – an imperative and an opportunity". In M. Thurian (ed.), pp. 163-174.

Küppers, W. 1968. Rezeption. Prolegomena zu einer systematischen Überlegung". In *Konzile und die ökumenische Bewegung*. Genf: Ökumenischer Rat der Kirchen, pp. 81-104.

Lanne, E. 1982. "The Problem of 'Reception'". In M. Kinnamon (ed.) *Towards visible unity: Commission on Faith and Order*. Geneva: World Council of Churches.

Lategan, B. & Vorster, W. 1985. *Text and reality: aspects of reference in Biblical texts*. Philadelphia: Fortress Press.

Lengfeld, P. & Stobbe, H.G. (Hrsg.). 1980. *Ökumenische Theologie. Ein Arbeitsbuch*. Stuttgart: Kohlhammer.

Lengfeld, P. 1981. "Ökumenische Spiritualität als Voraussetzung van Rezeption". In P. Lengfeld & H.G. Stobbe (Hrsg.), pp. 97-109.

Lengfeld, P. & Stobbe, H.G. (Hrsg.) 1981. *Theologischer Konsens und Kirchenspaltung*. Stuttgart: Kohlhammer.

Limouris, G. 1991. "Historical background to apostolic faith today". In *Confessing the one faith*, pp. 105-111.

Lindbeck, G. 1978. "Rezeption und Methode. Überlegungen zum ökumenischen Auftrag des LWB". In P. Hojen (Hg.), pp. 31-48.

Loewe, H. 1988. "Die Kirchen vor der Aufgabe der Rezeption von Ergebnissen ökumenischer Gespräche und Verhandlungen. In J. Rohls & G. Wenz (eds.), pp. 637-651.

Lossky, N (ed.) 1991. *Dictionary of the ecumenical movement*. Geneva: WCC Publications.

Lyotard, J.F. 1984. *The postmodern condition*. Manchester: Manchester University Press.

McGrath, A.E. 1990. *The genesis of doctrine*. London: Basil Blackwell.

Mehlhausen, J. 1995. "Die Rezeption der Barmen Theologischer Erklärung in den evangelischen Landeskirchen nach 1945". In W. Pannenberg & T. Schneider (Hrsg.) *Verbindliches Zeugnis II: Schriftauslegung – Lehramt – Rezeption*. Göttingen: Vandenhoeck & Ruprecht, pp. 219-244.

Meyer, H. 1980. "Anerkennung – Ein ökumenischer Schluesselbegriff". In P. Mans (Hrsg.) *Dialog und Anerkennung. Beiheft zur Ökumenische Rundschau* Vol. 37, pp. 25-41.

Meyer, H. 1981. "Wer ist sich mit wem worüber einig? Überblick über die Konsenstexte der letsten Jahre". In P. Lengfeld & H.G. Stobbe (Hrsg.), pp. 126-134.

Meyer, H. 1983. "'Reception' – vom Konsens zur Gemeinschaft". In H. Fries (Hg.) *Das Ringen um die Einheit der Kirchen*. Düsseldorf, pp. 169-175.

Meyer, H. 1986. "Der Einfluß des konfessionellen und kirchlichen Eigenverständnisses auf dieRezeption des BEM-Dokumentes und die Konsequenzen einer solchen Rezeption". In *Europäischer Kontext und die Rezeption des Lima-dokumentes. Bericht des vier Studienkonsultation über BEM der Konferenz Europäischer Kirchen 1984-1985*. Genf: Konferenz Europ. Kirchen, pp. 34-44.

Meyer, H. 1988. "Eine Gemeinschaft in Gegensätzen? Streit um Rezeption und ökumenischer Minimalismus?" *EvKom* Vol. 21, pp. 260-264.

Meyer, H. 1989. "Rezeptionsproblematik und Konsensstruktur. Bemerkungen zum DÖSTA-Arbeitspapier 'Theologie der Ökumene – ökumenische Theoriebildung' und zur Rede von Einer Gemeinschaft in Gegensätzen". *ÖR* Vol. 38, pp. 200-207.

Naudé, P.J. 1994. "Doxology and praxis: The ecumenical significance of religious experience in a South Africa of the 1990's". In J. Mouton & B. Lategan B (eds.) *The relevance of theology for the 1990's*. HSRC: Pretoria, pp. 421-434.

Naudé, P.J. 1996. *Is God hovering above the nineteenth floor? Doing theology in a post-disciplinary context*. UPE: Inaugural address D38.

Naudé, P.J. 1997a. "Die Belharstryd in ekumeniese perspektief". *NGTT* Vol. xxxviii, No. 3, pp 226-243.

Naudé, P.J. 1997b. "Regaining our ritual coherence: The question of textuality and worship in ecumenical reception". *Journal of Ecumenical Studies* Vol. 35, No. 2, pp. 235-256.

Nissotis, N. 1986. "Eine glaubwürdige Rezeption des BEM-Dokumentes auf jeder Ebene des Verständnisses, des Gottesdienstes und der Praxis in den Kirchen". In *Europäischer Kontext und die Rezeption des Lima-Dokumentes*. Genf: Konferenz Europ. Kirchen, pp. 131-152.

Neuer, P. & Wolfinger, F. (Hg.). 1982. *Auf Wegen der Versöhnung. Beitrage zum ökumenischen Gespräch* (FS H. Fries). Frankfurt: Frankfurt am Main, pp. 138-163.

Pemsel-Maier, S. 1993. *Rezeption – Schwierigkeiten und Chancen*. Würzburg: Echter Verlag.

Pesch, O.H. 1993. "Rezeption ökumenischer Dialogergebnisse". *ÖR* Vol. 42, No. 4, pp. 407-418.

Pioch, E.E. 1986. *Ökumene in der Gemeindepraxis: ein Arbeitsbuch zu den Konvergenzerklärungen von Lima*. Breklum: Breklumer Verlag.

Rodger, P.C. & Vischer, L. 1964. *The fourth world conference on Faith and Order* (Montreal 1963). London: SCM.

Rohls, J. & Wenz, G. (eds.) 1988. *Vernunft des Glaubens. Wissenschaftliche Theologie und kirchliche Lehre* (FS W Pannenberg). Gottingen: Vandenhoeck & Ruprecht.

Rusch, W.G. 1984. "'Baptism, Eucharist and Ministry' – and Reception". In J. Gros (ed.), pp. 129-143.

Rusch, W.G. 1988. *Rezeption: An ecumenical opportunity*. Philadelphia: Fortress Press.

Sauter, G. 1987. "Konsensus". In H. Krüger, W. Löser & W. Müller-Römheld (Hg.) *Ökumenelexikon. Kirchen – Religionen – Bewegungen*. Frankfurt, pp. 718.

Schatz, K. 1991. "Die Rezeption ökumenischer Konzilien im ersten Jahrtausend – Schwierigkeiten, Formen der Bewältigung und verweigerte Rezeption". In Beinert (Hrsg.), pp. 93-121.

Scheele, P.W. 1989. "Die Rezeption ökumenischer Dokumente als geistliches Geschehen". In K. Aland & S. Meurer (Hg.) *Wissenschaft und Kirche. FS E. Lohse*. Bielefeld, pp. 259-277.

Schmeider, T. 1979. "Jungend und Ökumene". *ÖR* Vol. 28, pp. 293-305.

Schmidt-Clausen, 1978. "Die Rezeption ökumenischer Konsensustexte durch die Kirchen. Erwägungen zu künftigen Aufgaben der ökumenischen Bewegung". *ÖR* Vol. 27, pp. 1-13.

Schultz, F. 1983. *Die Lima-Liturgie : die ökumenische Gottesdienstordnung zu den Lima-Texten: ein Beitrag zum Verständnis und zur Urteilsbildung*. Kasel: J. Stauda.

Schultz, F. 1987. "Die Rezeption der Lima-Liturgie". In *JbLH* Vol. 31, pp. 1-37.

Seils, M. 1981. "Die Problematik der Rezeption aus der Sicht evangelischer Kirchenleitung". In P. Lengfeld & H.G. Stobbe (Hrsg.), pp. 110-114.

Sieben, H.J. 1979. *Die Konzilsidee der alten Kirche*. Paderborn: Schöningh.

Smit, D.J. 1992. "Kerkeenheid in die ekumene". *Apologia* Vol. 7, No. 1 & 2, pp. 43-52.

Smit, D.J. 1994. "Etiek na Babel? Vrae rondom moraliteit en die openbare gesprek in Suid-Afrika vandag". *NGTT* 1994, No. 1, pp. 82-92.

Smit, D.J. 1995a. "Etiese spraakverwarring in Suid-Afrika vandag". *NGTT* 1995, No. 1, pp. 87-98.

Smit, D.J. 1995b. "Het Suid-Afrika 'n gemeenskaplike morele taal nodig?" *HTS* Vol. 51, No. 1, Maart 1995, pp. 65-84.

Smit, D.J. 1995c. "Oor die skepping van 'n grammatika van saamleef". *HTS* Vol. 51, No. 1, Maart 1995, pp. 85-107

Smit, D.J. 1996a. "Oor die kerk as 'n unieke samelewingsverband". *Tydskrif vir Geesteswetenskappe* Vol. 36, No. 2, pp. 119-129.

Smit, D.J. 1996b. "Oor die unieke openbare rol van die kerk". *Tydskrif vir Geesteswetenskappe* Vol. 36, No. 3, pp. 190-204.

Stobbe, H.G. 1980. "Konfessionelle Identität, ökumenische Bewegung und Macht". In Lengfeld & H.G. Stobbe (Hrsg.), pp. 215-237.

Stobbe, H.G. 1981. Konsensfindung als hermeneutische Problem". In P. Lengfeld & H.G. Stobbe (Hrsg.), pp. 31-51.

Stout, J. 1981. *The flight from authority*. Notre Dame: University of Notre Dame Press.

Sundermeier, T.H. 1986. "Konvivenz al Grundstruktur ökumenischer Existenz heute". In W. Huber, D. Ritschl & T.H. Sundermeier (Hrsg.) *Ökumenische Existenz heute 1*. München: Kaiser, pp. 49-100.

Taylor M-K. 1990. *Remembering Esparanza: A cultural-political theology for North America*. New York: Orbis.

Thurian, M. (ed.). 1983. *Ecumenical Perspectives on Baptism, Eucharist and Ministry*. Geneva: World Council of Churches.

Tillard, J.M.R. 1986. "The ecclesiological implications of bilateral dialogue". *Journal of Ecumenical Studies* Vol. 23, No. 3, pp. 412-423.

Tracy, D. 1978. *Plurality and ambiguity: Hermeneutics, religion, hope*. San Francisco: Harper and Row.

Van Niekerk, A.A. 1992. *Rasionaliteit en relativisme: Op soek na 'n rasionaliteitsmodel vir die menswetenskappe*. Pretoria: RGN.

Vischer, L. 1974. "Von Christi versöhnender Kraft zusammengeführt und zusammengehalten". In R. Groscurth (Hg.) *Wandernde Horizonte auf dem Weg zur kirchlichen Einheit*. Frankfurt: O. Lembeck, pp. 11-44.

Vischer, L. 1978. "Zur Methode und Rezeption interkonfesionelle Dialoge". In P. Hojem (Hg.), pp. 49-62.

Vischer, L. 1983. "Rezeption in der ökumenischen Bewegung. Die Texte über Taufe, Eucharistie, und Amt der Kommission für Glauben und Kirchenverfassung". *KuD* Vol. 29, pp. 86-99.

Vischer, L. 1984. "The process of 'reception' in the ecumenical movement". *Mid-Stream* Vol. 23, pp. 221-233.

Wainwright, G 1984. "Reception of 'Baptism, Eucharist, and Ministry' and the apostolic faith study". In J. Gros (ed.), pp. 71-82.

WCC. 1981. *One in Christ*, Faith and Order Paper 107. Geneva: WCC.

WCC. 1991. *Confessing the one faith*. Faith and Order Paper 153. Geneva: WCC.

WCC. 1996a. *Towards sharing the one faith*. A study guide for discussion groups. Geneva: WCC.

WCC. 1996b. *Constitution, Rules, Regulations and By-laws*. Geneva: WCC.

Welker, M. 1994. *God the Spirit*. Minneapolis: Fortress Press.

Welker, M. 1995. *Kirche im Pluralismus*. Gütersloh: Gütersloher Verlagshaus.

Wieacker, F. 1967. *Privatrechtgeschichte der Neuzeit unter besonderer Beruecksichtigung der deutschen Entwicklung*. Göttingen: Vandenhoeck u Ruprecht.

Willebrands, J. 1989. "Der ökumenische Dialog und seine Rezeption". In J. Willebrands (ed.) *Mandatum Unitatis. Beitrage zur Ökumene*. Paderborn: Bonifatius, pp. 279-290.

Willes, D. 1984. "Baptism, Eucharist, and Ministry, Reception and the Bilaterals". In J. Gros (ed.), pp. 96-106.

Wolfinger, F. 1977. "Die Rezeption theologischer Einsichten und ihre theologische und ökumenische Bedeutung: Von der Einsicht zur Verwirklichung". *Cath* Vol. 31, pp. 202-223.

Wolfinger, F. 1987. "Rezeption – ein Zentralbegriff der ökumenischen Diskussion oder des Glaubensvollzuges? Ein Vergleich zweier Veröffentlichungenn. *ÖR* Vol. 27, pp. 14-21.

1.2 REGAINING OUR RITUAL COHERENCE

The question of textuality and worship in ecumenical reception[1]

"Has the 'verbal ethos' of Faith and Order, its focus upon the written word as bearer of theological meaning, limited its understanding of worship and its importance in the search for Christian unity?"[2]

This important question asked recently by the Ditchingham group should be answered in the affirmative. The aim of this contribution is to explain why, from both a theoretical and a practical perspective, Faith and Order has fallen into the trap of "textualism" and, despite commendable efforts, is struggling to accept the role of liturgy and worship in its theological efforts. The framework is the wider issue of ecumenical reception[3] in which Faith and Order plays such a critical part.

I take my cue from the two elements of the question raised above. The "verbal ethos" and "focus upon the written word" are dealt with in the first section. I first attempt to highlight the well-known but neglected insight on the role of the receptor from post-structural New Testament hermeneutics, after which the relation between ritual and textual coherence is explained by drawing on the insights from oral theories and studies on the history of writing.

The limited "understanding of worship and its importance in the search for Christian unity" is dealt with in the second section. The crucial role of liturgy and the understanding of ecumenical theology as doxology form the basis for a critical analysis of how Faith and Order missed opportunities to apply its own insights on liturgy and worship.

It will emerge that reception is hampered by the present mode in which ecumenical work is produced and mediated. Part of the response to the problem is expressed in the title of this essay. Reception may have a greater chance of success via a regaining of the church's "ritual coherence".

---

1 This essay was first published in the *Journal of Ecumenical Studies* 35/2 (1998), 235-256.
2 The consensus statement of a Faith and Order working group, which met in Ditchingham, England, in 1994, was published in 1995 under the editorship of Best and Heller.
3 As technical theological term "reception" is of recent origin. One of the earliest works is Yves Congar's "La 'réception' comme réalité ecclésiologique" (1972:369-403). The first dictionary entries are in the middle 1980s. The matter to which it refers, however, dates back to the time of canonisation and the ecumenical councils of the early church. Good work on the historical developments are Rusch (1980), Kuhn (1983), Beinart and Fischer (1989), and Kilmartin (1984). In the modern ecumenical movement there is a definite move away from the juridical notion of reception to seeing it as an encompassing process (see Gassmann 1974:319-320) whereby results of ecumenical encounters are "received" at different levels and in different stages. Simply put: "Ecumenical reception is the comprehensive process by which the churches make their own the whole range of results of their encounters with each other" (WCC 1991:173). For a very basic description, see Houtepen (1991). For criticism on the vagueness of the term, see Fischer (1989).

1. RECEPTION AND TEXTUALITY

A cynical view of the ecumenical movement might be that it is comprised of a few professional theologians, mainly from the West, who gather at regular intervals to produce texts of which they themselves are the primary and only real receptors. Although one must consider its full context, it is fair to say that the most important theological results of the WCC as represented by Faith and Order, and the pivotal axis of bi- and multilateral dialogues, are indeed the production of texts. The problem lies with their reception. This is highlighted by a few randomly chosen examples. The mere "paper status" of the first ever document produced by Faith and Order in 1937;[4] the repeatedly expressed frustration over a lack of responses from churches (see Vischer 1984:221), or the slow process involved in getting a reply (up to ten years!), with the added problem that consensus reached by representatives is not necessarily accepted by member churches;[5] and the lack of progress in church unification, even within the same confessional tradition.[6]

How can a fresh look at the concept of textuality assist us to overcome some of the problems inherent to "the ecumenical production of paper" (Loewe 1988:649, my translation), which lends ecumenism an elitist character, thereby denying an integral ecumenism (May 1988)? I shall briefly, more by way of suggestion than definitive statement, examine insights drawn from reception theory in New Testament hermeneutics and studies regarding orality and the history of writing.

1.1 New Testament hermeneutics

Although some (like Beinert 1989:7-8) refer to reception theories in communication models, nowhere in the consulted literature is it seriously considered as making a contribution to our understanding of ecumenical or ecclesial reception. Even a superficial reading of reception theories in specifically New Testament studies does hint at exciting prospects. I focus explicitly on the shift from the historical and structural to the reception dimension of texts, drawing mainly on *Text and Reality* by South African New Testament scholars, Bernard Lategan and Willem Vorster (1985), specifically Lategan's contribution.

A trajectory of hermeneutical theories over the last few decades shows that "we find ourselves in the aftermath of an intense struggle between the historical method and the structuralist approach to the interpretation of biblical texts" (Lategan and Vorster 1985:4). An important shift occurred from the middle of the 1970s (see references in Lategan and Vorster 1985:5). In terms of the well-known communication model developed by Roman Jakobson (1960:350-377), linguistic communication is dependent on six factors (speaker, hearer, medium, code, situation and message) that correlate to six functions of language (emotive, conative, phatic, meta-linguistic, referential, and poetic). Moving beyond an exclusive focus on historical and structural elements, attention shifted from the left-hand side and middle of the model (sender

---

4   It was titled *Declaration on Divine Grace*.
5   See, for example, the Anglican-Roman Catholic dialogues (ARCIC) and documentation in Hill and Yarnold (1994) as repeatedly referred to by Evans (1996).
6   A good South African example is the painful process of receiving the Belhar confession as part of the unification between the Dutch Reformed Church and the Uniting Reformed Church of Southern Africa. See my analysis in Naudé (1997).

and medium) to the right-hand side (receiver). Most significantly, the receiver was awarded equal status to that of the sender, thereby emphasising that in the case of written communication one may talk about a cooperative enterprise between "author" and "reader". The completion of the process of understanding subsequently lies in the reception of the text (varied individual or communal appropriation of meaning) by the reader (Lategan and Vorster 1985:13,73). In terms of Schmidt's distinction between text production, text mediation and text reception, one has to accept that the latter is an integral part of the process of communication (Schmidt 1975:403), extending Gadamer's concept of *Wirkungsgeschichte* to *Rezeptionsgeschichte* (Jauss 1974:25-27), and developing a "Hermeneutik der Entfaltung" (Japp 1977:47) in the light of the polysemic, open-ended nature of texts.

If equal status is granted to the receiver, and if understanding is not complete without appropriation, it becomes imperative for the producers of ecumenical texts (text production; sender) to communicate these texts (text mediation) in such a way that the texts become part of the life of the church in the encompassing sense of the word (text reception). This is especially the case where the producers of a text are also its first receivers. There is the danger of creating a closed circle of intra-communication on the basis of an understanding that the texts produced by ecumenical dialogues are already "consensus texts" through the participation of official representatives from the different churches (see Fischer 1989:40,41). To borrow the technical distinction between an implied/real author and an implied/real reader (see Lategan and Vorster 1985:70-75), it is imperative that Faith and Order theologians (for example) do not stifle the open communication process by an (unintended) identification between the real author and the real/implied reader.

The equal status of the receiver does not imply, as Schmidt suggests (1980:534), that a text has as many meanings as it has readers. Appropriation of meaning is not a purely private enterprise that is wholly reliant on the reader. The receiver is subjected to at least two constraints: first, the constraint imposed by the text itself, because the text serves as the *Gegenüber*, "which is not only interpreted by the reader but which, in its turn, interprets and shapes the reader" (Lategan and Vorster 1985:16); second, in any "theological" reading, the constraint of the community of believers, which constitutes the pneumatological space in which reception must be justified. The first constraint guards against an over-extension of reception in a form of relativistic readings and highlights the public nature of hermeneutics. The second guards against forms of denominationalism and even sectarianism by highlighting the intersubjective nature of hermeneutics. Both constraints are crucial to the theological process of ecumenical reception.

In this light one should welcome the recent appointment of a commission from within Faith and Order to develop an ecumenical hermeneutic specifically related to the Canberra Assembly of the WCC meeting in 1991, which appropriated "koinonia" as the hermeneutical key for understanding church unity. In its first report, "Auf dem Weg zu einer Hermeneutik für eine wachsende Koinonia", as discussed by Konrad Raiser (1996:402-403), the church is described as a hermeneutical community; reception is specifically seen as more than the reception of texts, but as a broad hermeneutical process that includes inter- and transcultural communication.[7]

---

7   A discussion of the hermeneutics involved in the meeting of "strangers" with application

We shall have to wait and see how this will affect the work of Faith and Order in the next few years. There are encouraging signs that reception in the real sense is being adapted to the call of several theologians that it should increasingly be treated as more than "just assenting to a text" (Rusch 1984:49, my translation) but as "internalising what is to be received into all aspects of the church's life" (Beinart 1991:17, my translation). This is obviously supported by such efforts as the inclusion of a liturgy to accompany and mediate the Lima text, and the suggestion that churches who do not share the Nicene creed should seriously consider making it part of the church's life – even if only at special occasions (*Confessing the one faith* 1991a:4, see my critical discussion under liturgy below).

In short, ecumenical reception is neither the signature on a contract nor the distant reception of a text, but an embrace of love among sister churches (variation on Houtepen 1983:153). The production of texts, although theologically complex, is the easier part of the process. As much energy should go into the mediation and reception of texts, precisely because the status of the church as receptor is taken seriously as constitutive part of "textual communication".

Let us now briefly turn to the field of oral theories and the history of writing to conclude our investigation on the relation between textuality and ecumenical reception.

1.2. Oral theory and the history of writing

For the purposes of this essay, I am not primarily interested in the technical discussions about the so-called Parry-Lord thesis or the oral formulaic theories related to Walter Ong and others.[8] The cumulative impact of work on "orality" and history of writing is fruitful in a discussion of textual reception in ecumenical theology. Whatever the criticisms are against the various oral theories,[9] two general perspectives (at least) remain valid. The first is the social stratification constituted by the literate-illiterate dichotomy in societies where oral ("functionally illiterate") and literate people live side by side, which may be extended to the situation in the world at large. The second is the historical development from ritual- to textual-based cultural coherence (see Assmann below), which might be linked to the concept of theological authorship and authority in the modern era (see Thiel below).

---

to interreligious dialogue lies beyond the scope of this paper. Theo Sundermeier's recent *Hermeneutik des Fremdens* (1996) is a noteworthy and original contribution in this regard.

8   It is obviously not possible or necessary to give a wide-ranging publications list here. My own thinking on orality has primarily been shaped by AB Lord's *Singer of Tales* (1960), the many publications by Walter Ong, the groundbreaking field work on oral poetry and theoretical studies by Ruth Finnegan, the hermeneutical studies by New Testament scholar Werner Kelber, and the methodological work by John Miles Foley. My five years in a predominantly "oral society" in Venda, Northern Transvaal, South Africa, and field work among rural ZCC communities have indelibly shaped my thinking. In two articles, one on Zionist theology (1993) and the other on oral theology (1996b) I attempted a theological appropriation of these insights.

9   Valid criticism has been expressed from various perspectives against the sharp dichotomy between orality and literacy (Finnegan 1990; Tanner 1982); the easy generalisations from "oral forms" in texts to an "oral culture", which is itself a problematic idea; the shallow and elusive conceptual foundations of orality (Halverson 1994); and an over-evaluation of alphabetic writing in ancient Greece (Assmann 1992:300).

1.2.1 From "orality" to "literacy": A social stratification

The literate-illiterate dichotomy, with its built-in bias against oral people, has been neglected in the social analysis even of liberation theologians (of all persuasions) who profess the preferential option for the poor (see Naudé 1996:22, 25-26). There are millions of Christians (especially in the Third World) who have no access to the gospel or the tradition or ecumenical documents other than by the means of oral transmission via mnemonic devices of various sorts or, where available, the authority of a literate person. Depending on their context, they may have reason to be suspicious about written documents. This is explained by Jeff Guy from a South African perspective:

> The written word was part of conquest in South Africa. It was the medium whereby the conquerors communicated and organised resources, policies and tactics. The written treaty confirmed the right of the conqueror to the land, giving the act of conquest permanency over time and in space, and the history of South Africa is replete with accounts of the efforts of literate invaders to persuade, cajole, demand that the oral rulers, traditional rulers, touch the pen (Guy 1991:398).

The category "illiterate" is thus more than a description of people unable to read; it is a social category of marginalised people excluded from a world that assumes literacy. It has a specific application to the world of theology and ecumenical dialogue. For example, the registration of Independent African Churches in the past created enormous problems because of legal requirements pertaining to creeds and constitutions – obviously in written form.

If the WCC, by virtue of its commission for Justice, Peace and the Integrity of Creation, takes seriously its 1990 commitment (*Grundüberzeugung*) in Seoul, namely that God is on the side of the poor (second of ten affirmations), the question of ecumenical conversation and text mediation must be reconsidered. If not, the ecumenical movement may, by its very modes of operation, maintain a form of ecclesial repression and be a vehicle of theological imperialism. Let us explain these two dangers.

First, John May's observation is correct:

> When missionaries from a universalist tradition with a canonical literature encounter tribal peoples with oral cultures, the whole idea of discussions designed to facilitate the disinterested pursuit of religious truth becomes slightly absurd. Yet, such is the model of dialogue that Western Christians, at least, tend to presuppose, whether it be applied to meetings of religious leaders that are more symbolic than substantial or literary exchanges between highly articulate scholars (May 1988:578).

It is exactly this presupposition that harbours the element of repression, because this is the model that has become institutionalised in most of our ecumenical efforts.

Second, Stephen Sykes noted that, in situations of religious controversy, the theologian (or ecumenical organisation!) that is steeped in the compartmentalisation of Western intellectual life needs to realise the potential of a "tyranny of intellectuals, with their superior articulacy and natural concern for the epistemology of the arguments" (Sykes 1984:285). He referred to the "imperialistic instincts of the intellectual tradition" (Sykes 1984:32), which must, as we shall see later, be kept in balance by a dialectic between theology and worship.[10]

That there is some sensitivity to this, although from a different perspective, emerges from Mary Tanner's presentation to the recent Faith and Order meeting in Santiago. She referred to the Latin American delegation, who "called for a deconstruction of the classical Faith and Order method, stressing the need to begin with the experience of Christians gathered together in base communities" (Tanner 1994:26). She then referred to the relation between taking into account the continuity with the apostolic community (history, tradition) and learning from contemporary experiences of Christians. The challenge in Faith and Order is "to find an ecumenical method which lives more in the 'in between', constantly living the tradition handed on through the ages and constantly open to new ways of understanding and living the faith of the church in today's world". What we need is a more inclusive process and community. "We need to ask who is missing from our circle – and whom do we silence *within* our circle? ... Faith and Order also has a duty to represent those who have no voice within the structures[11] of the World Council of Churches" (Tanner 1994:26,27, her emphasis). This is crucial, one may add, because the Southern churches now represent the majority of Christians and will increasingly do so, while the theological and ecumenical centre points still remain in the North and West; the latter Christians should therefore open themselves up to experiences of faith and theological reflection not rooted in Western culture.

May's references to "canonical literature" and "disinterested pursuit of truth" link directly with our second point, pertaining to the history of writing.

1.2.2. From ritual to textual coherence

In his *Das kulturelle Gedächtnis*, Jan Assmann, the well-known German Egyptologist, described how early cultures – such as the ancient Egyptians, the Israelites and the Greeks – developed means of maintaining cultural coherence. In the case of ancient Egypt, the "Ort des Wissens" (site of knowledge) or "Überlieferung eines Wissensgebaüde" (transmission of a body of knowledge) was intrinsically part of the rituals. In both Judaism and Greek religion, however, rituals were relativised by the interpretation of texts as the primary mode of cultural coherence. The site of knowledge is now no longer the rituality where knowledge is carried forth in the form of holy recitation of texts, but in the exposition of texts. This is what Assmann call the "Übergang von *ritueller* zu *textueller* Kohärenz " (transition from ritual to textual coherence, Assmann 1992:87-88, his emphasis).

---

10 Attentive readers will realise that Syke's primary context is not the literate-illiterate distinction, but rather that between doctrine and worship. His discussion of literacy in the Roman Empire and Paul's authority arising from his writing abilities (231), as well as the insistence on "words" in religious conflict (32, 280-281), are enough to transpose his views to the present context. See the discussion in the next few paragraphs.

11 The bylaws of Faith and Order (Appendix V:309-313) do make provision for non-member churches to be represented on the Commission and study groups. Persons act in their personal capacity, but must be acceptable to the church from which they come. I have no information as to implementation of this provision.

It is not writing as such which leads to the transition from ritual to textual coherence, argued Assmann, but the canonical inscripturalisation of tradition. Ritually based cultural coherence is fundamentally repetitive and cyclic. Texts do function here, but as holy texts that are not so much interpreted as recited. Textually based coherence, on the contrary, allows for variation based on the on-going interpretation of canonical texts (1992:7-34). In short, it is a transition from "ritengestützter Repetition" (rite-based repetition) to "textgestützter Interpretation" (text-based interpretation, 1992:96). Because of this continual need for "Deutung", a new class of intellectual elites arose, the "Literatokratie" (1992:299) such as, for example, the Israelite Sofer, the Jewish rabbi, the Hellenistic *philologos* and the Islamic mullah. A social differentiation occurred where religious or text authorities occupied independent positions *vis-à-vis* politicians, jurors or trades people, and a certain institutionalisation was accomplished as in rabbinical schools or in Plato's academy, for example.

Based on a critical interpretation of EA Havelock's work (made known in Germany via Luhmann's work), Assmann has argued that Western thought – specifically its rationalistic nature, which includes critical distancing and variation on received ideas, that is, philosophy – must be linked historically to Greek scriptural culture (1992:200ff). The principle of "hypolepsis" expresses the reality that, in a text-based cultural situation, one never starts from scratch but is always already part of a preceding communication process. This hypoleptic process occurs via textuality[12] and the frameworks of interpretation, which are characterised by the constant approximation of truth (Assmann, "Annäherrung der Wahrheit", 1992: 207). What does this entail for our present discussion of textuality and the ecumenical reception process? We need another step to clarify the acute relevance of Assmann's description. This brings us, merely by way of reference, to the relation between literacy and veracity, on the one hand, and literacy and theological authority/authorship, on the other.

In his detailed work *The History and Power of Writing* French historian Henri-Jean Martin carefully constructed the advent of printing and the reign of the book (1994:182-282). In his discussion of the Reformation, he noted that Luther's *Betbuchlein* and Bible translations spread rapidly because the Germany-speaking areas had a relatively high literacy rate at the end of the fifteenth century and were the "motherland of printing" (Martin 1994:253). He then inferred: "The works gained in prestige from the mere fact of being printed; printing gave them something like a palpable existence and an implicit verity", which he ascribed to the fact that "reading was like a revelation hitherto known only in restricted circles which had transmitted no more than glimpses of it in sermons and readings during the Mass" (Martin 1994:254).

From a very interesting theological viewpoint John Thiel, in his *Imagination and Authority*, explained the major shifts that occurred between the Middle Ages and the

---

12 "Textualität entsteht dort, wo die Sprache sich hinreichend aus ihrer praktischen Einbettung in Situationen (d.h. soziokulturelle Interaktionstypen, 'Sitze im Leben') gelöst hat, um als Text eine unabhängige Gestalt zu gewinnen" (Assmann 1992:203). See my discussion of Ricoeur's extension of textuality to include human actions as studied in the social sciences (Naudé 1996a) and Aleida Assmann's reference to the difference between "Sprachkompetenz" and "Sinnkompetenz" (Assmann 1990:14).

modern period. He notes that modernity is characterised by a greater disciplinary self-awareness, an explicit historical orientation, a turn to the subject in the post-Kantian era, and – most important for this discussion – a shift in understanding the theologian's task:

> In a manner analogous to understandings of the practitioner in artistic and literary endeavour, theologians conceived of themselves as authors and measured the authority of their work ... not only in terms of its faithfulness to ecclesial tradition but also in terms of its creativity, its resourcefulness in explicating the contemporary meaning of ancient religious truths (Thiel 1991:9).

According to Thiel, the notion of individual theological authorship as we know it today did not exist overtly in the classical paradigm, because the theologian was mostly a mere representative of the ancient authoritative tradition. Distinctiveness and originality were not valued traits; more important was "soundness, or 'orthodoxy' in ecclesial terms" (Thiel 1991:16). In the modern era a note of authorship was born that exists "in this ascription of authorial ability, and thus authority, to the individual theologian" (Thiel 1991:21). One could add that the Roman Catholic idea of orthodoxy and tradition[13] was fundamentally challenged and altered by the Reformation because the Reformers relativised the status of interpretation of the canon in view of the canon itself. This had – and still has – the effect of producing greater variation, freedom, and a more intense hermeneutical struggle.

Theologians – everywhere, not only in the West – should make explicit their literary position that they assume implicitly and understand what one may call the "ethics of writing". This, one hopes, will lead to sensitivity to the social marginalisation experienced by churches (ordinary people) with a predominantly oral base.[14] We as literate theologians should view ourselves in the mirror of history to realise how elaborately we have institutionalised our position as members of the "Literatokratie" (Assmann) and how the present-day ascription to written texts of verity (Martin) and authority (Thiel) is an integral part of the history and theological development in the West that is all too easily universalised.[15] Is the whole cultural heritage of textual coherence – in terms of our present discussion – not strengthened by the set-up and predominant methods of Geneva? (see May and Sykes and the examples below).

This is obviously not a naive plea for the abolishment of textual communication. One cannot undo a cultural revolution, and the obvious advantages of the written word should not be minimised by a form of oral romanticism. It is, however, a warning against an ecclesial memory (in terms of Assmann's "cultural memory") that is obsessively text-based. The church must regain its constitutive ritual coherence[16] by keeping a healthy tension between holy texts (rite) and canonical texts

---

13 Jan Assmann made the very interesting observation that the rabbinical idea of an "oral torah" and the Catholic concept of tradition may historically be linked to the conviction "dass die Wegweisung genau so geheiligt wird wie die Text selbst" (1992:296).
14 Is this perhaps why the African Independent Churches have hitherto withstood efforts to make them part of the South African Council of Churches?
15 Is Sundermeier (1983:36ff) not correct in describing African humanity in terms of participatory, not discursive, thought and as *homo ritualis*?
16 A remarkable historical feature which attests to this is the dynamic development since the fourth century of the Byzantine rite that is prevalent in all Eastern Orthodox churches

(interpretation). In the latter format, remarked Assmann, texts are easily divorced from the real-life situations and have a limited capacity to carry communicative meaning (Assmann 1992:91).

The identity of Christianity (see Section Two), with its obviously indispensable canonical reference, is and has always been mediated pluriformally via hymns, sermons, prayers, catechesis, sacraments, ornaments, buildings, etc. This is exactly the argument in our next section, which considers reception in relation to liturgy, the nature of ecumenical theology and the identity of Christianity. Our way to liturgy and worship has been mapped by a discussion of the importance of receptors in textual communication, the ecumenical marginalisation of oral Christians, and the danger of an exclusively textual coherence. The ecclesial realm where most of these insights and concerns can be addressed is that of liturgy and worship.[17]

2. RECEPTION AND WORSHIP

The history of Faith and Order and the WCC generally is integrally linked to studies on worship and actual acts of worship. The very aim[18] of Faith and Order[19] is *inter alia* described in terms of worship: "The functions of the Commission are: (a) to study such questions of faith, order *and worship* as bear on this task and to examine such social, cultural, political, racial, and other factors as affect the unity of the church" (Appendix V in Best and Gassmann 1994, my emphasis).[20] Let us examine this more closely.

---

today. Meyendorff (1991:624) makes the startling observation that "it reached its present form by the 15th century, *after which the fixity brought by the printing of books effectively halted its further development*" (my emphasis).

17 The terms "liturgy" and "worship" are normally linked and even interchanged as "the public, common action of a Christian community in which the church is both manifested and realized" (Meyendorff 1991: 623). The Orthodox and Anglican communities would restrict "the Liturgy" to eucharistic fellowship. At the other end of the spectrum would be an identification between liturgy and worship to include any form of Christian worship (even private devotion). In a general discussion like this, it would suffice to understand liturgy as the elements (prayers, hymns, sacraments, etc.) in the public worship of Christian communities constituting the rite of a particular tradition (like the "rite" of the Eastern or Western Churches). For finer distinctions, see the *Report on Worship* submitted to Montreal in 1963, Faith and Order Paper 39:15ff or Saliers (1994:16ff).

18 "The aim of the Commission is to proclaim the oneness of the church of Jesus Christ and to call the churches to the goal of visible unity in one faith and one eucharistic fellowship, *expressed in worship* and in common life in Christ, in order that the world may believe" (Best and Gassmann 1994, my emphasis).

19 For the history and interpretation of "order" in the context of Faith and Order, see Smit (1991).

20 One of the earliest publications of the Faith and Order movement is entitled *Prayer and Unity* (Brochure No. 15, 1913). Since its incorporation into the WCC, a number of studies have been produced. The most important stages may be described as follows: the stage of a comparative and descriptive approach in *Ways of Worship*, prepared for the Faith and Order meeting of Lund (1952); the shift to the attainment of unity through worship was published as *Worship and the Oneness of Christ's Church* (Montreal 1963); a concentration on the problems of worship in a situation of secularisation (discussed at WCC, Uppsala 1968), published as *Worship Today*, emanating from the Faith and Order consultation in Geneva, 1969. Further works published in Geneva by the WCC are the link between

2.1. Reception and liturgy

It might be useful to utilise the well-known *lex orandi-lex credendi* principle to evaluate the history and present position of liturgy and worship as means of reception in the ecumenical movement. This expression has outgrown its original context of *ut legem credendi lex statuat supplicandi* (explained in Wainwright 1991) to depict the relation between worship and faith (theology). There are good exegetical and historical arguments for stating that the initial stages of the church (from canonical times till beyond the fourth century) were characterised by a movement from *lex orandi* to *lex credendi*.

The vast majority of early Christian literature is liturgical in nature, and the link between baptismal formulas and (later) creeds is especially evident. Paul Meyendorff (1991:624) has remarked: "As people worship, so they believe. Not surprisingly, *the liturgical assembly itself eventually became a source of theology*, particularly from the fourth century, when the Christian faith had to be explained to the masses of new converts who flocked to the church after the peace of Constantine" (my emphasis). In his ground-breaking *Doxology*, Geoffrey Wainwright argued convincingly that the recognition of Christ's divinity[21] (Chapter 2), the Trinitarian doctrine based on the threefold pattern of baptism (Chapter 3), and the Marian dogmas (formulated on the basis of popular devotion) all grew from worship. "In all three cases, worship practice was in advance of doctrinal decisions" (Wainwright 1980:250).

On a normative level, one could argue that worship not only "precedes" theology, but should in fact govern theology and creeds. However, "it soon emerges that it is too simple, both descriptively and normatively, to attribute priority to 'praying' over 'teaching', or at least to see the shaping and controlling influence as flowing only in one direction" (Wainwright 1991:600). A diversification of purposes beyond the formative years of the church's history (worship, apologetics, internal controversies and formal theological reflection, for example) led to a differentiation in language usage (Wainwright 1991:601) and a reciprocity between worship and theology.

---

worship and bilateral dialogues (*Confessions in Dialogue*, 1972), the extension of worship to include even the life of Christians outside the church (*The Worship of the Congregation*, 1978), and the expression of theological convergence by liturgical means (Lima 1982 and the WCC meeting in Vancouver, 1983). Recently, there has been a renewed effort to make the interrelation between worship and *koinonia* more explicit (Faith and Order in Santiago de Compostela, 1993), which culminated in the Ditchingham consultation in August 1994, which was published as *So We Believe, So We Pray* in 1995. The most significant renewals in liturgy and the theology of worship came via the Constitution on the Sacred Liturgy (*Sacrosanctum Concilium* 1963, Second Vatican Council), the vast influence of the Orthodox Churches that joined the WCC in 1960, and the Dutch liturgical movement, which led to the formation of the *Societas Liturgica* in 1965. In recent years an important impetus has come from Southern Churches and the feminist movement (Harling 1995:2-4). Some of the noteworthy worship-related achievements of the ecumenical movement are the annual Week of Prayer for Christian Unity, the Common Lectionary (1983) and a revised version of common prayers in English, *Praying Together* (1989; see Allen 1991). For more details and bibliographies, read the articles "Liturgical movement" and "Worship in the ecumenical movement" by Teresa Berger (1991a, 1991b).

21 He argued specifically for the establishment of the *homoousious* conviction of the Nicene creed on the basis of prayers and praise to Christ (see also Wainwright 1991:601).

In terms of our present discussion, it is easy to discern why worship is such an important locus for reception. Where "texts" arise from the practice of worship, their reception has in a sense been guaranteed by the worshipping community. Where texts are produced by theological reflection and subsequently brought into worship, the process also contributes to reception. In the context of liturgies such texts are situated in an extended intertextual situation; the hermeneutics of such texts are extended to include the "interpretation" (mostly tacitly) of non-textual elements such as symbols[22] (the cross, the altar, icons), oral witnesses, prayers and hymns, somatic movements, silence and meditation, etc. The church can thus give full credit to Assmann's idea of textual coherence, while retaining the renewing impulse of ritual coherence.

Despite this fundamental congruence, members at the Ditchingham consultation lamented the fact that "the vital connection between the two 'rules' has become weak; and the practice of theology and the practice of worship are not each nourishing the other as they should" (Best and Heller 1995:x; see Lathrop 1995). They considered their efforts as perhaps the first common exploration of theology and worship. How is this possible after so many years of reflection and so many reports? The answer is not easy to find; perhaps there are various explanations.

One could refer to the internal preoccupation with secularisation in the late 1960s and 1970s, which put discussions on worship in a sharply defensive and apologetic context. One could mention the obvious but often overlooked factor that, in situations of conflict and dispute (such as the ecumenical movement), both the Catholic and Reformed traditions are overtly biased toward the conceptual apparatus of a doctrinal tradition, because it furnishes "the sharpest tools known to us for making distinctive meaning as unambiguous as possible" (1984:32). Theologians instinctively turn to the precision of existing words (creeds and so forth) or the careful construction of new words whose meaning is delineated to the last detail (Sykes 1984: 231).

This obviously links with our discussion in the previous section and will be refined further below. In the context of this essay I wish to argue that the almost exclusively textual concentration of Faith and Order led to the loss of vision that worship may,

---

22 In a very informative article on the relation between worship and ethics, with a South African focus, Dirkie Smit (drawing on Woltersdorff) rightly points to the typical emphasis of Reformed liturgy on the preference for the ear over the eye. Whereas the Roman tradition seeks to see God, the Reformed tradition, since Calvin, accepts our blindness: "We are to hear God. This led to the contrasting liturgies until today" (Smit 1997:4) Without analysing the differences (and some growing convergences) between the Orthodox, Catholic or Reformed traditions or their variations in non-Western contexts, I am less sceptical about the eye – especially the eyes of those who have answered God's call. I find some support in Schlink's view on the differences but also the complementary aspects of "Hören" and "Sehen" (1961:77), and in Sykes's correction of the typically Protestant treatment of "Christianity as though Christian iconography or liturgical ritual was of no, or only of minor, significance" (1984:29). It reminds me of Per Harling's account of an old Lutheran theologian who participated in a symbolic (and, for him, strange) act of hammering sins to a wooden cross during the WCC mission and evangelism conference in San Antonio, Texas, in May 1989, and who attested to the experience as deeply moving: "Not even a Lutheran is only a soul with ears!" (Harling 1995:1). My own experience of liturgical renewal would support an understanding of liturgy as involving all the human senses as the Word is carried in multiple fashion – extending the ear!

in fact, even in our day, contribute significantly to theological convergence. Two decisions by Faith and Order itself illustrate this point. The first is from Montreal (1963) where *Worship and the Oneness of Christ's Church* states clearly:

> The study of worship has often been regarded as one of the 'compartments' of ecumenical conversation. It has often been controlled by theological assumptions not directly related to the actual worshipping life of the Church. But if theology is to reflect the whole faith of the Church, and if (as we believe) it is in *leitourgia* that the Church is to find fulfilment of its life, then *it is essential that we let leitourgia speak for itself*. It is of crucial importance that we should investigate its forms and structures, its language and spirit, in the expectation that this process might *throw new light* upon various theological positions and affirmations, *perhaps even lend new meaning* to them, and thus open new possibilities in ecumenical dialogue" (Rodger and Vischer 1964:69, par.107, my emphases).

The second is from Louvain (1971), where the conviction is expressed that:

> In all Faith and Order studies the importance of considering the subject in close relation to its expression in worship should continually be remembered. Indeed sometimes *such expression may form basic material without which the study cannot yield fruitful results*. We have in mind in particular any future studies on catholicity, on the preparation of a common declaration of faith, on the unity of mankind in relation to social questions, and to the diversity of races and cultures" (Faith and Order Paper 59:218, my emphasis).

These decisions clearly state the principle that *lex orandi* should, in fact, materially influence *lex credendi*; *leitourgia* must be able to speak for itself without the negative control of theological assumptions, and *leitourgia* may clarify and deepen the meaning of theological positions. Moreover, worship may indeed be the basic material from which theological results may be constructed.

This vision was never fulfilled. Faith and Order clearly opted for the one-way flow from theological agreement to "liturgical expression" of such agreements. Where worship itself became the object of theological reflection, the actual acts of worship in the many churches were out of focus. This is convincingly illustrated by both the Lima liturgy and the project on common faith. With all the positive points raised in favour of Lima – as well as the recent emphasis on its contextualisation – I agree with the verdict from Ditchingham:

> It ought also to be noted that the Lima liturgy is received chiefly as printed text. It is the work of theologians [notably Max Thurian: PJN]; it was intended in part to celebrate particular doctrinal convergences. There are dangers in this: it may lead us away from the primary purpose of any liturgy, worship of God. The main purpose of liturgy cannot be catechesis[23] (Best and Heller 1995:23).

---

23 In his argument for the importance of liturgy, Sykes noted that the function of liturgy was "not to determine with precision what shall be thought by all, but to unlock the prison doors of conventional and mundane habits of mind. The Church's educational

With regards to *Confessing the One Faith*,²⁴ a twofold opportunity was missed. The first relates to the history of the common-faith project. One of its immediate precursors was the study of *Giving Account of the Hope that is within Us*, initiated at the Louvain (Belgium) Commission meeting in 1971, and concluded at Bangalore (India) in 1978. It started as project to inject into the universal church dynamic contemporary expressions of faith found all over the world. Exciting material from the heart of the churches' worshiping life was collected,²⁵ opening the possibility of seeing the unity of the church through these diverse expressions of faith. "In the event the opportunity was missed, and the exercise if 'Giving Account of the Hope that is within Us' has become a forgotten byway en route from Montreal" (Falconer 1993:49). To express the unity of faith, attention was turned away from this diversity; it was then decided instead to go back in history to the period before the schisms and utilise Nicea as the source for unity in the apostolic faith (see Brinkman 1996:59ff; Falconer 1993:48-49; Limouris 1991).

Despite the fact that major ideas for the Nicene text itself arose from the liturgical life of the early church, the Louvain suggestion, specifically on a common declaration of faith (see above), was not followed. This led to a second missed opportunity. The text and commentary were published in 1991, followed the workbook for churches,²⁶ but (apart from the call to recite the creed at special occasions) without any inclusion of liturgical material that could facilitate the reception of the creedal expression, which was alien for many churches. We ask again why these opportunities were missed. In a revealing and hope-giving statement by the Ditchingham group (paragraphs 56-57,54; Best and Heller 1995:18), the root of the problem is detected by way of a rhetorical question:

> Has the *'verbal ethos'* of Faith and Order, its focus upon the written word²⁷ as the bearer of theological meaning, limited its understanding of worship and its importance in the search for Christian unity? If Faith and Order is to engage the issue of worship seriously, it must become more sensitive to visual settings and non-verbal forms of communication. This suggests that Faith and Order should explore new means of communication with a wider audience. And if Faith and

---

    task is certainly aided by liturgy, but liturgies should never be conceived of as primarily instruments of instruction" (1984:280).
24 For an excellent discussion of the link between BEM and this project, see Wainwright (1984).
25 The results were edited by Choan-Seng Song (Faith and Order Papers 81 and 86). See also the reports of the meetings at Accra and Bangalore (Papers 72 and 92) and the depiction of a "countermovement" to look back historically as described by Brinkman (1996:61).
26 Published by the WCC as *Towards Sharing the One Faith*, Faith and Order Paper 173, 1996.
27 It prompts one to ask whether Faith and Order ought to engage in a self-imposed moratorium on the production of paper(s) and ponder the wide convergences already recorded? This is not an idle question if one takes Falconer's account (Falconer 1993) of at least three important studies which gathered dust and became "forgotten paths" since Montreal: the study on the relation between science and religion and the tension between creation and redemption (*God in Nature and History*, 1967); the relation between state and church (*Church and State: Opening a New Ecumenical Discussion*, 1978): and Lukas Vischer's study *Intercession* (1980) on prayer from an ecumenical perspective. All three are still crucial theological themes today which should be addressed by the church in an radically changing environment. However, if your agenda is overloaded and if you have created a production mode of continual cycles, time for reflection on achievements is rare.

> Order wishes to do justice to local churches' contributions, it means that in listening more carefully to the regions, Faith and Order must take serious account of their worship life, and not only their formal theological statements (my emphasis).

If these and other insights from Ditchingham could be implemented, it would usher in an exciting era for the Faith and Order work on liturgy specifically and the reception of their work in general.

In concluding this section, I now leave the arena of material ecumenics and make three brief statements: one from a phenomenological perspective (with reference to Smart), the other two from a methodological perspective (with reference to Schlink and Sykes). All three contribute to an understanding of ecumenical theology as fundamentally doxological and undergird the argument for a constitutive link between worship and reception.

2.2. Ecumenical theology as doxology

First. As a result of his rejection of a common essence in all religions, and because of the fundamentally pluralist nature of religion, Ninian Smart does not attempt a formal definition of religion. In his *The World's Religions*, he instead sketches a seven-dimensional portrait[28] of religions "to make sense and to discern some patterns in the luxurious vegetation of the world's religions" (1989:12). These are the practical/ritual, experiential/emotional, narrative/mythic, doctrinal/philosophical, ethical/legal, social/institutional, and the material dimensions. Phenomenologically, these dimensions overlap, and not all of them are equally well developed in various religious movements. They do, however, argued Smart, enable one to characterise and give a balanced description of the various religions of the world. The argument above is thus deliberately intended to reinstate the practical/ritual with its concomitant experiential[29] dimension as a justified aspect of the profile of Christianity and to guard against a minimalising approach that would enhance the doctrinal/philosophical dimension as the ultimate perspective.

Second. In his influential article, "Die Struktur der dogmatische Aussage als ökumenisches Problem" (1957), reprinted in *Der kommende Christus und die kirchlichen Traditionen*[30] (1961:23-79), the German ecumenical theologian Edmund Schlink began with the observation "that members of the divided churches find it much easier to pray and witness together than to formulate common dogmatic statements" (1967:16; 1961:24). The reason, he argued, was not that prayer and witness were less "theological" than doctrines, but that they "format" the content of the gospel differently. He clarified that the answer to God's call in the gospel is the answer of faith. This answer (*Glaubensaussage*) is expressed in five basic forms: prayer,

---

28 This model has become instructive for discussion about the relation between worship and theology as is evident from the fact that both Wainwright (1980) and Sykes (1984, see below) draw on it to highlight the importance of the practical dimension of Christianity.

29 Drawing mainly on Schleiermacher, I have previously argued for an exploration of the ecumenical potential of religious experience, especially in a divided society such as South Africa. See Naudé (1994).

30 The English translation was published in 1967 as *The coming Christ and the coming Church*. I will quote from this translation with page references to the original German version.

doxology, witness, didache and confession. These elementary faith expressions are to be seen in all their forms as theological expressions, because they say something about God. These theological expressions may then lead to dogmatic expressions (*dogmatische Aussagen*) that are of a twofold nature: doctrine (*Aussage des Dogmas*, narrow meaning as derived from confessions) and, ultimately, dogmatics (*Aussage der Dogmatik*, broader meaning, as in systematic theology).

This morphological exposition and Schlink's extensive discussion (furthered in his *Ökumenische Dogmatik*) complement and deepen the arguments above from at least two perspectives He succeeds in explaining the vital ecumenical value of doxology as one of the *Grundformen* of faith, and he develops a methodologically constitutive link between doxology and ecumenical theology.

How important doxology is in the construction of Schlink's overall theology stems from the fact that he assigned doxology a separate place distinct from prayer as *Grundform* of faith. Based on Claus Westermann's refining of Gunkel's well-known *Formgeschichtliche* classification of the Psalter, Schlink observes that doxology neither expresses prayers on behalf of the person who prays, nor refers to God's deeds in particular; it concerns God for the sake of Godself. He infers from the linguistic structure of doxological passages (such as Is 6:3; 1 Tim 1:17; Rev 4:8, 7:12) that references to the believer and God as second person are often omitted:

> If in the doxology the divine 'Thou' gives way to the 'he', the 'I' of man who utters the doxology is bound to disappear as well ... The basic form of doxology is not, 'God, I praise Thee', but 'Let God be praised'. It is not, 'God, I glorify Thee', but 'God is glorious'" The reason is plain: "God Himself is the one and only subject in doxology. Hence doxological statements appear to be supremely objective.[31]

This is linked to the praise offering of the Old Testament, which is reinterpreted in a priestly context by the letter to the Hebrews (Heb. 13). "The 'I' is sacrificed in doxology. Thus doxology is always sacrifice of praise" (Schlink 1967:22; 1961:28-29, see also Schlink 1983:725-742).

Ecumenical progress is often made in the engagement with others not only as "official representative of church A or B" or "dogmatic tradition Y or Z", but also in the sphere of an engagement with God where the "I" humbly retreats in an "objective" praise of God. To clarify the ecumenical significance of this insight, it is worthwhile to repeat the oft-quoted witness by Yves Congar about the bilateral dialogues[32] by the Group de Dombes in France:

> More than once at the Dombes meetings an impasse has been reached in the discussion, but then after we have prayed together again a way forward has opened up. A level is attained at which the spirit

---

31 Schlink qualifies this "objectivity": "That a person keeps silent about him/herself in doxology is not an 'objectifying' of God but an expression of the full yielding to God. In these expressions God is everything" (1983:65, my translation).

32 There are many cases where worship played an important role in ecumenical dialogues. Another significant example is the way in which the Eastern Orthodox and Oriental Orthodox (Armenian, Coptic, Syrian) churches' dialogue on the difficult dogmatic questions of Christ's two natures and two wills was facilitated by their nearly identical liturgical life (see Nissiotis 1975:223).

of self-justification and rivalry disappears. One of the dangers of intellectual work, and even more of engaging in theological dialogue, is that we become trapped in an attitude of self-assertion. Prayer delivers us from this. For here a third factor, beyond myself and the other, a factor which is Reality and not pure Idea and which is shared by us both, is disclosing possibilities which we have failed to perceive ... As we dispose ourselves humbly in God's presence and before others, we prepare ourselves to receive the illumination and secret anointing of one and the same Holy Spirit. Theologians like to affirm that this Spirit is the same in Christ as in his members: it is he who establishes the unity of the body. And it is also in him that all glory is rendered back to the father: in unitate Spiritus Sancti. *Doxology is at the beginning and at the end of all striving for unity. It also accompanies it at every stage of the way* (Congar 1975:228-229, my emphasis).

Let us turn to the relation between doxology and theology. Schlink's morphology clarifies *Aussagen des Dogmas* and *Aussagen der Dogmatik* as second-order reflections on the primary morphologically diverse *Glaubensaussagen*. Yet, consonant with his 1957 article, he was able to describe theology in his *Dogmatik* as doxology. This was not a relation of identification but a constitutive and methodological relation. It relies on the historical observation[33] that the early creedal expressions in both Testaments and the creeds of the ancient church were doxologically expressed, whence the doctrines and systematic reflection developed. This leads to a methodological consideration:

> If the doxological moment in confessions is one of the most important roots of dogma, it must specifically be attended to in the dogmatic teaching about God. This teaching comes from doxology. Although dogmatics is not itself doxology, it can, as teaching about God, certainly not separate itself from doxology and become autonomous without damaging itself. It should therefore stay close to the structure of doxological expressions." And the ecumenical implication is clear: "Without reclaiming the Grundform of doxology, no shared doctrine of God is possible amongst Christians (Schlink 1983:65, my translation).

The flow from doxology (and the other forms of faith replies) to theology[34] is, in terms of this exposition, now self-evident. It constitutes the very structure of theology.

---

33 See the interesting discussion of how the worship context that is still evident in the Nicene and Apostolic creedal formulations shifted to a more doctrinal approach in Chalcedon, Athanasius and later the *Confessio Augustana*, where the liturgical setting is completely absent, for historical reasons and a shift in mode of expression. "Thus the element of worship and doxology which was included in the original acts of confession, is completely absent from this confession of faith. This explains why the Reformation Confessions were not used in worship but remained operative as 'confessional documents'" (Schlink 1967:36; 1961:39-40).

34 This in no way implies that Schlink was arguing for a one-way movement from *lex orandi* to *lex credendi*. He explicitly warned against an anti-dogmatic attitude in the ecumenical movement, based on the assumption that matters of doctrine can be avoided by a flight into worship and ethics, which leads to a phenomenology of religious experience and a kind of mystagogy wherein liturgical formulas replace dogmatic decisions (see Schlink 1983:53-54; 1961:46).

This reinforces the earlier arguments about the two principles and links with the vision of Faith and Order expressed in Montreal and Louvain that was, apparently, rekindled at Ditchingham.

Third. What is at stake in a discussion on worship and theology and the perennial problem of their interrelation is nothing less than the identity of Christianity. The argument by the Anglican theologian Steven Sykes in his inspirational work *The Identity of Christianity* is that Christianity can best be described as having an externality tradition and an inwardness tradition: "By externality, I mean the tradition which sees the identity of Christianity as lodged in certain external features, especially in the external dimensions we have listed;[35] by the inwardness tradition, I mean the reiterated appeal to that inner, spiritual reality of personal lives being transformed by God" (231). In terms of our discussion, the external forms relates to doctrines and the results of theological reflection, whereas the inward element relates to the "interior movement of the heart represented by the Church's public worship" (280).

Taken by themselves, each tradition is not merely inadequate; it is impossible (in the light of the full reality of what we call Christianity) to express the identity of Christianity via one of these alone. Conversely, it is a gross distortion of the reality of Christianity if any one of these becomes dominant (and we have seen that the temptation is mostly in the direction of a propositional bias). As Christian identity is not a state but a process, it entails a relation of dialectical restlessness between these two dimensions (285). Explicitly formulated, "It is in the *process of interaction* between this inward element and the external forms of Christianity that the identity of Christianity consists" (261, my emphasis).

Whereas Congar and others witnessed how ecumenical theologians engaged in dialogue were, through joint worship, delivered from attitudes of self-assertion and a spirit of self-justification, Sykes (1984:280-285) has made a statement about theologians' position in general.[36] If one applies this to our present discussion about reception and worship, one must heed the crucial point that the possible tyrannical use of intellectual power by ecumenical theologians, who assume that the reality of Christianity as a whole is subsumed under its intellectual content, can only be reined in if theologians actively participate in communal worship. This is where theology is not in charge but is a humble participant and where, in fact, theologians are educated by the Christian community.

However, which community's worship is cardinal for reception? Without denying the positive witnesses about worship and "internal" reception emanating from ecumenical encounters, the ecumenical movement is not the church. Part of the

---

35 Sykes describes the external features on the basis of John Henry Newman's threefold distinction between the dogmatic, devotional and practical areas which constitute Christianity "all at once", with explicit reference to the seven-dimensional model of Ninian Smart (27-28). Although Sykes uses the word "ritual" in a number of different (conflicting?) ways (see pages 278-283), it is clear that the ritual element of Christianity forms part of the externality tradition, because of its reliance on texts. This is slightly different from my definition above. Worship is consistently linked to the inwardness dimension, inter alia, because of its inclusion of nonverbal elements.

36 Sykes' discussion of the position of theologians – especially their potential to misuse their intellectually privileged position – is a fascinating "sub-plot to the central theme" (7) of his *The Identity of Christianity* (1984).

problem in the reception of ecumenical texts is the perception that the ecumenical movement has inadvertently acquired the status of an autonomous tradition. It employs its own theologians, has developed a set of technical theological terms unique to itself, maps itself via a dazzling array of references which serve as a kind of theological geography – and Geneva is a metaphor which functions on a par with Rome, Canterbury, and others as centre of authority[37].

The argument for reception via worship thus extends beyond the worship at ecumenical meetings. That is the easier step. "External" reception will only be effected if the ecumenical movement operates from the realisation that the power to preserve the identity of Christianity belongs properly to the church community as a whole. Here, Faith and Order is in an extremely awkward position. No internal reform will increase reception of its work unless it relativises itself in the light of a radical understanding of the etymological sense of *leitourgia* as public service. The path plotted thirty-five years ago is still the right one: "If it is in *leitourgia* that the church is to find fulfilment of its life, then it is essential that we let *leitourgia* speak for itself".[38]

BIBLIOGRAPHY

Allen, H.T. 1991. "Common liturgical texts". In *Dictionary of the ecumenical movement*. Geneva: WCC, pp. 622-623.

Assmann, A. 1990. "Vom Gewicht des Ungesagten". In Huber, Petzold, Sundermeier (Hrsg.), pp. 13-18.

Assmann, J. 1992. *Das kulturelle Gedächtnis: Schrift, Erinnerung und politische Identität in frühen Hochkulturen*. München: C.H. Beck.

Beinert W. & Fischer, H (Hrsg.) 1989. *Verständigung auf dem Prüfstand. Zum Problem von Rezeption und Verbindlichkeit oekumenischer Texte*. Berlin: Wichern Verlag.

Beinert, W (Hrsg.) 1991. *Glaube als Zustimmung. Zur Interpretation kirchlicher Rezeptionsvorgänge*. Freiburg: Herder.

Berger, T. 1991a. "Liturgical movement". In *Dictionary of the ecumenical movement*. Geneva: WCC, pp. 616-618.

---

37 After writing this essay, I found some welcome support in a recent article by Dietrich Ritschl (1996:428-429). He analysed the major ecumenical themes, then asked: "Geht von Genf eine autonome Theologie aus?" – obviously a question which surpasses mere pragmatics. It has direct bearing on one's understanding of the relation between "ecumenical" and "theology" on the one hand and the nature of the link between church and theology on the other. Ritschl has constantly opted for an integral ecumenical theology with no supra-confessional character such as a kind of "Übertheologie"(see Ritschl 1994:7).

38 I have limited the scope of this article to the "Ditchingham question". A general discussion of reception and worship could include at least three further important elements not considered here. First is the exciting concept of "the liturgy after the Liturgy" as an expression of the vital link between the order of liturgy (specifically the Eucharist) and the order of life (see Ion Bria 1987 for discussion and references). Second is the link between liturgy and ethics. For views from within the WCC, see Niles (1992); for an excellent discussion of a wide range of works by, for example, Hauerwas, Gustafson, Huber, Tödt, Wainwright and Woltersdorff, see Smit (1997). Third might be the hitherto underestimated value of a "spirituality of reception".

Berger, T. 1991b. "Worship in the ecumenical movement". In *Dictionary of the ecumenical movement*. Geneva: WCC, pp. 1107-1112.

Best, T.F. 1993. "The issues beyond the issues". *The Ecumenical Review* Vol. 45, pp. 55-65.

Best, T.F. & Gassmann, G (eds.) 1994. *On the way to fuller koinonia*. Geneva: WCC.

Best, T.F. & Heller, D (eds.) 1995. *So we believe, so we pray. Towards koinonia in worship*. München: Kaiser.

Bria, I. 1987. "The liturgy after the liturgy". In M. Thurian & G. Wainwright (eds.), pp. 213-221.

Brinkmann, M.E. 1996. *Progress in unity. Fifty years of theology within the WCC: 1945-1995*. Louvain: Peters Press.

Cohen, R. (ed.) 1974. *New directions in literary history*. London: Johns Hopkins University Press.

Congar, Y. 1972. "La 'réception' comme réalité ecclésiologique". *RSPhTh* Vol. 56, pp. 369-403.

Congar, Y. 1975. "Common prayer". In Ehrenstrom and Gassmann (eds.), pp. 226-229.

De Villiers, D.E. (ed.) 1997. *Scriptura 62.* Christian Ethics in South Africa.

Ehrenstrom, N. & Gassmann, G (eds.) 1975. *Confessions in dialogue. A survey of bilateral conversations among world confessional families 1959-1974*. Geneva: WCC.

Falconer, A.D. 1993. "En route to Santiago". *The Ecumenical Review* 45, pp. 44-54.

Finnegan, R. 1990. "What is orality – if anything?". *Byzantine and Modern Greek Studies* Vol. 14, pp. 130-149.

Fischer, H. 1989. "Rezeption in ihre Bedeutung für Leben und Lehre der Kirche". In W. Beinart & H. Fischer (Hrsg.), pp. 35-57.

Frawley, W. (ed.) 1982. *Linguistics and literacy*. New York: Plenum.

Gassmann, G. 1974. "Rezeption im ökumenischen Kontext". *ÖR* Vol. 26, pp. 314-327.

Gassmann, G. 1984. "Die Rezeption der Dialoge". *ÖR* Vol. 33, pp. 357-368.

Gassmann, G. 1993. *Documentary history of Faith and Order 1963-1993*. Geneva: WCC.

Gros, J. (ed.) 1984. *The search for visible unity*. New York: Pilgrim's Press.

Guy, J. 1991. "Literacy and literature". In E. Sienaert (ed.), pp. 395-413.

Halverson, J. 1994. "Oral and written gospel: A critique of Werner Kelber". *New Test. Studies* Vol. 40, pp. 180-195.

Harakas, S.S. 1991. "Must God remain Greek?" *The Ecumenical Review* Vol. 43, pp. 194-199.

Harling, P. (ed.) 1995. *Worshipping ecumenically. Orders of service from global meetings with suggestions for local use*. Geneva: WCC.

Harling, P. 1995. "The liturgy of the world: Ecumenical worship with all senses". In P. Harling (ed.), pp. 1-26

Hill, C. & Yarnold, E. (eds.) 1994. *Anglicans and Roman Catholics: The search for unity*. London: Society for Promoting Christian Unity.

Hood, R.E. 1990. *Must God remain Greek? Afro-cultures and God-talk*. Minneapolis: Fortress Press.

Houtepen, A. 1983. "Reception, Tradition, Communion. In M. Thurian (ed.) *Ecumenical perspectives on BEM*. Geneva: WCC.

Houtepen, A. 1990. "Ökumenische Hermeneutik. Auf der Suche nach Kriterien der Kohaerenz im Christentum". *ÖR* Vol. 3, pp. 279-296.

Houtepen, A. 1991. "Reception". In *Dictionary of the ecumenical movement*. Geneva: WCC, pp. 844-845.

Huber, W. & Petzold, E. & Sundermeier, T. (Hrsg.) 1990. *Implizite Axiome. Tiefenstruktur des Denkens und Handelns*. München: Kaiser.

Jakobson, R. 1960. "Linguistics and poetics". In R.T. Sebeok (ed.) *Style in language*. Cambridge MA: MIT Press, pp. 350-377.

Japp, U. 1977. *Hermeneutik: der theoretishe Diskurs, die Literatur und die Konstruktion ihres Zusammenhanges in den philologischen Wissenschaften*. München: Fink.

Jauss, H.R. 1974. "Literary history as challenge to literary theory". In R. Cohen (ed.), pp. 11-41.

Kilmartin, E.J. 1984. "Reception in history: An ecclesiological phenomenon and its significance". In J. Gros (ed.), pp. 34-54.

Kuhn, U. 1983. "Reception – an imperative and an opportunity". In M. Thurian (ed.), pp. 163-174.

Lategan, B. & Vorster, W. 1985. *Text and reality: aspects of reference in Biblical texts*. Philadelphia: Fortress Press.

Lathrop, G. 1995. "Knowing something a little: On the role of the *lex orandi* in the search for christian unity". In Best & Heller (eds.), pp. 39-48.

Limouris, G. 1991. "Historical background to apostolic faith today". In *Confessing the one faith*, pp. 105-111.

Loewe, H. 1988. "Die Kirchen vor der Aufgabe der Rezeption von Ergebnissen ökumenischer Gespräche und Verhandlungen. In J. Rohls & G. Wenz (eds.), pp. 637-651.

Lossky, N (ed.) 1991. *Dictionary of the ecumenical movement*. Geneva: WCC Publications.

Martin, H.J. 1994. *The history and power of writing*. Chicago: University of Chicago Press.

May, J. 1988. "Integral ecumenism". *Journal of Ecumenical Studies* Vol. 25, pp. 573-591.

Meyendorff, P. 1991. "Liturgy". In *Dictionary of the ecumenical movement*, pp. 623-626.

Mouton, J. & B. Lategan, B (eds.) 1994. *The relevance of theology for the 1990s*. HSRC: Pretoria.

Naudé, P.J. 1993. "Towards a local Zionist theology?" *Scriptura* Vol. 45, pp. 29-46.

Naudé, P.J. 1994. "Doxology and praxis: The ecumenical significance of religious experience in a South Africa of the 1990's". In J. Mouton & B. Lategan B (eds.), pp. 421-434.

Naudé, P.J. 1996. *Is God hovering above the nineteenth floor? Doing theology in a post-disciplinary context*. Inaugural address D38. Port Elizabeth: University of Port Elizabeth.

Naudé, P.J. 1996b. "Theology with a new voice? The case for an oral theology in the South African context". *JTSA* Vol. 94, pp. 18-31.

Naudé, P.J. 1997a. "Die Belharstryd in ekumeniese perspektief". *NGTT* Vol. xxxviii, No. 3, pp. 226-243.

Niles, D.P. (ed.) 1992. *Between the flood and the rainbow*. Geneva: WCC.

Nissiotis, N.A. 1975. "A worshipping ecumenical movement". In Ehrenstrom & Gassmann (eds.), pp. 221-224.

Ritschl, D. 1996. "Der Richtwert ökumenischer 'Grossthemen' und das Wachteramt des DOSTA". ÖR Vol. 45, No. 4, pp. 415-431.

Raiser, C. 1996. "Hermeneutik der Einheit". ÖR Vol. 45, pp. 401-414.

Ringbom, H. (ed.) 1975. *Style and text. Studies presented to NE Enkivst*. Stockholm: Spraaktoerlaget Skriptor.

Rodger, P.C. & Vischer, L. 1964. *The fourth world conference on Faith and Order* (Montreal 1963). London: SCM.

Rohls, J. & Wenz, G. (eds.) 1988. *Vernunft des Glaubens. Wissenschaftliche Theologie und kirchliche Lehre* (FS W Pannenberg). Gottingen: Vandenhoeck & Ruprecht.

Rusch, W.G. 1988. *Rezeption. Eine ökumenische Chance*. Stuttgart: Kreuz.

Saliers, D.E. 1994. *Worship as theology. Foretaste of divine glory*. Nashville TE: Abingdon.

Schlink, E. 1961. *Der kommende Christus und die kirchlichen Traditionen*. Göttingen: Vandenhoeck und Ruprecht (English translation: see Schlink 1967).

Schlink, E. 1967. *The coming Christ and the coming church*. Edinburgh: Oliver and Boyd. (German original: see Schlink 1961)

Schlink, E. 1983. *Ökumenische Dogmatik*. Göttingen: Vandenhoeck und Ruprecht.

Schmidt, S.J. 1975. "Reception and interpretation of written texts as problems of a rational theory of literary communication". In H. Ringbom (ed.), pp. 339-408.

Sienaert, E. (ed.) 1991. *Oral tradition and innovation: new wine in old bottles?: Selected conference papers*. Durban: University of Natal.

Smart, N. 1989. *The world's religions*. London: SCM.

Smit, D.J. 1991. "Order". In *Dictionary of the ecumenical movement*. Geneva: WCC, pp. 747-750.

Smit, D.J. 1997. "Liturgy and life? On the importance of worship for Christian ethics". In D. E. de Villiers (ed.), pp. 259-280.

Song, C. (ed.) 1976. *Giving account of the hope today*. Geneva: WCC.

Song, C. (ed.) 1978. *Giving account of the hope together*. Geneva: WCC.

Sundermeier, T. 1988. *Nur gemeinsam koennen wir leben. Das Menschenbild schwarzafrikanischer Religionen*. Gütersloh: Gütersloh Verlag.

Sundermeier, T. 1996. *Den Fremden verstehen. Eine praktische Hermeneutik*. Göttingen: Vandenhoeck und Ruprecht

Sykes, S.W. 1984. *The identity of Christianity. Theologians and the essence of Christianity from Schleiermacher to Barth*. London: SPCK.

Tannen, D. 1982. "The myth of orality and literacy". In W. Frawley (ed.), pp. 37-50.

Tanner, M. 1994. "The tasks of the world conference in the perspective of the future". In Best & Gassmann (eds.), pp. 19-28.

Thiel, J.E. 1991. *Imagination and Authority. Theological authorship in modern tradition*. Minneapolis: Fortress Press.

Thurian, M. (ed.) 1983. *Ecumenical perspectives on the BEM*. Geneva: WCC.

Thurian, M. & G. Wainwright, G. (eds.) 1987. *Baptism and Eucharist. Ecumenical convergence in celebration*. Geneva: WCC.

Vischer, L. 1984. "The process of 'reception' in the ecumenical movement". *Mid-Stream* Vol. 23, pp. 221-233.

Wainwright, G. 1980. *Doxology. The praise of God in worship, doctrine and life*. London: Epworth.

Wainwright, G. 1984. "Reception of 'Baptism, Eucharist, and Ministry' and the apostolic faith study". In J. Gros (ed.), pp. 71-82.

Wainwright, G 1991. "Lex orandi, lex credendi". In *Dictionary of the ecumenical movement*. Geneva: WCC, pp. 600-604.

WCC. 1991a. *Confessing the one faith*. Geneva: WCC.

WCC. 1991b. *Signs of the Spirit. Official report. Seventh Assembly*. Geneva: WCC.

WCC. 1996. *Towards sharing the one faith. A study guide for discussion groups*. Geneva: WCC.

1.3 DOXOLOGY AND PRAXIS

The ecumenical significance of religious experience in South Africa of the 1990s[1]

Events in recent months prove that our own society is in a crucial transitional phrase. A contribution to the moulding of a new society lies, *inter alia*, in the rethinking of our theological enterprises.

The aim of this paper is to highlight some implications for (systematic) theology should it wish to facilitate the ecumenical potential of religious experience in the process of unifying Christians in South Africa during the next few years. I limit the discussion to positive and communal (see William James's classic on individual religious experiences) religious experiences within a specific Christian context (see Prozesky 1987 for negative experiences). The intention is that the observations below should not only be about experiences – I hope that they might lead us back to a form of mutual spirituality. Each of the three main sections is introduced by a thesis which is then motivated with reference to the history of Western theology (especially Schleiermacher and Schlink) and aspects of a South African theology.

> *Thesis 1: The ecumenical potential of religious experience will only be realised if the overt recourse to experience as a reaction against rationalism-idealism is complemented by the natural development of theology from an experiential community.*

The first part of the thesis has a direct bearing on Western theology in the post-Enlightenment period (strongly, perhaps too strongly, represented by the vast majority of the theologians in South Africa, including myself), whereas the second part refers to the development of (a poorly represented) African theology.

It would be impossible to discuss all the different traditions of European theology represented in South Africa. My aim is to identify a certain (experiential) trend in post-Enlightenment European theology which might be applicable to a broad spectrum of theological orientations.

No discussion of experience in Western theology can afford to ignore the profound influence of the German philosopher, Immanuel Kant. As the epitome of the Enlightenment, his philosophy – as fundamentally rational philosophy – discredited a reputable appeal to experience in at least two ways.

First: In the first of his critical works, *Kritik der reinen Vernunft* (1781), Kant succeeded in proving the epistemological possibility of transcendental knowledge based on the categories of pure reason. The *a priori* formulation of synthetic judgements meant that, for the first time, pure knowledge was possible without recourse to empirical experience.

Second: In the establishment of his ethical ideas (see his *Grundlegung zur Metaphysik der Sitten* published in 1785 and *Kritik der praktischen Vernunft* published in 1788), Kant

---

[1] This essay was first published in 1994 in Mouton J. (ed.) *The relevance of theology in South Africa in the 1990s*. HSRC: Pretoria, pp. 421-434.

likewise emphasised the notion that the formulation of the categorical imperative (Werke 6:1ff) is attained without any recourse to experience. Any moral prescription that relies on empirical grounds may be a practical rule, but can never be a moral law (Werke 6:13). Duty and morality are derived from the idea of a will which is determined by *a priori* reason, i.e. *vor aller Erfahrung*. This implies that all moral ideas originate *völlig a priori in der Vernunft* (see Werke 9:127-129).

For theology it is important to note that religion and the idea of God are a function of morality insofar as the categorical imperative is endowed with the authority of "will of God". The three regulative ideas (freedom, immortality and God), which serve as postulates of practical reason, are fully embedded within the *a priori* character of morality. Kant thus rightly speaks about *Die Religion innerhalb der Grenzen der blossen Vernunft* (title of his first post-critical work dated 1793; see Kant 1978) – religion lies within the boundaries of pure reason.

One reference would suffice to illustrate how Kant rejects experience as basis for the Christian faith.

In his discussion of the catholicity of the church, Kant distinguishes between "historical faith" and "pure religious faith". The first has only limited value for the church, because of its limited validity (*Gültigkeit*) and its utter contingency (*Zufälligkeit*). And the reason for this? Because historical faith is based on revelation as experience (*Offenbarung als Erfahrung*)! The church as general (catholic) church should rather be seen in relation to pure religious faith (*reine Religionsglaube*). The essential character of such a faith is precisely that it is grounded in pure reason! (Kant 1978:126).

One could thus argue that Kant "dis-reputed" experience in both his epistemology and in the founding of his morality. And it is especially this last aspect which so profoundly influenced the further development of theology in Europe. Broadly speaking, the Kantian heritage left European theology with only two options: either to accept the terms set by a rationalistic approach, or to pave the way for genuine knowledge about God in a completely different fashion.

The latter option, initiated by especially Friedrich Schleiermacher (see below), set in motion a strong tradition of theology which takes its point of departure in some form of human experience. These Western theologies may all be seen as a "reaction" to the rationalistic tendencies which marked the birth of the Enlightenment. Two examples – one from a Protestant (Schleiermacher) and the other from a Catholic (Rahner) background – are briefly explained as illustration of this point.

It is generally accepted that Schleiermacher's *The Christian Faith* is "the first truly systematic account of Protestant theology since Calvin's Institutes" (Clements 1987:43; see Heron 1980:22-23; Holleman 1988). Although it is dangerous to draw major theological conclusions from biographical details, there is broad consensus that Schleiermacher was profoundly influenced by two movements: theological pietism (see his relation with the Hernhutters) and philosophical Romanticism (see his relationship with Friedrich Schlegel) (Clements 1987:11-19).

The important point is that both these movements may be viewed as *counter-currents* to the Enlightenment. Schleiermacher's theology was consequently without doubt an enterprise directed *gegen den kalten Rationalismus der Aufklärung* (Gadamer 1972:59;

see Heron 1980:24). And how did Schleiermacher accomplish such a counter-theology? For the purpose of our discussion two remarks are made in this regard.

Schleiermacher firstly rejected the notion that knowledge about God "arise(s) exclusively in the moral sphere" (Schleiermacher in Clements 1987:93). And secondly, he "located" such knowledge in contemplative affection and piety as "sense for the infinite" (Schleiermacher in Clements 1987:83, 85). A close reading of especially his second speech in *On Religion* and extracts from *The Christian Faith* (see Clements 1987:76-95, 99-107) reveals that the essence of his reaction against rationalism lies in the recourse to religious experience as the foundation and basis of all other experience.

Schleiermacher's theology is thus no less anthropocentric than Kant's epistemological construction, but whereas the latter rejects human experience as too contingent for knowledge about morality and God, the former grounds his entire theology precisely on the "feeling of being utterly dependent" (Clements 1987:99; see Heron 1980:25-26).

Let us turn to a second example as further confirmation of the thesis that a theological reaction to rationalism is often marked by an emphasis on human experience as religious experience:

Apart from the so-called Catholic Tübinger Schule, the neo-scholastic theology of 1850-1930 showed signs of isolation with regards to the philosophy of the Enlightenment by retaining the *Theologie der Vorzeit* (Metz 1984:16-17). The essence of the challenge facing Catholic theology since the 1930s was to develop a theology "which retains the sense of things medieval in a mode which is fully aware of the Kantian and the Enlightenment temper" (Johns 1976:129).

It is within this context that Rahner developed his transcendental-anthropological theology (see Rahner 1969:41-42 for this relationship with Kant). It is a *transcendental* theology because Rahner emphasises the preconditions for possible knowledge about God's revelation. And it is *anthropological* insofar as this knowledge is ontologically linked to the understanding of human existence. The essential character of man's spirit is the *absolute Offenheit für Sein überhaupt* (1969:55), but, in the light of God as Absolute Being, this "openness" constitutes an ontological *Offenheit auf Gott* (1969:133).

The paradoxical implication is that Rahner's attempt to take the Kantian heritage seriously leads him back to an analysis of human existence where human experience is the transcendental experience of God: knowledge of God lies in the knowledge of human existence as *Vorgriff auf Gott* (Metz 1984:61).

Although from a completely different angle than Schleiermacher, the theological "reaction" to Kantian rationalism is formulated in terms of human existence with its corollary of experience as religious experience (*transzendentale Erfahrung Gottes*, see *Schriften zur Theologie* V1:293). Both theologians, however, illustrate that a great deal of post-Enlightenment theology in Europe might be explained in terms of recourse to some form of religious experience in the light of the rationalistic strain established by Kant. This includes, for example, influential theologians such as Otto, Tillich and Bultmann.

The position of *South African Black Theology* is quite interesting at this point: that it is developed from the experience of oppressed and exploited black people is a truism. The crucial question is how this experience is being interpreted.

During the first phase of its development in the early 1970s South African black theology stood firmly within the Black Consciousness tradition, with its emphasis on race analysis as a basic socio-political tool. Theological attempts had an introductory character: they were "polemic and definitional with some passing allusions to method" (Motlhabi 1986:xiii).

How did a methodological "maturity" enter the interpretation of oppression? The answer is clear: "The introduction of Marxist analysis introduces an element in method. To this extent and to the extent that there will be progress in black theological reflection once more, we may say that phase two of black theology in this country has begun" (Mothlabi 1986:xiv-xv).

This more mature phase in black liberation theology was initiated by a very specific paradigm switch: in the "conflict between Hegelian Idealism and its Marxian rebuttal, which could be called Realism" (i.e. materialism), a definite choice for the latter took place. Sebidi states further: "We, therefore, wish to suggest that there seems to be a very close relationship between the idealist approach and the race-analysis paradigm, on the one hand, and the materialist approach and the class-analysis paradigm, on the other hand" (Sebidi 1986:23,24).

Although the concept of "racial capitalism" is sometimes employed to make room for both approaches, it clearly emerges from the essays in *The unquestionable right to be free* that Black theologians embraced class analysis as primary analytical instrument of history and present-day society. This is confirmed by the *Kairos document* which utilises structural Marxism in its social portrayal of the South African situation.

It is not my present concern to comment on this choice either positively or negatively. What is important in the present discussion is that the position of most contemporary black liberation theologians in South African confirms the thesis above: *the interpretation of experience related to the oppression and exploitation of black people takes places within a post-Enlightenment, European framework*. The theological rejection of exploitation mainly originates as a reaction against the rationalistic-idealistic tendencies inherent in Kantian and Hegelian philosophy. In this respect there is perhaps an unexpectedly close relationship between the experiential theologies in Western Europe (on the one hand) and liberation theologies in Latin America and South Africa (on the other).

If we wish to explore the full ecumenical potential of religious experience in the development of a truly South African theology, we need to take a closer look at the contribution from African theology in this regard. Just as European and liberation theologies encompass a large variety of theological approaches, sub-Saharan African theology includes a variety of approaches. In distinction to a socio-economic or socio-political approach which has very close ties with Black Theology, I use the term in a religio-cultural sense. It refers to "an attempt to verbalise African reflection about Divinity (do theology) from the perspective of African grassroots background and culture" (Setiloane 1986:35).

At this stage it is important to note that African theology does not "react" to a preceding form of rationality to "take recourse" to religious experience as constitutive element of such a theology. The difference between the interpretation of experience in the theologies referred to above and African theology in the sense used here is that the latter must be seen in a pre- or rather non-Enlightenment context. It is obvious that this does not at all imply a derogatory sense of "primitive" or "quasi-rational".

Although open to sentimentality and idealisation, it still holds true that much of African theology stems from an experiential religio-mythical world view. I think it was Mbiti who stated: I am religious, therefore I am! For the African, therefore, "to live is to be caught up in the religious drama. This is fundamental, for it means that man lives a religious universe" (Mbiti 1974:15-16). Stanley Mogoba refers to the fact that there is no appropriate word for "religion" in many African vernaculars, "because all of life is religion" (Mogoba 1985:6). How does this determine what is usually referred to as "spirituality"?

The very nature of African spirituality has as its principal feature "experiencing rather than formulating and expressing religion in set terms" (Setiloane 1986:30). The AACC conference in Lusaka (1973) describes African theology as based on biblical faith and "expressed in the categories of thought which arise out of the philosophy and world view of Africans" (see Setiloane 1986:34), and the latter is fundamentally experiential in nature.

This is confirmed in the comprehensive account of African philosophy by Ruch and Anyanwu (1984): "So, we must commence the study of African Philosophy by examining the *meaning of experience* ... (84, my emphasis). And to even think of a detachment between religion and experience (77-78), is to misunderstand the cultural world of total integration" ("unitary view of reality", 98) in which experience addresses itself "to the totality of a person's faculty" (87).

This implies that African theology, as a rational (i.e. interpretative) expression of the gospel in terms of specific cultural thought forms, will in essence be an experiential theology. Its emphasis on religious experience will be a natural development of an integrated religious experience and not primarily a reaction against a rationalistic-idealistic heritage.

The distinct contribution of this kind of theology is still at a very early stage of development in South Africa. Our theological scene has been dominated by Western and liberation theologies. A truly ecumenical South African theology, based on religious experiences, will have to allow African spirituality to set the "atmosphere" in which theology is done.

Thesis 2: The emphasis on experience in theology opens the possibility to reclaim the nature of systematic theology as doxology. Set in this "genre", theology loses most of its divisive attributes and contributes to the establishment of a catholic community of believers.

To illustrate the second thesis, it is necessary to reinterpret Schleiermacher's concept of the construction of theology to include a constitutive doxological element.

The structure of his theological enterprise is aptly described in his notion that "Christian doctrines are accounts of the Christian religious affections set forth in speech" (Schleiermacher in Clements 1987:134). For the sake of the present argument, attention is directed at the last section of the statement, i.e. "set forth in speech".

The important point which emerges is that religious emotions reach the point where "they manifest themselves outwardly". These expressions may take on different forms ranging from bodily gestures to sacred signs and symbolic acts (Clements 1987:134). In this regard speech plays a vital role both as a form of "inward thought" and as mode of outward (public) expression.

The Christological inclination of Schleiermacher's theology is evident from the fact that the self-communication by speech of Jesus' self-consciousness forms the very foundation of all other expressions of Christian experience. The latter is structured in three types of speech, namely poetic, rhetorical and didactic, all of which complement one another in the expression of the underlying religious self-consciousness (Clements 1987:134-135). The formulation of doctrine is thus a secondary act which takes place in terms of the three expressive forms of speech.

Although Schleiermacher himself does not (as far as I could ascertain) relate his description explicitly to "doxology", I wish to state the case that his reference to a "poetic" type of speech may be interpreted as such.

If the religious self-consciousness is precisely God-consciousness, if the pious affection is a revelation of the infinite in the finite, then the poetic form of speech is the expression (logos) of the glory (*doksa*) of God (doxology). The spontaneous structure of doxological passages in Scripture (see below) brings Schleiermacher's poetic form very close to the realm of doxology: "For when anyone finds himself in a state of unusually exalted religious self-consciousness, he will feel himself called to poetic description, as that which proceeds from the state most directly" (Schleiermacher in Clements 1987:136).

This poetic expression is then a constitutive element in the formulation of a *Glaubenssatz* (tenet of faith = doctrine), which in turn forms the content of kerygmatic and confessional statements. Schleiermacher's rediscovery of religious experience as constitutive for theology has therefore a fundamental influence on the constructive process which leads to "doctrine" and dogmatics.

It is clear that the doxological character of dogmatics (even if it is considered as a historical discipline) is guaranteed by the very poetic expression of religious experience. As Schleiermacher himself writes: *"it is clear that the figurative language which is always poetic in its nature, had the most decided influence upon the dogmatic language, and always preceded its development"* (Clements 1987:138, my emphasis).

In the light of this exposition, one may characterise Schleiermacher's theology as doxological without, I believe, doing an injustice to his own systematic-theological enterprise. Let us now turn to another example which illustrates the same point in a slightly different fashion.

From his experience in the ecumenical movement the German theologian Edmund Schlink observed that members from different churches pray and witness together much more easily than they formulate common dogmatic statements. One of the reasons for this is a reduction of the manifold morphological structures (*Grundformen*) underlying dogmatic statements to only one, namely formulae of doctrine (*Lehraussagen*).

It is thus for Schlink of crucial importance to understand the structure of dogmatic assertions from their basic forms. His argument, set out in his influential article, *Die*

Struktur de dogmatische Aussage als ökumenisches Problem (1957), is important for our discussion and is summarised below.

The answer to God's call to us in the gospel of Jesus Christ is that of faith. And this answer (*Glaubensaussage*) is expressed in five different basic forms: prayer, witness, doxology, didache and confession. The content of the gospel can only be expressed by all these forms collectively and they constitute the nature of dogmas (*Aussage des Dogmas*) and ultimately dogmatics/systematic theology (*Aussage der Dogmatik*).

One could thus say that dogmatics as second-order reflection relies on the underlying faith-expressions of which doxology is an important one. There are at least two characteristics of doxology which makes a constitutive relation with dogmatics possible and necessary.

First, doxology has God and the divine reality at its centre – one does not so much pray to God as that one is taken up in the praise of God with complete self-surrender. Doxology presupposes the offering of the self as a praise offering: "Das Ich wird in Doxologie zum Opfer gebracht. Doxologie ist immer zugleich Lobopfer" (Schlink 1957:256). This implies the essential theological character of doxology in its determination of dogmatics where the believing I interprets his/her faith.

Second, the very expression of doxological statements reveals a certain objectivity due to the fact that it is often set in specific kerygmatic formulae where the reference to the believer(s) is omitted. The basic form of doxology is not "God, I (we) praise thee", but "God be praised" (255, see examples of relevant Scriptural passages such as Is. 6:3, Rom. 11:33-36, 1 Tim. 1:17). This has the important implication that doxological expressions are closely related to liturgy and teaching, which are the roots of creedal formulations/dogmas and ultimately of dogmatics.

Instead of the theoretical misuse of dogmatics, which instigates the shift from praise to God as "last sayings" to theoretical premises about God as "first saying", systematic theology should honour doxology as one of its constitutive *Grundformen*. Why? Because theological statements, although themselves statements-about-experience (Schlink 1957:272), should never deny their own source in the *Situation des Betroffenseins* (270), where salvation is experienced and doxologically expressed.

This view of dogmatic statements is but a formalising of a crucial aspect of how "doctrine" was developed in earliest Christianity. The insights gained from form and tradition criticism point to the fact that the *Sitz im Leben* of many New Testament writings is related to preaching, worship and cathechesis.

In his excellent book *Doxology* (1980) Geoffrey Wainwright develops this into a systematic theology on the basis of *lex orandi, lex credendi* (1980:161, 218ff, 251ff). The role of worship in the development of doctrine is evident in, for example, the recognition of Christ's divinity (see Chapter 2); the Trinitarian doctrine based on the threefold pattern of baptism (see Chapter 3) and the Marian dogmas which were formulated on the basis of popular devotion. "In all three cases, worship practice was in advance of doctrinal decision" (Wainwright 1980:250).

Why is this so important in the South African context? Because it does point to at least one escape route from the ecumenical deadlock in a divided country. I shall return to the ideological-political nature of the problem below. In this context, one has to call for a return to communal doxology – not to fall into the trap of escapism, but precisely to open up new possibilities of ecumenical confessions and actions. Meeting one another in the liturgical context where "objective" doxology is practised, instead of meeting formally as representatives of A or B with the aim of formulating joint statements, might be the kind of experience which leads to an ecumenical breakthrough.

That this is a real possibility in South Africa emerges from two points (chosen at random).

Firstly, one should realise that African theology has a tremendous potential to "bring back the joy into Christianity – and I don't mean only into black Christianity, but all Christianity", because of its richness of symbolism and celebration (Mogoba 1985:9). Participation in and contribution to the innate spirituality of African theology may foster the fundamental affirmation that "we are Africans". Of course, this does not imply a monotonous uniformity of worship, "but it goes a long way if first of all, you feel affirmed and you know that you are an African" (Mogoba 1985:16).

Secondly, the publication of John de Gruchy's book of meditations, reflections and prayers (doxology!), *Cry Justice!* (1986), is an encouraging sign. Despite the many different Christian traditions in South Africa, "they all converge in enabling true worship and discipleship" and thus contribute to "unify" instead of divide.

Perhaps all of us – and especially church leaders and theologians – should again heed the well-known evangelical motto: A family that prays together, stays together. With an apology to Harvey Cox: It is in the dance that we shall not only meet God, but also one another.

Translated into theological terms: theologians who construct their theologies from shared doxological experience stand a good chance of contributing to the normalisation of ecumenical and inter-personal relations in South Africa.

Thesis 3: The emphasis on experience in theology is itself constitutive of a shift to the primacy of praxis. This brings the problem of "exclusive" experiential paradigms to the core of the ecumenical debate and necessitates an adapted theological agenda in South Africa.

To a certain extent this thesis is just an elaboration of the second, but its formulation leaves room for important insights not explicit in the second thesis. Concerning the first section of this thesis, I have extensively defended the view that the primary connotation of the term "praxis" is not so much "action", but experience-as-basis-for-action-and-reflection (see Naudé 1987:120-130). A theology constructed from the underlying faith-experience is in this sense a "praxis-theology"; a shift to experience is itself a shift to praxis.

This has already been illustrated by two aspects of Schleiermacher's theology. He (firstly) explicitly states that experience (i.e. praxis) always precedes dogma/dogmatics. And (secondly) his structuring of theology as discipline shows strong resemblances with other theologies which overtly claim to be "praxis-theologies" (see Clements 1987:139, 46).

The second part of this thesis brings important epistemological questions to the fore. One should start with the truism, easily overlooked, that there is no such thing as pure or un-interpreted experience. Experiences are always interpreted, but there are obviously different degrees of interpretation (Smart 1978:14). "This mediated aspect of all our experience seems an inescapable feature of any epistemological inquiry … which has to be properly acknowledged if our investigation of experience … is to get far" (Katz 1978:26).

If I understand it correctly, this is the point on which much (existential) phenomenology rests. The call *Zurück zu den Sachen selbst!* (Husserl), is a call to return to the "original" experience of the world. Phenomenology is aimed at *de restituer a l'experience son poids ontologique* (Luijpen 1969:113-114). The implicit pre-reflective consciousness always precedes the explicit reflection, e.g. consciousness of Z is preceded by consciousness (of) Z or Z-consciousness. The moment of irréfléchi is thus the constant (mostly unnoticed) ontological source of knowledge.

A vital implication of this phenomenology of knowledge is what one may call the anticipatory element of all experience. The forms of consciousness which are brought into a situation will determine the parameters of what will be experienced, and rule out in advance what is "inexperiencable" in the given, concrete context. In a very real sense, then, all experience is fundamentally *contextual* experience.

Applied to theology, it follows that radically different and politically opposing experiential contexts within the boundaries of one region lead to different theologies. This may enrich the theological scene with a variety of local theologies (see Schreiter 1984), but the "God" of Soweto and the "God" of Sandton may also be so different that ecumenical dialogue is inhibited. The forms of consciousness underlying the religious experiences which lead to the two theologies are so different that it leads to the "inexperiencability" of two entities.

On a structural level the respective "worlds" that inform different experiences are not only conceptually (or pre-conceptually) different, but to a great extent physically exclusive. The "ultimates" which underlie a normative system often conflict with "vital interests" which are institutionally legitimised in terms of an existing ideology (see Nürnberger 1988:137ff). The pre-consciousness brought to experience and which is the epistemological cornerstone of an eventual "theology" is from the outset formed in different worlds.

The ultimate question, then, is as follows: Are these radically opposing experiential paradigms incommensurable?

Although Thomas Kuhn's well-known work has direct bearing on paradigms in the natural sciences, it is worthwhile noting one of the reasons he stipulated as an explanation for the difficulty of inter-paradigmatic communication: proponents of different paradigms may look at the same reality, but because they operate in different worlds (where the same concepts acquire different meanings), they "see" different realities. This is, according to Kuhn, the "most fundamental aspect of the incommensurability of competing paradigms" (see Kuhn 1970:148-150).

And how does a switch eventually take place, if at all? Despite factors such as superior problem-solving ability and even aesthetic appeal, it is a religious concept to which Kuhn reverts to describe this transfer of allegiance: it is a conversion experience! (Kuhn 1970:151).

Along which avenues should we then seek for a solution? I make a few suggestions within the framework of the third thesis above.

1. Too many Christians and theologians are not yet even aware that the fundamental "problem" concerning religious experience in the South African context is precisely the prevailing experiential sectarianism which precludes the "seeing" of the problem.

Traditional Reformed theologians will have to realise that the relation between experience and theology is of equal epistemological importance to the relation between theology and Scripture/tradition. And some liberation theologians should avoid relying on a kind of "ineffability" to defend their way of doing theology as the only legitimate way.

The Gestalt switch (Kuhn) to "see", is in itself an important first step to a solution. We suffer from the old sin to see and yet not to see.

2. If one accepts, with Schleiermacher, the fundamentally communal nature of religious experience (see Clements 1978:38) as well as the close relation between statements of faith and kerygmatic statements, the church as primary context of experience comes to the fore. Apart from exegetical and dogmatic arguments towards greater church unity in the specific broader ecumenical sense, a radical openness to different (religious) experiences is a prerequisite for the possibility of inter-paradigmatic dialogue. Nürnberger (1988:295) is worth quoting on this point:

The sin of our disunity does not lie in our differences, not even in the tensions between us, but in our refusal to expose ourselves to the highly uncomfortable, challenging and transformative encounter with our enemy brothers and sisters, refusal to suffer them as Christ has suffered, the refusal to forgive the unforgiveable, to accept the unacceptable.

The unwillingness to open ourselves up to experience the "unexperiencable" is the old problem of refusal to be converted to the totally unacceptable by the inclusive grace of God (see Jonah 4:1-3, Luke 15's story of the older brother and Peter's dilemma in Acts 10). This lies at the heart of the church as truly catholic church and its missionary character as communion of (all!) the saints.

3. If systematic theology as theology from and about praxis is preceded by a Gestalt switch and a new (ecclesiological) interchange, it must redefine its primary task in the South African context.

On a theological level (first-order reflection) it must take upon itself the task of conscientisation precisely with the aim of changing the agenda of theology. This will bring the whole "process" which is the subject of this essay into focus and indelibly stamp theology as fundamentally ecumenical, i.e. relating to others in the clearest possible terms the experiences and corresponding theological concepts (see e.g. Albert Nolan 1988).

On the meta-theological level, theology as reflection from and about praxis will have to redefine its own presuppositions. This might lead *inter alia* to the insight that the retreat to experience is an equally fundamental problem as the retreat to commitment in the debate about the rationality of theological statements (see Van Huyssteen 1986).

4. I have argued elsewhere (Naudé 1988) that a new theological paradigm does not necessarily originate because of a progressive problem-solving ability. It is often preceded by "a very personal spiritual experience" (Küng 1984:64, my translation)

which accounts for its "irrational" mystical foundation. Ultimately our hope lies in the third Person of the Trinity to transform us through religious experience, which has its origin in spiritual experiences as experiences of the Spirit.

BIBLIOGRAPHY

Clements, K.W. 1987. *Friedrich Schleiermacher. Pioneer of modern theology*. London: Collins.

De Gruchy, J. 1986. *Cry Justice!* New York: Orbis.

Gadamer, H.G. 1972. *Wahrheit und Methode*. Mohr: Tübingen.

Heron, A.I.C. 1980. *A century of Protestant theology*. Philadelphia: Westminster.

Johns, R.D. 1976. *Man in the world: The political theology of Johann Baptist Metz*. Missoula: Scholars Press.

Kant, I. 1968. *Schriften zur Anthropologie, Geschichtsphilosophie, Politik und Pädagogik* (Werke 9). Darmstadt: Wissenschaftliche Buchgesellschaft.

Kant, I. 1968. *Schriften zur Ethik und Religionsphilosophie* (Werke 6). Darmstadt: Wissenschaftliche Buchgesellschaft.

Kant, I. 1978 (1793). *Die Religion innerhalb der Grenzen der blossen Vernunft*. Hamburg: Felix Meiner.

Luijpen, W. 1969. *Nieuwe inleiding tot de existentiële fenomenologie*. Utrecht: Het Spectrum.

Mbiti, J.S. 1974. *African religions and philosophy*. London: Heinemann.

Metz, J.B. 1984. *Glaube in Geschichte und Gesellschaft*. Mainz: Matthias Grünewald.

Mogoba, S. 1985. "Christianity in a Southern African context". *Journal of Theology for Southern Africa* Vol. 52, pp. 5-16.

Mosala, I. & Thlagale B. (eds). 1986, *The unquestionable right to be free. Essays in Black theology*. Johannesburg: Skotaville.

Mouton, J (ed.) 1988. *Paradigms and progress in theology*. Pretoria: HSRC.

Naudé, P.J. 1987. *Ortopraksie as metodologiese prinsipe in die sistematiese teologie*. Unpublished DTh. Stellenbosch: University of Stellenbosch.

Naudé, P.J. 1988. The limitations of problem-solving as criterion for paradigms in theology. In Mouton (ed), pp. 142 – 151.

Prozesky, M. 1988. "Methodological issues arising from the experience of religion as oppressive". In Mouton (ed.), pp. 259-270.

Rahner, K. 1969. *Hörer des Wortes: Zur grundlegung einer Religionsphilosphie*. München: Kösel-Verlag.

Ruch, E.A. & Anyanwu, K.C. 1984. *African philosophy. An introduction to the main philosophical trends in contemporary Africa*. Rome: Catholic Book Agency.

Schlink, E. 1957. "Die Struktur der dogmatische Aussage als ökumenisches Problem". *Kirche und Dogma* 3, pp. 251-360.

Schreiter, R.J. 1985. *Constructing local theologies*. London: SCM.

Sebidi, L. 1986. "The dynamics of the black struggle and its implications for Black theology". In Mosala & Thlagale (eds.), pp. 1-36.

Setiloane, G.M. 1986. *African theology. An introduction*. Johannesburg: Skotaville.

Smart, N. 1987. "Understanding religious experience". In S. Katz (ed.) *Mysticism and philosophical analysis*. London: Sheldon, pp. 10-21.

Wainwright, G. 1980. *Doxology. A systematic theology*. New York: Oxford University Press.

Witvliet, T. 1984. *A place in the sun. An introduction to liberation theology in the third world*. London: SCM.

1.4 CONFESSING NICEA TODAY?

Critical questions from a South African perspective[1]

In terms of its constitution, the World Council of Churches aims "to call the churches to the goal of visible unity in one faith and in one eucharistic fellowship expressed in worship and in common life in Christ, and to advance towards that unity in order that the world may believe" (Constitution III.1). This is echoed in the aim of Faith and Order "to proclaim the oneness of the Church of Jesus Christ and to call the churches to the goal of visible unity in one faith and one eucharistic fellowship, expressed in worship and in common life in Christ, in order that the world may believe" (Bylaws 3.1).

The question of "visible unity in one eucharistic fellowship" was addressed in the well-known Baptism-Eucharist-Ministry project (BEM), which culminated in the 1982 Lima declaration and its accompanying liturgy. The issue of "visible unity in one faith" relates to the study project *Towards the common expression of the apostolic faith*, officially launched in Lima, and taken further in subsequent conferences to produce a study guide on the explication, recognition and common confession of the one faith as expressed in the Nicene-Constantinopolitan Creed (NC). The study was published in 1991 by the WCC as a Faith and Order document (Paper 153) entitled *Confessing the one faith*. Whereas BEM could be construed as the "order" side of the search for unity, this initiative relates to the "faith" side of a visibly united church (Neuner 1997:163).

1. THE CHOICE FOR NICEA

The choice for NC as expression of the apostolic faith is explained in the Lima document, which states that "it is impossible to disregard the special place of the Nicene Creed. It is the one common creed which is most universally[2] accepted, as formulation of the apostolic faith by churches in all parts of the world, where it primarily serves as the confession of faith in the eucharistic liturgy" (Link 1985:216-217). This relates to the so-called double consensus that accompanied the self-understanding of the early Councils already expressed in the 5th century, namely *consensio atiquitatis et universitatis*, or vertical and horizontal consensus (see Sieben 1979:515). Its historical significance, universal acceptance and liturgical use confirm that NC expresses "the fundamentals of the apostolic faith" (*Confessing the one faith* 1991:4) as one of the few threads which can still hold a divided Christian church together (Kelly 1972:208).

---

[1] This essay is an adapted version of a lecture delivered at the Theological Society of Southern Africa at the University of the Western Cape (20-22 June 2001). The essay originally appeared in *Scriptura* 79 (2002), 47-54.

[2] NC was accepted by the Eastern church as baptismal creed from 451. It became part of the Western church's eucharist liturgy at the Synod of Toledo (Spain) in 589 and became part of the Lutheran, Anglican and Reformed Churches' heritage even after new confessional documents were accepted. In practice, though, the Apostolicum occupies a far more prominent place in Reformed liturgies than Nicea (Link 1998:34-35).

The question arises how South African churches and theologians should view the One Faith process. Adopting a polemical approach, I wish to state a few problems – some general and others more related to our context – regarding the project in our contemporary situation. As a member of the Dutch Reformed family of churches (DRC),[3] my remarks are strongly influenced by the situation in that specific family.

2. QUESTIONS FROM A SOUTH AFRICAN PERSPECTIVE

2.1. Does the NC as a doctrinal formulation of orthodoxy have more than a limited value in contributing to visible church unity today?

No one can doubt the historical and theological importance of NC as the first formal expression of faith assigned the authority of "orthodoxy". In his illuminating discussion of confessions as communicative acts of faith Edmund Arens divides the history of confessions in the church as follows: The *Sitz im Leben* of the earliest confessions was the liturgy, i.e. baptism, confession of faith and confession of sin. From Nicea onward a new genre of "Lehrendes Bekennen",[4] linked to synods and councils, becomes established. Arens sees the confessions (Bekenntnisschriften) of the Reformation period with their strong "teaching" character in the same light. This is then followed by "Situatives Bekennen"[5] (a somewhat unfortunate term) like Barmen and other declarations of the 20th century.

The question is whether the genre of formal faith confession as such is helpful in establishing greater church unity – apart from the question of whether Nicea specifically can/should play such a role.

One thinks of the many non-creedal or more independent types of churches which – rightly or wrongly – consider confessional statements as unwarranted intrusions between the Scriptural Word and the believer (Horgan 1988:64). Or of churches that harbour a much more individualist and prophetic understanding of the Holy Spirit. Or of groups such as the many African Independent Churches that operate in an oral context where the inscripturation of faith is in principle not a practical option, and may indeed be experienced as alienating. The interesting point is that empirical data about church demography in South Africa (see Hendricks 1996) demonstrate that it is precisely these churches – and not the historical mainline ones – that show growth. And they are not part of the broader ecumenical movement, which is seen by some as dominated by the concerns of the older churches for whom the early church and its doctrinal decisions carry a normativity not easily transferred to younger churches (see Neuner 1997:165).

---

3 See the recent very informative issue of *Scriptura* (September 2001) dedicated to a discussion of the DRC in the transition to democracy in South Africa.
4 "War auch bisher das Moment der rechten Lehre schon im Bekennen präsent ... kam darüber hinaus mit der *regula fidei* bereits der Zusammenhang von Bekennen und rechter Lehre zum Ausdruck, so wird mit dem Konzil von Nizaea das Bekenntnis selbst zum Lehrbekenntnis" (Arens 1989:265).
5 This is a somewhat unfortunate term as it unwittingly implies that the earlier creeds, as well as confessions from the time of the Reformation, were not "situation bound"?

In South Africa where "creedal" churches do in fact share a common confession of NC, the complexities of the situation (our political and church histories, our diverse cultures and languages, our socio-economic divides), make achieving church unity a slow and painful process, because the divisions are much more than creedal confession (although not unrelated to issues of faith and confession).[6] The DRC family, which has had six shared symbols of faith – including NC – over a period of more than a hundred years, is a case in point. Even without the complication of the 1986 Confession of Belhar, a common confession of the NC has been and is – to say the least – not of any help in fostering greater unity.

2.2. Is the language (thought form) of – as well as the issues addressed by – Nicea helpful in the processes of church unification?

One should obviously read NC in its context and see its great significance in what it set out to achieve in the fourth century church. But the valid question asked by Robert Hood in his book *Must God remain Greek? Afro-cultures and God-talk* needs to be echoed in a South African context. The agenda to talk about God, Christ and the Spirit on the basis of the NC assumptions "threatens the survival and integrity of Christian identity in this world of many and varied cultures" (Hood 1990: xi). It excludes or makes the intellectual contribution of African and other cultures very difficult, and represents a form of ecclesial neo-colonialism by Eurocentric and American churches, which control the ecumenical movement (see Hood 1990:247-248 and Stanley Harakas's reply in Harakas 1991).

The same could obviously be said about the Ancient Near Eastern (OT) or Greco-Roman (NT) context of the Bible. There is, however, a clear distinction between the Bible as canon and *norma normans* of the church and subsequent efforts to express the Christian faith. For the first, everyone everywhere should show great hermeneutical patience; for the second, one should be far more open to ongoing, varied expressions of faith in different contexts and different thought forms rather than attempt to take everyone back to the fourth century. "The confessional heritages may have a continuing life in the united Church, as long as they nourish the witness of the local church and do not diminish its capacity for responding to the needs of the people whom it is called to serve" (From: *A fellowship of local churches truly united* 1976, as printed in Gassmann 1993:74).

Apart from the "ethnocentric philosophical ideas" from the fourth century (Hood), one could also ask questions about the issues addressed by NC. No responsible theologian can underestimate the intricate and delicate doctrinal decisions represented by creeds and confessions that have become part of the church's precious heritage. Nicea itself was – in the context of the fourth century – described as a wonder (Sieben 1979:514). But it is quite another issue to launch a project by which those formulations and decisions – now almost an unconscious part of our tradition – are put before the whole church as the apostolic faith for today. Yes, it can and must – just like any classic document – be explicated for today as in the

---

6   See my discussion on how to deal theologically with so-called "non-theological" factors in an ecumenical situation (Naudé 1999).

WCC study document. But, as I will show below, this has its own limitations, which depend on who does the interpretative work.[7]

We in South Africa who now live from the fresh and contextual language of the Belhar confession and who are faced with urgent life-threatening issues not addressed in NC, would rather opt for a reclaiming of a specific Scriptural passage/passages or the open-endedness of new faith expressions in which the apostolic faith is set forth today. If American (Horgan 1988) and German (Staats 1996:305) Christians explain the uniqueness of their respective ecclesial contexts and how difficult it is to implement the NC project, an African statement is even more appropriate.

2.3. What influence did the Nicea process itself have?

One could raise the ethical question related to the cost of 300 theologians involved in 18 conferences all over the globe to produce a document of some 130 pages. One could ask whether the whole project is not a form of "ecumenism from above" driven by professional ecumenical theologians with very little resonance in grassroots Christian communities themselves. I would, however, rather accept the limitations of the ecumenical process and pursue the question of a "missed opportunity".

I refer here to the process of "Giving account of the hope that is in us", which commenced with the Faith and Order conference in Louvain in 1971. The "common expression of our faith" was here linked to "giving account of our hope" *and not to a formulation of a confession*: "The study will not aim at the formulation of a creed or confession; it will rather be an effort to give account of our faith today" (Faith and Order Paper 59:239). This led to a magnificent array of witnesses published in the well-known volumes by Choan-Seng Song *Giving account of our hope today* (Song 1976) and *Giving account of our hope together* (Song 1978).

The difficulty of finding a common point of reference[8] in such a multitude of witnesses, on the one hand, and the relative success of a common statement on BEM, on the other, led to a historicising counter-movement. And it (un?)intentionally started from a kind of *principium qiunquesaecularis* of a pristine and undivided church, easily forgetting the political and theological strife subsumed under common formulations from the early church (Brinkmann 1996:61,62). *The choice was clearly for a historical confession instead of an openness to confess the faith anew in different contexts and with different images that could subsequently have be en tested for their "consensus catholicus"*.

2.4. How does Nicea relate to the basic apostolic faith?

Despite the express intention of the study guide *Towards sharing the one faith* that "the point of the text is not the Nicene Creed itself but engagement with the basic issues of the Christian apostolic faith" (Falconer 1998:179), the whole project in practice condenses the apostolic faith to the NC and accords this creed unparalleled status.

---

7   One in any case wonders whether NC would have engendered such great interpretative interest if it were not for the *filioque* question – that is actually the only outstanding "issue" for the older churches to resolve today. See Oberdorfer (2000:129ff) for an elaborate history of the *filioque* problem.
8   Is this search for a common denominator a kind of modernist urge for ecclesial control, or perhaps a lack of trust in whither the wind blows?

The very concept "apostolic faith" has a variety of meanings in the context of the WCC. George van der Velde (1988) points to six such aspects including unity of apostolic faith, which exists "in the pluriformity of Christian traditions in a great diversity of contexts" (point 4). It is, however, interesting to note that before the Scriptures are mentioned as fundamental criterion (*norma normans*) in point 6, Van der Velde notes that "apostolic faith" is linked by the WCC to the NC "as the ecumenical symbol par excellence" (point 5). This is understandable for the historical reasons mentioned above, but there are formulations in *Confessing the one faith* that point to NC itself being a criterion for other, modern expressions of the apostolic faith, e.g. "The Nicene Creed thus serves to indicate whether the faith *as set forth in modern situations* is the same faith as the one the church confessed through the centuries" (par 12, my emphasis; see also par 16). This suggest a canonising function that is normally assigned to Scripture alone (Brinkmann 1996:72-73) and represents a narrowing down of the apostolic faith so eloquently expressed in Van der Velde's point quoted above.

Neuner reckons that this "Rückbesinnung auf die frühe Kirche, ihre Ordnung und Lehrentscheidungen" can be explained from both the method adopted for the confessing project and ecumenical politics at Lima: "Es ist offentsichtlich, dass sich hier die orthodoxen Tradition, die in Lima stark repräsentiert war, durchsetzen konnte. Für the Orthodoxe ist es unabweislich, dass eine Einigung nur auf der Basis der frühen Kirche erfolgen kann" (Neuner 1997:165; see Brinkmann's note on the "historicising approach" of the Eastern church, 1996:73-74).

2.5. How should we interpret the concept of ecumenism today?

I have up to now remained within the paradigm of the ecumenical movement as represented by the WCC and Faith and Order. The danger is, however, that the very concept of "ecumenism" could be restricted to its inner-ecclesial meaning of "relationships among churches belonging to the WCC".

Etymologically speaking, we all know that *oikumene* refers to the "inhabited earth" initially understood to be the Roman empire (see Luke 2). After the fall of this empire, *oikumene* acquired a "churchly" meaning with reference to the universal, i.e. ecumenical councils. In the 20th century the reference to the ecumenical movement again shifted the meaning to efforts of church unity later represented by the WCC. But as early as 1951, in the so-called Toronto declaration, the WCC itself declared that the term "ecumenical" be used as expression of the whole work of the whole church in the proclamation of the gospel in the whole world. The unity of the church is not an aim in itself, but directed at testimony and service to the world (see Frieling 1992:6).

If this "outward-looking" understanding of *oikumene* is regained, it opens the way for a different paradigm of ecumenics. Wolfgang Huber develops this idea by observing that we have reached a point in history where the experience of one world (*oikumene*!) is a reality. But this reality is filled with paradoxes and the knowledge of huge discrepancies. The search for unity, therefore, is fundamentally ethical, directed "zu einem vorrangige Kriterium für eine christliche Praxis, die sich an der Aufgabe orientiert, für die Überwindung dieser Widersprüche zu arbeiten und zu kampfen" (Huber 1980:48). Apart from an ethical unity, ecumenical theology's dialogical nature should be extended from inner-Christian confessional dialogues to an ecumenism of religions and nations (1980:71) to truly include "the world" as ethically one world.[9]

Huber does not – as far as I could gather – work out the implications of an ethical ecumenism for our understanding of the apostolic faith. The apostolic faith is without doubt carried forth in the church through normative common creeds and confessions. In Episcopal churches the magisterial episcopacy functions as normative teaching office to guard and set the apostolic faith forth. But is it not also valid to claim that discipleship of Jesus Christ and following Him in acts of love, justice and peace in solidarity with the poor and marginalised are equally normative expressions of the apostolic faith? A holy and liberating life is – according to the Scriptures – at the heart of prophetic and apostolic fidelity (see Horgan 1988:65).

Without in any way devaluing the NC or any other creed, it must be clear, in the light of HIV/AIDS, the unfinished project of reconciliation, radical and growing poverty, signs of moral disorientation and anomie in a society in transition (see Durkheim 1963:252-253) that *the churches in South Africa today will follow Jesus Christ better by an authentic ecumenical praxis than by a careful and drawn-out explication of the creeds*. This is not anti-dogmatism nor a non-creedal view; it is a judgement of our present situation where a specific choice is made for a specific mode of the apostolic faith (normative praxis) without losing sight of other modes (normative creeds and confessions) that inevitably inform and are informed by our praxis.

2.6. Is Nicea helpful in the urgent task of re-establishing the public role of theology in SA?

In the context of the so-called "public theology" debate in the USA, Cady focuses on three issues: Which publics are addressed? How are they addressed, i.e. what mode of presentation is appropriate? And are timely issues adequately addressed? (See Cady 1987.) Let us examine the *Confessing the one faith* project from this perspective.

Which publics?

It seems obvious that the only public that will be served by such a project is the church itself. Contrary to the original context where NC and other later creeds and confessions assumed huge public and specifically political importance far beyond the boundaries of the church, an explication of NC today will at most serve the awareness of active church members (which is obviously not to be disregarded). Such a process might also gain some prominence in the public of academia, but then probably confined to theology, which is in our context not really an alternative public to the church.

What mode?

It is highly unlikely that a text designed for both restraining heresies in the fourth century and as a creedal-liturgical expression is in its "format" appropriate for witnessing to a society such as ours. A fruitful engagement with different publics

---

9   See also the effort at a paradigm switch by Konrad Raiser (1989) and Schwöbel's discussion from a Trinitarian perspective (Schwöbel 1997:322ff).

in an open, democratic sphere requires different modes of communication ranging from lobbying for legislation to networking with NGOs and writing letters to the newspaper. In a country where some of the church formations still resist unification, the world is not waiting with huge expectation for a delayed unity, which in itself would have been a mode of witnessing to true reconciliation in Christ. Even within the church, very few ordinary members will naturally be excited by the language of Nicea – especially where the creed is "on the books" in Reformed churches, but rarely used liturgically (but this might change through repeated use).

Which timely issues?

Nicea has – like any ancient text – obvious potential for an interpretation that takes contemporary issues into account. My contention is that the *filioque* is not one of them (as it appears with only one cursory reference in par 210 of *Confessing the one faith*!). The Confessing study is nevertheless a limited sign of such interpretation. Limited, because it is apparent that the primary context at which the interpretation is aimed is a Western, modern, secular society under ecological threat (par 84-89, 205, 258, 270, 276) and where the core polemical issue is the acceptance of a reality beyond the physical world which allows for faith in a transcendent God (see par 7, 21, 23, 28 and Hebblethwaite 1996:68).

The interpretation is not only limited in scope, but also in its judging of an issue such as gender-sensitive readings of the Bible – and this from an almost fundamentalist, ahistorical perspective: "We may not surrender the language of 'Father' for it is the way in which Jesus addressed, and spoke of, God and how Jesus taught his disciples to address God ... The language of 'Father' and 'Son' links the Christian community through the ages and binds it in a communion of faith. Moreover, it is the language which expresses the personal relationships within the inner life of the Trinity, and in our relations with God" (par 50, despite a statement on language as only allowing approximate description of God in par 49!).

One could obviously write an explication on "reading the Nicene creed in South Africa today". But once completed, and with the construction of a public theology in mind, what do you do with it? From my perspective, it is doubtful that such interpretation will move beyond the circle of professional theologians into the public sphere. And even the theologians might ask: Why not rather address the timely issues (as is expected from good public theology) directly from Scripture with its rich variety of themes and perspectives, and obvious advantage of both canonical status in the church and relative knowledge among the public at large?

3. CONCLUSION

No one from the creedal churches would argue against the retention of NC as part of our rich heritage of witnesses to the apostolic faith. Very few from (South) Africa, I think, will argue that its common explication – the starting point of the WCC project – is the most urgent witness of the church to that common, apostolic faith. Even fewer will propose its explication as credible service to the world today.

The apostolic faith in South Africa today is not carried forth primarily through prophetic witness but rather through quiet, dedicated priestly service (Rom 12:1-2;

Heb 13). Pure and genuine religion before God is to take care of orphans and widows in their suffering (James 1:27).

This is whither the wind blows. Softly, sometimes incognito (Matt 25), but nevertheless authentic.

BIBLIOGRAPHY

Alston, W.A. & Welker, M. (eds.) 2003. *Reformed theology. Identity and ecumenicity II. Biblical interpretation in the Reformed tradition.* Grand Rapids: Eerdmans.

Arens, E. 1989. *Bezeugen und Bekennen. Elementare Handlung des Glaubens.* Dusseldorf: Patmos.

Brinkmann, M.E. 1996. *Progress in unity? Fifty years of theology within the WCC: 1945-1995.* Louvain: Peters Press.

Cady, L.E. 1987. A model for public theology. *The Harvard Theological Review* 80, pp. 193-212.

Confessing the One Faith: An Ecumenical Explication of the Apostolic Faith as It Is Confessed in the Nicene-Constantinopolitan Creed (381). 1991. Geneva: WCC.

Durkheim, E. 1963 (1897). *Suicide. A study in Sociology.* Glencoe: The Free Press.

Falconer, A. 1998. *Faith and Order in Moshi. The 1996 Commission meeting.* Faith and Order Paper No. 177. Geneva: WCC.

Gassmann, G. 1993. *Documentary history of Faith and Order 1963-1993.* Geneva: WCC.

Frieling, R. 1992. *Der Weg des ökumenischen Gedankens. Eine Ökumenekunde.* Göttingen: Vandenhoeck & Ruprecht.

Harakas, S.S. 1991. "Must God remain Greek?" *The Ecumenical Review* Vol. 43, pp. 194-199.

Hebblethwaite, B. 1996. *The essence of Christianity: A fresh look at the Nicene creed.* London: SPCK.

Hendriks, J.H. 1995. "South African denominational growth and decline 1911-1991". *JTSA* Vol. 91, pp. 35-58.

Hood, R. 1990. *Must God remain Greek? Afro-cultures and God-talk.* Minneapolis: Fortress Press.

Horgan, T.D. (ed.). 1988. *Apostolic faith in America.* Grand Rapids: Eerdmans.

Huber, W. 1980. *Die Streit um die Wahrheit und die Fähigkeit zum Frieden. Vier Kapitel ökumenische Theologie.* München: Kaiser.

Kelly, J.D.N. 1972. *Early Christian creeds* (3rd edition). London: Longman.

Link, H. 1998. *Bekennen und Bekenntnis.* Göttingen: Vandenhoeck & Ruprecht.

Naudé, P.J. 2003. "Reformed confessions as hermeneutical problem. The case study of the Belhar confession". In W.M. Alston & M. Welker (eds.) *Reformed theology. Identity and ecumenicity II. Biblical interpretation in the Reformed tradition.* Grand Rapids: Eerdmans, pp. 242-260.

Neuner, P. 1997. *Ökumenische Theologie. Die Suche nach der Einheit der christliche Kirche.* Darmstadt: Wissenschaftliche Buchgesellschaft.

Oberdorfer, B. 2000. *Filioque. Geschichte und Theologie eines ökumenischen Problems*. Göttingen: Vandenhoeck & Ruprecht.

Raiser, K. 1989. *Ökumene im Übergang: Paradigmenwechsel in der Ökumenischen Bewegung*. München: Kaiser.

Schwöbel. C. 1997. "Ökumenische Theologie im Horizont des trinitarischen Glaubens". ÖR Vol. 46, pp. 321-340.

Sieben, H.J. 1979. *Die Konzilsidee der alten Kirche*. Paderborn: Ferdinand Schöningh.

Song, C. 1976. *Giving account of our hope today*. FO Paper 81. Geneva: WCC.

Song, C. 1978. *Giving account of our hope together*. FO Paper 86. Geneva: WCC.

Staats, R. 1996. *Das Glaubensbekenntnis von Nizea-Konstantinopel. Historische und theologische Grundlagen*. Darmstadt: Wissenschaftliche Buchgesellschaft.

Vandervelde, G. 1988. "The meaning of 'apostolic faith' in World Council of Church's documents". In Horgen, T. (ed.), pp. 20-25.

Towards sharing the one faith. 1996. Faith and Order Paper No. 173. Geneva: WCC.

Towards the common expression of the apostolic faith. 1978. Geneva: WCC.

WCC Constitution, Rules, Regulations and By-laws. 1996. Geneva: WCC.

1.5 IDENTITY AND ECUMENICITY

How do we deal theologically with so-called "non-theological" factors?[1]

The theme of this conference is – at least for me – not merely an interesting academic one. I am an ordained minister of the Dutch Reformed Church in South Africa (DRC), which for many years identified itself so strongly with the aspirations and ideological interests of the Afrikaner people that it almost lost its identity as a truly Christian church by providing moral justification for apartheid policies.[2] As a young theologian I had to notice and live through the growing ecumenical isolation started in the early 1960s and only partially restored by the World Alliance of Reformed Churches after the last synod of the DRC in October 1998. My views on identity and ecumenicity below should consequently be seen in the light of this mainly negative experiential context.

One of the perennial problems in the ecumenical movement is the strained relations between churches' self-understanding and the aim "to call the churches to the goal of visible unity in one faith and one Eucharistic fellowship expressed in worship and in common life in Christ" (Best and Gassmann 1994:2) The problem may be restated in the theme of our deliberations as that between (ecclesial) identity and (holy) communion. The great ecumenical theologian Geoffrey Wainwright declares: "At stake in the understanding of unity and schism, of continuity and discontinuity, of integrity and fragmentation, is precisely the *identity of the church* and therewith the nature and substance of truth and the conditions of its *authoritative expression*" (1983:190; see also Wainwright 1984:71-75).

Apart from a "theological" identity (e.g. Reformed, Lutheran, Catholic), the self-understanding of a church is also shaped by "non-theological" factors such as geography, language, culture and a particular history. The role that these factors play was alluded to in the early stages of the modern ecumenical movement. Already the Second World Conference of Faith and Order in Edinburgh (1937) refers to socio-political and historical factors such as nationality, race, class and self-preservation that hinder the unification process among churches.[3]

---

1   This paper is an adapted version of a lecture at the International Conference on Identity and Ecumenicity (Systematic Theology) sponsored by Princeton Theological Seminary and held at the Ruprecht-Karl University, Heidelberg, Germany (21 March 1999). The essay was originally published in Wallace M. Alston and Michael Welker (eds.) *Reformed theology. Identity and ecumenicity* (2003) Eerdmans: New York, 435-449.

2   This is described and analysed in many works, notably in de Gruchy's outline of Afrikaner Calvinism (1991:1-46). For an informative overview of Reformed churches in South Africa, see Smit 1992.

3   See Faith and Order Papers, Old Series No. 84. I broadly follow Heinz-Günther Stobbe's historical overview (1980:194ff). This issue of "non-theological factors" emerged again at the Third World Conference of Faith and Order (Lund 1952), where churches were called upon to give special attention to the schismatic influence of social and cultural factors. An interdisciplinary commission was set up to advise the Fourth World Conference in Montreal (1963) with a follow-up document, *Spirit, Order and Organisation*, submitted to the Faith and Order Commission at Louvain. At that stage the Lutheran World Council set up a theological commission (1969) to study the same theme. The commission refers

Identity and ecumenicity

The significance of the problematic relation between theological and non-theological factors has grown during the last two decades. Lukas Vischer observes that "(t)he divided churches live today in a state of powerful inner contradiction. Years ago they greeted the ecumenical era with enthusiasm. … But now years have passed and the situation has changed. Today the churches stress their own identity and tradition". The process of reception in the ecumenical movement has indeed stumbled over this negative flight into an isolationist "identity".

> Frequently, confessional positions are not defended by a concern for the purity of their teaching. *The real motive is often simply preservation of one's identity which has developed over the course of history.* … These may be matters of language, ethnic identity, national pride, or other things. For this reason the *ecumenical movement must pay attention to these ancillary factors.* By breaking through these secondary barriers – which are no less resistant for all that – the church will win the freedom for its process of reception (Vischer 1984:221, 232, my emphasis; see also Loewe 1988; Fischer 1989).

Günther Gassmann refers to these "nicht-lehrhaften Faktoren" that exercise an essential influence on attempts at achieving greater unity and communion among churches. He seeks an explanation for diverse replies to the Lima text from churches that share the same confessional (e.g. Lutheran) tradition in contextual factors: Is the church a minority – or state church? Is the main dialogue partner the Catholic or Orthodox or Protestant free churches? These issues all contribute to the self-understanding of a specific church – apart from its narrow "theological" character (1984:366-367).

The problem of identity preservation, i.e. in the negative sense of self-sufficiency and exclusivity, has become enhanced over time. Because, says the seasoned Anglican theologian, GR Evans, over a longer period the habit of separateness determines identity to such an extent that the self-definition over and against others (in-group versus out-group) accepts separation as normal and as legitimate ground for continued or even further separation (see Evans 1996:42, 54), with a resultant loss of vision for communion.[4]

A remarkable feature of this problem is referred to in passing by Stobbe: The acuteness of "non-theological factors" have been recognised specifically in churches from the Protestant tradition (Stobbe 1980:196). There is no room to analyse this in more details, but it seems an almost typically Reformed feature to constantly ask "identity questions". This may be linked to Calvin's original impulse to proclaim the Word in a socially active, world-formative manner derived from a wider vision of God's kingdom (see Wolterstorff 1983:21). It may be the result of the dictum *theologia*

---

to misunderstandings created by the term "non-theological factors" and proposes "secular factors" as substitute (see the report *Mehr als Einheit der Kirche* 1970.) Specific reference is later made to the "kirchentrennende Wirkung der Sekularen Faktoren" in a study entitled *Ökumenische Methodologie* commissioned by the executive committee of the Lutheran Council for its August 1973 meeting.

4 See my extensive analysis of this problem in relation to the DRC's inability to come to grips with the challenge posed by the Belhar Confession of the Uniting Reformed Church (1997:226-243).

reformata et semper reformanda, as explained by Moltmann. The question constantly being asked is: What is Reformed theology?

> Das ist in gewisser Weise typisch für reformierte Theologie, den sie gründet nicht in ein für alle Mal festgelegten Bekenntnissen wie die lutherische Theologie im Konkordienbuch und auch nich in einer Tradition unfehlbare. … Lehrentscheidungen wie die römisch-katholische Theologie. Sie gründet in der 'Reformation' der Kirche 'nach dem Wort Gottes' (Moltmann 1998:157).

And this implies a constant reformation encompassing life, church and world.

In short, where God is taken seriously as God of all spheres of life (the world as theatre of God's glory) and where the Word of God is taken seriously as prophetic Word for each new situation (life as *coram Dei loquendi*), the problems related to "contextuality" and "rootedness" loom larger. The struggle for identity and therefore for ecumenicity is a broad issue intensified in Reformed theology by its nature as a constantly reforming theology.[5]

The question now remains: How does one address the "non-theological", "non-dogmatic", or "secular" factors to break through "secondary barriers" on the way to fuller koinonia? It depends, first, on the perspective from which one approaches this question; second, on the process followed; and third, on the normative reference point utilised.

1. A THEOLOGICAL PERSPECTIVE

One may attempt to fathom the impact of "non-theological" factors by relying on any one or a combination of the social sciences such as sociology, social psychology, political science or history and then clarifying how a group (in this case a church) has been determined by so-called "non-theological" factors.

This approach reveals the difficulty in accepting the term "non-theological", as the latter assumes the theological perspective as point of reference with other factors as "not-from-theology". Even if a theological perspective is assumed, the "other factors" must in some way be honoured in their own right. For the sake of this essay I prefer the term "social factors" – although somewhat vague, it does avoid some of the pitfalls of terms used hitherto.

The approach to understanding the reasons for both church divisions and church union from social sources[6] must be welcomed as an important facet of contextual analysis crucial to theology. It does assist the theologian to understand the historical, economic and cultural factors at play in the struggle for the visible unity of the local

---

5   See Boesak and Fourie (eds) for a recent contribution on the issue of Reformed identity from a South African context. Dirkie Smit, a leading Reformed scholar, writes in the introduction: "There is apparently something in the Reformed soul that constantly impels us to ask these self-investigative questions about our own identity … To ask this type of question is already part of our identity" (1998:21, my translation).

6   Compare the well-known work of H. Richard Niebuhr on *The Social Sources of Denominationalism* (1929) with Robert Lee's book, *The Social Sources of Church Unity: An Interpretation of Unitive Movements in American Protestantism* (1960) to see two sides of the coin. For references see Stobbe 1980.

(regional) and universal church. But these insights must be interpreted theologically to make a lasting impact on bilateral or multilateral dialogues. I will explain this from both the global and local ecumenical perspectives.

The Catholic ecumenical theologian J.M.R. Tillard states in his discussion of the ecclesiological implications of bilateral dialogue that one should refuse "to consider the so-called non-theological factors sufficient to explain the main divisions between Christians". He rightly points out that the ruptures between Rome, on the one hand, and Constantinople, Canterbury and Wittenberg, on the other "happened not only for theological reasons, but religious, theological, racial, political, cultural and economic factors were deeply entangled". He argues that during the process – and definitely in the mind of the next generation – "theological factors came to the foreground and have gradually been considered the implicit cause of rupture". Therefore, it is the dogmatic factors of division that must form the essence of bilateral dialogues and not the "easy solution" of non-theological factors (Tillard 1986:416,417).[7]

In the local South African context the struggle for church unification among the (Dutch) Reformed family of churches can indeed be viewed from a multitude of "social sources". Historical, political and economic factors[8] illuminate the stumbling blocks in the way of church unification. But these must be interpreted theologically, clarifying the crucial questions about God,[9] Christ's reconciliation, the interpretation of Scripture,[10] and the nature of the church[11] and its confessional character.[12] To put it bluntly, to understand apartheid as an oppressive social system in conflict with universal human rights is politically significant; to understand apartheid as a matter of theological *status confessionis*, sinful in its essence and not merely in its

---

7   It is interesting to note how Tillard moves from his insistence on dogmatic issues to an engagement with strategic (i.e. non-theological!) issues. He expresses an opinion that bilateral dialogues between the old churches of the Catholic tradition (including the Anglicans), on the one hand, and those between Protestant and new churches, on the other hand, could, if successful, in fact be a tragedy. Why? Because "it would finally divide Christianity into two competitive and strong (if not hostile) camps" (1986:419). This is a clear statement on a church-political power struggle which is in itself not a purely dogmatic issue.
8   For wide references on the intricacies of the South African situation, see de Gruchy (1991:4-13) and Smit (1992; 1998:3-16).
9   The struggle for church unification in the Dutch Reformed family is an immensely theological one. See the ongoing debates about the nature of God's concern for the poor as expressed in the Belhar Confession in Smit (1984), and my own recent analysis (1998:86-88).
10 The unification struggle is basically a hermeneutical struggle. For a succinct view of the matter from within the Dutch Reformed Church, see Loubser (1987).
11 It is significant that that the influential and prophetic DRC systematic theologian from Stellenbosch University, Willem D. Jonker, started the ecclesiological debate in the context of mission churches as early as 1962. It has remained a very important aspect of the family dialogue up to this day – especially in the light of the design of a new church order. An example of the debate in the 1970s is the collection of essays *Die eenheid van die kerk* (1978).
12 The acceptance by the Uniting Reformed Church of the Belhar Confession as a fourth confessional document apart from the Three Symbols of Unity (including the Heidelberg Catechism) added a dramatic dimension to the unification struggle. For an overview and analysis of the Dutch Reformed reaction, see my contributions (1997; 1998).

application, is what is ecumenically significant.[13] And obviously one cannot speak of dichotomies here, but rather of complementing perspectives supporting each other's validity in a complex and multifaceted interplay.

Social factors in the broad sense must be dealt with theologically, but not by way of sublimation. This exactly strengthens their power to ruin processes of dialogue and unification. When the question of preserving the Afrikaans language in a new unified Reformed church was raised by the now moderator of the Dutch Reformed Church and the Synod of the Northern Transvaal (1997), it was easy to explain from a historical, political and cultural perspective.[14] What has been crucial, however, is to clarify the language issue from the perspective of the church as exemplified in the Second Testament and confessed in the Reformed tradition – bearing in mind what important role language plays in the formation of a people's identity! This is pastorally sensitive, prophetically truthful and ecclesiologically significant.

The theological perspective on social factors enables one to understand the fundamentally ambivalent nature of "context". Calvinism in its various social formats – English, Dutch, French and Afrikaner; Reformed spirituality as Scottish Pietism, Dutch neo-Calvinism, Black and feminist theologies – all harbour within themselves the tension that has been expressed ecumenically as the relation between Tradition and traditions.[15] The root of the ambivalence lies in the walking of the tightrope to keep Tradition (for Reformed Christians primarily the Scriptures) and traditions (interpretation of Scripture in one's own context) in a healthy tension. Tradition alone is silent; traditions alone are heresy.

The gospel is in its very nature linked to the "social sources" of ancient Near Eastern and Greek-Roman societies, and has always been part of the "social sources" of

---

13 The World Alliance of Reformed Churches set this as a condition for re-acceptance of the DRC as a member. At its last synod (October 1998) the formulation about apartheid as sinful in its essence was approved by the synod. This opened the ecumenical doors after sixteen years of isolation.

14 The Afrikaans language developed from mid-seventeenth-century Dutch after the colonisation of the Cape in 1652. It was suppressed by the later English governments, but gained momentum from 1880 onwards with formal recognition in 1925 as one of two official languages. The rise of Afrikanerdom and Afrikaner identity was deeply shaped by this language – specifically through the translation of the Bible in 1933 (not unlike Luther's contribution to the German language). One of the historical markers in the black liberation movement was the Soweto student uprisings in 1976 directed against forced tuition in and of Afrikaans. After the democratic elections of 1994 Afrikaans became one of eleven official languages and lost most of its previous exclusive privileges. It is understandable that the Dutch Reformed Church would be tempted to see itself as one of the vehicles for maintaining Afrikaans, which was at one point (quite unnecessarily) seen as being threatened by church unification. The theological question is one about the task and nature of the church and not about the cultural value of a specific language: the tension between a biblical version of the church's "identity" and the temptation of a civil religion serving the needs of a *volk's* identity.

15 I do not offer a detailed discussion on the history of, and the technical distinctions between, the Tradition/traditions theme in Faith and Order. It is sufficient to refer to the Montreal distinction (1963) between Tradition (the gospel itself, transmitted from generation to generation in and by the church, Christ himself present in the life of the church) and tradition (both the diversity of forms of expression and also the confessional traditions). See Rodger and Vischer (1964:59), and Falconer (1993:45-47).

societies through the ages. There is no such thing as "pure" gospel without social trappings. This is the essence of the hermeneutical struggle, and we have many examples where the Christian tradition in general and the Reformed tradition in particular failed to remain true to Tradition. "The Reformed tradition, like any other, *can be seduced by social and cultural forces* that undermine its witness and keep it captive" (De Gruchy 1991:13, my emphasis). Thus remarks John de Gruchy in the context of his discussion of Afrikaner Calvinism, a prime twentieth-century example of how the gospel was smothered and concealed by social sources.[16]

It is thus no wonder that most discussions of social forces in ecumenical dialogues are predominantly negative (see quotations above). The question of how to deal with these ambivalent forces now comes to the fore. *How* in this case means: what process could be suggested in cases where dialogue partners find it difficult or impossible to make progress?

2. A THERAPEUTIC PROCESS

It seems that the most fruitful approach to social factors in a "stuck" bilateral/multilateral union process is a narrative, therapeutic one.[17] The partners should be allowed to reveal their identity by relating their story to each other through the telling of story fragments ("Einzel-Stories"). Ritschl dealt extensively with this issue in his *Story als Rohmaterial der Theologie* (edited with Hugh Jones, 1976) and later in his *Zur Logik der Theologie* (1984). The link between Story and identity is clarified as follows:

> Mit 'Stories' kann etwas ausgedrückt warden, wofür andere Idiome ungeeignet wären. Vor allem kan durch 'Stories' die Identität eines einzelnen oder eine Gruppe artikuliert werden. Menschen sind das was sie in ihren Story über sich sagen (bzw. was zu ihnen gesagt wird) und was sie aus dieser 'Story' machen. … Jeder von uns hat seine unverwechselbare Story, jeder *ist* seine Story (1984:45).

The narrative mode reveals[18] the perspective[19] or close-knit perspectives that determine "reality" in the act of a "seeing-as"[20] by each partner. In this process one

---

16   The conclusion regarding faith communities as formulated by the Truth and Reconciliation Commission in South Africa reads as follows: "In most cases, faith communities claimed to cut across divisions of race, gender, class and ethnicity. … However, contrary to their own deepest principles, many faith communities mirrored apartheid society, giving the lie to their profession of a loyalty that transcended social divisions" (Vol. 4, p. 65, paragraph 29).
17   I herewith engage in a free adaptation of some of Dietrich Ritschl's fascinating ideas based on his combination of insights from psychoanalysis, analytical philosophy and the earlier Chomsky's theory of language acquisition.
18   "Die Stories, die unser Leben ausmachen (einzeln und in Gruppen), sind die Träger unserer Perspektiven" (1984:58).
19   "In der sozialen Wirklichkeit sind Gruppen und Gemeinschaften durch gemeinsame Perspektive-Bündel gekennzeichnet, die in gemeinsamen Stories und Lebenshaltungen Ausdruck finden können" (1984:56).
20   A reference to the insight from phenomenology that objects are perceived "as something" and not "in themselves". This determines Ritschl's definition of perspectives as "die Weise, in der wir die Diknge sehen, den wir sehen Dinge immer im Modus des 'Sehen-

moves in various ways from the "surface level" to the "deep structure" of the conflict. If the process is allowed to continue, it will unearth that which will ultimately ("letzlich") steer the partners' thoughts and actions, namely "implicit axioms". "Das ist ja das Wesen von Axiomen, dass sie einfach da sind, dass sie funktionieren, ohne uns zu erlauben, sie wirklich begründen zu können, so, als stünden wir hinter oder über ihnen. Sie stehen aber hinter oder über uns, sie steuren uns" (Ritschl 1986:148). Upon close examination, the central axioms (normally few in number)[21] are revealed, with the possibility of understanding their hierarchical ordering (some are more important than others) and reciprocal interchange ("Vernetzung").[22]

What is crucial to this process is its *dialogical nature*. Not only is one partner telling her story (revealing identity, perspectives and implicit axioms), but her story is reciprocally *being told*.[23] In this way isolationism is overcome, because the neurosis[24] of a privatised language and world is opened up for a therapeutic resymbolisation (1986:158) that is a fundamental hermeneutical[25] (re-interpretative) process (1986:151).

One of the problems in ecumenical circles is to ensure that Stories are allowed to be told and thereby identities revealed in a truly dialogical process. Storytelling is no naïve retreat with romantic connotations, because it touches on the sensitive issue of power relations.[26] Mary Tanner, in her speech to the Fifth World Conference on Faith and Order, questions the very method and structures of Faith and Order, precisely to ensure that everyone is heard:

> For that we need a more inclusive community for reflection and interpretation, open to every culture and ecclesial tradition. We need to

---

Als'" (1984:56).

21 It is *inter alia* on this basis that Stephen Sykes argues that part of the link between the "essence" debate in theology and Ritschl's thinking is that both are driven by the motive of simplification (1990:268ff). The value of this for a complicated lateral/multilateral union is obvious: it simplifies the various conflicting perspectives under a more fundamental and more manageable entity or entities.

22 This is such an important aspect of Ritschl's thought that he notes in brackets and in the small print on page 145: "Mit dem Wort 'Vernetzung' oder einfach 'Netze' habe ich als mögliche Titel für dieses Buch gespielt" (reference to *Zur Logik*). For an instructive discussion of implicit axioms as "Grundkonzept" see Welker (1990:30-39).

23 My involvement in a forum for interchurch dialogue in Port Elizabeth has taught me the value of this. White theologians who benefited from the politico-economic system and who formed a self-understanding in isolation must go through the (especially painful!) process of "being told" our own story. The therapeutic value of stories has been amply proven – especially during the submissions to the Truth and Reconciliation Commission in South Africa. See the contribution of Gerald West (1995:213) on the issue of "speaking with" and the problem of a "hidden transcript" adapted from James Scott's "Don't Stand on My Story" (1997:6-8). See also Naudé (1994:421-434) on the experiential basis of ecumenical relations.

24 Building on A. Lorenzer's *Sprachzerstörung und Rekonstruktion*, Ritschl notes "dass sich z.B. Neurosen in privatisierter Sprache zeigen, nicht notwendig und sehr selten in unverständlichem Reden" (1986:159; see also 1984:142).

25 Ritschl does not, as far as I know, pursue the hermeneutical issue in this context. Wolfgang Huber suggests that the transition from an analytic to a hermeneutic process occurs precisely when one's implicit axioms are questioned by a dialogue partner (1990:20).

26 The view "from power" in the ecumenical movement is extensively developed and defended by Heinz-Gönther Stobbe. See Stobbe (1980a; 1980b).

ask who is missing from our circle – and whom do we silence *within* our circle? ... Faith and Order has a duty to represent those who have no voice in the structures of the World Council of Churches (1994:26, 27).

Storytelling as therapeutic process is indeed no easy process. It does in no way imply that the dialogue partners will always come to "see" their differences as surface expressions of the same deep structure or "Ur-Anliegen" (Ritschl 1994:58) as Ritschl seems to assume in his analysis of dogmatic differences (see 1986). Huber shows that it is possible to follow a type of axiomatic reasoning:

> ... der gerade nicht auf die Tiefengrammatik mögliche Einheit, sondern auf die Tiefenstruktur von Differenz zielt. ... Denn gerade in ihrer doppelten Verwendbarkeit hat die These von der impliziten Axiomen im Blick auf die ökumenische Situation der Gegenwart eine erhebliche diagnostische Kraft (1990:29).[27]

This therapeutic process, which marks theology as wisdom, allows for both a critical and healing ("zärtliche") engagement (Ritschl 1984:340) between dialogue partners. If allowed to grow, it will reveal if and how social sources (history, class, language, race) assume the status of implicit axioms that steer us, stealthily and often unconsciously, in such a way that despite dogmatic and textual[28] agreements, union still eludes us. More than that – and very difficult to untangle – a healthy therapeutic process will reveal to what extent social factors masquerade as "theological positions", imparting to them an ideological effect.

But what will serve as normative reference point in this therapeutic process? What leads theology to be a wisdom theology? We turn to this in our last section.

3. SCRIPTURES AS REFERENCE POINT

One does not have to argue the point that the heart of our Reformed identity is the centrality of the Word of God in its various manifestations as revelation, Scripture and proclamation. This was reinforced at a recent worldwide consultation of

---

27 Huber, in an ethical reinterpretation of axioms, also argues that they may not only be pre-linguistic assumptions ("schön immer Vorausgesetzten"), but also the result of (ethical) reflection that in the end accept certain basic insights as "implicit axioms" (1990:23ff).

28 One of the most graphic examples to prove that agreement on theology and wording does not guarantee reception is my proposal to the Eastern Cape Synodical Commission on Dogma and Ethics (Leer en Aktuele Sake) that our Synod should at least express support for the content of the Belhar Confession as accepted by the Uniting Reformed Church. One of the commission members, deeply embedded in the traumatic history of ecumenical isolation in the Dutch Reformed Church ("an attack on us from politically inspired churches"), said the following: "I stood on my knees before God and must say that not a single word of the Belhar confession is in contrast to the Gospel. But I will never be able to sign it". My proposal was accepted by the Commission, but rejected by the Synod. This problem is also referred to by Evans in her discussion (with examples) of the fallacious belief that if we understand, we would agree (1996:196). See my elaborate discussion on the value of liturgy and ritual in ecumenical reception processes (1998:235-256).

Reformed theologians published as *Zur Zukunft der Reformierten Theologie. Aufgaben – Themen – Traditionen.* The introduction already makes very clear:

> Der ökumenische Beitrag der reformierten Theologie besteht darin, dass sie sich ruhig und beharrlich, kritisch und konstruktiv *den vielen Versuchen widersetzt, das Wort Gottes zu entleeren* und es unter die Herrschaft von Metaphysik, Moral, Mystik oder unter das Diktat eines 'Zeitgeists' zu bringen (Welker and Willis 1998:10, my emphasis).

To restate the point in terms of this paper: the ecumenical contribution of Reformed theology lies in resisting the temptation to disempower the Word by letting it fall under the spell of social sources.

This is pointedly displayed in the writings of Heidelberger systematic theologian Michael Welker, one of the important voices in Reformed theology today. This is not the place for an extensive exposition or analysis, but in simplified terms one could argue that Welker takes up the double tasks of reinterpreting traditional faith symbols (*dogmatic loci*) from a strong biblical-theological perspective (Welker 1994, 1995a, 1995b, 1997) as well as providing an orientation in the face of highly complex modern and postmodern developments. He develops a "realistic theology" (Welker 1995b:12-13, 33-34; 1994:x-xii, 46-47, 49, 97; see also Oberdorfer 1997:63-83) that mediates between human reality and God's reality by "acquiring clarity concerning those traits that are characteristic and unavoidable for the appearance of God's reality and God's power *in the midst of* the structural patterns of human life (1994:xi, my emphasis).

In this mediation the multifaceted biblical text serves as criterion and reference point: "Die Heilige Schrift ist das Wort Gottes, an dem wir unsere Traditionen, Normen und Überzeugungen *immer neu zu messen haben*" (Welker and Willis 1998:176, my emphasis).

The implication of this Reformed thrust, "Reformierte Theologie ist als reformierende Theologie biblische Theologie" (Moltmann 1998:172), is that the therapeutic process discussed in the previous section cannot be seen in isolation. The Story that we *are* as Reformed Christians is to be understood in relation to the Bible in a double sense of the word. First, telling our story (revealing identity in an ecumenical encounter) is to acknowledge that the story itself has been shaped by the Bible (in its various manifestations such as preaching, worship, and catechesis) as well as various other social factors such politics, geography, sex, race and class. But secondly, the reference point and criterion of our story is always the Scripture as canonical Story, canon as "yardstick" of Christian authenticity and truthfulness.

This is the way pointed to by the biblical narratives[29] themselves. Two powerful passages from the Pauline literature serve as illustration

The Christian identity of local churches in Galatia was threatened by the insistence of some that non-Jews could only be saved by keeping the prescribed Jewish customs (Gal. 3:1-14; 4:8-11). Further tensions grew because of the pluralistic background of the members and the social forces shaping society. The danger was that the church

---

29 One could interpret the covenant history in the First Testament as a struggle between being the people of God or following the gods as stated in the first of the Ten Commandments.

might allow these social forces – including Jewish religious legalism – to disempower the gospel message of Jesus Christ summarised in the well-known exhortation: "You are all sons of God through faith in Jesus Christ, for all of you who were baptised into Christ have been clothed with Christ. There is neither Jew nor Greek, slave nor free, male nor female, for you are all one in Christ Jesus" (Gal. 3:26-28). Faith and baptism in Christ become the criteria by which members are measured. And of crucial importance: social forces such as nationality, class and sex are not denied, but seen relative to the new reality of life in Christ who, because he gave himself up, has the power to bring unity in the church (Eph. 2:11-22).

If it then does emerge that a non-theological factor (even a religious one like the will to preserve Afrikaner identity through a form of Calvinism) serves as a hierarchically important implicit axiom, its ecclesiological relativity must be shown in the light of the catholicity and biblical vision of the church. This is one way to see the struggle among Reformed churches in South Africa. It was and is a hermeneutical struggle to interpret the biblical text and take it so seriously that the social forces of political allegiance, cultural identity, race and class are "overpowered" (radically relativised) by the gospel, by Christ himself. If the biblical text, the canonical Scripture, loses this role, the Reformed – no – the Christian identity of the church is at stake.[30]

This is how one might interpret Paul's letter to the Philippians. In his explanation of righteousness through Christ, he explains his own identity formation by enumerating an interesting mixture of theological and social factors,[31] i.e. his birth as a Benjaminite and circumcision on the eighth day (Jewish origin), his party allegiance to the Pharisees (politics), his meticulous keeping of the law and persecutions of Christians (religion) (Phil. 3:1-6). All these factors are then "taken into account" but dramatically relativised: "But whatever was to my profit, I now consider loss for the sake of Christ. What is more, I consider everything a loss compared to the surpassing greatness of knowing Christ Jesus, my Lord, for whose sake I have lost all things. I consider them rubbish, that I may gain Christ" (Phil. 3:7-8). He then asks the Philippians to follow his example (v. 17) and not see themselves as citizens of the world: "Our citizenship is in heaven. And we eagerly await a Saviour from there, the Lord Jesus Christ" (v. 20).

It is clear: *non-theological/social factors in their negative determination of identity (neurosis in therapeutic terms; righteousness through the flesh in biblical terms) are only "overcome" through a radical reorientation to Christ (re-symbolisation in therapeutic terms; conversion in biblical terms) that works a new self-understanding in the light of Christ's second coming (reinterpretation in therapeutic terms; expectation in biblical terms).*

The growth of various identities toward greater ecumenicity must be seen in pneumatological terms. As Welker has shown, the outpouring of the Spirit gives

---

30 "If, for whatever reason, the trust in the Bible as God's living Word is threatened – and this is a world-wide process on various levels – the Reformed tradition itself is at stake" (Smit 1998, my free translation).

31 I am obviously aware of the vast "distance" between our perception of society with its various spheres and pluralisms and the pre-modern view reflected in biblical texts. The point about "identity" is, like all exegesis, merely a plausible construction!

rise to a unity that is not so much an illusory homogeneity as a cultivation of differentiations that do not contradict justice.

> The Spirit gives rise to a unity in which the prophetic witness of women is no less important than that of men, that of the young is no less significant than that of the old, that of the socially disadvantaged is no less relevant than that of the privileged. The promised Spirit of God is effective in that differentiated community which is sensitive to differences, and in which the differences that stand in opposition to justice, mercy, and the knowledge of God are being steadily reduced (Welker 1994:22).

This, I believe, is the art of sound ecumenical practice, taught by the Spirit-teacher.

The Holy Spirit convinces of sin – also the sin of closed identities. The Spirit pours the charisma of love into our hearts. This promises ecumenical acceptance, not so much of texts or liturgical orders or dogmatic positions, but of one another – hopefully in full communion – as children in the one household of God.

BIBLIOGRAPHY

Beinart, W. and Fischer, H. (eds.) 1989. *Verständigung auf dem Prüfstand*. Berlin: Wichern Verlag.

Best, T.F. & G. Gassmann, G. (eds.) 1994. *On the way to fuller koinonia*. WCC: Geneva.

Boesak, W.A & Fourie, P.J.A. (eds). 1998. *Vraagtekens oor Gereformeerdheid*. Belhar: Lus Uitgewers.

Botha, J. en P.J. Naudé, P.J. (eds.) 1998. *Op pad met Belhar*. Pretoria: J.L. van Schaik.

Brandt, S & Oberdorfer, B. (eds.) 1997. *Resonanzen. Theologische Beiträge Michael Welker zum 50. Geburtstag*. Wuppertal: Foedus.

Brandt, S, Suchocki, M.H. & Welker, M. 1997. *Sünde: Ein unverständlich gewordenes Thema*. Neukirchen: Neukirchener Verlag.

Cloete, G.J. & Smit, D.J. (eds) 1984. *'n Oomblik van waarheid?* Kaapstad: Tafelberg.

De Gruchy, J. 1991. *Liberating Reformed Theology: A South African Contribution to an Ecumenical Debate*. Cape Town: David Philip.

Evans, G.R. 1996. *Method in Ecumenical Theology: The Lessons So Far*. Cambridge: Cambridge University Press.

Fischer, H. 1989. "Rezeption in ihre Bedeutung für Leben und Lehre der Kirche". In W. Beinart and H. Fischer (eds.), pp. 100-123.

Gassmann, G. 1984. "Die Rezeption der Dialog", ÖR Vol. 33, pp. 357-368.

Gros, J. (ed.) 1984. *The Search for Visible Unity* New York: Pilgrim Press.

Falconer, A.D. 1993. "En route to Santiago". *The Ecumenical Review* Vol. 45, pp. 44-54.

Huber, W, Petzold E. & Sundermeier, T (Hg.) 1990. *Implizite Axiome. Tiefenstrukturen des Denkens und Handelns, FS Dietrich Ritschl*. München: Kaiser

Huber, W. 1990. "Ökumenischer Realismus. Zur theologischen Bedeutung impliziter Axiome". In W. Huber, E. Petzold & T. Sundermeier (Hrsg.), pp.19-29.

Lee, R. 1960. *The Social Sources of Church Unity: An Interpretation of Unitive Movements in American Protestantism*. New York: Abingdon.

Lengfeld, P. & Stobbe, H.G. (Hrsg.) 1980. *Ökumenische Theologie. Ein Arbeitsbuch*. Stuttgart: Kohlhammer.

Loewe, H. 1988. "Die Kirchen vor der Aufgabe der Rezeption von Ergebnissen ökumenischer Gespräche und Verhandlungen. In J. Rohls & G. Wenz (eds.), pp. 637-651.

Loubser, J.A. 1987. *The Apartheid Bible: A Critical Review of Racial Theology in South Africa*. Pretoria: J.L. van Schaik.

Lorenzer, A. 2000. *Sprachzerstörung und Rekonstruktion: Vorarbeiten zu einer Metatheorie der Psychoanalyse*. Frankfurt: Suhrkamp Verlag.

Meiring, P. & Lederle, H.I. 1978. *Die eenheid van die kerk*. Kaapstad: Tafelberg.

Moltmann, J. 1998. "Theologia reformata et semper reformanda". In M. Welker & D Willis (eds.), pp. 157-172.

Mouton, J. & B. Lategan, B. (eds) 1994. *The Relevance of Theology for the 1990s*. Pretoria: HSRC.

Naudé, P.J. 1994. "Doxology and Praxis: The Ecumenical Significance of Religious Experience in a South Africa of the 1990s". In J. Mouton & B. Lategan (eds), pp. 421-434.

Naudé, P.J. 1997a. "Die Belharstryd in ekumeniese perspektief". *NGTT* xxxviii/3, pp. 226-243.

Naudé, P.J. 1997b. "Regaining our ritual coherence: The question of textuality and worship in ecumenical reception". *Journal of Ecumenical Studies* Vol. 35, No. 2, 235-256.

Naudé, P.J. 1998. "Belhar se ontvangs in die NG Kerk". In J. Botha en P.J. Naudé (eds.), pp. 86-88.

Niebuhr, H.R. 1929. *The Social Sources of Denominationalism*. New York: Holt.

Oberdorfer, B. 1997. "Biblisch-realistische Theologie. Methodologische Überlegungen zu einem dogmatischen Programm". In S. Brandt & B. Oberdorfer (eds.), pp. 63-83.

Ritschl, D. 1984. *Zur Logik der Theologie. Kurze Darstellung der Zusammenhänge theologischer Grundgedanken*. München: Kaiser.

Ritschl, D. 1986. *Konzepte. Ökumene, Medizin, Ethik. Gesammelte Aufsätze*. Gesammelte Aufsätze. München: Kaiser.

Ritschl, D. & Ustorf, W. (Hg.) 1994. *Ökumenische Theologie – Missionswissenschaft*. Stuttgart: Kohlhammer.

Ritschl, D. 1994. "Ökumenische Theologie". In D. Ritschl & W. Ustorf (Hg.) *Ökumenische Theologie – Missionswissenschaft*. Stuttgart: Kohlhammer. pages?

Rodger, P.C. & L. Vischer (eds.) 1964. *The Fourth World Conference on Faith and Order*. London: SCM.

Rohls, J. & Wenz, G. (eds.) 1988. *Vernunft des Glaubens. Wissenschaftliche Theologie und kirchliche Lehre* (FS W Pannenberg). Gottingen: Vandenhoeck & Ruprecht.

Scott, J. 1997. "'Don't Stand on My Story'. The TRC, Intellectuals, Genre and Identity". *Journal of Theology for Southern Africa* 98, pp. 6-8.

Smit, D.J. 1984. "'n Oomblik van waarheid?". In G.J. Cloete & D.J. Smit (eds). Kaapstad: Tafelberg, pp. 39-48.

Smit, D.J. "As Voorwoord: Gereformeerde identiteit?" In W.A. *Boesak, & P.J.A. Fourie (eds)*, pp. 1-21.

Smit, D.J. 1992. "Reformed Theology in South Africa: A Story of Many Stories". In *Acta Theologica* Vol. 12, No. 1, pp. 88-110.

Stobbe, H. G. 1980a. "Konflikte um Identität. Eine Studie zur Bedeutung von Macht in interkonfessionellen Beziehungen und im ökumenischen Prozeß". In P. Lengfeld & H.G. Stobbe, pp. 190-237.

Stobbe, H.G. 1980b. "Konfessionelle Identität, ökumenische Bewegung und Macht". In Lengfeld & H.G. Stobbe (Hrsg.), pp. 215-237.

Sykes, S. 1990. "'Essence of Christianity' versus 'Implicit Axioms'". In W. Huber, E. Petzold & T. Sundermeier (Hrsg.), pp. 263-276.

Tanner, M. 1994. "The Tasks of the World Conference in the Perspective of the Future". In T.F. Best & G. Gassmann (eds.) *On the way to fuller koinonia*. WCC: Geneva.

Tillard, J.M.R. 1986. "The Ecclesiological Implications of Bilateral Dialogue". *Journal of Ecumenical Studies* Vol. 23, No. 3, pp. 416, 417.

Towards an Ecumenical Consensus on Baptism, the Eucharist and the Ministry. Geneva: WCC 1977 (Faith and Order Paper, No. 84).

Truth and Reconciliation Committee in South Africa (vol. 4, p. 65, paragraph 29).

Vischer, L. 1984. "The Process of 'Reception' in the Ecumenical Movement". *Midstream* Vol. 23, pp. 221, 232

Wainwright, G. 1983. *The Ecumenical Moment: Crisis and Opportunity for the Church*. Grand Rapids: Eerdmans.

Wainwright, G. 1984. "Reception of 'Baptism, Eucharist, and Ministry' and the Apostolic Faith Study". In J. Gros (ed.), pp. 71-75.

Welker, M. 1990. "Implizite Axiome. Zu einem Grundkonzept von Dietrich Ritschls 'Logik der Theologie'". In W. Huber, E. Petzold & T. Sundermeier (Hrsg.), pp. 30-39.

Welker, M. 1994. *God the Spirit*. Minneapolis: Fortress Press.

Welker, M. 1995a. *Kirche im Pluralismus*. Gütersloh: Kaiser.

Welker, M. 1995b. *Schöpfung und Wirklichkeit*. Neukirchen: Neukirchener Verlag.

Welker, M. & Willis, D. (eds.) 1998. *Zur Zukunft der Reformierten Theologie, Aufgaben. Themen. Traditionen*. Neukirchen: Neukirchener Verlag.

West, G. 1995. *Biblical Hermeneutics of Liberation*. Pietermaritzburg: Cluster.

Wolterstorff, N. 1983. *Until Justice and Peace Embrace*. Grand Rapids: Eerdmans.

1.6 THE BELHAR STRUGGLE IN ECUMENICAL PERSPECTIVE[1]

> Bekennen kann man nicht, weil man bekennen möchte in der Meinung, dass Bekennen eine gute Sache wäre. Bekennen kann man nur, wenn man bekennen muss (Karl Barth).

> The pretences for separation may be innumerable but want of love is always the real cause (John Wesley).

The events of the past few years[2] have shown that the unification process in the DRC family is seriously hampered by differences over the Belhar Confession. A perspective from the wisdom of ecumenism might contribute towards clarifying the unification process, and specifically the problems with the adoption of the Belhar Confession. For pastoral reasons the involvement of an "outsider" is often beneficial for resolving a deadlock situation. Perhaps the metaphorical person of "ecumenism" can free us from overheated emotions and from the captivity of our own histories, and can help to give air to the process and to resolve it.

This contribution consists of two parts.

Firstly, the discussion within the DRC family is described in technical terms peculiar to the ecumenical movement. Built into this are the perspectives that open such an objectifying[3] descriptive analysis of the current crisis.

Secondly, four problems with the acceptance of Belhar from the DRC perspective are spelled out in the context of the ecumenical discussion on reception. The focus is specifically on non-theological factors, with the identity issue as the most prominent point.

---

1. The essay "The Belhar Struggle in ecumenical perspective" is an English translation of the article "Die Belharstryd in ekumeniese perspektief", first published in 1997 in *Ned Geref Teologiese Tydskrif* xxxviii/3, pp. 226-243.
2. I refer to the fact that the decision-making bodies within the DRC, namely the General Synods of 1990 and 1994 and eleven regional synods in 1995, were not prepared to accept Belhar as a confession, as well as the events of October 1996, when the General Synodical Commission of the URCSA set the unconditional acceptance of the Belhar Confession by the DRC as a non-negotiable requirement for the continuation of the discourse on church unity.
3. Enough time has passed since the initial impact of Thomas Kuhn's paradigm-shift theory and related developments in the philosophy of science for us to know that "objectivity" is a loaded term that has first been threatened from within positivism and currently (of course, in a different manner) from within certain areas in post-modernism. The intention here is to create a certain "distance" by placing the Belhar discourse within the wider category of ecumenism. Readers may later judge for themselves whether categorising is "objectivising". In fairness I also declare my own interest: as a member and minister of the DRC I have a definite sympathy (empathy) with the DRC. I am convinced that we have to adopt Belhar as a confession and also proposed this as a member of SCDPA (Eastern Cape). The proposal was not endorsed by the Synod. This paper is an attempt to reflect on the matter theologically.

Each section is concluded with a brief summary, which must again be read in the context of the essay as a whole.

1. AN ECUMENICAL DESCRIPTION OF THE BELHAR DISCUSSION

It is enlightening to describe the current discussion within the DRC family with technical terms from the *ecumenical movement* as a *multilateral, intra-confessional unification discourse* strongly built around the *reception* of the Belhar Confession. Each of the terms printed in italics will be scrutinised in an attempt to view the Belhar discourse within a broader perspective.

The *ecumenical*[4] *movement*[5] specifically refers to the World Council of Churches[6] and the work done by Faith and Order[7] to accomplish the overall goal[8] of church unity between all Christian churches.

The *multilateral* nature of the discourse refers to the fact that more than two independent churches are involved in this. The impression that this is actually about the DRC and the URCSA is not factually correct, since at least the RCA should also be considered in the process, unless they themselves were to decide to withdraw from the dialogue or the association. The issue whether other churches of the former DRC family (churches in Zimbabwe, Namibia and Zambia) will also be involved

---

4   We should remind ourselves that the word "ecumenism" is related to the concept of *oikein*, which means the "inhabited earth" or "whole world". Originally it referred to the political scope of the Greco-Roman Empire. The adjective *oikoumenikos* was translated in Latin as *universalis* or *generalis* and was adopted as an ecclesiological concept. It refers to the universal validity (description of councils as ecumenical) or to the church all over the earth (gaining acceptance in modern ecumenism). See Bouwen 1991 for more detail.

5   Per Harling (1995:2) makes the interesting observation that the 20th century is characterised by four major movements in the church, namely the missionary movement, the liturgical movement, the charismatic movement and the modern ecumenical movement. I will later argue that the DRC has maintained an essentially negative relation to the latter movement that has narrowed its insight into the "wider shape of the Christian story" (Evans 1996:77, see 2.4 below).

6   The WCC was founded in Amsterdam on 23 August 1948 and had grown from 147 member churches to about 320 members by 1991. Since the involvement of the Roman Catholic Church (without formal membership), the WCC can justifiably be considered the most important ecumenical body. It was formed through the merger of four independent units, namely Faith and Order and Life and Work (both involved in the founding), with the International Mission Board (1961) and the World Council for Christian Education (1971) that joined later. Since its founding, the full assembly of the WCC has met 7 times already, including the founding meeting.

7   As mentioned in footnote 6, Faith and Order (FO) is older than the WCC. Its first world conference took place in Lausanne (1927) and the second in Edinburgh (1937). Under the auspices of the WCC, more conferences were held in Lund (1952), Montreal (1963) and Santiago de Compostela (1993). This is undoubtedly the main arm through which theological discourse on unification within the WCC takes place. For the meaning of "Order" see Smit (1991).

8   Faith and Order's mission is officially formulated as follows: "The aim of the Commission is to proclaim the oneness of the church of Jesus Christ and *to call the churches to the goal of visible unity in one faith and one eucharistic fellowship* expressed in worship and in common life in Christ, in order that the world may believe" (Appendix V, Best and Gassmann, 1994, pp. 309-313, my emphasis).

later will not be considered for the time being, but this issue is included in principle if the name "URC" is taken seriously: it is meant to include Reformed churches in *Southern* Africa. This does not at all imply that the historical and practical importance of the DRC is being underestimated in any respect. And to the extent that the DRC will decide independently on the status of Belhar and about joining the URC, the current discourse also bears the characteristics of a bilateral dialogue, of which there are many examples[9] in the ecumenical movement.

The question whether the Belhar struggle is about an *intra-confessional* discourse is particularly interesting. Since the Orthodox Church (1961) and Catholics (1968) joined the activities of the WCC, there has been a dramatic increase in inter-confessional discourses. It is clear that "confessional" in the strict sense of the word is used to refer to the historical traditions such as Catholic, Orthodox and Protestant, including all the nuances that occur within these traditions. Apart from theological deliberations and theological contacts between specific confessions, the overall work of Faith and Order is, of course, inter-confessionally tinted. Two contemporary examples of this are the documentation of preliminary consensus on baptism, eucharist and ministry,[10] and the attempt to accept the Nicene Creed[11] as a common confession in its original form.

In this light, the Belhar discourse is an intra-confessional matter. Through the Belhar Confession, however, an undeniable "confessional" element is involved in the narrower sense. However, this does not concern the exceeding of confessional boundaries (in this case, Reformed), but the continuing testimony of faith in a particular historical situation. In the opinion of the then Mission Church (1986), and followed by the DRC in Africa (1990) and of course the subsequent URCSA, this testimony had to be expressed in the strongest form, namely in a confession within the Reformed tradition.

The discourse within the DRC family is a *unification discourse*. Although it sounds obvious, in ecumenical terms these "dialogues of union" bring into focus factors that are not necessarily present in the "dialogues of unity". The former is the strongest form of ecclesiastical bonding; it is the last step of a usually laborious path and it

---

9   Consultations regularly take place under the auspices of the "Forum on bilateral Dialogues", which is published as Faith and Order Papers (see a.o. Ehrenstrom and Gassmann 1975). It is remarkable to see how much work has been done in the six forums since the 1960s to 1994. For an overview of the past decades, see the reports of the fourth (1985), fifth (1990) and sixth (1994) forums as published in Paper numbers 125, 156 and 168 respectively (with a historical overview since 1965 by Günther Gassmann as an appendix to 156). The Cento Pro Unione in Rome publishes a biannual bulletin with a Bibliography of Inter-church and Inter-confessional Dialogues. The Information Service of the Vatican regularly issues a French and English version of dialogues involving the Roman Catholic Church under the leadership of the Pontifical Council for Promoting Christian Unity (contact with WCC). An accessible source of information is the "Survey of Church Union Negotiations", which has been published biannually in *The Ecumenical Review* since 1954.
10 The dialogue and documentation on this are known as BEM (Baptism, Eucharist, Ministry). Literature on this is vast. The original publication under the same title (BEM) was published by the WCC in 1982 (FO Paper 111) and a study guide was edited by William Lazareth (1982, FO Paper 114).
11 See *Confessing the one faith* (1991, FO Paper 153) and the accompanying study guide *Towards sharing the one faith* (1996, FO Paper 173). For a discussion, see Brinkmann (1996).

is, of course, the deepest expression of the New Testament metaphors that describe the unity of the church. Between 1945 and 1990 about 60 churches established a new structural unity through unification processes, with approximately 20 million members (Kinnamon 1991:1033). Despite differences, visible structural unity – within one association[12] or across boundaries[13] – is one of the characteristics of these unifying or unified churches. They occur mainly in former colonised areas, where the historic confessional divisions are not as prominent. In most cases it is about more clearly expressing "the need for a common Christian witness" in a local context (Kinnamon 1991:1033-4).

In the simplest terms, *reception* as a theological concept[14] refers to the ecclesiastical acceptance of the outcome of ecumenical dialogue (see Houtepen 1991). However, it is not that easy to explain reception, partly because of its historical complexity. In a simplified way, the development of the concept of reception may be described on the basis of three historical phases.[15]

In the canonical phase concepts such as *lambanein* (receive) and *dechestai* (accept) point towards the deed of faith, namely acceptance of the gospel (Mark 4:20, Acts 2:41) or Christ himself (the well-known verses in John 1:11-12). Paul uses technical rabbinic terms (*paradidonai* and *paralambanein*; see, for example, 1 Cor 11:23) to explain the reception and handing down of the tradition of Communion. And the whole process of canon formation in the early church, where certain writings were accepted as authoritative, may be described as a reception process (see Kuhn 1983:166 and discussions by Loewe 1988:639, 1984:223 and Vischer 1984:223).

In the conciliation phase of the pre- and post-Constantine time, reception technically refers to the process by which local or regional churches announced their decisions by way of synodical letters to other churches, and the signifying of the process as authentically ecumenical through this reception. The councils[16] played a significant role in this. The confirmation of council decisions was a legal-institutional matter which synchronically confirmed that decisions were diachronically consonant with the apostolic tradition. In short: "Reception means the recognition of a *consensio antiquitatis et universitatis*" (Houtepen 1984:145).

---

12 For example, the United Methodist Church in the USA and, of course, our own URCSA.
13 For example, the Church of Christ in Zaire, the United Church of Christ in Japan and the United Church of Canada, where Congregationalists and Methodists were brought together.
14 The concept of reception was adopted by biology, legal science and literary science, and from the latter it found its way to post-structuralism in Biblical Studies. For the latter, see Lategan and Vorster (1985).
15 The most accessible overviews are the work of William Rusch (1988 originally in English) and Edward Kilmartin (1984).
16 The first four councils were of crucial importance for the Christological and Trinitarian doctrines. Nicea I (325) was directed against Arius and confessed Christ's hypostatic union with the Father. Constantinople I (381) confessed the divinity of the Spirit. Ephesus (431) was directed against Nestorius and confessed the unity of Christ's person. Chalcedon (451) confessed the two natures in the one person of Christ as opposed to monophysitism. Another three councils (Constantinople II and III in 553 and 680-1; and Nicaea II in 787) are usually considered as belonging to the undivided church (recognised by churches both in the East and the West).

With the advent of the modern ecumenical movement, reception has gradually been used as a differentiated concept to describe the comprehensive and gradual process of interchurch acceptance. In his illuminating review William Rusch offers the following definition:

> Ökumenische Rezeption umfasst alle Phasen und Aspekte eines anhaltenden Prozesses, durch den eine Kirche die Resultate bilateraler oder multilateraler Gespräche unter der Leitung des Heiligen Geistes zu einem Teil ihres Glaubens und Lebens macht, weil sie anerkannt hat, dass diese Resultate mit den Lehren Christi und der apostolischen Kirche, d.h. mit dem in der Schrift bezeugten Evangelium, übereinstimmen (1980:24).

This differentiation in the modern ecumenical movement exceeds the formal juridical meaning of the conciliation period and highlights, among other things, the *process*-character of reception, which involves all phases and aspects of the unification process. The *dialogic* character of reception is confirmed by emphasising that results are derived from bilateral and multilateral talks. The *pneumatological* dimension is evident in the conviction that *pardosis* and reception are essentially the work of the Spirit.[17] The *spiritual* or qualitative dimension emphasises that whatever is received will be part of the faith and life of the church (see Gassmann 1974:319-320; 1984:366) and, in the case of texts, will not have mere paper status (Loewe 1988:649). The *criteriological* component is related to the distinction from within Scripture and tradition, as summarised in our apostolic faith (and, of course, as interpreted differently from within different traditions).

When can we then talk about "acceptance by the church" or "reception"? There are different answers to this question, based on different views of the "authority of the church". These range from churches where episcopal succession and ecumenical councils are decisive, through the synodical processes in Protestant churches, to the so-called non-confessional churches, where there resides, at least in principle, much greater decision-making power in the local church or independent groupings. Of course there are determining theological decisions behind these differences, which explains why even ecumenical processes in themselves are (apart from content) problematic.[18]

The content of what should be accepted also differs from case to case and is usually related to the process in which the churches are involved. Examples range from an ecumenical consensus document (such as BEM or the study of Nicea), the change in status of a "statement" that becomes a "confession" (Barmen), a jointly formulated confession of sin (Stuttgarter Schulderkenntnis[19]), a concord of religious truths

---

17 For a creative ecumenical pneumatology, see Müller-Fahrenholz (1995).
18 Here it is important to note the study *Councils and conciliarity* on the relationship between the modern ecumenical movement and the councils of the early church, and the meaning of the conciliar process today (see summary and reports in Gassmann 1993, Part IV). It is clear that major breakthroughs in ecumenism will probably be achieved only by an Ecumenical Council. Such a request was recently repeated at the Faith and Order conference in Santiago de Compostelo (1993), but the awarding of conciliar status to such a meeting will be extremely difficult, especially from an Orthodox and Catholic angle.
19 This confession was formulated at the end of the Second World War by the Evangelical Church to confess its share in the atrocities of the war. Leading figures from the

(Leuenberger Konkordie[20]), to a church order that guides unification (DRMC and DRCA). From an ecumenical perspective, a unification dialogue that includes the reception of a confessional document is more complex than usual, but of course not impossible. In the case of Belhar, a further complicating factor is the fact that the confession is not the result of reciprocal discourse, but had already acquired the status of a confession[21] because of the particular situation in which it originated, and because it was preceded by a partial unification within the same family.[22]

Two examples in the confessional context can further clarify the reception process: Nicea and Barmen.

In an effort to join all the churches in a common expression of faith, Faith and Order decided to return to the period before the great schisms of 1034 (East-West schism) and 1521 (Rome-Reformation schism), when there was greater consensus in the church (the so-called *consensus quinquesaecularis*). It was decided to use the Nicene Creed as a starting point, since it already enjoyed the widest ecumenical acceptance. The text with commentary was sent as *Confessing the one faith* to all member churches (including the Catholic Church) in 1991, along with a study guide in 1995 to serve as a guide for study at a local level. The process is still underway and comments are being awaited for subsequent evaluation and conclusion.

Two obstacles had to be overcome. First there was the contentious issue of the *filioque*.[23] This later addition to the original confession of the church in the West led to years of debate and serious study of the church fathers. Consensus has been reached that, for ecumenical purposes, the text should be used in its original form (*filioque*

Confessing Church, such as Otto Dibelius and Martin Niemoller, played a big role in this. The confession was finalised in Stuttgart on 18-19 October 1945.

20   This "agreement" was formulated by the Protestant Churches in Europe (mainly Germany) and was accepted in Beuenberg (Bern) in March 1973 by 50 churches as a consensus on central matters of faith, without assuming the status of a confession. The intention was to establish a "church community": "Kirchengemeinschaft im Sinne der Konkordie bedeutet, dass Kirchen vershiedenen Bekenntnisstandes aufgrund der gewonnenen Übereinstimmung im Verständnis des Evangeliums einander *Gemeinschaft an Wort und Sakrament* gewähren und eine möglischt grosse *Gemeinsamkeit in Zeugnis und Dienst* an der Welt erstreben" (Konkordie, point 29, my emphasis; see Lohff 1985 for introduction and text). The churches of the Konkordie still meet regularly and new members from Protestant backgrounds have joined them over the years.

21   It is not suggested that the DRC and RCA would, for example, confess together if Belhar were to be submitted simultaneously as a confession. The history of Belhar itself (e.g. status confessionis on apartheid) at any rate made it impossible for the DRC to give serious attention to the confession as a confession. See my analysis under point 2. I simply remark that a confession that has already been accepted in one church complicates a unification process with another church.

22   The strenuousness which characterised the unification of the DRMC and DRCA (even to the point of declaratory court orders) should not be underestimated. Of course, other factors are present in the DRC that make such a process even more complex. Nevertheless, the establishment of the URCSA should serve as an ecumenical model of a source of hope. It can be done.

23   This means "and the Son" and was added to the confession on the Spirit by the church in the West, to emphasise that the Spirit is of both the Father and the Son (*ekporeuomenon*) in an effort to combat all forms of subordination of the Spirit. See Lukas Vischer (1981) for documentation on this, and *Confessing the one faith* (78-79).

therefore omitted) without sacrificing the theological importance of the relationship between Christ and the Spirit (*filioque* retained for own use[24]).

Secondly, there are many churches that do not feel themselves bound to the language or dated issues (among others, the *homo-ousios*) as contained in the Nicene Creed. It may even be experienced as a foreign confession.[25] The process was organised in such a way, however, that Nicea could possibly enjoy wide acceptance. The distinction between "recognition" and "reception" is of great importance here. Where the text is not accepted as a confession, it can still be "recognised" as an expression of the same apostolic faith that everyone shares. This "recognition" is the result of an "explication" through which the biblical, historical and contemporary meaning of the confession is explained. Assuming that the preceding process runs smoothly, "common confession" will follow after "explication" and "recognition": "Common *explication* and *recognition* of the apostolic faith provides a basis for a common *confession* of the same faith. This confession will ultimately require the mutual recognition of baptism, eucharist and ministry and the common structures for decision-making and teaching authoritatively" (*Confessing the one faith*: 6, my emphasis). This does not necessitate the formal acceptance of Nicea as a confession,[26] although the desired result would be to concretely express the unity of the church around the world.

With regard to Barmen, it is instructive to note that initially (1934), for historical reasons, it did not have the status of a confession. From the beginning, however, it was regarded as a document of exceptional significance – also by those who were not originally involved in the composition of Barmen. In time it was accepted as confession by a great number of Landeskirchen[27] in Germany. This is therefore a good example of the adoption of a document from within one historical context, its "recognition" as a contemporary expression of the apostolic faith and, in some cases, its total "reception" with its being granted confessional status in a different historical context.

We may conclude this analysis of the Belhar discourse in an ecumenical context with some summarising remarks.

1. The reception of Belhar is subject to the recognition that it is an integral part of a process that includes more than the adoption of a text. *The unification process between churches is a comprehensive whole.* "Church union, in other words, is viewed not as

---

24 This ecumenical attitude is apparent in, among other things, the fact that the new hymn book of the Evangelical Churches in Germany contains a footnote indicating that the *filioque* is omitted at ecumenical events.
25 See the book by Hood 1990 with the significant title, *Must God Remain Greek?*, especially 247-248 and the reaction of Stanley Harakas (1991).
26 There is particular sensitivity towards the so-called "non-credal churches" and the commission explicitly states that its study "does not mean to demand acceptance and use of the Nicene Creed", but expresses the hope that, because these churches share the same faith, they will be able to confess together during special ecumenical events (*Confessing the one faith*:4).
27 The declaration was accepted by these churches at the first synod in Wuppertal-Barmen on 31 May 1934 (based on preliminary work by Hans Asmussen, Thomas Breit and Karl Barth). Some Lutheran churches also recognise Barmen but do not accept it as a confession.

an all-or-nothing, one-time achievement, but as a process of gradual growth that allows the churches to strengthen their commitment to each other through interim steps" (Kinnamon 1991:1035). It is about reception of each other (with everything we bring with us) within the context of one new church (and all that goes with it). It is about histories, spirituality, liturgies, differences in theological emphasis, canonical arrangements,[28] pension funds and last but not least, about self-concepts and mutual concepts about each other (see section 2 below).

2. In this case, it also about a text. And this text is not merely a declaration or an agreement or a catechesis. At least in ecumenical terms, it is about the exceptional case of *a text with confessional status* that has already been accepted by one party to the dialogue and offered to other churches for reception. Precisely for that reason there must be so much sensitivity about the *dialogic moment*. Unlike political parties, churches may not relinquish one another. The future unifying church will also not benefit much if Belhar only enjoys paper or church-order status, without growing[29] in the hearts and deepest religious lives of all the members.

3. The URC insists on full reception and joint confession in one church. Ecumenism opens up the possibility for the DRC to attempt to make progress through an intermediate step. This intermediate step[30] towards the acceptance of a confession must at least be *common explication*[31] with formal *recognition*[32] ("recognition") by the DRC.

---

28 The central theological significance of a new church order should not be underestimated here. See Busch (1996). Dirk Smit notes that this is one of the biggest challenges on the agenda of the Reformed churches (1992:101).

29 Such a growth process is, of course, strengthened through the act of confessing the confession and does not have to precede it. The "forcing" down of a confession, as we will see later, will harm the spiritual (qualitative) dimension to which Rusch refers.

30 As is evident in the following footnote, the DRC missed its chance of such an interphase. Very little has happened regarding Belhar since the 1990 Synod. If we were sensitive to ecumenism, the 1994 Synod would have been an excellent opportunity for "recognition". Now we are left with an all-or-nothing situation, and there are serious doubts about the bona fides of the DRC.

31 The DRMC and URC theologians have already done excellent work. I am not sufficiently involved in the inner discussions to be able to judge whether something of this joint explication, also after the transformation of our country, was fully realised. From a URC perspective, the time for this has probably passed. It remains a good way to follow, though, and it requires special attention, "because it is *the presupposition* for reaching the goal of a common recognition and confession of the apostolic faith in our time" (*Confessing the one faith*: 3, my emphasis).

32 To date, the official response of the DRC still does not comply with the ecumenical principle of recognition. It involves more than "acknowledging" that the DRMC has "the fundamental right" to adopt a fourth confession (recommendations 2 and 3 of 1994). It also involves more than "acknowledging" that Belhar "in itself is not in conflict with the Three Formularies of Unity" (Recommendation 5). It involves "acknowledging" that the same apostolic faith which we share with the Catholic Church is reflected in the Belhar Confession, and to measure "how much in its own life and commitment it is faithful to the apostolic faith and how far it is confessing it in its own words and deeds" (*Confessing the one faith*:6, under "recognition"!). Thus, "recognition" as an intermediate step is not an easy solution: it is a serious matter and it confirms the intrinsic, biblical relationship between self-examination and confession. Only in this way, as ecumenism teaches us, can the participants in the dialogue be convinced of one's seriousness about the matter.

4. For the DRC earnest attention to the *criterion of the apostolic faith* – and theologically speaking nothing else – appears to be of key importance. It is time that the normative status of Belhar's origin history[33] is relativised in the light of biblical and theological assessment of Belhar "in itself" (Synod 1994, finding 5, see discussion under section 2.1). If problems are then identified, this should be an open part of the unification discourse.

5. In the meantime, this unification process asks of all participants to make an obedient commitment to the Holy Spirit who leads the church in truth and who wants to join the DRC family into one church. This commitment is not a pneumatological extra or a cheap methodism, but a theological *sine qua non* for the unification process.

Below, the specific problems which the DRC experienced with the adoption of the Belhar Confession will be explained and analysed from an ecumenical perspective.

2. THE DRC'S RECEPTION PROBLEM FROM AN ECUMENICAL PERSPECTIVE

Without presenting a detailed historical overview, I offer general perspectives that may possibly fulfil a wider heuristic function.

2.1. The chances of reception are poor if a defensive hermeneutic of suspicion[34] determines the strategy

The core problem is not the general trend or specific formulas of the Belhar Confession. The formulation of God as the God of the poor and the wronged (recommendation 8, 1994 Synod) is in terms of the URC's own point of departure in section 2 of the church ordinance (the confession is open to better insights from within Scripture), not an insurmountable obstacle. *Kerk en Samelewing* contains formulations that should be included in the debate. The 1990 Synod of the DRC has already, although in a negative formulation, judged that the Belhar Confession in itself is not in discord with the Three Formularies (recommendation 5). Positively, therefore, they acknowledge that Belhar is in accordance with the Scriptures[35] and Reformed tradition.

What is clear, though, is that the DRC adopted a defensive tone from the beginning because it experienced the "rejections" of the confession as directed against itself.

It is true that the accompanying letter clearly states that the confession is not aimed against a particular person, church or churches, and that no one should abuse the

---

33 Formulated in brief: less Boesak, more Bible.
34 In my explanation it is clear that I do not use 'hermeneutics of suspicion' here in the technical sense in which it was developed as criticism of ideology, and thus as an aid towards understanding. Marx, Nietzsche and Freud are often referred to as the "masters of suspicion" (see Naudé 1996a:19). In this case it is about suspicion as an obstacle towards understanding.
35 Let us learn from Barth. As one might expect, he discusses religious confessions in his study of God's Word. He is recklessly focused on the issue that the only source of authority for a confession should be the revelation of God as it is testified in Scripture. "Die Konfession stellt sich also mit ihrer Autorität nicht über und auch nicht neben, sondern als kirchliche Konfession *unter* die heilige Schrift" (KD 1/2:694; see his definition and detailed discussion on pages 693 to 739).

confession for political purposes. The mere fact that the DRMC mentions this as a statement in the letter that accompanies the confession shows that the political and church relations of the time created the opportunity for such an abuse. And it is through this lens that the DRC also read it. This explains why two of the nine points of the 1990 decision were formulated as a defence (see recommendations 6 and 7).

This is accompanied by suspicion. As a result, the Belhar text is not read according to its own theological merits.[36] Instead of focusing on its content, its problematic origination history[37] is pointed out. The November 1996 letter from the AC (DRC) unequivocally states that for those who oppose the confession, the relationship between the *status confessionis* and actions of certain persons with political agendas places Belhar within the framework of liberation theology.[38] And because we in the DRC have not yet succeeded in reading liberation theologies with the required discernment, this perception is sufficient to sink the confession.

2.2. The contribution that worship and liturgy can make towards reception is largely neutralised if worship itself is a point of contention or has an individualistic character

The relationship between doxology and reception has already been established thoroughly in the practice of ecumenism[39] and as a theme in ecumenical theology[40] (see Naudé 1997 for a detailed discussion). These possibilities were seriously compromised long before the emergence of Belhar, because joint use of the sacraments and joint worship have been so deeply embedded in the schism history of the DRC's relationship with its former "daughters". It is, of course, irresponsible to make random connections in history. But the question remains whether 1857 and

---

36 That is why reference is frequently made to the fact that the Belhar Confession "in itself" is not problematic. This implies that there are major problems because Belhar is *not* read "in itself"! It has been pointed out by reception theorists that texts are indeed read along with baggage. But then honesty (and good hermeneutics – according to Bultmann already!) requires that the baggage must be *declared*.

37 Barth writes about this with wisdom and insight. He indicates that there are almost always problems with the origin history of confessions, including Augsburg and Dordt. One should try to act in a church-like manner as far as possible. But no matter how "bedauerlich" the origin may be, its authority and acceptability must always be *measured against Scripture*. It cannot be formulated more clearly than this: "Gibt es keine Konfession, deren Autorität im Licht ihrer Entstehungsgeschichte nicht gefährdet erscheinen könnte, so gibt es auch keine, deren Autorität nicht trotz ihrer Entstehungsgeschichte das Zuegnis des Heiligen Geistes für sich haben könnte" (KD 2/1:715).

38 This is not the opinion of the General Synodical Commission, but only an explanatory note on perceptions within the DRC. The General Synodical Commission itself believes that Belhar cannot simply be dismissed as a liberation-theological document (letter of 8 Nov. 1996, point 2).

39 It is possible to indicate how this theme has been central to the work of Faith and Order from as early as 1913. The most recent summit on this took place in August 1994 in Ditchingham (England) and was published by Mary Tanner and Günther Gassmann (1995) as editors in *So we believe, so we pray*. For complete information see Naudé 1997.

40 The most prominent theologians who are specifically engaged with doxology and liturgy as a theme are Edmund Schlink (1961, 1983), Stephen Sykes (1984), Geoffrey Wainwright (1980, 1991), Dietrich Ritschl (1984) and Don Saliers (1994). For an excellent overview of the relationship between liturgy and ethics, see Smit (1997a).

1982 are not negative images of each other, although on totally different grounds. In both instances, brothers and sisters were divided by the Communion, instead of being brought together. First the Cape church excluded "coloured members", and then the same controversy was experienced at the Ottawa[41] meeting of the World Alliance of Reformed Churches, where the *status confessionis* on apartheid was accepted.

Furthermore, the by now familiar analysis of television sermons by Müller and Smit (see 1991 and 1994) indicates that liturgical themes in the DRC in the 1980s were characterised by a fundamental individualism and pietism. Issues such as unity, reconciliation and justice that form the basis of Belhar, were up to that stage not part of the public worship of the DRC. It is hard to say whether this has changed since then. Yet it attenuates the possibility that Belhar will easily find a liturgical home in the DRC. Although the General Synodical Commission (letter 11 Nov. 1996, item 7) asks that "prayerful attention" must be given to the confession, the context is limited to "church meetings", which rules a growth process from within the congregation out of order. This misses a central understanding of ecumenism.

2.3. Even in the case of intra-confessional dialogue, the chance of reception is impeded if participants practice their theology from radical social positions

The DRC and URC have so much in common. We come from the same theological tradition dating back to the 16th century; we belonged to the same church from 1652 to 1882 (DRMC) and 1910 (DRCA); we largely share the same language; we are Christians in the same country. Yet the distance between us is so great!

The reason for this lies in the many faces of "Reformed theology" in South Africa (see de Gruchy 1991; Smit 1992), which can be explained (though not exclusively) by the radically opposing social positions from which social reality is constructed. Without resorting to social determinism, the evidence from the North-South tension in the ecumenical movement and from our own context is overwhelming: epistemological priorities are determined and theological viewpoints are chosen from social positions.

This is evident in the 1990 decision (point 4) of the DRC:

> The General Synodical Commission appreciates that the Belhar Confession has been handled and accepted with great earnestness by the synod of the Reformed Mission Church *and that the content deals with matters that are of crucial importance to the Dutch Reformed Mission Church in particular* (my emphasis).

In a country on the brink of social collapse, where thousands of people have lost their lives, where members of Christian churches were at war with each other, the

---

41 The report-back from Ottawa took place among great interest in the Stellenbosch Seminary Hall. There were more people in the hall than during the early morning prayer meetings. When the then dean, Prof. David de Villiers asked Prof. Jonker to resign, he,[de Villers? Jonker?] made a brief impromptu speech. He noted, among other things, that "the DRC should listen to the voice of the universal church. That is the voice of the Holy Spirit calling us all" (freely quoted from memory). This left a lasting impression on me about our isolation and it convinced me that a secluded theology is a dangerous theology.

DRC declares that issues such as unity among Christians, reconciliation and justice are matters of great importance *for the DRMC in particular*. Of course, one must take into account the DRC's own documentation on South African society, such as *Ras, Volk en Nasie* and (by 1986) *Kerk en Samelewing*. Yet the decision displays some "social blindness" that can be explained only by the obvious fact that the DRC simply did not view the situation in the same serious light. For outsiders it creates the impression that, as far as matters of confession are concerned, the "foreign" topics[42] associated with Marcionism, Arianism, Epicureanism and Pelagianism (Belgic/Netherlands Confession of faith) or Arminianism (Dordt) are for the DRC closer to the core of faith than unity, reconciliation and justice.

It may also indicate that the DRC has a certain vision of the Three Formularies which implies that the existing confessions apply as canonical *corpora doctrinae* that need not be expanded[43] in the ongoing reformation of the church. This confirms a fundamental orientation towards Europe[44] – specifically the anti-liberal tradition (see Smit 1997b) – and an inability to articulate the suffering of others theologically, because we observed the world from the "top of history". We may agree with Barth: it is because we did not hear (or see?) the "No"[45] of the confession that we can also not confirm its "Yes" (KD 1/2 :705-706).

2.4. Reception is often hindered because relatively non-theological factors[46] factors are assigned a crucial role

From ecumenism it has become clear over the years that correspondence with a text or clarification of theological differences still does not lead to reception. Evans speaks

---

42 This is not an attempt to relativise the central religious value that was confessed against various heresies. Pelagius, for example, always threatens – in different guises – redemption through free grace alone. The intention is only to show that the issues that Belhar addresses in our past, current and future context should be the issue of confession of each Christian church.

43 There are poignant examples of new contextual confessions, as collected in Song 1976 and 1978. Of course, it is a big and historically significant step – hence the particular importance of Barmen and Belhar as the first new confessions since the Reformation, but ecumenism shows the positive effects of such new symbols of faith.

44 Of course, it is impossible and unwise to sever or to deny our theological ties with Europe. It depends on which traditions from Europe we fall back on and whether our "mindset" remains European or not. Compare Jonker's (1989) good review. Also see my criticism – on liberation theologies as well – from insights in the so-called "oral theory" that help us to recognise our African connectedness (Naudé 1996b).

45 It is clear from confession history that confessions always dismiss something as well in the light of which the truth is confessed as "Yes". The "No", according to Barth, is the basis of the factual distinction between different confessions.

46 This is an unsatisfactory concept. Social scientists could complain about the implicit subordination of factors to theology; theologians could argue that non-theological factors actually assume the character of theological factors and should be named as such (thus: bad theology!). See my discussion later. One could also talk about "secular" (Lutheran World Federation 1970) or "social" factors (R. Niebuhr). The issue of non-doctrinal factors in ecclesiastical relations have been on the agenda since the second world conference of Faith and Order (Edinburgh 1937). For information and literature up to the late 1970s, see Stobbe (1980:194-196). In his discussion of Reformed theology in South Africa Dirk Smit refers to the same problem: "Church unification is notoriously difficult. Even where churches truly want to unite, *practical and historical difficulties* often

of "the errant belief that if we understand we would agree" (1996:196). Günther Gassmann, former secretary of Faith and Order, states "dass auch sogenannte nicht-theologische oder besser nicht-lehrhafte Faktoren einen wesentlichen Einfluss auf die Rezeption der Dialoge haben können" (Gassmann 1984:266). Peter Stobbe interprets these factors from the (cynical) angle that it is about power,[47] without which confessional schisms – historically as well as today – cannot be conceived. Such an interpretation was also applied especially to the mission policy[48] of the DRC. The well-known thesis by JC Adonis shows that the mission policy, in spite of its theologically well-formulated ideals, in practice serves as an instrument of oppression, where black and white are not regarded and treated as equals (Adonis 1982:196). The numerous examples from mission practice (Adonis 1982:205-206) show that a clerical form of white supremacy and black subordination manifests here. Adonis describes missiology as a form of preserving white power in accordance with the policy of apartheid.[49]

In the light of the unification process referred to above, it is better[50] to focus on the question of identity. Numerous studies show that "questions of polity and the *fear of losing a sense of ecclesial identity* are the most stubborn obstacles to union" - especially where structural unification implies the forming of a new ecclesial identity[51] (Kinnamon 1991:1034, my emphasis).

---

    prove insurmountable" (Smit 1992:101, my emphasis).

47 "Wenn zu Begin dieser Abhandlung gesagt wurde, die Konfessionen verdankten ihre Existenz im wesentlichen dem Bündnis mit der politischen Macht, so ist jetzt, im Lichte des vornehmlich am Beispiel der katholischen Kirche Erlaueterten, hinzufügen, dass auch ihr Fortbestand zum allergrössten Teil durch die Wirksamkeit von Macht garantiert sein" (Stobbe 1980:214). He indicates that this does not only apply to Catholics. Church division becomes part of "der programmatischen Selbstdefinition der konfessionellen Systeme" which gradually grows "zu einem identitätsstiftenden un stabilisierenden Merkmal" (also of individual members). To illustrate this, he tells the story of the Lutheran who is stranded on an island after a shipwreck. He immediately builds two churches: the one he visits faithfully each Sunday; the other he refuses to enter!

48 Johann Kinghorn's analysis of the Federal Mission Policy of 1935 and 1947 is compulsory reading for anyone who still doubts the deep connection between white guardianship (power!), segregation and the theological motives of the DRC. He shows that this policy played a role that cannot be overestimated – very soon it was used for more than just a guide for missionary activities. In the absence of a socio-theological criterion in the church, it was also involved in assessing political ideas and, of course, the issue of apartheid (Kinghorn 1986:87, see the entire Chapter 5).

49 This is a harsh judgment. Of course, one cannot apply it to every missionary, and one cannot deny the pastoral and spiritual motives which run the mission documents. History, however, shows what the socio-political consequences were.

50 With this I do not deny the link between this particular confessional identity and power. Stobbe discusses it on the basis of the great historical traditions. He suggests that the WCC is actually a paradoxical phenomenon. Here confessionality and the power (see his definition 196-198) that goes with it are confirmed and at the same time seen as obstacles to church unity. See Stobbe (1980:215 ff).

51 Although I will focus on the so-called non-theological dimension of identity below, the core question of ecumenism is undoubtedly the ecclesiological (i.e. theological) question about the identity of the church. "At stake in the understanding of unity and schism, of continuity and discontinuity, of integrity and fragmentation, is precisely the *identity of the Church* and therewith the nature and substance of *truth* and the conditions of its *authoritative expression* (Wainwright 1983:190, his emphasis).

It is worth noting Lukas Vischer's insight on identity: "Frequently, confessional positions are not divided by a concern for the purity of their teaching. *The real motive is often simply preservation of one's identity which has developed over the course of history* ... These may be matters of language, ethnic identity, national pride, or other things. For this reason the ecumenical movement must pay attention to these ancillary factors. By breaking through these secondary barriers – which are no less resistant for all that – the church will win the freedom for its process of reception" (1984:232, my emphasis; see also Loewe 1988:646; Fischer 1989:48). With this, Vischer establishes the link between identity and additional ("ancillary") factors that may serve as obstacles in the quest for church unity.

It is no simple task to write about the "identity" of a church. Apart from the theological factors that ideal-typically and historically determine a church (traditional four marks, Reformed, etc.), there are also the socio-political and cultural factors that are also constituting the church as a social institution[52] (language, relation with a nation or a particular group, European, etc.). The key question is how these theological and social (non-theological) factors are constructively integrated into the practical realisation of the "self-concept" of a church. If non-theological factors become decisive and normative, identity is determined in a negative (i.e. theologically destructive) manner, with negative implications for ecumenism.

What non-theological factors contribute significantly to the DRC's self-understanding? I note – more on the basis of intuition than empirical studies – four brief points, while acknowledging that others[53] have already undertaken such a study in a more extensive (and better motivated) manner. The first is a (familiar) historical point, the second an ecumenical one, and the last two specifically relate to the current socio-political situation since 1994.

First. The adoption of a romantic concept of nation, intense empathy with the socio-political development of the Afrikaner and Kuyper's romantic view of history that was connected with the theological transformation of Warneck's idea of *Volksmission* by means of a *corpus christianum* (see Kinghorn 1986, Chapter 3). This led to a constitutive relationship between Afrikaners and the DRC (apart from existing *Hervormde* and *Gereformeerde* Churches), which was only relativised with the secession of the Afrikaans Protestant Church. The practice of having different churches for different peoples was carried through up to congregational level, where congregational borders coincided with the borders of separate residential areas, often with the additional result of a class division within one church (still observable today).

---

52 Bohoeffer, in his famous *Sanctorum Communio* (1960) makes the assumption that a sociological examination of the church is a dogmatic issue (see *Vorwort*). He distinguishes between the church as an empirical community and community "von Gott gestiftet" (1960:191) and indicates that sociological categories are exceeded in the community character of the church as "Gemeinschaftsgestalt *sui generis*, Geistgemeischaft, Liebesgemeinschaft" (1960:204). There is not sufficient space to discuss this matter further here.

53 See the lists of literature in earlier works such as De Gruchy (1979), Kinghorn (1986) and the more recent contributions by Smit (1992, 1996). A continuation of these studies – especially from within the DRC itself – is urgently necessary to give new theological direction.

Second. Due to the active involvement of the WCC and other ecumenical bodies in the issue of race in South Africa, the DRC has been increasingly isolated, either on its own initiative or as a result of the decisions of others. The withdrawal of the WCC (internationally) closed the door to the SACC (nationally), and the suspension of membership of the World Alliance left the DRC in the ecumenical wilderness.[54] This confirmed its self-understanding as a wronged[55] church that was dependent on itself,[56] as the WCC and SACC were seen over the years as politically motivated organisations deliberately attempting to isolate the DRC.

Third. In a radically changing South Africa the DRC has lost its prominence. It has become a peripheral church. Moreover, the historical and social factors which so profoundly shaped its identity have collapsed,[57] with the consequent deep crisis that goes with this. Choices that are made now and directions that are now taken will fundamentally determine the role of the DRC in the next century. And at the moment things do not look promising. Despite a declaration that racism is a serious error, and despite a (somewhat unwilling?) acceptance of the Rustenburg Confession, the attitude towards objectors in the URCSA in the Free State and Northern Cape, confusing signals regarding the Truth and Reconciliation Commission, and the reluctance concerning the Belhar Confession all indicate to the observer that this is a church that has not yet radically broken with its past. This deprives the DRC of its moral and prophetic authority, which is indispensable for making a contribution as a public church[58] in a democratic dispensation, and it forces the DRC further to the edge of the church landscape in South Africa.

Fourth: The shock of radical social change and a relatively peaceful political revolution also has an effect. This makes the church a safe haven, at least for some. Here, in the familiarity of its own socio-religious environment, things can continue

---

54 The events since 1948 (founding meeting of WCC, Amsterdam) by Cottesloe (1960), the Programme to Combat Racism (from 1969) and Ottawa (1982) are systematically discussed by Etienne de Villiers (1986) and tell a story of growing isolation and alienation.

55 This explains the initiative of the DRC to resign from the WCC and even the Reformed Ecumenical Synod (1985), for example.

56 Economic sanctions can force a country to change; "church sanctions" often achieve little more than strengthening a sectarian spirit.

57 What Smit still saw as a possibility in 1992 – and which he describes with so much passion – is now reality: "It may be that the white Reformed churches are also experiencing a serious crisis of identity. In terms of Peter Berger's sociology of knowledge, the walls of both the objective, physical world and the socio-historically constructed, internalised world they knew so well and in which they were so much at home, are falling. They experience themselves as 'homeless minds'. They no longer know who they are, where they come from and where they are going. In particular, their 'sacred canopy' has fallen. The religious legitimization of everything they were and all they did, has itself become suspect. They face 'an heretical imperative'. They find themselves at the crossroads. They are forced to choose: new destinies, new lifestyles, new values, a new religion" (1992:100).

58 For the DRC the new political dispensation implies a shift from de facto "state church" to one among a range of religious groupings in South African "civil society". This has radical implications for its public role. If this transition is not made, there remain only the ways of secularism and (in cohesion or in opposition) the piousness of a civil religion. In his opening address to the *Gesellschaft für Evangelische Theologie* in Munster, Germany (17 February 1997), Wolfgang Huber strikingly formulated that only a church characterised by "Offenheit" has any impact in the "Öffentlichkeit".

as they did in the past. Here a piece of self-determination is retained for Afrikaans-speaking[59] members of the church. Here the issue of survival, specifically ecclesial survival, forces the issue of church unity low on the agenda.

The cumulative result of these factors is the establishment of the DRC as an example of a denominational[60] church which is at the same time trying to find congruence with its radically new environment

In the light of the particular circumstances the DRC is obviously not unique. Our struggle is a familiar battle. The well-known Anglican church historian and ecumenical theologian, GR Evans, notes that, based on a mixture of purely human and ecclesiastical factors, "people find the well-defined and familiar most comfortable and will continue for that reason to gravitate towards it rather than risk the ecumenical step into the unknown" (Evans 1996:58-59). It is extremely difficult to admit that one was wrong (confession of guilt and confession of faith always go together!). The easy option is to give in to "denominational inclinations (which) tend to lead to self-sufficiency and exclusivity" and which lead to a loss of insight into "the wider shape of the Christian story" (1996:77). Why is this so dangerous? *Because isolation of a denominational church in the long run determines its identity so profoundly that separation is experienced as normal and even becomes a legitimate basis for continued isolation* (see Evans 1996:42, 54).

Unfortunately there are two strong factors that reinforce this exclusivity. On the one hand, in the wider context of churches around the world, Vischer notes that – after the first successes of the ecumenical movement – there is a loss of vision of unity because of an almost spontaneous return to the familiar, because "churches suddenly long for the relative security of their own traditions, and emphasise again their own identity" (Vischer 1984:221).[61] It could be argued that this is related to the emergence of new nationalisms since the collapse of totalitarian systems – especially in Eastern Europe and the former USSR – and that it is reinforced by the spirit of pluralism inherent in a post-modern society.

At a local level the URC ultimatum of October 1996[62] will have the same medium-term effect. Evans makes it clear that ecumenical theology is not a kind of clerical diplomacy where parties try to outwit each other. Without the principles of "non-adversiality" (24) and "rapprochement" (75), and enough time to let the process to

---

59 The debate over Afrikaans in a uniting church, as formally decided by the Synod of Northern Transvaal, is of course not innocent at all, in the light of our history and the new language consciousness among Afrikaans speakers. Hence the sharp response. This is a good example of what is discussed below as non-theological factors.

60 It is clear that I use this concept in the negative sense of the word, as meaning "encapsulated in one's own denomination". In the USA in particular many studies have appeared on the topic of "denominationalism". Some of the pioneering work was done by HR Niebuhr, *The social sources of denominationalism* (1954) and the collection edited by RE Richey entitled *Denominationalism* (1977).

61 See also his view of the discrepancy between ecumenical agreements and church practice (Vischer 1981:294-295).

62 The General Synodical Commission considers the unconditional acceptance of the Belhar Confession by the DRC as a non-negotiable requirement for the continuation of the discussion on church unity (General Synodical Commission Minutes, 15.1.3). Since then the URC Synod has amended this position on the discourse, although the requirement of Belhar for church unification was not lessened in any way.

run its course, bilateral talks are doomed. Her experience in the Anglican-Catholic dialogue has taught her that unification processes take decades[63] rather than years. This is confirmed by studies of unification processes: "Most are the result of decades of negotiation and planning", writes Kinnamon (1991:1033).

And what should be decisive in this process? "(R)espect for the other's liberty makes it a requirement that nothing shall be imposed on any party in ecumenism" (Evans 1996:49). Least of all when it comes to confession. Karl Barth had already realised: "Bekennen kann man nicht, weil man bekennen möchte in der Meinung, dass Bekennen eine gute Sache wäre. Bekennen kann man nur, wenn man bekennen muss" (KD, 1/2: 698[64]).

We end this section with a few conclusions.

1. There are a number of problems (hermeneutical, liturgical, social and identity factors) which *together* make the reception of the Belhar Confession extremely problematic for the DRC.

2. From an ecumenical viewpoint, the fact that it is about a *confession* which has *already been accepted by others* is a complicating factor on the way to church unity. The ultimatum that the URC set in this regard is understandable in the light of the frustration with a lack of progress, but is not reconcilable with sound ecumenical practice.[65]

3. The self-understanding of the DRC, which was formed in a normative manner by non-theological factors, establishes it as a *denominational church*. Acceptance of the Belhar Confession and expeditious unification with the URCSA is a *contra-decision* for the DRC, which cannot easily be reconciled with its self-construed identity.

Seen in the context of ecumenism, the DRC indeed stands before a particularly difficult choice. It is not without reason that Jaap Durand remarks that Belhar is the touchstone for the real and complete conversion of the DRC (*Insig* 1997). It can also be one of the most significant steps out of isolation and in the direction of a more truly catholic church. As in the case of all conversions, the price is high, but the

---

63 There is a distinct difference from context to context, and timeframes cannot be determined generally and normatively. One could indicate that unity talks between members of the former DRC family were already actively in progress in the 1970. Belhar itself is older than a decade. Ecumenism teaches us that unification takes a longer rather than a shorter time. My feeling – as spelled out here – is that the DRC's "delay" is linked to non-theological factors rather than to theological factors. And those are the hardest to deal with.

64 The context is Barth's discussion of the insight of a confession as gifted insight, as a gift of the Holy Spirit. The church that confesses does not so much find truth, as the church is found by truth. It is born of the need and compulsion of the Word. "Credo im Sinn der kirchlichen Konfession sagt die Kirche erst, wenn alle ihre anderen Möglichkeiten erschöpft sind, wenn man, auf den Mund geschlagen, nichts anderes mehr sagen kan als eben Credo ... Credo hat sie ja gesagt und eben damit ihre Aussagen als solche charakterisiert, deren Inhalt sie zwar niemandem aufdrängen kann noch will, mit denen sie aber jedermann zur Stellungname, zur Entscheidung auffodert" (KD 1/2:698-699).

65 Evans makes the interesting observation that a setback often paradoxically also implies progress, because at least it is not a backward step to the very beginning! See her discussion of "the winter of ecumenism" (1996:1-18). Hopefully the absolute seriousness of the URC regarding the confession is emphasised.

outcome is guaranteed by God: *"The price of true catholicity may well be the death and resurrection of the churches that we know – in the faith that God has greater things in store for his people than we can remember or even imagine."*[66]

BIBLIOGRAPHY

Barth, K. 1948. *Kirchliche Dogmatik 1/2*. Zürich: Evangelische Verlag.

Best, T.F. & Gassmann, G. (eds.) 1994. *On the way to fuller koinonia*. Geneva: WCC.

Best, T.F. & Heller, D. (eds). 1995. *So we believe, so we pray. Towards koinonia in worship*. München: Kaiser.

Bonhoeffer, D. 1960. *Sanctorum Communio. Dogmatische Untersuchung zur Soziologie der Kirche*. München: Kaiser.

Bouwen, F. 1991. "Ecumenical councils". In N. Lossky (ed.), pp. 336-339.

Brinkmann, M.E. 1996. *Progress in unity. Fifty years of theology within the WCC: 1945-1995*. Louvain: Peters Press.

Busch, E. 1996. "Die Kirchenordnung als Bekenntnisfrage". *Una Sancta* Vol. 4, pp. 329-341.

De Gruchy, J. 1991. *Liberating Reformed theology*. Grand Rapids: Eerdmans.

De Villiers, E. 1986. "Kritiek uit die ekumene". In J. Kinghorn (red.), pp. 144-164.

Ehrenstrom, N. & Gassmann, G. (eds). 1975. *Confessions in dialogue. A survey of bilateral conversations among world confessional families 1959-1974*. Geneva: WCC.

Gassmann, G. 1974. "Rezeption im ökumenischen Kontext". *ÖR* Vol. 26, pp. 314-327.

Gassmann, G. 1984. "Die Rezeption der Dialoge". *ÖR* Vol. 33, pp. 357-368.

Gassmann, G. 1993. *Documentary history of Faith and Order 1963-1993*. Geneva: WCC.

Gros, J (ed.) 1984. *The search for visible unity*. New York: Pilgrim's Press.

Harakas, S.S. 1991. "Must God remain Greek?" *The Ecumenical Review* Vol. 43, pp. 194-199.

Harling, P. (ed.) 1995. *Worshipping ecumenically. Orders of service from global meetings with suggestions for local use*. Geneva: WCC.

Harling, P. 1995. "The liturgy of the world: Ecumenical worship with all senses". In P. Harling (ed.), pp. 1-26

Hill, C. & Yarnold, E. (eds.) 1994. *Anglicans and Roman Catholics: The search for unity*. London: Society for Promoting Christian Unity.

Hood, R.E. 1990. *Must God remain Greek? Afro-cultures and God-talk*. Minneapolis: Fortress Press.

Houtepen, A. 1983. "Reception, Tradition, Communion. In M. Thurian (ed.), pp. 140-160.

Houtepen, A. 1990. "Ökumenische Hermeneutik. Auf der Suche nach Kriterien der Kohaerenz im Christentum". *ÖR* Vol. 3, pp. 279-296.

Houtepen, A. 1991. "Reception". In N. Lossky (ed.), pp. 844-845.

Jacobsen, R. 1960. "Linguistics and poetics". In R.T. Sebeok (ed.), pp. 350-377.

---

66   Albert Outler, as quoted in Wainwright (1983:220, my emphasis).

Huber, W, Petzold E. & Sundermeier, T. (Hg.). 1990. *Implizite Axiome. Tiefenstrukturen des Denkens und Handelns, FS Dietrich Ritschl*. München: Kaiser

Huber, W. 1990. "Ökumenischer Realismus. Zur theologischen Bedeutung impliziter Axiome". In W. Huber, E. Petzold & T. Sundermeier (Hrsg.), pp.19-29.

Jonker, W.D. 1989. "Suid-Afrika se verbondenheid met Europa: Die teologie". *Tydskrif vir Geesteswetenskappe* Vol. 29 No. 2, pp. 146-158.

Kilmartin, E.J. 1984. "Reception in history: An ecclesiological phenomenon and its significance". In J. Gros (ed.), pp. 34-54.

Kinghorn, J. (red.) 1986. *Die NG Kerk en apartheid*. Johannesburg: Macmillan.

Kinnamon, M. 1991. "United and Uniting Churches". In N. Lossky (ed.), pp. 1032-1036.

Kuhn, U. 1983. "Reception – an imperative and an opportunity". In M. Thurian (ed.), pp. 163-174.

Lategan, B. & Vorster, W. 1985. *Text and reality: aspects of reference in Biblical texts*. Philadelphia: Fortress Press.

Lengfeld, P. & Stobbe, H.G. (Hrsg.). 1980. *Ökumenische Theologie. Ein Arbeitsbuch*. Stuttgart: Kohlhammer.

Limouris, G. 1991. "Historical background to apostolic faith today". In *Confessing the one faith*, pp. 105-111.

Loewe, H. 1988. "Die Kirchen vor der Aufgabe der Rezeption von Ergebnissen ökumenischer Gespräche und Verhandlungen. In J. Rohls & G. Wenz (eds.), pp. 637-651.

Lohff, W. 1985. *Die Konkordie reformatorischer Kirche in Europa: Leuenberger Konkordie*. Frankfurt am Main: Otto Lembeck.

Lossky, N (ed.) 1991. *Dictionary of the ecumenical movement*. Geneva: WCC Publications.

Mouton, J. & Lategan, B. (eds.) 1994. *The relevance of theology for the 1990's*. Pretoria: HSRC.

Müller, B.A. & Smit D.J. 1991. "Godsdiens in die openbaar. Tendense in die Afrikaanse godsdiensprogramme van die SAUK". *NGTT* Vol. 4, pp. 652-665.

Müller, B.A. & Smit D.J. 1994. "Public worship. A tale of two stories". In J. Mouton & B. Lategan (eds.), pp. 385-408.

Müller-Fahrenholz, G. 1995. *God's Spirit. Transforming a world in crisis*. Geneva: WCC.

Naudé, P.J. 1994. "Doxology and praxis: The ecumenical significance of religious experience in a South Africa of the 1990's". In J. Mouton & B. Lategan B (eds.), pp. 421-434.

Naudé, P.J. 1996a. *Is God hovering above the nineteenth floor? Doing theology in a post-disciplinary context*. UPE: Inaugural address D38.

Naudé, P.J. 1996b. "Theology with a new voice? The case for an oral theology in the South African context". *JTSA* Vol. 94, pp. 18-31.

Naudé, P.J. 1997. "Ecumenical reception as theological process". Unpublished presentation for Systematische Societät, Heidelberg (Germany), 12 February.

Ritschl, D. & Jones, H.O. (eds.) 1976. *"Story" als Rohmaterial der Theologie*. München: Kaiser.

Ritschl, D. 1981. "Zur Geschichte der Kontroverse um das Filioque und ihre theologischen Implikationen". In L. Vischer (Hg.), pp. 25-42.

Ritschl, D. 1984. *Zur Logik der Theologie. Kurze Darstellung der Zusammenhänge theologischer Grundgedanken.* München: Kaiser.

Ritschl, D. 1986. *Konzepte. Ökumene, Medizin, Ethik. Gesammelte Aufsätze.* Gesammelte Aufsätze. München: Kaiser.

Ritschl, D. & Ustorf, W. (Hg.) 1994. *Ökumenische Theologie – Missionswissenschaft.* Stuttgart: Kohlhammer.

Ritschl, D. 1994. "Ökumenische Theologie". In D. Ritschl & W. Ustorf (Hg.) *Ökumenische Theologie – Missionswissenschaft.* Stuttgart: Kohlhammer.

Rodger, P.C. & Vischer, L. 1964. *The fourth world conference on Faith and Order* (Montreal 1963). London: SCM.

Rohls, J. & Wenz, G. (eds.) 1988. *Vernunft des Glaubens. Wissenschaftliche Theologie und kirchliche Lehre* (FS W Pannenberg). Gottingen: Vandenhoeck & Ruprecht.

Rusch, W.G. 1988. *Rezeption. Eine ökumenische Chance.* Stuttgart: Kreuz.

Saliers, D.E. 1994. *Worship as theology. Foretaste of divine glory.* Abingdon: Nashville, TE

Saliers, D.E. 1994. *Worship as theology. Foretaste of divine glory.* Nashville TE: Abingdon.

Schlink, E. 1961. *Der kommende Christus und die kirchlichen Traditionen.* Göttingen: Vandenhoeck und Ruprecht.

Schlink, Edmund 1983. *Ökumenische Dogmatik.* Göttingen: Vandenhoeck und Ruprecht.

Sebeok, R.T. (ed.) 1960. *Style in language.* Camgridge MA: MIT Press.

Smit, D.J. 1991. "Order". In N. Lossky (ed.), pp. 747-750.

Smit, D.J. 1992. "Reformed Theology in South Africa: A Story of Many Stories". In *Acta Theologica* Vol. 12, No. 1, pp. 88-110.

Smit D.J. 1996. Covenant and ethics? Comments from a South African perspective. *Annual of the Society of Christian Ethics,* pp. 265-282.

Smit, D.J. 1997a. "Liturgy and life? On the importance of worship for Christian ethics". In D. E. de Villiers (ed.) *Scriptura: Christian Ethics in South Africa* Vol. 62, pp. 259-280.

Smit, D.J. 1999. "Modernity and theological education – crises at 'Western Cape' and 'Stellenbosch'?" *Journal of African Christian Thought,* Vol. 2, No. 1, pp. 34-44.

Song, C. (ed.). 1976. *Giving account of the hope today.* Geneva: WCC.

Song, C. (ed.). 1978. *Giving account of the hope together.* Geneva: WCC.

Stobbe, H.G. 1980. "Konflikte um Identität. Eine Studie zur Bedeutung von Macht in inter-konfessionellen Beziehungen und im ökumenischen Prozess". In P. Lengfeld & H.G. Stobbe (Hrsg.), pp. 190-237.

Sykes, S.W. 1984. *The identity of Christianity. Theologians and the essence of Christianity from Schleiermacher to Barth.* London: SPCK.

Sykes, S. 1990. "'Essence of Christianity' versus 'Implicit Axioms'". In W. Huber, E. Petzold & T. Sundermeier (Hrsg.), pp. 263-276.

Thurian, M. (ed.). 1983. *Ecumenical Perspectives on Baptism, Eucharist and Ministry.* Geneva: World Council of Churches.

Tillard, J.M.R. 1978. "Element of unity in recent ecumenical discussion". *One in Christ* Vol. 14, pp. 94-105.

Tillard, J.M.R. 1986. "The ecclesiological implications of bilateral dialogue". *Journal of Ecumenical Studies* Vol. 23, No. 3, pp. 412-423.

Vischer, L. (Hrsg.) 1981. *Geist Gottes, Geist Christi: ökumenische Überlegungen zur Filioque-Kontroverse: Bericht und Vorträge zweier Tagungen auf Schloss Klingenthal*. Frankfurt am Main: Otto Lembeck.

Vischer, L. 1984. "The process of 'reception' in the ecumenical movement". *Mid-Stream* Vol. 23, pp. 221-233.

Wainwright, G. 1980. *Doxology. The praise of God in worship, doctrine and life*. London: Epworth.

Wainwright, G. 1983. *The ecumenical moment: crisis and opportunity for the Church*. Grand Rapids: Eerdmans.

Wainwright, G. 1984. "Reception of 'Baptism, Eucharist, and Ministry' and the apostolic faith study". In J. Gros (ed.), pp. 71-82.

Wainwright, G 1991. "Lex orandi, lex credendi". In N. Lossky (ed.), pp. 600-604.

WCC. 1991. *Confessing the one faith*. Geneva: WCC.

WCC. 1996. *Towards sharing the one faith. A study guide for discussion groups*. Geneva: WCC.

Welker, M. 1990. "Implizite Axiome. Zu einem Grundkonzept von Dietrich Ritschls 'Logik der Theologie'". In W. Huber, E. Petzold & T. Sundermeier (Hrsg.), pp. 30-39.

1.7 BELHAR – FOR SOUTH AFRICA, NORTH AMERICA AND WORLDWIDE[1]

You stand at the threshold of a very important decision regarding the confessional basis of the Reformed Church in America. If the proposal before this Synod is adopted, the path is cleared for the Belhar Confession to become a provisional – and in two years' time, a permanent – part of your church's faith foundation. This is potentially a momentous event. The date of the last confession, the Canons of Dort, is 1619, almost 400 years ago! It is amazing that Reformed churches could for such a long time refrain from a confession that declares the gospel anew, addressing the challenges of different times and contexts.

1. EXPLICATION, RECOGNITION AND CONFESSION

In ecumenical circles we talk about a threefold process in the reception of important ecumenical documents such as creeds and confessions: from common explication to common recognition and finally to common confession.

The first stage is common explication. I am impressed with the thorough work done over the last decade not only to study Belhar in the Reformed Church in America, but also to allow others, including the Uniting Reformed Church of Southern Africa, to bring their perspectives with regular intervals to your General Synods, to send Belhar back to the congregations before a final decision is taken.

The second stage is common recognition. The big question Reformed Christians ask when they receive a new confession is: "Do we recognise in this confession the truth of the apostolic faith?" There are two ways to determine this. Test the confession for consonance with Scripture and then judge the confession against our earlier confessions. Only if the test against Scripture is passed, do we "recognise" the truth. There are numerous references in the study documents that Belhar speaks the Word of God for our times. Belhar is the truth, because it is in accordance with the gospel of Jesus Christ as revealed in the Holy Scriptures. Belhar also confirms our earlier confessions. There is a deep consonance between Belhar and the Heidelberg Catechism, the Belgic Confessions and the Canons of Dort. A detailed study also shows the strong bonds between Belhar and the most ecumenical of creeds, the Constantinopolitan-Nicene Creed from 381.

However, true to the nature of confessions, they do not merely repeat Scripture and earlier confessions, but they speak anew. They provide us with new insight into both the heresies and truths of our time. Belhar speaks with, but also beyond, our earlier faith heritage. The way in which unity, reconciliation and justice are confessed has

---

1   This essay is an adapted version of an address delivered at the General Synod of the Reformed Church in America in Pellah, Iowa, USA (8 June 2007). The essay originally appeared in 2008 in *Perspectives. A Journal of Reformed thought*. May, pp. 17-21. Russel Botman was the other South African speaker at the synod where the Belhar confession was provisionally adopted with an overwhelming majority. It was a strange but joyful experience to see Belhar's adoption on "foreign" soil whilst we in the Dutch Reformed Church could up to that point not reach this decision.

never been done like this before. Our forbearers could not speak like this, because they were true to the demands of the gospel in their own time, as Belhar is true to our time.

The third stage is common confession. Actual confession can only happen if the prior explication and recognition have been sufficiently achieved. There is no logical or necessary movement from stages one and two to stage three. Many churches reflect on Belhar and recognise in it the gospel for our day, but nevertheless do not confess. There are a multitude of reasons for not confessing.

We confess because we have no other option. We confess because God has hit us on the mouth and we cry out: Credo! (Barth)

Let us be reminded that "confession-making" is a particularly Reformed activity. The greater part of the Christian family (like the Lutherans, Catholics, and Orthodox sisters and brothers) can in their view not accept new creeds or confessions. Others, in principle, do not accept confessions at all (like the Free- and non-creedal churches). With the rise of the Pentecostal and charismatic movements, confessions have moved even lower on the agenda of the church.

There are also non-theological reasons for not confessing, although they tend to be presented, and sometimes camouflaged, in theological language. Some see in Belhar a political witness, true to the times and in accordance with Scripture. It should be read in conjunction with, and on the same level as The Witness to the Peoples of South Africa from 1968 and the influential Kairos Document from 1985, but not on the level of a confession. Others see Belhar as too contextual, too specifically focused on the South Africa of the 1980s to qualify as a confession of the ecumenical church. For them Belhar is an important declaration, like Barmen and the Leuenberger Concordie, from which we learn how churches spoke in their specific situation, but it is not necessarily to be more widely confessed. There are Reformed Christians who state that Belhar does not witness to the whole gospel, as the Heidelberg Catechism does, for example, but only highlights important themes from the gospel. It is therefore a partial reflection of the gospel like a good sermon, but it is not a confession.

The act of confessing is a gift and a miracle. It happens because the Spirit is like a wind. You hear its sound, but you do not know wither it will blow. We confess, Karl Barth taught, not because we think it is a good thing to confess. We confess because we have no other option. We confess because God has hit us on the mouth and we cry out: Credo! (I believe).

2. THE SOUTH AFRICAN CONTEXT

Why is it so important that you move beyond recognition to common confession? Let me attempt to explain this from four contexts: the church in South Africa, the United States, the broader ecumenical family of churches, and specifically, the context of the Reformed Church in America.

I am glad to report that Dutch Reformed churches in South Africa have recently renewed their common commitment to reunification in one church after the establishment of separate churches for different race or cultural groups in 1881, 1911 and 1952. At its General Synod in 2007 the Dutch Reformed Church in South Africa clearly said that the debate around unity is no longer about "if" but about "how".

Belhar has no doubt complicated that process as those who might resist reunification can use Belhar as an insurmountable obstacle. "We cannot so easily reunite with a church that now stands on a different confessional basis", claim opponents of reunification. From those in the Uniting Reformed Church of South Africa, which has accepted Belhar, the counter-claim is clear: "No reunification is possible without Belhar". The reunification is now planned to include Belhar in the bigger reunited church, although it will not be required that every pastor sign the confession on the first day. We are sure that the confession will grow in the new church through preaching, liturgy, catechesis and experience.

If the Reformed Church in America would decide to confess Belhar, it would give our long and painful process a great impetus. It would, apart from the Verenigde Protestantse Kerk in Belgie, be the first full adoption of the confession outside South Africa. This will send a powerful message that Belhar has been judged to be worthy of acceptance on equal footing with our existing Reformed heritage. It will say that semper reformanda, so often repeated, does also include the reformation and renewal of our confessional basis.

Although South Africa has undergone a relatively peaceful transition to democracy and we have a stable constitutional state, the challenge of unity, reconciliation and specifically economic justice still loom large. Your confession would show that South Africa and its new challenges are not forgotten by the churches in the Northern Hemisphere. Your confession would be a sign of solidarity that you stand with us in the new struggles we face, as you and others stood with us in our struggle against apartheid theology.

3. THE AMERICAN CONTEXT

I have had the privilege of being a research guest in the United States for the past six months. This nation is too vast and complex for me to make quick and general conclusions. But allow me in all humility to say why I believe you in North America also need to confess the issues taken up in Belhar.

The freedom on which the United States has been built has turned into a libertarian spirit in the church. Unity and reunification among those churches that could and should belong together are not pursued with the necessary vigour. Schismatic actions and denominational divisions are not seen as counter-witness to the prayer of Christ in John 17, but rather as expression of religious freedom. Mission is replaced by market competition among churches, where new Christians are not brought in, but existing Christians simply are "re-circulated". Religious consumerism can supersede sound theology in a scramble to attract people and satisfy their religious and experiential needs.

The sensitivities of Belhar, that Christ has only one body and gave his own flesh to bring unity and that visible unity in freedom is both a gift and a task, are urgently needed among churches in North America. Recent events have shown the deep social divisions remaining. Racism is "still endemic to our society" and there is a general denial of history under the cloak of a sentimental, Hollywood-style "universal culture", states William H. Willimon (1997:485-490). There is still the continued need for a "black history month", and black bodies are, according to James Cone, still lynched today "whenever a people cry out to be recognised as human beings and society ignores them" (2007:47-55). The proclamation of Belhar that reconciliation is possible in Christ and that cultural and other "natural" differences are gifts for the building up of church and society, should be heard loudly and clearly all across America.

As the undisputed economic, military and technological leader of the world, a huge responsibility rests on the US to use its immense power wisely. There remains, therefore, a crucial task for theologians, ethicists and church leaders in the US to urge the political powers of the day to actively support global ecological initiatives, and in a rational manner renegotiate the terms of global trade toward a fairer and more just system. Let us be reminded that the linking of security, politics and religion has shown itself to be the main building block of inhuman "Christian" ideologies in the 20th century. Apartheid is an infamous example of this.

4. THE GLOBAL CHURCH

If the churches in the world cannot show greater visible unity, the world will not believe that God sent Christ as the saviour of all humankind (John 17). Church union and reunion dialogues, as well as dialogues among the great traditions of the Christian family with a view to celebrating common baptism and communion, are absolutely crucial in a world that yearns for signs that unity is possible amidst diversity and deep historical separations. If we do not achieve more, Christ is divided and the power of the gospel denied.

If the churches in the world do not demonstrate that we are "alternative" societies where there is no longer Jew and Greek, man and woman, boss and slave, how will the world believe in the power of reconciliation in Christ? If the churches are merely mirror-images of societal divisions between rich and poor, black and white, man and woman, educated and illiterate, we have become cultural-religious clubs that play church, but do not practically demonstrate God's embracing love (Galatians 3:26-28). I often marvel at the fact that sociology ("birds of a feather …") is stronger than theology ("body of Christ") when it comes to the practice of being church.

If the churches in the world merely accept global economic, cultural and ecological injustices, as if the powers behind these new configurations are blind and immutable laws of economics and politics, how will justice be established? Have we resigned ourselves to the fact that many humanist efforts and non-governmental organisations (NGOs) with a clear vision have supplanted the churches in the spheres of public life?

5. THE CONTEXT OF THE REFORMED CHURCH IN AMERICA

A confession without action is like faith without works. The best way to disempower Belhar is to accept it as a confession and then make no changes in your life: to see Belhar as an interesting, exotic product "out of Africa" with some curiosity value, but not as transformative Word of God. Confessing Belhar will raise serious questions for the RCA. You are best able to formulate them. My restricted view suggests the following questions:

- Do you love the unity of Christ's body more than your own tradition and history? Or have you become a typical denominational church that sees the boundaries of your church as the boundaries of the kingdom and of your own Christian identity?

- Are you willing to become a truly multicultural church that openly witnesses against racism, sexism and xenophobia no matter who is involved, and no matter how sensitive such witness may be politically?

- Are you a rich, blessed and middle-class church in the North, willing to stand where God stood in Christ – with the outcast and socially marginalised members of American society and elsewhere in the world?

- Are you willing to follow Christ, who did not cling to his Godhead, but humbled himself even unto the cross? Are you willing to be a kenotic church, a doulos (slave) church for the sake of others?

6. CONCLUSION

Confessions in the earliest church did not start with dogmatic statements after careful deliberation by a synod commission. No, they were doxological utterances in reaction to the resurrected Christ.

The early church did not "think up" the idea of Jesus Christ as Lord. This earliest confession was a reaction of praise and worship to their encounter with the post-Easter Jesus. They could not foresee what the ecclesial, political and economic consequences of that kurios confession would be. In a sense, the act of confession is, humanly speaking, an irresponsible action because you never know what might follow.

When the Dutch Reformed Mission Church confessed in 1982, they – and we in the Dutch Reformed Church also – did not know what would follow. It was politically dangerous and seen by some as ecclesial schism. We now know it was indeed a prophetic witness. We in South Africa, and elsewhere, wait eagerly to hear the good news from the Reformed Church in America.

BIBLIOGRAPHY

Cone, James. 2007. "Strange Fruit: The Cross and the Lynching Tree". Harvard Divinity Bulletin (Winter 2007), pp. 47-55.

Naudé, P.J. 2004. "Confessing the One Faith: Theological Resonance Between the Creed of Nicea (325 AD) and the Confession of Belhar (1982 AD)," Scriptura Vol. 85, pp. 35-53.

Willimon, W.H. 1997. "Why We All Can't Just Get Along: Racism as a Lenten Issue". Theology Today Vol. 53, No. 4, pp. 485-490.

1.8 EDMUND SCHLINK (1903-1984)

Telling his story from a South African perspective[1]

It is a huge and almost impossible task to "tell the story" of one of the greatest ecumenical theologians of the 20th century. I will, nevertheless, attempt to give some insight into his life and work in three sections below. Although Edmund Schlink does not himself utilise an overt "narrative" form of theology, it is possible to give a theological account of his life story and his work, and to draw some conclusions from that "narrative" for our theological narrative in South Africa.

Section one gives a biographical overview of Schlink's life to provide the context in which he made his theological contributions.[2] Section two outlines his specific view of an ecumenical dogmatics.[3] Section three provides a brief exposition of one recurring theme in his writings – the unity of the church. The essay is concluded with a short statement on the significance of his work and life for South African theology in the 21st century. The four sections therefore move from a theologically interpreted life story via a synthesis of core ideas in Schlink's work (ecumenics and church unity) to a critical reflection on our (my?) theological story in this country.

My own encounter with Schlink started quite late in my theological research. Unlike most contributors to our colloquium, who have spent a life of study on a particular theologian, I only "discovered" Schlink whilst on a sabbatical at the University of Heidelberg in Germany in 1997-1998. I saw his picture on the wall above the library and immersed myself in the many interesting works collected in the Ecumenical Institute, where Schlink spent the longest part of his career. Ever since that time he has been a constant partner in my own ecumenical journey. It is a great pleasure to introduce him to a wider English speaking audience.

---

1 This essay is an adapted version of a lecture – "How are they telling the story? Edmund Schlink as ecumenical theologian" – delivered at a conference on 20th-century theologians at the University of the Western Cape, led by Ernst Conradie (25 October 2007). The essay was first published in 2008 in Scriptura, Vol. 97, 122-136, under the title "On Edmund Schlink".

2 For the first section I gratefully acknowledge the use of Eugene M. Skibbe (1999), although some of the interpretations are my own. See also the abbreviated CV of Schlink in Eber (1993:278-279).

3 Schlink's massive Ökumenische Dogmatik of more than 800 pages (referred to as ÖD below) is my primary source for sections two and three. Some of the material was published earlier – some of these also in English. I will refer to the new edition of Schlink's work, where his Dogmatik appears as Band 2 of Schriften zu Ökumene und Bekenntnis (2005). Unfortunately this major work, originally published in 1983, and receiving more than 30 reviews in academic journals around the world, has never been translated into English, depriving many theologians and church leaders of his influence. For a full list of Schlink's 246 publications, excluding unpublished sermons, see Eber (1993:274-289). For the sake of brevity, I have not cited the growing number of secondary studies on Schlink's work.

Edmund Schlink (1903-1984)

1. BIOGRAPHY AND CONTEXT

Edmund Schlink was born on 6 March 1903 in Darmstadt. He completed a broad, classical school education before studying mathematics, philosophy and physics at various universities, eventually settling in Marburg. His parental home was Christian oriented, with his father from a Catholic and his mother from a Protestant (Hernnhut Pietist) background. By late 1925 – in the aftermath of the First World War – he experienced a deep "Sinnkrise" and attempted to find meaning from the works of Dostoyevsky and Nietzsche. "Why live at all?" was the basic existential question that took him to work on a farm in Silesia in an attempt to find direction in his life. In January 1926 – influenced by the witness of Christians from a mystical Lutheran background – he made a personal conversion to Christ and decided to study theology.

His parents insisted that he complete his science studies in Marburg. He did, however, change direction to psychiatry and in 1927 completed a doctorate in clinical psychology with an empirical analysis of religious experience: *Persönlichkeitsänderunge in Bekehrung und Depressionen: Eine empirisch-religions-psychologische Untersuchung. Nebst kasuistischen Beiträgen zur Psychologie des Gotteserlebens als Anhang.*[4]

He started his college-level theological education at Bethel Theological School near Bielefeld, but soon decided to go to Münster for a full university education, drawn there by the presence of Professors Barth (dogmatics) and Stählin (practical theology). Barth had already published his *Prolegoma zur Christlichen Dogmatik* in the summer of 1927 and would commence his work on the KD in 1931. Barth taught on ethics at Münster (1928-1929) and Bonn (1930-1931) at the same time that Schlink approached him to work on a doctorate in theology.

Barth's radical theological and Christological approach to ethics and anthropology (the human being under God's Word) seemed to contradict both the empirical method and subject matter of Schlink's work on religious experiences. Schlink in the meantime became active in the Lutheran church, entered the seminary in Friedberg, and was ordained as pastor in 1931. He nevertheless completed his theological doctorate under Barth in 1930 on the topic *Emotionale Gotteserlebnisse: Ein empirisch-psychologischer Beitrag zum Problem der natürlichen Religion.*

Barth's early influence on Schlink is evident from the fact that there is a clear emphasis on a theo- and Christocentric interpretation of anthropology as studied through an empirical analysis of religious experiences (see Schlink 1931:152-168). Schlink discusses the reality of purported "God-experiences" in relation to the classical questions of natural religion and the tension between general and specific revelation. The only plausible "explanation" for human experiences of God, asserts Schlink, is God's work of grace through Scripture and Christ. Knowledge of God is – as Luther argued – not attainable through experience or rational enquiry (1931:164), nor without God's self-revelation (1931:153).[5] In his commendatio of the doctoral

---

4   Marburg dissertation (1927); partially published in 1929, Archiv für die gesamte Psychologie (70:81-118).
5   Schlink writes that the question of truth in relation to "emotionale Heilserlebnisse ist theologisch als die Frage nach der Wirklichkeit einer Erkenntnis der göttlichen Gnade oder – *da Gotteserkenntnis ohne Gottes Offenbarung nicht möglich ist* – nach der Offenbarung

dissertation, Barth notes that Schlink's scientific analysis of "nature" leads us to be confronted with "grace", as there is no point of contact in nature for God's radical grace (Skibbe 1999:22).

This Christocentricity is further evident in Schlink's Habilitationsschrift, published in 1936 as *Der Mensch in der Verkündigung der Kirche: Eine dogmatische Untersuchung*. The date of publication sets the dramatic context for this theological contribution, where Schlink forcefully argues that not the human being, but only God working through Scripture, is the content and criterion of the church's proclamation. What was at stake was the simple but absolutely fundamental question: How do we know God?

Two important "audiences" should be assumed. The first was liberal theologians who saw anthropology – knowledge of the human person and his/her experience – as the starting point for knowledge of God. And the second the rising tide of German Christian theologians – many of them Lutheran – who claimed that historical events (such as the messianic significance of Hitler) constitute a new revelation of God. In typical Barthian sense, Schlink re-states that God is known through God's self-revelation in Christ and the gospel. And – drawing on his Lutheran roots – he asserts in his earlier Habilitation lecture[6] that God is hidden in history. One should therefore be careful to declare a historical situation a kairos moment, as this can easily turn the voice of people into the voice of God, and shift normativity from God's Word to history.[7] Revelation and truth emanate only from God's Word, proclaimed as law and gospel.[8]

Reflecting on the conclusion of Schlink's formal academic work, Eugene Skibbe asserts that "the earliest, most dominant drive in Schlink's life work was to create a Lutheran articulation of Barth's theology of the Word" (Skibbe 1999:22).

Schlink's biography would – in the next decade – be deeply affected by the rise to power of the National Socialists. He was appointed as teaching assistant at the small University of Giessen, but after only one semester his application for a full

---

der göttlichen Gnade in den emotionalen Heilserlebnissen zu bestimmen" (1931:153, my emphasis).

6   "Die Frage der Erkenntbarkeit göttlichen Handelns in der Geschichte", published in *Evangelische Theologie 1* (1934:257-277), and later included in the well-known collection *Bekennende Kirche und Welt* (1947:26-42).

7   One can sense the passion with which Schlink writes that there is a huge difference between finding God's Word in history (revelation) and discerning God's Word for history (discipleship): "Für den Christen gibt es kein Gebot der Stunde, keine Forderung der Geschichte, keinen Anspruch eines irdischen Du. Für ihn gilt nicht: Volkes Stimme ist Gottes Stimme. Er kann in all dem keine Norm erblicken. Er hört nicht mehr auf die Stimme der Situation, sondern hört auf das Gotteswort für die konkrete Sitauation, - für die Stunde, für die geschichtliche Lage, für die Stellung zum Du und zum Volk. Alles, alles muss Gott untertan warden" (Schlink 1947:42, emphases in the original). He earlier wrote that the basis of concrete historical knowledge is not history itself, but God's Word.

8   Revelation as law and gospel is a core theme in Schlink's later work and a point of continued difference between Schlink and Barth. This fascinating debate is not pursued here. See the long exposition in his discussion of the Lutheran confessions (Schlink 1961:67-139), his interpretation of the second article of the Barmen declaration from the perspective of law and gospel (Schlink 1937:97-102, as well as 2005: 234-250 (law) and 416-443 (gospel). See also Eber (1993:79-96).

appointment in March 1935 was denied by the Nazi-oriented Ministry of Culture. He was invited back to Bethel Theological School, where he taught and wrote what – up to this day – became his best known book, *Theologie der lutherischen Bekenntnisschriften* (completed 1938, published 1940).[9]

After the outbreak of the Second World War in 1939 the government increased its clampdown on dissident voices and Bethel School was ordered to close. Schlink was served with a gagging order and he returned to pastoral work and Bible study in Westphalia, where in April 1940 he was again forbidden to speak in public. His application for exemption from military service was fortunately granted on the basis of his assumed indispensable service as wartime substitute pastor in the Westphalia region. When he was called or sought calls from churches, the Gestapo intervened on the basis that Schlink was not seen as loyal to the German Christian Church. He was – with other pastors – required to sign the oath of loyalty to Hitler on two occasions (1938 and 1941).

This was a matter of great tension and controversy. Schlink signed the oath as interpreted theologically by Karl Koch, who was present at the Barmen Synod and had signed the Barmen declaration, but who sought a compromise position between the views of the Bekennende Kirche and the Nazi government. Through this interpretation (and reflected in Schlink's own work) the ultimate loyalty to Christ was maintained, whilst he was able to officially serve in the church during the war.[10] After the invasion of France in June 1940 the Protestant and Catholic theological faculties in Strasbourg were closed. The Lutherans created their own seminary, the Thomasstift, and invited Schlink to become Director of Studies, where he worked part-time – travelling between Germany (Bielefeld) and France (Strasbourg) – over the next four years.

After the war he was called to help reconstruct the theological faculty at Heidelberg University, where he went as Professor of Dogmatics and Ecumenical Theology in 1946. Under the leadership of philosopher Karl Jaspers and other notable theologians such as Hans van Campenhausen (church history), Günther Bornkamm and Gerhard von Rad (Old Testament), Schlink played a crucial role in re-establishing the university and the theological faculty specifically. His leadership was acknowledged with his election as rector for the 1953-1954 term.[11]

His major contributions during his Heidelberg years were his work in the ecumenical movement and in establishing systematic theology as a fundamentally ecumenical enterprise. Schlink's theological studies in Münster had already shaped his ecumenical cast of mind. At a predominantly Catholic faculty, he was

---

9   The reason for this book's fame is to be explained from its wide use as a textbook in Lutheran seminaries and its translation into English as Theology of the Lutheran Confessions in 1961.
10 See my discussion of this decision in the closing section below.
11 Schlink's inaugural lecture is an absolute joy to read. Drawing on Luther's Heidelberg disputations from 1518, he makes an argument that the university should promote wisdom rather than folly – as reflected in the title, *Weisheit und Torheit* (Schlink 1953). This can only happen if science is approached from faith in Jesus Christ, as in this manner reason is brought under the control of love (Luther!) and the whole of reality can truly be seen in all its richness and paradoxes under the Lordship of its Creator (see especially pages 21-22).

taught by Catholic, Reformed and Lutheran teachers, and had to develop his own Lutheran convictions in open dialogue with others. The war – especially in the aftermath of massive air raids over Germany in 1943 – forced a pastoral situation upon clergy from different traditions to work in the tragic situation of mass burials of unidentified people. Pastor Schlink also served the Holy Communion to slave labourers from Ukraine and soldiers from different backgrounds. He later reflected on this and asked why such inter-confessional encounters cannot be maintained outside of crisis situations. "What in crisis situations in the church shines as the truth cannot in normal situations become untruth" he remarked (see Skibbe 1999:48 and footnote 179).[12]

When he moved to Heidelberg after the war, Schlink played a major role in setting up various academic channels in the service of a thoroughly ecumenical awareness.

- He was appointed to the first chair in Germany where Dogmatics and Ecumenical Studies were officially combined.

- Soon after his arrival in 1946, he set up what would become the famous Heidelberg Ecumenical Institute (predating the WCC Bossey Institute by a few months!). The primary aim was "to examine carefully the consonance and differences among Christian churches and the numerous efforts toward Christian unity in our time" (as quoted by Skibbe 1999:72; for original source, see Skibbe's footnote 245, page 146).

- He assisted in establishing the first German language journal for ecumenical thought, *Ökumenische Rundschau*, and published the opening article in the first edition on "The task and danger of the World Council of Churches".[13]

- Schlink played a leading role over a period of 34 years (1945-1979) in the so-called Jäger-Stählin Circle[14], a confidential dialogue group between Catholics and Lutherans that shaped his theological thinking on ecumenical relations with the Roman Catholic Church.

In addition to his theological studies, pastoral work and academic activities in Heidelberg, Schlink gradually became a leading figure in the ecumenical movement and played a crucial role over many years. There were hardly any major events in which he did not participate in some manner.

In the reconstruction of the Protestant churches after the war, Schlink was instrumental in the success of very delicate negotiations amongst different factions in the Lutheran Church and amongst Lutheran, Reformed and United churches that eventually formed the EKD in 1948. He was official delegate of the EKD to the founding of the WCC in Amsterdam in that same year and became a leading member of Faith and Order.

---

12   See how Schlink – in a sermon in the Marienkirche in Dortmunt (1941) – reflects on the unnatural deaths that war brings. He speaks of the *Widernatürlichkeit* of so many young people dying, but still links this to facing God's judgment (Schlink 1947:99).
13   Included as a chapter in the English translation of collected essays *The coming Christ and the coming church* (1967).
14   Lorenz Jäger, the Catholic archbishop of Paderborn, and Wilhelm Stählin, the Lutheran bishop in Oldenberg, set up the dialogue group in the early 1940s.

His stature in the WCC was confirmed when he – following his teacher, Karl Barth, who spoke in 1948 – was invited to be one of the opening speakers at the second meeting of the WCC in Evaston (1954). The theme was "Christ – the hope of the world". Schlink developed an eschatological view on ecumenism, reminding members that hope of God's new order includes a realisation of the provisional nature of the church, its outward form, its church orders and its dogmatic formulations. "The church too will be transformed. In the new creation there will be no temple", he reminded his audience, "for 'the Lord God Almighty and the Lamb are the temple'" (Rev xxi.22) (see Schlink, The coming Christ 1967: 268).[15]

A crucial contribution was Schlink's attempt to develop an ecumenical hermeneutics. His article "Die Struktur der dogmatischen Aussage als ökumenisches Problem" (1957; see also The coming Christ 1967:16-84) later became a core part of his major work, Ökumenische Dogmatik (see especially Chapter 3). This analysis of primary faith response forms serves – in my view – as methodological basis for his whole ecumenical theology (see Section Two below).

There were two further ecumenical endeavours that fundamentally shaped Schlink's thought and contributed to his mature ecumenical theology by 1983.

The first was his direct and extensive involvement in convincing the Russian Orthodox Church to apply for membership of the WCC in 1958.[16] The second was his status as official observer at Vaticanum II, where he noted the intense debates amongst Catholic theologians. He wrote 60 reports and more than 400 shorter analyses of these debates, and published Nach dem Konzil in 1966 (translated as After the Council 1968). It is no wonder that he was appointed – along with inter alia WA Visser't Hooft, Nikos Nissiotis and Lukas Vischer – to a joint task force to set up a closer link between the WCC and the RCC (see Skibbe 1999:90-98).

Schlink's intimate knowledge of the great faith traditions gradually led him to the conviction that the Lutheran church is well placed to play a significant ecumenical role.

Lutherans stand at a mid-point within ecumenical relationships – with the Anglican, Catholic and Orthodox churches to the right, and with the Reformed, Congregationalist, Quaker and Baptists churches to the left. With its focus on the irreducible core of the gospel and the actual preaching of the living Word, the Lutheran tradition is able to see Christ in others and therefore strive for the unity of the church beyond the limits of Lutheranism.[17] Although Schlink was undoubtedly

---

15 Schlink makes clear that there are two intertwined acts of hope: the preaching of the gospel and "accepting responsibility for the just ordering of society" (1967:261-267, 262). God is not only Creator but also Sustainer. "God demands that we take responsibility for the preservation of all human life regardless of whether that life be a Christian or not, that we take responsibility for all men [sic], regardless of their nationality, race or social status, and He also demands that we accept responsibility for their freedom" (1967:263).

16 For an overview of the four-part role that Schlink played, read Skibbe (1999:83-89) and see Schlink (1958).

17 See his paper prepared for the Third World Conference of Faith and Order in Lund (1952) on Die Weite der Kirche nach dem lutherischen Bekenntnis, where he argues – in typical Lutheran fashion – that unity without confessional documents is possible as long as the pure gospel is preached and the sacraments celebrated accordingly. See also his discussion of the church in Theology of the Lutheran Confessions (1961:194-225).

a Lutheran theologian, his ecumenical spirit led him to a much broader vision of Christ's work beyond the boundaries of Lutheranism. A Copernican revolution in ecclesiological thinking occurs when Christ is thought of as the centre with different churches circling with one another around that centre (Schlink 1968: 248; 2005:xxv, 695-6).

2. ON AN ECUMENICAL DOGMATICS

Schlink is well aware of the various adjectives that are available to describe dogmatics: Christian, Catholic, Reformed, Orthodox or (as with Barth) Church Dogmatics. Many claim to call their work "ecumenical" in the sense that dogmatics is a reflection on the faith of the one people of God. Schlink, however, finds this claim unsatisfactory: A mere claim to be ecumenical is not enough. What is needed is a specific scientific endeavour ("eine besondere wissenschaftliche Bemühung", 2005:51) to construct an ecumenical theology with distinctive features.

The key to Schlink's ecumenical method lies in his well-known exposition of primary faith responses ("elementäre Grundformen"), first published as "Die Struktur der dogmatischen Aussage als ökumenisches Problem" (1957) and included in his ÖD as chapter III.

Our response to the gospel, argues Schlink, is directed to God as well as to others, and takes on the following primary forms: prayer, doxology, witness, teaching and confession. After a careful analysis of these forms (2005:33-39), he concludes that all the forms are present in a condensed way in confessions. To avoid morphological impoverishment through the tyranny of one faith response (such as teaching) – resulting in a hardening of belief systems – all these primary forms need to be kept alive in faith communities and in the personal lives of believers (2005:40,47).

Because all of these responses are concerned with God, they are all theological expressions ("theologische Aussagen", 2005:40-41) Schlink therefore does not define theological expressions as second-order reflections upon God, but exactly these primary faith responses directed toward Godself.

"Dogmatic statements" are then to be understood as either statements of dogma or statements of dogmatics. The first is interpreted in the restricted sense, where a church makes a statement of dogma (orthodox belief) that it requires for its life of faith. A confession[18] in the technical sense is such a statement of dogma. The second (dogmatics) is to be understood in a wider sense as including dogma, but extending reflection to other faith responses such as prayer, doxology and witness. History of theology ("Theologiegeschichte") is more than the history of dogma ("Dogmengeschichte", 2005:42). In the light of these distinctions, an ecumenical dogmatics studies how the great deeds of God are responded to in an array of primary faith forms in the whole church of God.

---

18   See Schlink's discussion of the nature of confessions as the church's normative exposition of Scripture in his analysis of the Lutheran confessions (1961a:xvi). He states that a study of the confessions is the actual prolegomena to dogmatics (see whole introductory section of 1961a).

Edmund Schlink (1903-1984)

For Schlink the shift from one form to the other (e.g. doxology to confession) and the translation of one form into the other (prayer into witness) are both historically and theologically important. Historically, because this explains the structural shifts arising in the various epochs as churches responded to different needs at various stages of history. Theologically, because the primary focus of ecumenical dogmatics is not to find exact word agreements (consensus on dogmas, confessions), but to see consonance in content amongst various (seemingly unconnected) faith expressions, and to help churches in ecumenical dialogues to find a surprising unity amidst their diversity.

He then proceeds to explain an ecumenical dogmatics in negative terms (2005:52-53):

- Ecumenical Dogmatics does not take the teaching of your own church as reference point and then seek to find partial representation of this true church in others from whom you are disunited in those instances where their teachings happen to agree with yours. In this way a true understanding of the other church – which also understands itself as the "whole" church – is impossible. It furthermore fails to recognise the plurality of ways in which the richness of Christ finds expression in churches beyond the boundaries of your own.

- Ecumenical Dogmatics does not restrict itself to the ancient church's consensus as expressed in the first five centuries. This is a great temptation, as most churches that were formed up to and including the Reformation in fact acknowledge the decisions of the early Councils. But since the 17th century many new faith communities in a variety of cultures were formed. For them the early consensus is not a part of their tradition. They find the nurturing Word of God and a strong missionary focus as adequate for their identity formation. Their presence and reality should be incorporated into a contemporary ecumenical dogmatics.

- Ecumenical Dogmatics cannot be restricted to a comparative study of contemporary differences amongst churches in order to find some middle ground of convergence. These comparisons are helpful as dogmatic pre-work, but are in themselves not dogmatic work yet. Such a "comparative dogmatics" (2005:57) would lead to an ecumenical minimalism and would not contribute to re-uniting the churches. No, ecumenical theology must show the courage to be "maximalist" in converging churches around the apostolic faith.

- Ecumenical Dogmatics should also not occupy itself merely with a phenomenological analysis of pious religious experiences – even if they result from exciting ecumenical encounters. This approach would never appeal to dogmatic-founded churches; it denies the importance of common truth statements for church unity, and it opens the ecumenical process up to misuse by political and social currents of the day, so that unity itself becomes an exponent of contemporary worldviews. What then are – in positive terms – the core methodological components of an ecumenical dogmatics? (see 2005:54-57)

- Ecumenical Dogmatics needs to acknowledge the rich plurality of Scriptural witnesses to the same saving acts of God. A specific act of God – including descriptions of Godself as Father, Son and Spirit – is not only expressed in a rich variety of metaphors and names, but is also witness to the rich variety of historical situations in which the biblical narratives arose.

- Ecumenical Dogmatics needs to acknowledge the rich plurality of dogmatic statements ("dogmatische Aussagen", 2005:54) within the boundaries of one church tradition and obviously amongst churches of different traditions. Understanding the specific historical situations in which these convictions were formed is crucial for a proper understanding of their content. We do not need exactly the same formulations to express the same content, because the same truth can be expressed differently in the various primary forms ("Grundformen") of faith responses expounded above; and the same formulation can sometimes signify a different content to people reading them from different contexts.

- For Schlink the core task of an ecumenical dogmatics is "translation" work, i.e. to translate from and into various primary forms, and from and into various historical contexts in order to establish surprising connections between faith responses that might at first glance be viewed as exclusionary or contradictory (see 2005:57-58).

- Once an ecumenical dogmatics reconstructs the plurality of contemporary dogmatic views as historical developments of the "urchristlichen Bekenntnisaussagen" (2005:55), two conclusions are possible. First, one is able to see a unity amidst the plurality of seemingly contradictory viewpoints (they are all historical developments of the ancient Christian faith). Second, one is able to reconstruct these different views as manifold witnesses of the Spirit through the ages – just as there are many gifts in the church, appropriate for each situation.

- Ecumenical Dogmatics needs to focus on the actual role of dogma in the life of the churches. Churches tend to make implicit choices for certain dogmas or even certain parts of the canon. Churches which profess no formal confession may in actual fact be upholding strong dogmatic views in the practical life of the faith communities (liturgy, pastoral and mission work). Conversely, so-called "dogmatic" churches may in their faith communities not actually care so much about the orthodoxy they confess on paper.

- Ecumenical Dogmatics also focuses on confessions in the churches and understands these as conceptual concentrations ("begriffliche Konzentration", 2005:55), where the whole of the faith is expressed in a few words. Confessions are therefore always less than the fullness of faith or the multiformity of Scripture, and show legitimate historical differentiation as a result of the development of faith in different traditions. For example, the Christologies of the East are shaped by the epiphany, whereas in the West they are shaped by the cross. They are thus both legitimately based on Scripture, despite their different emphases.

- Ecumenical Dogmatics does recognise the enormous potential to develop new dogmas as the gospel spreads over the earth into new cultures and spiritual climates. Ecumenical dogmatics cannot restrict itself only to already existing dogmas – specifically those that create disunity amongst churches – it must (in the light of the riches of Scripture!) be open to and willing to develop new confessions about Christ who not only came, but who is coming again (2005:56).

3. ON CHURCH UNITY

It is to be expected that the unity of the church would play a significant role in Schlink's ecumenical theology.[19] His ideas are represented in summarised form in three short sections:

- What is the theological starting point for reflections on church unity?
- How do schisms amongst churches develop?
- How do we recognise the one church in a disunited Christianity and what are the crucial presuppositions in our striving for visible unity?

Theological starting point

It would be fair to represent Schlink's starting point on church unity as Trinitarian but with a Christological focus. All Christian communities are encapsulated by two acts of God: they were all founded on the basis of God's salvation in Jesus Christ and are all therefore grounded in grace. And they all are moving toward the judgment of God expected in the parousia of Christ. All churches live between cross/resurrection and second coming.

The thrust behind and the deepest ground of the ecumenical movement lie not in socio-political or pragmatic factors, but must be viewed as God's work through the Spirit: the ecumenical movement is a pneumatic movement (2005:683). Only God's Spirit can overcome ecclesial self-satisfaction, boasting in self-righteousness, laziness of theological thought and lack of creative love that resist unity in the church.[20]

Because the church is God's creation and because God keeps the church, a fundamental presupposition in seeking greater unity in a disunited Christianity is that the church is at all times the one, holy, catholic and apostolic church. No schism can diminish the always presupposed unity of the church. Yes, this unity may be made invisible or only partially visible by disuniting churches, but the unity can in principle not be negated, because it is a gift of God based on the unity of Father, Son and Holy Spirit (2005:684).

The primary task of churches is not to re-establish unity, but to make two movements – and in this specific sequence: acknowledge the unity amidst a disunited Christianity, and then realise this unity in the re-establishment of church communion. If these two tasks are inverted, the very theological ground for seeking unity is destroyed and churches strive for unity no longer based on the indicative of grace but on the imperative of a self-defined ecumenical task (2005:685).

---

19 The primary source of Schlink's ecclesiology is his exposition of the church in *Theology of the Lutheran Confessions* (1961:194-225). It is interesting to note that the church follows the discussion of gospel and sacraments, and is presented in the context of the struggle between the kingdom of the devil and the kingdom of Christ. Jochen Eber's carefully written dissertation Einheit der Kirche als dogmatisches Problem bei Edmund Schlink (1993) is imperative secondary reading, especially pp. 126-149.

20 The original German is beautiful and is impoverished by my (poor) translation: "Nur Gottes Geist vermag die Selbstzufriendenheit, die Rechthaberei, die Faulheit im Denken und den Mangel an Phantasie der Liebe zu beseitigen, die der Einheit entgegenstehen" (2005:685).

The Christological concentration of Schlink's presupposed theological grounds for unity emerges from two specific passages.

In his exposition of the marks of the church (2005:585-589) Schlink clarifies that these marks are a description of the church as it is in Christ. The church's unity (for example) is not a characteristic of Christians, but derived from their being in Christ. The unity of the Church is Christ's unity that cannot be denied by our disunity.

In his discussion of how we could recognise the one church amidst a disunited Christianity, Schlink's often quoted passage about a Copernican paradigm shift further clarifies his Christological focus. Ecumenical relations are not promoted as long as one's own church serves as reference point and criterion in the light of which all other churches are judged. "Wir haben die anderen christlichen Gemeinschaften nicht mehr so anzusehen, als ob sie sich um unsere Kirche als Mitte bewegen, sonder wir müssen erkennen, dass wir mit den anderen Gemeinschaften zusammen gleichsam wie Planeten um Christus als die Sonne kreisen und von ihm das Licht empfangen" (2005:696). This radical Christocentric ecclesiological shift is a prerequisite for any real ecumenical progress, because it shifts the focus and criterion from any one church to Christ and the apostolic witness.

How do schisms develop amongst churches?

"Dass die Christenheit mit ihren Trennungen und Gegensätzen der Welt dasselbe Schauspiel bietet, wie diese im Neben- und Widereinander der Völker und Staaten, ist ein Skandal" (2005: 683)

With his many years of practical ecumenical dialogue and thorough knowledge of theological history, Schlink make some perceptive remarks. He first demonstrates that disunity rarely if ever arises from outside the church. No, the drive for ecclesial self-preservation is the root of disunity. What happens is that the gifts for the preservation of the church – the canon, dogma and church order – are paradoxically the very factors that operate in disuniting the church.

The gospel of the canon, the living Word of God, is reduced to a mere prescribed reading of the Bible or a source of teachings, without the freedom of witness and prayer in the liturgy. The doxological[21] and biblical roots of dogma as living response to God are stifled into strict orthodox statements about God. The variety of ministries emerging in New Testament times is fixated into neat hierarchical categories of laypeople versus church officials. The sad irony, says Schlink, is that all these things happen in the name of preserving unity, but they are often nothing more than self-preservation of a specific church tradition, cutting the church off from others and from God's call in the contemporary world to which it owes its service (2005:675).

Once self-preservation sets in, the scene is set for the rest of the disuniting factors to play their role. If we accept that a schism is only to be considered when Christ

---

21 There is no room to expound the importance of doxology in Schlink's construction of an ecumenical dogmatics. Doxology already appeared as a primary ground-form of faith responses (1957); and doxology both introduces and closes his doctrine of God (2005:725ff, 790-792). Schlink does acknowledge Wainwright's *Doxology*, which appeared about a year before his publication of ÖD in 1983. For the link between doxology and reception of ecumenical documents; see Naudé 1998:252-254.

is denied ("Abfall von Christus" or "Verleungung Jesu Christi", 2005:682), this legitimate reason is extended to present other factors in the same light by portraying them also as a fundamental denial of Christ. Schlink remarks that one has to carefully distinguish between historical reasons for a schism, and its a posteriori theological legitimisation! (2005:682).

If you see your church as the only true church, you increasingly use dogmatic means to re-ensure your difference with others, masking the many factors that unite you with them. You quickly enhance one point of difference into the whole gospel, blinding yourself to the work of Christ beyond the boundaries of your own church. If you then do seek reunification, it is based on the assumption that the other must become and believe as you do. The schismatic situation amongst Christians denies that Christ has conquered the world, and gives the world justification for its own schisms and enmities. This is a scandal (2005:683).

How do we recognise the one church in a disunited Christianity and what are the crucial steps in our striving for visible unity?

Based on his strong Christological starting point, Schlink first argues that we should recognise the one church exactly in the disunited Christianity. Even if Christ judges disunity in the church, He is able to work even in and through a disunited Christianity. He does not allow disunity in the church to disunite Himself (2005:699).

Once we see Christ represented in a variety of ways in the whole church, it leads us to self-critique and confession of our part in disuniting the church. If we confess our sins by turning to Christ, we are at the same time converting ourselves to one another. Instead of suspicion and focusing on the past reasons for disunity, we then turn to other churches in hope – the hope to find in them a witness to Christ and a gift of the Spirit absent or marginalised in our midst (2005:695).

The way toward one another is via bi- or multilateral ecumenical dialogue based on both a hierarchy of truth[22] and a hierarchy of church life. The Catholic Church and the WCC agree that belief in the Triune God and the acceptance of Christ as Saviour are the core of the Christian faith. In church life there is – according to Schlink – a difference between specific church orders regulating officials' status and the preaching of the gospel of Jesus Christ. The inordinate energy spent on "ministries" in ecumenical dialogues clearly inverts the order of importance that the Bible presents to us.

Schlink then lists seven practical ecumenical steps[23] that are required to establish the visible unity of the church (see 2005:700-708).

1. There must be a striving for confessional consensus. As stated earlier, this must not be restricted to traditional dogmatic differences and should be addressed on the basis of the core truths of the apostolic faith – seeking to find and strengthen the many agreements already existing.

---

22 Schlink was deeply influenced by both Luther's idea of the "main articles" of faith and the Second Vatican Council's idea of a hierarchy of truths – distinguishing between core and marginal dogmatic statements (see 2005:697).
23 This section may be related to Schlink's excellent paper (13 October 1954) on "The task and danger of the World Council of Churches" (see Schlink 1967:3-15).

2. The reciprocal recognition of faith expressions even where these are not accepted by all in the exact wording of shared formulas. These faith expressions are recognised on the basis of the rich diversity of language used in the canon to describe the great deeds of God.
3. Reciprocal recognition of God's work in the practical life of other churches, specifically the way in which the salvation acts of God are expressed in a variety of liturgies. Once you accept that God is at work in the liturgy, the door is opened to recognising the ministry of another church as well.
4. The repeal of mutual condemnations ("Anathematismen", 2005:704) is a requirement for unity. Even though consensus might not be possible in each and every theological question, an anathema constitutes a fundamental contradiction to church unification.
5. The necessity of self-corrections by reinterpreting already accepted dogmas and by being open to reformulate faith in the light of new situations. Fear of a disintegrating and plural identity is overcome by holding on to Christ to whom all faith formulations point.
6. The establishment of a shared faith community ("gottesdienstliche Gemeinschaft", 2005:706), including the invitation to holy communion by forgiving one another at the table of the Lord. There is no need to give up distinct liturgical identities as the pluriformity of prayer and worship is a testimony that God gives gifts appropriate for each time and context.
7. The shared growth toward unity, because unity is a continuous imperative based on a growth toward Christ and spurred on by the Holy Spirit. The Spirit creates in us the urgency for a greater visible unity in the church, and gives us the gifts of growing together in faith and love.

I conclude this section by referring (once again) to the eschatological horizon within which Schlink presents his ecumenical dogmatics. He admits that the church grew older than the apostles and their followers had expected. But this does not mean that the church should lose its character as being called out of the world to live as the eschatological people of God. This does not mean any diminished sense of Christ's return to judge everything in heaven and on earth – including the church.

The real schism in the church will only be revealed in Christ's end judgment. As is evident from Jesus' parables, the theological distinction between the visible and invisible church makes sense from the eschatological critique of the church by the coming Christ. And that schism – much more fundamental than the human schisms we have created – will cut across all churches: no part of Christ's body will be spared the schism of the true church from the false; the separation of the weed from the true harvest (2005:685-687).

4. CONCLUSION

Edmund Schlink followed a different path than two of his better known contemporaries. Unlike Bonhoeffer who actively resisted National Socialism and paid for that with his life, Schlink decided to work against National Socialism from within the church and under the rules of the state.[24] Unlike Karl Barth who rejected the Hitler regime as an outright evil, Schlink decided differently. He did not embrace mainstream Lutheran thinking that all governments – regardless of their stance – are creation orders instituted by God. But whilst professing his ultimate loyalty to Christ, he did hold on to the possibility that an evil state could be the mask behind which God acts, and that God could act – as in the case of Pharoah – against those very authorities to fulfil God's saving acts in history.

Looking back on his fundamental theological contributions to the Confessing Church[25] and his rich ecumenical heritage, we might admit that there are different paths of faithfulness to God.

Schlink was recognised in his lifetime by being awarded three honorary doctorates from the University of Mainz (1947), Edinburgh (1953) and the St Sergius Institute for Orthodox Theology in Paris (1962). He lived in Heidelberg, the basis of his major ecumenical and academic endeavours; he died there on 20 May 1984, a year after the first publication of his major book, *Ökumenische Dogmatik*. The re-publication of his writings in the first decade of the 21st century is a most fitting reminder that the way beyond sectarianism and fundamentalism lies in a deep commitment and openness to others. This is superbly exhibited in the ecumenical spirit that fills the life and work of Edmund Schlink.

The question now remains: How does the 'story' of Schlink's life and work shape my and our narrative in South and Southern Africa? I would suggest three fundamental insights from Schlink that might assist us in our ecumenical and theological endeavours.

First. Schlink's endeavour to establish a methodological base for an ecumenical dogmatics, and his actual construction of such a dogmatics – whether "successful" or not – has significance for us. An ecumenical theology does not take as its starting point some vague supra-confessional position or meta-Christological Archimedes point from whence all other traditions are judged.

---

24 In 1979 Schlink – who knew and met Bonhoffer a few times – said that "the kind of resistance was not the same, but we knew ourselves to be united in resistance" (Skibbe 1999, footnote 130).

25 A number of Schlink's contributions were published in *Theologische Existenz Heute*, and to see the intensity of the church struggle as waged by Schlink, it is imperative to read *Bekennende Kirche und Welt*, which contains lectures and sermons from the period 1934-1945 (Schlink 1947). See, for example, his dramatic words from a lecture in Bonn in 1934 (published the next year in *Th Existenz Heute*, Heft 20). Speaking on how Israel rejected Christ, Schlink makes an almost direct application to the German situation: "Aber so wie damals über der Gabe der allwirkende Geber vergessen wurde im Ruhm der eigenen Gerechtigkeit, so wird auch heute der dreieinige göttliche Geber vergessen über seinen Gaben, und die Geschichte wird anstelle Christi, und Blut und Rasse werden anstelle der Heiligen Geist gerühmt und geehrt". He calls this the paganism that has entered the German church and warns that the Bible is clear that God can take away the place of whole churches if they persist in idolatry (Schlink 1947:10).

An ecumenical theologian is rooted in a specific tradition, but she is able to relativise, critique and appreciate that tradition from the perspective of Christ, the apostolic faith, and the rich plurality of Christian beliefs and practices in other traditions. An ecumenical theologian actively addresses those theological questions pertaining to the visible unity of Christ's body and practical demands of the gospel in her specific context, but also on a catholic scale. Such a theologian is actively engaged in ecumenical bodies and practices, building networks of trust and love conducive to greater theological consensus.

It would be fair to say that – for historical reasons – Reformed theology[26] dominates the public, academic scene in South Africa. It is therefore crucial that the spirit of these theologies is imbued with the ecumenical thrust of their origin in the Protestant Reformation, and that theologians from this tradition relativise themselves and their work in the light of Christ and other expressions of the faith in our context. Exactly because of their dominant position, sectarian Reformed theologies remain a temptation to avoid for the sake of Christ and the truth.

Second. The TRC report (1996) on faith communities in South Africa states that despite their professed faith to the contrary, these communities in fact were mirror images of the socio-economic divisions of an apartheid society. The church struggle tells an ambiguous story on two levels. Not only were churches divided amongst themselves about resistance to apartheid, but many churches who actively resisted and protested against the system of racial division were themselves (and in some cases are still today) racially divided. Much has happened after 1994 in the political, social, sports and economic spheres to create visible signs of a shared citizenship based on the values and prescriptions of the South African Constitution. And in the churches much has happened to bring about greater visible unity amongst, for example, Apostolic Faith, Lutheran and Dutch Reformed churches. But much still remains to be done.[27]

There is – as Schlink argued – absolutely no theological reason why visible church communion amongst the traditional faith communities could not be realised. (Have we silently accepted these traditional schisms as "normal"?) With the dramatic growth of churches under the broad banner of Pentecostalism in South and Southern Africa, the issue of ecumenicity becomes more complex and at the same time more urgent. As Schlink reminds us, the eschatological critique of the church and her identity as "tent-pilgrims" should destroy all self-satisfaction or even self-righteousness in our midst. The scandal of disunity and the lack of enthusiasm for (re)unification sometimes stand in sharp contrast to secular attempts in realising a united South Africa. The question is whether a commitment to human rights and democratic political ideals is more powerful than the cross and resurrection of

---

26   There are obviously many different forms and emphases of "Reformed" theologies in South Africa, as Dirk Smit rightly points out (see Smit 1992). See also De Gruchy's well-known reinterpretation of this multifaceted tradition in the South African context (De Gruchy 1991).

27   From my own limited position in the DRC family, I understand the step-like processes toward reunification, but fear that our vision is too restricted to focus on this family alone. There are many churches in Africa to the north of us who belong in one church. And there are many other (Reformed) churches with whom some form of greater visible union is possible and important.

Jesus Christ, whose physical body was broken for the sake of unity in his ecclesial body? A Christological concentration – the knowledge that we are one in Christ and should therefore become one, and that all churches circle around Christ as the centre – remains the only antidote to a laid-back attitude concerning the visible unity of the church.

Third. There is little doubt that an ecumenical awareness and ecumenical practices were the most powerful bases of the struggle against apartheid. How can we forget the role of the WCC, the LWF, the WARC, and locally the Catholic Bishop's Conferences, the SACC and the DRMC in providing a fundamental critique of apartheid theology in order to erode the moral basis of a race-based political system? The question is: Where is that same ecumenical commitment and enthusiasm for the new struggles against HIV/AIDS, neoliberal capitalism, ecological destruction, disregard for human rights in Africa and elsewhere, and abject poverty amidst a growing economy and surplus state funds? The "single enemy syndrome" and the obvious moral rightness of the struggle against apartheid played an "energising" role in the ecumenical efforts up to 1994.

We need an awakening of the Spirit to unite once again on issues that might not be politically correct, that might not reach the front pages of newspapers or the attention of TV crews, and that might challenge the policies of our democratic political leadership. The gospel of righteousness, with its imperatives superseding the significant normative guidelines of human rights,[28] did not suddenly change in 1994.

BIBLIOGRAPHY

De Gruchy, J. 1991. *Liberating Reformed theology. A South African contribution to an ecumenical debate*. Grand Rapids: Eerdmans.

Eber, J. 1993. *Einheit der Kirche als dogmatisches Problem bei Edmund Schlink*. Göttingen: Vandenhoeck & Ruprecht.

Naudé, P.J. 1997. "Regaining our ritual coherence: The question of textuality and worship in ecumenical reception". *Journal of Ecumenical Studies* Vol. 35, No. 2, pp. 235-256.

Naudé, P.J. 2007. "Between humility and boldness: Explicating human rights from a Christian perspective". *NGTT* Vol. 48, pp. 139-148.

Schlink, E. 1929. "Persönlichkeitsänderunge in Bekehrung und Depressionen: Eine empirisch-religionspsychologische Untersuchung. Nebst kasuistischen Beiträgen zur Psychologie des Gotteserlebens als Anhang". *Archiv für die gesamte Psychologie* Vol. 70, pp. 81-118.

Schlink, E. 1931. *Emotionale Gotteserlebnisse: Ein empirisch-psychologischer Beitrag zum Problem der natürlichen Religion*. Leipzig: Johann Ambrosius Barth.

---

28 For a discussion of the relation between human rights and Christian theology, see Naudé 2007, where I argue that human rights need to be affirmed and sustained by Christians, as long as their limitations vis-à-vis the gospel are also kept in mind. To freely give your life (goods, gifts, time) for others – a basic call in the gospel – is obviously far more radical than a striving for autonomy, human dignity and self-affirmation based on the right to equality.

Schlink, E. 1934. "Die Frage der Erkenntbarkeit göttlichen Handelns in der Geschichte". *Evangelische Theologie* Vol. 1, pp. 257-277.

Schlink, E. 1936. *Der Mensch in der Verkündigung der Kirche: Eine dogmatische Untersuchung.* München: Kaiser Verlag.

Schlink, E. 1937. "Das Lutherische Bekenntnis und die zweite These der Barmer theologischen Erklärung". *Theologische Existenz Heute,* Heft 53, pp. 97-102.

Schlink, E. 1940. *Theologie der lutherischen Bekenntnisschriften. Einführung in die evangelische Theologie.* Bd8. München: Kaiser.

Schlink, E. 1947. *Bekennende Kirche und Welt: Vorträge und Predigten aus den Jahren 1934 bis 1945.* Tübingen: Furche Verlag.

Schlink, E. 1953a. Die Weltkirchenkonferenz in Lund. ZW Vol. 24: 443-448.

Schlink, E. 1953b. "Weisheit und Torheit" (Rektoratsrede). *Kirche und Dogma* Vol. 1, pp. 1-22.

Schlink, E. 1957. "Die Struktur der dogmatischen Aussage als ökumenisches Problem". *Kerygma und Dogma* Vol. 3/4, pp. 251-306.

Schlink, E. 1958. "Zur neuesten ökumenische Stellungnahme des Moskauer Patriarchates". ÖR Vol. 7, pp. 127-140.

Schlink, E. 1961a. *Theology of the Lutheran Confessions.* Philadelphia: Muhlenberg.

Schlink, E. 1961b. *Der kommende Christus und die kirchlichen Traditionen.* Göttingen: Vandenhoeck & Ruprecht.

Schlink, E. 1966. *Nach dem Konzil.* Taschenbuchreihe Vol. 75. München: Siebenstern.

Schlink, E. 1967. *The coming Christ and the coming church.* Edinburgh: Oliver & Boyd.

Schlink, E. 1967. "The task and danger of the World Council of Churches". In *The coming Christ and the coming church.* pp. 3-15.

Schlink, E. 2005. *Schriften zu Ökumene und Bekenntnis. Band 2. Ökumenische Dogmatik.* Göttingen: Vandenhoeck & Ruprecht.

Skibbe, E.M. 1999. *A quiet Reformer: An introduction to Edmund Schlink's life and ecumenical theology.* Minneapolis: Kirk House.

Smit, D. 1992. "Reformed theology in South Africa: A story of many stories". *Acta Theologica* Vol. 12, No. 1, pp. 88-110.

Wainwright, G. 1983. *Doxology: The praise of God in worship, doctrine, and life – A systematic theology.* London: Epworth Press.

PART 2 –
ESSAYS IN AFRICAN, LIBERATION AND FEMINIST THEOLOGIES

2.1 THEOLOGY WITH A NEW VOICE?

The case for an Oral Theology in the South African context[1]

The aim of this exploratory paper is to highlight the possibilities of studies in orality for (systematic) theology. The paper is developed in two broad sections. Section one gives a brief outline of the development of so-called oral theory on the basis of which the case for an "oral theology" is defended. Section two is an attempt to explain why the development of oral theologies in South Africa with literally thousands of oral Christian communities has been delayed up to now.

SECTION ONE

Oral theory was developed from the innovative studies in classical philology by Milman Parry in the 1930s. Through careful analysis of the text, and putting aside the assumptions of literate expression and transmission, he concluded that Homer constructed the *Iliad* and *Odyssey* in formulaic fashion, i.e. he used standardised formulas grouped around equally standardised themes. In this way questions were raised about the mode of expression, performance and transmission of material in a society still in the mindset of primary orality.

The specific Homeric question and the assumptions about orality were subsequently tested by Milman Parry and Albert Lord in the context of living oral traditions in Yugoslavia. In the process the Homeric question became the oral tradition question brilliantly espoused in the influential *The Singer of Tales* published by Lord in 1960. By a comparative application of the analyses of living oral traditions in Yugoslavia (South Slavic epics) to earlier literatures only accessible via texts, he illustrated by analogy the traditional oral forms of those literatures. Again the so-called oral formulaic density of texts was seen as an important indicator of their oral quality.

The methodological shift in the narrow field of philology soon developed into a discipline (Foley 1988:57-93) and spread into various fields ranging from folklore studies, social anthropology, oral history to biblical studies. The oral theory, or more specifically the oral-formulaic theory, aroused wide academic interest as is evident from the more than 1 800 entries in John Miles Foley's bibliography, *Oral-Formulaic Theory and Research* published in 1985 and the journal *Oral Tradition*, which deals specifically with issues related to oral theory.

Despite some disputes on issues about performance, mnemonic devices and memorisation, the degree of differences between an oral and literate mindset, a number of important insights gradually emerged from studies in orality. Based on the work of especially Walter Ong and Ruth Finnegan, I wish to highlight some of them. Moreover, I wish to show how these insights might be fruitful for the development of the concept (terminology) and practice (hermeneutics) of an "oral theology".

---

1   This essay is an adapted version of a lecture given in 1995 at the Society for the Scientific Study of Religion held at Albuquerque in New Mexico, USA. The essay originally appeared in the *Journal of Theology for Southern Africa* 94 (1996), pp. 18-31.

Why is this so important? Because the broad impact of the oral theory has up to now been virtually absent from (systematic) theology or theology in the wider sense of the word. Whereas biblical studies – both Old and New Testament – were perceptive to the fundamental insights of oral studies (see Foley 1988:84-86 for the initial years and my more specific discussion in section two below), (systematic) theologians have not yet reflected on the impact for theology as such.

An interesting attempt to understand the early Christian creeds and controversies about the Trinity from an orality-literacy perspective has been made by Thomas J. Farrell (1987a). This is comparable to the textual analysis with which the oral theory commenced and relies perhaps too much on the stark difference between the mentalities of oral and literate people respectively. It is, however, the actual development of an oral theology from living Christian communities which concerns me here.

What issues could be of assistance in developing both the concept and practice of an "oral theology"? In a summarised fashion, I refer to two broad areas of fruitful debate: firstly, problems relating to terminology, and secondly, problems relating to hermeneutics.

Terminology

The first area relates to the terminological problems involved with the term "oral literature". For the sake of our discussion, two issues may be listed: the implied paradox between oral presentation and literature, and the ambiguity of the term "orality".

In his *Orality and Literacy* (1982) Walter Ong, following the categorical approach of the Parry-Lord thesis and earlier work by McLuhan (see McLuhan 1967), distinguishes quite sharply between an oral (verbomotor) culture (see Ong's reference to Jousse on page 68 and Ong 1967:195-207), a chirographic (writing) culture and a typographic (printing-electronic) culture (1982:2). He employs the term *primary orality* as referring to persons totally unfamiliar with writing (1982:6), and argues for the tenacity of orality and the residually oral mentality of people who have been exposed to, but have not yet interiorised, the literacy mode of thought (1982:11, 56).

Based on this assumption, it is quite understandable that Ong has serious problems with the term "oral literature". He sees this "strictly preposterous term" as the ideological product of the relentless dominance of textuality. It is based on the false assumption "that oral verbalization was essentially the same as the written verbalization" and "reveals our inability to represent to our own minds a heritage of verbally organised materials except as some variant of writing, even when they have nothing to do with writing at all" (1982:10,11). Writing is an imperialist activity and the etymology of the term "literature" is carried through so that "it appears quite impossible to use the term 'literature' to include oral tradition and performance without subtly but irremediably reducing these somehow to a variant of writing" (1982:12).

In line with his assumption of two contrasting periods – orality versus literacy – he finds it unacceptable to explain a phenomenon (orality) by starting with the subsequent secondary phenomenon (literacy). He therefore suggests terms like "verbal art forms" or "purely art forms" and hopes that "oral literature" will lose more and more ground.

A slightly different opinion is expressed by Ruth Finnegan, who has done extensive work on orality from a social anthropological perspective. If one reconstructs her thought, one could argue for the retention of the term "oral literature" from two perspectives:

First, she is highly critical of the postulation of two ideal types of society reminiscent of *Gemeinschaft* and *Gesellschaft*: she argues that societies of primary orality hardly exist and that this notion is based on an assumption which is then empirically generalised. "One has to face the unromantic truth that few or none of these (texts) are directly recorded from the extreme type of primitive culture envisaged in the common dichotomy" (1977:48,254-260). The ideal type society is both sociologically no longer tenable, and is in a certain sense the continuation of the traditional folkloristic approach of the Romantic era (1977:30-41).

The strong emergence of studies questioning the deep divide between orality and literacy (see, for example, Tannen 1982), as well as the many indications of "transitional texts" (see Bäuml 1984 for a proposal of a third theory), adds considerable weight to Finnegan's arguments. This corresponds with shifts to a more liberal view even amongst adherents of the Parry-Lord theory (see Finnegan 1992b:119-120).

Second, Finnegan extends her initial argument that the term "literature" may outgrow its etymological roots (borne out by the wide usage of the term in oral studies) to the more fundamental question of what counts as literatures or texts. Is it true that the label "non-literate" necessarily implies "without literature"? And must literature necessarily be written?

Finnegan argues from the point of view that so-called oral culture produces similar artistic forms as known to us from a literate perspective. Her point is that we should rather extend the term "literature" to include "the unwritten forms of millions of people throughout the world, now and earlier, who do not employ writing" (Finnegan 1973:117), whilst retaining the insight that there are obviously considerable differences in performance and transmission. It is clear that for something to be locally accepted as literature (and the local appreciation is what is relevant here), there is no need to rely solely on the particular convention of the printed page (1973:122).

This relates to what may count as "text". Must a "text" necessarily be written with a fixed connotation? In the Midland edition of her *Oral Poetry* (1992a) Finnegan states:

> There is now a general development across a number of disciplines away from older views of text as hard-edged, spatial, fully comprised by its verbal components, existent independent of its performance, analysable separately from other texts or other aesthetic media, or finally the form in which artistic expression quintessentially exists and should be analysed (1992a:x).

Instead of the older model of a finalised a-social product, one should perhaps look upon a text as an emergent process with all its connotations of co-text, meta-text, con-text, pre-text, sub-text, inter-text and after-text (see Finnegan 1992b:21 and the discussion of Hanks 1989).

This notion of text-as-process opens up the possibility to speak about an "oral text" whilst doing justice to the dynamics involved in the creation and transmission of oral or verbal art forms. (And one could even muster some etymological support from text as referring to "weaving" in the sense of weaving songs together!)

A last terminological remark relates to the ambiguity of the term "oral". At first sight it obviously refers to unwritten or partially unwritten. But – as Finnegan points out – it also implies a reference to more-than-just words! In terms of poetry she says:

> The performance of any poem almost necessarily also involves delivery arts and stylistics – not to speak of audience dynamics – which take us beyond purely verbal text in the narrow sense of that term. So when we say "oral" we paradoxically, and almost by definition, mean something more than just verbal (1992a:xi-xii).

Read in conjunction with the above paragraphs, this dual and paradoxical understanding of the term "oral" further strengthens the argument for the retention of the designation "oral literature" under the conditions set out above.

It is in relation to this debate that the case for the term "oral theology" may be argued for. Two recent publications highlight the relation between theology as a discipline and the act of writing/authorship with the concomitant conferral of authority.

From a historical perspective, Henri-Jean Martin's seminal *The History and Power of Writing* (1994, original 1988), carefully constructs the advent of printing and the reign of the book (1994:182-282. See Assmann 1992 for a discussion of the effect of writing on corporate cultural identity in earlier civilisations). In relation to, for example, the spread of Luther's Reformation (e.g. the *Betbuchlein* and Bible translations), he notes that Germany had a relatively high literacy rate at the end of the fifteenth century and was the "motherland of printing" (253). He subsequently suggests that "The works gained in prestige from the mere fact of being printed; printing gave them something like a palpable existence and an implicit verity". This he ascribes to the fact that "reading was like a revelation hitherto known only in restricted circles which transmitted no more than glimpses of it in sermons and readings during the Mass" (254).

From a *theological* perspective, John Thiel, in his *Imagination and Authority* (1991), argues persuasively that "modern theology" constituted a paradigm shift in relation to the classical Middle Ages. This was achieved via a greater disciplinary self-awareness, an explicit historical orientation, a turn to the subject in the post-Kantian era and – for our purposes the most important feature – a shift in understanding the theologian's task:

> In a manner analogous to understandings of the practitioner in artistic and literary endeavour, theologians conceived of themselves as authors and measured the authority of their work ... not only in terms of its faithfulness to ecclesial tradition but also in terms of its creativity, its resourcefulness in explicating the contemporary meaning of ancient religious truths (1991:9).

In the classical paradigm the notion of individual creative authorship did not exist, as the theologian was a mere representative of the ancient authoritative tradition. As a reaction against Enlightenment rationalism, a romantic notion of theological authorship was born "in this ascription of authorial ability, and thus authority, to the individual theologian" (Thiel 1991 21).

This inextricable link between theology, authorship and authority is still entrenched today as an invisible but powerful assumption of theologians' self-understanding – one reads theology and one writes theology and one interprets/studies theology in the sense of texts handed down in writing. This view of theology – strongly entrenched in the West since the Enlightenment – was fundamentally questioned by the emergence of (third world) liberation theologies since the 1960s. The paradigm switch (Kuhn) implied a shift from theory to praxis (Metz 1979 and others), from orthodoxy to orthopraxis (Leonardo Boff 1978), from mere contemplation to action, from Hegelian idealism to Marxian materialism (Sobrino), from theology as first act to theology as second act (Gutierrez 1983).

But despite these fundamentally important shifts, theology remained primarily based on literary assumptions and theologians retained their chirographic bias. The voice from the underside of history was never heard as a dynamic *oral* voice, but as the secondary literate voice of the (Western) trained liberation theologian. That is why theology in a new key (Brown 1978) needs to be complemented by theology with a new voice (*vox* relating to speech).

But this implies a further fundamental shift in the answer to the question: What is theology? If the term is to be retained (and I think it should – also for strategic reasons), we shall have to understand the religious expressions in manifold forms of oral communities (i.e. illiterate or functionally illiterate communities) as proper theology, i.e. oral theology.

Literally millions of Christians all over the world – and especially in the so-called third world – have no other access to the gospel and tradition but via oral means of memorisation, performance and transmission. And their prophets, healers, poets and preachers are the theologians of their societies and churches.

In conjunction with the shift in perceptions about "texts" as a dynamic process, "theology" should no longer only be viewed as fixed literary products with the latter as *the* form in which the intellectual expression of faith (*fides quaerens intellectum*) exists. Added to the con-text of liberation theologies comes the insight of poli-textuality which warns us that all productions of theological texts – especially oral texts – are distortions because of the limiting funnel effect in the fixed textual representation of theology-as-process.

This relates directly to the positive ambiguity of the term "oral". In conjunction with theology, it consequently refers to non-written forms of religious expression, but also to non-verbal aspects which constitute the total performance of oral theologies. The variations of voice tone, the active audience interaction (see the call-response structure of many art forms), the music and dance – they all add up to "voicing" theology-as-process in distinction to "writing" and "doing" theology.

The question may now arise: Why bother so much with terminology? Is oral theology not just another term in the long row of labels for theology including contextual, indigenous, popular, inculturalised or even local theology? (See Schreiter 1985:1-6.) The answer is that it is not. This is explained in relation to the second area of concern which arose from oral theory and subsequent studies in orality, namely the notion of an oral hermeneutic.

Hermeneutics

The whole development of oral theory may be seen in a hermeneutical light. No matter whether one accepts or relativises the difference between oral and literate cultures, there is general consensus that verbal art forms must be interpreted in a *sui generis* fashion. And this is possible because certain specific features of oral performance, memorisation and transmission are detectable even in a fixed oral text and should be understood from the perspective of an oral hermeneutic.

There is no room to develop a full oral hermeneutic within the confines of this essay, and it is not necessary to repeat what more competent scholars have said (see references to Kelber in Section Two). My own extensive field work amongst two separate oral Christian communities in Venda have shown that many "nonsensical" features of oral texts – as seen from a print-orientated hermeneutic – become exciting expressions of meaning from an oral perspective: the variability of "texts" without an "original" authentic version; the manifold repetitions and recurrent phrases (very "pale" if represented in writing); the interplay between audience and performer (sometimes overtly structured in caller and community response); the mnemonic devices to "preserve" the "text"; and the "illogical" connection between divergent categories – all these and many more are only "meaningful" if the paradigm of linearity so intimately bound to writing and a print-orientated hermeneutic is shifted in the direction of vibrant oral speech unconnected by time and space (Kelber 1985:32-34. See Ong 1982:31-77; Finnegan 1973:136ff; Finnegan 1977: Chapters 3-5 and 7).

The point is that the representation and interpretation of oral religious expressions must take serious note of the fundamental insights pertaining to an oral hermeneutic. My field work in the Saint Engenas Zion Christian Church (South Africa) is ample illustration of the salient theological implications if an outsider wishes to "hear" the voice of oral theologians (Naudé 1993, 1995). It is only an oral hermeneutic that can guard one against misunderstandings such as "repetition of a phrase implies its importance for the performers"; "the caller is the actual theologian because she leads the congregation", "the intimate relation between the leader and God/Christ illustrates their syncretistic views" and so forth.

If this is properly understood, the introduction and retention of the term "oral theology" not only makes sense – it becomes a necessity to preserve the integrity of oral theologians and to open the universal church to their enriching insights.

Definitions are sometimes arduous, but may be helpful heuristic devices. In the light of my arguments above, I suggest a two-tier definition. First-order oral theology refers to the varied religious expressions of an oral community based on their underlying faith experiences. And second-order oral theology is the systematic reflection upon the manifold expressions of first-order oral theology in the specific light of an oral hermeneutic.

A few explanatory remarks need to be added to this suggestion. First-order oral theology relates to the emic perspective of the insider. And it is called theology because the religious expressions do represent an insight into and understanding of the underlying faith tradition, although not "systematised" in a fashion to which literates are accustomed. To take the latter as the natural yardstick to which all others should strive (Finnegan 1973:143-144) is to show a remarkable lack of historical and comparative perspective as well as an (unintended?) snobbery so deeply ingrained in literates – including theologians.

Second-order oral theology may be done by both insiders and outsiders, but is a specific literary activity (like this essay itself!) and usually involves an etic perspective. Here we move closer to the traditional perception of theology. The difference with contextual or popular or local theologies, however, lies in the respect for first-order oral theology as *oral,* as becomes evident from the adoption of an oral hermeneutic.

We can now move on to Section Two, where I attempt to understand the reasons for the absence of oral theologies in their second-order manifestation from the South African theological scene. Perhaps some readers might find the reasons cogent enough to serve as "diagnosis" on a wider front beyond the Southern African context.

SECTION TWO

The burning question is why the exciting possibilities that oral theory opened did not impact on the South African theological scene. Why, in a country with countless oral Christian communities and an abundance of first-order oral theologies, has the development of second-order theologies been absent? The answer, I would argue, is manifold and may be explained from the following perspectives:

1. The specific focus of theologies developed in response to the oppressive political system in South Africa;

2. The limited hermeneutical perspective in the few cases where oral material was in fact analysed as basis for theology;

3. The specific route that oral theory followed to enter the systematic theological arena via biblical studies – specifically the New Testament.

I hope that my discussion of these points will serve as implicit argument for redirecting at least some of our (the outsiders!) theological energy to the field of oral theologies. The last perspective does provide some hope for the future in this regard.

1. It is quite understandable that the theological focus in South Africa from the 1960s fell on undermining the moral base of a theologically justified apartheid policy. A number of theologies united in the struggle against apartheid: black theology, African theology, feminist theology, English "progressive" theology and critical voices from within the Afrikaans-speaking churches (including the DRC and old Mission Church now united with the DRC in Africa as the Uniting Reformed Church).

It would be unfair to oversimplify the varied responses to expressions from these theologians. Generally speaking, however, the categories employed as analysis of the situation moved from racial discrimination (black versus white) to a class analysis (poor versus rich; socialism versus capitalism) with a strong emphasis on the "gospel of the poor". This was an extremely fruitful period of theologising in South Africa as is evident from numerous publications including declarations, public statements, theological documents (*Kairos, The Road to Damascus*), the groundbreaking Belhar confession, anthologies, articles in local journals such as *JTSA* and *Scriptura* as well as several monographs by, for example, Allan Boesak, Desmond Tutu, John de Gruchy, Charles Villa-Vicencio, Klaus Nürenberger, Adrio König, Johann Kinghorn, Dirkie Smit, Etienne de Villiers and others.

But one important aspect of the oppressive situation has hitherto been neglected, namely the strong literate-illiterate dichotomy (or rather the oral/non-oral distinction). As a result of the (legitimate) focus of the contributions mentioned, and because of the text-based hermeneutical model employed, a lack of sensitivity was revealed to the fact that the very products of a liberatory theology were in a sense reinforcing the dominance of Western trained, highly literate theologians. The voice of the oral peoples was not heard, despite noble intentions.

This is illustrated by the legitimate and creative reclaiming of the traditional theological resources ranging from Calvin and Luther, to Kuyper, Barth and Bonhoeffer. A good example is *On reading Karl Barth in South Africa* under the editorship of Charles Villa-Vicencio (1988). The contributors to this volume use the insights of black and liberation theology to reread traditional theologies in order to reclaim them as "important resources in our struggle for spiritual and political liberation" (1988:xi).

In his introductory chapter Villa-Vicencio remarked that theology in recent times had been revolutionised by the fact "that the theological reflection of oppressed people has penetrated the theological marketplace, and this kind of theology is very different from that expressed by theologians who have emerged from the dominant class" (1988:3). He is, however, completely oblivious to the fact that he (and others) inadvertently sustained a new kind of exploitation, namely the inability of oral people to enter this "marketplace" now dominated by highly literate and prolific liberation theologians!

This is apparent from his emphasis on rereading the Bible from the location of the poor. His important call on theologians to "work in close proximity with the oppressed people of society, to hear their questions, to respond to their needs, and, as far as possible to fear their fears and dream their dreams that emerge from their oppression and poverty" (1988:4) excludes the experience of being oral and unable to be heard in a literate theological world.

And what makes this exclusion so serious is the historical and social context of oppression in South Africa that overlooked the literate-illiterate dichotomy. One paragraph from an illuminating article by Jeff Guy (1991) makes the point:

> The written word was part of conquest in South Africa. It was the medium whereby the conquerors communicated and organised their resources, policies and tactics. The written treaty confirmed the right of the conqueror to the land, giving the act of conquest permanency over time and in space; and the history of South Africa is replete with accounts of the efforts of the literate invaders to persuade, cajole, demand that the oral, traditional rulers, touch the pen (Guy 1991:398).

Yes, the creation of the category "illiterate" is simultaneously the creation of a vulnerable social group with ever increasing opportunities for discrimination and exploitation. Illiterates have been, in the South African context, not merely those unable to read: they are the category of marginalised people, excluded – for many years by law – from education and access to the world of literacy that controlled their lives through documents (pass laws) they could not even read. The current debates on land redistribution and reconstructing education in a new South Africa have their roots inter alia in the dichotomies created by the oral-literate social construction in our history. And theologians who take social analysis seriously must take this matter seriously precisely to avoid a continuation of this condition.

Villa-Vicencio (and others) thus make two mistakes: their concern for the poor and oppressed is a selective one, omitting any acknowledgment of the oppression of a literate society, and they continue this oppression by the very fruits of their labour. Until liberation theologians go out and really listen to the first-order oral theologies (and not only to influential traditional voices), millions of poet- and prophet-theologians are kept in silence (if seen from a second-order perspective). (Perhaps we need their voices more than they need ours – they will in any case not read what we write about them!).

I fully respect and endorse a reclaiming of the tradition and a theology of the poor. And one must see the important work by Villa-Vicencio and others within the context to which it responded as well as that of further developments since 1992. But the time has come to utilise the perspectives of oral theory in order to develop a fuller picture of a truly South African theology.

2. In retrospect it emerges that the development of a second-order oral theology has also been hampered by people who attempted to take oral texts seriously. The basic problem is that where oral expressions were analysed as the proper source of second-order oral theology, they were seen as texts and not read from an oral hermeneutical perspective. I briefly refer to works by GC Oosthuizen, Absolom Vilakazi and John de Gruchy as examples of this.

The most remarkable of these is Oosthuizen's *The Theology of a South African Messiah* (1976), which is an analysis of the hymnal of the Church of the Nazarites published in the 1940s. (It must be pointed out that Oosthuizen, a world-renowned expert on the Independent Churches, has since the early 1970s already alluded to the unwritten theology of people in freely sung hymns, prophecies and sermons. I am heavily indebted to his influence on my own thinking).

It is impossible to do full justice to this work. In the context of oral theory, I want to make several observations.

Despite the acknowledgement that Shembe I, the founder of the Church of the Nazarites, was illiterate, the whole presentation is from the viewpoint of literate authorship with Shembe I "writing" the hymns and being the "author" (in the literate sense) of a "hymn book" (Oosthuizen 1976:1).

This viewpoint has at least two broad negative effects, i.e. on Oosthuizen's theological evaluation and his actual analysis of the hymns.

First, Oosthuizen has a very specific theological interest and his whole analysis is aimed at uncovering the "theology implied in the hymnal" (1976:i) and the "theological disposition" of the Shembe movement (1976:145). Despite an openness to learn from movements like this, Oosthuizen adopts a very closed perspective based on the tradition of the Church:

> Every religion has a creed, a cult and a culture, and as far as the creed is concerned, no borrowing is possible for Christianity unless one wishes to establish a new religion. The cult and the culture could be taken into possession and regenerated through the work of the Holy Spirit, but the Christian creed cannot be changed (1976:10).

I suggest that an understanding of oral theory would have opened new hermeneutical possibilities and would have assisted Oosthuizen to see, for example, the identification of Christ and Shembe (1976:36-7, 56, 150), or the Spirit and Shembe (152), from the noetic perspective of orality. The hymnal is not in the first place "the Catechism of the movement" (1976:6), thus implying that we have a systematic theological statement before us. No, it is an oral religious document and the constructed theology should respect it on its own terms and not be judged in the light of an "unchanged Christian creed".

Secondly, because of his thorough understanding of traditional Zulu religion, Oosthuizen is able to see some of the structural features of traditional songs in the hymnal. He refers to the call-response structure (1976:8), repetition, the rhythm, the concreteness of content (1976:154-155) and the non-analytical nature of these hymns (1976:152). But instead of relating these features to oral transmission and performance with the concomitant hermeneutical possibilities, he merely ascribes them to aspects of the "pre-Christian Zulu religion" (154).

It becomes obvious that proper understanding of oral theory opens exciting possibilities poorly understood by Oosthuizen at the time of writing his book.

Closely linked to this perspective is that of Absolom Vilakazi in Shembe, *The Revitalization of African society*, published in 1986. In his discussion of the hymns by Isaiah Shembe, he explains the categories of Shembe songs including hymns in the style of Zulu indigenous singing called *isikegle* (song and dance).

Vilakazi then makes an important observation:

> Izikegle ... are automatically exposed to an oral tradition, and their words are hardly sung according to the written letter. In Zulu folk music the beauty of a musical text lies in its semantic meaning rather than in its verbal precision, and the improvisation of the words is therefore permissible (1986:154).

It is clear that Vilakazi understands almost intuitively that oral performances are of a different kind than the Western-styled hymns also composed by Shembe. But because Vilakazi operates from a literate point of view, he foregoes the opportunity to understand these folk-type music and texts on their own terms. This forces him into a defensive mode so that the improvisation of the words (so crucial to oral performances!) becomes an embarrassment and is consequently described as "permissible".

Of all the good books that John de Gruchy published, his *Cry Justice* comes closest to the purpose of this essay. From the foreword and introduction it emerges that de

Gruchy wishes to overcome the dichotomy between sacred and secular by relating Christian spirituality to social transformation. It is evident that de Gruchy is very well aware of the

> six million members (who) belong to the various indigenous churches in South Africa, that is, to churches which have in varying degrees related their Christian faith to traditional spirituality. Although suppressed within the mainline churches, elements of African spirituality and culture have always been present even if sometimes dormant, and in our time a renaissance has begun that is of considerable significance (1986:41).

This anthology of thirty-one sets of readings does not include an analysis of the material drawn from various sources. They are clearly understood as readings (1986:20), but the author should be commended for at least including in the remarkable variations of sources, material from the indigenous oral Christian communities (see, for example, the witness and hymn of Ntsikana, 56-59 and many others). From the perspective of developing an oral theology, this anthology for personal and communal devotion at least points to the fact that orally transmitted material is taken seriously in a doxological context. The time has come to bring them into the centre of our "doing theology in (the South African) context", which is, incidentally, the title of an anthology of articles published in 1994 by de Gruchy and Villa-Vicencio.

The concern in this recent volume is to overcome the perception that theology is merely a discipline of reading and studying. Therefore the emphasis falls on *doing theology*, because "studying theology has significance only in so far as it enables us to do theology today with better insight and greater faithfulness to the gospel" (de Gruchy 1994:2-3).

Here the author echoes the valid claim for a praxis-orientated theology – the intimate relation between reflection and action. My plea in this essay is that we introduce another category into our theological education in South Africa, namely "voicing theology" and "hearing theology", which complement "reading" and "doing" theology.

The epistemological break brought about by a shift from idealism to materialism should now be extended to relativise the literate-analytical categories from an oral-aural noetic position espoused in the context of oral studies. The implications of this are too manifold to explore here, but would include a serious rethinking of our curricula and what has traditionally been included under "practical theology".

We now turn to what I perceive to be the last reason for the weak focus on an oral theology in the South African context.

3. As outlined above, oral theory developed in the specific area of classical linguistic studies and only later became a distinguishable discipline in its own right, crossing the boundaries into various other fields such as anthropology, folklore studies and history.

The immense energy created by oral theory eventually also impacted on biblical studies. Since the 1960s oral-formulaic theory was applied to Old Testament studies.

Robert Culley, for example, worked on the Psalms (1967), William Urbrock on Job (1972, 1975) and Whallon (1963, 1969) and Yoder (1970, 1971) on Hebrew poetry (see Culley 1976 for an overview and references).

In the meantime the validity of the traditional approaches in form and tradition criticism were questioned. Oral theory cast doubt on the assumption of mechanical transmission of "oral units", where the norms of transmission are derived from textuality. It subsequently claimed that the interpretative approach to these "oral units" as primarily literary products is a disproportional print-orientated hermeneutic and should be replaced by an oral hermeneutic.

The breakthrough (in the words of Farrell 1987b) came with Werner Kelber's illuminating New Testament study, *The Oral and the Written Gospel* in 1983. It is imperative reading for anyone interested in oral theology. Much has been written about this book and it need not be repeated here. For our purpose this reference is important, for it is the subsequent work of people in the New Testament Society of South Africa which placed oral theory firmly on the broad theological agenda. Other disciplines such as history and anthropology show the influence of oral theory since the mid-1980s. The prolific work of Pieter Botha (Unisa) since 1990 on ancient communication, reinterpreting letter writing and the relation between folklore and New Testament studies should be mentioned specifically (see bibliography).

Three notable articles sensitive to orality appeared independently in different editions of *Scriptura* during the same year (1993). I refer to Loubser, myself and Cochrane, who all happen to be involved in local Christian communities in different areas of South Africa.

A tentative bridge between New Testament studies and a more systematic Christology has been attempted by JA Loubser in *The Oral Christ of Shembe: Believing in Jesus in oral and literate societies.* It is based on an analysis of "the oral conventions of traditional African society" in 23 sermons from the Shembe church and attempts to explain the "unorthodox christology" emerging from these sermons in terms of Ong's work on orality. Oral theory provides us with the interpretative framework in which the identification of Sheme and Christ may be explained; i.e. the oral conception of time; the situational thinking and participatory style of narrative which eradicate the distance between Christ and Shembe (Loubser 1993:73-76). Although Loubser acknowledges his dilemma in developing "theological criteria for evaluating the Shembe theology" (77), he does relativise earlier studies operating in a "literate" framework and leading to accusations of heterodoxy and even syncretism.

My own work on more than 50 hymns from the Saint Engenas Zionist Christian Church must be read in the context of oral theory (see Naudé 1993). It led to some methodological observations (how does an outsider construct a so-called local theology? 30-38), provisional reconstructions in theology and Christology (The God of Engenas and Jesus as *nanga*, 41-43), as well as criteria for evaluating oral theologies (40-44). It is an attempt to take seriously the theological voicings (in this case hymnal performances) of oral poets/musicians on their own terms, namely as oral performances and not as fixed textual products.

The third contribution is that of James Cochrane. I refer to his *God in context. The symbolic construction of a religious universe in a base Christian community* (published in

1993) and his contribution to De Gruchy and Villa-Vicencio: *Doing theology in context* (1994), entitled *Theology and faith: Tradition, criticism and popular religion*.

Although Cochrane's work does not at this stage show evidence of a strong relation to oral theory, he does expand the traditional English liberal or liberationist perspective to include local theologies and popular religion. He wishes to speak *with* the local communities and he understands that they (in this case referring to women from Mpophomeni township near Howick in Natal) are semi-literate and theologically untrained (1994:30).

As I read him, he has not yet seriously grappled with an "oral theology" in the sense defined in this essay. The reason is that his concern at this stage lies not with the semi-literate but with the theologically untrained: how can the theology of ordinary untrained people be taken seriously when they do their own theology. "They draw on powerful oral traditions which may not be scripturally located" (1994:30). This "incipient" theology may yield results which are "not necessarily orthodox theology, but it is real theology" (1994:31).

Despite the absence of specific oral analyses, Cochrane succeeds in clarifying some important methodological issues (see "interpretative strategies" (1993:39) and the "*Gestalt* of theological construction" (1994:35-37)) and expands the understanding of "doing theology" in the South African context.

CONCLUSION

It is clear: our work as second-order oral theologians has just begun. If we accept the terminology and practice of "oral theology" (Section One); if we expand our understanding of oppression, broaden our hermeneutical perspective and leave our comfortable desks to listen to theology (Section Two), exciting prospects open up. Our advantaged location amidst oral communities in South Africa, a new openness after the apartheid era, growing interest from African and local theologians, set the scene for a creative hearing-theology in the South African context. The voice of the hitherto marginalised "voicings" must be heard!

BIBLIOGRAPHY

Assmann, J. 1992. *Das kulturelle Gedächtnis: Schrift, Erinnerung und politische Identität in frühen Hochkulturen*. München: C.H. Beck.

Bauml, F.H. 1984. "Medieval Texts and the Two Theories of Oral-Formulaic Composition: A Proposal for a Third Theory". *New Literary History*. Vol. 16, No. 1, pp. 31-49.

Boff, L. & Rahner, K. (ed.) 1977. *Befreiende Theologie. Der Beitrag Lateinamerikas zur Theologie der Gegenwart*. Stuttgart: Kohlhammer.

Boff, L. 1978. *Jesus Christ Liberator: A Critical Christology for Our Time*. New York: Orbis.

Botha, P.J.J. 1990. "The task of understanding the Gospel traditions Werner Kelber's contribution to New Testament research". *Hervormde Teologiese Studies*. Vol. 46, No. 1 & 2, pp. 47-70.

Botha, P.J.J. 1991. "Mark's story as oral traditional literature Rethinking the transmission of some traditions about Jesus". *Hervormde Teologiese Studies* Vol. 47, No. 2, pp. 304-331.

Botha, P.J.J. 1991. "Orality, literacy and worldview exploring the interaction". *Communicatio* Vol. 17, No. 2, pp. 2-15.

Botha, P.J.J. 1992. "Letter Writing and Oral Communication in Antiquity". *Sciptura* Vol. 42, pp. 17-34.

Brown, R.M. 1978. *Theology in a New Key*. Philadelphia: Westminster Press.

Cochrane, J. R. 1993. "God in Context. The Symbolic Construction of a Religious Universe in a Base Christian Community". *Sciptura* Vol. 12, pp. 35-56.

Cochrane, J. R. 1994. "Theology and faith Tradition, criticism and popular religion". In De Gruchy & Villa-Vicencio (eds.)

Culley, R.C. 1976. "Oral Tradition and the OT. Some recent discussions" *Semeia* 5. pp. 1-33.

De Gruchy, J. 1986. *Cry Justice*. New York: Orbis.

De Gruchy, John & Villa-Vicencio C. (eds.). 1994. *Doing theology in context: South African perspectives*. Cape Town: David Philip.

Foley, J.M. 1988. *The Theory of Oral Composition History and Methodology*. Bloomington: Indiana University Press.

Farrell, T.J. 1987a. "Early Christian creeds and controversies in the light of the orality-literacy hypothesis". *Oral Tradition* Vol. 2, No. 1, pp. 132-149.

Farrell, T.J. 1987b. "Kelber's breakthrough". *Semeia* Vol. 39, pp. 27-45.

Finnegan, R. 1970. *Oral Literature in Africa*. Oxford: Clarendon Press.

Finnegan, R. 1970. "Literacy versus Non-literacy The Great Divide?" In H. Robin & R Finnegan (eds.), pp. 112-144.

Finnegan, R. 1977. *Oral Poetry. Its nature, significance and social context*. Cambridge: Cambridge University Press.

Finnegan, R. 1991. "Tradition, but what tradition and for whom?" *Oral Tradition* Vol. 6, No. 1, pp. 104-24.

Finnegan, R. 1992a. *Oral Poetry Its nature, significance and social context*. Bloomington: Indiana University Press.

Finnegan, Ruth. 1992b. *Oral Traditions and the verbal arts: A guide to research practices*. London: Routledge.

Gutierrez, G. 1983. *The Power of the Poor in History*. London: SCM.

Guy, J. 1991. "Literacy and literature". In E. Sienaert (ed.), pp. 395-413.

Hanks, W. F. 1989. "Text and textuality". *Annual Review of Anthropology*. Vol. 18, pp. 5-127.

Lord, A.B. 1964. *The Singer of Tales*. Cambridge: Harvard University Press.

Loubser, J.A. 1993. "The Oral Christ of Shembe". *Sciptura* Vol. 12, pp. 70-80.

Martin, H.J. 1994. *The History and Power of Writing*. Chicago: The University of Chicago Press.

Metz, J.B. 1979. *Zur Theologie der Welt*. London: Routledge and Kegan Paul.

Naudé, P.J. 1993. "Toward a local Zionist Theology? The role of the outsider theologian". *Sciptura* Vol. 45, pp. 29-46.

Naudé, P.J. 1995. *The Zionist Christian Church in South Africa: An experiment in oral theology*. Ontario: The Edwin Mellen Press.

Ong, W.J. 1967. *The Presence of the Word*. New Haven: Yale University Press.

Ong, W.J. 1977. *Interfaces of the Word Studies in the evolution of consciousness and Culture*. Ithaca: Cornell University Press.

Oosthuizen, G.C. 1976. *The Theology of a South African Messiah. An analysis of the hymnal of the Church of the Nazarites*. Leiden: Brill.

Schreiter, R.J. 1985. *Constructing Local Theologies*. London: SCM.

Sienaert, E. (ed.) 1991. *Tradition and Innovation: New wine in old bottles*. Durban: University of Natal, Durban.

Sobrino, J. 1977. "Theologisches Erkennen in der europäischen und lateinamerikanischen Theologie". In L. Boff & K. Rahner (eds.), pp. 123-143.

Robin, H & R Finnegan, R. (eds.) 1970. *Modes of Thought Essays on Thinking in Western and Non-western Societies*. London: Faber & Faber.

Tannen, D. 1982. "The Myth of Orality and Literacy". In F. Williams (ed.), pp. 37-50.

Thiel, J.E. 1991. *Imagination and Authority Theological authorship in modern tradition*. Minneapolis: Fortress Press.

Vilakazi, A. 1986. *Shembe The Revitalization of African Society*. Johannesburg: Skotaville.

Villa-Vicencio, C. (ed.). 1988. *On Reading Karl Barth in South Africa* Grand Rapids: Eerdmans.

Williams, F. (ed.) 1982. *Linguistics and Literacy*. New York: Plenum Press.

2.2 TOWARD A LOCAL ZIONIST THEOLOGY

The role of the outsider theologian[1]

Quite a number of important studies have appeared over the years on the theological and socio-political significance of the hymnal traditions in African independent churches (see e.g. Kruger 1971; Oosthuizen 1976; Vilakazi 1976; Cargie 1988; Blacking 1981; Lukhaimane 1981). The study of oral traditions is well established in the so-called Anglo-American school of literature studies, where the basic work by Milman Parry and Albert Lord and subsequent work on orality by Marshall McLuhan, Walter Ong, Ruth Finnegan and Jack Goody led to an upsurge in studies on the oral genre as such. In history, especially African history, oral traditions have earned a respected place (see the standard work by Vansina, 1985) and such an approach has become part and parcel of historical-critical investigations in biblical studies (e.g. tradition and form criticism).

During 1989 I did extensive field work in the Saint Engenas Christian Church (ZCC) of Itsani, a small peasant village about 15 km from Sibasa in Venda (Northern Transvaal). The oral material I collected consisted of 52 freely sung hymns, which were transcribed, translated and interpreted. The aim was to construct what could be the outline of a local Zionist theology. (The results were submitted to the HSRC under whose auspices the project was executed; see Naudé 1992).

Based on this work, the purpose of this paper is to reflect on the role of the foreign or outsider theologian in the construction of a local theology. Although references to matters of "content" are made (see creedal formulation below), the primary concern is one of method: what is the "methodological position" of an outsider in his/her endeavour to grasp a "foreign" theological tradition expressed in oral format?

I shall (1) explain concisely the concept of local theology; (2) offer a note on the importance of cultural analysis; and then (3) proceed to elaborate on the various "functions" of the outsider theologian.

I hope that this will shed some methodological light on the important task of South African theologians to record the oral theology (people's theology?) of which millions of believers are the subject, but which is poorly represented in academic theology.

1. THE CONCEPT OF LOCAL THEOLOGY

The realisation of the "locality" of theology opposes the traditional perception that Western theology is "theology" with an implied universalist strain, whereas other theologies are "adjective theologies", e.g. liberation theology, African theology, Asian theology, and so forth. It seems more appropriate to speak of theologies in the plural – especially where the enculturalisation of the gospel is discussed.

---

1 This essay is an adapted version of a paper on Zionist theology as systematic theology delivered in Pretoria in 1989 at the Theological Society of Southern Africa. The essay was first published in *Scriptura* 45 (1993), 29-46.

The concept of "local theology" to describe the product of the dynamic interplay between gospel, church tradition and culture is excellently explained by the Catholic scholar, Robert Schreiter, in his *Constructing local theologies* (1985). (See an early discussion of the so-called Chicago effort in Joseph Spae 1979). I accept his reasons for adopting the term, especially with its connotation of *ecclesia particularis*, which reflects the contribution of the local church in developing a culturally relevant theological response to the gospel (Schreiter 1985:5-6).

The task of constructing a fully developed local theology is a very broad and complex task to execute. In the case under discussion the "source of information", namely freely sung hymns, is perhaps too narrow a basis from which to proceed. But in a sapiential context, where theology is more wisdom (*sapienta*) than sure knowledge (*scientia*) (see Schreiter 1985:85-87), and with the example of liberation and African theologies in recent years (see Schreiter 1992), the way to a genuine local theology is not *via* the highway of impressive system building. It is the following of a number of small footpaths – perhaps unimpressive from a traditional systematic theological perspective – that leads to the creation of a theology which corresponds to the experience of the community in which it arises (see Penoukou's Christological construction aptly described as Christology in the village).

From this perspective the results of any study by an outsider may be an important "footpath", expressing the religious experiences of the relevant community in theological terms, albeit partially and inadequately. I say partially, because there are other sources such as sermons, prayers and prophecies that must be consulted to draw a fuller picture of a local theology in action. And I say inadequately, because an extensive cultural analysis is needed to interpret hymns (or any other source material) within their historico-religious framework.

2. ANALYSIS OF CULTURE AS STARTING POINT?

The importance of such an analysis is stated very clearly by Schreiter:

> Ideally, for a genuinely contextual theology, the theological process should begin with the opening of the culture, that long and careful listening to a culture to discover its principal values, needs, interests, directions and symbols (1985:28).

He says this on the basis of the semiotic approach of the American anthropologist, Clifford Geertz, where both culture and religion (as part of culture) are defined in terms of symbols that constitute webs of significance which are to be interpretively analysed (see Geertz 1975:5; see also his reliance on Gilbert Ryle's notion of a "thick description" of culture, and the definitions on pages 89-90ff).

According to Schreiter, a local theology is developed from cultural texts which need not be overtly religious. Once the sign system of a culture is understood, a selection of cultural texts is made "that will become the focus of theological reflection", so that the religious domain may be brought into relation to the other semiotic domains. Once this is established, the dialogue with the broader church tradition commences (1985:73-74).

Within the limitations of this project, no elaborate, autonomous cultural analysis was attempted. Certain broader cultural considerations were, however, introduced to explain expressions and references which occurred in the hymns. Being an "outsider", one has to suppose that many of the broader underlying cultural symbols were just not "seen" and were thus omitted. A fuller interpretation would possibly arise in conjunction with members of the community and a well-trained anthropologist.

In the interplay between culture, gospel and tradition (Schreiter), I took the second, namely the interpretation of the gospel (verbalised in freely sung hymns), as my point of departure. Despite the strong point made by Schreiter (cultural texts as *starting* point), I believe this to be a fruitful theological avenue for two reasons.

First, there is nothing in Geertz's definition of culture and religion respectively that precludes an "entrance" to the former *via* the latter. He understands culture to be

> an historically transmitted pattern of meaning embodied in symbols ... by means of which men communicate, perpetuate, and develop their knowledge about and attitudes toward life (1975:89).

And what is the function of religious symbols? Precisely to synthesise a people's ethos and world-view, thus formulating

> a basic congruence between a particular style of life and a specific metaphysic (1975:90).

If the most comprehensive idea of order is being expressed in religious symbols, and if there is a reciprocal sustaining relation between lifestyle and metaphysics, the identification of a set of religious symbols may open the door to understanding the lifestyle/ethos of a cultural group.

Second, if this is accepted, the "doorway" to these religious symbols is *inter alia* by way of the poets, prophets and composers in a community. They express the (religious) experiences of the community through the creation of (religious) symbols in a variation of genres (see Wainwright's systematic theology based on doxology, 1980). Von Allem describes this process in terms of the New Testament in his illuminating article, "The birth of theology" (1975). I quote his general conclusion:

> The theologian has no right to fear the spontaneous manner in which the church sometimes expresses the faith. If the apostles had been timorous and shut the mouths of the poets through fear of heresy, the Church would never have found footing on Hellenistic soil. Thus the way things happened in the primitive church teaches us that in the Church the life of faith is the primary thing. Missionaries do not preach a theology but rather the Gospel. Nor is the response of faith yet theology, but rather worship or hymns proclaiming the mighty deeds of God in Jesus Christ (44).

Because of the interrelation between religious and other cultural symbols, the latter are important, even essential, but (contrary to Schreiter's notion[2]) need not necessarily serve as starting point for a local theology.

---

2 In all fairness, it must be stated that Schreiter is not dogmatic about this. Throughout his book, and drawing on wide experience, he constantly urges an openness to allow

These few paragraphs inevitably lead to the question of how the "outsider" professional theologian would proceed to contribute to the construction of a local theology. This will explain my own function *vis-à-vis* the Itsani congregation and will bring us to the point where the first (systematic) theological results emerge.

3. THE ROLE OF THE OUTSIDER-THEOLOGIAN

In anthropology and other social sciences the differentiation between an etic or emic perspective is well established. This has a direct bearing on the image and relative distance between the researcher and participant (see Mouton and Marais 1988:81ff; Geertz's reference to Kohut's differentiation between experience-near and experience-distant; and important studies on field work such as Burgess 1984, Lofland 1971, Denzin 1978, Becker & Geer 1984).

As long as one is aware of one's position as outsider with the concomitant "etic" perspective, there is, from a researcher's point of view, no fundamental exclusion of important insights and even positive contributions to an understanding of the matter under discussion.

Schreiter points out that the "explanations" of an emic perspective tend to remain within the system:

> hence, if the questioner does not already understand the system, the explanations are not of much help – they are not really translations into another mould, but variations within the same range of discourse (Schreiter 1985:57).

Outer descriptions (etic), on the other hand, often have the advantage of being phenomenological with a very specific concern for explanation. And they are executed on the basis of "translating the reality to another mode of discourse or into another sign system" (1985:58).

Far from being an imperialist intrusion, an etic perspective may contribute to the self-understanding of the "insiders", and, if "translated" well, provides the essential basis for intercommunication and cohesion.

Knowing well that one can never fully understand the symbols of a foreign culture – including the religious symbols – the "outsider theologian" still has a number of important functions which are – in my view – indispensable for the construction of a local theology. Despite the fact that the development of such a local theology requires a rootedness in the community not attainable by the outsider, and although the community itself is (in this case) the key source for the expression of "theology", the outsider "can sometimes hear things going on in the community not heard by a native member of the community" (Schreiter 1985:19).

---

for a variation of approaches – even the one adopted here! (See 1985:84.) See also his exposition of semiotic domains as the assemblage of cultural texts (1985:69-70). In terms of his own exposition, I would, for instance, defend the view that the dominant semiotic domain in rural Venda, in communities such as Itsani, is the religious one. And the root metaphors in this domain provide the major linkage between the sign systems of the culture as a whole.

Both the insider and the outsider need to engage themselves in this very complex process.

The different stages of the outsider theologian's role may now be summarised and described. In practice such a neat distinction is not always possible, but the exposition will at least clarify the process of the development of a local theology as viewed by the outsider.

3.1. The task to listen and discern

Listening to the poet-theologians entails far more than the physical art of making sound or video recordings. It includes a "being-present" in the community so that a sound relationship of trust is built. It entails the development of perceptive skills not naturally developed in the course of (systematic) theological training: to "see" what is "veiled" to a superficial observance. It requires an openness to experiential expressions and (as observed by Schreiter) perseverance in the long and careful listening to a culture. To listen is in a certain sense an art at which not many Western (and liberation!) theologians, including myself, excel.

To play a constructive role in the development of a local theology, the outsider is compelled to listen with discernment. And in this context it implies a very definite hermeneutical framework. The process of distilling theological insights from transcribed hymns in fact starts with the transcription and translation. My creation of the categories into which the different hymns were "classified" (e.g. Christology, ecclesiology, Engenas, biblical figures, prayer, etc.) was an important step: this interpretative "grid" – not inherent to the hymns or their performance as such – may be viewed as a "contamination" of the original performances and be seen as undesirable. But it served the important function of discerning recurrent themes of an oral-formulaic nature in which certain symbols play a central role (see Ong 1982:31-77).

This not only led to the discernment of traditional Christian symbols such as father, saviour, the cross, the shepherd or the Spirit, but a number of exciting new ones. It cannot be denied that Engenas, Thabakgona, Moria-Zion and *nanga* are powerful new symbols abstracted from a very specific cultural and religious experience. Once the themes and symbols have been brought to the surface, the second phase of the theologian's task commences.

3.2. The task of ordering and translation

The next few paragraphs will make evident why it is very difficult to separate the two aspects of ordering and translation. As I rely to a certain degree on Geertz and Schreiter, a few remarks are needed to clarify the nature of the theologian's task in this regard.

Geertz advocates the use of the term "interpretative anthropology" to explore the implications of a semiotic approach to human nature (see Umiker-Sebeok (1977) for an informative overview of related approaches in the semiotics of culture). He relies (per definition) on the concept of "symbol" to set out his own interpretation of culture, including its religious dimension. (In line with this approach I usually employ "symbol" rather than what are generally known as metaphors in theology.

I am aware that "symbol" has a somewhat negative technical connotation in metaphorical theology as set out by, for instance, Sallie McFague. No further definition of metaphor, model, paradigm and related terms is attempted here.)

And what is a symbol? It is a tangible formulation of a notion, an abstraction from experience fixed in perceptible form, a concrete embodiment of an idea or belief. Symbol is used, says Geertz,

> for any object, act, event, quality, or relation which serves as a vehicle for a conception (and) the conception is the symbol's "meaning" (Geertz 1975:91).

According to him, the essence of human thought lies in the perception of the structural congruence between one set of processes and another set for which it acts as a programme, so that the programme can be taken as a symbol of the programmed (1975:94). Religion is thus a system of symbols whose "meaning" is, *inter alia*, derived from their interrelation within a web of significance. And to endeavour an interpretation is to involve oneself in sorting out the structures of significance.

The implication of this project is clear: the mere isolation of symbols (listening and discerning) is not enough. They need to be "ordered" so as to create a specific interrelation which makes a higher level of interpretation possible. My view is that such an "ordering" occurs precisely in the act of translation as explained below.

Translation is used on two senses: the first is the ordinary act of expressing ideas set out in one language in another language. The transcription and translation of hymns with interpretative footnotes in the original project were the first steps in this process of uncovering the significance of related symbols. Mere observation (implied interpretation) became overt interpretation.

But in a semiotic context translation entails more than a mere transposition from one language to another. It may include the creation of an alternative, but comparative, sign system or mode of discourse precisely with the aim to enhance the interpretative possibilities of the original symbols.

An allusion to music theory will perhaps illuminate this point: one set of notes is often rewritten, i.e. transposed, in a different key. It is also possible to rewrite a musical piece (combination of notes) originally intended for one instrument to be suitable for performance on a different instrument – often with exhilarating effect! The latter example is perhaps an analogy to what I attempt on a theological level.

Within the context of this project, I had an overt systematic theological interest. The first step of translating the hymns into a different mode of discourse was executed by the creation of (mostly) traditional systematic theological categories such as Christology, pneumatology and ecclesiology. As with any intercultural interpretation, a "foreign" schematic representation is not only inevitable, but necessary to make a new "reading" possible.

These systematic categories contributed to the identification as well as an understanding of the relation among different symbols (e.g. the relation between father and Engenas; shepherd and saviour, Zion and Thabakgona, and so on). But there is a further stage of ordering which makes a further representation of the symbols possible. This representation is an attempt to answer a simple question: in what "format" has the church through the ages "ordered" her religious symbols?

The answer is abundantly clear: in the "symbols" which embodied the church's creedal formulations and to which a definite dogmatic-juridical status of orthodoxy was later assigned. These creedal formulations, often hymnal in character, of the New Testament (discerned in passages such as Phlp 2; Col 1; Rom 10 and 1 Cor 15) received in the course of time different stereotyped formats. And as the church found a definite formulation necessary for the sake of unity, the resultant text became known as a "symbol", e.g. the *Symbolum Romanum* or the Apostolic symbol.

The important question that now arises is which of the many "symbols" (here used in the sense of a collective formulation of accepted and well-known individual symbols) would be suitable to serve as alternative mode of discourse? Which "symbols" would have a universal intercommunicative value as well as (on a secondary level) a normative function?

I believe that the Apostolic symbol (*Apostolicum*, or the twelve articles of faith) is an excellent choice in this regard. This may be motivated from different angles.

First, apart from its universal acceptance, it has, historically speaking, roots in the Western, Eastern and African churches (e.g. Carthago and Hippo). It thus avoids the criticism of representing (Western) theological imperialism or (Western) rationalistic expression. Second, its pre-history through the *Symbolum Romanum* until the final formulation (starting from the second and ending between the fourth and seventh centuries AD) is a clear example of creedal *formation* (see Doekes 1975:12ff), very applicable to the situation of the ZCC. Third, the *Apostolicum* may assist us greatly in the difficult task of introducing a critical element, namely a criterion or criteria for what may be called "Christian identity". This relates to the critical function of the theologian as discussed below.

The next step in the process of translation is now clear: the representation of the Zionist hymnal symbols in a creedal formulation on the basis of the *Apostolicum*. Based on the content and interpretation of the transcribed hymns, as well as the categories created, the following creedal formulation may serve as representation and (for purposes of interpretation) final "translation" of the religious symbols into an alternative mode of discourse.

There is obviously no intention to present the formulation below as a serious suggestion for the ZCC to accept. If one understands how this church functions and how the liturgy is organised, such an ideal would be out of place. The history of creedal formation in the church in any case denies the suggestion of a "finished product" being "presented" to a church for acceptance or refusal. It is nothing more than a representation to bring a new interrelation of new and old symbols into existence and to make a certain kind of intercommunication possible.

A constructive *Apostolicum* from the Itsani Zion Christian Church could perhaps read as follows:

> We believe in the God of Engenas, Jehovah;
>
> who instructs us to pray;
> and who as the holy Father stops the fighting of this world.

> We believe in the Lord Jesus, our Saviour, the Son of God;
> who died on the cross;
> who is the Shepherd;
> who as *nanga* of the spirit controls our lives;
> who is the Messiah on his way;
> and who will return at the sound of the horn.
>
> We believe in the Holy Spirit who blesses us;
> who as Good Spirit fills our hearts.
>
> We believe in the pardoning of offences through the blood of the Lamb.
>
> We believe in Engenas as father of the nation, the chief of all chiefs;
> who gives us rain and who heals;
> we accept Moxwadube who dances luimbo,
> who preaches the gospel,
> and about whom everyone speaks.
>
> We believe in the truth that Moria, the holy mountain of Engenas is for all;
> we believe that in Zion, whence we are called by prayer, everybody will be pardoned and healed.
>
> We believe in the unity of the church, based on peace and love which come from the Lord Jesus;
> and we believe that the Father makes the emblem of Moria shine.
>
> We believe in heaven, eternal life before God, where we shall praise the name of Jesus.
>
> Amen.

It is essential to read the translation *cum* interpretations of hymns in the original report to understand the "roots" and significance of the formulation above. It is the end of a laborious process and must be read as such. I do not include any interpretive remarks here. The only reason for its inclusion is to clarify the role of the outsider theologian in practical terms.

Now that the ordering-translating role of the theologian has been described, the last phase of his/her involvement comes to the fore, namely to relate and evaluate.

3.3. The task of relating and evaluating

As with the other stages described above, the aspects of relation and evaluation are closely connected and no strict sequence should be assumed on the basis of the exposition that follows. In the process of constructing a local theology many questions ultimately arise.

In this section two kinds of questions are discussed. Firstly, questions relating to the ecumenical context: what contribution, if any, does the Itsani congregation make to the universal church's understanding of the gospel? Is there a strong enough basis to relate the symbolic expressions of the local community of saints to the catholic church?

Secondly, there are critical (i.e. evaluative, normative) questions: are the symbols and their representation congruent with what may be called the "Christian identity?". When is a call of syncretism or dual religious system justifiable, and how should a local Zionist theology be judged?

Let us commence with the perspective of the interrelation between the local and the universal church: convinced of the basic nature of theology as an ecumenical enterprise, I consider the responsibility of inter-communicator to be one of the gravest for the professional (outsider) theologian.

The theologian who stands in a certain tradition – itself an example of "local theology"! – and gains a view of an alternative tradition, has, for the sake of truth, to engage the two worlds by *inter alia* commencing genuine dialogue. In this way an interrelation may be created which opens all the exciting possibilities of reciprocal enrichment and expansion of the Christian tradition.

> In so doing, the theologian helps to create the bonds of mutual accountability between the local and world church (Schreiter 1985:18).

How does one establish a bond of mutuality? In the concrete case of this project, it would – at least initially – be premature to immediately compare the Itsani *Apostolicum* (IA) with the standardised one (A), point out what is being omitted in IA and then wait for their "reply". (The latter will in any case not be forthcoming!). It is premature for a number of reasons.

Firstly, such a comparison denies the methodological way (meta + hodos) travelled above: if the starting point is the faith experience of an oral (mostly illiterate) community based on the work of a specific indigenous religious leader and expressed in their own cultural thought forms, an end product identical to A is obviously highly improbable. In fact, the high degree of similarity (although constructed) between A and IA is astonishing and may point to a stronger reliance of the Zionist church on the traditional Christian paradigm than might have been expected (see historical notes above).

Secondly, room should be made for the process of creedal formation, i.e. the extension/alteration of the present symbolic world. The original forms of A were much shorter than the final product. Its cradle is the New Testament creedal formulations. Many reformulations occurred resulting in different complementary "symbols" in Europe and North Africa. Eventually the *Symbolum Romanum* was formulated, seven additions[3] responding to different questions were accepted until the present *textus receptus* of the *Apostolicum*. The latter functioned in the church from the eighth century, but was officially accepted by the Roman Catholic church only in the twelfth century! (See Doekes 1975:16.)

---

3   These additions are as follows: (i) *creatorem coeli et terrae* (already present in some Eastern creeds); (ii) in terms *passus* and *mortuus* (part of the cathegesis of the church); (iii) instead of born from the Holy Spirit, *qui conceptus Est de Spiritu sanco*; (iv) *descendit ad infernos* (prevalent in the Syrian church); (v) the further explanation of the church as the *catholicam* and (vi) as *communion sanctorium*; (vii) the important reference to eternal life (*vitam aeternam*). See Doekes (1975:17-19).

This creates an open-ended perspective with regard to the *Apostolicum* and allows for the voice of the ZCC to be heard. Because of the dynamic process of theology-in-the-making in the ZCC (changing leadership; high interaction between different religions; creation of new hymns and "forgetting" old ones; rapidly changing cultural conditions), as well as the expressed universalist strain in some of the hymns, one may accept that during the performances there will be a continuous extension of the present symbolic representation. And part of this extension may come about through ecumenical dialogue, for which there is a growing openness.[4]

Perhaps it is too bluntly formulated, but the point of departure is not the one-to-one comparison of IA and A, but the process of creedal formation in the context of the living experience of faith underlying religious symbols.

Let us now turn to the critical-normative perspective: whether IA is, generally speaking, accepted as a remarkable recontextualisation of the Christian truth, a serious form of syncretism or even a dual religious system, will depend on how broad or narrow the evaluative starting point is.

Authors differ considerably on this issue, and understandably so. To mention but a few. Von Allem (1975:50) takes a narrow but very definite stance in accepting the confession of the Lord Jesus Christ who died and was raised for us as the focal point of faith from which any authentic theology must start ever anew. HB Beeby (1973:37) sees the biblical revelation (Old and New Testaments) as norm and foundation of any indigenous theology, whereas Eugene Nida takes God's redemptive love in Jesus Christ resulting in redemptive lives as the basic criterion to judge whether the Good News has been communicated (quoted by Taber 1978:77).

Others introduce a broader criteriology. Charles Taber (1978:69-76), for example, lists seven delimitations or criteria for indigenous theology: it must be biblical, affirm the transcendence of God, be Christological and prophetic, dialogical, open-ended and subject to the Holy Spirit. Robert Schreiter offers five criteria that cumulatively give a reasonable guarantee of "Christian identity": the cohesiveness of Christian performance, the test of theology in the worshiping context, the praxis (fruits) of the Christian community and the Christian performance, the judgement of other churches and (lastly) the challenge of the local theology to other churches (1985:118-120).

One cannot expect to reach agreement on this matter. Schreiter admits that

> this remains the most difficult area in developing local theologies, at least from a theoretical perspective. But it is also one of the most important (1985:121).

---

4   I was quite amazed when I was approached by a prominent and well-educated member of the Saint Engenas ZCC in Venda who asked me to give him some examples of Christian creedal formulations. I then learnt that he was not even aware of a document such as the *Apostolicum*, but that the ZCC wants to enhance its theological standing by adopting a kind of creedal formulation. Obviously, a mere acceptance of A would be very superficial and will amount to mere tokenism, neglecting the rich symbols already present in the ZCC. As a document it will in any case have little or no influence on the ordinary church member: many of them are not even aware of the Church's constitution (and why should they be?).

As my concern is not only to point out certain theoretical considerations, this "most difficult" task must be approached head-on.

With the specific methodology employed in this study, and with the representation of religious symbols from one genre (hymns) to another (creedal formulation), I have already moved in a certain direction. Without pretending to present a full "evaluation", the following three questions may now be explained as a kind of "model" for assessing the quality of presenting the Christian identity.

The first critical question is whether the symbols and their interrelation as presented here as a result of theological reflection adequately express the underlying religious experience of the community from which they arose in the first place.

Here the position of the outsider theologian is very tenuous. For the theologian "adequate expression" is normally used as an analytical criterion: have I taken account of all the recurring symbols? Have I been consistent in my semiotic translation? And so on. There are obviously some empirical data which may point in a certain direction: the growth in membership and the liveliness of worship might confirm that the isolated symbols (in varying degrees of importance) are indeed an adequate expression of the underlying religious experience.

But this criterion has perhaps to be applied far more intuitively and existentially – and this can only be done by the members of the local community themselves, and be tested by theologically trained people from the community.

The second critical question is whether there is a congruence between the symbols inherent to a local theology, on the one hand, and the symbols which have become an accepted part of the broader Christian tradition (itself an accumulation of a series of local theologies!), on the other? This is what Schreiter refers to as cohesion; i.e.

> if the theological formulations find themselves clearly at odds with the rest of Christian doctrine or require a radical shifting of large parts of it, there is a very good chance that it is not well-formed Christian performance[5] (1985:118; see Taber's notion of a dialogical theology).

Here the outsider theologian plays an essential role. In this specific case I have (for reasons set out above) chosen the *Apostolicum* as the "grammar" of Christian tradition in terms of which the (constructed) "performance" of the Itsani congregation may be evaluated. With the comments above in mind, a few remarks are made which point the way for a full evaluation, which is not attempted here.

---

5   The background of this statement lies in Schreiter's reworking of Noam Chomsky's theory of language acquisition (Schreiter 1985:114ff). Highly simplified, Chomsky's theory of transformational grammar proves that language competence and the concomitant language performance in a certain sense "preceded" the grammar which was traditionally seen as creating language. Applied to theology, faith relates to language competence; theology to language performance, and orthodoxy (e.g. creeds) to grammar. Just as the multiplication of language performances on the basis of language competence eventually leads to the development of a grammar to have a normative function, faith and theologies may be (and are in fact) developed "independently" of orthodoxy. But they must eventually allow the latter to serve as a normative boundary; just as not every sentence is correct, so not every theology is "equally well performed".

For any meaningful and creative enculturalisation of the gospel to occur, one should not expect an exact duplication of all the traditional religious symbols and metaphors. As already stated: a one-to-one comparison with a resultant list of omissions or additions proves very little. New symbols and metaphors are welcomed – they enrich our understanding of the gospel and allow the local church to contribute to the universal church.

Let me use the notions of God as the God of Engenas and Jesus as *nanga* as illustrations of the second critical question: to describe Him/Her as the *God of Engenas* is obviously a novel expression of God's identity. A fundamentalist approach would regard this as unacceptable. But the question is whether the meaning of this symbol (which can be determined hermeneutically) contradicts the notion of God when described in terms of (fore)fathers such as Moses, Abraham, Isaac and Jacob.

In the light of the interpretation of the hymns above, the answer to the question of a contradictory depiction of God is negative: for the ZCC members Engenas is the founder of their faith, and in terms of the clan idea prevalent in their thinking, it is a natural identification of the God they came to know.

The other references to God clearly identify the God of Engenas *inter alia* as the Jehovah of the Old Testament, the One who sent His Son, and as the One in Whose presence eternal life is lived.

Cumulatively it becomes clear: this is the same God known and confessed by the universal church, although presented in a culturally creative way.

Another new symbol is the title of *nanga* assigned to Jesus. Superficially one might be drawn to the conclusion that this is a denial of Christ as He is humiliated by being placed in the context of sorcery or witchcraft; or it may be seen as a syncretistic portrayal of Jesus because elements of traditional religion determine the content and meaning of the symbol. A number of suggestions are necessary to come to some sort of "evaluative judgement" on this issue.

First, a brief remark about the history of Christological titles makes abundantly clear that the mere "influence of culture" is not a pivotal factor in a conception of syncretism. In an article written a long time ago CFD Moule points to the influence of circumstances in the early church to give reasons "for the appearance and disappearance, for the advance and retreat, of one title and another" (Moule 1959:165).

One tends to forget that the present, accepted symbols to portray Christ (Jesus, Son of Man/God; Lord; Divine Logos; Christ itself) are all drawn from the prevalent cultural settings in which they were formulated. They have become so "universal" that their particularity has been forgotten: new symbols only appear to be more culturally conditioned in the light of this "forgotten history".

Second: is the point not that syncretism (negatively understood) arises when a foreign culture determines the context and meaning of the traditional Christian symbol? To answer this, let us take the well-known Johannine Logos as an example.

John clearly relies on two cultural traditions in his depiction of Christ as the Logos. First, the Logos concept is steeped in Hellenistic thought. It carries the association of the rational principle in the ordering of the universe from Heraclitus through the Stoics to Philo's interpretation of logos as mediation between God and the universe.

In the Jewish tradition logos is related to the *dabar* (word) of Jahwe and as the fashioner of all things within the context of the wisdom literature.

Is John not dangerously close to "syncretism" in his employment of the logos concept? How would a Greek or Jewish reader understand his prologue? Is the understanding of Christ not (negatively) determined by foreign cultures?

The answer is yes and no: yes, because there is no other way to explain the gospel than to use existing cultural concepts. And this always implies a certain "determination" of meaning. But also no, because there is also a transcendence of these cultural concepts, which explains the uniqueness of the gospel. In John's case one could refer to the radical reference in the prologue of a logos who became flesh. This places the interpretation of the logos on a totally different level unparalleled in (but still related to) Hellenistic and Jewish thought.

This example hopefully illustrates the process involved in the enculturalisation of the gospel. Christianity, as Schreiter points out,

> has a long history of absorbing elements from the cultures in which it has lived: but this is precisely how it developed its incarnate character (Schreiter 1985:151).

Returning to the question of Jesus as *nanga*, two remarks are now relevant. It is obviously a concept derived from the Venda cultures with overtones of *vuloi* (witchcraft) and the manipulation of the forces in the cosmos (see Van Rooy 1978:24ff). In this sense it does "determine" the meaning of Jesus. But in a semiotic approach the relationship among symbols is of paramount importance in "determining" meaning. If *nanga* is read in relation to *Morena* (Lord), *mulauli* (controller), *Yesus* (Jesus) and *murwa Mudzimu* (son of God), the distinctiveness of the gospel is confirmed (there is no other *nanga* like this!). But – and this is very important – the meaning of the gospel is also enhanced (Jesus is a *nanga* of the spirit!).

In view of this, it becomes clear that a fruitful discussion of syncretism has to bear two considerations in mind. On the one hand, the struggle of the local church to understand the gospel in its own cultural context is just as important as the dogmatic certainties of the universal church. On the other hand, what is termed "syncretism" may, from a semiotic analysis of culture, only be a stage in the long process of one culture's way of coming to grips with an advancing culture, resulting in the emergence of a conjunctive sign system (see Schreiter 1985:144ff).

I hope these examples illustrate the manner in which the second question of the relation between the local and "universal" church may be addressed. This is obviously an ongoing process which should involve both insiders and outsiders.

The third (and last) critical question that remains to be asked with regard to local theology as well as the Christian tradition, centres on the paradigmatic and normative role of the Scriptures, where the root metaphors and symbols of the Christian tradition are expressed. If a better understanding of these symbols in new contexts requires the tradition to be refined – even on the level of creedal formulations – the process of reformulation on the basis of consensus (agreement in the discerning of the Spirit) should be set in motion.

It is important to remind ourselves of the fact that we are dealing here with the oral expression of faith from a largely illiterate community. This has, in relation to the last question, several implications.

A second-order reflection on Scripture as Scripture should not be expected. The "theological material" which reflects the psychodynamics of an oral noetic position makes such analytic categories highly improbable (see Ong 1982:31-77).

A first-order expression of Scriptural passages will not take the form of exact quotations. This is the case because the majority of singers do not have access to a textual Scripture for an exact memorisation to take place. Even more important is the realisation that oral performances are creative activities resulting in different representations of "texts" in every performance (there is no original!). This was evident in the comparison of the same hymns that were never performed in exactly the same manner (see original report) despite the strong conserving influence of music as mnemonic device.

One should perhaps in this regard ask what the empirical relation was between the *Sola Scriptura* of the Reformation and the rise of "literacy" as a result of the translation of the Bible into various indigenous languages. In the case under discussion, one could only speak of the implicit role of Scripture in shaping the freely sung hymns.

The broader church community, however, has over the ages been convinced that the *Apostolicum* is in congruence with the Scriptures. The church accepts that this is an adequate expression of the root symbols in terms of different religious experiences. In this context the omission of reference to God's creative work or the resurrection of the body (to name but two aspects) are important, for they form an essential part of the biblical witness to God and the Christian faith.

The challenge for the ZCC in general and the Itsani congregation in particular is to allow their experiences to be increasingly shaped by the Scriptures (itself largely an orally based document). This will allow the constant renewal of their symbols in the amazing way verbalised in their hymns, and (ultimately) in their theology.

In the meantime the broader church should not close herself off as if the "final truth" has been attained once and for all. It is the work of the Spirit to lead the church in the truth. The basis for theological intercommunication in South Africa lies, *inter alia*, in the third Person of the Trinity. He opens the eyes of insiders and outsiders to understand "alien" spiritual experiences as experiences of the Spirit.

A humble listening to the theological voice of the ZCC hymns will add important notes to the symphony of the universal church's doxology before God.

BIBLIOGRAPHY

Becker, H. & Geer, B. 1984. "Participant observation: the analysis of qualitative field data". In Burgess (ed.), pp. 239-250.

Beeby, H.D. 1973. "Thoughts on indigenizing theology". *South East Asia Journal of Theology* Vol. 14, No. 2, pp. 34-38.

Blacking, J. 1981. "Political and musical freedom in the music of some black South African churches". In L. Holy & M. Stucklik (eds.), pp. 35-62.

Burgess, R.G. 1984. *In the field. An introduction to field research*. London: Allen & Unwin.

Cargie, D. 1988. *Xhosa Zionist church music*. city: University of Zululand.

De Gruchy, J. 1986. *Cry Justice*. New York: Orbis.

Denzin, N.K. 1978. *The research act*. Second edition. New York: McGraw-Hill.

Doekes, L. 1975. *Credo. Handbook voor de Gereformeerde symboliek*. Amsterdam: Ton Bolland.

Geertz, C. 1975. *The interpretation of cultures*. London: Hutchinson.

Holy, L & Stucklik, M. (eds.) 1981. *The structure of folk models*. London: Academic.

Kruger, M.A. 1971. *Die Zion Christian Church – 'n religieuse Bantoebeweging in 'n tyd van ontwrigting?* Unpublished MTh. Potchefstroom: Potchefstroom University:

Lofland, J. 1971. *Analyzing social settings. a guide to qualitative observation and analysis*. Belmont: Wadsworth.

Lukhaimane, E. 1981. *The Zion Christian Church of Ignatius (Engenas) Lekganyane, 1924-1948: an African experiment with Christianity*. Pietersburg: Unpublished MA. city: University of the North.

Moule, C.F.D. 1959. "The influence of circumstances on the use of Christological terms". *JTS* Vol. 10, pp. 247-263.

Mouton, J. & Marais, H.C. 1988. *Basic concepts in the methodology of social sciences*. Pretoria: HSRC.

Naudé, P.J. 1992. "Religious experience and local theology. An analysis of some ZCC-hymns within the framework of an ecumenical theology". Unpublished report. Pretoria: HSRC.

Ong, W.J. 1982. *Orality and literacy. The technologizing of the word*. London: Methuen.

Oosthuizen, G.C. 1976. *The theology of a South African Messiah. An analysis of the hymnal of the Church of the Nazarites*. Leiden: Brill.

Penoukou, E.J. 1992. "Christology in the village". In Schreiter (ed.), pp. 24-51.

Schreiter, R.J. 1985. *Constructing local theologies*. London: SCM.

Schreiter, R.J. (ed.) 1992. *Faces of Jesus in Africa*. London: SCM.

Spae, J.J. 1979. "Missiology as local theology and interreligious encounter". *Missiology: An international review* Vol. xii, No. 4, pp. 479-500.

Sundkler, B.G. 1961. *Bantu prophets in South Africa*. Second Edition. London: Oxford University Press.

Taber, C. 1978. "The limits of indigenization in theology". *Bible Studies* Vol. 70, pp. 54-79.

Umiker-Seboek, J.D. 1977. "Semiotics of culture: Great Britain and North America". *Annual Review of Anthropology* Vol. 6, pp. 121-135.

Van Rooy, J.A. 1978. *The traditional world view of Black people in Southern Africa*. Potchefstroom: Instituut vir die bevordering van Calvinisme.

Vansina, J. 1985. *Oral tradition as history*. London: James Currey.

Vilakazi, A. 1986. *Shembe. The revitalization of African society*. Johannesburg: Skotaville.

Von Allem, D. 1975. The birth of theology. *Bible Studies* Vol. 68, pp. 37-52.

Wainwright, G. 1980. *Doxology. A systematic theology*. New York: Oxford University Press.

2.3 JESUS AS NANGA?[1]

Christological enrichment from a Zionist perspective[2]

The overall impression one gains of Prof. Hennie van der Merwe is one of a man with a good ear. I came to know him during our discussions in the Northern Transvaal branch of the Theological Society of Southern Africa. He would listen intently, and when he spoke, it was with great insight and humility. This is one of the rare, but essential qualities of any theologian who works in an African context.

It is therefore appropriate to share with him, and others, a small glimpse of the "listening" I have done in the Venda context. What follows is an adapted excerpt from a pilot study during 1989-91 under the auspices of the HSRC's centre for methodological research.

1. ORAL RESEARCH AS BASIS FOR CREEDAL FORMULATION

One of the basic assumptions of this project is that creedal formulations do not "fall from the sky", but are expressions of a community's experience of the gospel in a concrete situation. To determine the "content" of a community's faith, one has to listen carefully to the various expressions of their faith.

The insights gained from form and tradition criticism point to the fact that the *Sitz in Leben* of many creedal formulations in both the Old (e.g. Jahwe as God of history) and New Testaments (e.g. Christ is Lord) are related to worship, preaching and catechism.

In his excellent book *Doxology* (1980) Geoffrey Wainwright develops this into a systematic theology on the basis of *lex orandi, lex credendi* (1980:161, 218ff, 251ff). The role of worship in the development of doctrine is evident in, for example, the recognition of Christ's divinity, the Trinitarian doctrine based on the threefold pattern of baptism, and the Marian dogmas which were formulated on the basis of popular devotion. "In all three cases, worship practice was in advance of doctrinal decision" (Wainwright 1980:250).

One of the most important liturgical elements in the New Testament is the hymn. Apart from brief acclamatory confessions (normally introduced by ὁμολόγειν, e.g. Rom. 10:9) and longer creedal forms (introduced by πιστεύειν, e.g. 1 Cor. 15:3-5), "New Testament writers find it valuable to draw on the known hymns of the Christian community when they are themselves establishing doctrine" (Wainwright 1980:258).

The creedal process started by the doxological (i.e. hymnal oral) expression of being touched by the gospel, leading to the formulation of doctrinal expressions, and ultimately to confessions and systematic theology, is in a sense re-enacted by the research referred to above.

---

1 Note that in the original language, *nanga* is spelt with a dot on the initial n.
2 This essay originally appeared in *Theologica Viatorum*, September 1992, 127-141.

The starting point was to take an example of "creedal formation" from an independent black church. Of the 43,2% Christians in Venda, almost half (19.3%) belong to an independent church, with the Lutheran church as largest "historical" church, representing a mere 7.1% (HSRC 1985:23). The major question was: What kind of creedal formulations or "theology" would emerge from their single most important liturgical activity, namely the free singing of hymns in the local and other languages?

The low level of (functional) literacy amongst people in rural Venda ensured a strong reliance on oral tradition and the utilising of hymns as mnemonic devices (see Vansina 1985:16). My inquiries led me to the Saint Engenas Zion Christian Church at Itsani, a peasant village about 12 km from the Sibasa-Thoyandou area. Tape recordings of hymns were made during 1989. The laborious transcription and translation work was completed during 1990 and interpretation/re-presentation took place during 1991. (A full description of field work and research design is included in the original report. See Naude 1995).

More than fifty hymns were recorded and classified into seven theological categories. The Christological category appeared to be the most important – both in terms of numbers (20 hymns) and with regard to content. A very rich Christology emerged from these hymns and it is perhaps fruitful to mention a few reasons for this:

In the context of the history of independent churches/movements, one is struck by their specific messianic character. This is especially evident from studies on the *Izihlabelelo* (hymnal) of the Shembe church (see Oosthuizen 1976; Sunkler 1961:275ff). The motivating forces for messianism (interpreted more widely than a purely futuristic expectation) are numerous and very complex (see Kruger's (1971) references to authors such as Barrett, Hayward, Schlosser, Martin and Häselbarth).

If one takes the history and context of the ZCC into account, the following important factors arise: the establishment of churches under indigenous leadership; messianism as an answer to the power of witchcraft or the search for general material and especially physical wellbeing. It might be seen as an attempt to synchronise the message of Christianity with traditional beliefs, or as a form of religious escapism from the harsh socio-economic realities in which many members find themselves.

One of these motives, namely the search for general wellbeing, comes to the fore in hymns about Jesus as Healer. This is a small but significant section of the overall Christological expressions detected in the recorded hymns where mention is made of Jesus as the One to follow; the Saviour, the Shepherd and the coming Messiah (see creedal formulation below).

Only the hymns on Jesus as Healer are now presented with interpretative explanations in the footnotes. (Readers may ignore the numbering as they refer to the place on the tape recording. S refers to the call of the soloist, and C to the response from the community).

2. TRANSCRIPTION, TRANSLATION AND INTERPRETATION OF HYMNS ON JESUS AS HEALER[3]

B3.   YESU U A RI LAULA (Venda)

S: Yesu u a ri laula
     Jesus' controls us

C: Yesu ndi mulauli
     Jesus is the controller

S: Yesu ndi mulauli
     Jesus is the controller
                    (x2)

S: na fhano hayani Yesu u a ri laula
     Even here at home, Jesus controls us

C: Yesu ndi mulauli
     Jesus is the controller

S: ndi mulauli Murena, Yesu u a ri laulu
     the Lord is the controller, Jesus controls us

C: Yesu ndi mulauli
     Jesus is the controller
                    (x6)

S: ndi nanga[4] ya muya, Yesu ndi nanga ya muya
     He is the healer of the spirit, Jesus is the healer of the spirit

---

3   There is no doubt that faith healing and divine healing have been the single most important factors for the growth of the ZCC – especially in rural areas where very few clinics or hospitals were available. "It has been calculated that about 80% of Engenas's followers joined the Church because of illness or some other difficulties, 15% by natural process, and 5% out of mere conviction" (Lukhaimane 1981:63). It is interesting to note the similarities between the ZCC and the Church of the Nazarites in this regard: stories about the healing powers of Engenas (see Lukhaimane 1981:72) and Shembe respectively and healing are regarded as the basic growth factor in both churches (see Vilakazi 1986:41-45), who also states (58) that investigations showed "that all the people who joined the church as adults … did so because of illness". Whereas some followers believe in the healing powers of just looking at Shembe's picture (Sundkler 1961:285), Engenas's followers would roll on the ground where he has passed to receive healing or blessing (Lukhaimane 1981:43). This section on Christ as healer points to a certain "Christological concentration" in the ZCC not evident from the studies on the Shembe church. The section on Engenas (not represented here) contains surprisingly little on his healing powers.

4   Van Rooy's remarks from a traditional Venda perspective are worth noting: "The *nanga* is the person who is initiated into the laws of manipulating the forces in the cosmos. Anyone who knows a herb with healing properties, and uses it, practices *vhunanga*, but only those who, by long training, and by endowment with powers of divining, are able to determine the cause of the harm done to their patients, and have the power to avert and redirect those harmful influences, can rightly be called *nanga*" (1978:26). That Jesus is called the *nanga* of the spirit is thus loaded with meaning: if the cornerstone of the traditional Venda world view is constituted by a "hierarchy of forces, each with a fixed place in the totality, and exercising influence and power on each other" (Van Rooy 1978:3), Jesus as *nanga* has the power to redirect these forces. To call Him the *controller* is thus a very real description of His work as *nanga*.

C:	Yesu ndi mulauli Jesus is the controller[5]
S:	ndi nanga ya muya, Yesu ndi nanga ya madi He is the healer of the spirit, Jesus is the healer of water[6]
C:	Yesu ndi mulauli Jesus is the controller
S:	nangwe ro dzula, Yesu u a ri laula even when we are seated, Jesus controls us
C:	Yesu ndi mulauli Jesus is the controller
S:	nangwe ro dzula, Yesu u a ri laula even when we are seated, Jesus controls us (repetitions)
S:	ndi nanga ya madi, Yesu ndi nanga ya muya He is the healer of water, He is the healer of the spirit
C:	Yesu ndi mulauli Jesus is the controller
S:	ndi nanga ya muya, Yesu ndi nanga ya madi He is the healer of the spirit; He is the healer of water
C:	Yesu ndi mulauli Jesus is the controller (repetitions)
S:	nangwe ro lala, Yesu u a ri laula even when we are asleep, Jesus controls us

Core contents[7]

Jesus controls us. He is the controller.
The Lord is the controller.

---

5 The enumeration of the different spheres of life where Jesus acts as controller (in difficulties; at home; concerning the spirit/inner life; when we are seated or when we are asleep) is very closely related to Ps 139, where almost the same "categories" are mentioned. From a Venda perspective, this acquires the meaning that all forces affecting life are (re)directed by Him.

6 Water plays a central role as a means of faith healing in the ZCC. Firstly, the immersion during baptism is seen as having a healing function. Secondly, water blessed by Engenas or the local minister is used as *meets a thapelo* in a variety of ways: to sprinkle homes or businesses in order to ward off misfortunes; to drink warm water (previously blessed) every morning and evening (called *mogabolo*); to purify after a funeral or after any event causing impurity (see Lukhaimane 1980:66-67 and the broader discussion by Oosthuizen 1968:285-288). The reference to Jesus as the *healer of water* is perhaps related to the many Johannine sections (including Revelation) on this theme. It does provide a strong Christological interpretation of a custom steeped in African traditional religion and taken over by many independent churches. (The only form of healing/blessing which I witnessed at Itsani was the laying on of hands with blessed pieces of paper).

7 This is a beautiful example of the call-response structure which is so typical of many African hymns. The rich content provided by S is continuously reinforced by *Yesu u a rilaula*. Conversely, the meaning of the C lines is enriched from different angles as a result of the changing contexts created by S. See Psalm 136 for a biblical example of a

Jesus is the healer of the spirit.
Jesus is the healer of water.
Even when we are seated, Jesus controls us.
Even in difficulty, Jesus controls us.
Even when we are asleep, Jesus controls us.

B17.   YESU NDI DZINA LAVHUDI (Venda)

C: Yesu ndi dzina lavhudi
Jesus is a good name
la murwa Mudzimu
of the son of God[8]
li a difha dzindevheni
it is sweet in the ears
dza vha mu tendaho
of those who believe in him

dzina heli li na maanda
this name has power[9]
a kunukisaho
an amazing power
na vhane vha vhaisala
even those who are ill
vha nga fhodzwa ngalo
they can be healed by it
ri tshi swika makoleni
when we reach heaven[10]
phanda ha Mudzimu
before God

tshine ra do rimba tshone
what we shall sing
ndi dzina la Yesu
is the name of Jesus

Core contents

Jesus is a good name of the Son of God –
It is sweet in the ears of those who believe in Him.
This name has an amazing power,

---

hymn with a similar structure.

8 It is theologically significant that the title *son of God* is used in connection with the healing power of Jesus: this is precisely in line with some of the Gospel traditions which state that Jesus' miracles were performed "that you may believe that Jesus is the Christ, the Son of God, and that believing you may have life in his name" (John 20:31).

9 The power attached to Jesus' name is evident from the early church. Luke's account of the healing of the man at the gate of the temple makes Peter say that the healing takes place in the name of Jesus of Nazareth (Acts 3:6). Jesus' own words to the disciples as reported by different gospel writers emphasise that healing and casting out of demons take place in His name. Amongst people whose world view is closely related to the cosmic balance of powers, the *amazing power* of Jesus' name is of great importance.

10 An eschatological perspective which emphasises the importance of Jesus' name: this will be the "content" of the song sung before God. See hymns 18-20 below.

even those who are ill can be healed by it.
When we reach heaven before God,
what we shall sing is the name of Jesus.

B11.   SIZOMBONGA NGANI[11] (Zulu)

S: Sizombonga ngani?
        how can I thank him?

S&C: sizombonga ngani, uMesia wame?
        how can I thank him, my Messiah?
                    (x2)

S: hamba Lekganyane
        Lekganyane must go

S&C: hamba Lekganyane u ya ruta evangeli
        Lekganyane must go and preach the gospel
                    (x2)
                (several repetitions)

S: ngatola simayo mazioni
        Zionist, you do not give thanks

S&C: ngatola simayo modimo wa mazioni
        I received healing from the God[12] of the Zionists.

Core contents

How can I thank Him?
How can I thank Him, my Messiah?
Lekganyane must go;
Lekganyane must go and preach the gospel.
Zionists you do not give thanks,
you do not give thanks to God.
I received healing from the God of the Zionists.

C4.   SIZOMBOMGANA NGANI (Zulu/Venda)

S: sizomobonga ngani
        how can we thank Him?

C: sizomobonga ngani, uMesia wami
        how can we thank Him, my Messiah
                    (x2)

S&C: ho dzhena tshimangadzo
        there entered a miracle

---

11 Note that this song is included in the Engenas section as well. (Not included in this article).
12 If the initial section is interpreted as praise for healing (as is also suggested by the alternative version in the next hymn), a close relation between *Messiah* and the *God of the Zionists* is assumed. Note that this song refers to three important figures in the context of healing: the Messiah, Lekganyane and God. (The second section on Lekganyane's preaching the gospel may be a 'non-related' interpolation that does not entail a strict healing relation).

C: ho dzhena tshimangadzo mudini wa Zion
there entered a miracle in the house of Zion[13]
(x2)

Core contents[14]

How can I thank Him, my Messiah (Zulu)
There entered a miracle in the house of Zion (Venda)

3. THE COMPLEX TASK OF "DOING" THEOLOGY

The question now arises: What does the (systematic) theologian do with these hymns? And can he/she do anything as an outsider and foreigner? Let us answer the last question first

In anthropology and other social sciences the differentiation between an etic or emic perspective is well established. This has direct bearing on the image of and relative distance between the researcher and the participant (see Mouton & Marais 1988:81ff). As long as one is aware of one's position as an outsider with the concomitant "etic" perspective, there is, from a researcher's point of view, no fundamental exclusion of important insights into the matter under discussion, and positive contributions to an understanding are even possible.

Robert Schreiter points out that the "explanations" of an emic perspective tend to remain within the system; "hence, if the questioner does not already understand the system, the explanations are not of much help – they are not really translations into another mode, but variations within the same range of discourse" (Schreiter 1985:57). Outer descriptions (etic), on the other hand, often have the advantage of being phenomenological with a very specific concern for explanation. And the latter is executed on the basis of "translating the reality into another ode of discourse or into another sign system" (1985:58). Far from being an imperialist intrusion, an etic perspective may contribute to the self-understanding of the "insiders", and, if "translated" well, provides the essential basis for intercommunication and cohesion.

The question of what function the (outsider) theologian fulfils may now be answered: It is the task of the theologian to *listen* to the poet-theologians of the community. Secondly, he/she must *discern* (isolate) the religious symbols expressed by the community. Thirdly, these symbols should be ordered in some or other systematic form. Fourthly, an *evaluation* of these symbols take place in the light of the Scriptures and broader Christian tradition (universal church). And lastly, the theologian has the duty to foster an *ecumenical* spirit where the contribution of the local church to the Christian tradition is brought into focus.

There is no room to elaborate in detail on each of these "functions". Very cursory remarks are offered to illustrate them with regards to the hymns on Jesus as Healer.

---

13 As explained above, healing plays a central role in the attraction to Moria. Note the typical biblical expression to describe the ZCC at Moria, namely the *house of Zion*.
14 A comparison with the previous hymn provides a good example of a variation on the same theme as well as the alternation of languages to express the same ideas. An 'aetiological' study on one or more of these hymns could yield interesting results.

1. Listening to the poet-theologians entails far more than the physical act of recording hymns: it includes a thorough and patient listening to the cultural context in which the community finds itself. "Ideally, for a genuine contextual theology, the theological process should begin with the opening up of culture, that long and careful listening to a culture to discover its principal values, needs, interests, directions and symbols" (Schreiter 1985:28). And let us admit it: not many theologians are skilled in cultural analysis. Questions such as world-view (a closed universe of power and counter-power?) and needs (physical and spiritual wellbeing; freedom from witchcraft) play a vital role in understanding why Jesus is depicted as having amazing power that controls all aspects of life (see footnotes above).

2. If one takes a symbol to be an abstraction from experience fixed in a perceptible form, it implies that any object of relation which serves as a vehicle for a conception may be termed "symbolic" (see Geertz 1975:91). The Christian tradition is rich in symbols such as the cross or the shepherd, or terms such as Messiah or Lord. They sprung from the cultural world of the Old and New Testaments. In the case of the ZCC, a strong symbol is created by calling Jesus the *nanga* of the spirit. It serves as an excellent vehicle for the conception of Jesus as the One who controls powers and protects us "even when we are asleep" (see elaboration in footnote 3 above).

3. The ordering of symbols is not possible within the confines of this article. This is a complex process whereby the genre in which the symbols appeared (hymnal form) is transformed into an alternative mode of discourse. In the original project, the latter refers to a representation of symbols in the creedal formulation of the *Apostolicum*. The result, which includes the present Christological symbol, reads as follows:

We believe in the Lord Jesus, our Saviour, the Son of God;
who died on the cross;
who is the shepherd;
who as nanga of the spirit controls our lives;
who is the Messiah on his way
and who will return at the sound on the horn.

4. An evaluation of Jesus as *nanga* should entail at least three vital questions (answers are not attempted here!).

Firstly, is the symbol an effective vehicle of the Christological conception in terms of the experience of the local church? (Almost impossible to be answered by the outsider).

Secondly, is the symbol (in)commensurate with traditional Christological symbols? A new symbol normally shifts the boundaries of meaning: does the presentation of Jesus as *nanga*, seen within the cultural context, move so far that it exceeds the boundaries of what may be called the "Christian identity?" Or is it an ingenious enrichment of our understanding of the Christ mystery?

Thirdly, and most importantly, does the concept of the *nanga* confirm or deny the foundational symbols which represent Christ in the Biblical texts?

5. The theologian serves as bridge-builder: the laborious work of listening, discerning, ordering and evaluating must culminate in the search for the ecumenical truth. The mystery of God's will has been revealed in Christ (Eph. 1:9-10). This revelation has

through the ages found a firm root in different cultures and in different churches. It is precisely through the church that the *manifold* wisdom of God is now made known (Eph 3:10).

Perhaps the confession of Jesus as *nanga* of the spirit unlocks a new dimension of Jesus, "the image of the invisible God" (Col 1:15). Whether accepted or rejected, the art of listening to unlock the wealth of a hitherto unwritten theology is fruitful and essential in the development of a broader South African theology.

BIBLIOGRAPHY

Geertz, C. 1975. *The interpretation of cultures.* London: Hutchinson.

HSRC. 1985. *Religion, intergroup relations and social change in South Africa.* Pretoria: HSRC.

Kruger, M.A. 1971. *Die Zion Christian Church – 'n religieuse Bantubeweging in 'n tyd van ontwrigtig?* Unpublished MTh dissertation. Potchefstroom: University of Potchefstroom.

Lukhaimane, E. 1981. *The Zion Christian Church of Ignatius (Engenas) Lekganyane, 1924-1948: an African experiment with Christianity.* Unpublished MA dissertation. Pietersburg: University of the North.

Mouton, J. & Marais, H.C. 1988. *Basic concepts in the methodology of the social sciences.* Pretoria: HSRC.

Naude, P.J. 1995. *The Zionist Christian Church in South Africa: An experiment in oral theology.* Ontario: The Edwin Mellen Press.

Oosthuizen, G.C. 1968. *Post-Christianity in Africa. A theological and anthropological study.* London: C Hurst.

Schreiter, R.J. 1985. *Constructing local theologies.* London: SCM.

Sunkler, B.G.M. 1961. *Bantu prophets in South Africa.* Second Edition. London: Oxford University Press.

Van Rooy, J.A. 1978. *The traditional world view of Black people in Southern Africa.* Potchefstroom: Instituut vir die bevordering van Calvinisme.

Vansina, J. 1985. *Oral tradition as history.* London: James Currey.

Vilakzi, A. 1986. *Shembe. The revitalization of African society.* Johannesburg: Skotaville.

Wainwright, G. 1980. *Doxology. A systematic theology.* New York: Oxford University Press.

2.4 THE 'PREGNANT' CHRIST: A FEMINIST REINTERPRETATION

The role of women in the 1990s[1]

Chairlady, allow me to make two comments before I start formally with my paper. Firstly, the fact that this conference needed to be organised is indicative of the fact that sexism, the mother of all oppression, is still very much part and parcel of South African society. I can hardly imagine that a conference would be organised with the theme "The role of men in the 1990s". Secondly, it does indicate the fact that women are not accepting this situation and that they understand the value of reflection on the role of women in the 1990s. Hopefully this will lead to appropriate action in the aftermath of this conference.

My topic could be rephrased to state that the role of women in the 1990s is to reclaim the Judeo-Christian religious tradition so as to unmask the oppression of sexism and consequently to lead all people, men and women, to a new and inclusive society. This is obviously based on the assumption that religion can indeed play a constructive role in the forging of a new and inclusive society in South Africa. In the short fifteen minutes available I would like to present a few ideas in the format of five statements, where the fifth functions as a practical illustration of the preceding four. I will not have the time to explain them fully, but during question and discussion time we might pursue a few of these issues.

The first statement is that there is an ontological relation between authentic language and reality, with the implication that language not only reveals but also transforms reality

Here I will loosely interpret the language ontology of the German existentialist philosopher, Martin Heidegger. His ontological starting point is the unique existence of human beings – *Sein* as *Dasein*, or "being" as "being there". A human being brings an understanding of reality to the fore through language, so that language is not a mere description of a reality out there, or an accidental complement to reality out there. It is in fact constitutive of reality itself. Heidegger writes that "die Sprache is das Haus des Seins" (1963). One could loosely translate this that speech is the "house of reality" or "speech harbours reality". This means that language is essential for the revelation of reality. From a critical perspective language is equally essential for the *transformation* of reality. Obviously not every usage of language has this revealing and transforming function. Heidegger refers to inauthentic or conventional language, which he calls *das Gerede* ("empty talk"). Such language leads to a kind of collective blindness in which people are stuck in empty talk. Language loses its revealing and transformative function through the blind repetition of the status quo. (In terms of the conference today, I might then point out that the whole drive for more inclusivist language – also in the academic world – is more than a mere fad. Language can play a very important role in transforming sexist perceptions.

---

[1] This essay was first published by the Institute for Planning Research, 3-14 (1994) University of Port Elizabeth. It is an adapted version of a lecture delivered at the Institute for Research Planning on "The role of women in the 1990's" in Port Elizabeth in 1989.

The second statement is that authentic religious language expresses and transforms the underlying religious experience, which may be called an experience of God.

It is important to realise that we do not have direct access to God or the reality of God. We only know God indirectly via the symbols and metaphors which we employ to describe the infinite richness of God and our God-experiences. I specifically follow Max Black's exposition of the interactive view of metaphor in this regard. When a metaphor is used, we have two thoughts with different references coming together, and the "meaning" of the metaphor results from the *interaction* of the two ideas. Religious language can become inauthentic (in Heidegger's terms) when the metaphors and symbols we employ to describe the reality of God become "dead". They no longer unlock that reality, or they become completely incompetent to express or transform a fundamental underlying religious experience.

The third statement is that feminist theologians have opened our eyes to the androcentric patriarchal cultural bias of the Scriptures from where we derive our main metaphors to talk about God, and they claim that these are thus an inadequate expression of a womanist experience of God.

To put it very bluntly: the Scriptures were written by men and mostly reflect the experiences of men. This is perfectly understandable within the cultural context of the Ancient Near East and the Greek/Roman world in which the Old and New Testaments were formed. Contrary to the revolutionary or radical feminists (e.g. Naomi Goldenburg and Mary Daly), I follow the road of the reformist feminist theologians (e.g. Rosemary Reuther, Letty Russell, Elizabeth Schlüsser-Fiorenza), who assume that the Judeo-Christian tradition as reflected in the Scriptures is not to be rejected offhand and be replaced by a completely different, one could almost say "Goddess", religion. It is indeed possible to *reinterpret* the tradition in such a way that it again becomes an authentic expression of total human experience, including the womanist experience of reality.

The fourth statement relates precisely to this re-interpretation of the Judeo-Christian tradition with its patriarchal bias. To salvage this tradition and to create an inclusivist vision of a new humanity, the Scriptures as language of that tradition should be *critically, creatively and liberatively re-interpreted.*

Perhaps I should repeat that the hermeneutical act involved in the reclaiming of the Judeo-Christian tradition is a critical, creative and liberative act of re-interpretation.

The first one then, the *critical* re-interpretation, refers to the unmasking or the unveiling of the patriarchal bias of the Scriptures. When God is consistently described as father, as king or as judge, it refers to the fact that "He" is described in culturally biased metaphors that lose their function to express the womanist experience or to create an inclusivist society.

Secondly, the *creative* part of such a hermeneutical act refers to the coining of new, fresh metaphors to talk about God. One could, like Sallie McFague, speak about God as our friend or lover, God as our mother and Jesus not so much the Son of God but a *child* of God. Alternatively, one could creatively reinterpret existing images as I will endeavour in point five below.

The third, the *liberative* aspect of hermeneutics refers to the fact that interpretation is concluded only in the practice of action. The term "praxis" refers to the constant, critical interplay between theory and practice so that one could speak of a praxis-orientated hermeneutics. The critical and creative phases of re-interpretation should lead to liberative actions. These include the deconstruction of the ecclesiastical structures which for many years have been an important sign of the sexist practice of the churches. They must also include active resistance to the oppression of women in society at large as expressed by other speakers today. It is important to understand that this hermeneutical spiral of critical, creative and liberative readings is distinguishable only in theory; in practice the three facets may form one important "act of re-interpretation".

The fifth and last statement is merely an example of what I refer to as a reclaiming of the Judeo-Christian tradition. An example of such a critical, creative and liberative reading may perhaps be the re-interpretation of the birth image in both the Old and the New Testament.

It is noteworthy that in some of the Priestly codes birth and the physical aspects associated with birth were subjected to all sorts of purification laws and acts. After the start of the menstruation period a woman would be regarded as unclean for seven days, which amounts to about one quarter of her productive adult life. Intercourse would defile you until the evening and it necessitated a purificatory bath. It is also interesting to read in Leviticus 12 that a mother would be unclean for seven days after birth, and that the period of purification would last for 33 days. The argument that these were merely health codes is put in proper perspective if one notes that these periods were doubled in the case of the birth of a girl! During this period a woman may not touch any hallowed object and she may not enter the sanctuary.

Now if one thinks of this as the context in which the birth image functions in the Old Testament, it is important to reclaim this very seminal and profound experience of many women, namely giving birth, in the context of a new hermeneutics. I refer to a number of points in this regard.

Firstly, the incarnation of Jesus Christ and the whole of salvation history could be re-described in terms of birth and birth images. I think it would be perfectly appropriate to refer to Christ as the "pregnant Christ".[2] I use the word "pregnant" in the sense of a significant event or an event full of promise. It is interesting that Jesus was born "in the fullness of time". Just before his crucifixion He refers to the fact that "the time has come" – the time of birth has arrived. The "pregnant Christ" has reached the point where the transformation of life and the birth of a new life is at hand. (In his case it didn't take nine months but probably some thirty years!). One may also refer to the anguish and the pain in Gethsemane and on the cross, which are from this perspective, nothing other than the pain of a new birth.

It is also interesting that resurrection in the New Testament and early church were linked to baptism. Death and the resurrection of a new life were symbolised by the immersion into water. The water baptism could be referred to as "the breaking of the water", which inaugurates new birth. It is then not surprising to find that very often

---

2   My "inspiration" for this metaphor came from listening to a paper by Prof Mary-Henry Keane in Cape Town in August 1993. The exposition is my own.

in the New Testament, especially in the Pauline writings, new life is being referred to in creation terms. To cite one example, 2 Corinthians 5:17 refers to the fact that when somebody is in Christ, such a person is a new creation.

A second example apart from the incarnation and salvation history is the fact that Jesus reclaims the birth image, given that (in terms of a certain tradition in the Old Testament) birth leads to impurity, to describe precisely the process of spiritual awakening and purification: in John 3:3-6 He explains that to enter the kingdom of God one has to be reborn; one has to go through a process of rebirth. He hereby completely inverts the associations attached to the image of birth and childbirth in parts of the Old Testament.

A third example from the Old Testament itself is, significantly, drawn from Deutero- and Trito-Isaiah (I mean by this the second and third parts of the book of Isaiah, which was written during and after the time of the exile). For the Jews in Babylon the exile was a period of total hopelessness. They lost their city, they lost their leaders, they were no longer close to the temple, and they had no idea what to expect in such a situation of hopelessness. It is precisely in the second part of Isaiah and in the promises of the third part that God is projected as a mother who gives birth to Judah (see Isaiah 46 and 66); God promises release from exile in terms of a birth-image. How can a mother who is on the brink of giving birth not give birth? Jerusalem will be the place where the exiled people will again drink from the breasts of the mother. They will be fed and be given the comfort that they so dearly needed during the period of the exile. Now this is quite interesting, because it refers to the birth image not merely as a personal spiritual awakening but as a *social* reality. It refers to the fact that in a situation of hopelessness the promise of God is specifically verbalised in terms of womanist experiences, namely a mother who gives birth, a mother who comforts, and Jerusalem as a mother who breastfeeds the people of Israel.

The last example of a re-interpretation of the birth image would be the constant references of Jesus during his last teachings. In John 16:20-22 He refers to the fact that the disciples and the believers will wait in pain, like the agony of a woman awaiting the birth of her child, until He returns with the second coming. This implies that not only the incarnation, but the whole period between Christ's first and second coming, is nothing other than the story of the pregnant time and the pregnant grace until the agony and the pain of our human, earthly existence will be completely taken up in the full glorification at the end of history: the birth of a new time.

I conclude. At this very critical juncture in the history of our country, with a violence-torn society, the reclaiming of this powerful religious tradition by adopting new metaphors (such as, for instance, the illustration of the birth image) may bring us new hope. This is not only hope in theory, but in practice, because we may take up the promise of our mother God who said: "Shall I bring to the brink of birth and not deliver the child?"

BIBLIOGRAPHY

Ackermann, D. 1988. "Feminist Liberation Theology". *JTSA* Vol. 62, pp. 14-28

Ackermann, D. 1993. "Critical Theory, Communication Actions and Liberating Praxis". *JTSA* Vol. 82, pp. 21-36.

Anderson, G.H. & Stransky, T.F. (eds.) 1979. *Mission Trends Vol. 4*. New York: Paulist Press.

Black, M. 1962 *Models and Metaphors*. New York: Cornell University Press.

Du Rand, J.J.F. 1993 "Theology and Resurrection – Metaphors and Paradigms". *JTSA* Vol. 82, pp. 3-20.

Fiorenza, E.S. 1979. "Feminist Theology as a critical theology of liberation". In G.H. Anderson & T.F. Stransky (eds.), pp. 188-216.

Fiorenza, E.S. 1988. *In memory of her*. New York: Crossroad.

Heidegger, M. 1963 *Sein und Zeit*. Tübingen: Max Niemeyer.

McFague, S. 1985. *Metaphorical Theology*. London: SCM Press.

McFague, S. 1987 *Models of God*. London: SCM Press.

Mollenkott, V. 1979. "Women and the Bible: A challenge to male interpretations". In G.H. Anderson & T.F. Stransky (eds.), pp. 221-233.

Smit, D.J. 1986. "The symbol of reconciliation and ideological conflict in South Africa". In W.S. Vorster (ed.), pp. 79-112.

Vorster, W.S. (ed.) *Reconciliation and Construction*. Pretoria: Unisa.

2.5 CAN OUR CREEDS SPEAK A GENDERED TRUTH?

A feminist reading of the Nicene Creed and the Belhar Confession[1]

The aim of this paper is to explore the potential of the Nicene Creed (381) and the Belhar Confession (1986) "to speak a gendered truth",[2] i.e. their openness toward a feminist hermeneutic and re-reading. I will proceed in two parts: the first is a short methodological orientation on feminist scholarship, and the second is an actual attempt at a feminist interpretation of the two texts under discussion.

PART ONE: A SHORT METHODOLOGICAL NOTE

Christian feminist scholarship has matured in recent years and represents a complex array of approaches that may be "modelled" in quite a variety of different ways. Traditionally Christian feminism has been categorised as radical (revolutionary), reformist and womanist.[3] *Radical* feminists represent those scholars who view the Judeo-Christian canon itself, the *Wirkungsgeschichte* of its interpretation, as well as its institutional form in the church as irredeemably androcentric, and in principle and practice oppressive toward women. This led to attempts to develop an alternative religious framework to set up a paradigm of text, interpretation and institutions liberating to women. Well-known exponents of this paradigm are Mary Daly, Naomi Goldenburg and Carol Christ.[4]

Reformist feminists[5] agree on the androcentric nature of the canon, its interpretation and ecclesial practices flowing from such male-dominated views, but agree that a

---

1. This paper was originally read at the annual conference of the Theological Society of Southern Africa at Hammanskraal, July 2003. It was later published in *Scriptura* 86 (2004), 201-209, and partially included in Naude's monograph, *Neither calendar nor clock*, published by Eerdmans in 2010.
2. The idea of a truth shaped by the perspective of gender is in principle not a novel one. It could be construed as involving the same procedure as the construction of a truth from the perspective of, for example, race or class or disability or culture. In recent South African scholarship it emerged in relation to an analysis of "truth" as sought by the Truth and Reconciliation Commission. See Van Schalkwyk's penetrating article, and also De Gruchy, who states that one of the difficulties "in getting at the truth had to do with the male-dominated structure of the Commission and the fact that the majority of those who appear before the TRC were black women" (2002:157).
3. There are more such "categories" such as, for example, socialist feminists who strongly relate sexist and classist oppression, or the differentiation between exclusive and inclusive feminism. For an orientation from a South African source, read Landman (1984). In my brief orientation no further refinement is pursued.
4. See McFague (1982:156-158) and Walker (1989) for a discussion and literature.
5. This group is probably the biggest and is represented by authors such as Letty Russell, Sallie McFague, Rosemary Radford Reuther (all USA), Catharina Halkes (The Netherlands) and Elisabeth Moltmann-Wendel (Germany). In South Africa the work of Denise Ackermann (Practical Theology), Christina Landman (Church History and recently Pastoral Theology), Annalet van Schalkwyk (Missiology) and Elna Mouton (New Testament) could all be seen as attempts at a reformist reinterpretation of Scripture and the androcentric tradition.

careful feminist re-reading of the canonical text yields sufficient potential to accept its liberating power for both men and women.

The *womanist* movement[6] within feminism may be described as an attempt by African-American and African theologians to emphasise the particular oppressive structures under which black (generically speaking) women suffer. According to them, this warrants a distinctive voice, complementing "Western" feminism, but drawing specific attention to the racist and classist dimensions attached to and supported by sexism in church and society.

Recently a second interesting "modelling" of feminism emerged that takes various epistemological[7] presuppositions as its point of departure. A threefold distinction is then proposed.

Feminist *empiricism* presupposes a form of positivist epistemology, where empirical observation of sexism in church and society is the basis for a feminist critique that implicitly accepts the possibility of an Archimedes point from which objectivity and truth are constructed. Feminist *standpoint epistemology* is more open to the cultural conditioning of knowledge – including "feminist" knowledge. It sets the androcentric and feminist constructions up as opposing views with the latter as the more liberative option because it represents an "oppressed" truth.

Feminist *postmodernism* (post-structuralism) points out that empiricism presupposes an impossible "outsider" viewpoint, and standpoint theories – whilst rejecting anthropocentrism as one "universalism" – introduces feminism as another universalism, therewith retaining a form of modernist meta-narrative that grows from a so-called "common or universal woman's experience" that is oblivious to the complexities and paradoxes of so-called "women" experiences. In the light of this criticism post-modern feminism, following Lyotard (1979), rejects the possibility of meta-narratives and a rationality posited on a subject-object dualism that only accepts discursive forms as valid expressions of truth. Instead, for post-modern feminists truth is much more pluralistic and fragile, speaking in a multiplicity of voices including lesbian, African, Western and Eastern, assuming different approaches such as Marxist, structuralist, phenomenological, and moving beyond the boundaries of Christianity to include important inter-religious voices from, for example, Judaism and Islam.

This is not an essay in feminist methodology. The preceding paragraphs are intended to illustrate the complexity of a notion such as "gendered truth" in the title of this paper. To avoid methodological paralysis, a few remarks are necessary to frame the work attempted in part two below.

---

6   The volume edited by Ursula King, *Feminist theology from the Third World* (1994), gives an interesting overview of some womanist approaches. For a specific theological and hermeneutical orientation, see the contributions of Oduyoye and Ackermann in Maimela and Konig (1998:349-372). Other well-known representatives of this group are Dolores Williams, Katie Cannon and bell hooks (sic).
7   Epistemological typologies are often used in philosophy of science or research methodology discussions. See, for example, Babbie and Mouton (2001:19-46), who work with positivist, phenomenological and critical-emancipatory approaches. The specific application to feminist theory was developed by Pamela Sue Anderson, to whom I was introduced via the excellent Master's thesis of JA Trisk (2002:4ff). At the time of writing this essay I did not have access to Anderson's original work.

Despite different approaches and contrasting epistemologies, *one could safely assert that much of feminist scholarship is focused on language and its constitutive relation to reality*. And although this variety of views has an obvious effect on how language itself is understood, one could posit that feminism has made a decisive contribution to Christian theology by showing the powerful relation between religious language (metaphors) and ecclesial-societal realities. Although expressed differently by, for example, existentialism and structuralism, it is accepted that reality is itself constituted by language with the consequence that a great deal of feminist hermeneutics is iconoclastic in nature. For radical feminism this means the rejection of androcentric metaphors and the creation of an alternative symbolic world; for reformists and womanists it means the transformation of metaphors and an archaeology of the construction of meaning based in existing canonical texts.

Whereas much creative work has been done on the canon, *the creeds and confessions have not yet received as much attention*. The reasons are simple: the canon (although itself contested) is the founding document of the Christian church and the obvious site of hermeneutical struggle for a feminist reinterpretation. The creeds and confessions are secondary expressions of the church's insights at a particular point in time and directed at particular heresies primarily (though not exclusively) relevant to that time. The creeds such as Nicea, Athanasius and the Apostolicum are indeed ecumenical in nature, but still not universally accepted nor liturgically practised in the same way in different traditions. Confessions such as Augsburg, Belgica, Barmen and Belhar are strongly tradition-bound and seen as a specific expression of the Protestant tradition.

It is thus natural for feminist scholarship to focus on the canon. As this paper attempts to illustrate, creeds and confessions speak the truth of the apostolic faith at a specific time and thus become part of the church's tradition. They are therefore important texts – often cited personally or in community – that require close scrutiny from a feminist perspective. It would be strange to develop a critical feminist reading of the canon, but allow the liturgical texts of the church their assumed androcentric freedom!

This shifts the hermeneutical struggle from the canon to these secondary texts. And for the purposes of this essay, the question rises from a reformist hermeneutical view: If we accept the voice of the church at a specific moment in history, but already know the androcentric bias of the church through the ages, do these texts yield the potential to speak a "gendered truth"? Are they able to liberate us from sexist and related forms of androcentric oppression? The answer will be found only in a close reading of the texts from a feminist perspective.[8]

---

8   As a male reader I am obviously limited in my abilities to construct a feminist perspective. However, I consider myself a Christian feminist in the sense that I attempt to be sensitive to sexism, resist forms of male domination in church and society, and believe the gospel is an inclusive message of liberation.

Can our creeds speak a gendered truth?

PART TWO: READING NICEA AND BELHAR

2.1. The choice of texts

The reader may rightly ask: Why these two texts?

The choice of the Nicene-Constantinopolitan Creed arises from the primordial ecumenical significance of the Nicene creed in early and contemporary church history, as recently exemplified in the WCC project on *Confessing the one faith* (see WCC 1991). The choice of Belhar arises from its crucial significance in the theological struggle against apartheid in South Africa and its growing ecumenical[9] significance as a clear confession of faith for our time.

In a recent paper (Naudé 2003a) I dealt with the history and textual construction of these two documents extensively and provided full bibliographical details of a selection of the most important work done on Nicea and Belhar. Suffice it to say: Nicea was an attempt to address a complex set of heresies, but was initially motivated by Arian ideas[10] about the relation between God and a subordinate Second Person in the Trinity, and later by the so-called pneumatomachians in their denial of the Godhead of the Spirit. In three sections it consequently focuses on the unity of the Father, Son and Spirit (with confessions about the church, baptism, resurrection and the world to come included under the latter).[11]

Belhar grew from a history[12] of the church struggle against apartheid which culminated in the *status confessionis* declared by the LWF (1977) and WARC (1982). The text[13] is divided into five parts. After an introductory statement on the Trinity and the church, the three middle articles deal with unity, reconciliation and justice respectively, followed by a statement that the church is called to confess and do all these things even in the face persecution.

2.2. A feminist perspective on Nicea

Considering its early date in the history of the church, the Greco-Roman culture from which it sprang, the fact that delegates (bishops) to Nicea/Constantinople excluded women, and considering the political motives of the emperor, one would expect the language of Nicea to reflect an androcentric bias. And indeed: the dominant androcentric and "dominion" metaphors of the canon are the main ones employed to express the unity in God and the relation amongst Persons of the Trinity: God is called *"Father"*,[14] *"the Almighty"*; Jesus is called *"Lord"*, *"the only Son of God"*, *"of*

---

9 See Naudé (2003) for the reception of Belhar in the ecumenical church and its relation to recent ecumenical developments.
10 See Ritter (1978) for an in-depth discussion of Arianism.
11 For the Greek text and authorised English translation, see WCC (1991:10-12).
12 The history has been extensively analysed in a paper dealing with the close link between Belhar and antecedent church witnesses such as the Cottesloe Declaration (1960), The Message to the People of South Africa (1968) and others (Naudé 2002a).
13 For the English version and excellent essays, see Cloete and Smit (1984). The subdivisions of the text in the discussion below are my own to make easy reference possible.
14 "God is Spirit and has no gender. The Father is revealed as the Father of the Son, but 'Father' and 'Son' are metaphors. Scripture uses motherly metaphors for God as well. But God is not a mother in the sense that the world or humankind is generated

one Being with the Father" and as *"seated at the right hand of the Father"* whence he will return as judge to establish his kingdom that will have no end. The Spirit is called *"Lord"*, *"who proceeds from the Father"* and *"Who, with the Father and the Son, is worshipped and glorified"*.

Does this mean the text is irredeemably sexist? Below I seek to show that Nicea indeed has the potential to speak the truth in a more inclusive way.

God

In the article on God, God is metaphorically depicted as "Father" and "Almighty", but God's creative work is clearly inclusive of all reality: *"maker of heaven and earth, of all that is, seen and unseen"*. Thus, despite the androcentric bias in naming God, God's work encompasses all reality not only in a spatial sense (*"heaven and earth"*), but also in an ontological sense (*"all that is"*), including empirical and non-empirical realities (*"seen and unseen"*).

If we accept that God's character is derived from God's work in creation and salvation, the inclusivity of God's creative acts is clearly "violated" by the exclusive, biased metaphors used to name God. Seen from its context, Nicea had no cultural or feminist theological sensitivity to "naming God" as we have today, so that its article on God speaks in paradoxical terms about God's inclusive work, but bearing an exclusive Name. Or, interpreted more favourably, Nicea corrects/complements its androcentric bias in naming God with a remarkably inclusive statement on the creative acts of God, thereby leaving room for all of reality and all persons to be included in God's creative and continued providential acts.

Jesus Christ

The article on the Second Person equally shows potential for an inclusivist interpretation. Three points seem relevant.

First. The mediation of Jesus Christ in creation – inclusively described in the article on God – is expressed clearly in its relation to Christ: *"Through him all things were made"*. Christ, in fact, is the One through which the inclusive spatial, ontological and (non-)empirical reality was brought into being, again superseding a closed, androcentric understanding of "the only Son of God".

Second. Nicea has in this article a remarkable *pro nobis* character. Why would Christ do all these things? It was *"For us all and for our salvation"* (*di' hemas tous anthropous kai dia ten hemeteran sooterian*), and *"For our sake"* (*huper humoon*) that Christ was crucified and suffered under Pontius Pilate. The Greek link between *"hemas"* and *"anthroopos"* clearly indicates an inclusive humankind on whose behalf the whole of Christ's life and work is interpreted and confessed. Although caught up in the exclusive "we" of the original Nicene formulation, both its intention of being a confession for the one, holy, catholic church, and its generic inclusion of all humankind in the cited formulations, set the creed free to speak *"for us all"* – men and women in one church.

---

from a divine womb or is an extension of God's own being". This quotation from the Presbyterian Church's *Draft Confession of Faith* (2003) is *in nuce* an explanation of some of the interpretive issues involved here.

Third. I am quite aware that the article on *"the Virgin Mary"* might be constructed as depicting women as subservient and allowing them to be oppressed in silence. Nevertheless, the whole purpose of God's act of salvation in Christ is expressed in two powerful statements, namely that for us all *"he came down from heaven"*. This is followed by the manner in which this was made possible, i.e. *"by the Holy Spirit he became incarnate from the Virgin Mary, and was made human"* (generically understood from "enanthroopesanvta"). Just as Christ mediated an inclusive, encompassing creation, Mary mediated God's inclusive salvation (*"For us all"* and *"For our sake"*). That she could do only in and through her womanhood and physical motherhood. But the latter – far from being merely a sexist, oppressive state – made possible and affirmed an inclusive salvation far beyond the dualism of man/woman and including whoever wishes to claim salvation in faith and profess: *"For us all ... Christ became incarnate from the Virgin Mary."*

Holy Spirit

The article on the Holy Spirit leaves at least two options open for a potentially inclusive interpretation.

First. The magnificent description of the Sprit as *zoo-poion*, giver of life (or the One who makes alive), is clearly open to such reinterpretation. If read in its creation sense, all life finds its origin in God's inclusive creation which is mediated through Christ, and now find its life, its breath (see *ruah* in Old Testament) from the Holy Spirit. If read in the sense of "enliven" (making alive that which is spiritually dead), the strong cluster of birth metaphors comes to the fore, linking the new life in the Spirit to being reborn of the Spirit. As in the description of God, we find an ambiguity here: *"Life-Giver"* is juxtapositioned by naming the Spirit *"the Lord"* which is normally uncomfortably accepted as a "dominion-metaphor" (McFague) by feminists. If one keeps the heresy and political context in mind from which the church spoke in Nicea, the *kurios* is understandable – even unavoidable. Nonetheless – probably beyond the intentions of the original authors – a feminist reading could find comfort in believing the Spirit as *Life-Giver*, a metaphor with a strong maternal and inclusivist ring to it.

Second. The Spirit, Nicea teaches, is the One *"who has spoken through the Prophets"*. The prophetic tradition of the Old Testament was undoubtedly androcentric, despite a few examples to the contrary and the potential to interpret the prophetic tradition from an alternative perspective. Embedded in this tradition, which found its way into the New Testament, is the eschatological vision that a time will come when God's Spirit is showered upon all people, so that sons and daughters can act as prophets; so that old and young people will see visions and dream dreams. It is significant that this vision – expressed *in nuce* by Joel (2:28-32) and repeated by Peter to interpret the Pentecost (Acts 2:14ff) – is a powerfully inclusive vision where gender (sexism) and age (ageism) are transcended in God's pneumatological community. This community is filled with the Spirit – exactly the One, according to Nicea, *"who has spoken through the prophets"* – and who keeps on calling us all into the prophetic community where women and men are free to speak "about the great things that God has done" (Acts 2:12).

Church

The nature of this community is described in the article on the church in which unity (one church against divisions of gender, culture and class) and catholicity (inclusive generality) appear in the foreground, despite sexist and exclusivist practices up to this day. We enter this community through *"one baptism"*, through which all receive forgiveness of sins (including the sins of sexism). There is further the inclusive eschatological expectation of resurrection (based on no bias but God's fair judgement) and the life of the age to come (a time when all dualisms or other forms of divisions will be transcended because God will be everything in everyone).

Provisional conclusion

More interpretative work needs to be done. But if the church is sensitive to the potential of the Nicene creed to address all forms of oppression – including sexism – and back that up with liberating liturgical practices, it might be possible for women and men (and for that matter old and young, rich and poor, literate and illiterate) to co-confess with the apostolic church through the ages. This we will do whilst taking into consideration the ambiguity of the text with both its limitations and potentialities to speak a liberating word beyond its own time and become the confession of the whole faith community.

The acid test is who the confessing "we" of the Nicene creed includes or could include.

2.3. A feminist perspective on the Belhar Confession

Let us look at the potential of Belhar for a liberative, feminist reading by focusing on the three middle articles regarding unity, reconciliation and justice.

Unity

It is clear from the rejection statements of the unity article that Belhar, true to its history and context, has the racial and cultural divisions of the church in mind in its positive declaration of the church's unity. In Belhar's time the danger was not perceived as sexism or gender discrimination, and thus no explicit rejection of this is found in the text. But the text has just too many explicit statements about an inclusive unity to be disregarded.

See 2.3, for example, which claims that *"this unity must become visible so that the world may believe that separation enmity and hatred between people and groups is sin which Christ has already conquered"*. It then clearly opens up an inclusive interpretation by saying *"anything* ("alles" could also be *"everything"*) *which threatens this unity may have no place in the church of Christ and should therefore be resisted"*. This finds an echo in 2.4, where the community of believers is called upon to *"fight against all which may threaten or hinder this unity"* as differences amongst people (language, culture, background) and their gifts are – because of Christ's reconciliation – *"opportunities for mutual service and enrichment within the one visible people of God"*.

Although the gender issue is not specified – and this is a pity – the text is clear in its intention *to resist all forms and causes of disunity* in the one church of Christ.

Reconciliation

This article is even stronger in its focus on racial non-reconciliation, as emerges from 3.3 (*"forced separation of people on racial grounds"*, echoed in 3.4) and the rejection statement about *"the forced separation of people on the grounds of race or colour"*. But these references are embedded in more inclusive and general views on the church as salt and light, as peacemakers and as eschatological community that are witnesses through word and deed to the new heaven and the new earth in which righteousness reigns (see 3.1). This is followed by the confession of God's reconciling power through God's *"life-giving Word and Spirit"* that overcame *"non-reconciliation and hatred, bitterness and enmity"*, which enables God's people to live as an example of a reconciled community in the world (see 3.2).

The fact that these fundamental expressions of God's reconciliation finds application in one specific area of human life (race and culture) in no way precludes its application to other forms of non-reconciliation such as gender oppression. The same could be confessed about gender conflict and androcentric prejudices, namely *"that any teaching which is not prepared to venture on the road of obedience and reconciliation, but rather, out of prejudice, fear, selfishness, and unbelief, denies in advance the reconciling power of the gospel, must be considered ideology and false doctrine"* (see 3.4).

Justice

There is no doubt that Belhar's true potential for an encompassing liberation lies in this article (whilst keeping in mind the close relation amongst the articles). The reason is that this article transcends the narrower application to race and culture evident in the former articles (and to be explained from Belhar's context). Although God is named via sexist metaphors, God is described *"as the One who wishes to bring about justice and true peace amongst people"*. How does God achieve this? By being *"in a special way the God of the destitute, the poor and the wronged"* ("verontregte" in the original Afrikaans). The examples in this passage – drawn from Scripture and the Lukan focus on the poor – explicitly mentions the widow and the orphans twice!

I am aware that even this might not be read as specifically gender-sensitive, but generically as a symbol for all those who are without legal recourse and legitimate voice in society. But the fact of the matter remains: even in patriarchal societies, the message of a faultless religion before God (James 1:27) is to stand by the orphans and widows in their suffering. This surely opens the possibility to extend the categories of wronged peoples to include women (and children, and other voiceless ones who are physically poor or in other ways socially marginalised and shunned).

This is reinforced as the church is called to witness against "any *form of injustice*" (4.2) and against "*all the powerful and the privileged that selfishly seek their own interests and thus control and harm others*" (4.3). The rejection clause ending article 4 is equally emphatic and inclusive of "any ideology *which would legitimate forms of injustice and any doctrine that is unwilling to resist such an ideology in the name of the gospel*" (my emphases to illustrate a wider application).

The concluding article 5 is a source of encouragement for all who struggle against gender injustice: *"The Church is called to confess and do all these things, even though the authorities and human laws might forbid them and punishment and suffering be the consequence"*. I can see no reason why *"authorities and human laws"* – apart from referring to the socio-political order – could not also include ecclesial authorities, ordinances and practices that continue to contradict both a confession and presumed commitment to gender equality in the church.

Provisional conclusion

In this way Belhar, despite its limitations in terms of the narrow focus and sexist theological metaphors, can indeed be a powerful tool to proclaim the church's true unity, God's encompassing reconciliation and gendered justice in society.

3. CONCLUSION

This essay has argued that, despite a complex array of feminist approaches, the crucial battle for language is a common concern amongst Christian feminist theologians. In line with a feminist reinterpretation of the canon, it was argued that important secondary texts such as creeds and confessions warrant the same critical reading to explore their liberative potential. *A cursory reading of both the Nicene creed and the Belhar confession points to an ambiguity in both texts: the presence of traditional androcentric metaphors for the Trinity is in subtle ways "redeemed" by inclusive language and references that show the potential for an emerging gendered truth.*

Whether documents like these are in actual fact confessed by all – specifically by marginalised women – will not depend on a hermeneutic alone, but on the liturgical practices and rearrangement of institutional power relations in the church itself.

We still have a long way to go.

BIBLIOGRAPHY

Ackermann, D. 1998. "Feminist and womanist hermeneutics". In Maimela & König (eds.), pp. 349-358.

Babbie, E. & Mouton, J. (eds.) 2001. *The practice of social research*. Oxford: Oxford University Press.

Cloete, G.D. & Smit, D.J. (eds). 1984. *A moment of truth*. Grand Rapids: Eerdmans.

De Gruchy, J. 2002. *Reconciliation. Restoring justice*. Cape Town: David Philip.

King, U. (ed.) 1994. *Feminist theology from the Third World: A reader*. New York: Orbis Books.

Landman, C. 1984. "A profile of feminist theology". In W.S. Vorster (ed.) *Sexism and feminism in theological perspective*. Pretoria: University of South Africa, pp. 1-29.

Lyotard, J.F. 1979. *The postmodern condition*. Minnesota: University of Minnesota Press.

Maimela, S & König, A. (eds.) 1998. *Initiation into theology. The rich variety of theology and hermeneutics*. Pretoria: Van Schaik.

McFague, S. 1982. *Metaphorical theology. Models of God in religious language*. London: SCM Press.

Naudé, P.J. 2002. "Confessing Nicea today? Critical questions from a South African perspective". *Scriptura* Vol. 79, pp. 47-54.

Naudé, P.J. 2003a. "The theological coherence between the Belhar confession and some antecedent church witnesses in the period 1948-1982". *Verbum et ecclesia* Vol. 42, No. 1, pp. 156-179.

Naudé, P.J. 2003b. "'A gift from heaven – the reception of the Belhar Confession in the period 1982-2000 and its ecumenical significance today". *NGTT* Vol. 44, No. 3 & 4, pp. 407-420.

Naudé, P.J. 2004. "Confessing the one faith: Theological resonance between the creed of Nicea (325 AD) and the Confession of Belhar (1982 AD)". *Scriptura* Vol. 85, pp. 35-53.

Oduyoye, M.A. 1998. "African women's hermeneutics". In S. Maimela & A. König (eds.), pp. 359-372.

Ritter, A.M. 1978. "Arianismus". *TRE* Vol. 3, pp. 693-719.

Trisk, J.A. 2002. *Who do I say I am? Identity as a construct and its implications for Christian anthropology*. Unpublished MA Thesis. Cape Town: University of Cape Town.

Van Schalkwyk, A. 1999. "A gendered truth. Women's testimonies at the TRC and reconciliation". *Missionalia* Vol. 27, No. 2, pp. 165-188.

Vorster, W.S. (ed.) 1984. *Sexism and feminism in theological perspective*. Pretoria: University of South Africa.

WCC. World Council of Churches 1991. *Confessing the one faith* (new revised version). Faith and Order Paper 153. Geneva: WCC.

2.6 LIBERATION THEOLOGY AS ORTHOPRACTICAL THEOLOGY

A methodological evaluation[1]

The intention of this presentation is to briefly explain the core of the methodological claim within Latin American liberation theology in terms of the "orthopractical primate". This claim is then evaluated from two viewpoints: firstly, the truth concept associated with such an orthopractical theology is investigated; secondly, liberation theologians' representation of the relationship between orthodoxy and orthopraxis is questioned in the light of their relationship with Karl Barth. The discussion is wrapped up with a brief summarising conclusion.

1. CLAIM OF METHODOLOGICAL INNOVATION

The main claim of Latin American liberation theology (henceforth: liberation theology) is undoubtedly made at the level of theological methodology. In their struggle for independence alongside traditional European theology, liberation theologians are not primarily focused on defending substantive renewal, but rather to show that their work is concerned with the *"reformulation* of the preconditions, presuppositions and *methods* of doing theology at all" (Míquez-Bonino 1979:260). The liberation theological venture therefore involves the "inwijden van een *nieuwe methodologie* van christelijke bezinning vanuit en over de geloof als gegeven historische praxis" (Vidales 1974:128).

This methodological claim is grounded primarily in a reformulation of the theory-praxis relationship to design a theology from the "primate of praxis" (Gutierrez 1975:48; Boff 1978a:122-123). The choice of praxis (experience/transformative act) as a starting point and goal of theory (theological reflection) is philosophically derived from the leftist Hegelian tradition (particularly Marx) and is theologically translated in terms of the *priority of orthopraxis over orthodoxy*.

In terms of this, the epistemological rift between liberation theology and Europe is embedded in an appeal to two opposing philosophical traditions, namely those of Kant and Marx. According to liberation theology, this philosophical tension gives rise to two kinds of theology, namely an *abstract orthodoxy* (Europe) and a reality-engaging *orthopraxis* (Sobrino 1977:123ff; 1985:21-27). "The 'orthodoxy' of the Christian message has been reduced traditionally to its theoretical formulations or to the purity of its oral proclamations. Now we can no longer restrict the meaning of the term 'orthodoxy' to 'right thinking' or 'right speaking'. We must recover the full dimensions of the term, and its basic meaning of 'right doing'" (Vidales 1979:37-38, see also Boff 1978b:46; Schillebeeckx 1977:693). In short, *methodological renewal means that a theology that was focused on "Orthodoxie und Reinheit von Formeln"* (Boff 1978a:120) *is replaced with a theology that gives priority to orthopraxis, or correct action.*

---

[1] This essay is an English translation of "Bevrydingsteologie as ortopraktiese teologie: 'n Metodologiese evaluering" and was first published in *Ned. Geref. Teologiese Tydskrif* 19/2 (1988), 236 – 245, as an adapted version of a paper delivered at the Theological Society of Southern Africa on Liberation Theology and Methodology in Pretoria (1987).

As mentioned above, the objective is to question the methodological claim of liberation theology from two angles. Firstly, it is argued that liberation theology, despite its valid criticism of traditional theology, deals with a truth concept which is unacceptable for various reasons. Secondly, the representation that some liberation theologians make of the relationship between orthodoxy and orthopraxis is tested against their relationship with the "orthodox" theology of Karl Barth.

1.1. Orthopraxis as operational truth

To understand the debate between liberation theology and Europe, it is essential to take account of the fact that we are dealing with a predominantly Catholic inclination that reacts against the design of a "scholastic theology". Scholasticism displays a rationalist character and is narrowed to *scientia conclusionum*, i.e. an ahistorical system of Godly truths. These truths receive the status of infallibility, so that the function of theology as an ecclesiastic science constitutes a dialectical reproduction of formal jurisdictionally arranged "orthodoxy" (see Rossouw 1973:204, 205).

The main criticism of liberation theology against this exclusive relationship between "truth" and "orthodoxy" is the relativising of action (acts) to secondary "consequence" or "derivation" of truth, but not in itself as constitutive of truth. The traditional notion of truth as *adaequatio rei et intellectus* means that truth is construed as "Wahrheit von vornherein als Korrelat rein theorethischer Vernunft", or as a product of absolute reflection (Metz 1984:57). In this way truth becomes a self-contained, autonomous domain and "die Erkenntnis ein Wert in sich: Wahrheit um der Wahrheit willen" (Girardi 1974:20). As an unchangeable premise, truth stands aprioristically fixed – formulated as infallible dogmas – and every discrepancy between truth and reality is regarded as an "imperfect application" of truth, so that any change of the status quo (historical reality) is constantly opposed from the position of "truth". Theology as a scientific reflection of dogmas has indeed attempted to maintain contact with reality through moral theology, but "it was a non-temporal moral theology remarkably similar to the civic morality required by established society" (Segundo 1979:250).

In this concept of truth, the most important criterion for truth is the correct formula/dogma as juridically organised by the church. The "orthodoxy" is therefore not only a consolidation of the doctrinal truths, but in itself also the verification criterion which is used to distinguish between true and untrue. *In terms of theory and praxis, traditional theology implies that verification is by definition theoretical in nature and that it rests upon the correspondence between the contents of dogma and the tradition that was handed down.*

In the light of the constitutive relationship between truth and method,[2] a change in the concept of truth and coherent verification simultaneously implies "a real conversion in methods" (Segundo 1976:281). This "conversion" is interpreted in terms of the shift from orthodoxy to orthopraxis; and in order to give form to the latter, liberation theology designs an *operational-historical* concept of truth with an associated *social verification*.

---

2   There is no distinction between method as "way of truth" and truth itself: "The method used in arriving at the truth is itself a forward step within the bounds of truth. Our methodological approach, then, is the truth as it is being unveiled" (Vidales 1979:42).

In close correlation with Marxist epistemology,[3] truth is connected to historical praxis (transformative act) and verification is located in the "liberation effect" of such an act: "Truth is the name given by a historical community to those acts which were, are and will be effective for the liberation of man" (Hennely 1979:105, footnote 44; see also Assmann 1975:56-57). In other words: "A knowledge of reality that does not lead to changing that reality is an unverified interpretation: it does not have the consistency demanded by truth" (Gutierrez 1975:44-45). Reflection does not constitute any "own world" and is a contemplation of praxis, with the effect that "haar wereld en haar waarheid in haar eigen praxis zitten" and that every "-logy" which is not a "-logy" of praxis is rejected (Assmann 1975:54).

Theologically speaking, this does not involve a mere reformulation of the correlation between "truth" and "dogmatic content", as if liberation theology exchanges the latter for "praxis". As orthodoxy in traditional theology contains the content as well as the verification of the content, liberation theologians formulate the "orthos" of praxis *in terms of the praxis*. This means that "no single dogma can be studied with any other final criterion than its impact on praxis" (Segundo 1979:250). Not orthodoxy (correct doctrine), but "a real, and even material, success in a historical liberation" is the pre-eminent feature (Segundo 1976:281-282), and theological language is verified "in and through its engagement in the liberation of the poor" (Gutierrez 1978:247). Truth is therefore not so much "handed down", as "invented" or "established" in history as interested truth (preferred option for the poor).

To summarise, it can be stated that orthopraxis is a reference to those acts that make an effective contribution to the liberation of the poor. Truth is established where this liberation comes into existence, and falsehood is revealed where liberation is resisted and where oppression continues.

There can be no doubt that liberation theology provides valuable criticism of traditional theology in this manner. It indeed expands the meaning of "fallacy" or "heresy" from heterodoxy to heteropraxis, because "de gevaarlijkste ketterijen voor de kerk zijn altijd de praktische ketterijen geweest, als een leer die formeel naijverig juist was, samenging met de verloochening ervan in openlijke samenspel met de mensen die de mens verdrukten" (Assmann 1975:61). Or, vice versa: the heresy that essentially threatens any form of religion from its very origin is the *gnosis*: "Zij versmalt het christendom tot een theoretisch heilsleer – die, gezien het uitgangspunt consequent de wereld laat voor wat ze is – tot een hermeneutische bestaansverheldering, zonder interesse in daadwerkelijke vernieuwing van wereld of menselijk bestaan!" (Schillebeeckx 1969:142). A believer who actively engages in transformative praxis may therefore be "more orthodox" than the so-called "orthodox" Christian who prides him- or herself on "orthodoxy", as the criterion for truth has shifted to "de inwerking van de evangelieverkondiging aan de armen op de menselijke geschiedenis en de grad van effectiviteit van die bevrijding van de verdrukten in onze dagen" (Gutierrez 1974:133).

Yet, on theological-dogmatic grounds this methodological shift from orthodoxy to orthopraxis, as expressed in the operational concept of truth, cannot be accepted without criticism. To stimulate discussion, two related points of criticism are plotted

---

3   One of the best summaries of Marx's concept of truth is his well-known second thesis against Feuerbach. For a discussion, compare Van den Oudenrijn (1972:14-15).

in broad terms: *firstly*, the acceptance of Marxist epistemology implies that the primary correlation between faith and theology is replaced in an unacceptable way by a correlation between love and theology; *secondly*, the absolutising of "effective liberation" as the final criterion for dogma (amongst others) results in a devaluation of other theoretical criteria for systematic theology.

1.1.1. *Theology as scientia caritatis?*

Marxist epistemology leads liberation theology to understand theology not so much as *scientia fidei*, but rather as *scientia caritatis*. The principle of "truth is act" (Alves 1969:80) means that there is no place for an independent noetic moment in the relationship with God. God is not known through a (theoretical) profession of faith, but through obedience: "Obedience is not a consequence of our knowledge of God … obedience *is* our knowledge of God" (Míquez-Bonino 1976:40). Faith as knowledge of God is dismissed in an identity relationship with love as a way of knowledge leading to God, and the appeal of liberation theology to the *fides quaerens intellectum* of Anselm (see Segundo 1979:250) could be changed from "faith seeking understanding" to "love seeking efficacy". Not faith, but love-as-praxis is the primary correlating partner of theology: "Liebe (ist) freilich nicht der Ertrag einer Theologie, sondern ihr *Ausgangspunkt. Liebe aber ist Praxis und keine Theorie, Entscheidung für die Armen*" (Boff 1977:58, my emphasis). As a theory of effective love, the praxeological nature of the theology is guaranteed: as theo-praxis, theology is the "logos" of the "praxis" (see Zwiefelhofer 1976:77-78; Frieling 1972:28).

The problem with this methodological resolution in favour of orthopraxis is the fact that the choice for praxis (love) as a premise of theological reflection is based on an unacceptable relationship between faith, salvation and deeds. It is not sufficient that we are saved by faith alone (in which a certain knowledge of Christ and his benefactions is assumed) and that faith works through love (Galatians 5:6). No, "man darf nicht glauben, die Werken seien nur *Ausdruck* (original emphasis) einer ihnen vorausgehende Wesenheit. Es sindt viel mehr die Werke selbst, die konkret diese Wiesenheit, die Gnade *konstituieren*" (Boff 1983:175, my emphasis). Of course, faith without love is dead (James 2), but Boff also argues that *love without faith* is possible and that it makes sense because love (praxis for the sake of the poor) is identified with salvation: "Da die Agape als Entscheidung zur existentiellen Heilsebene gehört, *ist sie das Heil selbst* in seiner historischen Gestalt" (Boff 1983:175-176, my emphasis).

This high premium on human acts beyond faith is also defended by Gutierrez. By advocating that a quantitative-extensive concept of salvation be replaced with a qualitative concept of salvation, he is not merely shifting the emphasis in order to make salvation possible outside the church as well: "The very heart of the question was touched in the search for a means to widen the scope of the possibility of salvation: man is saved if he opens himself up to God and to others, even if he is not clearly aware that he is doing so. This is valid for Christians and non-Christians alike – for all people. To speak about *the presence of grace* – whether accepted or rejected – in all people implies, on the other hand, *to value from a Christian standpoint the very roots of human activity*" (Gutierrez 1983:151, my emphasis).

Salvation is therefore not alien to this world. Rather, it gives to the world "its own autonomy, because *salvation is already latently there*" (my emphasis) and makes it possible to grant salvation status to human acts, independent of faith, because of the classical relationship between nature and grace (*natura propria*) (Gutierrez 1983:151-152).

The methodological choice for a *scientia caritatis* is therefore derived from a dogmatic framework in which the autonomy of faith is threatened and the constitutive relationship between salvation and faith is exchanged for the relationship between salvation and love.

1.1.2. A *second* problem with the indicated operational-social verification is the fact that liberation theologians tend to transfer criteria that determine the credibility of faith exclusively to theology as a science. Put another way, this means that traditional[4] liberation theologians identify the epistemological mode of theology with the existential-practical mode of faith, and then transfer the truth criteria of the latter to the former.

By developing credibility as a *noetic* category, the impression is reinforced that acting/love is the *basis* of knowledge of God, with the result that the being-known-by-the-Shepherd (John 10) and knowledge as a gift from God (1 John 4:20) lose their a priori position. Of course, a true Christian theology will display an engagement with reality. The doxological quality of theology, however, cannot be verified solely against such engagement. Even if a traditionally "orthodox" theology may result in practical heresy, it does not mean that the "orthopractical" theology is elevated above dogmatic (orthodox!) fallacy.

Confession, regardless of how much it is an *act*, remains relevant to confession as a *formula of faith*.[5] A conclusive or actionist communion with God in which the practice of faith (love) stands opposite the confession of faith, and in which the proclaiming of acts is set against the proclaiming of Scripture, results in an anti-confessionalist doxopathy or doxopraxis which attempts to deny the essential connection with the normative condition of doxology, namely *orthodoxy*: "Not everyone who says to Me 'Lord, Lord' shall enter the kingdom of heaven, but only he who does the will of My Father in heaven". But this does not make the confession superfluous. On the contrary: meaningful communion with the Lord is only possible when we can also say who and what He is. Likewise, doxopraxis is only possible on the basis of doxology, Christian morality on the basis of Christian confession (Rossouw 1973:208).

In addition to this fundamental importance of orthodoxy, the scientific nature of theology is also subject to *other theoretical criteria* such as its critical, problem-solving ability (Van Huyssteen 1986:187-205) or its intrinsic coherence. By absolutising "effectiveness in praxis" as a criterion for systematic theology, "liberation" becomes more important than theology (to put it harshly) and theo-*logy* is dismissed in theo-*praxis*. The impression exists that the liberation-theological epistemology narrows the indispensable reality involvement of systematic theology to a unilateral operative contextuality.

---

4   As far as a refinement of the theological theory is concerned, there is a clear break between authors such as Clodovis Boff and Jose Miguez-Bonino and the vast majority of liberation theologians. How much influence this new theoretical awareness has is difficult to determine at this stage.

5   Just as the "theoretical element" in "praxis" cannot be denied, the "orthodox" specificity of "orthopraxis" cannot be disregarded. Put differently: the *fides qua creditur* is not possible without a *fides quae creditur* (see Schillebeeckx 1969:137-139; Metz 1984:177).

In a situation of glaring injustice and oppression, the theologian is tempted on two sides. On the one hand, there is the tendency to position the comfort of "pure thought" opposite self-sacrifice in service of the poor. On the other hand, compassion with socio-economic hardship often leads to participation in liberation without theologically ethical criteria. In both cases the dialectic relationship between orthodoxy and orthopraxis is relinquished, with negative consequences for theology as well as for the poor who cry for deliverance.

Apart from the unacceptable manner in which the irrational concept of truth is theologically realised, a second critical remark is to be made concerning the methodological claim of liberation theologians. In their relationship with Karl Barth it will become evident that there is *no causal relationship between the methodological construction of a theology and its so-called "praxis involvement"*.

1.2. Liberation theology and Karl Barth

In the current debate about the interpretation of Barth two poles can be distinguished, according to Van Niekerk (1984:3). The first pole represents a "church-centred" interpretation with the emphasis on the "supernatural" character of its theology, as though this theology is untouched by contemporary thinking. The second pole emphasises the social and philosophical specificity of Barth's thinking, and this falls into two groups: on the one hand, there are the "bourgeois" theologians who interpret Barth in terms of the liberation idea of the Enlightenment, and on the other hand, there is an interpretation from socio-political dialectics with or without the class struggle as a component.

The references to Barth in liberation theology[6] vary according to the intention of the author in question. In the context of the struggle dialogue with Europe, Barth obviously is perceived negatively and he is portrayed as "neo-orthodox" (Torres and Fabella 1978:xiv) or "bourgeois" (Brown 1976:xxii), although Protestants are positive towards his penetration of the "bankruptcy of liberal ideals and the illusionment of liberal theology" through an emphasis on Christology and Scripture (Couch 1978:200-201). Where the emphasis is on the struggle for the poor and socialism as socio-political ideals, Barth (together with Bonhoeffer[7] and Tillich[8]) is, however, presented as an ally of liberation theology, and he is interpreted in accordance with the basic tenets of latter liberation theologies (see Brown 1976:xxii-xxiii and Gutierrez 1978, 1983).

---

6   Beatrice Couch (1978:200-201) (with reference to Emilio Castro) makes some historical remarks on the influence of Barth on the Spanish world. Barth initially became famous because of the references to him by the Spanish philosopher Miguel de Unamuno, whose work was published in Latin America, as well as through the publications of Ortega y Gasset in the philosophical journal *Revista de Occidente*. In theological circles there are references to Barth from as early as 1938 in *Luminar*, an evangelical magazine in Mexico. The breakthrough came with the 1956 edition of the Argentine paper *Cuadernos Teologicos*, which was entirely devoted to Barth.

7   For a discussion of Bonhoeffer, see Gutierrez (1978:250) and the article by Julio de Santa Ana (1976).

8   Tillich is valued positively primarily because of his religious socialism. Compare Brown (1976:xxiii).

Methodologically speaking, Gutierrez's (1978) comparison between Barth and Bultmann is the most fruitful example of the extent to which liberation theologians motivate their positive appeal to Barth. In the context of theologies that originated in the struggle of the poor and oppressed, Gutierrez writes:

> It is instructive in this context to contrast the theologies of Barth and Bultmann. *Barth* (my emphasis), the theologian primarily of God's transcendence, seemingly theologically unconcerned with the human hearers of God's word, was pastor in a working-class milieu. His experiences there led him to a well-defined and lifelong socialism (see Husinger and Marquart). However his politics may have influenced his theology, he remained sensitive to the evil of human exploitation. *Bultmann* (my emphasis), on the contrary, concerned with the great questions of contemporary life and with modern humanity's incomprehension of the gospel message, was nevertheless limited by bourgeois ideology: his theology is oblivious to the oppression created by and for the very people who were the objects of his theological concern.

From this Gutierrez concludes the following:

> So the theologian who started from "heaven" was deeply aware of those who lived in "hell on earth", whereas the theologian who started from earth seemed oblivious to human exploitation.

Then follows the explanation:

> There is no real paradox here. An authentic and profound sense of God does not preclude awareness of the poor and the questions they raise. "Spirituality" does not preclude "social conscience". The real incompatibility is between bourgeois individualism and spirituality (Gutierrez 1978:249).

It is impossible to spell out all the implications of this interpretation. For our methodological discussion it is essential to note that Gutierrez deals with a very difficult situation here: how is it possible that this neo-orthodox theologian nevertheless displays an openness to human need (praxis!)? How is it possible that "orthodoxy" can be so much focused on "orthopraxis", if the entire methodological venture of liberation theology precisely intends to prove the opposite? The point is that in his answer to this question, Gutierrez – because he is thinking about "theorising" from the assumption of an irreversible relation between "orthodoxy" and "foreign to reality" – *does not at all honour the methodological structure of Barth's thinking.*

This becomes clear from two important remarks that precede the above comments. *Firstly*, Gutierrez explicitly states that "the primary difference" between traditional and liberation theology "is political, grounded in social inequity" (242). The empathy for the poor in Barth's theology is therefore (according to Gutierrez) not concerned with theological methodology, but must be interpreted in terms of his choice of "lifelong socialism". On the basis of this *political choice* Barth – in contrast with Bultmann, who is *ideologically* committed – therefore is acclaimed in liberation theology: the "primary difference" between the two theologies has been dismissed.

Secondly (and crucially), Gutierrez explains the unique nature of liberation theology by referring to the fact that "commitment" to the poor precedes theologising; and "liberation theology's second central intuition is that God is a liberating God, revealed *only* in the concrete historical context of the poor and oppressed" (247, my emphasis). When he states in the citation that the important correspondence with Barth and the difference from Bultmann lies in *spirituality* ("an authentic and profound sense of God"), his statement is seriously compromised. The first question is whether Bultmann's existential theology (although expressed in individualistic terms) is not also a revelation of a "profound sense of God" after all, and whether it can therefore also lay claim to "spirituality".

The key question, however, is whether Gutierrez takes into account at all the radical break between him and Barth regarding the way they reflect on God and his revelation ("revealed only in the historical context"). Thus, the real incompatibility is *not* between bourgeois individualism and spirituality, but between *spirituality and spirituality*.

In other words, in the light of the close relation between spirituality and methodology, the big shortcoming in Gutierrez's interpretation is the fact that he does not take the structure of Barth's thinking into consideration at all. In this regard, Van Niekerk points out that the tendency to indicate analogies between Barth's thinking and a practical context that was theorised beforehand can "prove" almost anything: "This is because a *methodological exposition* of Barth's theology is incontrovertibly necessary to the current debate ... What is needed is a *methodical inquiry* into the theological merits of *Church Dogmatics* as 'part of the work of human knowledge'" (Van Niekerk 1984:4,11; my emphasis).

Even a superficial comparison between Barth[9] and liberation theology reveals the fundamental methodological differences.

(a) Contrary to liberation theology, the "premise" of dogmatics is not the "experience at the bottom of history", but God's acting revelation in His Word,[10] namely Jesus Christ (incarnate Word), Scripture (written Word) and the proclamation of the church (proclaimed Word) (CD 1/1:88-124; Barth 1985:7, 13; Van Niekerk 1984:46, 50-51). Through this the fundamental epistemological difference between Barth and liberation theology is revealed. Whereas the latter derives knowledge of God from "effective liberation", Barth construes his theology on the fundamental principle "that God is knowable by God and by God alone" (Van Niekerk 1987:29). Because of the irreversible relation in which God stands with people, knowledge of God is therefore knowledge *by the grace of God* on the basis of His Self-knowledge (Van Niekerk 1987:23, 29).

(b) The context in which the dogmatics arises is not historical praxis, but the *church* as "the place, the community, charged with the object and the activity with which dogmatics is concerned – namely, the proclamation of the Gospel" (Barth 1985:9-10, see CD1/1:47-87; Van Niekerk 1984:36).

---

9   I am aware of shifts in Barth's thinking, but for the sake of the discussion I work with the CD, in which his methodology is explicated.

10   Actually it is more correct to say that the starting point is God Himself: "God Himself is He who is revealed as God" (Barth 1985:30).

(c) As in liberation theology, dogmatics (systematic theology) is for Barth also a *critical science*, but with the exception that the origin and context differ; there is for Barth – as opposed to the liberation theological "impact on praxis" – no *criterion* for dogmatics other than Scripture and (in a derivative sense) confession ("non-binding authority") (Barth 1985:13; 1933:12, 13).

(d) Contrary to liberation theologians, who assign a constitutive methodological position to the social sciences, Barth's concept of truth leaves no room for such a contribution: the truth of God in Christ is *the prima veritas* as well as the *ultima veritas* (Barth 1985:26) and the theological task is formulated in a such way that other sciences can be viewed only in the context of their relative importance in terms of theology (Van Niekerk 1984:77, 242; 1987:31).

It would be possible to continue along this vein, but I think that this simplified indication of a few differences is of such a fundamental methodological nature that liberation theology's appeal to Barth – even where they can find citations to support their position – is out of order in principle. The same words do not necessarily convey the same meaning and for Barth the methodological structure of liberation theology would be nothing more than extreme natural theology. The fact that liberation theology easily joins Barth in terms of its claim of the "orthopractical primate",[11] not only contradicts their own typification of his theology as "neo-orthodox", but also leaves the impression that theological partners are selected on the basis of *political* grounds (choice of socialism) rather than *theological-methodological* grounds (relationship between orthodoxy and orthopraxis).

2. CONCLUSION

This brings us to a summarising assessment of the methodological claim of liberation theology. An orthopractical primate on the basis of a renewal of the theological concept of truth should be welcomed. Indeed, this fact represents the main component of the paradigm shift that liberation theologians brought about within theology.

Yet it has been indicated that the way in which the orthopractical primate is created is not unproblematic. From a Reformed perspective in particular, orthopraxis as developed by liberation theology on dogmatic grounds cannot be accepted unconditionally. From a broader scientific-theoretical framework, orthopractical verification results in a narrowing of the criteria for systematic theology, and theology would benefit by maintaining orthopraxis only (and precisely!) in a dialectical relationship with the implied orthodoxy. Liberation theologians' appeal to Karl Barth furthermore indicates that the relationship between orthodoxy, orthopraxis and methodology is much more nuanced than is generally supposed.

---

11   The reason why liberation theology so easily identifies with Barth possibly has to do with the fact that both derive political directives from theology in a direct way, albeit from exactly opposite angles. Whereas liberation theology is concerned with theology (theory) in the world/politics (praxis) (thus, approaching theology from the context of the world), Barth is concerned with the world (creation) in theology (Christology). Both approaches are unacceptable: in the former too little weight is given to theology, while Barth in turn expects too much of theology. Compare Kuitert (1985:106-111) for a discussion of Barth in this regard.

In the light of the fact that the orthopractical primate is a *theoretical primate* and in any case dependent on a particular "doxa" for the "orthos", it can justly be asked whether liberation theology in its current form should not be regarded as a new form of late 20th-century orthodoxy. An on-going study of liberation theology is essential – precisely for the sake of its "orthodox" value within a universal context that calls for liberation – including a liberation from theological traditionalism.

BIBLIOGRAPHY

Alves, R. 1969. "Theology and the liberation of man". In Committee on Society, Development, and Peace (eds.), pp. 75-92.

Ana, J. 1976. "The influence of Bonhoeffer on the theology of liberation". *The Ecumenical Review* Vol. 22, No. 1, pp. 1-15.

Assmann, H. 1975. *Onderdrukking-Verzet: Een uitdaging aan de christenen*. Baarn: Ten Have.

Bakker, J.T. et al (eds.) 1973. *Septuagesimo anno: Theologische opstellen aangeboden aan Prof. Dr.G.C. Berkouwer*. Kampen: Kok.

Barth, K. 1933. *Theologische Extenz heute*. München: Kaiser.

Barth, K. 1975. *Church Dogmatics 1/1*. Edinburgh: T&T Clark.

Barth, K. 1985. *Dogmatics in outline*. London: SCM.

Bettscheider (Hrsg.) 1974. *Theologie und Befreiung*. Bonn: Steyler.

Boff, C. 1983. *Theologie und Praxis. Die Erkenntnistheoretischen Grundlagen der Theologie der Befreiung*. München: Kaiser.

Boff, L. 1977. "Theologie der Befreiung – die hermeneutische Voraussetzung". In C. Modehn, K. Rahner & H. Zwiefelhofer (Hg.), pp. 46-61.

Boff, L. 1978a. *Erfahrung van Gnade: Entwurf einer Gnadenlehre*. Düsseldorf: Patmos.

Boff, L. 1978b. *Jesus Christ Liberator: A critical Christology for our time*. New York: Orbis.

Brown, R.M. 1976. "A preface and a conclusion". In Torres & Eagleson (eds.) *Theology in the Americas*. New York: Orbis.

Committee on Society, Development, and Peace (eds.) 1969. *In search of a theology of development*. Cartigny: SODEPAX Conference.

Couch, B.M. 1978. "New visions of the church in Latin America: A Protestant view". In Torres & Fabella (eds.), pp. 193-226.

Frieling, R. 1972. "Die lateinamerikanische Theologie der Befreiung". *Materialdienst des Konfessionskundlichen Instituts* Vol. 23, No. 2, pp. 26-35.

Gibellini, R (ed.) 1979. *Frontiers of theology in Latin America*. New York: Orbis.

Girardi, G. 1974. "Theologie der Befreiung". In Bettscheider (Hrsg.) *Theologie und Befreiung*. Bonn: Steyler, pp. 12-38.

Gutierrez, G. 1974. "Bevrijdingsbewegingen en theologie". *Concilium* Vol. 10, No. 3, pp. 122-134.

Gutierrez, G. 1975. "Faith as freedom. Solidarity with the alienated and confidence in the future". *Horizons* Vol. 2, pp. 25-61.

Gutierrez, G. 1978. "Two theological perspectives: liberation theology and progressivist theology". in Torres & Fabella (eds.), pp. 227-255.

Gutierrez, G. 1983. *A theology of liberation: History, politics and salvation*. London: SCM.

Hennely, A. 1977. "Theological method: The southern exposure". *Theological Studies* Vol. 38, pp. 709-735.

Kuitert, H.M. 1985. *Alles is politiek, maar politiek is niet alles: Een theologisch perspectief op geloof en politiek*. Baarn: Ten Have.

Metz, J.B. 1984. *Glaube in Geschichte und Gesellschaft: Studien zu einer praktischen Fundamentaltheologie*. Mainz: Matthias Grünewald.

Miguez-Bonino, J. 1976. *Christians and Marxists: The mutual challenge to revolution*. Grand Rapids: Eerdmans.

Modehn, C, Rahner, K & Zwiefelhofer, H. (eds.) 1977. *Befreiende Theologie. Der Beitrag Lateinamerikas zur Theologie der Gegenwart*. Stuttgart: Kohlhammer.

Rossouw, H.W. 1973. "Doksologie, ortodoksie en ekumene". In J.T. Bakker et al (eds.), pp. 203-212.

Schillebeeckx, E. 1969. "Het 'rechte geloof', zijn onzekerheden en zijn crieteria". *Tijdschrift voor theologie* Vol. 9, pp. 12-149.

Schillebeeckx, E 1977. *Christus und die Christen*. Freiburg: Herder.

Segundo, J.L. 1976. "Statement by JL Segundo". In Torres & Eagelson (eds.), pp. 280-283.

Segundo, J.L. 1977. *The liberation of theology*. Dublin: Gill and Macmillan.

Segundo, J.L. 1979. "Capitalism versus socialism: crux theologica". In Gibellini (ed.), pp. 240-259.

Sobrino, J. 1977. "Theologisch Erkennen in der europäischen und der lateinamerikanischer Theologie". In C. Modehn, K. Rahner & H. Zwiefelhofer (Hrsg.), pp. 123-143

Sobrino, J. 1985. *The true church and the poor*. London: SCM.

Torres, S. & J. Eagleson, J. (eds.) 1976. *Theology in the Americas*. New York: Orbis.

Torres, S. & Eagleson, J. (eds). 1981. *The challenge of the basic Christian communities*. New York: Orbis.

Torres, S. & Fabella, V. (eds.) 1978. *The emergent gospel*. New York: Orbis.

Van den Oudenrijn, F. 1972. *Kritische Theologie als Kritik der Theologie: Theorie und Praxis bei Karl Marx – Herausforderung der Theologie*. München: Kaiser.

Van Huysteen, W. 1986. *Teologie as kritiese geloofsverantwoording: Teorievorming in die sistematiese teologie*. Pretoria: RGN.

Van Niekerk, E. 1984. *Methodological aspects in Karl Barth's Church Dogmatics*. Pretoria: Unisa.

Van Niekerk, E 1987. "Methodological aspects in Karl Barth's Church Dogmatics". *Theologia Evangelica* Vol. XX1, pp. 22-36.

Vidales, R. 1974. "Kroniek van enkele recente latijnsamerikaanse publicaties over de theologie van de bevrijding". *Concilium* Vol. 10, No. 6, pp. 124-134.

Vidales, R. 1979. "Methodological issues in liberation theology". In Gibellini (ed.), pp. 34-57.

Zwiefelhofer, H. 1976. "Theologie der Befreiung – Versuch einer 'Zwischenbalanz'". *Orientierung* Vol. 40, No. 7, pp. 76-80.

2.7 THE POOR AS HERMENEUTICAL SUBJECTS IN LIBERATION THEOLOGY[1]

The most suitable approach to a discussion of the hermeneutics of Liberation Theology is to view to view such hermeneutics as fundamentally part of the distinctive theological methodology developed by liberation theologians. To deal with the poor as hermeneutical subject in Liberation Theology, the subject is developed in four parts.

In the first part the intimate relation between methodology and hermeneutics is defended in the light of the fact that the *locus theologicus* constitutes the hermeneutical subject. The methodological starting point of Liberation Theology and the hermeneutical point of departure (the faith of the poor) thus coincide.

The second part deals with two implications of the poor as hermeneutical subject, namely the reinterpretation of presuppositions in view of the inevitable ideological nature of faith, and the relative position of Scripture with regard to the status of socio-analysis as alternative "text".

The third part deals with the relation between the canonical text and the present context as basis for liberation theologians' rereading of Scripture in the light of the experience of poor people.

To conclude, a few critical questions are enumerated in the fourth part, dealing, *inter alia*, with the revelatory status of "the signs of the time" and the methodological position of Scripture in Liberation Theology.

New Testament professor: You would not find the slightest reason in the New Testament for what is practised as Theology of Liberation.

Student: Professor, do you not think that there are more important issues to discuss during the visit of the US president than NATO?

Professor: But why? The unity of NATO is definitely threatened.

Student: And the systematic exploitation of the Third World? Now it is clear to me why nothing is said in the New Testament about the Theology of Liberation.

Professor (astonished): What, then, is the relation?

Student: Hermeneutics, professor, pure hermeneutics (my free translation and adaptation from Assmann 1969:236).

Since the 1960s a current of so-called "Liberation Theologies" has attracted a fair amount of attention on the theological scene. I believe that the most fruitful approach

---

1 This paper was read at the second annual conference of the Department of Biblical Studies, University of Venda, 7 October 1985. It was later published in *Scriptura* 17 (1986), pp. 15-34.

to these theologies is to discern them within the oppression-liberation binary and draw their respective characters from the nature of the oppression in question: Black Theology intends to liberate from racism, Feminist Theology liberates from sexism, and African and Asian Theologies are struggling with cultural, class and racist oppression.

For the sake of this essay attention is focused on Latin American Liberation Theology for the obvious reason that a socio-economic class distinction is of fundamental importance for these theologians' comprehension of the Latin American situation. In no other liberation theology does the oppression-liberation theme emphasise the rich-poor contrast as is the case in this theology. And our concern will be to look at some of the hermeneutical consequences of such a theology.

The student of hermeneutics is immediately tempted to shed light on the hermeneutics of Liberation Theology by means of a (contrasting) comparison to major approaches in European Theology.[2] One could, for example, refer to Rudolf Bultmann as contrasting partner, who draws on the existentialist philosophy of Martin Heidegger to mediate hermeneutics on the way to a better self-understanding. Liberation Theology draws on the historical-materialistic philosophy of Karl Marx to mediate hermeneutics on the way to structural change. This approach does display the sound educational principle of moving from the known to the unknown and makes for exciting reading. But it would precisely be the approach so strongly rejected by liberation theologians themselves, namely to be interpreted from a Eurocentric point of view.

This comparative approach lies implicit in the apologetic parts of Liberation Theology, and "European" terms like presuppositions, surplus meaning and merging of horizons are in fact taken over and adapted. To embark on a discussion of the hermeneutics of Liberation Theology by employing these concepts as starting points would, however, only render "secondary" comprehension. *The soundest approach to a responsible discussion of the hermeneutics of Liberation Theology is to view the latter as fundamentally part of the distinctive theological methodology of Liberation Theology.*

This essay will deal with the subject along the following lines: in the first part the intimate relation between methodology and hermeneutics is defended in the light of the fact that the *locus theologicus* constitutes the hermeneutical subject. The second part deals with two implications of this: the reinterpretation of presuppositions in view of the inevitably ideological nature of faith and the relative position of Scripture with regard to the status of socio-analysis. The third part deals with the relation between the canonical text and the present context, and in the last part some critical questions which could serve as basis for further discussion are raised.

1. RELATION BETWEEN METHODOLOGY AND HERMENEUTICS

Since its formulation Liberation Theology has emphasised that it views theology as a "critical reflection on Christian praxis in the light of the Word" (Gutierrez 1974:13).[3]

---

2   John Goldingay (1983:133-137), for example, starts his article with the differences between traditional scholarship and the approach of LT.
3   See related definitions in his articles (1975:37; 1976:67).

This has led to a distinctive methodological approach which may be simplified in the way indicated below.[4]

Theology starts with a thorough analysis of the de facto reality and assigns an important place to the social sciences in this regard. This is the socio-analytical mediation of theology. Secondly, the analysed reality is interpreted in the light of faith using Scripture and tradition. This constitutes the hermeneutical mediation of theology. Thirdly, pastoral actions are derived from a combination of the first two procedures in order to modify reality to correspond more closely to the principles of God's Kingdom. Numerous very interesting dogmatic implications follows from this description of theology, but only those relevant to the topic are mentioned here.

The *locus theologicus* is not represented by the desks of academic theologians, but refers to the socio-historical praxis of Christians. It is their faith that seeks understanding (*fides quaerens intellectum*). But in view of the situation analysis whereby Latin America's position of dependence and exploitation is explicated,[5] the point of departure is specifically "the life of faith on the underside of history" (Gutierrez 1983:90), resulting in a theology "springing up out of the poverty, the oppression, the heartrending conditions under which the great majority of Latin Americans live".[6] The authenticity of this theology is thus closely related to the degree in which it succeeds in being a theology of the poor (and not merely for the poor). Theology is a reflection of the poor upon their faith (Gutierrez 1983:90-91). And a clear commitment to the poor is nothing less than a methodological presupposition: "From the start liberation theology has maintained that active commitment to liberation comes first and theology develops from it" (Gutierrez 1978:247). To formulate the same point in slightly different terms, one could say that Liberation Theology starts with praxis, but is not an indiscriminate praxis: "It is not enough to know that praxis must precede reflection, we must realise that the historical subject of the praxis is the poor" (Gutierrez 1978:247).[7]

The very important question that follows is whether methodology and hermeneutics are related closely enough to justify an identification of the theological and hermeneutical *subjects*. The definitions of theology as critical reflection in the light of faith, and of hermeneutic mediation as the relation between Liberation Theology and the traditional Christian sources, have already pointed to the methodological importance of hermeneutics. But one could even transcend this fact and state that liberation theologians come very close to an *identification* of theology and

---

4   This summary is present in almost every work by liberation theologians. See as examples the whole structure of the excellent work *Theologie und Praxis*, by Clodovis Boss (1983) and the book by the Boff-brothers (Clodovis and Leonardo) (1984:27). The documents of bishop-conferences like Medillin and Puebla are structured in the same way.

5   Articles by leading Latin American social scientists on dependence are to be found in Henry Bernstein (1973).

6   R.M. Brown in the preface to Torres and Fabella (1978:2). See also his discussion (in Torres and Fabella 1978:60-62) where he states: "Liberation theology has a different starting point. Its starting point is the poor. ... The marginalized, the poor, comprise the great majority of the human family. And it is with them that theology must start; not with theories, not with views from above, but with 'the view from below'".

7   See also Manfred Hoffmann (1978:126), who states: "Die Praxis ist nicht irgendeine unbestimmte Praxis. ... Der Andere/Arme steht in der Mitte der Befreiungspraxis. Es geht um de Praxis des Armen und für den Armen".

hermeneutics, as also happens in the works of the European theologians Gerhard Ebeling and Ernst Fuchs (Stuhlmacher 1972:192-196).

The best example of this is *The Liberation of Theology* by J.L. Segundo. This book is hailed for its methodological insights, but see how Segundo formulates his intention: "In this book I am going to try and show that an approach which attempts to relate past and present in dealing with the word of God has to have its own special methodology. I shall give this methodology a pretentious name and call it the hermeneutical circle" (Segundo 1977:8). Methodology as such is thus called a hermeneutical circle. This is confirmed by the conclusion of Manzanera: "Das eigentümliche dieser Theologie besteht darin, ... dass die Hermeneutik der Befreiung zur Hermeneutik *der Theologie selbst* wird" (1975:52). This is possible because of the praxis-theory-praxis structure of Liberation Theology, that is, the dynamic, dialectical relation between praxis (starting point) and theory (Segundo 1977:8).

Segundo, however, does refer to the hermeneutical circle in theology[8] and thus falls short of an identification between hermeneutics and theology, which would in any case make a hermeneutic *mediation* of theology impossible. But there is, I believe, a strong enough basis for an identification of the theological and hermeneutical subjects, namely the poor. "Solidarity with the poor, commitment to the liberation of the exploited classes ... led *to a re-reading of the gospel*" (Gutierrez 1975:42, my emphasis). But this re-reading in terms of the poor (hermeneutics) relies on an analysis of the socio-historical situation of the poor (methodology).

The methodological starting point of theology in general (analysis of the context in view of the poor on the underside of history) thus *coincides* and has a profound significance for the hermeneutics of Liberation Theology.

2. TWO IMPLICATIONS OF THE POOR AS HERMENEUTICAL SUBJECT

2.1. The first implication of the poor as methodological (i.e. theological) subject of Liberation Theology is that the generally accepted notion of inevitable presupposition (so eloquently developed by Bultmann 1957:145ff) is taken over but expounded with far greater politico-ideological awareness.

It is impossible, says Beatriz Couch (1976:304), to approach Scripture with an "original naiveté" as if a disengagement from cultural, philosophical and ethical presuppositions could take place in a "pure" application of Scripture to reality. This is confirmed by Leonardo Boff: "We do not want to be naive from the hermeneutic standpoint. Our question (referring to the meaning of Christ in an oppressive situation) is prompted by a very clear and well defined interest" (1979:102).

The concept of ideology as used in this context is not intended in the pejorative sense (a set of ideas held not for its inherent truth, but for the interests it legitimises), but as a reference to "the system of goals and means that serves as the necessary backdrop for any human option or line of action" (Segundo 1977:102).[9] And the fact that methodology starts with an analysis of reality (mostly with a critical recourse to

---

8 Compare Segundo's definition of the hermeneutical circle (1977:8) with the first two points of the simplified methodology above.
9 See his exposition of the intricate relation between faith and ideology (1977:102ff).

Marxist categories), enables Liberation Theology to emphasise the political character of all theologies, even of those who do not think in political terms.

But if the methodological starting point is also the starting point of the hermeneutical circle, it follows that a critique of theology becomes constitutive of a *hermeneutics of suspicion*. "A hermeneutical circle in theology always presupposes a profound human commitment, a partiality that is consciously accepted – not on the basis of theological criteria, of course, but on the basis of human criteria" (Segundo 1977:9).[10] In Latin America this profound commitment is the preferential option for the liberation of the poor and every theology (and resultant hermeneutic) is judged in the light of the oppression-liberation criterion. It is impossible to avoid ideologies and presuppositions, but liberation theologians believe that in the serious situation of Latin America one bias is not as appropriate as another. The question is whose interests theology serves (Wells and Baum 1984:81-87), and these interests are revealed by a hermeneutics that is suspicious of any commitment (and resultant exegesis) which does not take the poor as starting point.

The ideological suspicion which revealed the Latin American situation as one of oppression and dependence (and *not* underdevelopment) leads to a hermeneutical suspicion where Scripture is re-read in the light of the option for the poor. In other words: "From its point of departure in the anguish of the poor of the world, the whole biblical message emerges as a proclamation of liberation" (Boff and Boff 1984:26). Liberation becomes the semantic axis for a rereading of Scripture. It is not my purpose to give an account of the exegetical work done by liberation theologians,[11] but it is important to discuss *the theological motives for the poor as hermeneutical subject*.

2.1.1. The first motive is directly related to God's *revelation* in Jesus Christ. The kenosis of Christ reveals a "lesser God" (Sobrino 1985:148) in a twofold sense: not only did Christ become man, He became one of the poor and lived in solidarity with the marginalised. Thus, the conception of Karl Rahner that anyone seeking God has already found Him must be qualified: the privileged locus for an experience of God is the poor. "The question is not whether someone is seeking God or not, but whether he is seeking Him where God himself said he is" (Sobrino 1985:149). A presupposition for a liberative hermeneutic is a radical conversion to God in Christ, that is, a commitment to the oppressed: "gloria Dei, homo vivens" becomes "gloria Dei, *pauper vivens*" (Sobrino 1985:152).

2.1.2. A second motivation is found in *ecclesiology*.[12] The life of faith on the underside of history is the source of Liberation Theology, and this is where the church of the poor is constituted. This church is more than a theologically democratised "people of God"; it is more than a church that shows some compassion for the poor: it is a church of and from the poor.

---

10   See Segundo (1977:34), where he refers to WH van der Pol, who emphasises the a priori character of any point of departure.
11   The works of J.S. Croatto and J.P. Miranda are the best examples of excellent exegetical work.
12   For the important ecclesiological contribution of Latin America in this regard, any of the major theologies may be consulted. Anthologies which give an overview are *Concilium* 11 (1975) and Torres and Eagleson (1981). I draw mainly on the insights of the recent book by Jon Sobrino (1985).

"The Church of the poor is a Church the social and historical basis of which is to be found amongst the poor. ... It is these poor, therefore, that are said to constitute the very basis of the Church" (Sobrino 1985:135). The important point for our purpose is not merely to understand the nature of the church, but to grasp the relation between the members of this church and hermeneutics. And Sobrino cannot be clearer when he states: "The poor within this church become the *hermeneutical principle* for a primary concrete expression of important Christian concepts and realities" (Sobrino 1985:137)[13]. This leads to a total reformulation of all the important theological loci and, liberation theologians believe, to a new view on the task of the theologian (C. Boff 1981:108-132): the reading of books and deduction of new theological principles and mere intellectual insights are replaced by the task of listening to the poor in the light of their epistemologically privileged position to inquire about the message of God.

2.1.3. A third motive for the partiality in hermeneutics relates to Liberation Theology's *view of Scripture* itself, which will be discussed in greater detail below. What is important is the point of departure that Scripture as documentation of God's historical revelation is ideological, and therefore partial, in at least two respects: it is *partial experience* of God in a specific situation by a specific individual/group *and a partial written representation*. The experiential event is interpretatively and selectively documented (Croatto 1983:150) and although the canon (as part of the hermeneutical process) has paradigmatic value, the notion of a universal God who reveals Himself to a universal man must be rejected as a residue of Greek thought (Segundo 1977:33). The profound experience of liberation which underlies the text formation and traditions of Israel asked to be creatively reinterpreted in a new situation from an inevitably partial point of view, namely the poor in the Latin American context. This partiality has always been implicit in hermeneutics and is only criticised because it challenges the powerful and reveals the oppressive nature of traditional theology. "Partiality is justified because we must find, and designate as the word of God, that part of divine revelations which today, in the light of our concrete historical situation, is most useful for the liberation to which God summons us" (Segundo 1977:33). This objective *nature* of Scripture is complemented by the *contents* of Scripture to legitimise the preferential position of the poor. "Der Arme ist der bibelhermeneutische Ort für die Botschaft der Befreiung ... Sie (die Bibel) ist am richtigen Ort – bei sich selbst – wenn sie am Ort des Armen ist und von Armen her gelesen wird" (Hoffmann 1978:52).

2.2. Let us turn very briefly to the second implication of the poor as methodological and hermeneutical subject: the relative position of Scripture in view of a situation analysis which leads to a hermeneutics of reality or a hermeneutics of history.

Because they view theology as theo-praxis, liberation theologians understand the call to go "back to the sources" not only in the light Scriptures and tradition but, in line with their inductive methodology, as including the socio-analytical "text of

---

13 Cf. the remark of Croatto: "Its (the people's) reading of the Bible is mediated by that of specialists (the theologians, the biblicist) or else by that of the powerful (church authority). And yet, whenever the people take up this oft-forbidden book, it discovers a wealth of unsuspected possibilities. This is what occurs in the process of liberation ... in which the people or community is the agent of both a history and a reading of the biblical kerygma" (1983:153).

reality" (Boff and Boff 1984:9).[14] Liberation Theology has matured considerably since Rual Vidales wrote (1979:48): "Though still in its initial stages, liberation theology is already breaking new ground in hermeneutics. It is obvious that we need a different hermeneutic key, one which will enable us to deal with other 'texts'...", which include history as complementary to the traditional Bible. Because both Scripture and tradition must always be historically mediated (thus there is no "direct" recourse to them), a reading of the signs of the times, as word of God to us today, is just as important as an understanding of the "word" as canon and tradition, and the "Word" who became flesh (De Valle 1979:85). "God's summons to us – God's word today – arises out of communal analysis of historical data and historical happenings as praxis" (Assmann 1979:134).

Parallel to what has been said, the *relative* value of Scripture lies in the fact that it reveals no eternal unhistorical truths which can be directly applied to a new situation. Forms of praxis in the times of Scripture are relative to forms of praxis today. The latter can only by discerned in terms of a socio-analytical "reading". But this relativisation of Scripture must not be rejected outright as a diminishing of the value of Scripture in hermeneutics.

Firstly, as Scripture bears a contextual message, it asks to be re-contextualised *precisely to honour its message* (Croatto 1983:164). To merely repeat the culturally conditioned language of Scripture would be hermeneutically naive and would doom Scripture to silence. To say the *same*, something *different* must be said. Thus the false security of an "absolute and infallible Word of God" must be unmasked in the light of radical *historical* hermeneutics.

Secondly, Scripture reports the foundational and paradigmatic event which serves as normative basis for the interpretation of the present situation. Liberation Theology is more than a theologised sociology – its Christian character is guaranteed by the fact that reflection on praxis occurs in *the light of the Word*. Liberation theologians thus believe that the relative position of Scripture does not lead to relativism, because the normativity of the canon serves as a kind of objective control, so that the text ultimately serves as conditioning factor in exegesis. How this happens will be clarified in the section that follows, where I will deal with the text-context relation.

3. THE RELATION BETWEEN TEXT AND CONTEXT

Some liberation theologians present the relation between Scripture and context in an almost fundamentalist way: the Bible is taken literally and a direct correspondence between Latin America and the reported event is sought. God then only speaks in so far as an archetypal event coincides with a present reality.[15] This is, however, strongly

---

14 See Hugo Assmann (1969:232-233), who emphasises the structural analysis of reality ("Strukturanalyse der Wirklichkeit") as a source of theo-praxis. Compare also Miquez-Bonino (1975:93), who stresses the indispensable role of socio-analysis as part of hermeneutics: "We are not concerned with establishing through deduction the consequences of conceptual truths, but with analysing a historical praxis which claims to be Christian".

15 See L. Boff's article in Gibellini (1979:103), where he works implicitly with a correspondence model: "That world (in which Christ lived) was strikingly similar to our own Latin world; it was a world suffering from oppression both from within

criticised by the majority of Latin American scholars. Míquez-Bonino describes such an effort of direct correspondence as a dangerous short cut and definitely not as the purpose of socio-analysis (1975:102). The clearest example of an alternative model is that of Clodovis Boff in *Theologie und Praxis* (1983). A correspondence of concepts where "oppressed Hebrews" and "the exodus from Egypt" are seen as direct parallels of the "oppressed Latin Americans" and "liberation from dependence" leads to a kind of hermeneutical positivism or copying,[16] where the uniqueness of the original context is levelled down and the present political concern becomes the exegetical point from which the text is read.

What should happen, says C. Boff, is not a correspondence of *concepts* or situations, but a correspondence of *relations* ("Korrespondenz der Relationen") (1983:241-249). The Bible must be viewed as a hermeneutical habitus where a certain *relation* exists between context and message. Not the "what" of the context/message is important, but the "how" of their reciprocal *relation*. It is the relation that is hermeneutically of vital importance for a creative reading of Scripture in a new situation.

The relation between text and context as expounded by liberation theologians may be summarised in the following three points.

3.1. Methodologically speaking, the relation between praxis and theory is translated in hermeneutical terms and leads to a reformulation of the hermeneutical circle. As stated above, the point of departure is the praxis of the poor, which is then interpreted in the light of the Word in order to lead to pastoral action and a transformation of the historical praxis. But this is precisely what is meant by the hermeneutical circle: "It is the continuing change in our interpretation of the Bible which is dictated by the continuing changes in our interpretation of the present-day reality ... And the circular nature of this interpretation stems from the fact that each new reality obliges us to interpret the word of God afresh, to change reality accordingly, and then go back and reinterpret the word of God again, and so on" (Segundo 1977:8).

This has lead liberation theologians to change the concept of the hermeneutical *circle* to one of hermeneutical *circulation*:[17] a circle conveys a "closed" and "finished" image whilst the open dialectics of praxis-theory-praxis[18] is expressed by *circulation*. The implication for hermeneutics is profound: as a hermeneutics of engagement a mere rereading of Scripture does not suffice. In the final analysis *exegesis of the Word* takes place in the *transforming actions of real life* (Gutierrez 1975:47).[19] A reading of the poor

---

and without".

16 C. Boff (1983:238): "Nach dem Modell der Korrespondenz der Begriffe werden die Begriffe, die man benutzt, dadurch miteinander verglichen, dass man sie parallel setzt. Man braucht dann nur noch den Sinn des ersten Bruchs auf den Zweiten zu übertragen – eine Art *hermeneutischer Kopie*".

17 The "hermeneutical circle" stems from Martin Heidegger who developed this concept in his existentialist ontology, whereas Liberation Theology refers to the French theologian Georges Casalis, for its use of "hermeneutical circulation" (I could find no reference to the original of the latter author.)

18 There is no room to explicate the terms "theory" and "praxis". Strictly speaking, "praxis" refers to the dialectical process *as a whole*, and must not be equated with "practice". See J.C. Scannone (1977:77-96) for a good overview.

19 See also L. Boff (1979:100-103), where the sole criterion for hermeneutics becomes its efficacy in the present situation.

compels action for and by the poor. "Das Neulesen, die 'Relectura' der Schrift aus der Perspektive des Armen, führt zu einer Re-aktualisierung des Wortes Gottes ... Aus der Perspektive der Armen müssen daher *das Neulesen der Bibel und das Neuschaffen der Praxis* erfolgen" (Hoffmann 1978:144-145, my emphasis). Thus, *formally* speaking, the dialectical hermeneutical circulation guarantees the relation between text (present situation), text (rereading of canon) and text (transformed situation).

3.2. A second factor in the relation between text and context is Liberation Theology's view of the canonical text itself. Far from rejecting the critical methods of exegesis, the liberation theologians emphasise the fact "theological hermeneutics cannot forgo the effort to gain access to the text by means of critical instruments which the sciences of interpretation have created" (Míquez-Bonino 1975:101-102). This is imperative in determining the "context-backward" of the text, but it is very easy to be confined to all sorts of questions related to the pre-canonical text, or to view the text as a deposit of meaning coinciding with the intentions of the author or final redactor.[20]

It is of the utmost importance to view the text as a *reservoir* of meaning with a "context-forward" that opens a world of meanings by virtue of the surplus of meaning which stems from the potentiated polysemy of every text. This is explained by Croatto in terms of the well-known transmitter-receiver and common context analogy: as soon as the text appears in *written* form "the meaning-closure imposed by the transmitter is converted into an openness. The narrator is now the text itself" (Croatto 1983:144). This constitutes the openness of the text and is the basis for a rereading in a new context as is evident from Scripture itself: the exodus event is reinterpreted in different contexts and at different stages of the history of Israel; the resurrection of Christ becomes much more than a mere historic event in its theological reinterpretation. And the local or dated character of the original text is not an impediment in this regard, but a *necessity* without which no reinterpretation would be possible. "Der Text der Christlichen Schrift ist voll von möglichen Bedeutungen, die durch den Kontakt mit der historischen Aktualität ans Licht kommen" (C. Boff 1983:235).[21]

This forms the basis for Liberation Theology to state unequivocally that to be true to the *text itself* a rereading from the present context (the poor in Latin America) is not only possible, but necessary. Rereading is thus not a repetition of meaning but *creative production of meaning* in a new context (Croatto 1983:147).[22] And this synthetic productive hermeneutical act where the merging of horizons takes place (Gadamer's "Horizontverschmelzung") ensures the relation between text and context.

Is any possible ingenuity now permissible? The answer is an emphatic no. The polysemy of the text is delimited by the text itself – that is precisely the value of historical exegesis. "One cannot make the text say something. It says what it permits itself to say" (Croatto 1983:165). The penetration of the original historicity is a guarantee that certain parameters are respected. The other side of the coin is equally

---

20 Croatto calls this the trap of exegetical historicism (1983:145). Of all the critical methods it is only redaction criticism that takes the final form of the text as well as the theological intent of the author into account.
21 The importance of the present situation is strongly defended by Boff: "Die gegenwart is nicht nur das, was man liest, sondern auch das *wodurch* man liest. Dies ist die Voraussetzung für die Möglichkeit jeder Lektüre und nicht ihre Hindernis" (1983: 234, my emphasis).
22 According to him every exegesis *must* be a form of *eisegesis*!

important: a rational analysis of the present situation serves as hermeneutical control. Not every interpretation of the Latin American context is equally illuminating, and not every locus is equally suitable for hermeneutics. It is on this basis that Liberation Theology defends the hermeneutics of the poor.

3.3. Thirdly, the relation between the two texts is also seen in the light of the revelation of the triune God: God's continuous revelation in Christ and the Spirit. The canon in its final form is the codex of the paradigmatic message about God's revelation and serves in tradition as a *norma normata normans* and (more precisely) as a *norma normans ut normata* (C. Boff 1983:233). The epiphany of God as recorded in Scripture is the paradigmatic reading of an *unfinished salvation history* (Croatto 1983:162-163).

In accordance with post-Vatican II theology, Liberation Theology accentuates the radical historical character of God's revelation with the abolishing of any dualism between salvation history and secular history.[23] This implies that God's revelation in Christ and the Spirit is complemented by his revelation in the socio-economic realities of Latin America. Through faith, the theological element of the apparent secular events must be discerned: "In these realities, considered to be secular, there is a real but hidden, theological element. Only faith enables one to see this element present within the economic, the political and the educational. It is the task of Christian reflection to unveil and extract this hidden theological element" (C. Boff 1983:17). The struggle for liberation has revelatory power: God liberates when man acts on behalf of the poor: temporal progress is the coming of the Kingdom.

It is this revelatory relation between text and context that serves as basis for the productive hermeneutical act by the present reader. And this relation has a specific Christological (Vidales 1979:50) character: "The hermeneutical synthesis is not so much a datum as a person: Jesus Christ. More specifically, here it is Christ in the person of our lowliest human beings".

Just as Christ's incarnation is the mediation between God and man, He is, hermeneutically spoken, the axis of the relation between God's word and the human word. In communion with the *nous Christou* (1 Cor 2:16), a spiritual insight is gained. The Spirit of God was given precisely to reveal the truth of Christ's work, and the recognition of God in the present situation is a charismatic gift, the *diakrisis pneumaton* (1 Cor 12:10). The spirit makes the present events comprehensible "as obviously belonging to the same divine revelation" (Segundo 1977:120). Pneumatologically the original text and the present "text" are embedded in the same epiphanic history. Hermeneutics, then, is nothing other than the discernment of God's revelatory presence in the liberation struggle of the poor in Latin America.

4. CRITICAL QUESTIONS

Some concluding critical questions must be raised in the light of the exciting hermeneutical challenge posed by Liberation Theology. These are directed to evoke a response and do not pretend to be full-fledged criticism.

---

23 One could, for example, summarize Gutierrez's whole theology as anti-dualistic. See Part IV of *A theology of liberation* (1974).

1. Are all hermeneutical differences ultimately of a *political* nature? If so, what reconciliatory power does Scripture have in a deeply divided situation?

2. If Scripture is methodologically relegated to "second position", does hermeneutics determine praxis or does praxis determine hermeneutics? (Or both?)

3. Is commitment to the poor primarily a political commitment based on rational analysis of the situation, or is it the result of Scriptural studies?

4. The "signs of the time" have revelatory status. By which criteria are two conflicting "revelations" in the same society judged?

5. Is there a *formal* difference between reading Scripture from the perspective of "justification by faith alone" and a reading in terms of "the liberation of the poor"?

6. The relevance of these questions to our present situation in South Africa is abundantly evident. Would it be an exaggeration to state that the reconciliation of Christians and a peaceful future are ultimately a question of hermeneutics?

BIBLIOGRAPHY

Anderson, G.H. & Stransky, T.F. (eds.) 1976. *Mission trends Vol. 3*. Grand Rapids Eerdmans.

Assmann, H. 1969. "Die situation der unterentwickelt gehaltenen Länder als Ort einer Theologie der Revolution". In E. Feil & R. Weth (eds.), pp. 218-248.

Assmann, H. 1979. "The power of Christ in history". In Gibellini (ed.), pp. 133-150.

Bernstein, H. (ed.). 1973. *Underdevelopment and development: the Third Word today*. University of Texas: Penguin.

Boff, C. 1981. "Gegen die Knechtschaft des retionalen Wissens". In H. Goldstein (ed). *Befreidungstelogie als Herausfordering*. Düsseldorf: Patmos Verlag, pp. 108-138.

Boff, C. 1983. *Theologie und Praxis*. München: Kaiser.

Boff, L. 1979. "Christ's liberation via oppression". In Gibellini (ed.), pp. 100-131.

Boff, L. & Boff, C. 1984. *Salvation and liberation*. New York: Orbis.

Brown, 1978. "Preface". In Torres and Fabella (eds.), pp. 1-9.

Bultmann, R. 1957. "Is exegesis without presuppositions possible?" In S.M. Ogden (ed.), pp. 145-153.

Couch, B. 1976. "Statement". In S. Torres & J. Eagleson (eds.), pp. 304ff.

Croatto, S. 1983. "Biblical hermeneutics in the theologies of liberation". In S. Torres & V. Fabella (eds.), pp. 140-167.

De Valle, L. 1979. "Towards a theological outlook starting from concrete events". In Gibellini (ed.), pp. 79-99.

Feil, E. & R. Weth, R (eds.) 1969. *Diskussion zur "Theologie der Revolution"*. München: Kaiser.

Gibellini, R. (ed.) 1979. *Frontiers of theology in Latin America*. New York: Orbis.

Goldingay, J. 1983. "The hermeneutics of liberation theology". *Horizons in biblical theology* Vol. 5, pp. 133-161.

Goldstein, H. (ed). 1981. *Befreidungstelogie als Herausfordering*. Düsseldorf: Patmos Verlag.

Gutierrez, G. 1974. *A theology of liberation*. London: SCM.

Gutierrez, G. 1975. "Faith as freedom solidarity with the alienated and confidence in the future". *Horizons in biblical theology* Vol. 2, pp. 25-61.

Gutierrez, G. 1976. "The hope of liberation". In G.H. Anderson & T.F. Stransky (eds.), pp. 64-69.

Gutierrez, G. 1978. "Two theological perspectives: liberation theology and progressivist theology". In S. Torres & V. Fabella (eds.), pp. 227-255.

Gutierrez, G. 1983. *The power of the poor in history*. London: SCM.

Hoffmann, M. 1978. *Identifikation mit dem Anderen*. Lund: Berlings.

Manzanera, M. 1975. "Die Theologie der Befreiung in Latinamerika und ihre Hermeneutik". *Theologische Akademie* Vol. xii, pp. 52-78.

Miguez-Bonino, J. 1975. *Doing theology in a revolutionary situation*. Philadelphia: Fortress.

Modehn, C, Rahner, K & Zwiefelhofer, H. (eds.) 1977. *Befreiende Theologie. Der Beitrag Lateinamerikas zur Theologie der Gegenwart*. Stuttgart: Kohlhammer.

Ogden, S.M. (ed.) 1957. *Existence and faith*. London: SCM.

Segundo, J.L. 1977. *The liberation of theology*. Dublin: Gill & Macmillan.

Scannone, J.C. 1977. "Das Theorie-Praxis-Verhältnis in der Theologie der Befreiung". In Modehn, C, Rahner, K & Zwiefelhofer, H. (eds.) (eds.), pp. 77-96.

Sobrino, J. 1985. *The true Church and the poor*. London: SCM.

Stuhlmacher, P. 1979. *Vom Verstehen des neuen Testaments*. Gottingen: VandenHoeck & Ruprecht.

Torres, S. & J. Eagleson, J. (eds.) 1976. *Theology in the Americas*. New York: Orbis.

Torres, S. & Eagleson, J. (eds). 1981. *The challenge of the basic Christian communities*. New York: Orbis.

Torres, S. & Fabella, V. (eds.) 1978. *The emergent gospel*. New York: Orbis.

Torres, S. & Fabella, V. (eds.) 1983. *Irruption of the Third World*. New York: Orbis.

Vidales, R. 1979. "Methodological issues in liberation theology". In Gibellini (ed.), pp. 34-57.

Wells, H. & Baum, G. 1984. "Political theology in conflict". *The Ecumenist* Vol. 22, pp. 81-87.

2.8 PREACHING FROM THE OLD TESTAMENT

A perspective from Liberation Theology[1]

1. INTRODUCTION

The assignment to address this meeting on the topic stated above can be executed if at least three important limitations are kept in mind. It is (firstly) impossible to give a perspective from "liberation theology" as this term covers a wide variety of theological currents from different geographical areas with distinctive emphases. It would lead to an oversimplification to subsume (e.g.) approaches from feminist theologians under the same "perspective" as those from Latin America, North America, black theologians or the Minjung theology from Korea. There are even distinctive patterns within these different currents.

To overcome this problem, I shall concentrate mainly on some of the best known liberation theologians from Latin America, with special emphasis on Severino Croatto, 1 an accomplished Old Testament scholar.

The second limitation is that actual sermons (i.e. "preaching") are rarely published and this forces the reader to construe how these theologians, to be consistent, would view preaching from the Old Testament in general. This is, however, not a difficult task in view of the pastoral nature of the literature drawn from liberation theology.

The third limitation is of a personal nature: I am not an Old Testament specialist and am open to correction and assistance from colleagues who are well versed in this regard.

The essay is developed in three stages. I shall first explain that an understanding of preaching from a liberative angle is only possible if the close unity between the methodological structure of liberation theology and its hermeneutical approach is kept in mind. The implications that this unity has for preaching is consequently discussed and this is followed by a few evaluative remarks, which may form the basis for further discussion.

2. THE UNITY OF METHODOLOGY AND HERMENEUTICS

Every Christian theology is compelled to "interpret" Scripture, tradition and the context in which it is developed (Tracy 1975:22ff).

This necessitates a "theory of interpretation", i.e. a hermeneutical approach which is explicitly developed or implicitly assumed. The thesis I wish to defend is that the methodological structure of (liberation) theology determines its hermeneutical key.

In Latin America theology is defined as a "critical reflection both from within, and upon, historical praxis, in confrontation with the word of the Lord as lived and experienced in faith" (Gutierrez 1983a:60). This definition embodies the most

---

[1] This paper was read at the meeting of the Theological Advisory Council (DRCA) in Pretoria on 18 October 1988. It was later published in 1989 in *Theologica Viatorum* 17, pp. 63-73.

important claim by Latin American theologians: their way of doing theology leads to a "reformulation of the preconditions, presuppositions and methods of doing theology at all" (Míquez-Bonino 1979:260; see Vidales 1974:128).

This methodological claim is based on the reformulation of the theory-praxis relation where theology is constructed from the "primacy of praxis" (Gutierrez 1975:48; Boff 1978a:122-123). This philosophical "inversion" is then theologically translated in terms of the priority of orthopraxis over orthodoxy (Naudé 1987:239-323).

This distinctive methodological approach may be simplified as follows: theology starts from an experience and thorough analysis of the present situation and assigns an important place to the social sciences. This is the socio-analytical mediation of theology. The analysed situation is subsequently interpreted in the light of faith/Scripture. This constitutes the hermeneutical mediation of theology. Lastly, pastoral actions are derived from a combination of the first two procedures in order to modify reality to correspond more closely to the principles of God's kingdom. This may be referred to as the pastoral mediation of theology (Boff 1983; Boff and Boff 1984:27).

The important point is that this methodology as such may be described as a hermeneutical circle. J.L. Segundo, whose work *The liberation of theology* has been hailed for its methodological insights, formulates his intention as follows: "In this book I am going to try to show that an approach which attempts to relate past and present in dealing with the word of God has to have its own special methodology. I shall give this methodology a pretentious name and call it the hermeneutical circle" (Segundo 1978). In the preface to the revised edition of his *Exodus* which is an "essay in hermeneutics", Croatto explicitly states: "I want to contribute to the epistemology of the theology of liberation" in the light of the need "to go more deeply into the methodology of liberation" (Croatto 1981:iv, vi). This confirms the conclusion of Manzanera that the distinctive feature of liberation theology lies in the fact that "die Hermeneutik der Theologie selbst wird" (Manzanera 1975:2).

The methodology of liberation theology is thus not only developed via hermeneutical mediation: it is in fact developed in terms of a hermeneutical circle. The precise nature of this hermeneutical "circulation" which constitutes the crux of the way (meta & hodos) in which liberation theology is constructed, will unfold as the discussion on the nature of preaching proceeds (see below).

3. IMPLICATIONS OF METHODOLOGY FOR UNDERSTANDING OF PREACHING

As stated above, the work of Severino Croatto serves as basis for this exposition. He has, apart from original work done by José Miguez-Bonino and Clodovis Boff, developed the most refined theory interpretation among the ranks of liberation theologians. The "implications for preaching from the Old Testament" were obviously not set out by Croatto, but I believe these are logical extensions of his (and other writers') ideas.

3.1. Preaching is a profoundly experiential event in more than one sense of the word

The experiential nature of preaching as proclamation of the Word is, firstly, related to the nature of the Word of God as "text".

According to Croatto, a text always has its point of departure in some form of experience which constituted a particularly meaningful event. This event (experience) is resumed in words (oral or written) which have a selective and interpretative role *vis-à-vis* the event. The "word" unfolds the "reservoir of meaning" in the event and the event is recharged with meaning through successive rereadings which, in the end, say "more" than merely repeating the original event (Croatto 1981:13-14; 1983:150).

Croatto relies on Gadamer's well-known insight – set out in his *Wahrheit und Methode* – that a human event generates other happenings because of its "historical effect" (Croatto 1981:1). Instead of perceiving the historical distance between event and interpretation as barrier for interpretation, Gadamer's emphasis lies on the "wirkungsgeshichtliche" growth of meaning. The text is not "closed", but open to the future, where the dialogue between text and interpreter implies a "merging of horizons" ("Horizontverschemelzung") constituting a transcendence of the original meaning (Gadamer 1965:286-289).

If Scripture itself is the interpretation of God's salvific events, it did not only originate in experience, but is itself a report of the existential rereading by Israel and the early church of certain foundational events (Croatto 1983:150). The text is thus by its very nature "proclamation" or "message" (Croatto 1981:14) and must be re-proclaimed from a new existential encounter between reader (preacher) and text.

The second sense in which preaching is intimately related to experience is liberation theology as a critical reflection from and about "praxis" (see Assmann 1975:17; Gutierrez 1975a:46-48). Despite multiple ways in which "praxis" is employed, a careful analysis (Naudé 1987:120-130) proves that the relation between experience and praxis is prior to that between action and praxis. This is confirmed by both Gutierrez and Galilea, who emphasise that a contemplative experience at the underside of history (the faith of the poor) precedes the theology of liberation and makes the latter possible (Gutierrez 1983b:225; Galilea 1981:56).

Theology as *fides quaerens intellectum* is nothing more than an interpretation of the faith of experience of the poor. The theologian and preacher (see 3.3: Preaching as community activity) who do not share the experiential basis of liberation theology will not be able to understand this theological current. But even more: outside the locus of the poor, preaching ceases to be liberative preaching because of the "foreign" (normally oppressive) experiential context from which it arises. If not poor himself, the preacher must be urged to make an existential commitment to the poor.

Preaching as experiential activity does not refer to a superficial psychological "Erlebnis" or cheap emotionalism (Boff 1978:59-62). It stems from the hermeneutical view of Scripture as "word-about-foundational-event" and the methodological prerequisite or a co-experience with the poor.

3.2. Preaching as pistic (faith) event has a promissory and exclusively contextual character

The exclusive contextual character of preaching may partly be derived from the semiotic basis of Croatto's hermeneutics. When language ("Sprache") as system of signs with polysemous words becomes speech ("Sprechen"), a definite closure of meaning takes place in order to say "something to someone about something" (Croatto 1983:143). This closure of meaning is a prerequisite for any real communication between the transmitter and receiver sharing a common context.

As soon as a foundational event becomes a written exemplary passage, the original transmitter, receiver and horizon are no longer present. "Now the meaning-closure imposed by the transmitter is converted into an openness", makes room for a rereading and allows the new addressee to enter the text with and from his own context (Croatto 1983:144-145).

The point is that a creative rereading again "closes" the meaning of the text. The sermon, an existential encounter with the exemplary passage (canon), necessarily excludes other readings in a twofold manner. It (firstly) originates from and takes place in a specific (exclusive) context and it (secondly) produces exclusive meaning by reducing the polysemous possibilities to "one" interpretation.

It is clear that Croatto and liberation theology in general reject the traditional view that the task of the preacher is to understand the text in its original context (explication) and then apply it to the present situation (applicatio).

This view, a form of "exegetical historicism", focuses on the "context backward" of the text by focusing on the pre-canonical phase. Although liberation theologians do not reject modern critical methods (see Miranda 1974 and Míquez-Bonino 1975:101-102), they do not reject the assumption that the text is a closed deposit of meaning so that the only "correct" reading is the one which coincides with the intention of the author (Croatto 1983:142-145). Not only is it impossible to speak of "the author" of many books in the Old Testament, it is also hermeneutically naive to understand *sola Scriptura* in such a way that the inevitable presuppositions (Bultmann) are denied.

The preacher has to make sense of the exemplary passage by producing meaning within the "context forward" of the text. In this sense exegesis is impossible without *eiseqesis* (Croatto 1983:157-159). I bring my own world to the world of the text – not impose a new meaning on the text, but precisely to honour the polysemous nature of the text. In this way my interpretation is exclusive and contextual.

In what sense is liberative preaching from the Old Testament an act of faith? Based on the intimate relation between methodology and hermeneutics, preaching is a proclamation on the faith of the poor which is being contemplated in theology (see Gutierrez 1975:26, 52). If theology is a second-order activity arising from faith, preaching is the third-order activity proclaiming the intuitive truth of the religio-sided popular (faith of the people).

Preaching is, secondly, an act of faith because it re-proclaims the "message" of the exemplary event as perceived in present historical events (see 3.4). When the event is "contemplated from within the perspective of faith", the "memory" of the event and the "message" of the past becomes "promise". The sermon is then a proclamation of the promise and an enjoinment of the people to prolong the event into the present situation (Croatto 1981:14-15, see 3.5).

It is important to understand the socio-analytical mediation of liberation theology as a prelude to the hermeneutical mediation. The "sociological" (Marxist) analysis of the oppressive situation is complemented by a "reading of the signs of the time" as a discernment of faith, which is a gift of God's Spirit. Preaching as liberative preaching is thus an act from and through faith.

3.3. Preaching is a communal event as it occurs from and for the community of believers

It is well-known that liberation theology is a reflection of the poor upon their faith and that "it is not enough to know that praxis must precede reflection; we must realise that the historical subject of that praxis is the poor" (Gutierrez 1983:90-91; 1978:247). The ecclesiological implication of this is the identification of the "people of God" with the poor. The church is more than a church that shows compassion for the poor: it is a church of and from the poor.

The important point for our purpose is to grasp the relation between the members of the church and hermeneutics as "community-based hermeneutics" (Croatto 1981:11). Jon Sobrino states unequivocally: "The poor within this church become the hermeneutical principle for a primary concrete expression of important Christian concepts and realities" (Sobrino 1985:137). The preacher who merely engages in the academic study of commentaries denies himself the opportunity to be "evangelised" by the people who constitute the primary "readers" of the text.

But the "communal" character of preaching is also embedded in the hermeneutical conviction that the Bible (and specifically the Old Testament) can best be interpreted from the perspective of the poor and oppressed. Because the Old Testament is itself the proclamation of liberation, the oppressed are epistemologically privileged readers: they "more than anyone else" are the addressees of the "kerygmatic nucleus" of Scripture (Croatta 1983:v,156-157). The preacher, if not poor him/herself, will have to enquire about God's message where God is most likely to be found: among the poor, the people of Gold, the holy community of believers.

3.4. Preaching as liberative event is specifically drawn from the Old Testament in the light of the exodus event as semantic axis of Scripture

A lot has been written about the exodus motif in liberation theology (e.g. Sauter 1981; Loader 1987; Oosthuizen 1988). There is no need to repeat what is already well known, except to indicate that Croatto (and others) look upon the exodus event as the foundational event and the paradigmatic experience from which the whole Bible – creation, the prophets, the ministry of Jesus and Paul's letters – must be approached (Croatto 1981; Gutierrez 1974:153-178). It would be no exaggeration to say that liberation theology has "reclaimed" (Gowan 1981:v-vi) the Old Testament for the church of our day in a very forceful and imaginative way.

Not all liberation theologians have done this rereading in an hermeneutically sound way. In reaction against an undue spiritualisation (Gutierrez 1974:166), the exodus is often taken with a direct (fundamentalistically based) correspondence between

Egypt and Latin America. Leonardo Boff, for instance, writes: "That world (in which Christ lived) was strikingly similar to our own Latin world; it was a world suffering from oppression both from within and without" (1979:103).

An alternative example, close to the one proposed by Croatto, is put forward by Clodovis Boff in his *Theologie und Praxis* (1983). Hermeneutics is not based on the correspondence of two similar situations, but on a correspondence between the relation of context and message in the Bible as "hermeneutical habitus" (Boff 1983:241-249). The creative rereading of the sermon is thus a re-enactment of this relation from an (inevitably) different situation.

This kind of "selective" reading of the Old Testament is not peculiar to liberation theologians. The question of the "Mitte" (centre/focal point) of the Old Testament has been part and parcel of Old Testament theology for more than two centuries (Hasel 1975:117ff). Well-known examples of these "central concepts" are the covenant (Eichrodt), the holiness of God (Sellin), communion (Vriezen) and salvation history (Von Rad).

None of these authors had the deliberate intention to select only those passages from the Old Testament that "fit the scheme". On the contrary – the very existence of these influential works points to the fact that a "selective" reading of such a rich document is essential and contributes considerably to our understanding of the Old Testament. The expansion of a liberative reading to include the Wisdom literature and Job (Gutierrez 1987) is part of an ever-increasing illumination of the Old Testament from a (I believe) valid hermeneutical focal point.

3.5. Liberative preaching as pastoral preaching is directed at transformative praxis as final act of exegesis

It is clear that the hermeneutical circularity of liberation theology's method takes "praxis" as its starting and its (always provisional) point of termination (see introduction to this essay). The praxis of the poor (experience of oppression), the concrete reality of Latin America which led to a rereading of the gospel (hermeneutics of suspicion), must now be changed by transformative action (Segundo 1977:8, Gutierrez 1975:47-48).

This must be seen in the light of liberation theologians' view that the sources for theology are no longer solely determined by Scripture and tradition, but include a "structural analysis of reality" (Assmann 1969:233-234, my translation). The "text" of reality is reread in the light of the Scriptural "text", which leads to transformation of the initial "text".

This radicalisation of James' "doers of the word" implies that a preacher must decide, in close relation with the community, on appropriate action (normally political in nature) to "liberate" or to maintain liberation. The final exegesis only takes place if the socio-political "text" embodies the principles contained in the commitment to the poor and a reading of Scriptures from the perspective of the liberation of the poor.

This implies that the pastoral nature of preaching may not be interpreted individualistically; the sermon has a pastoral basis, is constructed pastorally (communally) and is finally executed through pastoral action (see Nogglar 1977).

Perhaps we can learn a way out of the impasse of a "domineeskerk" by appropriation of the fundamentally pastoral character of the preaching event and the liturgical changes resulting from it!

4. Conclusion and critical questions

There is no doubt in my mind that we must accept liberation theology as a worthy partner in our search for the relevance of the Old Testament for the church today. We must release this theology (which is alive and well in the hearts of many South African Christians) from its position of anathema and take its proponents seriously as brothers and sisters in search of liberation. But we must not be trapped in refined paternalism by abstaining from entering into serious debate. The quality of this debate and the love among its participants constitute a transformative action in itself. We must be liberated for a genuine engagement with liberation theology!

To foster such an engagement I list a few relevant questions which may serve as the basis for further discussion.

1. Is there any formal difference behaviour between reading Scripture from the perspective of "justification by faith alone" and reading in terms of "the liberation of the poor?"

2. Is it true that the exodus (and other) traditions undergo a creative rereading in the course of Israel's history? A specific rereading may, however, be a distortion of the exemplary event as is witnessed in some of the prophets (and even more forcefully in Jesus' encounters with his contemporaries). How does a "self-critical function" operate within a liberative tradition?

3. In what way does the "objectivity of the text" exclude certain possible readings, if such a reading is exclusive in a threefold sense (from exclusive experience, reading as exclusive determination-of-meaning and towards exclusive pastoral action), or should such "objectivity" be abolished in principle?.

4. If socio-economic reality as "text" is assigned revelatory status, by what criteria (other than pure ideological commitment) are conflicting "revelations" judged?

5. Is it true that any reading of the Old Testament is (to some extent) selective? How are passages about the joy of marriage love (Song of Songs) or God's inclusive grace (Jonah) "included" in the exodus perspective? Should our call to proclaim the full salvation of God not make us less satisfied with a selectivity as proposed by liberation theologians (or any other theological current)?

BIBLIOGRAPHY

Assmann, H. 1969. "Die Situation der unterentwickelt gehaltener Lander als Ort eine Theologie der Revolution". In E. Feil & R. Weth (eds.), pp. 218-248.

Assmann, H. 1975. *Onderdrukking – Verzet: Een uitdaging aan die christenen*. Baarn: Ten Have.

Boff, C. 1983. *Theologie und Praxis: Die erkenntnistheoretischen Grundlagen der Theologie der Befreiung*. Munchen: Kaiser.

Boff, L. 1978. *Erfahrung von Gnade: Entwurf einer Gnadenlehre*. Dusseldorf: Patmos.

Boff, L. 1979. "Christ's liberation via oppression. An attempt at theological construction from the standpoint of Latin America". In R. Gibellini (ed.), pp. 100-132.

Boff, L. & Boff, C. 1984. *Salvation and liberation: In search of a balance between faith and politics*. New York: Orbis.

Croatto, S. 1981. *Exodus – a hermeneutics of freedom*. New York: Orbis.

Croatto, S. 1983. "Biblical hermeneutics in the theology of liberation". In S. Torres & V. Fabella (eds.), pp. 140-167.

Feil, E. & R. Weth, R (eds.) 1969. *Diskussion zur "Theologie der Revolution"*. München: Kaiser.

Gadamer, H.G. 1965. *Wahrheit und Methode. Grundzuge einer philosophischen Hermeneutik*. 2. Aufl. Tübingen: Mohr.

Galilea, S. 1981. *Following Jesus*. New York: Orbis.

Gibellini, R. (ed.) 1979. *Frontiers of theology in Latin America*. New York: Orbis.

Gowan, D.E. 1980. *Reclaiming the Old Testament for the Christian pulpit*. Edinburgh: T & T Clark.

Gutierrez, G. 1975. "Faith as freedom: Solidarity with the alienated and confidence in the future". *Horizons* Vol. 2, pp. 25-61.

Gutierrez, G. 1978. "Two theological perspectives, liberation theology and progressivist theology". In S. Torres & V. Fabella (eds), pp. 227-255.

Gutierrez, G. 1983a. *The power of the poor in history. Selected writings*. London: SCM.

Gutierrez, G. 1983b. "Reflections from a Latin American perspective. Finding our way to talk about God". In S. Torres & V. Fabella (eds), pp. 222-234.

Gutierrez, G. 1987. *On job. God-talk and the suffering of the innocent*. New York: Orbis.

Hasel, G. 1975. *Old Testament theology. Basic issues in the current debate* (revised edition). Grand Rapids: Eerdmans.

Loader, J. 1987. "Exodus, liberation theology and theological argument". *JTSA* Vol. 59, pp. 3-18.

Manzanera, M. 1975. "Die Theologie der Befreiung und ihre Hermeneutik". *Theologische Akademie* Vol. XII, pp. 52-78.

Miguez-Bonino, J. 1975. *Doing theology in a revolutionary situation*. Philadelphia: Fortress.

Miguez-Bonino, J. 1979. "Historical praxis and Christian identity". In Gibellini, pp. 260-284.

Miranda, J.P. 1974. *Marx and the Bible: A critique of the philosophy of oppression*. New York: Orbis.

Modehn, C, Rahner, K & Zwiefelhofer, H. (eds.) 1977. *Befreiende Theologie. Der Beitrag Lateinamerikas zur Theologie der Gegenwart*. Stuttgart: Kohlhammer.

Naudé, P.J. 1987. *Ortopraksie as metodologiese prinsipe in die sistematiese teologie*. Unpublished OTh thesis. Stellenbosch: University of Stellenbosch.

Noggler, O. 1977. "Theologie oder Pastoral der Befreiung". In C. Modehn, K. Rahner & H. Zwiefelhofer (Hrsg.), pp. 97-105.

Oosthuizen, M.J. 1988. "Scripture and context. The use of the Exodus theme in the hermeneutics of liberation theology". *Scriptura* Vol. 25, pp. 7-22.

Sauter, G. 1981. "'Exodus' and 'Liberation' as theological metaphors: A critical case study of the use of allegory and misunderstood analogies in ethics". *Scottish Journal of Theology* Vol. 34, pp. 481-507.

Segundo, J.L. 1977. *The liberation of theology*. Dublin: Gill and Macmillan.

Sobrino, J. 1985. *The true church and the poor*. London: SCM.

Torres, S. & Fabella, V. (eds.) 1978. *The emergent gospel*. New York: Orbis.

Torres, S. & Fabella, V. (eds.) 1983. *Irruption of the Third World*. New York: Orbis.

Tracy, D. 1975. *Blessed rage for order: The new pluralism in theology*. New York: Seabury.

Vidales, R. 1974. "Kroniek van enkele recente latijnsamerikaanse publicaries over de theologie van de bevrijding". *Concilium* Vol. 10, No. 6, pp. 124-134.

PART 3 –
ESSAYS IN
REFORMED THEOLOGY

3.1 IS THERE A FUTURE FOR SCHOLARSHIP?

Reformed theological scholarship in a transforming higher education environment[1]

1. INTRODUCTION

In discussing the future of Reformed churches in South Africa during a conference[2] in March 2001, John de Gruchy *inter alia* referred to the legacy of scholarship stemming from Calvin as a Christian humanist. "Such scholarship is not narrowly theological but encompasses all branches of knowledge and culture ... I fear, however, that there is a decline[3] in Reformed scholarship today that bodes ill for the future. *Where are the Reformed theologians and biblical scholars, the church historians and practical theologians? Certainly not in great abundance!*" (2001:43-50, my emphasis).

There are many empirical reasons for this decline: historical churches are losing members[4] and qualified pastors – new *and* old – are often without placement in the church,[5] with the result that fewer students enrol for degrees in theology. New academic positions are very rare, existing ones are on hold and sometimes not filled, faculties of theology close or lose their status as faculties.[6] And with the demise of religious education in schools, the traditional religious studies departments are on the brink of collapse as independent units. The social status traditionally associated with academia is on the decline. There are few black role models left in theology,[7] and bright new black and women scholars in all disciplines find much

---

1 This essay originally appeared in *Journal of Theology for Southern Africa* 119 (2004), July, 32-45.
2 The conference was held in Stellenbosch under the auspices of the University of Hamburg study group on the role of religion and specifically the Dutch Reformed Church in the transition to democracy. The papers were published in *Scriptura* 76 (2001/1).
3 The immediate context of De Gruchy's remark suggests "decline" in both the number of scholars (where are the future scholars?) as well as in quality (where is the spirit of humanism?). I try to address both in my exposition below.
4 The Centre for Religious Demographic Research at the University of Stellenbosch has become known for its empirical work on trends in church membership. See Hendriks and Erasmus (2001:41-65), where they indicate the steady decline of mainline churches and the growth of the AICs and Pentecostal/Charismatic Churches (see their Tables 8-11).
5 This is a topic for another time, but I find it heartbreaking that pastors with PhDs in theology from, for example, the DRC lose their church positions as a result of financial issues without some drastic intervention from the church in broader terms (circuit, synod). It is not strange to find doctors of theology selling insurance policies, repairing computers or starting a nursery. These examples do not create confidence in potential candidates for both the ministry and the academy.
6 Example of closure is the faculty at Rhodes university after 52 years of distinguished work, with serious question marks over faculties established at historically black institutions like the University of the North and Qua-Qua (merged with UOFS). The faculty at Fort Hare is now a department in the Faculty for Africa and Democracy Studies.
7 Many of the leading figures of the 1980s are either in politics or in university management positions. They might do excellent work where they are (the kingdom is bigger than theology or the church!), but they do leave a vacuum that is very hard to fill. The strongest

more lucrative offers in the private and public sectors that are under legal pressure to promote equity.

But there is a much more profound reason for the declining scholarship in theology specifically and the pressure on the social sciences/humanities in general. It relates to the very influential "knowledge production" debate set forth in the work of Gibbons, Scott and others, and the fact that in a global so-called "knowledge economy", knowledge itself has become a commodity. This in turn has been informing the transformation of higher education in South Africa with serious implications for the way in which scholarship is regarded.

Let us examine this in detail.

2. NEW KNOWLEDGE FORMS, MARKETISATION AND HIGHER EDUCATION TRANSFORMATION

In a remarkably influential book, *The new production of knowledge. The dynamics of science and research in contemporary society* (1994), Gibbons and others distinguish between mode 1 and mode 2 knowledge. The first relates to traditional knowledge production in the preferred social space of the university; it follows the canons of established disciplines or specialised sub-disciplines; it is verified and quality-assured by peers, and its possible application, if relevant at all, is left to others beyond the boundaries of the academic world. It is then argued that this type of knowledge no longer reflects developments in our post-industrial and post-modern societies.

Mode 2 knowledge is produced in a variety of social settings, of which the university might or might not be part, and "internet-ed together". Because it bears the character of problem solving on the move, it takes on inter- and post-disciplinary cognitive forms pursued in problem-solving teams. The quality of knowledge is ultimately judged by the users of the knowledge, because the distinction between "theory" and "application" is collapsed whilst knowledge is produced in the context of application itself.[8] This means that "the notion of accountability is 'inside' the research design ... shaping the epistemological and methodological processes for producing 'good' science" (Scott 1997:36).

In the meantime, a "networked" knowledge economy developed where industrial success and market share depend heavily on "Vorsprung durch Technik". In almost all spheres of the economy, ranging from computer technology, automobile manufacturing to financial services, pharmaceutics and the mining industry, access to and development of cutting-edge knowledge is of the utmost importance. Many companies have research budgets that universities and scientific boards can only dream of. More than this: higher education itself has become a commodified service industry, listed on the stock exchange, with many private universities and business schools setting up shop all over the world or via the internet, or creating partnerships with established universities to maximise knowledge output valuable to the relevant industry.

---

contemporary voice is that of Tinyiko Sam Maluleke. His appointment for African and black theology at UNISA will hopefully remedy the situation in the future.

8 See how these views are directly corroborated by Clyde Barrow's study on universities in the light of global competition in a post-industrial society, quoted by Chopp (2002:469).

These are exciting developments with enormous impact on the very idea of a university. There is a clear shift away from universities as ivory-tower institutions of learning, privileged by society to pursue knowledge for its own sake and of its own choice. In her presidential address to the American Academy of Religion in 2001, Rebecca Chopp explained these transformative forces acting upon the university in the metaphor of three cities. In the *village* scholars stand in an organic community of town and gown, and serve the public through educated debate in the village commons. In the *metropolis* scholars are entrenched in disciplinary boundaries with discourses turned inward toward academic guilds. In the emergent *global city*, driven by technology, interdisciplinarity and internationalism, a new breed of boundary-crossing scholar is emerging with changing intellectual assumptions and much greater public engagement.[9]

If one accepts the intimate relation between theology, church and society, there are good reasons why theology has, and can, in many ways operate in mode 2 knowledge forms, or that it can indeed adapt to scholarship far more open to other disciplines and communities beyond itself. Instead of seeing these developments as threats, theological scholarship – and therefore the very structures of the academy – need to be responsive to, and in fact lead, these developments. That this is easier said than done relates to both the values underlying transformation in South African Higher Education, and to theology's own inability to reshape itself institutionally and epistemically.

Some aspects of the "modes of knowledge" debate have informed the transformation of higher education in SA over the past seven years.[10] There have been very necessary and laudable forms of transformation as the university system had reflected our apartheid past in its very set-up and constellation. I have elsewhere written a case study on the various stages of HE transformation (Naudé 2003). Here I just point out that we had the moral obligation to transform *politically* for the sake of legitimacy and democratic participation. The stream of African students to formerly white institutions and the fact that we need to give greater credence to our position on this continent required an *academic* transformation toward access and responsiveness. Keeping our scarce resources in mind, the *financial* transformation toward efficiency and sustainability was almost a natural outcome of the foregoing processes.

There are, however, two aspects of this transformation that I judge to be detrimental to higher education in general and theology in particular: the marketisation of universities, and a pragmatist notion of relevance that is almost exclusively defined by perceived needs outside the university.

---

9 See Chopp (2002:461-474). In her view, the village is represented by small, liberal arts colleges, the metropolis by most discipline-structured and bureaucratic contemporary universities, and the global city by units and centres in universities with a much more flexible, strategic, publically engaged and project-driven approach.

10 It is unimaginable that higher education would not be part of the democratic transformation of our country. This is evident from a regular stream of incisive policies from the National Council on Higher Education Report and South African Qualifications Authority Act in 1995 through the White Paper (third edition) and subsequent Higher Education Act of 1997, and the recent National Working Group on reconfiguring the institutional landscape of higher education *inter alia* through mergers, take-overs and closures.

Instead of a "scholarship" or "learning community" view of the university, a "market idea" is emerging with universities funded by the state (or private concerns) obliged "to give a return on the investment" in terms of applicable and required knowledge to provide society (or the company) with its human resources needs. The whole language game (Wittgenstein) has altered: the rector becomes the CEO; students become clients who demand a good service, with high throughput rates, and instructed in knowledge forms that are "relevant to the world of work". If we take Heidegger seriously and accept that *"die Sprache ist das Haus des Seins"*, this linguistic shift with regard to universities reflects not only an epistemological, but also an ontological transformation of our institutions. This is indeed reflected in terms like the "entrepreneurial university" or a "socially engaged university", neither of which is problematic on the face of it, except if narrowly interpreted in market terms.[11]

The curriculum price we pay for this marketisation rhetoric is high. There is an underlying policy hostility toward modules and courses that do not fit the pragmatic shape of "preferred knowledge" (leaving aside the fact that education is a "futuring" exercise) and driven by an idea that "science and technology"[12] are really all that we need. In this atmosphere you do not need a lot of imagination to see that the type of knowledge traditionally developed in theology[13] (or the humanities) will not be in great "demand", and that these disciplines will be forced silently to the epistemological margins. To keep a faculty of specifically Reformed theology[14] going in a country with a secular constitution and separation of state and church[15] is unthinkable for some.

We have reached a point where a spirit of pragmatism and a rationality of application-driven education are destroying *the function of the university as custodian*[16] *of knowledge*

---

11 In these terms, an entrepreneurial university is not so much one that allows minimal bureaucratic restraints and rewards creative, critical scholarship, but one that maximises its profits from selling its knowledge in a variety of ways. And in market terms, an engaged university is not so much one that dialectically interacts with its environment in relative autonomy, but one that is externally determined by the economic and political agenda of the day.

12 Nobody with even a rudimentary understanding of economic growth (like myself) will deny the importance of e.g. vocationally oriented, skills-based education and training; nor that no country can afford not to try and keep up with technological advances. My problem lies with the values communicated along with this emphasis. Have we forgotten so soon that it was an understanding of truth, reconciliation, constitutionality, equity and justice that brought us our new country, and that we need to sustain history, African languages, the arts and other seemingly "non-utilitarian" knowledge forms to build a united nation?

13 According to some, a general knowledge of religions (especially Islam) might be useful, humanistic ethics is definitely in "because we need more morality", but Christian theology actually does not belong in the state university at all, because it serves a sectarian interest group whilst it draws on taxpayers' money.

14 The traditional faculties of Reformed theology at Potchefstroom, Pretoria, Bloemfontein and Stellenbosch have all been actively engaged in efforts to broaden their base toward a more open, ecumenical approach.

15 The separation of church and state in South Africa has a particular meaning and has not taken on the shape it has in, for example, the United States. See the remarks by Lombaard (2001:21-22) and his reference to some political uneasiness with Christian faculties in state universities.

16 The core criticism against this view of custodianship of tradition is that it is not necessary

traditions: We therefore train lawyers without proper grounding in legal philosophy and without a reading knowledge of Latin; we deliver psychologists who have mastered interviewing techniques without knowing the masters of suspicion: Marx, Nietzsche and Freud; we design a more compact curriculum for theology without a proper base in the social sciences such as philosophy, sociology or anthropology (and will one of these days face the question whether the biblical languages are really necessary, as so few pastors actually use them in the ministry, and you can in any case buy an inter-linear translation off the shelf).

3. THE CHALLENGES FOR REFORMED THEOLOGICAL SCHOLARSHIP

It is clear from the above that there is a huge challenge for theology to ensure a critical, inter-disciplinary and creative scholarship base in SA – preferably in the university, and only by absolute necessity outside of it[17]. Let us look at each of these attributes of scholarship in relation to Reformed scholarship in the context of the Dutch Reformed Church:

Concerning *critical scholarship*, two remarks – one theological and the other hermeneutical – are relevant: In an interesting paper on the relation between SA and Europe, Willie Jonker observes that the DRC never fully understood the combined effect of World War Two and the Second Enlightenment represented by the critical theories of Horkheimer, Adorno, Marcuse and Habermas. What happened, says Jonker, is that the DRC relied on an earlier, pre-critical European theology (in the form of romantic and self-satisfied neo-Calvinism) exactly at a time when ideology-critique was accepted as an indispensable part of any theoretical construct. This delayed the DRC's full confrontation with new European theological trends and led to its almost total intellectual and ecumenical isolation: "From the view of the outside world as a whole, the theology of the Afrikaans churches is too uncritical, too naive with regard to the ideological presuppositions of our thoughts, too much oriented to a period in the *Geistesgeschichte* that has passed, and shows too little willingness to accept the implications of the Enlightenment" (1988:154, my translation).

It lies beyond the scope of this paper to show how many – Jaap du Rand (1985), Willie Jonker (1988), and recently Russel Botman (2001, 2002) and myself (Naudé 2001) – have indicated that the theological roots of a critical theology lay with Karl Barth, who was, until the mid-eighties, not appropriated in DRC theology due to

---

in an African context where other demands are to be met. I agree that the worst possible dream would be to recreate a Cambridge or Princeton or Heidelberg in South Africa. But unless we take a radical stance on what an "African university" is (perhaps nurturing indigenous knowledge forms and seriously elevating African languages apart from Afrikaans to a scientific level), we shall have to heed the Western tradition of sciences that we inherited in relation to our context. Note the emotional debate about Africanisation at UCT in the late 1990s and how it explicitly markets itself as "a first-class African university". The core questions are what effect this African orientation has on the curricula and who decides what "first class" is.

17 The Northern Cape Synod of the DRC accepted a resolution to set up an independent church seminary due to a perceived diluted Reformed orientation at Stellenbosch, and loss of appointment powers by the church. This was rejected by the recent General Synod of Oct 2002. See Conrad Wetmar's well-argued case for theology education in the university (1996:473-490).

perceived problems with his views on revelation, Scripture, baptism and election. One can now add: the invigorating theologies of liberation (black, African, feminist) that started to emerge in the early seventies with their overt ideological-critical[18] approach and fresh insight into the message of the Bible, could in principle not be heard in a church and society defending themselves meticulously against such revolutionary forces that "mix religion and politics" in an unacceptable way.[19]

I am not sure that the DRC – struggling with its very Reformed identity – has in the meantime developed a critical theological universe of discourse, or what such a universe would look like (see below). Without some framework, our scholarship might be interesting, and even grow in quantity, but will decline in its ability to lead the church and South African society toward a new future. (Or have we, victimised by our past, given up such lofty ideals for theology all together?)

The hermeneutical remark stems from Bernard Lategan. He argues that Reformed hermeneutics in general suffered from a structural deficit in its inability to deal with the question of history as posed by the Enlightenment. Whereas the Lutheran tradition could accept critical historical ideas, utilising the *was Christum treibet* principle and practising internal *Sachkritik,* Reformed scholars developed a dogmatic resistance against *Geschichtlichkeit* in their construction of Scriptural authority and infallibility on the assumption of truth as historical truth (i.e. correspondence between historical events recorded in Scripture and their actual occurrence). "This necessitated the defence of biblical history as historically correct" and as precondition for its truthfulness. Except for textual criticism, "there was no natural uptake and exploiting of the historical family of hermeneutical methods – historical criticism, tradition criticism, redaction criticism, composition criticism and the like" (2001).[20]

I have indicated earlier (Naudé 2001:85-98) that biblical scholarship in South Africa – probably our most enlightened group of scholars with high international standing – destroyed the impact of their critical scholarship in a number of ways. This was summarised by Elizabeth Schussler-Fiorenza (1988:4) with regard to biblical

---

18   This type of thinking emerged in the circles of ABRECSA, whose charter and supplementary declaration (1981) are a brilliant reclamation of the Reformed tradition in answer to the crucial question of how it is possible to be black and Reformed (related to the title of Allan Boesak's well-known book). Although one could question the almost naive re-appropriation of Marxist ideology-critique by most forms of liberation theologians, it does not diminish their role in focusing theological attention on "the underside of history" (Gutierrez). Reformed liberation theologians were consequently able to develop a credible alternative hermeneutical key to "justification by faith alone" in their insistence on the epistemological privilege of the marginalised and the poor. One of the Belhar confession's important achievements is that it was able to draw these two lines together in one confession – look at the inner consistency and "logic of grace" in the movement from the first to the highly contested fourth article. Up till now our mainline scholarship has not been able to take the second line seriously. For text and discussion, see GD Cloete and DJ Smit (1984).
19   This is clearly illustrated in my analysis of why the DRC struggled to accept the confession of Belhar as confession: once it was popularly labelled as "liberation theology" its fate was sealed, despite even official denials from the DRC leadership. See Naudé (1997).
20   Lategan, following Nash, reconstructs the well-known Du Plessis case in terms of its implications for critical theological scholarship, which they believe shifted from the Stellenbosch Seminary to Philosophy (Kirsten, Rossouw) and Semitic Languages (Fensham, Deist).

scholarship in general: an assumed value-neutrality oblivious to the political context of interpretation; an inability to translate meaning beyond the historical investigation of the text; little or no consideration of ecclesial or confessional traditions; and the creation of a closed world of expertly scholarly inquiry which denies the interests and values underlying their communicative practice. I do not want to repeat the concrete examples here (Naudé 2001:97), but the broader critical effect of our biblical scholars was neutralised in advance by their "scientist ethos" (Botha 1992:179) and the fact that, despite their good intentions (see the foreword to the very first edition of *Skrif en Kerk*), biblical scholars usually found themselves extremely uneasy when engaging with the *wirkunsgeschichtliche* realities of the church and its confessions, avoiding the difficult question of what *sola Scriptura* could mean after the Enlightenment.

Their only option was to combine a highly critical biblical scholarship with a highly naive dogmatics, leaving the poor dogmaticians with both a naive theology and even more naive reading strategy.[21]

The chickens have now come home to roost in the two forms: Ben du Toit's book on faith in a post-modern age entitled *God? Geloof in 'n postmoderne tyd* (2000), and the surge of a so-called "second reformation" driven by critical biblical and classical scholars in alliance with the Jesus seminar. Critical scholarship has hit the streets and the pages of *Beeld*. (Did someone say any publicity is good publicity?).

Du Toit's book is the first attempt in Afrikaans Reformed circles to take critical scholarship to the heart of our confessional tradition.[22] His own roots lie in the critical realist school set up in South Africa by Wentzel van Huyssteen (1986) and appropriated hermeneutically by Ferdinand Deist (1994). In Ben du Toit's own thought, the lines of a methodologically post-Barthian systematic theology and a critical hermeneutic[23] come together in a very interesting genre that is more confession than formal dogmatics. This convergence has not happened before in our theology. This explains the ambiguous reaction of both rejection as obviously unorthodox, and acceptance as a liberative, post-modern account of faith. We need a lot more thinking in this regard.

A few remarks about the "second reformation": I am sure any reasonably informed theologian understands that the questions announced by our colleagues are indeed

---

21 See the very interesting remark by Bertie du Plessis, former NT scholar at Unisa, in his newspaper review of the *Festschrift* for Willie Jonker: "For the subject specialist the thoughts of Heyns (and Jonker) appear to be naive, because they do not reflect in any way the problems arising from the exegetical discipline". This is inter alia linked to a "*probleemlose* beroep op die Skrif" (my translation, emphasis original). I know that some biblical scholars also said that about Adrio Konig's systematic work ("more sermons than exegesis").

22 When I saw the unpublished manuscript, I sensed this *novum*, and immediately agreed to write the recommendation on the back cover despite the ambiguities in the argument. We realised that it would be difficult to find a publisher. It is a bit ironic that the Christelike Lektuurfonds (CLF) – known for its printing and distribution of more pietist literature – had the courage to take the project on.

23 See his book written with Van Huyssteen on the authority of Scripture in reaction to the Synod of Delft (Netherlands) report *God met ons* in 1979: JWV van Huyssteen and BJ du Toit (1982). The basic shift was away from a correspondence theory of truth to a relational, constructivist view of truth with obviously radical implications for an interpretation of Scripture and its authority.

nineteenth-century type questions about which we were informed all along (although the details obviously differ). But because of the failed ecclesial and confessional integration of biblical scholarship, referred to by Schüssler-Fiorenza, this now appears to ordinary believers as a "surprise" or a new freedom from an authoritative church, "who kept these things secret". The tragedy is that DRC synodical reports on both Scripture and ethical issues since the debate about women's ordination in the 1970s and around apartheid in the mid-1980s appear to deal with the issue of history in a very responsible and open manner. We have perhaps failed our *dominees* and congregants by not supporting them in making this paradigm shift, where "truth" and "history" are linked in a more complex but much more enhancing manner.

The dualism between exegesis (critical biblical scholarship) and dogmatics (confessional tradition) is now as glaring as ever. The "second reformation" will help us to face the difficult reflective task of greater theological and ecclesial coherence[24] – even if we have to admit to more pluralities of thought than we would feel comfortable with. The mark of truly critical scholarship is in any case a greater tolerance – no, in fact a promotion – of dissidence.

Concerning *inter-disciplinary scholarship*, theologians are notoriously turf-defending. The very entity we call "theology" has been divided into six neatly distinguished subject fields, with further refined distinctions into specialisation areas, institutionalised in departments as physical and epistemological spaces. What we, and other disciplines, have gained since the modern era of disciplinary development is now one of our greatest impediments: we struggle to go beyond intra-theological boundaries and very rarely succeed in post-disciplinary engagement around problems that require a spectrum of inputs from, for example, law, biology, economics, linguistics or history. There are impressive exceptions,[25] but mostly we are stuck in mode 1 knowledge production whilst the real world has moved on.

Is that perhaps why we are not taken seriously – *as theological scholars* – not in other faculties nor in society, because we are perceived as intellectual sectarians producing answers to questions that nobody really asks? (And we explain this by referring to outdated notions of secularisation and vague ideas about the privatisation of religion in general). John de Gruchy's reminder that the Reformation grew from the antecedent humanistic revival and encompassed all branches of knowledge[26] is not a day too late.

---

24 I have not read the book published by these colleagues, but from the website I was struck by the fact that each of them tries to draw up a kind of "statement of faith" to clarify their position. This is exactly the point: they realise you cannot deconstruct at will, without reconstructing your presuppositions. And these statements confirm my insistence that Bultmann's notion of *Vorverstandnis* always includes systematic theological convictions as well. (My first impression – probably corrected in the book – is that they urgently need a systematic theologian in their midst, if they can find one with enough courage).
25 Work produced in ethics lends itself more to this boundaryless approach, and obviously biblical scholars are in constant dialogue with literary theorists, historians and archaeologists.
26 Obviously this must be seen in its historical context. The ideal of the "great learned scholar", spanning science, languages, biology and theology, is clearly not possible in that sense today. This is all the more reason to work in problem-solving teams and develop a "corporate scholarship". Even in Germany the notion of a professor with his (sic) "school of thought" and admiring students, is on the decline, and replaced by much

To write about *creative scholarship* is obviously not easy – especially if you have a kind of artistic creativity in mind. Although there is much to say for the theologian as poet and the link between theology and aesthetics in general, I restrict creativity to a form of "courageous" scholarship that, on a first level, renews the content and focus of theology, and at a higher level, shifts the very epistemological presuppositions and boundaries of theology. In Kuhnian terms, one could situate this first-level creativity within the context of normal science, and the second-level creativity in the mode of revolutionary science, leading eventually to a Gestalt-switch or paradigm shift.[27]

What does this mean in concrete terms?

If we bring together the implications of mode 2 knowledge with the post-positivist philosophy of science developments in the work of Bartley, Popper, Lakatos, Laudan and others, an interesting convergence is noted: mode 2 knowledge is basically problem solving on the move, whereas post-positivist philosophy of science (in various ways) takes the relative problem-solving abilities of rival theories as measures of scientific progress. In the absence of a paradigm shift, it seems that creative scholarship is about problem identification and solving within the parameters of normal science.

If we now take one step further, and accept Kuhn's fundamental insight that paradigms are community constructs – the agreement amongst a group of scholars to "see the world in a certain way" and to ask the questions emerging from that world view – a fundamental issue is raised: Who is the one in our scientific community that will shape our "view of the world" from which the subsequent questions will emerge? *The first step in fostering creative scholarship is then not to rephrase questions, but to reshape the very community from which the questions are raised.*

And here one has to agree with Jim Cochrane in his editorial to *JTSA* 111 (Nov. 2001) in which a number of theological biographies are published: he admits that "the structural, systemic problem of theology in South Africa is painfully evident in the collection of papers we are able to publish ... The dominant theological paradigms and people of the past decades in South Africa have been white, male and Protestant". This is not to diminish the excellent scholarly contributions made by John de Gruchy, Charles Villa-Vicencio, Willie Jonker, Johan Heyns, Klaus Nürnberger, David Bosch, Ferdinand Deist and many others. The point is, though: in the present situation of dramatic power shifts and opening up of previously unknown possibilities inside South Africa and beyond our borders[28] we urgently need African, feminist/womanist, black and ecumenical theologians to extend our community of scholarship – not as interesting guests to give "alternative" input in order to legitimise our conferences, nor as affirmative action agents, *but as co-determinants of the very questions we ask and therefore co-determinants of our theological agenda.*[29]

---

    more open, but no less exciting, inter-disciplinary co-operation.
27 A paradigm switch rarely occurs in theology, but such judgement would depend one's definition of a paradigm. For a "paradigmatic" view of theology over twenty centuries, see Tracy and Kung (1986), and Kuhn (1962).
28 I obviously include theologies in the Northern hemisphere, Latin America and Asia. It would be a big error if we expand our local and African community in various ways, but lose the creative community of scholars in the greater ecumenical world. The power relations at stake in such an engagement is an issue we need to take seriously, though.
29 For a variety of reasons, some outlined above, this is easier said than done, unless we

Let me close the discussion on creative scholarship with a very brief remark about the second-level, paradigm-shifting kind of scholarship. I do this in relation to the inner-theological reality of the Dutch Reformed Church (which incidentally still has the most theologians active in the academy in South Africa today).

Highly simplified, the dominant paradigm of DRC theology[30] has been shaped by three forces from the nineteenth century: Abraham Kuyper's neo-Calvinism, Gustav Warneck's missiology, and Scottish Pietism. On a positive note: we gained a view of Christ's rule over the whole earth from Kuyper (a truly Calvinistic line). We gained a view of enculturalisation in mission from Warneck; and we gained a view of personal commitment to Christ and a holy life from Andrew Murray. These positive influences were, however, overshadowed and ultimately destroyed by the worst in each of these roots.[31]

Via his organically constructed general/special grace distinction Kuyper provided the grounds for the differentiation between the church as organism and as institute, thereby relativising the visible unity of the church to an eschatological reality, and actually constructing a subjectivist ecclesiology based on personal choice. Warneck's construction of *Volkschristianisierung* provided the grounds for the constitutive relation between *Volk* and church and separate churches for separate *Volke*. And pietism, with its personalist focus and anti-intellectual, almost fundamentalist, approach to Scripture, provided the grounds for a privatised religion without a real effect on the world.

What has happened to this paradigm? The demise of apartheid *as a theology* left us with a huge vacuum and loss of direction. The overarching and encompassing view of the Afrikaner people, a certain interpretation of the Bible, the church as basically *volkskerk*, and of society as segregated according to God's will – a kind of quasi-religious umbrella – collapsed. People are uncertain what "Afrikaner" means today (if you still need such a label); the Bible (if still read and not accessed via popular pious literature) is approached via either a modernist or naive reading strategy; the DRC congregations have evolved into a plurality of liturgical, geographical and organisational forms; and pietism has in many cases turned into forms of charismatic pentecostalism.

What is the implication of all this for DRC theology? Simply this: we are in a very difficult but exciting phase between two paradigms. We know the former one led us into a dead end, but are still clueless as to the emerging one. A few things, though, are perhaps clear already. I state them as "wishes" more than as generally accepted ideas.

---

    change our very view of scholarship and of what theology is. I am not sure what that really means and where it will lead us.

30   The best "overview" information about the development of DRC theology is found in Johann Kinghorn (1986), Ferdinand Deist (1994) and *Scriptura* 76 (2001), in which very insightful papers on the DRC and the transition to democracy were published.

31   I have in a recent paper, delivered at the University of Heidelberg (Nov. 2002), researched the negative effects of these three forces (see Naudé 2005). Extensive references to original and secondary sources pertaining to Kuyper, Warneck and Pietism are found in that paper and not repeated here.

We would like to remain Reformed, but in a non-authoritarian, pluralistic sense of the word. Therefore studies on our tradition (Augustine, Calvin, Barth) and confessions (Nicea, Three Formulae, Belhar) are as crucial as ever. The issues of *sola Scriptura* and a responsible hermeneutic need our urgent attention. And the lack of a coherent liturgical theology is already destroying parts of our heritage.

We would like to re-join the ecumenical church and take our cue for a theological agenda from them (whilst making our own creative contribution): the issue of a *processus confessionis* on economic justice; ideas of what an ecological church would look like; a renewed interpretation of justification by faith alone; promoting church unity confessing the apostolic faith, and many other themes.

We would like to become a distinctly African Reformed church. Therefore the theological and missiological questions of the rapidly growing independent churches must be on our agenda. Theological interpretations of an African renaissance and the power of a global market economy, together with the urgent need for a theology in a time of AIDS, will have to inform our thinking. The issue of a lay theology and all the questions related to what we call theological education will become more urgent as we move forward.

Will an overarching paradigm such as the previous one emerge? I think the answer is no. *We will learn to live in fragile, pluralist theoretical constructs, doing eclectic and not systematic theology.* Our theology will perhaps derive coherence only from the inner thrust of Reformed theology itself: *semper reformanda*.

There is a lot to be done.

If we needed good theology to lead us from apartheid to democracy, we now already know that we need even better theology to strengthen and sustain our democracy through a vigilant civil society in which the university and vibrant scholarship are crucial partners.

BIBLIOGRAPHY

Botha, J. 1992. "The ethics of New Testament interpretation". *Neotestamentica* Vol. 26, pp. 169-194.

Botman, R. 2001. "Belhar and the white DRC: Changes in the DRC 1974-1990". *Scriptura* Vol. 76, pp. 33-42.

Botman, R. 2002. "Is blood thicker than justice? The legacy of Abraham Kuyper for Southern Africa". In L.E. Lego (ed.) *Religion, pluralism and public life. Abraham Kuyper's legacy for the twenty-first century.* Grand Rapids: Eerdmans, pp. 342 -361.

Chopp, R.S. 2002. "Beyond the founding fratricidal conflict: A tale of three cities", *Journal of the American Academy of Religion* Vol. 70, No. 3, pp. 461-474.

Cloete, G.D. & Smit, D.J. (eds.). 1984. *A moment of truth.* Grand Rapids: Eerdmans.

Cochrane, J. 2001. "Editorial". *JTSA* Vol. 111, pp. 2-4.

De Gruchy, J. 2001. "The future of Reformed churches in SA – some random notes and reflections". *Scriptura* Vol. 76, pp. 43-50.

Deist, F. 1994. *Ervaring, rede en metode in Skrifuitleg. 'n Wetenskapshistoriese ondersoek na Skrifuitleg in die Ned Geref Kerk 1840-1990.* Pretoria: HSRC.

Department of Education. 1997. *Education White Paper 3: A programme for the transformation of higher education.* Department of Education: Pretoria.

Department of Education. 2001. *National Plan for Higher Education.* Department of Education: Pretoria.

Du Rand, J. 1985. "Afrikaner piety and dissent". In C. Villa-Vicencio & J. de Gruchy (eds.) *Resistance and hope.* Cape Town: David Philip.

Du Toit, B. 2000. *God? Geloof in 'n postmoderne tyd.* Bloemfontein: CLF.

Gibbons, M. 1994. *The new production of knowledge. The dynamics of science and research in contemporary society.* London: Sagen.

Hendriks, J & Erasmus, J. 2001. " Interpreting the new religious landscape in post-apartheid South Africa". *JTSA* Vol. 100, pp. 41-65.

Jonker, W.D. 1988. "Some remarks on the interpretation of Karl Barth". *NGTT* Vol. 29, pp. 29-40.

Jonker, W.D. 1988. "Suid-Afrika se verbondheid met Europa: die teologie". *Tydskrif vir Geesteswetenskappe* Vol. 28, pp. 146-157.

Kinghorn, J. (ed.). 1986. *Die NG Kerk en apartheid.* Johannesburg: Macmillan.

Kuhn, T. 1962. *The structure of scientific revolutions.* Chicago: University of Chicago Press.

Lategan, B. 2001. "History, historiography and reformed hermeneutics at Stellenbosch. A case study of an unsolved problem and possible alternatives". Unpublished paper delivered at a Centre for Theological Inquiry conference on *Reformed Identity and Ecumenicity,* Stellenbosch, April 2001.

Lombaard, C. 2001. "The left governing hand and the right governing hand". *JTSA* Vol. 109, pp. 17-24.

National Commission on Higher Education. 1996. *A framework for transformation.* Pretoria: NCHE.

Naudé, P.J. 1997a. "Die Belharstryd in ekumeniese perspektief". *NGTT* xxxviii/3, pp. 226-243.

Naudé, P.J. 2001. "The DRC's role in the context of transition in South Africa: Main streams of academic research". *Scriptura* Vol. 76, pp. 87-106.

Naudé, P.J. 2005. "From pluralism to ideology: The roots of apartheid theology in Abraham Kuyper, Gustav Warneck and theological Pietism". *Scriptura* Vol. 88, pp. 161-173.

Naudé, P.J. 2003. "From campus by the sea to a university for all. A review of curriculum transformation at the University of Port Elizabeth". In P.J. Naude & N. Cloete (eds.) *A tale of three countries. Curriculum transformation in the social sciences.* Cape Town: Juta.

Schussler-Fiorenza, E. 1988. "The ethics of interpretation: De-centring biblical scholarship". *JBL* Vol. 107, pp. 3-17.

Scott, P. 1997. "Changes in knowledge production and dissemination in the context of globalisation". In N. Cloete, J. Muller (eds.) *Knowledge, identity and curriculum transformation in Africa.* Cape Town: Maskew Miller Longman, pp. 17-42.

Tracy, D & Kung, H. 1986. *Paradigm change in theology.* New York: Crossroad Publishing Company

Van Huyssteen, J.W.V. 1986. *Teologie as kritiese geloofsverantwoording.* Pretoria: RGN.

Van Huyssteen, J.W.V. & Du Toit, B.J. 1982. *Geloof en skrifgesag*. Pretoria: NGKB.

Wetmar, C. 1996. "Wat het Athene met Jerusalem te doen? Enkele histories-sistmatiese gesigspunte in verband met die vraag of teologie aan die universitieit tuishoort". *Skrif en Kerk* Vol. 17, No. 2, pp. 473-490.

3.2 THE LIMITATIONS OF PROBLEM SOLVING AS A CRITERION FOR PARADIGMS IN THEOLOGY[1]

In dialogue with Wentzel van Huyssteen

The aim of this essay is to outline the use of problem solving as a criterion for paradigms in theology and to raise a few related limitations to the implementation of this approach. For the sake of this conference, the parameters for the discussion below are taken from the thought-provoking work by Prof. Wentzel van Huyssteen (1986), and it is hoped that the few arguments put forward here will contribute to a refinement of our normative judgements in theology.

1. PROBLEM SOLVING AS A CRITERION FOR SCIENTIFIC PARADIGMS

In his important study, *The structure of scientific revolutions*, Thomas Kuhn (1970b) established "problem solving" as the most important criterion for determining a new scientific paradigm.

> Probably the most prevalent claim advanced by the proponents of a new paradigm is that they can solve the problems that have led the old one to a crisis (Kuhn 1970b:153).

When persistently unsolved "puzzles" (constitutive for normal science) lead to a growing professional insecurity, and the former become "anomalies" that are viewed as "counter-instances", the possibility arises that an alternative paradigm, claiming to solve the crisis-provoking problems, may be accepted. Although not exclusively so, this acceptance is based on the scientists' belief in the "future promise" of the new paradigm, i.e. its comparative ability to solve problems (Kuhn 1970b:97, 153-158, 185).

Kuhn warns against a direct application of his views concerning the nature of natural science to other sciences (1970b:208). He refers to theology only once to explain co-option of a proposed new paradigm by reliance on an authoritative source (1970b:136). Kuhn's influence has, nevertheless, extended beyond the boundaries of natural science (see Gutting 1980). And Van Huyssteen has proved that important insights for systematic theology can be derived from *inter alia* an extended definition of rationality and truth, the role of commitments, and the nature of science as a group-based, sociologically determined activity (Van Huyssteen 1986:80-82).

One of the most important elements in Van Huyssteen's development of a critical realist model of theology is the appropriation of problem solving as a criterion for paradigms in theology (1986:187-206). "Theological assertions must critically identify and analyse real problems and formulate theories that render valid and adequate solutions to these problems" (1986:187, my translation). Problem solving is supplemented by relation-to-reality (*werklikheidsbetrokkenheid*) and the progressive nature of theological statements as basic criteria for the rationality of systematic theology.

---

[1] This essay was first published in 1988 in J. Mouton (ed.), *Paradigms and progress in theology*. Pretoria: HSRC, 142-151.

It is important to note that "criterion" is not used as an analytical concept to distinguish between two or more paradigms, but in a normative sense, i.e. to evaluate the comparative success of different paradigms (Van Huyssteen 1986:169; Pfürtner 1984:189). The defence of a critical realist model for theology is in itself an endeavour to promote a "better and more valid" model.

In the next few paragraphs a number of related limitations to the use of specifically problem solving as prescriptive criterion for theology are set out. I believe that this will not only clarify some ambiguous points in Van Huyssteen's exposition, but serve to enhance the possible application of this criterion in systematic theology. The references to specific examples in historical and contemporary theology serve as illustrations of different arguments and should be tested by detailed analyses not possible within the confines of this essay (see "historical" section in Küng and Tracy 1984).

2. THE LIMITATIONS OF PROBLEM SOLVING AS A CRITERION FOR THEOLOGICAL PARADIGMS IN THEOLOGY

1. The whole debate about "paradigms", "scientific revolutions", "problem solving" and "rationality" is part of a very specific tradition, namely the Euro-American philosophy of science. This tradition constitutes a specific scientific context that is not necessarily shared by all theologians and implies that the paradigm problem is itself paradigmatically determined.

To "see" the problem presupposes, at least for some non-Western theologians, a "*Gestalt* switch" which seriously impedes the application of "problem solving" as universal criterion for systematic theology. A few examples will suffice to illustrate that such a criterion may in some cases even be viewed as a form of scientific paternalism.

African theology as an alternative system of thinking is not a theology of the book (Setiloane 1986:36) that shares Western scientific or philosophical sophistication (28, 45). It views Western theology as a threat to the "soul of Africa" (44) and is in itself an attempt to express faith "from the perspective of African grassroots background and culture" (35). From this perspective "knowledge" and "rationality" are closely linked with an oral tradition (Setiloane 1986:1-2) and religious myths have an explanatory role normally reserved for natural science in the Western tradition (Koech 1977:118).

Liberation theologians from Latin America are suspicious about the "academic" character of Western theology (Assmann 1974:144-153; Miguez-Bonino 1975:xix; Segundo in Hennely 1979:xii). The latter has become a system of ideas addressing the cognitive problem of scientific and rational credibility stemming from the Enlightenment since Immanuel Kant (Sobrino 1977:124-128). Instead of engaging in meta-theological debates about a theory of progressive, cognitive growth, liberation theology is (at least initially) a spontaneous reflection on the experience of the poor in Latin America (Gutierrez 1983:76, 90).

In developing a theology from a Korean women's perspective, Kyung defines her own position as a second-generation liberationist who wishes to free theology from colonial and neo-colonial powers.

> We know that the most dangerous thing for an oppressed people is to become benumbed through internalizing alien criteria and ignoring our own gut feelings (Kyung 1988:28).

She then continues to explore the theological significance of the Han experience and "Han-pu-ri" as collective healing and therapy (Kyung 1988:34-36).

One may simply indicate that these examples, despite their different frameworks, precisely illustrate what Van Huyssteen means by the contextual determinations of theological problems (1986:189): African theology aims at solving the conceptual problems posed by the African world view; liberation theology is primarily directed at the problem of theological epistemology; and woman's theology from Korea tries to solve the empirical problem of suffering.

The point is, however, that these theologies do not understand themselves primarily as "problem-solvers" whereby scientific progress (if important at all) is normatively determined in terms of "cognitive growth". Laudan expressly states that these issues arise "because most people in the West draw the bulk of their beliefs about nature, and even about themselves, from the corpus of science" (Laudan 1977:6). In a cultural context where "rationality" is closely linked to folk tales and myths, and where the experience of the non-persons becomes the source for theology, "problem solving", as set out by Van Huyssteen, loses some of its appeal as a general criterion for systematic theology.

From a fundamental theological point of view, this very insight may be counted as constituting "progress" in any further debate on the issue of problem solving. In some theological contexts it is not the application of the criterion, but the nature of the criterion itself that needs to be highlighted, and discussion about the latter is the basis for an ecumenically acceptable application.

2. The manner in which Van Huyssteen implements the criterion of problem solving poses the danger of circular thinking. Following Larry Laudan, he distinguishes between empirical and conceptual problems. Empirical problems are constituted by anything about the natural world "which strikes us as odd, or otherwise in need of explanation" (Laudan 1977:15). Where empirical problems lead to first-order questions about substantive entities, conceptual problems are directed at higher-order questions about the "well-foundedness of the theories which have been devised to answer the first-order questions" (Laudan 1977:48). Internal conceptual problems arise from self-contradictions or logical inconsistencies/ambiguity of concepts within a specific theory. External conceptual problems are (*inter alia*) generated by logical inconsistencies and methodological conflicts between two or more competing theories (Laudan 1977:48-54).

The question of whether one paradigm solves problems better than its rival, says Van Huyssteen, is determined by Scripture, tradition and contemporary scientific thought, with Scripture as the most important factor (*basiskriterium*) (1986:193). There can be no doubt that the theologian's view of Scripture and related questions about hermeneutical presuppositions constitute an internal conceptual problem within a certain tradition. But the moment Scripture is implemented as a basic normative criterion to judge the problem-solving abilities of systematic theologies from different traditions, it becomes part of a methodological conflict. It thus constitutes an external conceptual problem where the definition of the science (what is theology?) is at stake (Kuhn 1970b:103).

The history of the debate between Catholic and Reformed scholars, for example, illustrates that the relative "weight" assigned to Scripture *vis-à-vis* tradition (Berkouwer 1967:331-386) will not be solved by simply stating that the former should be accepted as basic normative criterion in theology. Nor will a mere re-confirmation of Scripture (*vis-à-vis* social experience) as methodological source of theology (Naudé 1987:41-43, 313-314) solve the conflict between liberation theologies and a classic Reformed position. In both cases the methodological status of Scripture itself is the crux of the (external) conceptual problem and may (at least initially) not be employed as basic criterion to judge competing methodological claims.

No Christian theology would reject Scripture as a criterion for theology (Küng 1984:73-75), but from a fundamental theological perspective (Tracy 1981:54-79; Van Huyssteen 1986:2), the relative position of Scripture must be the focus of attention. This would limit circular thinking and open the way for ecumenical (inter-paradigmatic) consensus on the manner in which Scripture is employed as a criterion for theology.

3. It is doubtful whether the criterion of problem solving as implemented by Kuhn and Van Huyssteen takes the valid distinction between "theories" and "paradigms" adequately into consideration. The former refers to a specific theory serving as answer to an empirical or conceptual problem, whereas the latter is constituted by a number of conceptually or historically related theories. These may be called a "paradigm" (Kuhn), "research programme" (Lakatos 1970:133-134), "research tradition" (Laudan 1977:70) or *Verstehensmodell* (Küng 1984:41).

It is important to defend the view that although a constituent theory may play a decisive role in the process of paradigm rejection, the term "scientific revolution" or "paradigm switch" should be reserved for fundamental changes of research traditions only. This is the basis for a more discriminating application of problem solving as a normative criterion, because it allows a relative weighing of actual problems solved and avoids the assignment of equal scientific-theoretical importance to theories which prove to have different (i.e. "unequal") historical and methodological significance.

Answering his critics, Kuhn modifies his conception of a "scientific revolution" to transcend a purely empiricist notion of progress (1970b:92) in order to take sociological and psychological aspects into account (1970b:179-180; 1970a:21-22). It is only a new theory (solving an empirical anomaly), but also a "special sort of change involving a certain sort of reconstruction of group commitments", that constitute a revolution (1970b:181). Despite this reformulation, Kuhn still considers a very small-scale change to be a "revolution" (1970b:50,92,180-181) and underestimates the fact that even "normal science" is constituted by a continuous debate about foundational issues.

The basic problem is that Kuhn does not clarify the difficult issue of the relationship between a paradigm and its constituent theories, and does not allow for a corrective relation between a paradigm and contradicting data (Laudan 1977:74-74, 134-136). This "rigid" concept of a paradigm (constituted by an unchanging set of doctrines) makes it very difficult for Kuhn to acknowledge that research traditions may also evolve as a result of a change of some of its most basic core elements (Laudan 1977:96) without necessarily leading to a paradigm switch/scientific revolution.

Following Kuhn, Van Huyssteen states that a revolutionary stage in theology "needs not only be associated with prominent names like an Augustine, Calvin, Luther, Barth, Moltmann or a Pannenberg. On the contrary, a breakthrough or conceptual transformation in systematic theology is any special kind of change that can lead to the restructuring of the basic commitments (*grondoortuigings*) of a specific person or group or persons" (1986:83, my translation). Despite a later qualification (1986:213), Van Huyssteen's exposition leaves the ambiguous impression that the same theoretical status (i.e. "revolutionary") is assigned to the Reformation, on the one hand, and a new theory regarding the conquest of Canaan or the historicity of Jonah (1986:82-83), on the other.

4. Three remarks about the relation between "problem solving" and theological paradigms may highlight further limitations of the former and lead to its more refined application to systematic theology.

4.1. The philosophical argument for a stricter definition of a paradigm switch/scientific revolution (Laudan) is important for theology, for at least two reasons: firstly, because conversion to an alternative model is tied up with deep-seated beliefs and interests (see below); secondly, because continuation between successive theories is even more obvious than in the natural sciences.

In support of this point, Greinacher (1984:31-32) states that the co-existence of competing paradigms is an integral part of theological science. Unlike Kuhn's exclusive paradigm succession, a Hegelian *Aufhebung*, constituted by, among other considerations, a strong element of conservation (*Aufbewahren*), is a more adequate description of theology. Due to Scripture being the *Grund- und Urzeugnis* of all Christian theology, one may (paradoxically) speak of a paradigm switch on the basis of the permanence of the Christian message (Küng 1984:66). Küng feels so strongly about this that he even points to a certain resistance against the use of the concept "revolutionary" science in theology (1984:65).

Even when one limits the application of problem solving to a specific discipline in theology, one should be cautious not to view evolutionary developments as revolutionary transformations. Two examples, one from dogmatics and the other from hermeneutics, illustrate this point.

If Aquinas makes a radical anthropocentricity possible without relinquishing theocentricity, and Metz applies this to develop a "theology of the world", it is obvious that doing so does not involve a radically new *principium formale*, but only a new application of the existing thought form (*Denkform*) (Metz 1962:34-35, 47-50; 1979). If Schleiermacher develops a psychological relation between reader and original author, and Bultmann applies this insight in terms of an existential hermeneutics (Pannenburg 1971:97-101), doing so may be viewed as an evolutionary expansion of Schleiermacher's development without obtaining "revolutionary" cognitive status.

Apart from the strong element of continuation which should make one very cautious in assigning "revolutionary" status to a problem-solving theory, the perspective from which a certain theory or new theological current is viewed will ultimately determine the associated "problem" under discussion. This, in turn, will determine whether the (new) theory is described in "paradigmatic" terms or not.

A simple example will illustrate this point. If Latin American liberation theology is approached from the angle of solving the problem of the relation between theory and praxis (Lamb 1976), it does present us with such important methodological insights that "revolutionary" status may be assigned to this type of theology. . But if the same theology is analysed in comparison to other "experiential theologies", a basic continuation is found. The contextual (exclusive) experience of the poor is the source of a God-experience (knowledge of God) such as is found in (for example) Schleiermacher's "feeling of dependence", Bultmann's "existential decision" or Rahner's "transcendental secret" (Naudé 1987:150-152).

One should thus not only be hesitant in assigning revolutionary cognitive status to any problem-solving theory, but be very clear from what perspective such "problem-solving judgement" is performed. The final decision on any theology will obviously depend on the cumulative weight of particular arguments from more than one perspective (see Pfürtner 1984 on Luther and Thomas).

4.2 The issue of the relative status of problems solved may be addressed by utilising Küng's distinction between macro, meso and micro models (Küng 1984:43). This will undoubtedly lead to a positive refinement of the problem-solving criterion.

It is possible that certain changes in a part of the theological discipline may have far-reaching implications, e.g. a different doctrine of salvation (objective versus subjective) or alternative view of Scripture (fundamentalist versus historical-critical). But one must account for the fact that the restructuring of commitments in the choice for/against a Reformed research tradition is normally of a far more profound nature than the choice for an alternative theory regarding, for example, the conquest of Canaan. The former would almost always imply a "paradigm switch", whereas the latter would rarely lead to a scientific revolution in the stricter sense of the word.

If one accepts Küng's point that paradigmatic periods in theology (see Table, Küng 1984:25) are constituted by macro levels (*Gesamtlösungen*) only, and other problems solved belong to the "lower" status of meso or micro models (*Detaillösungen*), a relative value can be assigned to the problems solved by competing theological theories. An extension of the present formulation to include this instrument of "weighing" different problems will lead to more convincing results in the application of the criterion under discussion.

4.3 A last element (ignored by Van Huyssteen) which limits the application of the problem-solving criterion is the fact that this criterion cannot account for the "irrational" element related to theological paradigms.

Kühn's reference to a "conversion experience" (1970b:151) in the acceptance of a new paradigm is true in a very real sense in theology. One reason for this is that non-scientific factors introduce an "irrational" element on two levels.

First: If a "discernment of faith" (*Glaubensentscheidung*), common to all scientists, is reduced to an existential religious decision, a new paradigm may be resisted (or even shelved) despite a superior problem-solving ability or acceptance by a large scientific community. Küng (1984:58) refers *inter alia* to the continuous reliance on thirteenth-century Thomism up to Vaticanum II, despite its "refutation" by alternative paradigms.

Second: A theological paradigm does not necessarily originate in a new problem-solving theory, but is often preceded by "a very personal spiritual experience" (Küng 1984:64, my translation). Augustine is an excellent historical example that a new paradigm in theology may sometimes have an "irrational" mystical foundation (Kannengieser 1984:165), which can only be ascribed to the creative work of God's Spirit. The same Spirit may, even against "scientific" arguments, convince a theologian to accept a new paradigm as part of his/her obedience to God. A theologian hardly leaves the comfort of a study or university to do theology from the perspective of the poor because he/she is "scientifically" convinced!

It might be difficult to prove the last argument, but it does point to the fact that there are factors involved in the judging of competing theological theories which are not catered for by "problem solving" because they lie outside the scope provided by this criterion.

3. CONCLUSION AND SUMMARY

It seems as if the criterion of problem solving is relative to the cultural context in which a specific theology is developed and may not be universally suitable in its present formulation.

The indication of Scripture as the basic determining factor in the application of problem solving is relative to the confessional context and such application should form an integral part of the ecumenical problem-solving debate.

Because of the strong element of continuity between successive theories, and as a result of the perspectival nature of problem-solving judgements, problems solved by theological theories rarely imply a new paradigm. The problems solved might be part of the evolutionary development of an existing paradigm responding to issues raised in a specific area of theological science or responding to contemporary thought.

When the criterion of problem solving is employed as normative judgement, the more strict definition of a paradigm or research tradition should be taken into account and a *Gestalt* switch attributed mainly to the solving of external conceptual problems or problems on the level of macro models. A distinction between different levels of problem solving is imperative for the assignment of relative cognitive status to competing theories.

Application of the criterion of problem solving is limited by the fact that it is unable to account for the "irrational" element involved in the creation, resistance or acceptance of paradigms.

These indicated limitations do not necessarily entail the discarding of problem solving as valid criterion for theological paradigms. It does, however, call for some refinement and – as Van Huyssteen himself suggests – for supplementation by other criteria prior to a final decision on the theoretical merits of any theological model.

BIBLIOGRAPHY

Assmann, H. 1974. "Kritik der "Theologie der Befreiung". *Internationale Dialoz Zeitschrift* 7, pp. 144-153.

Berkouwer, G.C. 1967. *De heilige Schrift II*. Kampen: Kok.

Booth, N. (ed.) 1977. *African religions: A symposium*. New York: NOK Publishers.

Gutierrez, G. 1983. *The power of the poor in history*. London: SCM.

Gutting, G. 1980. *Paradigms and revolution. Appraisals and applications of Thomas Kuhn's philosophy of science*. Notre Dame: University of Notre Dame Press.

Hennely, A.T. 1979. *Theologies in conflict: The challenge of Juan Luis Segundo*. New York: Orbis.

Kannengiesser, C. 1984. "Origenes, Augustin und der Paragmenwechsel in der Theologie". In H. Küng & D. Tracy (eds.), pp. 151-167.

Koech, K. 1977. "African mythology: A key to understanding African religion". In N. Booth (ed.), pp. 117-139.

Kyung, C.H. 1988. "'Han-pu-ri': Doing theology from Korean women's perspective". *The Ecumenical Review*. Vol. 40, No. 1, pp. 27-36.

Kuhn, T. 1970. *The structure of scientific revolutions*. Second edition. Chicago: Chicago University Press.

Küng, H. 1984. "Paradigmenwechsel in der Theologie. Versuch einer Grundlagenerklärung". In H. Küng & D. Tracy (eds), pp. 37-75.

Küng, H. & Tracy, D. (eds). 1984. *Theologie – wohin? Auf dem Weg zu einem neuen Paradigma*. Zürich: Benziger.

Lakatos, I. & Musgrave (eds.), 1970. *Criticism and the growth of knowledge: Proceedings of the International Colloquium in the Philosophy of Science,* London, 1965. Cambridge: Cambridge University Press.

Lakatos, I. 1970. "Falsification and the methodology of scientific research programmes". In I. Lakatos & Musgrave (eds.), pp. 91ff.

Lamb, M.L. 1976. "The theory-praxis relationship in contemporary Christian theologies". In *Catholic Society of America: Proceedings of the thirty-first annual convention* 31, pp. 149-178.

Laudan, L. 1977. *Progress and its problems. Towards a theory of scientific growth*. London: Routledge and Kegan Paul.

Metz, J.B. 1962. *Christliche Anthropozentrik: über die Denkform des Thomas van Aquin*. München: Kosel.

Metz, J.B. 1979. *Zur theologie der Welt*. 4. Ufl. Mainz: Matthias Grünewald.

Miguez Bonino, J. 1975. *Doing theology in a revolutionary situation*. Philadelphia: Fortress.

Modehn, C, Rahner, K & Zwiefelhofer, H. (eds.) 1977. *Befreiende Theologie. Der Beitrag Lateinamerikas zur Theologie der Gegenwart*. Stuttgart: Kohlhammer.

Naudé, P.J. 1987. *Ortopraksie as metodologiese prinsipe in die sistematiese teologie.* Unpublished DTh thesis. Stellenbosch: University of Stellenbosch.

Pannenberg, W. 1971. *Grundlagen systematischer Theologie: Gesammelte Aufsätze.* 2. Aufl. Göttingen: Vandenhoeck & Ruprecht.

Pfürtner, S. 1984. "Die Paradigmen von Thomas und Luther. Bedeutet Luthers Rechtfertigungsbotschaft einen Paradigmenwechsel?". In H. Küng & D. Tracy (eds), pp. 168-192.

Setiloane, G.M. 986. *African theology. An introduction.* Johannesburg: Skotaville.

Sobrino, J. 1977. "Theologisch Erkennen in der europäischen und der lateinamerikanischer Theologie". In C. Modehn, K. Rahner & H. Zwiefelhofer (Hrsg.), pp. 123-143

Tracy, D. 1981. *The analogical imagination. Christian theology and the culture of pluralism.* London: SCM.

Van Huyssteen, J.W.V. 1986. *Teologie as kritiese geloofsverantwoording. Teorievorming in die sistematiese teologie.* Pretoria: RGN.

3.3 THE TWO FACES OF CALVIN IN SOUTH AFRICA

In honour of the 500th commemoration of John Calvin's birth[1]

1. INTRODUCTION

These reflections are a contribution to the festive commemoration of Calvin's birth around the world during 2009. The article was read as a paper to a German-speaking audience in the context of a lecture series by the University of Basel on the reception of Calvin in various parts of the world. Reflections were offered from such diverse settings as Hungary, the USA, China, Germany and South Africa.

Part one of the article offers a short historical background to the situation of *status confessionis* in general, but with a specific focus on the South African situation. The first face of Calvin is then sketched via the reception of Calvin in the mainly neo-Calvinist theology of Abraham Kuyper and his South African followers.

Part two of the article presents the second face of Calvin in relation to tensions in Calvin's own work, but more focused on the reception of the "liberative" Calvin in the works of theologians such as Allan Boesak, John de Gruchy, Beyers Naudé and Willie Jonker. This second reception of Calvin is subsequently linked to the rejection clauses of the three middle articles of the Belhar confession. The link to Belhar serves as a direct antithesis to the first reception of Calvin and provides the basis for a short conclusion on the future of Calvin theology in South Africa.

2. HERESY AND STATUS CONFESSIONIS

The church declares a state of confession when a situation arises in which neutral or mediocre matters (*adiaphora*) become issues of grave importance that threaten the very heart of the gospel message, and thus compel the church to witness and act against this threat. Although the threat may be "ethical" in nature, the church interprets this as a theological or doctrinal matter, and considers such threat to the gospel as a false teaching or heresy.[2]

During the 20th century three[3] such occasions arose.

---

1 This essay was originally published in two parts in the *Dutch Reformed Theological Journal* Vol. 30, No. 3 & 4, 607-613 and 614-619, as an adapted version of a paper delivered in Basel, Switzerland on 7 May 2009 in the context of the Calvin commemoration year. The topic for this public lecture on Calvin was provided by the University of Basel, which requested an analysis of "Rassismus als Häresie: Komplexe calvinistische Wirkungen in Südafrika".

2 For a conceptual and historical analysis read Smit (1984).

3 A quite recent example that has not yet reached full confessional status is the *processus confessionis* announced by the World Council of Churches on issues of economic and ecological justice. Although the World Alliance of Reformed Churches adopted the Accra Confession in 2004 as a fundamental critique against the "empire" of global capitalism and its devastating ecological impact, the Alliance itself recognises that Accra is not a confession in the traditional sense of the world. It could, however, become the fourth

First: In the German *Kirchenkampf* against National Socialism issues such as church structure, eligibility for church office and church discipline became matters that fundamentally threatened the credibility of the gospel and compelled the Confessing Church in Barmen to accept a new declaration of faith in 1934.

Second: The ecumenical rejection of racism – especially as legalised in South Africa – led the Lutheran World Federation in Dar es Salaam (1977) to declare a *status confessionis* on matters of race-based church membership and the political system of apartheid. This was followed by two further declarations on the same matter by the World Alliance of Reformed Churches in Ottawa (1982) and the Dutch Reformed Mission Church in South Africa (1982). It was this latter church that subsequently adopted the Confession of Belhar[4] (1986) against the heresy of a false gospel.

The third instance relates to the Reformierter Bund in Germany, which in 1982 announced a *status confessionis* on the possession of nuclear arms, as they judged that such arms fundamentally threaten the possibility of human life and put the core of the Christian faith at risk.

For the sake of this paper, I therefore focus on the second example of *status confessionis* referred to above: the declaration of racism as a heresy was primarily directed against the formation of separate Reformed churches for different races and a Christian gospel that supported a political and legal system of state-enforced racial separation.[5] The neutral matters of church membership and structure, as well as the political order of society, became matters of confession that relate to the core of the gospel message.

"But where does Calvin fit into this story?" one may ask. Let us make a short detour into South African history.[6]

The first permanent settlement of Europeans in South Africa in 1652 was of Dutch descent. As employees of the Dutch East India Company directed to set up a half-way station between Europe and the East, they brought with them a Christian faith that was primarily shaped by the Calvinist stream of the Protestant Reformation. The Dutch Reformed Church (DRC) was established under the auspices of the classis of Amsterdam, and held Scripture and the Three Formulae of Unity (The Belgium Confession, the Heidelberg Catechism and the Canons of Dordt) in high esteem.

As local people of mixed race and black people converted to the Christian faith, they were baptised into the one DRC church. As a result of social and language differences, as well as the missionary idea of *Volkskirchen*, the Cape Synod of the DRC decided in 1857 that separate communion services would be held for indigenous people. This eventually led to the establishment of new separate Reformed churches based on race. In 1881 the coloured Dutch Reformed Mission Church was established, followed by the black and Indian churches in 1963 and 1968 respectively. Together with the "white" mother church, these four churches formed the so-called "DRC family" of churches in South Africa.

---

example of a *status confessionis*.
4   For the confessional text, accompanying letter and insightful discussion see Cloete and Smit (1984).
5   For an analysis of the heresy debate read de Gruchy and Villa-Vicencio (1983).
6   One of the best theological interpretations of South Africa's history remains de Gruchy (1979).

The European people of Dutch (and later French) descent slowly built their own language and identity against the colonial powers of the day – whether Dutch or British. They increasingly saw themselves as Afrikaners ("from Africa and speaking Afrikaans") with nationalist ideals of political independence and self-determination. These nationalist ideals grew especially strong after the defeat in the South African War of 1899-1902 and the formation of the Union of South Africa in 1910. When the National Party won the white elections in 1948, the path was opened for grand apartheid and an intensification of racial separation.

The political situation at that point sadly mirrored the racial segregation in the DRC family and drew its moral legitimacy from a specific interpretation of the Christian gospel understood as Calvinism. This represents the first face of Calvin in South Africa. How could such a racial situation in church and society be derived from a call upon the name of Christ and the Calvinist tradition? To answer this question, we need to take a diversion to the Dutch theologian, Abraham Kuyper.

3. THE FIRST FACE OF CALVIN IN SOUTH AFRICA: INTERPRETATIONS OF ABRAHAM KUYPER

Abraham Kuyper (1837-1920), a self-professed (neo-)Calvinist since 1870, exerted enormous influence on church and society in the Netherlands during his lifetime.[7] Kuyper was a pastor, a brilliant scholar and theologian, as well as an active public figure who eventually became prime minister. He commenced his reflections on Calvinism with a series of Bible studies in which he worked out the basis for what became his formal dogmatic works published between 1888 and 1917.[8]

One should be careful not to draw a simple, direct line between Kuyper and Afrikaner Calvinism.[9] However, the weaknesses in Kuyper's theology did create the opportunity for interpretations that could legitimately call on his – and by implication on Calvin's – authority and blessing. In highly simplified terms, three elements of Kuyper's vast thinking are relevant here: his cosmology based on a specific interpretation of general grace, his ecclesiology, and his view of human and social development.

3.1. Cosmology embedded in general grace

One of the key thrusts of Calvin's own thought, and a driving force behind Kuyper's thinking, is its conviction that the whole world and all spheres of society exist under the reign of God in Christ. Christian faith, therefore, does not only have personal

---

7   For an overview and evaluation of Kuyper's life and work, read Lugo (2000) and van der Kooi and de Bruijn (1999).

8   The most comprehensive exposition of his thought is the broad overview of theology as a science in three volumes, *Encyclopaedie der Heiligen Godgeleerdheid* (1893-1894) and *De Gemeene Gratie*, also in three volumes (1903-1905). For fuller literature information see Velema (1989).

9   Kuyper's influence should be read in the wider context of other theological influences, as well as the socio-political history of the Afrikaners. It would perhaps be fair to say that Kuyper himself cannot be held responsible for the brand of Kuyperism that became the specific contextual theology for Afrikaans churches in South Africa in the first half of the twentieth century.

significance, but has social transformative power. In the words of Hesselink: "Calvinism can never be accused of having a God who is too small, or a vision that is too narrow. ... In contrast to Lutherism's quest for a gracious God, pietism's concern for the welfare of the individual soul, and Wesleyanism's goal of personal holiness, the ultimate concern in the Reformed tradition transcends the individual and his salvation. ... The concern is for the realisation of the will of God also in the wider realms of state and culture, in nature and in the cosmos" (Hesselink 1983).

One of many attestations to Kuyper's cosmological thinking is found in the second chapter of his well-known Stone lectures published as *Calvinism: Six lectures delivered in the Theological Seminary at Princeton. The L.P. Stone lectures from 1889-1899* (1899).

In line with this tradition, Kuyper's aim was to provide a theological basis for bringing the whole of reality under the rule of God. He accomplished this by constructing a cosmology in which there is a close analogy between Creator and creation, based on the notion of common grace (*gemeene gratie*). The created order is marked by a rich pluriformity and develops through time according to different particular life principles. There are God-willed orders of creation such as family, state and church that exist in sovereign spheres, but they are held together by God's common grace, which prevents the world from degenerating into chaos. General grace allows for the evolutionary development of the life streams inherent in creation. In this way creation, including the different peoples of the world, fulfils its potential under God's reign and to God's glory (see Velema 1989:58; Jonker 1981:93-94; Van der Kooi 1999).

Critique

Dutch theologian WH Velema's critique of Kuyper's over-emphasis on general grace is unambiguous: Velema argues that the dialectic relationship between common and special grace is an element of Kuyper's idealistic philosophy and cosmology couched in Calvinistic terms, but not drawing on the intentions of Calvin himself. The only way out of this idealistic system, says Velema, is a radical break from the notion of common grace in order to restore some of Calvin's Reformed intentions (Velema 1989:69).

This is confirmed by Kees van der Kooi from the Free University in Amsterdam. He refutes Kuyper's claim that he (Kuyper) merely developed Calvin's notion that some Divine indulgence remains beside the total corruption of creation and mankind. "It should be clear, however, that Calvin's point in speaking about general grace is entirely the opposite of Kuyper's. While in Calvin this general grace receives no further attention and the focus remains on mankind's total dependence on God's grace, Kuyper turns his attention to the subject of this common grace" (Van der Kooi 1999:97-98). Common grace in fact becomes a broad theory of culture based on an optimistic view of Western society, civilisation and scientific achievements (Van der Kooi 1999:98).

If through common grace God establishes orders of creation such as family, state and church, surely one can argue further that the existence, development and protection of different peoples – each as a separate people according to its own potential and law-stream ("*wetstroom*") – can be seen as the will of God? This is especially relevant if a people, such as the Afrikaners, who are Christians and who believe that it is through God's providence that they were planted on the southern tip of Africa to be bearers of the light of the gospel.

It does not require a lot of imagination to see why Kuyper's neo-Calvinist theology became so influential in Afrikaans South African churches of Dutch origin.[10] His own glowing respect for the Boers, who resisted British colonisation and who – inspired by God – trekked into the darkness of Africa to set up republics as a result of their Calvinistic heroism (Strauss 1995:13; Kuiper 1999:78), added a very personal dimension to this relationship. Afrikaners reinterpreted their own history as sacred history, analogous to the Israelite people of God. In short, "The blending of Afrikaner 'sacred history' and neo-Calvinism with its 'sovereignty of spheres' thus provided a powerful ideological base for Afrikaner nationalism and apartheid", writes John de Gruchy (1991:27).

3.2. Ecclesiology

It is important to note that for Kuyper the institutional (i.e. external) form of the church does not belong to its essence. This implies that the traditional marks of unity, holiness, catholicity and Christian, are marks of the unseen church that will only be realised eschatologically.

The formation of various institutional churches (as in the Netherlands after 1886) is thus no threat to the spiritual unity of the church. In fact, the search for external, institutional unity is a form of "churchism" (*kerkisme*) that is to be resisted. The freedom of people to form their own churches should not be diminished. Differentiation amongst peoples will naturally lead to the development of different institutional churches. "The people amongst whom the church is formed are not the same. They differ according to origin, race, country, region, history, potential and psychological orientation, and also do not stay the same, but go through various stages of development" (Kuyper 1904:223, my translation). Because of this, the differences that separate person from person had to form a wedge in the unity of the external church. This pluralistic church formation is "according to my firm conviction a phase of development to which the church should have come" (Kuyper 1904:231, my translation).

Critique

Willie Jonker, an influential South African systematic theologian in the period after 1960, notes that Kuyper constructs the pluriformity of the church not on the basis of Scripture, nor the intention of Calvin and the Reformation, but on his evolutionist and organic concept of history. Kuyper, under influence of nineteenth-century

---

10 As early as 1882 the Rev. S.J. du Toit attempted to translate Kuyper's ideas into the political and ecclesial situation at the time. After 1907 postgraduate students chose to attend the Free University in Amsterdam rather than the State University in Utrecht, and some of them returned to South Africa as avid Kuyperians. In the Gereformeerde Kerk Kuyper's ideas were carried forth by J.D. du Toit and H.G. Stoker, professors of theology and philosophy respectively. Among the Dutch Reformed Church academics F.J.M. Potgieter and A.B. du Preez, and church leaders J.D. Vorster and A.P. Treurnicht, became the most significant proponents of a neo-Calvinist revival in the 1930s and beyond (Kinghorn 1986).

individualism and idealism, introduces a subjectivist element into his ecclesiology. Church formation becomes an issue of personal choice and the exercise of personal freedom. This can lead to the conclusion that it is a normal and God-willed development to establish separate institutional churches for groupings based on culture, psychology or any other human factor. As Kuyper himself argues, these separate churches in no way detract from the unity of the church as a fundamental spiritual reality in Christ (Jonker 1981:91-94; 1989:16-18).

3.3. Human development

With regard to human and social development, Kuyper was a man of his times. He therefore shared the cultural biases of Europe in the latter half of the nineteenth century. Based on general grace, all people have a natural knowledge of God, and in principle the human race and all nations stand equal before God. This general grace forms the basis and stepping stone for special grace that leads to a higher knowledge of God in Christ. On the one hand, Kuyper follows Calvin by maintaining the unity of humanity based on God's counsel (Velema 1989:66). On the other hand, his conception of common grace allows him to see the confusion of the Babel events as setting forth each nation or people according to their own type and "law-stream" (Strauss 1995:12).

According to Kuyper, a hierarchy then follows. The first level consist of people (for example, in Africa) where natural or common grace has not yet developed to its full potential. Then there is a second level where one finds a greater impact of common grace, with pockets of developed areas, for example, in India and Japan. Following this, is a level of social systems where special grace dominates. This is the highest level of development, where there is a maximum Christian effect on the whole of society. The pivotal examples of this are the European and North American civilisations (see Strauss 1995:11 and a discussion of the Stone lectures by Kuiper 1999:74-75).

This differentiation amongst people based on their participation in levels of grace is the hermeneutical key to understanding, for example, Kuyper's view of the three children of Noah. They reflect the various developmental levels. The children of Shem received both common and special grace; those of Japhet benefited to a lesser sense from special grace; and the descendants of Ham show a lack of both forms of grace. Therefore, the descendants of Ham are to be temporarily subservient to the other groups until they have reached the same level of development and civilisation (see Strauss 1995:14 and the fine analysis by Kuiper 1999:74-78 based on original Kuyper sources).

Critique

Based on the analysis of Roman Catholic scholar, Alexandre Ganoczy, John de Gruchy (1991:32) points to the ambiguity of Calvin's life and work. On the one hand, there is the "young Calvin" with his positive, evangelical and liberating theology. On the other hand, we find the "older Calvin" who shows tendencies towards domination and constriction. The historically first reception of Calvin in SA – and dominant until at least the mid-1970s – was via "imperial Calvinism", which was in essence "fearful of spontaneity, openness, equalities and diversities" (Woltersdorff as quoted by de Gruchy 1991:18). The neo-Calvinism espoused by Kuyper found public expression in his political activities. Jan de Bruijn argues that Kuyper was a child of European Romanticism and that his Calvinist politics was in part imbued with his romanticising of the glorious Dutch past and a specific brand of Dutch nationalism (De Bruijn 1999:45-58). This nationalism was based on a theology that accorded undue weight to "a value of separateness" (Botman 2000:355). And because it was embedded in a hierarchical view of civilisations, it paved the way for Afrikaner nationalists to claim legitimate *voogdyskap* (rule over) black people in South Africa as an expression of God's will, as well as a practice of equal but separate justice. As in Kuyper's case, "circumstances claimed victory over doctrine" (Kuiper 1999:81).

When these ideas blended with the socio-economic position of the Afrikaner people after 1929,[11] the scene was set for the development of Kuyper's (and Calvin's!) legacy into a theologically guided ideology. This close link between Calvin, volk and church is quite evident in the journal series *Koers in Krisis* ("Direction in crisis") started by HG Stoker and FJM Potgieter in the mid-1930s. In the first editorial they write: "May this work be to the honour of God and the benefit of the volk, and may it conquer the heart of our volk. And may it unite all the Calvinists in South Africa, whatever their church, province or profession, to common Calvinist action in South Africa" (Stoker and Potgieter 1935:xii).

In this way Calvin's legacy provided the religious and moral legitimacy of apartheid theology and the policies of separate development after 1948. This is, however, not the full picture. There is a second face of Calvin in South Africa, to which we now turn.

4. THE SECOND FACE OF CALVIN: STATUS CONFESSIONIS AND THE BELHAR CONFESSION

Contrary to public perception, Calvin's legacy in South Africa is not only embodied in a theology supporting apartheid. His legacy also took another trajectory, namely the resistance against a theology that made separateness a God-willed principle of creation. This points to the ambiguities evident in the reception[12] of Kuyper in South

---

11 I refer here to the rapid urbanisation of Afrikaners when both economic depression and severe droughts forced them to turn from an agricultural economy to an industrial one. For this they were not skilled and they found themselves in an environment dominated by English capital. The well-known Carnegie Commission was set up to investigate the problem and make recommendations. It found that by the early 1930s about 300 000 Afrikaner people were living in poverty. (A similar study was undertaken for black people in the late 1980s.)

12 Kuyper has left a wide-ranging, complex and even contradictory legacy, which is, like any comprehensive oeuvre, open to more than one interpretation. No wonder that Russel H. Botman (2000:354) argues that Kuyper was indeed both liberative and oppressive! The bases in Kuyper's work for a liberative understanding of Calvinism must be read against the historical context and specific occasion for which they were constructed. See specifically the discussion of Kuyper's rhetorical strategies for American and French audiences by Kuiper (1999). The reclaiming of Kuyper for liberation in South Africa should also be seen in its rhetorical context of fighting Kuyperism at its worst with Kuyper himself. Whatever contrasting evidence, or even direct quotations, are found to support contrasting views, *it is the underlying and permeating structure of Kuyper's thought that should ultimately lead our interpretation*. I declare my South African Reformed presuppositions openly and probably err in the direction of a more critical, rather than

Africa. Scholars such as Alan Boesak (1984:87), John de Gruchy (1984:107) and Russel Botman (2000:354) clearly attempt to retrieve the liberating elements of Kuyper's theology in their struggle to turn Afrikaner civil religion against its own source. Let us look at a few of the important signposts along the way to the "other" Calvin.[13]

4.1. Examples of an alternative Calvin

Already in 1969 Beyers Naudé, well-known anti-apartheid activist, called Afrikaner South Africans back to the "real Calvin". He wrote a newspaper article entitled "What Calvin really stood for" in the *Rand Daily Mail* of 29 April 1969, and remarks: "If Calvin were to come alive and be in South Africa today, he would be the first to protest against and combat many of the concepts proclaimed by and posturing as Afrikaner Calvinism". Naudé made clear that a close reading of the *Institutes* (Book I, chapters 3, 5, 10 and 15) would find no support for the principle of diversity expressed in racial domination. What Calvin did profess was the unity of humanity created in the image of God and our solidarity in sin before God. Nor would Calvin support such a close and exclusive link between volk and church, and – despite being a leader in the Reformation – Calvin maintained a remarkably open ecumenical spirit, as exemplified in his relations with German and Swiss Lutherans, as well as his letter of 29 March 1552 to the Archbishop of Canterbury.

Beyers Naudé's reinterpretation of Calvin, his early writings (1962) about a confessing church in South Africa, as well as his own example in the Christian Institute after he officially broke with the white DRC in 1963, were powerful forces to build up an alternative view of Calvin and his work. In true prophetic spirit he wrote that, if only South Africans would heed the true message of another Calvin, "how vastly different our whole church and political life would be".

The very close link between Calvin, racism and heresy is exhibited in the contributions of Allan Boesak in the late 1970s and early 1980s. His work and leadership in the Dutch Reformed Mission Church and as president of the World Alliance of Reformed Churches in Ottawa provide perhaps the closest link between a reinterpretation of Calvin and the declaration of apartheid theology as a heresy.

In a speech at the South African Council of Churches conference in Hammanskraal north of Pretoria in 1979 Boesak speaks on the struggle of the Black Church for justice. He summarises the classic nature of a confession by saying: "The struggle is not merely *against* an oppressive political and exploitative economic system, it is also a struggle *for* the authenticity of the gospel of Jesus Christ" (1984:25). He then quotes at length from Calvin's commentary on Habbakuk to muster support for the oppressed against the actions of tyrants, because God hears the "cries and groaning of those who cannot bear injustice" (1984:26).

In the same year (1979) Boesak wrote an open letter to the then Minister of Justice to explain the actions of civil disobedience supported by black Reformed churches.

---

an appreciative, reading of Kuyper.

13 What is discussed here is obviously not an exhaustive list. There are many other important voices not mentioned here. For a fuller version of Calvin in anti-apartheid memory read Vosloo (2008:217-244). For a broader and incisive analysis of Calvin's reception in South Africa read Smit (2007:306-344).

He puts forward three fundamental ideas derived from Calvin: the Bible as Word of God that requires from us more obedience to God than to an unjust state (1984:40-41); the Lordship of Christ over all spheres of life, including political life (1984:37); and the notion that the state is called to justice and to serve its people. Boesak (1984:42) refers directly to Calvin's letter to Francis I (preface to the *Institutes*): "For where the glory of God is not made the end of government, it is not a legitimate sovereignty". The later call in 1985 for the fall of the National Party government was thus based on the idea of freedom so forcefully argued for by Calvin when he discussed the freedom to be indifferent to human, cultural, ecclesial and political obligations (*Institutes*, Book IV, chapters 8-12 and 20).

In 1986, the year in which the Belhar confession was formally adopted, John de Gruchy published an article entitled "The revitalization of Calvinism in South Africa". He made a strong argument, later developed into his well-known book, *Liberating Reformed theology* (1991), that Calvin's legacy needs to be appropriated via a critical, prophetic theology of social transformation that acts as vibrant alternative to the neo-Calvinist tradition that dominated South African church and political life for such a long time.

It is interesting to note how Willie Jonker undermined the notion of an elect people in the biological sense of the word with a clear argument based on Calvin's doctrine of election. Jonker rarely addressed issues of political concern directly. He did, however, undermine the edifice of Afrikaners' self-understanding as a specially elect people of God in his book on the covenant, *Uit vrye guns alleen* (1988).

With Augustine, Calvin maintained the notion of the total corruption of all people. He resisted the temptation of the semi-Palagians, who held that humans can and do work with God toward their salvation, and also rejected the Arminian position that our salvation is based on the fact that God foresaw our faith in advance and this faith is therefore grounds for our salvation (Jonker 1988:28,32). Calvin adheres to the notion of *sola gratia* and – according to Jonker – rightfully places election not in the doctrine of God but in soteriology – understood in a Trinitarian sense. Jonker (1988:50ff) also critically notes that Calvin in some respects falls back into a scholastic treatment of this subject by losing his Christological focus and therefore separates election and predestination. We are saved by the grace of God, shown to us in Christ and realised through the work of Holy Spirit.

Election therefore rests on nothing in human beings, but solely in "die onveranderlike en vasstaande keuse van God" (Jonker 1988:35). Consequently no single person – nor a specific biological people – can claim to have been elected by God in Christ by virtue of any trait in themselves (race or geography). Jonker specifically warns against an uncritical transferral of God's covenant with Israel to any historical group today, as such an argument wrongly reduces God's predestination and election to a covenant that does not encompass the grace of God as embodied in the church (Jonker 1988:215).

One can thus cumulatively argue that the same Calvin who was called upon to set up and defend a heretical gospel of racial separation, was called upon to witness and struggle against this heresy. The roots of the *status confessionis* in Dar es Salaam,

Ottowa and Belhar lie not only in the legacy of Karl Barth[14] and Dietrich Bonhoeffer,[15] but clearly also in John Calvin. There is thus a strong relation between the liberative Calvin and Belhar, written in October 1982 and formally adopted by the Dutch Reformed Mission Church in 1986.

4.2. The rejection clauses of the Belhar Confession

Let us immediately focus on the content of the rejection clauses attached to the three middle articles on unity, reconciliation and justice.

What does Belhar reject with regard to the unity of the church?

> *Therefore, we reject any doctrine which absolutises either natural diversity or the sinful separation of people in such a way that this absolutisation hinders or breaks the visible and active unity of the church, or even leads to the establishment of a separate church formation.*

Belhar does not deny the reality of "natural diversity" amongst people. To do that would be to deny actual empirical realities. Contrary to an interpretation of Calvin that absolutises diversity to the point of making separation a principle of creation and the gospel, this diversity of background, culture and convictions is seen from the perspective of reconciliation in Christ. It is Christ who turns diversity and pluralities from threatening divisions to opportunities for reciprocal service and enrichment within the one visible people of God. The establishment of separate churches for different races is a denial of Christ's reconciliation and therefore a sinful practice.

> *(We reject any doctrine) which professes that this spiritual unity is truly being maintained in the bond of peace whilst believers of the same confession are in effect alienated from one another for the sake of diversity and in despair of reconciliation.*

Belhar clearly witnesses against the inadequacy of a mere "spiritual" unity. Obviously unity in and amongst churches is of a spiritual nature, but when people share the same confession in the same country, their "bond of peace" requires a visible unity. If one goes the route of separation here, you make diversity an aim in itself and you show yourself to be in despair of Christ's reconciliation.

> *(We reject any doctrine) which denies that a refusal earnestly to pursue this visible unity as a priceless gift is sin.*

If an ecclesiology is built on the assumed God-willed differentiation in creation and a view of the church as cultural prolongation of this separation, there will be no need nor urgency to pursue unity. Unity in the church is a priceless gift from God that is to be embraced. A doctrine that teaches otherwise is sin and heresy.

> *(We reject any doctrine) which explicitly or implicitly maintains that descent or any other human or social factor should be a consideration in determining membership of the Church.*

---

14 For a discussion of Barth's relation to the Belhar confession read Naudé (2007) and the earlier article by Smit (2000).
15 The many contributions of John de Gruchy come to mind. See de Gruchy (1984).

The "weakness of some" not to receive Holy Communion with new converts from a different background, language and culture, and the missiological practice and method of converting people as an ethnic entity, became the principle for separate church formation. Once this ethnic or cultural principle comes to determine actual membership of the church, a false requirement beyond faith in Christ is set down. This doctrine is to be rejected as a false vision of the church in which human and social factors supersede our being in Christ.

What does Belhar reject with regard to reconciliation in society?

> *Therefore, we reject any doctrine which, in such a situation, sanctions in the name of the gospel or of the will of God the forced separation of people on the grounds of race and colour and thereby in advance obstructs and weakens the ministry and experience of reconciliation in Christ.*

Article 3 of the Belhar confession moves from the unity of the church to reconciliation in society. The rejection clause refers to "in such a situation" and draws on the earlier statement of forced racial separation in a country that claims to be Christian. Note that Belhar does not make any reference to apartheid as political system. Belhar remains at the level of Christian doctrine. If the Bible teaches that the message of reconciliation is entrusted to the church, and a new doctrine is professed that sanctions enmity and forced racial separation as being the will of God or even the good news of Christ, such a teaching should be rejected as heresy and ideology.

Such a false teaching takes as its assumption that people from different racial groups are in principle not to be reconciled, except by physical and spatial separation. In this way the very possibility to minister and actually experience reconciliation in Christ is obstructed in advance.

What does Belhar reject with regard to social and economic justice?

> *Therefore, we reject any ideology which would legitimate forms of injustice and any doctrine which is unwilling to resist such an ideology in the name of the gospel.*

Article 4 builds on unity and reconciliation to proclaim justice to the poor, to those who suffer, and to those who are treated unjustly. In this particular case Belhar rejects both an ideology and a false doctrine. It is not the task of a confession to write definitions. But one could infer with some certainty what the assumed notion of "ideology" in article 4 is, namely a belief system that legitimates and upholds a socio-economic dispensation that works for the unjust advantage of some and the exclusion of others from the basic necessities of life.

Belhar obviously addresses the specific situation of South Africa by around 1980. At that point the bitter irony of Afrikaner history had already emerged. Those who were poor and downtrodden under British rule and who built themselves up with enormous effort; those who drew in great piety on the spiritual resources of being an elect people of God in a country where they were predestined to proclaim the gospel: those very same people became oppressors themselves. Those who were in their own self-understanding "slaves in Egypt" used their newly gained political power after 1948 to intensify racial privileges through numerous laws that excluded black people from the land, the education system and the economy of South Africa.

Like Israel, whom they sought to emulate, the former "slaves" became masters of new slaves. The false doctrine in this case is to see such injustice as the will of God.

How do good Christian people turn injustice into justice? Keeping our discussion above in mind, this was possible on the basis of three inter-connected factors:

First, the understanding that white people were called by God to be guardians of the lesser black people and therefore should decide for them;

Second, the sense of justice that Afrikaners held and which they believed found best expression in equal rights, exercised in territorial separation so that blacks were not dominated by whites, but could actually develop to their full capacities;

Third, there is the universal problem that theological convictions are, but for the grace of God, to a considerable degree shaped and then determined by socio-economic and other "non-theological" factors.

The same theology that lifted Afrikaners up was, in a strange psychology of both sympathy and fear, used to keep black South Africans marginalised.[16] The isolation of apartheid meant that Afrikaners were not exposed to the spirit of the Enlightenment that promoted democracy based on universal human rights. In fact, when the rest of the free world accepted that view formally in 1948, the grand project of apartheid moved directly in the opposite direction.

If God reveals God-self to be in a special way the God of those who suffer, and if the church is called to stand where God stands, then a doctrine that legitimises separation and unjust privilege, and a gospel that is unwilling to resist such injustice, is a heresy.

5. CONCLUSION

The Belhar Confession ends with a call to obedience based on the Lordship of Christ. In the spirit of Calvin, it requires from us to witness against un-just human laws and earthly powers, no matter what may follow. Now that South Africa has gained political freedom, our task is not over. It has just begun.

What are our most urgent tasks?

We would do justice to the liberative legacy of Calvin, expressed centuries later in confessional form, if we continue our struggle for visible unity in the Reformed Church family; if we strive for reconciliation amongst the diverse peoples in our country as well as the foreigners who seek refuge with us; and if we let our deeds demonstrate a search for gender, ecological and global economic justice.

Calvin – no, the gospel of Jesus Christ as interpreted by Calvin in the sixteenth century – is as relevant as it was 500 years ago. But is also open to the constant danger of usurping ideological hermeneutics and powers. In the words of the New Testament injunction, we are called to vigilance and prayer.

---

16 See *The legacy of Beyers Naude* (2005:55-62) for an incisive and moving account of Beyers Naude from 1967 on why Afrikaners held the racial beliefs they did.

BIBLIOGRAPHY

Boesak, A. 1984. *Black and Reformed. Apartheid, liberation and the Calvinist tradition.* New York: Orbis.

Botman, R.H. 2000. "Is blood thicker than justice? The legacy of Abraham Kuyper for Southern Africa". In L.E. Lugo (ed.), pp. 342-361.

De Bruijn, J. 1999. "Abraham Kuyper as a Romantic". In C. van der Kooi & J. de Bruijn (eds.), pp. 45-58.

De Gruchy, J.W. 1979. *The church struggle in South Africa.* Cape Town: David Philip.

De Gruchy, J.W. 1984. *Bonhoeffer and South Africa: Theology in dialogue.* Grand Rapids: Eerdmans.

De Gruchy, J.W 1986. "The revitalization of Calvinism in South Africa". *Journal of Religious Ethics* Vol. 14, No.1, pp. 22-47.

De Gruchy, J.W. 1991. *Liberating reformed theology. A South African contribution to an ecumenical debate.* Grand Rapids: Eerdmans.

De Niet, J., Paul, H & Wallet, B. (eds). 2008. *Sober, Strict, and Scriptural: Collective Memories of John Calvin 1800-2000.* Leiden: Brill.

Cloete, D. and Smit, D.J. (eds). 1984. *A moment of truth. The confession of the Dutch Reformed Mission church 1982.* Grand Rapids: Eerdmans.

Hansen, L.D. (ed.) 2005. *The legacy of Beyers Naude.* Stellenbosch: Sun Press.

Hesselink, J. 1983. *On being reformed.* Servant: Ann Arbor.

Jonker, W.D. 1981. *Die Gees van Christus.* Pretoria: NG Kerkboekhandel.

Jonker, W.D. 1988. *Uit vrye guns alleen.* Pretoria: NG Kerkboekhandel.

Jonker, W.D. 1989. "Die pluriformiteitsleer van Abraham Kuyper. Teologiese onderbou vir die konsep van aparte kerke vir aparte volksgroepe?" *In die Skriflig* Vol. 23, No. 3, pp. 16-18.

Kinghorn, J. (ed.). 1986. *Die NG Kerk en apartheid.* Johannesburg: Macmillan.

Kuiper, D.T. 1999. "Groen and Kuyper on the racial issue". In C. van der Kooi & J. de Bruijn (eds.). 69-81.

Kuyper, A. 1899. *Calvinism: Six lectures delivered in the Theological Seminary at Princeton. The L.P. Stone lectures from 1989-1899.* New York: Revell.

Kuyper, A. 1904. *Die gemeene gratie III.* Amsterdam: Hoveker.

Lugo, L.E. (ed.) 2000. *Religion, pluralism, and public life. Abraham Kuyper's legacy for the twenty-first century.* Grand Rapids: Eerdmans.

Naudé, P.J. 2007. "Would Barth sign the Belhar confession?" *JTSA* Vol. 129, pp. 4-22.

Smit, D.J. 1984. "A status confessionis in South Africa?" *Journal of Theology in Southern Africa* Vol. 47, pp. 21-46.

Smit, D.J. 2000. "Social transformation and confessing the faith? Karl Barth's views on confession revisited". *Scriptura* Vol. 72, pp. 67-85.

Smit, D.J. 2007. "Views on Calvin's ethics: reading Calvin in the South African context". *Reformed World* Vol. 57, No. 4, pp. 306-344.

Stoker H.G. & Potgieter, F.J.M. (eds.) 1935. *Koers in Krisis I.*

Strauss, P.J. 1995. "Abraham Kuyper, apartheid and the Reformed churches in South Africa in their support of apartheid". *Theological Forum* Vol. XXIII, No. 1.

Van der Kooi, C. 1999. "A theology of culture. A critical appraisal of Kuyper's doctrine of common grace". In C. van der Kooi & J. de Bruijn (eds.)

Velema, W.H. 1989. "Kuyper as theoloog. Een persoonlike evaluatie na dertig jaar". *In die Skriflig* Vol. 23, No. 91, pp. 56-73.

Van der Kooi, C. & de Bruijn, J. 1999. *Kuyper reconsidered. Aspects of his life and work.* Amsterdam: VU Uitgeverij.

Vosloo, R. 2008. "Calvin and anti-apartheid memory in the Dutch Reformed family of churches in South Africa". In J. de Niet, H. Paul & B. Wallet (eds.), pp. 217-244.

3.4 A LETTER FROM JOHN CALVIN TO SOUTH AFRICAN CHRISTIANS – 500 YEARS ON[1]

FROM: John Calvin, saved by the grace of God; died into a blessed eternal life; now a member of the cloud of witnesses, and one of your grateful forebears in the holy faith.

TO: All Christian men and women in South Africa, gathered in humble commemoration of the good work which God elected to establish through my life and ministry.

Grace to you and peace from God our Creator and from our Saviour, Jesus Christ.

"Let this mind be in you which was also in Christ Jesus" (Phil 2:5)

INTRODUCTION

Not in my wildest dreams could I – and those who fought for the reformation of the medieval Catholic Church – have foreseen the many epistles of Christ around the world that grew from our ministry.

These epistles are the churches (whether officially called Reformed or not) in which the true gospel is preached, and in which the sacraments as installed by Christ are celebrated.

The spread of the true gospel through the Europe we knew, and later to the new world of the Americas, into Africa and the East, is a sign that these letters were written not with ink, but by the Spirit of the living God.

These churches are to be known in the first place not as Calvinist (God forbid!) or Reformed, as this might suggest that the church is proceeding from the plans of humans. No, these churches are indeed epistles of Christ (2 Cor 3:3) – they are *Christian* churches.

We have witnessed over the last 500 years that God who has begun a good work in you (and in those who stood in faith prior to you) is indeed completing it until the day of Jesus Christ (Phil 1: 6).

With St Paul, I pray that you will grow in love and knowledge so that you may discern the signs of the times, and focus on those things that are close to the mind of God (Phil 1:9-10).

The mind and holy will of God are no secret beyond human understanding. It has been revealed in and through Christ Jesus. Therefore I join brother Paul in calling upon you to adopt the mind of Christ. Christ's mind is expressed in a glorious manner in the hymn of the early church:

---

1   This essay is an adapted version of a sermon presented in the Stellenbosch Mother Church on the occasion of the 150th anniversary of the Theological Seminary (30 October 2009) and the 500th commemoration of the birth of John Calvin.

He was in the form of God, but did not cling to his status as equal with God. He humbled himself, he made himself of no reputation, by becoming a human being, serving others like a slave. He humbled himself even further and was obedient to God to the point of death, the cursed death on the cross (Phil 2:6-8).

But why would St Paul call on the Christians in Philippi to embrace the mind of Christ? As a discernment of the times in Southern Africa and the world today, I wish to point out that the mind and the attitude of Christ make possible – among other things – *unity amongst believers* and *justice in the world*.

St Paul had a very special relation with the Christians in Philippi. It is in that city that he and Silas were put in jail for bringing unrest via their preaching. In that city their prayers and worship miraculously opened the doors of captivity and they were set free to continue the work of Christ. Being sensitive not to appear to preach the gospel for his own material gain, Paul rarely received gifts and stipends from local churches. His special relation with the Philippians is evident in their continued material support for him (4:10-20) – even sending a congregant, Epaphroditus, to Rome (2:19-30). At the time of writing the letter Paul was under house arrest in the palace of the Roman emperor. He writes this letter partially as a thank you for all the support he received.

UNITY

But messages and rumours of disunity amongst the Philippians also reached Paul. He refers to this several times in this short letter – naming Euodia and Sintiche, amongst others, as partial to divisions in the body of Christ (4:2). He calls on them to stand fast in one spirit against false teachings (1:27), and to fulfil his joy by being like-minded – sharing one love, one heart and one striving (2:2).

Paul then points to the reasons for disunity and names them in unambiguous terms: disunity arises from selfish ambition, the seeking of honour for the self, from looking out for and promoting one's own interests, by striving to build a reputation or a name for yourself (2:3-4, 7).

Yes, unlike the common idea that disunity in the church and amongst churches as a rule arises from deep theological convictions, Paul points to minds focused on the self instead of adopting the mind of Christ. (One need only read the origins of the Church of England to understand this.)

You may accuse me and other reformers for being part of one of the greatest schisms in the history of church. Let me remind you that neither Luther, nor I, nor any other reformer ever in principle sought a schism in the church. In fact, we appealed to the authority of church and state at the time to hear us as people with no intention of bringing disunity, but as proclaiming the basic truths of the gospel openly. (My letter to the king of France printed in the Institutes is there for all to read. So are my comments on the unity of the universal catholic church.)

Even if disunity is, humanly speaking, forced upon us in a situation in which the very gospel itself is at stake, as in our case back then, or when a state of confession (*status confessionis*) is declared, we should never accept the outcome as normal – even if history proves us to be on the right side of the terrible battle between Christian and Christian.

In most cases, however, disunity arises from matters of culture, language, property ownership and pension funds. To hide these obvious matters of self-interest, we couch them in theological language so as to pretend that what divides us are matters of grave doctrinal concern. We find a theological reason which – taken by itself – looks important, but is only hiding the real reason for in-fighting and schism: the desire to further or maintain our own interests, which can even find expression in the pious-looking intent to build a missionary reputation for our denomination, be it Catholic, Dutch Reformed, Methodist or Lutheran.

Those who promote disunity inside congregations or amongst churches are enemies of the cross. They are spiritually immature, says St Paul. They are – in the graphic description of St Paul – people whose god is their belly (3:19) – that is they eat and eat to serve their own body and reputation. Their glory is in their shame, i.e. they turn what should be shameful into glory (literally: they practise a scandalous doxology).

Why would they do such foolish things? one may ask. The answer is clear: "they set their mind on earthly things" (3:19). Instead of adopting the mind of Christ, they think and act through selfish ambition.

Where Christians act outside and against the mind of Christ, there cannot be one love (because love of the self, obliterates love of the other); and there cannot be one mind (because each mind focuses on the flourishing of its own ambition). Sadly for those outside the church, there is then also no longer one Christ, and the very mission of the Son is obscured and rendered incredible (John 17).

The way to unity is thus via a deep self-knowledge that arises from being known by God, as I wrote at the very beginning of my Institutes. Like Isaiah, who saw the Lord and fell to the ground declaring: "I am finished!", we see our true selves only in the light of God's revelation.

Then, seeing Christ, one reckons the things that you are proud of – the factors on which your identity is built; the things on which your confidence is grounded – as nothing, as rubbish, in order to gain Christ (3:4-8).

Then Christ restores to us the use of our diverse gifts and histories – not as building blocks for our own reputation, but as means by which we follow Christ's mind in serving others (HC, Belhar).

Every act of unity is therefore a sign of Christ's mind. Indeed, Christ cannot be divided. God cannot be torn into different parts (Commentary on the Epistle to the Ephesians 5:5)

We humble ourselves before others from whom we are removed. We do not cling to our status as something we need to protect. We put our name and reputation and history and hymn book and liturgy and church law and theology to the service of others. We become slaves, willing to give up our very own lives as we actively seek their interest above our own, and as we actively love them more than we love ourselves.

This is the mind of Christ.

Insofar as South African churches in the Dutch Reformed family still remain divided – no matter what intricate histories lie behind this schism – so far the full consolation of Christ and the fellowship of the Holy Spirit is withheld from South African society. If you claim to stand in the tradition of the Reformation gospel for which I and others toiled under difficult circumstances, you will urgently and continuously strive to unite. You will enter into a pious conspiracy (*pia conspriatio*) to cultivate peace amongst yourselves (Preface to the Catechism and the Confession of faith 1538).

This you will only do if you esteem the other better than yourself; if you strip yourself of pride and have a lowliness of mind about your own reputation, and if – by the powerful work of the Spirit – you adopt the service-oriented mind of Christ.

My great wish for the churches of the Reformation all over the world is that their conduct toward one another would be worthy of the gospel of Christ (1:27). It would reverberate in the heavens if you could all become one, and – by the grace of God – re-unite even beyond your own confessional boundaries so that the glory of God be known in all the earth.

JUSTICE

Let me hasten to say a few words about justice, specifically social justice.

You would understand that I was a refugee myself and worked as pastor amongst those who fled their homelands because of religious persecution. We knew how it felt to be on the margins of society. Like many South Africans in the 20th century, we understood how political, economic and ecclesial power can combine into a seemingly omnipotent ideology, crushing beneath its feet those who dare to resist.

In your societies marginalisation has taken on new forms: huge inequalities, human rights on paper with no power to put them into effect, poorer nations outmanoeuvred in a global trade regime where "centre" and "margin" are clearly defined in euphemisms such as developed and under-developed nations, indigenous peoples (the few who are left in some cases) robbed of land and dignity, women and children living in fear of sexual and physical violence, and the almost obscene Olympian ideal of human beings rich, self-made and seemingly free to choose what to consume and where.

Let me then remind you that Paul himself wrote his letter from a prison. His preaching of the gospel of Jesus Christ brought him huge suffering and humiliation. Although a Roman citizen, he had little power over his own destiny. That is why he writes in such glowing terms about Epaphrodites.

Here is a man, Paul said, with a Christ-like mind. He left the security of his home town to come to dangerous Rome where his visit to a political prisoner in the house of the emperor was a life-threatening act. On top of that, he fell seriously ill to the point that Paul and others thought he could die in his mission to support a marginalised prisoner. For the sake of the work of Christ – serving others in need, seeking the interest of the lowest – Epaphroditus came close to death, not regarding his life in service of others (2:30).

To become servants of justice requires a radical redefinition of the life of faith. Before recounting the visit by Epaphroditus, Paul tells the Philippians: Your faith is a sacrifice in the service of God. His own life is poured out as a drink offering. God granted them the privilege not only to believe in Christ, but also to suffer for His sake (2:17; 1:29).

I am not suggesting that we constantly seek martyrdom in a masochistic sense of the word. But Christians and Christian churches who understand the life of faith as cheap grace (our brother Bonhoeffer saw this rightly), who see religion as social gain, will rarely – if ever – leave the comfort of their middle- or upper-class status for the sake of others.

They are so used to being served that the very idea of discipleship and suffering does not even occur in their minds.

Instead of seeing themselves as stewards of God's gifts and blessings so richly bestowed upon them (see my commentary on Gen 2:15), their very religious life becomes a means not to serve others but to build a reputation of a successful church. Sadly, such "success" is measured in terms of the flesh (the market ideology of the day) and not in terms of the mind of Christ.

Sadly, a church can herself become party to a beast that eats and gobbles up the poor and sucks their blood, instead of helping them and looking on them with fairness (see my Sermon XLIV on the harmony of the gospels).

I am amazed how many Christians make the will of God a difficult question. Scripture is the full revelation of God's will and states plainly and simply: gifts to those who suffer, visits to those in prison, generosity to strangers as if they were angels, and helping the widows and the orphans – these are all acceptable and pleasing sacrifices to God. These acts of service and discipleship are like a sweet-smelling aroma rising up to God's throne (Phil 4:18).

It is indeed not difficult to know what pleases God. It is only difficult if your religious life is a means to please yourself. The churches in South Africa are ideally placed by God to be living testimonies of doing justice in the world. Grasp this unique opportunity to live as self-donating churches that – in the words of the beautiful African confession (Belhar) – stand where God stands: against injustice and in a special way for the oppressed and the poor.

JOY

What will the mood and atmosphere be in churches that adopt and live by the mind of Christ? Many have turned my so-called "Calvinist" heritage into a very dark and almost depressive church. "Calvinist" means strict adherence to man-made laws and a frown on the forehead to show what serious Christians really look like.

This can never be the case. My symbol of faith was nothing other than a burning heart!

No other letter in the NT speaks so much about joy as this one by Paul. (Knowing the circumstances, it is not to be humanly expected). "Rejoice in the Lord!" is a recurring theme in the letter (Phil 3:1 *passim*).

Yes, where churches follow the mind of Christ in uniting with one another, making peace and overcoming even ages of separation, immense joy returns to the church.

Where churches follow the mind of Christ in serving others beyond their own boundaries, giving themselves away as slaves, risking their very own existence, there immense joy takes hold of the church.

This is the paradox of the gospel of Jesus Christ. Unlike the false prosperity gospel that proclaims cheap psychology and material reward for being faithful, Christian joy lies in the opposite direction of self-assertiveness and self-preservation. Joy is a gift of the Spirit to the church that walks in the Spirit (Gal 5).

Contrary to those who believe joy can be "produced" by changing the means of the liturgy (new instruments and new media), Scripture teaches that unity and justice are the sober but truthful and lasting building blocks of joy.

HOLY COMMUNION

It is time to close.

I am pleased that you will celebrate holy communion tonight. As you know, I called on the church to celebrate the supper of the Lord on a weekly basis.

The DRC family experienced the pain of separation at the table after 1857. This separation and enmity led to its exclusion from the ecumenical table in Ottawa in 1982. The heavens were quiet at the pain of those events. What should be a celebration of the one body of Christ – breaking one bread and drinking from one cup – has been deformed in history.

The way back toward one another is exactly via the regular celebration of the Lord's supper. The table is the place for sinners and schism-makers to meet each other in the presence of the Lord who gave his body so that we would be one.

Scripture is also clear that Holy Communion and justice belong together. We shall not eat the bread as long as others are hungry. We shall not drink the wine as long as others are thirsty. The table is the place to be reminded that all of creation is a theatre, reflecting the glory of the Lord. That glory shines forth if we strengthen our faith at the table to once again adopt the mind of Christ so that the weak will benefit from our generosity.

I thank you for the commemoration of God's work in my life. All honour belongs to Him alone.

May I remind the churches in South Africa that God shall supply all your needs according to his riches in glory by Jesus Christ (Phil 4:19).

Together with all the witnesses in heaven, we wish you peace and justice and joy in the Lord.

I sign this letter with my own hand.

Amen.

3.5 THE RECEPTION OF KARL BARTH IN SOUTH AFRICA 1960-1990 – SELECTED PERSPECTIVES[1]

One of the great tragedies in the development of Afrikaner Reformed theology in the three decisive decades of its evolvement (1930-1960) was that Barth's criticism of religion and natural theology was never really heard (Durand 1985:40).

1. INTRODUCTION AND EXPLANATORY NOTES

This paper explores a fairly narrow selection of receptions of the work of Karl Barth in the period 1960-1990. The aim is to highlight a few trends or paradigmatic readings of Barth emanating from this period. This is not even close to an exhaustive list of all "Barth readings" from this period. Names such as de Gruchy, Villa-Vicencio, Durand, Boesak, Maimela, (Pieter) Potgieter and others are missing, and would have to be incorporated if a richer tapestry of Barth receptions is to be constructed. In the end the choice was partially motivated by the interesting contrasting readings represented here.

A further limitation is that these readings are merely re-presented as contrasting receptions of Barth and they are not evaluated for their "correctness" against the original Barthian oeuvre, nor engaged with on the basis of the vast secondary Barth scholarship. In other words: this is like a collage of five Barth "pictures" simply put up against the wall, followed by an interpretative summary towards the end.

2. FIVE READINGS OF BARTH ...

One could demonstrate that each reading of Barth was prompted by a core leading question in the mind of the interpreter. Of course, this writer puts the question there as an inference drawn from the readings themselves! The readings and concomitant leading questions are put in historical order:

- FJM Potgieter: How must we understand the Bible as "inspired Word of God" and the "visible unity" of the institutional church in the light of "pluriform development" as the will of God? (1963, 1961, 1958);

- TA Mofokeng: How can a black Christology be developed that underpins the struggle for liberation in South Africa?[2] (1983);

- JWV van Huyssteen: How can theology be a rational science? (1973, 1986);

---

[1] Revised version of a presentation made on 13 May 2012 as part of a conference hosted by the Stellenbosch Faculty of Theology under the title: "The Reformed Churches in South Africa and the struggle for justice: Remembering 1960-1990". The essay was first published in 2013 in *Reformed Churches in South Africa and the Struggle for Justice* by Sun Media, Stellenbosch.

[2] In the introduction to this book (Mofokeng 1983), Mofokeng himself indicates what question led his theological work: "How can faith in Jesus Christ empower black people who are involved in the struggle for their liberation?"

- WD Jonker: How can theology respond to the challenges of the Enlightenment? (1987, 1988, 2008); and
- DJ Smit: How does justice for the destitute and the poor flow from God's radical grace?[3] (1988).

FJM Potgieter

In the period under discussion Potgieter, Professor of Dogmatics at Stellenbosch, engaged with Barth's thinking in two ways. He first wrote a highly critical article on Barth's controversial notion of divine inspiration of the Scriptures, and subsequently made a very short but telling reference to Barth in relation to the question of the visible unity of the institutional church (Potgieter 1961:273).[4] As shall be demonstrated below, the combination of these two framings of Barth provided a highly effective strategy to inhibit the positive reception of Barth for at least the ensuing fifteen years.

In relation to the inspiration of Scripture, Potgieter asks how we should we interpret 2 Timothy 3:16, the well-known passage that all of Scripture is inspired by God (*pasa grapha theopneustos*).

He commences by rejecting a number of viewpoints (Potgieter 1963:134-136):

- Mechanical inspiration, as if God directly wrote through the authors who are used as passive instruments, denies the human aspect of Scripture writing, he argues;
- Dualistic inspiration, as if Scripture is inspired with respect to matters of salvation but not in terms of history, chronology and geography, does not take seriously enough the notion that the whole of Scripture is inspired;
- The personalistic theory, as if divine inspiration refers to the writers of the Bible in their own person, but not to their actual words and the content they provide, is once again a limitation of the full inspirational character of Scripture.

Over and against these views, Potgieter – following Bavinck – carefully argues for an organic-verbal inspiration of Scripture (Potgieter 1963:136-137). He explains that verbal inspiration implies that each specific word in the Bible is inspired on condition that words are read in context and that inner-canonical writers could freely use earlier words of Scripture. This must be seen as complementary to organic inspiration, namely that the Holy Spirit inspired people through the use of their own talents and insights to actually write the Scriptures.

Having set out his view, Potgieter then rejects Barth's view on *theopneustos* on a number of grounds (1963:138-146). Barth does not see Scripture itself as object of the inspiration. He understands inspiration as the dynamic act of God's grace through the Spirit, who makes the human words of Scripture into the actual Word of God as it pleases God. The Bible, therefore, is not the Word of God; it becomes the Word of God. Barth perceives the biblical texts as fallible products of ordinary sinful human

---

3 I read Smit quite selectively in this era and do not take account of his prolific Barth scholarship in subsequent years.
4 The reference to Barth, Brunner and Van der Leeuw (all without motivation) is accompanied by a critique of Prof. AS Geyser, who defended the visible unity of the church based on his analysis of New Testament texts and the *Apostolicum*.

beings subject to the questions raised by higher criticism. These fallible words become God's Word via the miracle of the internal witness of the Holy Spirit.

Potgieter maintains that the texts are themselves the object of *theopneustos* and therefore constitute the infallible Word of God, including the historical information contained in them. If this view is not upheld, Potgieter sees the rise of full relativism as to the authority of Scripture. He employs the doctrine of the two natures of Christ as analogy to reconcile the human and divine dimensions of Scripture: "*Na sy wese is the Heilige Skrif Woord van God; na sy natuur is dit mensewoord*" (Potgieter 1963:143, italics in the original).

This brings us to Potgieter's second encounter with Barth from this period. In an essay on the visible unity of the institutional church published in 1961, Potgieter merely lists Barth as one of the authors who (in his view wrongly) defends the visible unity of the church (Potgieter 1961:273). This essay demonstrates a specific reading of Abraham Kuyper – whom Potgieter cites on numerous occasions – which should be read together with Potgieter's earlier article on pluriform development as the will of God (Potgieter 1958:6).[5] In short, Potgieter argues, that visible unity belongs to the wellbeing (*wel-wese*) but not the being/essence (*wese*) of the church (Potgieter 1961:274-275). This is argued from the perspective that the visible unity of the church is an eschatological and not a historical reality to be realised here and now. Race-based ethnic churches – separate in visible structures – is defended on the basis of pluriformity as principle of creation (Potgieter 1961:276-277). The differentiation amongst peoples is indeed caused by sin, but then blessed under God's general grace as his will in the course of human history. In a sentence that is difficult to translate, Potgieter writes that differentiated development is God's will for the interlude between creation and the second coming of Christ. This differentiation "vind sy aanleidende oorsaak in die sonde, maar sy bewerkende oorsaak in sy (God's) algemene genade" (Potgieter 1958:13). This pluriformity was clearly confirmed after the fall by God's general grace in history, notably in both the Babel and Pentecost narratives.

Potgieter goes further to state that an insistence on the visible unity of the institutional church is in fact a Roman Catholic idea (Potgieter 1961:275) as it grows from the conviction that the differentiated church is held together as one by the papal hierarchy, a view of church authority so clearly rejected by the Reformers.

Based on this cursory reading of some of Potgieter's essays one can therefore detect a two-pronged rhetorical strategy in his reading of Barth. By demonstrating that Barth deviates from the orthodox position on the inspiration of Scripture and by arguing that seeking visible unity for institutional churches is not only against the Bible, but actually Catholicism in disguise, Potgieter effectively relegated the critical and evangelical dimensions of Barth to the side-line of the mainstream Reformed tradition as it unfolded in South Africa during the period 1960-1985. What Durand (1985:40) observed about the period up to 1960 was re-confirmed for at least the next two decades, after which new voices started to speak on Barth.

---

5   This is probably one of the most coherent and well-defined defences of separate churches for different races and cultures.

One of those voices spoke from and toward South Africa via The Netherlands. Let us turn to Takatso Mofokeng.

Takatso Mofokeng

Mofokeng published his dissertation, supervised by JT Bakker in Kampen, in 1983 under the title *The crucified among the cross-bearers. Towards a black Christology*. His point of departure is that of Black Theology, understood as reflection on the black praxis of liberation in a situation of racist oppression and exploitation (Mofokeng 1983:19-20).

It is his intention to enrich Black theology by developing a distinctive Black Christology. The source from which he draws is the powerful combination of Steve Biko,[6] the father of Black Consciousness, and Black Theology, particularly as espoused by authors such as B. Goba, A. Boesak and M. Buthelezi (1983:17-27). What this combination of thoughts establishes is the rebirth and restoration of a black person as active and critical subject in history. Two further sources discussed in the dissertation are the influential book by the Latin American theologian, Jon Sobrino, *Christology at the crossroads* (1978), and the earlier work by James Cone, *A black theology of liberation* (1970). A major part of the dissertation, however, is spent on reading Karl Barth's doctrine of reconciliation as set out in the *Church Dogmatics*, IV (1956, 1958).

Mofokeng's reading of Barth is a deliberately tendentious reading. The hermeneutical starting point is to read Barth from a black theological perspective. He further follows the theo-biographical approach as established earlier by both Marquardt (1972) and Hunsinger (1976).[7] For Mofokeng, Barth's political biography is not merely a life narrative, but actually constitutes his theological methodology.

On the basis of these hermeneutical assumptions, Mofokeng asserts that Barth's famous break with liberal theology was prompted by his rejection of political liberalism as a result of his pastoral involvement with the poor, a class analysis of society, and a deliberate socialist choice, which was deepened by the crisis of World War I. For Barth the socio-political crisis of autonomous Western man in the early part of the 20th century mirrored the universal crisis of the relationship between God and man (Tillich), which in turn formed the socio-political basis for the theology espoused in the famous Romans commentaries of 1919/1921 (Mofokeng 1983:113-118).

Mofokeng further argues that the Christology as reflected in the doctrine of reconciliation (*CD* IV 1 and 2) was written just after the Second World War. Barth fundamentally questions liberal individualism in its existentialist form as (for example) set out by Rudolph Bultmann. In contrast, Barth moves to re-establish theology and society on the basis of the death and resurrection of the crucified Jew, Jesus Christ (Mofokeng 1983:126). God's identification with all people – specifically the poor and marginalised – can be interpreted as bringing hope for the black oppressed peoples of South Africa.

Mofokeng's critique of Barth is in line with these hermeneutical assumptions. Barth's move from Safenwil to the academy was a social move with limiting consequences for Barth's theology. Barth's strong belief in ideas, namely that on the basis of the "right theology" the "right action" will also be created, cannot be supported from

---

6 See discussion of, and references to, Biko (1983:6-17).
7 See discussion and references (1983:113-115).

the praxis views underlying all liberation theologies, including Black theology. Jesus Christ is indeed placed amongst the poor as God's incomparable action in this new man. But, according to Mofokeng, the poor themselves and their communal praxis are not properly accorded hermeneutical or theological significance by Barth. Christ's identification with the poor in His condescension is not matched with an equally privileged position when ascension is discussed. The poor therefore (in contrast to the leitmotiv of Black Consciousness) remain to be viewed as passive objects and not as active subjects. The "Christological concentration of man" (1983:195) in fact denies the actuality of human agency, more specifically the agency of oppressed peoples to become subjects in the transformation of history.

Barth sees God's revelation as an event. To have a relation to this revelation means to enter into this history of God's action (Mofokeng 1983:198). Mofokeng latches on to this revelation event and describes it as the dialectical relation between God's action in Christ and black liberation praxis. In the actualities of history there are times of identification between human action and God's action, and those actions carry God's blessing and affirmation. But there are also times of separation with an "utter distinction" between God and human (in)action, carrying God's judgment (1983:199). Despite this deep historical ambiguity to which all human action is subjected, Mofokeng still maintains the qualitative difference between the actions of the oppressed and those of the oppressors.

For Mofokeng the crux of the matter is that the over-might of God's action (so forcefully set out by Barth) does not preclude the human efforts of the oppressed, amongst whom Jesus is present. The cross of Jesus awakes those who are crucified under historical crosses, and their "plunging deeper into the cross" is a historical and provisional verification of the history of Jesus Christ (1983:223). Christ's resurrection awakens the oppressed people's insurrection against injustice and guarantees its outcome, seeking for verification of the resurrection (1983:259), despite them "living a long Good Friday" (Buthelezi 1979:225).

In this manner, the Crucified (Christ) is indeed amongst the (black) cross-bearers, constituting a powerful affirmation and re-interpretation of Barth's doctrine of reconciliation for the construction of a Black Theology in South Africa.

JWV van Huyssteen

The recurring Leitmotif of Van Huyssteen's work is to establish and extend theology as a rational account of faith.[8] To explore different notions of rationality, he builds on debates within the science of philosophy and then brings these insights to bear on the scientific nature of theology. His interest is therefore in meta-theological issues, questioning the epistemological and methodological claims made by theology in order to secure the intelligibility, accountability and relevance of theological statements.

Van Huyssteen (1986:15-22) explains how logical positivism takes the position that true knowledge is based on sense observation (empiricism), with the natural sciences as ideal norm. Meaning is therefore only attributable to empirical-logical

---

[8] This guiding interest is already evident in his dissertation published in 1970 under the title *Teologie van die rede. Die funksie van die rasionele in die denke van Wolfhart Pannenberg*, in which he made his first critical comments on Barth's methodology (see 13-23).

claims, thereby excluding the very possibility of cognitive content attributed to metaphysics (including theology). Objectivity is only realisable in the model set by a standard notion of science where the sequence of observation, inductive reasoning, and generalisation enables scientists to formulate the laws of science. The intention of positivism (as represented, for example, in the Wiener Kreis of Schlick and Carnap) is to strive for the unity of all science based on a similar theoretical and verification structure.

Van Huyssteen then sets out how the philosophical debate about knowledge and science is reflected in the well-known interaction between Heinrich Scholtz and Karl Barth. Scholtz takes positivism seriously and attempts to explain how evangelical theology is possible as a science (Scholtz 1931). He argues that minimum criteria for scientific knowledge also apply to theology: objectivity requires that what is claimed should in fact correspond with a described reality, and that such claims be open to control by others. Coherence requires that claims are at least non-contradictory.

Barth's response – as outlined by Van Huyssteen – was simply that the question of its scientific nature is in no way a life-question (*Lebensfrage*) for theology.[9] Barth attempts to overcome the grounding of theology in either history (Jesus research) or nature (general revelation) or personal experience (Schleiermacher, Bultmann) and shifts the ground of theology solely to God's revelation: God is the Subject that acts in his revelation. God is the "in sich selbst begründeten Grund, der nun wirklich in keinem Sinn 'Objekt' sondern unaufhebbares Subjekt ist" (Barth 1928:269). For Barth the fundamental qualitative difference between God and humanity implies humans' inability to gain access to God's transcendence via any human possibility other than God's "alien" revelation "from above".

Van Huyssteen's comment is that Barth falls into the trap of positivism by not recognising the mediated nature of all human knowledge, including claims about God's revelation. Barth's actual methodological starting point is not in God's revelation, but in Barth's conception of God, and his theology falls prey to the same subjectivity he tries to escape (Van Huyssteen 1986:27-28). Barth creates two realities: God (on the one hand) and history, human realities, nature (on the other) and – according to Van Huyssteen (1973:138-139) – he is not able to bridge this gap in a rational manner. Barth's "knowledge" claims are in fact simply an elaborate confession of personal (ecclesial) faith presented in the form of kerugma (Van Huyssteen 1986:31).

Van Huyssteen's response to this Barthian dilemma draws – in line with his own methodological approach – on developments in the science of philosophy. He refers to fruitful advances in the post-positivistic thinking of Karl Popper (all knowledge is theory-laden), William Bartley (the role of commitment and temptation of retreating into an ultimate commitment), and Thomas Kuhn (the paradigmatic nature of all knowledge, including scientific knowledge)[10]. In light of these developments, Van Huyssteen develops a theory of "critical realism" (1986:151ff). It takes into account a broadened view of rationality beyond empiricism and acknowledges the

---

9   This question "ist auf keinen Fall eine Lebensfrage für die Theologie" (Barth 1932:5).
10   See Van Huyssteen (1986:37-46 on Karl Popper; 47-62 on William Bartley; and 63-90 on Thomas Kuhn).

fundamental metaphorical or model type nature of theological language on the basis of which the intelligibility of theological truth claims can be advanced.

For Van Huyssteen the theology of Barth is therefore useful to demonstrate the negative consequences of naive methodology (he calls Barth's method "esoteric" (Van Huyssteen 1986:31)), resulting in a retreat to commitment which can only lead to "irrational" truth claims. What should be advanced is a "new natural theology" (Van Huyssteen 1973:142) that accepts the fundamental human character of all questions about "God".

WD Jonker

Willie Jonker came to know the work of Karl Barth through his South African teacher at the University of Pretoria, AB du Preez, and then during his stay in The Netherlands where he worked under Berkouwer and read the works of Schilder, Noordmans and Miskotte. Of all the authors discussed in this essay, Jonker interacted by far the most extensively with Barth's thinking during the period demarcated for this reflection. What is represented here is but a small part of Jonker's thinking around Barth developed in the mid-1980s, and focuses on explicit reflections on Barth's influence on his generation (1987, 1988). His quite lengthy Christological discussions of Barth are, for example, not taken into account at all (see for example Jonker 1977:118-125, 182-184).

Jonker is quick to point out the controversial aspects in Barth's thinking that would not be considered in line with positions generally held in the Reformed tradition. He refers to Barth's actualistic notion of revelation; his universalism; his somewhat reductionist reading of Scripture from a Christological perspective; and his rejection of infant baptism (Jonker 1988:30, 32). These aspects, however, in no way detract from the huge significance and influence of Barth's theology on Jonker's own thinking.

Jonker sketches a broad appreciation of Barth: God and theology are sources of joy because of the radical grace of God and objectivity of salvation. There is the centrality of Christ in line with the Pauline vision of the New Testament. Barth further exudes an evangelical enthusiasm for the proclamation of biblical truths and can – in a qualified and positive sense – be called an "orthodox" theologian (Jonker 1987:44-49; 1988:31).

For Jonker the crucial contribution of Barth lies in the fundamentally different response he gives to the challenges of modernity. For him Barth is a modern theologian in his own right and his theology "can only be understood against the background of the Enlightenment" (Jonker 1988:35). Far from being a positivist or retreating into a pre-modern position that tries to escape the difficult questions of historicity and freedom, Barth exactly addresses those questions, but he does so on the basis of a radically different paradigm. He shifts the basis of theology from the transcendental subjectivity of religious man (as put forward by the Cartesian theologies of Schleiermacher, Bultmann and Tillich) to the transcendental subjectivity of God. In the light of this starting point, Barth has no place for hermeneutical (prolegomena-type) questions and no room for apologetics: "It was not necessary to indulge in hermeneutics in order to help modern man, to understand the gospel. What he really needs to know is that God loves him" (Jonker 1988:34; 1987:45-46).

In Jonker's assessment, Barth provides a "hidden accommodation" of the modern critical mind through a radical Christological reinterpretation of core concepts such as freedom, autonomy and change. Barth in fact confronts the issues of modernity head-on, but from a quite distinct evangelical position which Jonker – despite some criticism – judges the most appropriate response in the early part of the 20th century (see the whole argument in Jonker 1987).

Jonker further expresses appreciation of the socio-political thrust of Barth's theology. Barth's "political" significance is derived from his Christological concentration, where (for example) the bodily resurrection of Christ points to the fundamental material (not only "spiritual") character of salvation, and prepares the ground for Barth's later emphasis on the humanity of God that in fact transforms social reality: "God's freedom in love also calls us to freedom in love, so that the humanity of God calls us to every form of action that will serve the humanization of society" (Jonker 1988:38).

Jonker specifically endorses the critical power of Barth's theology. This critical element "touched us in a special way" (Jonker 1988:30) and enabled a new generation of theologians to formulate their critique of the theology underlying the apartheid system.

He refers to the "self-satisfaction of some forms of neo-Calvinist theology with which we were acquainted", whilst neo-Calvinist theologians themselves "were all very critical about him (Barth)" (Jonker 1988:29). Barth also unmasked "the self-deception of the pietistic, Arminian and Methodist preoccupation with personal holiness and perfection which we were perpetually confronted within our circles", and assisted a new generation to be critical of "the religious familiarity with God which we knew all too well" (Jonker, 1988:31). For Jonker, Pietism is a complex historical phenomenon that at times provided direction to an overt objectivism in theology, but he judges the kind of pietism that mixed with neo-Calvinism in South Africa as too individualistic and too anthropocentric (Jonker 1987:35-37) – traits that stood diametrically opposed to the dialectical theology of Karl Barth.

Despite questions about controversial aspects of Barth's theology, Jonker found in Barth a source for critical engagement with the mainstream DRC theology of his time, and the most credible 20th-century response to the challenges of the first and second Enlightenment movements.

DJ Smit

With the acceptance of the Belhar confession in draft form by the then DRMC in 1982, a collection of explanatory essays, edited by Daan Cloete and Dirk Smit, was published as *A moment of truth* (1984). In this volume Smit made two invaluable contributions. He explained the dogma-historical origin and significance of a *status confessionis* (1984:7-32) and provided an exegetical rationale for the controversial claim in the Belhar Confession that God is in a special way the God of the destitute, the poor and the wronged (1984:53-65). The essay under discussion here was published in 1988 as part of a volume edited by Charles Villa-Vicencio under the title *On Reading Karl Barth in South Africa*. One could argue that this later essay by Smit provides the theological mirror image of the exegetical work done a few years earlier in his essay on the God of the destitute and the poor. For this theological rationale, Smit turns to Barth's doctrine of reconciliation (CD/IV) and specifically his exposition of Jesus as the royal man (CD IV/2) who performs miracles that are seen as "paradigms" of the kingdom of God. This kingdom is marked by God's radical grace, which liberates unconditionally from the destructive powers of evil.

Following Barth, Smit first states that Jesus, the royal man, exists analogously to the mode of God's existence (1988:23). The royal man – through his humiliation – shares fully in the destiny of humankind. Almost to the point of prejudice, the royal man shows remarkable affinity for the weak, the lowly and those who are poor in moral, economic, spiritual and social terms. This affinity is not based on any merit that might lie in the situation of the poor or in poor people themselves – love flows only because of God's infinite grace. The royal man thus affirms and reflects the divine YES to humanity, especially humanity in suffering. The cross can therefore be viewed as the triumph and coronation of the royal man (1988:25-27).

The miracles of Jesus, the royal man, are done toward those "with whom things are going badly"; for whom human life is "like a great hospital" (1988:29). Their suffering is mostly physical and the focus of the miracles is not primarily salvation from sin, but release from suffering, irrespective of their sin. This is a powerful demonstration of God's interest in humankind itself, in humans as cosmic beings, created by God. In the miracles God is placed on the side of humanity and against hostile powers, nothingness, evil and destruction that cause suffering and death (1988:31-32).

An interesting question now arises: Why did Protestantism miss this point? Barth's answer – affirmed by Smit (1988:33) – is that the message of the gospel was understood from the side of humanity, where sin and the need for forgiveness were seen as almost "meritorious" grounds for God's action. In contrast to this, the message must be understood from the view of the kingdom, i.e. from God's unconditional free grace toward humanity, not only understood as sinners, but as God's creatures in need of total redemption.

The "option for the poor" is therefore not a simple ethical matter or socio-economic description of a specific class of people – it is a deeply theological matter, steeped in the doctrine of reconciliation, because in this option we see "the astonishing light" of God's radical, free grace. "We can now conclude", writes Smit in line with his 1984 exegetical view, "that Reformed Protestantism finds in Karl Barth an important witness to testify that the God of Jesus Christ is indeed in a special way the God of the poor" (1988:42).

3. CONCLUDING INTERPRETIVE REMARKS

We surveyed five readings of Barth in the period 1960-1990. If we limit our view to this period and the works discussed, an interesting picture emerges.

There are two readings highly critical of Barth, though on completely different grounds. Potgieter resists Barth from the perspective of a theology of pluriformity and differentiation which at that time (in the early 1960s) reinforced the ideological nature of what could be described as an Afrikaner civil religion. In terms of the conference theme, namely "the struggle for justice", Potgieter overtly resisted the advancement of inclusive justice in both church and society. He did this by demonstrating Barth's heterodox views on inspiration and by labelling the visible unity of the institutional church (affirmed by Barth and Geyser) as a Roman Catholic ideal contradicting God's express will for pluriformity in creation and society.

Van Huyssteen's sharp critique of Barth flows from his methodological starting point in critical realism as a response to the fundamental epistemological questions emerging from the natural sciences. For Van Huyssteen the question about (social) justice was not the focus of his meta-theological reflection at the time. He does demonstrate a sensitivity to the contextual nature of theological reflection and specifically the personal and ecclesial dimensions of this contextuality (1986:173-186). He, however, did not directly address the theological-ethical questions facing the struggle for justice. Looking back, one could – in a positive interpretation of Van Huyssteen's work – refer to the fact that he opened up the hermeneutical question[11] of the very basis of theological reflection, which was indeed a prerequisite for self-critical reflection, unmasking the ideological nature of Afrikaner theology. But this he did "unintentionally" and not by calling on Barth, but rather via his own quest for the rationality and plausibility of theological claims as such.

The three other readings of Barth all draw on his work to define a theological rationale for the advancement of ecclesial and social justice. They, however, do so from three different angles and contexts.

Mofokeng reflects upon his experience of black suffering from being a pastor amongst "the scarred figures of the black congregation" (1983:ix) and then embarks on a socio-political reading of Barth, affirming the Christological focus of Barth's work, but transcending Barth by awarding a greater historical subjectivity to black oppressed people.

Jonker reflects on his experience in the context of a self-satisfied, neo-Calvinist tradition, which presents itself as genuinely Reformed, but at the same time not only affirms injustice and racial church separation, but shows no ability to respond to looming questions about freedom, autonomy and religiosity so powerfully raised by the first and second Enlightenments. He draws on Barth in a double movement, namely to unmask uncritical Afrikaner neo-Calvinism, and at the same time to formulate a satisfying theological response to the Enlightenment questions.

Smit straddles both the worlds represented by Mofokeng and Barth. He shares in the neo-Calvinist tradition of white Afrikaans churches, but he also lived and worked amongst the marginalised people of the Western Cape. He chooses not to follow the Mofokeng route of black liberation theology, nor did he – at that time – primarily attempt to wrestle with questions of modernity (so central to his later work). Smit reaches the same goal of a search for justice by standing in the confessional tradition of the Reformed faith which he shares with both Mofokeng and Jonker. He then draws on Karl Barth to confront the Reformed tradition with its own roots, namely a faith in Jesus Christ as Lord and establisher of God's kingdom, but then reinterpreted beyond personal justification by faith toward the liberation of the poor and the destitute.[12]

---

11   This is the view supported by Ferdinand Deist in his extensive historical review of the biblical interpretation in the reformed Churches in South Africa. See Deist (1990:202, 238). He notes that Van Huyssteen's epistemological questions brought a definitive shift ("beslissende wending") to the Biblical Sciences' debates of the 1970s to the 1990s.

12   This fulfilled an apologetic intent, namely to respond to early (and current!) criticism

One could safely say that the reading and reception of Karl Barth in the period 1960-1990 was no simple and neutral matter: it represented one of the most prominent sites of struggle for justice in South Africa. More work should be done on this.

Who said the reading of thick German books is not dangerous?

BIBLIOGRAPHY

Barth, K. 1928. "Die dogmatische Prinzipienlehre bei Wilhelm Herrmann". *Theologie und Kirche*. München; EVZ-Verlag, pp. 240-284.

Barth, K. 1932. *Kirchliche Dogmatik 1/1*. München: EVZ-Verlag.

Barth, K. 1956. *Church Dogmatics* IV/1. Edinburgh: T&T Clark.

Barth, K. 1958. *Church Dogmatics* IV/2 Edinburgh: T&T Clark.

Buthelezi, M. 1979. "Violence and the cross in South Africa". *Journal of Theology for Southern Africa*, Vol. 29, pp. 51-55.

Cloete, D. & Smit, D.J. (eds). 1984. *A moment of truth: The confession of the Dutch Reformed Mission Church, 1982*. Grand Rapids: Eerdmans.

Cone, J. 1970. *A black theology of liberation*. Philadelphia: J.P. Lippincott.

Deist, F.E. 1990. "Wetenskapsteorie en vakmetodologie". *Bybelwetenskaplike navorsing in Suid-Afrika Vol. 2*, Pretoria: RGN, pp. 202-238.

Durand, J. 1985. "Afrikaner piety and dissent". In C. Villa-Vicencio & J. De Gruchy (eds.), pp. 39-51.

Jonker, W.D. 1977. *Christus, die Middelaar*. Pretoria: NG Kerkboekhandel.

Jonker, W.D. 1988. "Some remarks on the interpretation of Karl Barth". *NGTT*, Vol. XXIX, No. 1, pp. 29-40.

Jonker, W.D. 2008. *Die relevansie van die kerk. Teologiese reaksies op die vraag na die betekenis van die kerk in die wêreld*. Wellington: Bybel-Media.

Mofokeng, T.A. 1983. *The crucified amongst the cross-bearers. Towards a black Christology.* Kampen: Kok.

Potgieter, F.J.M. 1958. "Veelvormige ontwikkeling: Die wil van God". *Die Gereformeerde Vaandel* (March), pp. 5-15.

Potgieter, F.J.M. 1961. "Die wese van die kerk van Christus. *Nederduits Gereformeerde Teologiese Tydskrif*, (December), pp. 271-277.

Potgieter, F.J.M. 1963. "Die teopneustie van die Heilige Skrif met besondere verwysing na Karl Barth". *NGTT*, Vol. 4, pp. 131-149.

Scholtz, H. 1931. "Wie ist eine evangelische Theologie als Wissenshcaft moeglich? " *Zwischen den Zeiten.*, Vol. 9, pp. 8-53.

Smit, D.J. 1984. "In a special way the God of the destitute, the poor, and the wronged". In D. Cloete & D.J. Smit (eds.), pp. 53-65.

Smit, D.J. 1988. "Paradigms of radical grace". In C. Villa-Vicencio & J. De Gruchy (eds.), pp. 17-44.

---

against the Belhar confession's article on justice.

Sobrino, J. 1978. *Christology at the crossroads.* New York: Orbis Books.

Van Huyssteen, J.W.V. 1970. *Teologie van die rede. Die funksie van die rasionele in die denke van Wolfhart Pannenberg.* Kampen: Kok.

Van Huyssteen, J.W.V. 1973. "God en werklikheid". *NGTT,* Vol. XIV, pp. 132-149.

Van Huyssteen, J.W.V. 1986. *Teologie as kritiese geloofsverantwoording; Teorievorming in die sistematiese teologie.* Pretoria: HSRC.

Villa-Vicencio, C. & J. De Gruchy, J. (eds.) 1985. *Resistance and hope. South African essays in honour of Beyers Naudé.* Cape Town: David Philip.

3.6 THE MARKS OF THE CHURCH IN SOUTH AFRICA TODAY

In dialogue with Jürgen Moltmann on his 80th birthday[1]

On 8 April 2006 we celebrated the 80th birthday of renowned German systematic theologian Jürgen Moltmann. To mark the occasion, two separate Festschriften, both edited by Michael Welker (Heidelberg) and Miroslav Volf (Yale), recently appeared. The two books, with distinct contents, both take the doctrine of the Trinity as their focus and were published as *God's Life in Trinity* (2006) and *Der lebendige Gott als Trinität* (2006).

Moltmann is considered as the most influential Reformed theologian in the second half of the twentieth century. Whereas Barth and Bonhoeffer – and to slightly lesser extent Paul Tillich – dominated the first half of the twentieth century, Moltmann stepped onto the theological scene with his remarkable *Theologie der Hoffnung* in 1964. This re-establishing of theology as future-oriented eschatology in a time of heightened tensions between East and West, the threat of nuclear war, the growth of regional conflicts and the realisation of the limits of our ecosystem, is compared to the ground-breaking direction given by Karl Barth's Römerbrief in 1918, directly after the First World War (Welker and Volf 2006a:9).

This was followed by *Der gekreuzigte Gott* (1972, English version *The crucified God* 1974), which reinterpreted and criticised theology from the radical perspective of the cross of Christ. "Either Jesus who was abandoned by God is the end of all theology or he is the beginning of a specifically Christian, and therefore critical and liberating, theology of life" (Moltmann 1974:4).

The openness to the future explicated in *Theology of hope*, and the political liberation expounded in *The crucified God* (see specifically 1974:317ff) provided a crucial impetus for what became known as liberation theologies in Latin America[2] and elsewhere, including South Africa.[3]

The third book of what grew into a coherent trilogy bore the title *Kirche in der Kraft des Geistes* (1975, English translation *The church in the power of the Spirit* 1977). Moltmann himself explains in the preface: "It looks as if I have now arrived theologically at the

---

1 This essay, a paper read at the annual meeting of the Theological Society of Southern Africa in Pietermaritzburg, 22 June 2006, was first published in 2006 in *Verbum et Ecclesia* 27/3, pp. 944-963.
2 Moltmann's imagery of an "exodus church" and his discussion of the political dimensions of the gospel, as well as the expressly "political theology" of Catholic scholar, JB Metz, clearly influenced Latin American theologians such as Gustavo Gutierrez and Jon Sobrino. They, however, developed their own interpretations and focal points, and later impacted on European theology as well. See Moltmann's references to Gutierrez in Moltmann (1977:364, 373, 400-401). On the theme of ecclesiology, Sobrino's *The true church and the poor* also discusses the four marks of the church and strongly draws on Moltmann's insights (see Sobrino 1984:98-124).
3 For a general discussion of Moltmann's influence on South Africa, see Dirkie Smit's contribution to the English Festschrift mentioned above (Smit 2006). He refers inter alia to Daniel Louw, Jaap Durand and the theological series on dogmatics published by Jonker and Durand.

Pentecost and the sending of the Spirit, having started from Easter and the foundation of the Christian hope and travelled by way of Good Friday and the exploration of God's suffering". All three books have to do with "the wealth of God's liberating dealings with the world. That is why I shifted emphasis from 'the resurrection of the crucified Jesus' in *Theology of Hope* to 'the cross of the risen Christ' in *The Crucified God*. Both perspectives would be incomplete if 'the sending of the Spirit', its messianic history and the charismatic power of its church were not added" (1977:xvi-xvii).

It is immediately evident that these early works of Moltmann advanced a renewed Christology from the perspectives of resurrection (hope) and cross (suffering), as well as a socio-historical interpretation of the Trinity. Even the third book on the church has a Christological subtitle: "A contribution to messianic ecclesiology".

It is argued in this paper, however, that Moltmann's implicit concern has been the church. He did not only turn to ecclesiology as an "afterthought" as though a focus on resurrection and cross did not also spell out a new vision of and for the church. In fact, one can show that the very intention of *Theology of hope* was ecclesiological.

After establishing the eschatological nature of revelation in critical dialogue with Kant, Barth and Bultmann (1977:45-68),[4] Moltmann explicates the promissiological character of the Old Testament as a "word of promise" (1977:102-105). He then turns to the New Testament and depicts the resurrection of Jesus as the opening up of a new future. Exactly because of the promise and hope, "the as yet unrealised future of the promise stands in contradiction to the given reality. The historic character of the reality is experienced in this contradiction, in the front line between the present and the promised future" (1977:225).

The crucial question is now: How will this contradiction between "promise" and "reality" be overcome? For Moltmann the answer lies in the church: "The promissio of the universal future leads of necessity to the universal missio of the Church to all nations". The very structure of Moltmann's historically conditioned eschatology precludes all ideas of narrow evangelical mission. The church comes about via the justification of the godless and this "leads immediately to the hunger for divine right in the godless world, and to the struggle for public, bodily obedience" (1967:225). In what would later become a dominant metaphor in liberation theologies, Moltmann concludes his great treatise on hope with a chapter devoted to the church as "exodus" community (1967:304ff).

In a poignant analysis of religion in a post-industrial, post-Enlightenment society, Moltmann shows the threefold adaptation of the church to the demands of society. The church stabilises – and is a servant of – this society by providing a private, romantic escapism ("the cult of transcendental subjectivity"), or by creating a small group of co-humanity, compensating for loss of community in a technocratic world ("the cult of co-humanity"), or by providing a stabilising role and some institutionally derived security to ensure meaning in closing, secularist world ("the cult of the institution").

---

4   Moltmann discusses the link between revelation and eschatology. He depicts his three dialogue partners as follows: Kant as developing a transcendental eschatology based on human reason, Barth as developing a theology of the transcendental subjectivity of God, and Bultmann as the transcendental subjectivity of man.

This socially imposed neutralising of the gospel's power is the basis for Moltmann's concept of the exodus church: "If Christianity, according to the will of him in whom it believes and in whom it hopes, is to be different and to serve a different purpose, then it must address itself to no less a task than that of breaking out of these socially fixed roles ... If the God who called them to life should expect of them something other than what modern industrial society expects and requires of them, then Christians must venture an exodus and regard their social roles as a new Babylonian exile" (Moltmann 1967:320).

The world is neither a hell of self-estrangement, nor yet finished. It is – in the light of a promissiological theology – a world of possibilities. "To disclose to it [the world, PJN] the horizon of the future of the crucified Christ is the task of the Christian Church" (Moltmann 1967:338). This is the last sentence in *Theology of Hope* – a fundamentally ecclesiological book.

The same ecclesiological theme can be detected in *The crucified God*. It may even be cited as the very reason behind the book. In the explanation of the theme at the beginning, Moltmann already writes that if people are to be freed from the facts of the present time and step into the freedom of a new future, "church and theology must turn to the crucified Christ ... This is essential if they wish to become what they assert they are: the church of Christ, and Christian theology" (Moltmann 1974:1).

He consequently argues for a dialectical instead of analogical theology, because God is known in his opposite, namely in the incarnation and crucifixion of Jesus of Nazareth.[5] Therefore the church must, "for the sake of its identity in the crucified Christ, reveal him (Christ) and itself, by following him, in what is different and alien" (1974:28). This is the only way to overcome the false oppositions in the church between "evangelisation" (verticalism) and "humanisation" (horizontalism) sometimes expressed as "the crisis of identity" versus "the crisis of relevance" (1974:25).

When he outlines the resistance of the cross against its interpretation, Moltmann explicitly refers to the following of the cross as the "active imitation of the crucified Christ" on the part of those who follow him (1974:53). The followers of Christ – because they are crucified with Christ and take up their cross – move beyond the purely private into the political realm. "The suffering of love for forgotten, despised and betrayed human beings wherever they are oppressed is concrete suffering in imitation of Christ, and in practice can be called taking one's cross upon oneself" (1974:64).

One could say that the Christological and Trinitarian expositions in the middle part of the book (Chapters 3-6) are the development of a dialectical theology of the cross that for Moltmann should determine the self-understanding of the church. The cross of Christ, embodied in the church of the crucified one, is the way toward both the psychological (1974:291-316) and political liberation of humanity (1974:317-340).

---

5   Moltmann shows clear affinity with Luther in this passage: "If the principle of analogy alone is followed, the result would be a *theologia gloriae*, applicable in heaven only". And then we hear Barth in the background: "It is the dialectical knowledge of God in his opposite which first brings heaven down to the earth of those who are abandoned by God, and opens heaven to the godless" (Moltmann 1974:28).

This political liberation (or rather liberations) is concretely expounded in Moltmann's moving and well-known five-fold "vicious circles of death" (1974:329-332) followed by "ways toward liberation" (332-335). It is worth quoting his expression of God's presence amidst these circles of death – only possible on the basis of a theology of the cross, and only mediated (at least partially) by a church of the cross:

> In the vicious circle of poverty it can be said: God is not dead. He is bread. In the vicious circle of force God's presence is experienced as liberation for human dignity and responsibility. In the vicious circle of alienation his presence is perceived in the experience of human identity and recognition. In the vicious circle of the destruction of nature God is present in joy and existence in peace between man and nature. In the vicious circle of meaninglessness and god-forsakenness, finally, he comes forward in the figure of the crucified Christ, who communicates the courage to be (Moltmann 1974:337-338).

Moltmann then closes this discussion (and the book as a whole) with a telling remark which may be construed as a bridge to the third volume in the trilogy: "In accordance with theological tradition it is possible to see this real presence of God, pointing beyond itself, as the history of the Spirit which comes upon all flesh. We understand it here as the process of the Trinitarian history of God" (1974:338).

Ecclesiology is clearly implied by this view. In Scripture the gift of the Spirit, "which comes on all flesh", is the fulfilment of a prophetic promise (Joel 2) that marks the birth of the New Testament church (Acts 2). From the creeds (both Nicene and Apostolicum) we learn that faith in the Trinitarian God is the foundation of our belief in the church whose mission is nothing other than the missio Dei, the embodiment of the crucified God amidst the suffering of history.

It is therefore understandable that the third book, *The church in the power of the Spirit*, makes its practical intention quite clear, namely "to point away from the pastoral church that looks after the people, to the people's own communal church among the people ... Missionary churches, confessing churches and 'churches under the cross' are fellowship churches, or inescapably become so. They do not stray into social isolation but become a living hope in the midst of the people" (1977:xvi).

The implicit ecclesiological theme of the two previous books is now taken up explicitly without losing sight of the Trinitarian foundation of the church. The church is the church of Jesus Christ (Christology, 1977:66-132);[6] it is the **church of the kingdom of God** (theology, 1977:133-196);[7] and it is the church in the presence and power of the Holy Spirit (pneumatology, 1977:197-336).[8]

---

6 "'Without Christ, no church'. This simple sentence expresses an incontrovertible fact. There is only a church if and so long as Jesus of Nazareth is believed and acknowledged as the Christ of God" (Moltmann 1977:66).

7 "Christian eschatology is not merely eschatology for Christians; if it is to be eschatology of the all-embracing kingdom, it must also be unfolded as the eschatology of Israel, of the religions, of human social systems and of nature" (Moltmann 1977:135; see also the footnote references to both Barth and Bonhoeffer on page 378).

8 "The church lives in the history which finds its substantiation in the resurrection of the crucified Christ and whose future is the all-embracing kingdom of freedom. The living remembrance of Christ directs the church's hope towards the kingdom. ... The

The exodus church, founded on the resurrection, carries hope in the world and opens the vista of a new future (Volume 1) exactly when it is the church of the cross (Volume 2) that lives in the power of the Holy Spirit (Volume 3). There is an inextricable link and theological coherence between Easter Sunday, Good Friday and the Day of the Pentecost.

Moltmann's discussion and reinterpretation on the marks of the church can be seen as the high point of his early theological development. His discussion of the marks not only closes the trilogy (Moltmann 1977:337-361), but harbours in itself and presupposes the rich theological foundations laid earlier. It must therefore not be read in isolation from this wider framework, a rough sketch of which has been attempted thus far.

I wish to highlight and reinterpret freely three remarks by Moltmann as preface to the discussion of the marks of the church in South Africa today.

1. The marks of the church are confessed as part of the creed. The structure of both Nicea and the Apostolicum sees the church as the result of the Trinitarian God's saving history in the world. Ecclesiology is always embedded in theology, and any discussion of the nature and mission of the church should be derived from the nature and mission of God in Christ and the Spirit. The marks are statements of faith in the characteristics of Christ, statements of hope about the coming of God's kingdom and statements of action (love) in the power of the Spirit that turns "normativities" into "realities" (Moltmann 1977:338-340).

2. The four marks of the church – unity, holiness, catholicity and apostolicity – serve as pointers to the essential, but have never been meant as restriction. Moltmann rightly points out that Luther – responding to the situation of his time – identified seven signs of the true church. This "gives us liberty to move other marks of the true church into the foreground in a changed world situation, and to link these to the traditional ones" (1977:340).

New contexts – in my view – require at least a fourfold hermeneutical movement: an interpretation of the church's "social and political *Sitz im Leben*"; the development of new, complementary marks of the church that are oriented to this situation; a reinterpretation of the traditional marks in the light of the first two interpretations; and last (or first!) a re-reading of the biblical traditions relevant to these signs.

---

present power of this remembrance and this hope is called 'the power of the Holy Spirit'" (Moltmann 1977:197).

If we do not engage in this process, the church "would be forsaking the cross of its Lord and would be turning into the illusionary church, occupied merely with itself" (1977:342).

3. The signs of the church serve a twofold purpose. They re-orientate the church inwardly toward its own origin and tradition. They help to reshape the church's identity in times of change and conflict. Secondly, they serve an "outward" purpose as the church's public witness to the world. Depending on the situation, both are important, but for Moltmann, "an ecclesiology oriented towards the conflict of the world situation of today" takes precedence (1977:342).

Moltmann then develops an extended version of the traditional signs: unity in freedom, catholicity in a partisanship; holiness in poverty, and apostolicity in suffering (1977:342-361). If we wish to remain true to Moltmann's charge to steer clear of an illusionary church, we should not merely repeat what he wrote in the context of Western Europe and the world of the late 1960s and early 1970s. Learning from him (and others), we should venture into our own hermeneutical tasks and construct our own relevant interpretations of the signs of the church in Africa and the South Africa of the early 21st century. It is obviously not possible to construct a full contextual analysis, declare all theological assumptions,[9] and reinterpret the doctrine of the church in South Africa in a short paper like this. But the greater task should not inhibit us from drawing a rough first sketch.

The method I follow is to first point out the most important questions facing us as South Africans. This reveals my reading of the situation[10] at the moment (Moltmann's social and political *Sitz im Leben*). Thereafter I (like Moltmann) will not develop new marks of the church, but – in close relation to select biblical traditions – rather extend and reinterpret the traditional ones as "responses" to the contextual questions posed.

The four suggested questions and related responses are presented below.

1. HOW DO WE CREATE COMMUNITY IN A SITUATION OF CONFLICTING INTERESTS AND IDENTITIES? THROUGH THE UNITY OF THE CHURCH.

The struggle against apartheid was a struggle for the right to be "the same". It was the dream for equality under a system that viciously misused differences of culture and language to divide and rule. The system received political legitimisation from a

---

9   One assumption needs clarification, namely that the church (still) matters. My personal conviction does not rely on positive experiences, but on the fact that I view the church from the perspective of the economic trinity. In some instances only the church in its institutional form can embody the marks of the church. Unity immediately springs to mind. In other instances the church as salt and light, i.e. ordinary Christians living in the world (sometimes outside the institutional structures), is able to make true the confessions about the church. The discussion of holiness and apostolicity below might fall into this category. Moltmann has been influenced quite strongly by his teacher, Otto Weber, and emphasises the local faith community as well as the institutional and ecumenical forms of the church (see Moltmann 1977:1-18).

10 When Steve de Gruchy discusses the church in a post-apartheid South Africa, he outlines "four key struggles" facing us now: national reconciliation, human sexuality and gender justice, pluralism in a secular state, and dealing with the promises and perils of globalisation (de Gruchy 2004:224-255).

neo-Kuyperian missiological theology that saw God as the great Differentiator and (consequently) the institutional church as a God-willed disunited church, reflecting racial and cultural "diversity" in its blessed seperatedness.[11]

Those who suffered under the system had a common enemy, with the consequence that for them identity questions were literally restricted to "black" versus "white". After 1994, Tinyiko Maluleke remarks, "Issues of culture are again acquiring a new form of prominence in various spheres of South African society. It is as if we can, at last, speak truly and honestly, about our culture. This is due to the widespread feeling that now, more than at any other time, we can be the subjects of our own cultural destiny ... we must recover our own selves" (quoted in Balcomb 1998:70).

This is echoed by Miroslav Volf from a wider perspective: "In recent decades the issue of identity has risen to the forefront of discussions in social philosophy. The liberation movements of the sixties were all about equality – above all gender and race equality – major concerns in the nineties seem to be about identity – about the recognition of distinct identities of persons who differ in gender, skin colour, or culture" (Volf 1998:23).

The question in a post-apartheid country is how we can assert the right to be different without succumbing to a debilitating, hierarchically structured pluralism nor giving up the notion of an emerging, shared South Africanism. One answer is to build precedent communities where the freedom to be different is upheld and celebrated in community. The unity of the church, a unity in freedom (Moltmann), points in this direction.

The prophetic vision of a peaceable kingdom in Isaiah 11 can be interpreted as the radical transformation of identities through a knowledge of the Lord, where "natural" divisions and enmities (wolf and lamb, calf and lion, child and viper) no longer lead to harm or destruction.

The creation of a prophetic community at the first Pentecost is equally powerful testimony that differences in gender, culture and age can become reciprocal gifts in the one church. Sons and daughters prophesy, the languages of the time (representing different cultures) are freely spoken and understood, the Spirit is poured out on all flesh, including both men and women, and old people dream dreams (Ac 2:17-21). But they all form part of one body where members devote themselves to *koinonia* (fellowship) and have everything in common (Ac 2:42-47). They were, in Pauline imagery, different members serving one another in one body (1 Cor 12).

We can refer to the Pauline vision that in Christ gender, cultural divisions and class do not disappear, but they are relativised in an egalitarian faith community where all become children of Abraham (Gl 3:26-28). The diverse and "naturally" divided faith community should now use their freedom to "serve one another in love" (Gl 5:13-15).

This unity in freedom and service is powerfully expressed in the Belhar confession. We believe, confesses Belhar, that unity in the church can only be embodied "in freedom and not through force". Difference and varieties of language and culture

---

11 See the detailed discussion of apartheid theology's origins in Kuyper, Warneck and Pietism by Naudé (2005a), as well as the extensive references to original sources.

"are opportunities to reciprocal service and enrichment in the one visible people of God" (Belhar 1986, statement 2, my translation).[12]

The critical question to the institutional churches in South Africa is whether we are indeed such precedent communities where difference-in-community is embodied. In my view, the answer is no, we are not. Churches who are structurally one harbour in themselves deep racial and class divisions. In many churches gender is still a basis for leadership discrimination. The dramatic growth of charismatic churches is often sadly accompanied by little concern for unity and a complete absence of a deeper and wider ecumenical vision. Historical churches built their identities so strongly on their distinctive histories, liturgical practices and doctrinal convictions that the only option that remains is to be different-in-disunity.

This is not just an innocuous institutional deficit. The shame of disunity and the inability to build communities – of difference – is a reflection on the very suffering of Christ. Moltmann rightly points out the unity of church is the unity of Christ (1977:338). And in Christ's last prayer, according to the Johannine gospel, unity amongst the disciples and those who would believe after them became the criterion of both the unity between Father and Son, and the one witness that may bring the world to believe in the mission of the Son (Jn 17). Our disunity is a re-crucifixion of Christ.

For many in South Africa the church (and therefore Christ) no longer provides hope for the growth of new identities in difference, freedom and service. Two other powerful public institutions have taken over this role: sporting bodies and corporate business. If ever there was a reason for secular faith, this is it.

2. HOW DO WE CREATE, SUSTAIN AND LIVE A SHARED VALUE ORIENTATION? THROUGH THE HOLINESS OF THE CHURCH.

Few debates after 1994 have been so recurring as the "moral regeneration" of South Africa. The well-known phrase that we need an "RDP of the soul" (Mandela) still rings loudly. The ANC has – in an effort to stem crime and lawlessness – dedicated state resources and portfolios at all three levels of government to address the issue of anti-corruption and rebuilding the moral fibre of the country. Despite a theoretical and legal consensus on those values that bind us together as expressed in the preface to the Constitution[13] and embedded in the Bill of Rights, the chasm between the rule of law and an anomic[14] society is growing. Not surprisingly, the churches (and other religious communities) are regularly called upon to make a contribution in this regard. Moral regeneration seems like the churches' only avenue to still claim public

---

12 For Belhar's original Afrikaans text, and an accessible, explanatory discussion, see Botha and Naudé (1998).
13 The Constitution was adopted as Act 108 of 1996. The preamble says: "We, the people of South Africa, believe that South Africa belongs to all who live in it, united in our diversity", and focuses on values such as democracy, social justice, freedom, and quality of life.
14 The term "anomie" ("no law") stems from French sociologist, Emile Durkheim, and describes a society with low social cohesion and a value disorientation due to abrupt social transitions. See Naudé (2005c:539, footnote 6 for an explanation and reference).

and political relevance in a situation where economics and law have usurped the power of theology to shape the nation.

There is a complex relation between narrative, education, religion and moral formation.[15] Instead of dealing with the flood of literature in this regard, let us simply look into the well-known Deuteronomic passage following the *shema* in Deuteronomy 6:4. Let us accept the canonical presentation of Deuteronomy (literally: "second law") as the farewell speech of Moses on the eve of the wandering people's enter into the promised land. He repeats the Ten Commandments in Deuteronomy 5 and then turns to the parent community: "These commandments that I give you today are to be upon your hearts. Impress them on your children" (Dt 6:6-7a).

How would such "impression" take place? The answer in the text is clear and gives an interrelated account of how "moral formation" took place: through verbal and written repetition of the law to children (6:7,9); through symbolic representation (6:8); through conduct/example shaped by the commandments (6:17-18); and through a recounting of the exodus narrative as explanation for liturgical expressions of the law (6:20ff). This "impression" would mark the distinctiveness of God's people as a holy people in a land of competing gods and alternative moralities.

Although not present in the same condensed form, the early New Testament church communities were communities of moral instruction and moral formation.[16] Christ is the church's holiness (1 Cor 1:30); early oral traditions and later written traditions served as memories of Him (Lk 1:1-4); those strong in faith are to serve as examples to others (1 Cor 8); moral injunctions to live according to the Spirit and be holy rest upon justification by faith (Gl 3:13-26; 1 Pt 1:13-16); and the sacraments served as symbolic representations of Christ's life and work (1 Cor 11:23-26).

These (and other) considerations bring the holiness of the church into fruitful relation with moral formation in post-apartheid South Africa. Instead of becoming a cheap political ally to a government clearly at loss over "moral regeneration", the church must know: democracy and the law of the land do not equal the law of God or the rule of Christ. Christians' greatest contribution to "morality" is to live in the various spheres of civil and public life as an ethical minority if required, whilst involving

---

15 In South Africa reflections on ecclesiology, liturgy, narrative and moral character were specifically prompted in dialogue with the work of American Methodist theologian, Stanley Hauerwas. He develops Christian ethics around themes of moral agency, community (church) and character (see an early example in Hauerwas 1983). At least five South African theologians – Neville Richardson, Nico Koopman, Robert Volsoo, Andrew Philips and De Wet Strauss – wrote doctoral dissertations on Hauerwas. They and others such as Dirkie Smit from Stellenbosch, and the Pretoria ethicist Etienne de Villiers, have since made solid contributions to what may broadly be termed a virtue ethic. For a short, informative overview of virtue ethics, see Jean Porter's contribution to the *Cambridge Companion to Christian Ethics* (Porter 2001). For an important view on the relation between ethics and ecclesiology in the ecumenical movement, see Best and Gobra (1997), where the notion of the church as "moral community" is made explicit.

16 See the well-known publication by Wayne Meeks (1983) on the moral world of early Christian communities, and the attempt by Allen Verhey (2002) to reconstruct a contextual ethics of Jesus based on the notion of instructing faith communities (see Verhey's discussions of remembrance and the early church as a community of moral discourse (2002:3-33)).

themselves continuously in the task of "impressing" the law and gospel upon the next generation.

Holiness does not imply an out-dated, conservative life shielded from the world behind church or monastery walls. It is life "set aside" for God exactly in the realities of the world. The church as *ecclesia reformata et semper reformanda* testifies to the coming *reformatio mundi* (Moltmann 1977:355). The "stabilising" contribution that politicians covertly hope the church would make to morality, may turn – as Moltmann aptly showed – into a "cult of institutionalisation". This cult needs to be resisted by the exodus church as she follows in the footsteps of Christ, living the values of the kingdom of God as presented by Jesus in his love for the convicts, the poor and the outcast. "The church is therefore sanctified where it participates in the lowliness, helplessness, poverty and suffering of Christ" (1977:355). This is a partisanship (Moltmann) that might be seen as destabilising and undermining the authority of the state.

3. HOW DO WE RESPOND TO GLOBALISATION? THROUGH THE CATHOLICITY OF THE CHURCH.

Globalisation may be seen as complex processes of culture, economics and politics that create an apparent unified, boundary-less world.[17] Through information technology the physical boundaries and limitations of geography and space are overcome. Through mainly the Anglophone culture and language, previous differentiations are homogenised, thus limiting communication boundaries. Through the "triumph" of capitalism after 1989 standardised ideas about development – predicated on the vision to bring third world nations up to the example of industrialised nations – have eroded the authority of autonomous states, as all are required to respond to the standardised commodification of life.

The unity of a global world is not a unity that results from the free choice of individuals or nations. It is the unity brought upon us in "a runaway world" (Giddens; see Smit 2003:307), creating a "one-way traffic" from mostly American and Western cultural-economic interests to the rest of the world. Globalisation in many senses creates a mirage of unity and community, but is in fact an intensification and acceleration of modernity's individuation.[18]

Yes, globalisation in its varied forms has brought enormous technological and information advances in the world. There are undoubtedly gains in efficiency and knowledge from which institutional and free churches also benefit, whilst they themselves become agents of globalisation. But one may speak of the Janus face of globalisation. The dark side of the face is evident in at least two phenomena: first on the surface level, the promise and advantages of globalisation are favouring

---

17 Renowned political scientist, David Held, analyses globalisation in terms of culture, economics and politics (see Held 2000). I follow the short but incisive exposition by Dirkie Smit (2003) who applies various insights into globalisation to the lack of urgency regarding "unity" in our South African context.

18 See Smit's reference here to the work of Peter Berger and Samuel Huntington who write: "If there is one theme that all different sectors of cultural globalisation have in common, it is *individuation* ...". See Smit (2003:308) for references. It is immediately apparent that the unity and catholicity of the church are two sides of the same coin.

the strong and marginalise weak nations, indigenous peoples and the non-human environment; second, on a deeper level globalisation provides a value-laden meta-narrative that usurps all counter-narratives as it establishes its authority through science, technology (especially the mass media) and digital capitalism.[19]

How does the confession of the church's catholicity[20] relate to these more destructive dimensions of globalisation?

Because God is "catholic" in the sense of being "universal", God's kingdom is equally catholic in its reach. The kingdom is meant to be established spatially in the entire world. But it is also meant to be established qualitatively in its wholeness (catholicity) or in its entirety. The church as first fruit of the kingdom is therefore called to establish this kingdom in the whole world and in its entirety.

The church "remains limited, non-universal and non-catholic until 'every rule and every authority and power' is destroyed (1 Cor 15:24)" (Moltmann 1977:350). This does not mean that the church should become a power amongst or against other powers (economic or political), but that its power – like that of Christ – lies in it powerlessness.

The church therefore combats the assumed and unchallenged authority of globalisation as "the only way", as the "true story", with the confession of Christ's universal (catholic) lordship. We follow the earliest Christians who confessed that not the Roman emperor (the global power of the day) but Jesus is the *kurios*. And this lordship is shown exactly where "the church as property of God stands where He stands, namely against all injustices and with the oppressed". The church must witness "against all powerful and privileged who selfishly seek their own interest whilst ruling over others and disadvantage them" (Belhar, statement 4).

Whilst this was a predominantly racial issue at the time of Belhar's formulation in the period 1982-1986, it has now become a more focused class issue. As the ANC government moved from RDP (Reconstruction and Development) to GEAR and now to ASGISA,[21] it has increasingly bought into the growth and development ideology of the global markets. As powerful politicians move into the private sector, a new elite and a relatively isolated middle class are created, establishing a clear line between weak and strong in this country, reflecting the same structure as global inequalities between North and South. With adequate resources,[22] but an inability to deliver at local level, the government faces rising protest action (more than 900 in 2005). There are too many South Africans who do not see and experience the benefits of the system.

---

19 See Naudé (2005c) for a discussion of the homogenisation implied by globalisation whilst apparently fostering differentiation, and the effect of this on ethics and identity formation.
20 For the various senses of "catholicity" in church history, see McGrath (2005:500-503).
21 This stands for *Accelerated and Shared Growth Initiative for South Africa* and falls directly under the control of the Deputy-President. The aim is to achieve a growth rate of 6% by 2008.
22 The notion of "adequate resources" is obviously contextually defined. I simply refer to the fact that just over R44 bn has been collected above budget in the 2005-6 financial year, and the numerous examples of unspent millions in socially sensitive departments such as housing and health care at provincial government level.

The church is partisan and particular precisely in order to demonstrate the universal love and reign of God. "Christian partisan support for the oppressed is intentional and its goal is to save the oppressor also. ... Christian universalism will therefore be realised in particular conflict situations in a partisanship of this kind; otherwise it is still in danger of being abstract" (Moltmann 1977:352).

This particular partisanship is an ecclesiological expression of glocalisation: we make God's global love concrete in specific local options for the oppressed.

4. HOW DO WE RELATE TO MARGINALISED PEOPLE AND OUR NON-HUMAN ENVIRONMENT? THROUGH THE APOSTOLICITY OF THE CHURCH.

The concept of marginalised or vulnerable people requires description in each specific society and may be identified on a more universal scale. An example of the latter is "indigenous peoples" scattered around the globe and presently the subject of intense United Nations activities.[23]

Who are the vulnerable and (in most cases) marginalised people in present-day South Africa? It will be difficult to reach full agreement on this issue. My understanding would include rural women; most people with HIV/AIDS; illiterate adults; unemployed people;[24] orphans; refugees within our borders; and people living below the poverty line as defined in our context.[25] A simple calculation would bring the number of people in these categories to around 8-10 million or roughly a quarter of our population. The current debates about eco-tourism and golf estates, nuclear power and renewable energy resources, and the retention of biodiversity clearly put our natural environment into the category of the vulnerable.

We may understand the apostolicity of the church as its foundation, namely that it is based on the testimony of the apostles, eyewitnesses of the resurrection. We may also understand it as the task or commission of the church, namely to participate in the apostolic mission of Christ (Mt 28:19-20; Ac 1:8).

Many churches in South Africa understand and show great enthusiasm for mission in the sense of teaching others "who have not heard of Christ" to convert to the Christian faith. This is undoubtedly a dimension of the church's apostolicity. But in the context of South Africa, where the gospel is widely known,[26] apostolicity

---

23 The UN estimates that about 6% of the world's population are "indigenous people" based on a combination of historical, cultural and geographical factors. The period 2005-2014 has been declared as the Second International Decade of the World's Indigenous People.

24 According to the Markinor survey of 2000, 30.7% of the adult population was unemployed at that stage. Economists differ about the very definition of "unemployment" and figures vary accordingly. See Erasmus and Hendriks (2003:94).

25 By 2000 the poverty threshold was set at R1 400 per month per household. An average of 64.4% of the population fell into this category (Erasmus and Hendriks 2003:93). Recent economic growth might have eased this figure, but the extent of absolute poverty is still vast.

26 See the regular updates on religious affiliation by the Unit for Religious and Demographic Research at the University of Stellenbosch. The association with Christianity is slightly in decline, but was still at a high 77% of the population in 2000. See Erasmus and Hendriks (2003) and references to their earlier work in footnote 1 (2003:80).

clearly requires much more. The answer lies in participating in Christ's mission in a specific manner.

To reduce Jesus' ministry to "the great teacher" is misleading. Jesus did not come only to proclaim or teach a new message. Yes, he undoubtedly preached and taught. But he saw himself in the prophetic tradition (Lk 4:14-21) and complemented his teaching in many different ways. He healed the sick who were marginalised by strict social and legal codes; he befriended the socially insignificant and despised; he dined with the enemies of the people; he empowered women who were socially and religiously marginalised through patriarchal gender relations and customs; he undermined religious customs through boundary-less love. In the words of an early hymn: He did not cling to the Godhead, but made Himself nothing; he humbled himself and became obedient to death on the cross (Phlp 2:6-8).

An apostolic church is a "nothing" church. It is a *doulos* (slave) church. It is a cross-bearing church. You find her and her members on the margins of society – because the church knows from Matthew 25 that Christ meets them in the clothing of half-dressed children and in the embrace[27] of those who die of AIDS without access to basic life-saving medical provisions.

5. CONCLUSION

In a situation of competing identities and conflicting differences, the one church is a precedent community of unity in freedom, joy and reciprocal service.

In a situation of anomie and moral bewilderment, the holy church engages in fruitful moral formation according to the law and gospel, and in a "destabilising" commitment to the values of God's kingdom.

In a situation of increasing globalisation, the catholic church confesses one lord, Jesus Christ, and practises his universal love in partisan service to the oppressed.

In a situation of so many marginal people and an exploited ecosystem, the apostolic church stands where God stands – against injustice and enslaving in its mission for the sake of the despised.

I close with a question:

If the marks of the church are inferred from the triune God, is this how God will be known in South Africa?

BIBLIOGRAPHY

Balcomb, T. 1998. "From liberation to democracy: Theologies of bread and being in the new South Africa". *Missionalia* Vol. 26, No. 1, pp. 54-73.

Best, T.F. & Gobra, M. (eds.) 1997. *Ecclesiology and ethics. Ecumenical engagement, moral formation and the nature of the church.* Geneva: WCC.

---

27 See Naudé's description – in dialogue with Miroslav Volf – of the church as "embracing and healing community" in the midst of the HIV/AIDS pandemic (Naudé 2005b:438-439).

Botha, J. & Naudé, P.J. (ed.) 1998. *Op pad met Belhar. Goeie nuus vir gister, vandag en môre.* Pretoria: JL van Schaik

Erasmus, J.C. & Hendriks, J. 2003. "Religious affiliation in South Africa early in the new millennium: Markinor's World Values Survey". *JTSA* Vol. 117, pp. 80-96.

Gill, R. 2001. *The Cambridge companion to Christian ethics.* Cambridge: Cambridge University Press.

Hauwerwas, S. 1983. *The peaceable kingdom: A primer in Christian ethics.* Notre Dame: University of Notre Dame Press

Held, D. 2000. *A globalizing world? Culture, economics, politics.* New York: Routledge

Meeks, W. 1983. *The first urban Christians: The social world of the apostle Paul.* New Haven: Yale University Press.

McGrath, A.E. 2005. *Christian theology: An introduction* (Third Edition). London: Blackwell

Moltmann, J. 1964. *Theologie der Hoffnung: Untersuchungen zu Begründung und zu den Konsequenzen einer christlichen Eschatologie.* München: Kaiser (English translation: see Moltmann 1967).

Moltmann, J. 1967. *Theology of hope. On the ground and implications of a Christian eschatology.* London: SCM (German original: see Moltmann 1964)

Moltmann, J. 1972. *Der gekreuzigte Gott: das Kreuz Christi als Grund und Kritik christlicher Theologie.* München: Kaiser (English translation: see Moltmann 1974).

Moltmann, J. 1974. *The crucified God. The cross of Christ as the foundation and criticism of Christian theology.* London: SCM (German original: see Moltmann 1972)

Moltmann, J. 1975. *Kirche in der Kraft des Geistes: ein Beitr. z. messianischen Ekklesiologie.* München: Kaiser (English translation: see Moltmann 1977).

Moltmann, J. 1977. *The church in the power of the Spirit. A contribution to messianic ecclesiology.* London: SCM (German original: see Moltmann 1975)

Naudé, P.J. 2004. *Drie maal een is een. 'n Besinning oor God vandag.* Vereeniging: CUM.

Naudé, P.J. 2005a. "From pluralism to ideology: The roots of apartheid theology in Abraham Kuyper, Gustav Warneck and theological Pietism". *Scriptura* Vol. 88, pp. 161-173.

Naudé, P.J. 2005b. "'It is your duty to be human': A few theological remarks amidst the HIV/AIDS crisis". *Scriptura* Vol. 89, pp. 433-440.

Naudé, P.J. 2005c. "The ethical challenge of identity formation and cultural justice in a globalising world". *Scripture* Vol. 89, 536-549.

Porter, J. 2001. "Virtue ethics". In R. Gill (ed.), pp. 96-111

Smit, D.J. 2003. Unity in church and society? Theological reflection on an ongoing challenge in South Africa today. *Scriptura* 83, 305-314

Smit, DJ. 2006. "Church unity in freedom". In M. Welker and M. Volf (eds.), pp. 73-92

Sobrino, J. 1984. *The true church and the poor.* Maryknoll: Orbis Books

Welker, M. & Volf, M. (Hrsg.) 2006a. *Der lebendige Gott als Trinität. Jürgen Moltmann zum 80. Geburtstag.* Gütersloh: Gütersloher Verlagshaus.

Welker, M. & Volf, M. (eds.) 2006b. *God's Life in Trinity.* Minneapolis: Fortress Press.

Verhey, A. 2002. *Remembering Jesus. Christian community, Scripture and moral life.* Grand Rapids: Eerdmans.

Volf, M. 1988. "'The trinity is our social program': The doctrine of the trinity and the shape of social engagement". *Modern Theology* Vol. 14, No. 3, pp. 403-423.

3.7 "PUBLIC THEOLOGY" FROM WITHIN THE CHURCH?

A reflection on aspects of the theology of W.D. Jonker (1929-2006)[1]

1. INTRODUCTION

Willem Daniel (Willie) Jonker was born on 1 March 1929 in the Lichtenburg district of the Western Transvaal, South Africa. He studied theology and languages at the University of Pretoria until 1951, completing a Bachelor of Divinity (BD) on how conceptions of God impact on the doctrine of forgiveness in the work of Schleiermacher, Ritschl and Brunner (Jonker 1951), and a Master's degree (MA) in translation studies on the translation of the gospel of Mark by Ulfilas (Jonker 1952), demonstrating his advanced knowledge of both Greek and Latin. He then departed for the Netherlands, where he completed his doctoral studies in dogmatics with distinction at the Free University of Amsterdam under Prof. Gerrit C Berkouwer between 1952 and 1955.[2]

Willie Jonker and his family returned to South Africa and he entered the ministry in the Dutch Reformed Church (DRC), serving various congregations in Johannesburg and Potchefstroom in the period 1955-1967. He quickly rose to prominence in the church and was elected Actuary of the Transvaal Synod in 1961, with Beyers Naudé elected as assessor of the same synod. He held a brief appointment as Professor at Unisa and then accepted a professorship in Practical Theology at Kampen University in the Netherlands, where he worked from 1968 until 1971. He accepted a call from the DRC as Professor in the Stellenbosch Theological Faculty in 1971, where he taught dogmatics until his retirement in 1994.

From this cursory biographical overview it is evident that Willie Jonker was a student and professor of theology in the most turbulent years of South Africa's transition from apartheid to democracy. Establishing random links tells the story. He completed his doctoral studies in the year of the Freedom Charter (1955). He was active in the DRC and its leadership during the Sharpeville and Cottesloe events (1960) and the Rivonia trial in 1964, when Nelson Mandela and others were sentenced to life imprisonment. He was Professor of the DRC theological faculty at Stellenbosch when this church in 1974 accepted its document *Ras, Volk en Nasie. Volkeverhoudinge in die Lig van die Skrif*, an exposition of a conception of pluriformity upon which separate churches for different cultures could be defended.

---

1 This essay is an adapted version of a lecture delivered at the Faculty of Theology at Stellenbosch University on 13 February 2013. The essay appeared in 2014 in *Verbum et Ecclesia* 35(1), Art. #1136, 8 pages. http://dx.doi.org/10.4102/ve.v35i1.1136.

2 *Mistieke liggaam en kerk in die nuwe Rooms Katolieke Teologie* is an eccesiological exposition and critical appraisal of the church as *corpus Christi mysticum* developed after World War I by French Catholic theologians such as Congar, Journet and De Lubac. This thesis prepared Jonker well for the many ecclesiological battles in ensuing years in the context of South Africa where, for example, an insistence on the visible unity of the church was portrayed as a Roman Catholic(!) tendency that stands in contrast to the Reformed tradition (see Potgieter 1961).

The Soweto uprisings of 1976 and increasing repression from the ruling National Party in the 1980s were mirrored by turbulent developments in the South African church struggle. One thinks of the Lutheran World Federation's declaration of apartheid as theological heresy (1977), the suspension of membership in 1982 of two Afrikaans white churches at the World Alliance of Reformed Churches in Ottawa, Canada (chaired by Allan Boesak), followed by the adoption of the draft Confession of Belhar by the Dutch Reformed Mission Church (1982), the Kairos document (1985) and *The Road to Damascus* (1989). Jonker was also part of the DRC's intense internal debates, which in the end led to a new stance on race relations by the DRC in 1986, expressed in the document *Church and Society*, revised in 1990. This change in direction was the direct reason for a split in the DRC, when the Afrikaanse Protestantse Kerk, a whites-only church of roughly 40 000 members at the time, was formed. A few years later the Rustenburg church conference (1990) was convened to talk about the role of the churches in South Africa's transition. In the year of Willie Jonker's retirement, we saw the reunification of the DRCA and DRMC to form the Uniting Reformed Church in Southern Africa, as well as – on 27 April 1994 – the first full democratic elections in South Africa.

Over this period Jonker played a critical role in the context of the DRC and wider church relations. Instead of merely enumerating these milestones along this journey, however, this essay attempts to frame Jonker's contribution to complement the "public theology" debates in South Africa and elsewhere.[3] This "framing" is, of course, somewhat asynchronic, as the debate about the "public" nature of theology as such was not overtly raised by Jonker and his contemporaries. As far as could be established, he never referred to himself as a "public" theologian. This, however, does not mean that some of the issues addressed in "public theology" discourses were not also on his mind, as his elegant exposition of the church in an age of modernity (Jonker 2008) demonstrates, and as interpreted by Nico Koopman, one of the foremost public theologians in South Africa today (Koopman 2008)[4].

For the sake of this discussion, the contribution of Willie Jonker to a South African public theology in the period 1955-1994 will be addressed from two perspectives: First: What is theology? And second: How can a focus on the public of the church have an effect on the publics beyond the boundaries of the church?[5] A quite simple conception of public theology[6] underlies this discussion: a public theology attempts

---

3   For an overview of these debates, see *Responsible South African public theology in a global era* (2011), a special issue of the *International Journal of Public Theology*. This journal addresses the need for theology to interact with public issues of contemporary society in dialogue with different disciplines such as politics, economics, cultural and religious studies. For an earlier article on the genre of public theology in South Africa in the same journal, read de Gruchy (2007).
4   This essay must be read in conjunction with Koopman's clear exposition of the Trinitarian motives in Jonker's public ecclesiology (Koopman 2008:165-168).
5   See Smit (2008a) for an excellent analysis of the philosophical (Habermas, Luhmann, Arendt) and theological (Marty, Tracy, Bellah, Welker) roots of public theology. He distinguishes between normative and descriptive notions of public theology, where the first refers to an ideal of theological reflection (ethical engagement with issues of public concern) and the latter an (empirical) recognition of the public role of the Christian faith in history and in our current societies (Smit 2008a:28-29).
6   For technical discussions on the definition of public theology, see the two influential essays by Breitenberg (2003, 2010). For critique on the very notion of a "public theology"

to address issues of public concern from a theological perspective and communicates this to appropriate publics in church and society.

2. WHAT MAKES A THEOLOGY "PUBLIC"?

The roots of a "public theology" lie in the conception of what theology actually is. In an article entitled "What is theology?" written for a 1976 consultation of the Reformed Ecumenical Synod, Jonker distinguishes four models of theology (1976a:3-7). These are (1) theology as mystical knowledge of God, constituting theology as "wisdom" (Augustine and the Eastern Orthodox tradition); (2) theology as rational knowledge about articles of faith (Aquinas and Roman Catholic scholasticism); (3) theology as knowledge of God via revelation in Scripture (the Protestant tradition inaugurated by Luther and Calvin); and (4) theology as knowledge of God via human experience or religiosity (Schleiermacher, Neo-Protestant and Pentecostal theologies).

Jonker then makes a conscious choice for the Protestant model because – according to him – the Scriptures are taken as source, object and criterion of theology in a more adequate manner than in the other models or traditions. In the mystical tradition Scripture is important up to a point, after which mystical reflections lead to a higher-order knowledge of God beyond the revelation in Scripture. In the Catholic tradition the doctrines and traditions of the church are seen as equally important sources of revelation compared to Scripture, and Scripture itself is not the actual object of study. Interestingly, Jonker considers the model of experiential theology the least attractive as he views this as an anthropocentric way of speaking about God with only a relative position assigned to Scripture, thereby in fact deserting the very modus of theological language (1976a:7).

Jonker goes further and positions himself in the specific Reformed tradition within broader Protestant theology.[7] He draws distinctions between Luther and Calvin, and argues that the valid insights from Luther should be maintained, but supplemented with the broader theological vision of John Calvin (Heyns and Jonker 1974:248-252).

Jonker obviously works in broad strokes here. In depicting the relationship between God and humans, Luther would emphasise the holiness of God and the sinful nature of the human being, whereas Calvin works on the basis of a Creator God in relation to a fallen creation, including fallen human beings. Justification for Luther is being saved from sin, whereas for Calvin justification encompasses the recreation of all of reality and God's saving act from sin and all destructive powers. Luther interprets the rule of Christ through the "two kingdoms" view, where the law has as primary role the revelation of sin, whereas Calvin views Christ's rule as a rule over all of reality in the one kingdom of God with the law as a guide to holiness and the transformation of society (Heyns and Jonker 1974:251-252).

This overt choice for the Reformed view in the tradition of Calvin is echoed in an important article on theology and social ethics (Jonker 1973b).[8] This was written

---

 in South Africa, read Maluleke (2011).
7 See Jonker's contribution in the Heyns and Jonker (1974:232-260) co-publication, *Op weg met die teologie*.
8 For a recent instructive discussion of Jonker's ethics, read Van Niekerk's (2011) exposition delivered as the Willie Jonker memorial lecture in 2011.

at a time when the social dimensions of ethics were under-represented and where pious people with a strong individual spirituality in fact "overlooked" the structural dimensions of the gospel in relation to apartheid society. Jonker differentiates between personal and social ethics. The former deals with the moral action of the individual, whereas the latter focuses upon the relation amongst people within the structures of society (Jonker 1973c:79).

He then points to the danger of over-emphasising the personal dimension of ethical questions. This tendency has its roots in both Pietism and the subject philosophies of the Enlightenment (Jonker 1973c:81). Social ethics has the advantage that it brings the "institutes" into critical focus (82-83). In line with his views on theology in general, Jonker points to the limitations of Luther's two kingdoms theory which – probably contrary to Luther's intention – prioritises the individual view and may lead to a mere acceptance and even sanctioning of existing social orders belonging to the "kingdom of the world". Jonker also judges the natural-law tradition as too weak to be a solid foundation for social ethics as – theologically speaking – this tradition is simply too optimistic about the natural consensus amongst people of good will and makes too much of general grace in distinction from God's saving grace in Christ (84).

Like so often in his work, Jonker returns to Calvin (1973c:84-85), whom he admires for developing a truly social ethics on the basis of Scripture as norm for all spheres of life. In this inclusive view the social institutes are themselves brought under the critique of God's Word – a welcome correction to the Pietism in South African Afrikaans churches in the mid-1970s.

To avoid a possible misunderstanding of the Reformed tradition as sectarian, Jonker emphasises that this tradition is "catholic" in a double sense of the word. It stands in continuity with the early church and the church through the ages, and it strives to understand and proclaim the "wholeness" of the truth as revealed in Scripture.[9] That is why the Reformed tradition takes the whole canon, specifically including the Old Testament, seriously as it perceives God in the history of creation, law and the covenant (Heyns and Jonker 1974:253-259).

The above interpretation of the nature of theology provides the first answer as to the roots of Jonker's public theology. He placed himself squarely within the Reformed tradition, interpreted via John Calvin[10] and Karl Barth,[11] as a theology that seeks to transform all of reality according to the will of God as revealed in Scripture. The notion that theology would not include all societal spheres or publics would be foreign to Jonker. He would, however, maintain – and this is important – *that the church, understood as local congregation, denomination and ecumenical church, is the gateway to the other publics.*

Let us turn to the church as a "public" of theology.

---

9   See the article by Smit (1989) for an exposition of the catholicity of Jonker's thought.
10 For the reception of Calvin in the work of Jonker, read Naudé (2010).
11 Read Jonker (1988a) for his critical though overtly positive interpretation of Barth. For a broader perspective on Jonker's interpretation of Barth, read Naudé (2013).

3. THE "PUBLIC" OF THE CHURCH

The question now is: How can a focus on the public of the church have an effect on the publics beyond the boundaries of the church? Jonker implicitly provides a number or pathways in this regard. For the sake of brevity, three aspects that link the church's life and work with broader society and other public spheres are discussed: preaching, confessing and public witnessing.

3.1. Theology and proclamation

There is a deep pastoral and practical intent in all of Jonker's theology:[12] every doctrine should serve the faithful, the church and God's honour in the world. His appointment in Kampen was in Practical Theology, and at that stage already he published on the "problem" of preaching in an increasingly secular environment (Jonker 1970b).

His short monograph *Die Woord as opdrag* (Jonker 1976b) was an Afrikaans version of his lectures in the Netherlands and has become a classic for guiding and informing preaching in a perceptive and accessible manner.[13] Let us look at just one excerpt from the book, namely the section dealing with the transition from "text" to "sermon": "Van die teks na die preek …" (Jonker 1976b:68-78).

In line with the Reformed model of theology, Jonker stands firmly on the fact that preaching is preaching of the biblical text, obviously in the context of the specific pericope or book, and in line with the whole biblical message. Jonker opposed both fundamentalism, which takes the text at face value without a historical or grammatical context, and he also avoided the trap of the different "criticisms" that may render the text mute, because the reader is forever caught up in presuppositions and hermeneutical methodologies. The role of proper exegesis is to check first impressions of the text and make sure the scope and kerugma of the text are determined in the context of the relevant book and the Bible as a whole.

For the text to be preached, Jonker guides his readers toward the importance of personal Bible study, which represents an existential dimension where the preacher is herself being addressed and where God is being met. This opens the preacher to both the pastoral situation of the church and the relevant topics of the day.[14]

Meditation upon the text is the axis point where the history of the text turns to the actual present situation in the light of the preacher's knowledge of theology and insights into the "spirit of the times". Here "text" (biblical) and "text" (context) meet, and the preacher should be both theologically and socially competent to ensure a proper communication of the gospel message in the realities of the world.

The task of the preacher is to formulate one clear message, clarified from different perspectives. Jonker warns against the danger of "thematic preaching" – even with

---

12   For a discussion of this pastoral intent with specific respect to the doctrine of election, read Naudé's (1991) comments on Jonker's book *Uit vrye guns alleen* (1988b).
13   For more academic reflections on the link between Scripture (exegesis) and dogmatics, read Jonker (1970c, 1973a, 1979), and for actual sermon outlines for the time of the Passion, read Jonker (1982).
14   For the actuality of preaching that addresses contemporary challenges – very much in current "public theology" language – read Jonker (1976b:109-126).

a biblical intent – as the preacher easily slips into no longer being a witness to the Word but an orator on a Christian topic (1982:76-77).

If the preacher then finally delivers the sermon, she trusts God who transforms the church and the world through Word and Spirit. Jonker therefore has the local congregation uppermost in his mind. However, it is clear that, when the Word is proclaimed, God transforms not only congregants, but – through them – the world beyond the boundaries of the institutional church. Although preaching seems highly existential and personal, it is in fact a public event with a transformative power both within and outside the church.

That this was true for Jonker's own preaching is evident from two examples, namely his Mission Week sermons in the Stellenbosch student church, published as *Die liefde van Christus dring ons* (1976c), and his weekly meditations in *Die Burger*, an influential Afrikaans newspaper, published over a period of many years (see collection in Jonker 1987).

There is a deep evangelical thrust to Jonker's conviction of the public nature of proclamation. In his recently published *Die relevansie van die kerk* (2008, original unpublished manuscript, 1983) Jonker deals with the typical question that informs much of the public theology discourse today. In short: How can the church (and theology) remain "relevant" in the light of the massive impact of both the first and second Enlightenments, where the "turn to the subject" in Descartes and Kant was followed by a fundamental critique of religion itself in the work of philosophers such as Feuerbach and Marx? (Jonker 2008:41).

After a significant discussion of various responses (and a critical choice for Karl Barth), Jonker comes to a sobering conclusion: The gospel is relevant as it is the good news from God. We need not make the gospel relevant. In fact, by attempting to make the gospel relevant, we as the church and theologians might exactly lose our relevance, as we take on the assumptions of a secular and anti-religious worldview, which can only lead to a weakening, if not betrayal, of the gospel (Jonker 2008:147-153).

Preaching is public theology in action as the echoes of the gospel are heard in the church and its effects felt far beyond the church – because it is God's gospel.

3.2. Confessions

The Reformed tradition – precisely because it takes the proclamation of the Word in every age seriously – developed confessions as ever new witnesses to the gospel of Jesus Christ as required by the signs of the time.

A confession is "a faithful and doxological repetition of Scripture".[15] Confessions derive their authority from Scripture because they are viewed as being in consonance with Scripture. Simultaneously, despite their gravity, they are always provisional, standing under the critique of Scripture and a better insight into the truth of the gospel.

Confessions play at least three important roles in the life of the Church and beyond (Heyns and Jonker 1974:200-203; see also Jonker 1994:8-15):

---

15 "… 'n gelowige en lofprysende *repetitio Sacrae Scripturae*, 'n naspreke van die spreke van die Skrif" (Heyns and Jonker 1974:200).

(1) Confessions as public documents in and beyond the church serve as witness to the world about the great deeds of God. Confessions are doxological in nature and praise God amongst the nations; (2) confessions serve the church via catechesis and pastoral care, and they shape the embodiment of faith inside the church and the Christian life in publics beyond the church; and (3) confessions act as a rule of faith to discern the truth from heresies and false gospels.

And although this last one seems like an "inward-looking" function of confessions, this is perhaps its most "outwardly" public face: the Barmen declaration (1934) does not mention National Socialism, nor does the Belhar confession (1986) mention apartheid by name. But what does occur is a fundamental exposure of the false theological bases on which both political ideologies were built. No wonder the authorities responded so quickly – they knew that seemingly intra-ecclesial doctrinal matters were of crucial public-political concern.

The difficult question then arises: Do the confessions not curtail the freedom of the theologian who in her scientific endeavours should in principle be open to explore new possibilities and question all inherited truths? Does a confessional theology not in principle make speaking in the public realm of science (understood in an encompassing sense) impossible? (Heyns and Jonker 1974: 205).

Jonker suggests that there are normally two opposing positions in this regard. The one position emphasises the scientific freedom of the theologian, who should not be restricted in any way to seek for the truth. The other position insists on the binding of the theologian to the confessions and therefore accepts certain *a priori* limitations in scientific research.

Jonker proposes a third way. A confession provides an open presupposition, which in any case is inevitable for all scientific enquiry as there is no such thing as value-free interpretation (see Heyns and Jonker 1974:208). Stating this presupposition does not limit the theologian any more than other scientists are limited by their respective presuppositions. However, the confession also provides a basis for the relationship between theologian and church so that the former is free to question (including those very presuppositions!) and the church is duly informed to judge what theology produces, whilst both theologian and church always remain open to new insights from Scripture (Heyns and Jonker 1974:210). *Semper reformanda*.

3.3. Public witness

The most "public" moment of Jonker's theological and church journey occurred at the Rustenburg church conference in 1990.[16] Jonker was asked by the organisers to speak on the obstacles to a united public witness amongst the churches in South Africa. He cites as the greatest obstacle the sinful division of the church (Jonker 1991b:88) and continues to observe that the social divisions of the country are sadly reflected in these church divisions (89). These vastly opposing social locations made a united witness very difficult (1991b:90).

Speaking only months after the DRC General Synod of October 1990 finally rejected the theology of apartheid and recommitted itself to unity amongst churches of the

---

16 See the publication by Albert and Chikane, *The Road to Rustenburg* (1991).

DRC family, Jonker confidently stated that apartheid was now no longer accepted by the DRC. In this light, he therefore has the courage to confess:

> I confess before you and before the Lord, not only my own sin and guilt, and my personal responsibility for the political, social, economic and structural wrongs that have been done to many of you, and the results of which you and our whole country are still suffering from, but vicariously I dare also to do that in the name of the DRC of which I am a member, and for the Afrikaans people as a whole (Jonker 1991b:92).

Jonker then asked: Is the task of the church reconciliation or resistance? (93) He referred to 2 February 1990 (the announcement of the release of political prisoners and unbanning of all political formations) and asked whether "theological positions which were geared to match the struggle will be softened and even changed?" (95). He acknowledged that South Africa had come through abnormal times in which the churches played an overt and more direct political role. He warned, however, that there were limits to the political task of the church. This task is limited to the proclamation of "God's general and abiding demands of justice, fairness and the protection of the weak and the poor" (95), but churches cannot play the role of political parties. Christians were called to be radical disciples of Christ whilst knowing that "political change alone can never make us free from inner bondage" (98).

Jonker later reflected on this public confession of sin (see Jonker 1991a). According to him, the space for a confession was created by the DRC which finally moved away from understanding itself as a "volkskerk", based on natural theology in the negative sense of the word, to a church of Christ, saved by grace alone (Jonker 1991a:99). A biblical, theological or moral defence of apartheid was no longer possible (Jonker 1991a:97, 98). This non-defence of apartheid was further enabled by the impact of the ecumenical movement (97) as well as the acceptance by the DRMC of the Belhar confession. The voice of the former daughter church turned around the DRC in its tracks (98).

Jonker had to confess publicly because of the special guilt of the DRC (1991a:101) concerning separate churches and its theological support for the policies of apartheid. Yes, there are various levels of individual guilt and collective guilt. The church as a collective, however, could not wait with a confession of guilt until each member was ready this will in all probability never happen. Therefore it is imperative for an individual to do this "vicariously" (*plaasbekledend*) on behalf of the collective (102).

With sharp foresight, Jonker suggests further that in this confession of guilt the DRC might assist other churches who now or in the future would stand before the same temptation of aligning the church too closely with political ideals, thereby compromising the gospel of Jesus of Christ.

This public witness (confession) elicited huge media exposure and received both widespread criticism and support from Christians. Jonker himself was vilified by many white (and suspicious black) Christians. It was specifically painful that the church council of Biesiesvlei, the town of his birth, rejected this confession of guilt in a letter to him, calling on him not to be manipulated by politics, but to remain true to the Word of God. His letter of explanation was, however, never read to the church council – a fact that saddened him deeply (Jonker 1998a:209-210).

Looking back, this confession was an important precursor to the Truth and Reconciliation Commission (1995-2002),[17] which played a determining role in the healing of South Africa's past. It, however, played its role in line with Jonker's view of public theology as reconstructed here – the socio-psychological and political impact of his witness was to be channelled via the public of the church itself – in this case the public of the ecumenical church.

Jonker always understood his role as primarily *theological* in the realm of the church and hesitated to play a "direct" political role for fear that the gospel might once again be compromised. This seemingly "conservative" position was in fact transformative in a quiet but fundamental way. Without his public theology, the struggle for unity, reconciliation and justice would have been longer, and we still draw on his legacy as we face the unfinished task of church reunification in the DRC family, inclusive of the Belhar confession.

4. BEYOND JONKER: WHAT ROLE FOR THE CHURCH IN SOUTH AFRICAN PUBLIC THEOLOGIES TODAY?

Looking back on the journey of Willie Jonker with the DRC and the churches in South Africa in general, the question may be asked: Is the approach he followed still valid for public theology today? This question cannot be answered with a simple affirmation or negation. The following remarks attempt to re-position some of Jonker's impulses in our current context.

4.1. Understanding a different socio-political situation

Willie Jonker and the theologians of his time – both liberation and apartheid theologians – were by default ensured of the public significance and impact of their work beyond the boundaries of the church because they worked in South Africa prior to the impact of the liberalisation and secularisation which swept over us like a whirlwind after 1994. There was a unity between the institutional church, on the one hand, and politics and public life, on the other, because apartheid was in fact a pseudo-religious system predicated upon a pre-modern conception of society.

What the institutional church did and decided, and what church leaders said, really mattered as there was a strong correlation between "theology" and "society". To decide that the unity of the church is not merely an invisible spiritual matter, but required outward and visible unification of the segregated Reformed family was a fundamental theological decision proposed by Jonker from the beginning of his theological and church life.[18] However, in the minds of many Christians this was – correctly – interpreted as eroding the very basis of a society built on legally segregated communities. As in the time of the early church, to say that "Jesus is Lord" was indeed "political" in a system where the reconciliatory power of Christ was upheld in theory but denied in practice.

---

17 The official report, *Truth and Reconciliation Commission of South Africa Report*, detailing the facts, findings and recommendations of the TRC was published in five volumes in 1998. See especially Volume 4, pp. 59-92, which deals with the faith communities.
18 See Jonker (1955a, 1962, 1964, 1967, 1986).

One must further consider that the liberation struggle found fertile tactical space in the church as a consequence of the banning of political leaders in the period 1964-1990. This opened the door for a "direct" political role by leaders such as Desmond Tutu, Allan Boesak, Beyers Naudé, Frank Chikane, Johan Heyns and others, who could "step back" after 1994.

As so ably demonstrated by a number of theologians after 1994,[19] it is quite a different matter to do public theology in the context of a liberal democracy with a more strongly defined distance between state and Christian church, equality of all faiths, secular human rights guiding the Constitution and public ethics, and with legitimate political representatives operating in an open society. In short, the kinds of developments in Western societies which initially informed the very debate about the public nature of theology have now arisen in this African context as well, though with different emphases and trajectories.[20]

Willie Jonker – shaped by European theology and philosophy – understood and saw these developments coming to our shores. He was faithful to the context and dynamics of his time and knew that others after him would have to face a different kind of constellation of "publics" in which theology and the church would have to live out their calling. Whether "the publics" and "the institutes" can be reached through the public of the church in the same way as Jonker and his contemporaries presupposed, however, is doubtful.

It is the responsibility of our post-liberation generation to chart new pathways on the fundamental assumption[21] that the Christian church as the bride of Christ to whom the ministry of reconciliation has been entrusted remains a crucial pathway for the gospel in the world.

4.2. Affirming the link between worship and the publics

The proclaiming and confessing local churches remain important to shape believers who act as "light and salt" in their everyday lives in other spheres of society.[22] Under conditions of a liberal democracy, faithful Christians rather than the formal institutional church are for many people – believers and non-believers – a more important and perhaps the only representative face of "the church". In this

---

19 See the work of Smit (2007a, 2007b, 2008a), de Gruchy (2007), Koopman (2009) and De Villiers (2011).
20 For example, South Africa is not "secular" in the same sense as European countries such as France, Belgium and the Netherlands. Also, our Constitution requires a strict separation of church and state as in the USA, nor do we have an official state church or churches as in the UK and Germany. We are a typical society in transition with its own dynamics of modernisation and secularisation, whilst at the same time harbouring fast growth in African Independent and Pentecostal-type churches or communities. For reflections on public theologies in South Africa as transitional society, read Koopman (2005) and the doctoral thesis by Kusmierz (2009).
21 This assumption can obviously be challenged. It rests upon a specific understanding that God, in God's wisdom, has chosen to bless the earth through Israel in the OT (Gen 12) and the church as proclaimed in the NT (see the various references in the Pauline letters), whilst also acknowledging that, if the church does not proclaim, the stones will call out.
22 See Smit (2008b) on six different meanings of "church", including the reference to Christians in everyday life.

sense the public nature of the liturgy[23] – as set out by Jonker – must be reinforced and confirmed.

4.3. Strengthening the prophetic channels of democracy

The institutional church must be seen to be a united ecumenical church and retain its prophetic role, but not exclusively via after-the-fact reactive media releases or the modus of synodical reports. The "how" question is important: churches for the most part have to take up the role of "silent prophets" who influence policy in the democratic process by taking hands with Christians in the spheres of the economy, politics, law and the public service. We are ill-prepared to work "beyond" theology in cross- disciplinary boundaries, and when we do engage in questions of public concern, we struggle to retain (like Jonker) the profile of our *theological* perspective in dialogue with others. Institutional churches and ecumenical bodies such as the SACC have proven that we are not well suited to operate in a society where – unlike for Jonker and his contemporaries – institutional and social power has shifted away from the institutional church, and an impact on the publics outside of the church should therefore be sought in part via participation in democratic structures.

4.4. Recognising the social and public influence of "Pentecostalism"

The public space of the institutional churches that fought for and against apartheid has been seriously challenged by the phenomenal growth of not only African Independent Spirit Churches, but also by the attraction of a young generation to non-denominational, multi-racial, "charismatic" churches. The latter group of churches seemingly speak much better in the language of our time and via new-media technologies than the historical churches.

These churches or local, informal faith communities no longer fit easy theological descriptions. Some are strong on social justice, some are strong on the teaching office and some take Scripture seriously beyond fundamentalism, so that the old criticisms of pietism, superficial experiential theology and ahistorical readings of Scripture no longer apply equally to all.

In his last academic publication Jonker (1998b) once again addressed the DRC. He asked the pertinent question about which of three possibilities the DRC will turn: Will it grasp back to its own past and endeavour to remain a *"volkskerk"*? Will it embrace Pentecostalism? Or will the DRC remain true to its Reformed roots? Jonker expressed the hope that the last option will be followed. In light of his fundamental critique of Pietism and "Cartesian" theologies with an anthropocentric experiential religiosity, the question arises whether our theological evaluations of "Pentecostal" communities need not show greater nuance in the light of current developments, where a one-size-fits-all view simply does not hold.[24] Perhaps Reformed churches

---

23 For a discussion on the link between worship and public theology, read part four of [rather insert specific detail here] (2007:423-469).

24 See the interesting article by Botha (2007:295-325). He judges the rise of the Pentecostal-charismatic movement since 1906 as of equal fundamental importance to the 16th-century Reformation. He further cites the reasons why this movement has grown to more than 600 million people by referring inter alia to its theological flexibility, its attraction to marginalised people, its high indigenisation capacities coupled with a strong missionary

should remind themselves that the very same Jonker told us: "Each sect is the unpaid bill of the church".[25]

Who knows? Perhaps the face of the public church in the 21st century South Africa might not look "Reformed" as traditionally understood at all?

4.5. Seeking justice for the weakest in society

There is no greater public task for the churches in this nation and on the African continent than to further their priestly role as disciples of Christ in the service of justice. To repeat Jonker at this point: the church has to seek "God's general and abiding demands of justice, fairness and the protection of the weak and the poor" (Jonker 1991b:95). Churches will have to play a more constructive public role – no longer from a relatively privileged social location, but as a humble but indispensable member of civil society, representing faith communities in action. Churches could lend their networks, expertise and infrastructure to address the current government's failures in education, health and caring for the most vulnerable. We could re-ignite capabilities to soften the blow of non-delivery to the most vulnerable in our society.

Let us remind ourselves that public theology is not about public relations on behalf of the church, or seeking cheap public attention for a well-spoken theologian, but it is about serving the most vulnerable when the left hand does not know what the right hand is doing.

The actual purpose of public theology – in whatever form – is well described by Jesus: "In the same way, let your light shine before others, that they may see your good deeds and glorify your Father in heaven" (Mt 5:16).

BIBLIOGRAPHY

Albert, L. & Chikane, F. (eds). 1991. *The Road to Rustenburg: the church looking forward to a new South Africa*. Cape Town: Struik Christian Books.

Bakker, J.L. (ed.). 1973. *Septuagesimo Anno. 'n Huldigingsbundel opgedra aan Prof GC Berkouwer*. Kampen: Kok.

Botha, E. 2007. "The new reformation: the amazing rise of the Pentecostal-Charismatic movement in the 20th century". *Studia Historiae Ecclesiasticae* Vol. 33, No. 1, pp. 295-325.

Breitenberg, E.H. 2003. "To tell the truth: Will the real public theology please stand up?" *Journal of the Society of Christian Ethics*, Vol. 23, No. 2, pp. 55-96.

Breitenberg, E.H. 2010. "What is public theology?" In D.K. Hainsworth & S.R. Paeth (eds), pp. 3-17.

Burger, C.W. & Müller, B.A. & Smit, D.J. (eds.). 1982. *Riglyne vir lydensprediking. Woord teen die lig*. Kaapstad: NG Kerk-Uitgewers.

Conradie, E.M. (ed.) 2007. *Essays in public theology*. Stellenbosch: Sun Press.

---

zeal, healing, use of media in worship as well as empowerment of ordinary believers in the loose leadership structures of these churches.

25 This is the author's recollection. Because Jonker had such an ecumenical orientation, he could – despite fundamental critique – remind us that those who break away in what the church calls "sectarian groups" always mirror a weakness in the church itself.

De Gruchy, J.W. 2007. "Public Theology as Christian Witness: Exploring the Genre". *International Journal of Public Theology* Vol. 1, No. 1, pp. 26-41.

De Villiers, E. & Kitching, D. (eds.) 1991. *Derdegelui vir môre: die NG Kerk voor die uitdagings van 'n nuwe tyd*. Kaapstad: Tafelberg.

De Villiers, D.E. 2011. "Public Theology in the South African Context". *International Journal of Public Theology* Vol. 5, No. 1, pp. 5-22.

Hainsworth D.K. & Paeth, S.R. (eds). 2010. *Public theology for a global society*. Grand Rapids: Eerdmans.

Heyns, J.A. & Jonker, W.D. 1974. *Op weg met die teologie*. Pretoria: NG Kerkboekhandel.

International Journal of Public theology. 2011. *Responsible South African public Theology in a Global Era*. Vol. 5, No. 1.

Jonker, W.D. 1951. *Die invloed van die leer aangaande God op die opvatting van die vergiffenis van sonde in die teologie van Schleiermacher, Ritschl en Brunner*, Ongepubliseerde BD-verhandeling. Pretoria: Universiteit van Pretoria.

Jonker, W.D. 1952. *'n Waardering van Ulfilas se vertaling van die eerste hoofstuk van Markus se Evangelie, met verwysing na enkele ander plekke*. Ongepubliseerde MA-verhandeling. Pretoria: Universiteit van Pretoria.

Jonker, W.D. 1955a. *Mistieke liggaam en kerk in die nuwe Rooms-Katolieke teologie*. Kampen: Kok.

Jonker, W.D. 1955b. "Genade en kerk". *Die Kerkbode* 14-21 Desember.

Jonker, W.D. 1962. *Die Sendingbepalinge van die Ned Geref Kerk van Transvaal*. Potchefstroom: Kerk en wêreld-studiegroep.

Jonker, W.D. 1964. "Die liberale kerkreg en die veelheid van kerke". *NGTT* Vol. 5, pp. 3-9.

Jonker, W.D.1967. "Volkskerk of belydende gemeente?" *NGTT* Vol. 8, pp. 20-26.

Jonker, W.D.1970a. "Vier preeksketse, in Werkgroep Kerk en Prediking". *Postille*. 'sGravenhage: Boekencentrum NV, pp. 45-57.

Jonker,W.D.1970b. "Heeft de preek een toekomst?" *Geref Weekblad* 13 November - 4 Desember.

Jonker, W.D.1970c. "Eksegese en dogmatiek". In W.D. Jonker, J.H. Roberts & A.H. van Zyl (eds.), pp. 157-179.

Jonker, W.D. & Roberts, J.H. & van Zyl, A.H. (eds.) 1970d. *Hermeneutica. 'n Huldigingsbundel opgedra aan prof. E.P. Groenewald*. Pretoria: NG Kerkboekhandel.

Jonker, W.D.1973a. "Dogmatiek en Heilige Skrif." In J.L. Bakker (ed.), pp. 86-111.

Jonker, W.D.1973b. "Heilige Skrif en sosiale etiek by Calvyn". *Bulletin van die Suid-Afrikaanse vereniging vir die bevordering van Christelike wetenskap* Vol. 39, pp. 31-37.

Jonker, W.D.1973c. "Die aktualiteit van die sosiale etiek". In P.A. Verhoef, D.W. De Villiers & J.L. De Villiers (eds.), pp. 78-107.

Jonker, W.D.1976a. "What is Theology?" In P.C. Schrotenboer (ed.), pp. 3-15.

Jonker, W.D. 1976b. *Die Woord as opdrag*. Pretoria: NG Kerkboekhandel.

Jonker, W.D.1976c. *Die liefde van Christus dring ons*. Pretoria: NG Kerkboekhandel.

Jonker, W.D.1977. "Die unieke karakter van die kerk". *In die Skriflig* Vol. 11, pp. 4-13.

Jonker, W.D.1979. "Die Ou Testament in die dogmatiek". In D.H. Odendaal, B.A. Müller & H.J.B. Combrink (eds.), pp. 75-85.

Jonker, W.D.1982. "Prediking in die lydenstyd". In C.W. Burger, B.A. Müller & D.J. Smit (eds.), pp. 7-20.

Jonker, W.D.1986. "Afsonderlike kerke vir afsonderlike bevolkingsgroepe?" *Scriptura* Vol. 17, pp. 1-14.

Jonker, W.D.1987. *Die hand wat my vashou*. Kaapstad: Lux Verbi.

Jonker, W.D.1988a. "Some remarks on the interpretation of Karl Barth". *NGTT* Vol. 29, pp. 29-40.

Jonker, W.D.1988b. *Uit vrye guns alleen. Oor uitverkiesing en verbond*. Pretoria: NG Kerkboekhandel.

Jonker, W.D.1991a. "Die noodsaak van skuldbelydenis". In E. De Villiers & D. Kitching (eds.), pp. 94-102.

Jonker, W.D. 1991b. "Understanding the Church Situation and Obstacles to Christian Witness in South Africa". In L. Albert & F. Chikane (eds.), pp. 87-98.

Jonker, W.D. 1994. *Bevrydende waarheid*. Wellington: Hugenote Uitgewers.

Jonker, W.D.1998a. *Selfs die kerk kan verander*. Kaapstad: Tafelberg.

Jonker, W.D.1998b. "Kragvelde binne die kerk". *Aambeeld* Vol. 26, No. 1, pp. 11-14.

Jonker, W.D.2008. *Die Relevansie van die kerk: Teologiese reaksies op die betekenis van die kerk in die wêreld*. Wellington: Bybel-Media.

Koopman, N.N. 2005. "After ten years. Public theology in post-apartheid South Africa – lessons from a debate in the USA". *NGTT* Vol. 64, pp. 149-164.

Koopman, N.N. 2008. "Suid-Afrikaanse kerke en die openbare lewe. Enkele lesse uit die teologie van Willie Jonker". In W.D. Jonker *Die relevansie van die kerk: Teologiese reaksies op die betekenis van die kerk in die wêreld*. Wellington: Bybel-Media, pp. 165-178.

Koopman, N.N. (ed.) 2008. *Opstelle oor geloof en openbare lewe: Versamelde Opstelle 2*. Stellenbosch: Sun Press.

Koopman, N.N. 2009. "Public Theology as Prophetic Theology. More than utopianism and criticism". *JTSA* Vol. 134, pp. 117-130.

Kusmierz, K. 2009. *Theology in transition. Public theologies in post-apartheid South Africa*. Unpublished doctoral thesis. University of Basel.

Maluleke, T.S. 2011. "The elusive public of public theology". *International Journal of Public Theology* Vol. 5, pp. 79-89.

Naudé, P.J. 1991. "Uit vrye guns alleen: Grondlyne vir 'n pastorale dogmatiek". *NGTT* Vol. 32, No. 1, pp. 110-118.

Naudé. P.J. 2010. "Op 'n mespunt. Die resepsie van Johannes Calvyn in die werk van Willie Jonker". *NGTT* Vol. 52, No. 3 & 4, pp. 82-91.

Naudé, P.J. 2013. "The reception of Karl Barth in South Africa 1960-1990 – Selected perspectives". In M. Plaatjies-VanHuffel & R. Vosloo (eds.), pp. 186-199.

Odendaal, D.H. & B.A. Müller, B.A. & H.J.B. Combrink, H.J.B (eds.) 1979. *Die Ou Testament vandag*. Kaapstad: NG Kerk-Uitgewers.

Plaatjies-VanHuffel, M. & Vosloo, R. (eds.) 2013. *The Reformed Churches in South Africa and the struggle for justice: Remembering 1960-1990*. Stellenbosch: Sun Press.

Potgieter, F.J.M. 1961. "Die wese van die kerk van Christus". *NGTT* Vol. 2, pp. 271-277.

Schrotenboer, P.C. (ed.) 1976. *Church and theology in the contemporary world.* Grand Rapids: Michigan.

Smit, D.J. 2007a. "No ulterior motive – and public theology?" In E.M. Conradie (ed.), pp. 139-156.

Smit, D.J. 2007b. "Revisioning during reconstruction? Contemporary challenges for the churches in South Africa". In E.M. Conradie (ed.), *Essays in public theology*. Stellenbosch: Sun Press, pp. 41-56.

Smit, D.J. 2008a. "Wat beteken "publiek"? Vrae met die oog op publieke teologie". In N.N. Koopman (ed.), pp. 3-34.

Smit, D.J. 2008b. "Oor die kerk as 'n unieke samelewingsverband". In N.N. Koopman (ed.), pp. 69-82.

Smit, D.J. 1989. "Om saam met al die heiliges Christus te ken". In P.F. Theron & J. Kinghorn (eds.), pp. 11-32.

Theron, P.F. & Kinghorn, J. (eds.) 1989. *Koninkryk, kerk, en kosmos: Huldigingsbundel ter ere van Prof W.D. Jonker*. Bloemfontein: Pro-Christo Publikasies.

Truth and Reconciliation Commission of South Africa. 1998. *Truth and Reconciliation Commission of South Africa Report*. Cape Town: Juta.

Van Niekerk, A.A. 2011. "Willie Jonker se Teologiese Etiek" (Sesde W.D. Jonker Gedenklesing, Kaapstad, 30 Oktober 2011), *NGTT* Vol. 52, No. 3, pp. 585-599.

Verhoef, P.A. & De Villiers, D.W. & De Villiers, J.L. (eds.). 1973. *Sol Iustitiae. 'n Huldigingsbundel opgedra aan B.B. Keet, J.C.G. Kotze, J.J. Müller, W.J. van der Merwe, T.N. Hanekom & F.J.M. Potgieter*. Kaapstad: NG Kerk-Uitgewers.

3.8 THE BELHAR CONFESSION (1982/1986) AND CHURCH AND SOCIETY (1986)

A comparative essay in five statements[1]

This essay offers a close comparative reading of the *Belhar confession* and the DRC witness document, *Church and Society*. It is argued (in the first statement) that, although there are many similarities in content between the two documents on the surface, they are in fact theologically quite different (statements two to five). It is hoped that the DRC's decision in 2011 to start a process of adopting the Belhar confession represents a return to its Reformed roots in the confessing church tradition.

The year 2011 was a significant one for the family of Dutch Reformed Churches in South Africa. In this year we commemorated the 25th anniversaries of two significant church documents, namely the *Belhar confession* and *Church and Society*. The Belhar document[2] was adopted as a draft confession by the then Dutch Reformed Mission Church in 1982 and subsequently formally included as confession in the church orders at the general synod in the suburb of Belhar close to Cape Town in October 1986. *Kerk en Samelewing*[3] (KS/CS) is a witness document accepted as policy guideline for the DRC at the General Synod, also in October 1986, and incidentally also in Cape Town.

The relative distance in time of 25 years allows for rich opportunities to reflect on the significance of these documents. This paper attempts to read the two documents in a comparative way. The aim, however, is to go beyond a mere comparison of content, which is addressed in the first section below. The intention is to rather investigate what the significant social and theological divergences were (and still are?) so as to understand why the DRC took a quarter of a century to resolve in principle to accept the Confession of Belhar.[4]

For the sake of clarity and progression of argument, this paper posits five statements which are then explained in the ensuing paragraphs. Each of these statements could have been an academic paper on its own. The weakness of this essay is therefore that huge topics will be presented quite concisely in the hope that what is gained in breadth will adequately compensate for the loss in depth at some points.

1. FIRST STATEMENT

On the face of it, there is a strong convergence in content between the Confession of Belhar (1982/6) and the DRC witness document Kerk en Samelewing (1986).

---

1   Revised and shortened version of a paper delivered on 31 October 2011 at the Theological Faculty of the University of the Free State and published the following year in *Acta Theologica* 32 (2), 147-161 (2012).
2   For a first theological discussion on the origin and intention of the Belhar confession, read Cloete and Smit (1984).
3   For this essay the original Afrikaans version of 1986 is used as basis, with English translations by the author. It should be noted that *Kerk en Samelewing* was revised in 1990.
4   For a definition and discussion of reception of church documents, read Naudé and Smit (2000). For a case study of the DRC's reaction to Belhar, read Botha and Naudé (1998:77-89), and for a more academic account, Naudé (2007).

One can easily draw two columns with Belhar formulations on the one side and those of KS/CS on the other and see that in many cases there are even exact verbal correspondences between the two documents. Because of its historical precedence, let us take the five sub-divisions of the Belhar confession as point of departure and do a brief comparative reading.

Belhar's first article confesses the Trinity and the belief that the church came into existence and is under the care of God through the Word and the Spirit.

In section 243 of KS/CS the DRC confesses that it forms part of God's unique, holy people who have been elected to eternal life through the Word and the Spirit (reflecting Heidelberger Catechism Question 45). That the church owes its existence and calling in the world to the gracious election by God is further emphasised with reference to the church and the new covenant through the miracle of recreation. The essence of the church is therefore determined by the Triune God. The church is – above all – God's people (see KS/CS sections 42, 46-8 and 82).

Belhar's second article repeats the creedal formulation from Nicea and the Apostolicum, namely a confession of one, holy, catholic church, and places emphasis on both the spiritual and visible unity of the church.

The unity of the church is also a core theme in KS/CS. The unity of the church is a reflection of the unity of the Trinity, and by living this unity the church is a window on God's new world (KS/CS, section 81). Just as in Belhar, the link between theology and ecclesiology is an intricate one. As a direct echo of Belhar's second article, KS/CS states:

> The church is from its inception one in the Triune God, but must seek, serve and make this unity visible in the midst of the diversity in God's creation and amongst God's people in this broken reality (section 82, my translation).

It is important to note that on the unity question KS/CS indeed corrects the traditional views of the DRC up to that point in two ways: diversity in creation is no longer used as argument for human and church divisions on the principle of pluriformity and, whilst acknowledging the theological (spiritual) origin and eschatological fulfilment of this unity, KS/CS clearly calls for *visible* unity, realised here and now. The notion of "unity in freedom" (Belhar, article 2) finds expression in the KS/CS statement that visible unity must not be forced upon people for the mere sake of outward demonstration (CS, section 94).[5]

Belhar's third article focuses on the conviction that the message of reconciliation has been entrusted to the church and that the church should embody this reconciliation amongst its own members and in society.

In its discussion of the essence and calling of the church in paragraph 11 (with 9 sub-paragraphs), KS/CS presents reconciliation from two perspectives. First, the priestly task of the church requires it to proclaim in word and deed the love and reconciliation amongst people (section 51). And secondly, it makes particular mention of the church as "reconciled community" (paragraph 11.7, section 77-80). As

---

5   See also sections 59, 62, 74, 76, 82-99 and the practical translation with regard to the DRC family in sections 257-8.

in Belhar, reconciliation is fundamentally seen as a gracious gift from God through the blood of Christ.

Once the church understands its own reconciliation and peace with God, part of its thankfulness is to take up the ministry of reconciliation, noted for its love and peace amongst people, and erecting visible signs of God's kingdom amidst the divisions of society (section 223). Racism is hence declared "a serious sin which no person or church may defend or practise" (section 112).

Belhar's fourth article confesses that God is a God of justice and peace who is in a special way the God of the sufferer, the poor and oppressed, and that the church is called to stand with God to ensure that justice and peace are established.

This has been the most contentious article of the Belhar confession and has been – and is today still being – used to discredit the confession as "liberation theology" built on the notion of a Marxist class struggle.[6] In its first reaction to the Belhar confession, the DRC stated that this section could have been formulated differently, and at that point put forward the view that KS/CS actually expresses the concern for justice more adequately.[7]

The point is not whether KS/CS is "better" than Belhar, but whether the DRC's witness can be seen as consonant with the Belhar confession in this specific regard.

A close reading of the KS/CS division on the church and relations amongst groups of people (division 12) reveals an astonishing and passionate plea for justice based on a careful analysis of the same biblical traditions cited in Belhar, namely the prophets and wisdom literature in the Old Testament, and the gospels and James in the New Testament. Justice is particularly expounded in relation to those whose rights have been violated. This is not only relevant on a personal level, but applies equally to the social structures in society (KS/CS, sections 136-137).

Believers are therefore called to stand up for the rights of the poor and the vulnerable. In deep consonance with Belhar, KS/CS states that where this happens, believers follow the example of God Himself. "He is indeed par excellence (*by uitnemendheid*) the One who stands for the case of the sufferers and those living under injustice" (section 144, my translation, referring to Ps 140). This is repeated in the NT, where especially the Lukan gospel describes God as "the One who especially cares for the less privileged and the vulnerable" (section 145, my translation). Indeed, because we are created in God's image, the Bible demonstrates "special sensitivity for those who are oppressed and exploited" (section 147, my translation).

It is clear that KS/CS uses the same biblical language with the same kind of emphases as we find in Belhar article 4. No reformulation nor discrediting of Belhar can be defended from the strong witness that speaks so clearly from KS/CS. Members of the DRC who still do this contradict the stance of their own church.

---

6   See the discussion about Belhar and liberation theology in Botha and Naude (1998: 86-88), and Smit's brilliant exegetical study on this article in Cloete and Smit (1984).

7   See the discussion of the DRC General Synod of 1990 decision (point 8 refers to Belhar's article 4) in Botha and Naude (1998: 83).

Belhar's last article is a call for embodiment of the confession, despite the actions of governments or the ordinations of men. It recalls the early church's confession that Jesus is Lord, and ends with a doxology to the Father, Son and Spirit.

In the context of South Africa in the early and mid-1980s the issue was indeed living the faith in the face of strong and sometimes violent state action. Readers are reminded of the controversial movement that prayed for the fall of the government in 1985.[8] How does one embody one's deepest confession if the state legalises injustice and upholds unjust laws in the name of the very Christ whom one confesses?

KS/CS is quite aware of this. The "Reformed" in the name of the DRC played an important role here. KS/CS distinguishes between the state (ordained by God) and the government of the day representing the state. The status of the government is dependent on its fulfilment of its calling to be servant of God by caring for all its citizens, and making sure that peace, order and wellbeing are promoted (sections 310-432).

In principle KS/CS agrees with Belhar: the Reformed tradition recognises the right to protest against and actively resist the political order of the day (section 323). The chief reason and justification for these actions of last resort – such as civil disobedience and peaceful resistance (section 328) – is if the government in itself demonstrates such a measure of injustice that its legitimacy is fully questionable (section 326).

It will be shown later that this agreement in principle (that obedience to Christ the Lord is a higher requirement than obedience to the government or state[9]) was not upheld consistently and in practice by KS/CS. Nevertheless, one may assert that on the face of it, KS/CS concurs *in theory* (see section 328) with Belhar, namely that one should rather suffer for your faith than to follow the stipulations of men (sic).

KS/CS ends – like Belhar – on a doxological note from Philippians 1:9-11, referring to our salvation through faith in Christ, and the eschatological hope that believers will be unblemished when Christ returns, to the honour and glory of God (section 383).

2. SECOND STATEMENT

The primary and most obvious divergence between the two documents is that they represent distinct theological genres with a distinct "status", namely an official church confession following a status confessionis (1977/1982) and, in the case of Church and Society, a synodical witness document following a rethinking of a previous DRC document called Ras, volk en nasie (1974).

Different church traditions respond in distinct ways to new situations in which a reinterpretation of the gospel is required. The best known of these ecclesial modes of speaking is the Roman Catholic encyclicals that from time to time provide pastoral and ethical guidelines for believers, whilst at the same time serving as the church's witness in the world.

---

8   See the SACC text that motivated the call for prayers to end unjust rule in Villa-Vicencio (1985:247-250).
9   Read the moving testimony of Beyers Naudé and others on the issue of the right to resistance by Christians in the context of the Schlebusch Commission appointment in 1972 to investigate the work of the Christian Institute (Naudé 1995:170-179).

It is also common knowledge that only the Reformed tradition developed the specific genre of confessions, namely witnessing to the gospel in a specific situation against a perceived heresy and for the truth of the apostolic faith.[10] But that does not happen often. In the normal course of events churches in the Reformed tradition (obviously with some variations) formulate their witness via the work of officially appointed commissions and synodical reports.

I will not aim to analyse the theological differences underlying the notion of truth, Scripture and authority emanating from dialogues among faith traditions. Within the Reformed tradition the view is clear: Scripture is the first and primary and ultimate "authority" for all forms of witness in the church. Following this, we find the credos of the early church, followed historically by confessions specific to the Reformation tradition that all derive their authority from Scripture and that they are always open to revision in the light of a subsequent better understanding of Scripture.

Commission and synod reports are the on-going witness of the church, subject to the same Scriptural truth. However, they do not carry the same "weight" as confessions, which are serious expressions of faith following a situation of *status confessionis* in which the truth of the gospel itself is at stake. Barth (1961:79) reminds us that no church can be in a permanent state of *status confessionis* – confessions are therefore rarer, and from the perspective of church law, take a prime position in the orders of the church, from where they flow into the life and ministry of the church.

The simple but – as we will see below – important difference between Belhar and KS/CS is that the latter was an updated witness of the DRC, revising its views of 1974 on core aspects of the faith in the context of South Africa in the early 1980s. In contrast stands Belhar as a confessional response to the very same situation, constituting a fundamental difference on the interpretation of the seriousness of threats to the truth of the gospel at that point.

What appears to be the same content as set out in the first statement above is not the full story.

3. THIRD STATEMENT

Part of the reason for responding differently to the situation of South Africa in the 1970s and 1980s is that the DRC interpreted the situation from an oppositional perspective compared to the DRMC. These oppositional perspectives have their roots in at least three factors pertaining to the DRC, namely socio-economic status, political ideology and natural theology.

3.1. Socio-economic status

There are quite a number of perspectives on how social factors determine our view of the world. The most prominent of these perspectives in theological circles is the Latin American liberation theologians' emphasis on the so-called "preferential option for the poor", which constructs reality "from the underside of history" and then takes the view of the poor as hermeneutical key to retrieve core themes in

---

10 For a broad historical overview of *status confessions,* read Smit's contribution on this topic in Cloete and Smit (1984). Read Naudé (2010:77-103) on the specific confessional character of the Belhar text in relation to the theology of Karl Barth.

Scripture from this perspective. In the broader field of hermeneutics and biblical studies, the same point regarding social location (from different angles) has been made by feminist scholars, materialist exegetes, black and African theologians, and those who privilege the "ordinary readers" of the Bible.[11]

Outside the field of theology, some of the most prevalent theories related to our perspective-dependent view of reality are related to Marxism[12] (the sub-structure of economic class determining the super-structure of religion, culture and politics) and the paradigm theory of Thomas Kuhn[13] (scientific interpretation is shaped by the "normality" accepted by a relevant community of scholars).

The South Africa of the period 1950-1980, from which the two documents under discussion emerged, was predicated upon a strict spatial, social and economic model of separation. White and coloured people in particular literally and metaphorically lived in different worlds through the implementation of the Group Areas Act, and it is therefore to be expected that their perspective on South African realities would be markedly different: one from the upper, and the other from the underside of history and power.

This is evident in many ways, but perhaps nowhere more poignantly reflected than in the DRC's official response to Belhar during the general synod of 1990. The right in principle of the DRMC to accept a new confession is granted. The DRC also noted that this acceptance was done "in great earnest (*met groot erns*)" and that the content addresses "matters that are of essential importance to the Mission Church" (Botha and Naudé 1998:83).

It is this last sentence that strikes one as the most revealing in viewing the world from different perspectives. Matters such as unity, reconciliation and justice (and the seriousness of a *status confessionis* associated with them) were just not on the radar screen of the DRC in the same way, simply because it is very, very difficult to jump over one's own shadow – in the case one's social location. Barth is right: If you do not see the no! of the confession, you will also not confess the yes! of the confession (Barth 1956: 630-631).

3.2. Political ideology

One could further argue that this social location of legal and practical separation, sprung from a political ideology which is unfortunately still present in aspects of KS/CS. In this particular sense KS/CS is an ambiguous witness.

It takes as point of departure (in the Calvinist tradition) that God rules over all of reality and all spheres of society (sections 42, 44, 50, 216). It then proceeds to state that love, justice and human dignity are the tests for any political model (309). But instead of logically moving forward to actually judge the politics of race-based separation from this perspective, KS/CS retreats into a supposedly "neutral"

---

11   For an accessible overview of different hermeneutical approaches with references to original literature, see Maimela and König (1998:257-450).
12   For a short statement on the interpretation of history as that of a class struggle, read Marx and Engels (1971, original 1848).
13   See Kuhn's highly influential study on paradigms in science (1962) and the theological interpretation of his views by Tracy and Küng (1986).

position, stating that it is not the task of the church to actually prescribe any political model or policy. It names apartheid openly, but instead of an unequivocal rejection, it says: "The DRC is convinced that the managing of apartheid (*hantering van apartheid*) as a political and social system that brings injustice to people and benefits one group unjustly above another cannot be accepted on Christian ethical grounds" (306). KS/CS continues to state that not all suffering of people can be attributed to apartheid only (307), admitting that (perhaps) some of the legal measures in place were experienced as hurtful and inhuman (339).

The same tension between "principle" and "practice", resolved in a supposedly neutral position, emerges from the section on the church and government. It was noted above that the KS/CS accepts the right to rise up against a government which – because of injustice (323) – has lost its legitimacy (326). But the DRC cannot support even cases of peaceful protest such as the call for sanctions or marches for freedom, because they bring greater suffering and lead to unrest and violence. The retreat into "neutrality" is the way out: "The DRC may not identify itself with existing or other political ideologies or attempt to be involved in politics via the drafting of political programmes or models" (332).

It is evidently clear: the DRC of the mid-1980s was politically just too compromised to clearly state that apartheid *as such* was not acceptable on ethical grounds, and that in fact the government of the day has lost all legitimacy in the eyes of the majority and in terms of the DRC's own ethical criteria. The dual power of social status and political ideology was too strong.

But again: that is not the full story. Theology was the real issue at stake.

3.3. Natural theology

The differences in social analysis and political ideology are not adequate to explain why KS/CS and Belhar seem so close in terms of content, but in fact stand quite far apart. It has to do with the theological point of departure as is witnessed in the interpretation of South African society at that time.

Chapter 1 in KS/CS (entitled: "Background") refers to the complex society in which the DRC finds itself. This complexity is constituted by the fact that there is a wide divergence of racial groups, and KS/CS gives exact percentages of the population for Zulu, Xhosa, White and Coloured people. This is followed by the remark that population growth amongst Whites is slower than amongst black peoples and will lead to Whites constituting a proportionally smaller part of the total population. Literacy amongst Whites is much higher than amongst blacks and this will play a role in economic differences between rich and poor. In summary: the issue which needs to be addressed by the church is the wide diversity related to "race, skin colour, *volk* and culture, language and education, politics and economics, religion and church coupled to a big difference in levels of development". If all these factors are present in one society, and one adds the strife between capitalism and communism as well as the struggle for world power, the potential for conflict is huge (KS/CS, section 29).

What is crucial to note is that this "background" is stated first, and then the principles of accountability (read: theology) follow in Chapter 2. This is not a simple question of whether contextual analysis precedes or follows theological reflection.

No, the real observation is that the DRC uses race differentiation and a philosophical principle of pluriformity as hermeneutical key to "frame" the subsequent theological response. When it is then stated that Scripture is the only criterion for judging the South African situation (section 36), the reading of Scripture is already embedded in a compromised principle of natural theology where God's revelation is seen in relation to the pluriformity in creation and recreation.

It is not in the nature of a confession to do extensive social analysis. In Belhar this "analysis" must be sought in the accompanying letter and in a few contextual references in the confession itself (e.g. article 3). What is immediately evident is a totally different spirit: Belhar approaches the South African situation from the perspective of whether the truth of the gospel is at stake or not. In other words, Belhar approaches the situation from a confessional starting point and not from any philosophical or political or language or race perspective. Yes, all these matters are indeed relevant in the confession of unity, reconciliation and justice – Belhar is far from neutral or objective – but it approaches the situation via a *status confessionis*.

In short: for KS/CS the "problem" is how to live together in a complex and diverse society. For Belhar the "problem" is a false gospel supporting the division in church and society on the basis of diversity.

If one adds this latter theological point to the socio-economic status and political arguments above, a fuller picture emerges of why KS/CS and Belhar hold oppositional views, despite the seeming concurrence in content.

4. FOURTH STATEMENT

Apart from the fact of situational interpretation, the DRC at that point did not actualise its claim of being a confessional church in the Reformed tradition, open to new revelation of the truth in dialogue with the ecumenical church, partially because of its ecumenical isolation, and more fundamentally because its theological identity was Reformed in the formal but not in the normative sense.

It is not surprising to note how often the DRC refers to itself as a confessional church in the tradition of the Reformation. That is what its name and history say!

The church is a confessional community that stands in the tradition of the New Testament church and the apostolic faith. In fact, the apostolicity of the church refers to a sound adherence to the teaching of the apostles (KS/CS sections 60-61). And the catholicity of the church refers to the unity of the one people of God on earth (sections 73-75). Truth arises from dialogue, and we must accept that no one has the monopoly on truth – openness to each other lets us know the full nature of truth (159).

In sections 245-264 the DRC positions itself in the widening circle of ecumenical relations from its own family to the Roman Catholic Church and separatist groups. The DRC states that it will strive for membership of ecumenical bodies "where the basis, aims and practical living of these are compatible with its own confessional viewpoints" (264).

The question then arises: If confessions of the apostolic faith are particular to the Reformed tradition, and if the truth is not held by any one church, but in openness in dialogue, why did the DRC, which claims to stand in this confessional tradition, not accept the confession of Belhar in the period between 1982/86 and 1990 – or even to this day?

There are many reasons – some of them implicit in the analyses of statements above. In this specific context a part of the answer lies in the innocuous-sounding end of paragraph 264: by 1986 the DRC was under huge ecumenical pressure to denounce the theology of apartheid.[14] It was a relatively lonely church that felt itself under attack from others who could not see how complex the situation was and how honest the DRC was in its intentions to respond theologically. Deep down was the conviction that if others believe and practice those beliefs differently, the confession held by the DRC was the truth.

And yes, church politics was a reality. But for the first years after 1982, and for some even up to this day, the confession could not be heard because it was seen as an attack on the DRC from both the ecumenical world (Lutheran World Federation and the WARC) and its own daughter church, the DRMC. The reaction in the first phase after 1986 was not humble co-confession but defence, because the DRC was no longer in the broader catholic and apostolic church, where the specific truths of unity, reconciliation and justice resided (see Naudé 1997).

There have been numerous studies on the theology which enabled the DRC to justify apartheid as church and political policy.[15] Dirkie Smit makes the distinction between being Reformed in the formal and normative senses of the word.[16] A church may have the right church orders and may officially subscribe to the right confessions, and even call itself "Reformed" without in fact being Reformed if judged by the normative criteria of this tradition. In actual terms, the DRC's identity in the first half of the 20th century was predominantly shaped by neo-Calvinist, missiological Pietism (Kuyper, Warneck, Murray) – a theology that was in principle open to confession but not in actual practice. The DRMC had its identity shaped by the normative Reformed tradition of Calvin, Kuyper (reinterpreted), and specifically Barth[17] in the confessing church tradition of Barmen and Bonhoeffer, and was as a church therefore much better prepared for the act of confession. It was Beyers Naudé, a son of the DRC, who first called for a confessing church as early as 1965 (Naudé 1965). But we know his voice was not heard for decades in his home church, because he spoke "too early".

---

14 For a discussion of the DRC's ecumenical relations in this period, see the incisive analysis by De Villiers (1986).
15 See Hexham (1981), De Gruchy (1979), Kinghorn (1986), and for a condensed version Naudé (2005; 2010:23-48). For recent contributions on the work of Ben Marais and Beyers Naudé as critical voices from within the DRC, read Coetzee (2011), and for an analysis of B. Marais and F.J.M. Potgieter, read the study by Engdahl (2006).
16 For a short exposition of this difference, see Smit (2009:221); and for an outline of the normative frame of being Reformed, see Smit (2010).
17 For the enormous direct influence of Barth in the Belhar synod of 1982, read Naudé (2010:77-83); and for a general assessment of Barth's value for confessional theology, read McCormack (2003).

5. FIFTH STATEMENT

The DRC's General Synod's recommendation that Belhar becomes a part of its confessional basis (despite significant legal obstacles) probably represents both a societal and a theological shift, and it has the potential to invigorate the truly Reformed roots of the DRC and make the visible reunification of the family possible.

A very difficult question to answer is: What changed in the DRC that its General Synod recently (October 2011) decided with a significant majority to recommend to its parishes the adoption of Belhar as fourth confession? The answer to the question is probably too complex to answer right now. And we are perhaps too close to the events to fully understand what is going on.

One could somewhat cynically argue that the DRC is just a very late arrival in the new South Africa, and had to wait for its members to adapt to the realities of losing social, political and some economic power. This awareness of relative social status is then transferred to the ecclesial realm, and members are more comfortable about accepting Belhar. Perhaps younger people (who according to reports played a significant role at the General Synod of 2011) do not know and are no longer emotionally blinded by the origins of Belhar and the leading figures of that time. They can read Belhar for what it says and not by whom it was said.

On the level of theology, one can argue that the DRC is currently a truly pluralistic church with no dominant paradigm: there are Pentecostal, Baptist, Congregational, Pietistic and various shades of Reformed strands all making up the complex and ever shifting theological self-understanding of the DRC. The most positive interpretation of the decision by the synod is to infer that the DRC has indeed returned – via a fairly lengthy detour of 130 years – to its normative, confessional roots. This inference will be tested in the lengthy process of confessional adoption, and we shall only know the answer with more certainty afterwards.

But it must be said with hope and joy: the structural and visible reunification of the DRC Family on the basis of an already shared tradition, complemented by the Belhar confession, will auger in a new and exciting theological and prophetic phase in the history of the Reformed churches in South Africa, and hopefully further into Africa, as we cannot rest until the visible unity of the church is realised in practice.

BIBLIOGRAPHY

Alston, W. & Welker, M. (eds.) 2003. *Reformed theology. Identity and Ecumenicity.* Grand Rapids: Eerdmans.

Alston, W. & Welker, M. (eds.) 2007. *Reformed theology. Identity and ecumenicity II. Biblical interpretation in the Reformed tradition.* Grand Rapids: Eerdmans, 242-260.

Barth, K. 1956. *Church Dogmatics I/2: The revelation of God.* Edinburgh: T&T Clark.

Barth, K. 1961. *Church Dogmatics III/4: The doctrine of creation.* Edinburgh: T&T Clark.

Botha, J. & Naudé, P.J. 1998. *Op pad met Belhar.* Pretoria: Van Schaik Publishers.

Cloete, G.D. & Smit, D.J. (eds). 1984. *A moment of truth: The confession of the Dutch Reformed Mission Church, 1982.* Grand Rapids: Eerdmans.

Coetzee, M.H. 2011. *Die "kritiese stem" teen apartheidsteologie in die Ned Geref Kerk (1905-1974)*. Wellington: Bybel-Media.

De Villiers, E. 1986. "Kritiek uit die ekumene". In J. Kinghorn (red.), pp. 144-164.

De Gruchy, J. 1979. *The church struggle in South Africa*. Cape Town: David Philip.

Engdahl, H. 2006. *Theology in conflict – readings in Afrikaner theology*. Frankfurt am Main: Peter Lang.

Hexham, I. 1981. *The irony of apartheid: The struggle for national independence of Afrikaner Calvinism against British imperialism*. New York: Edwin Mellen.

Kinghorn, J. (red.) 1986. *Die NG Kerk en apartheid*. Johannesburg: Macmillan.

Kuhn, T. 1962. *The structure of scientific revolutions*. Chicago: University of Chicago Press.

Maimela, S & Konig, A. (eds.) 1998. *Initiation into theology. The rich variety of theology and hermeneutics*. Pretoria: Van Schaik.

Marx, K. & Engels, F. 1971 (1848). *The communist manifesto*. New York: International Publishers.

McCormack, B. 2003. "The end for reformed theology? The voice of Karl Barth in the doctrinal chaos of the present". In W. Alston & M. Welker (eds.), pp. 46-64.

Naudé, B. 1965. "Die tyd vir 'n 'belydende kerk' is daar". *Pro Veritate* Vol. 15, 4 Julie, pp. 3-4.

Naudé, B. 1995. *My land van hoop. Die lewe van Beyers Naude*. Kaapstad: Human & Rossouw.

Naudé, P.J. 1997. "Die Belharstryd in ekumeniese perspektief". *NGTT* xxxviii/3, pp. 226-243.

Naudé, P.J. 2005. "From pluralism to ideology: The roots of apartheid theology in Abraham Kuyper, Gustav Warneck and theological Pietism". *Scriptura* Vol. 88, pp. 161-173.

Naudé, P.J. 2007. "Reformed confessions as hermeneutical problem. The case study of the Belhar confession". In W. M. Alston and M. Welker (eds.), pp. 242-260.

Naudé, P.J. 2010. *Neither calendar nor clock. Perspectives on the Belhar confession*. Grand Rapids: Eerdmans.

Naudé, P. and Smit, D.J. 2000. "Reception – ecumenical crisis or opportunity for South African churches?". *Scriptura* Vol. 43, pp. 175-188.

Nederduits Gereformeerde Kerk. 1986. *Kerk en samelewing. 'n Getuienis van die Ned Geref Kerk*. Bloemfontein: Pro Christo.

Smit, D.J. 1984. "In a special way the God of the destitute, the poor, and the wronged". In D. Cloete & D.J. Smit (eds.), pp. 53-65.

Smit, D.J. 2009. *Essays on being Reformed, Collected essays 3*. Stellenbosch: Sun Media.

Smit, D.J. 2010. "Trends and directions in Reformed theology". *The Expository Times* Vol. 122, No. 7, pp. 1-14.

SACC. 1985. "A theological rationale and a call to prayer to the end of unjust rule". In C. Charles Villa-Vicencio (ed.), pp. 247-250.

Tracy, D. & Kung, H. 1986. *Paradigm change in theology*. New York: Crossroad Publishing Company.

Villa-Vicencio, C. (ed.) 1985. *Between Christ and Caeser. Classic and contemporary texts on church and state*. Cape Town: David Philip.

3.9 THE DUTCH REFORMED CHURCH'S ROLE IN THE CONTEXT OF TRANSITION IN SOUTH AFRICA[1]

1. INTRODUCTION

The task assigned to me by the conference organisers was to establish the "concerns, approaches and results" of mainstream academic research emanating from the Dutch Reformed Church in the late phase of apartheid. This is a complicated task subject to a number of limitations, which must be addressed in advance to put the interpretation below into context.

Limitation of the period of transition

The period of transition, i.e. "the late phase of apartheid", has been taken as 1980-1994. The latter date refers to the democratic elections of 27 April 1994, which practically and symbolically brought the long preceding period of struggle on various fronts – including theological and church struggles – to a point of culmination. The first date allows for a long enough period to reconstruct an overview of a dramatic period in South Africa's history and theologically one of intense debate. As will be highlighted during the rest of this conference, a number of very significant events occurred during this period which require careful analysis.[2]

How would one establish the "main streams of academic research" which formed the thrust of work done by DRC theologians during this period?

Limitation of the academic basis

I followed the route of scanning the three journals *Ned Geref Teologiese Tydskrif* (Stellenbosch), *Fax Theologica* (Bloemfontein) and *Skrif en Kerk* (Pretoria) over the period 1980-1994. In this regard 1980 is quite significant as it was the commencement year of both *Fax Theologica* (which became *Acta Theologica* in 1989) as well as *Skrif en Kerk*. These journals, in conjunction with some other major publications, establish a firm albeit restricted base to view "DRC theology" over the chosen period. It would obviously be a much greater task to take account of every publication by every DRC-aligned academic (including Unisa and other universities) in all journals (nationally and internationally) over all theological disciplines.

Apart from the limited choice from a wider field of academic contributions, *academia* in itself limits the view of a specific theologian's contribution. Many names mentioned (or omitted) below worked in commissions of the church and in regional

---

1 This paper was read at the International Conference on Societies in Transition that was sponsored by Hamburg University and delivered at the University of Stellenbosch (March 2001). The essay was first published in Weisse and Anthonissen (2004).
2 One immediately thinks of the *status confessionis* of 1982; the Kairos-document in 1985; the Belhar confession in 1986; the DRC's revised policy document *Church and Society* in 1986; the split in the DRC with a loss of approximately 40 000 members to the APK in 1988; the Rustenburg conference in 1988; the DRC's first official reaction to Belhar at the General Synod of 1990 and many more.

and national synodical structures. Others published more popular articles in church and public media. Others may have been active as preachers with few formal publications listed to their credit. The impact of some of these contributions might even have been greater than the academic work underlying them. But in line with the assignment, the focus remains on the limited field of formal academic publications.

Limitation of interpretation

Like all overviews with their undeniable selection of what is significant and what not, what constitutes "contributions to transformation" and what is meant by this phrase, the outline below is linked to my own presuppositions and those implicit in the topic of the conference.

The most important of these is that theology as an academic discipline – like all other scholarly forms of inquiry – is a communicative practice that not only reflects, but also affects, interests, values and visions, so that one can speak about the "transformative power" of theoretical constructs, the public ethos of science and – more bluntly – the political context of scholarship (see Schussler-Fiorenza 1988:4ff).

I understand theory to be a form of social practice with the implication that academic research, including theology, is subject to at least three "concerns", i.e. contextual, ideological and ethical. All generation of knowledge reflects a contextual concern – even in the "denial" of its own contextuality. All generation of knowledge reflects/affects power relations linked to the researchers' social location. All generation of knowledge reflects implicitly or explicitly an ethical concern over the impact (or not) of such knowledge on the context (restricted or encompassing) in which it is practised (see point 6 below).

In this sense it becomes indeed possible to reflect on DRC theology and its contribution in shaping South Africa in its transition from an apartheid state to a democracy. A number of themes emerged from the period 1980-1994, some of which are listed and discussed below.

2. MAIN THEOLOGICAL THEMES

2.1. The struggle for the biblical/Reformed identity of the church

An amazing cluster of publications[3] around 1980 put the theme of the church high on the agenda in the DRC and in South Africa in general: J.D. Vorster: *Veelvormigheid en eenheid* (1978); Johan Heyns: *Die Kerk* (1977) and *Dogmatiek* (1978:352-374); P.F. Theron: *Die ekklesia as kosmies-eskatologiese teken*, completed as doctoral study under Heyns's supervision (1978); Piet Meiring and H.I. Lederle: *Die eenheid van die kerk* (1979); Piet Meiring: *Die kerk in die nuwe Afrika* (1979); W.D. Jonker and P.F. Theron:

---

3   For a fuller list and overview see Smit (1981). These publications appeared in the midst of important church conferences such as the March 1979 meeting of 16 churches in the first full consultation under the WARC banner since Cottelsoe in 1960 (see Boesak 1979), as well as the inter-denominational SACLA conference of over 6 000 Christian leaders and lay people in Pretoria in 1979.

Vreemde gemeenskap (1979); Allan Boesak: *Die vinger van God* (1979); Douglas Bax: *A different gospel* (1979) and John de Gruchy: *The church struggle in South Africa* (1979).

The implicit shared assumption of publications and church meetings from this era was that changes in the churches' view of themselves and their relations with one another would impact directly on the social structure of the broader South African society. De Gruchy puts it unambiguously with regard to the DRC: "Given this impressive position within society, and the access it brings to the corridors of power at the national and local level, *it can be argued that the DRC holds one of the keys to the future of South Africa*" (1979:70, my emphasis).

And almost a decade later, in his magnificent speech on obstacles to Christian witness at the Rustenburg Convention, Willie Jonker states as part of his motivation: "Our country will benefit if the Church as a whole could be united in its witness about socio-political matters" (Jonker 1991:88). Theologians of the late seventies and eighties knew this and understood the significance of their theological decisions – this explains the emotional and intellectual intensity of the debates.

The theological issue at stake was the character or identity of the church and specifically the relation between unity and pluriformity in the aftermath of the 1974 DRC decisions in *Ras, Volk en Nasie* (Ned Geref Kerk 1975). We need not repeat the background to this struggle as this has been ably done by others – specifically by Johann Kinghorn et al in *Die NG Kerk en Apartheid* (Kinghorn 1986). Kinghorn has argued convincingly that the romantic *volksidee* carried by Warneck's missiology and a specific interpretation of Kuyper's neo-Calvinism formed the core of mainstream thinking in the DRC.

In simplified terms: ecclesiology would either be constructed from creation or from recreation.[4] In this sense the interesting difference between Heyns, on the one hand, and both Theron and Jonker, on the other, is significant. Heyns was fundamentally influenced by the Calvinist philosophy of H. Stoker, whose conception of creation (*skeppingsidee*) provided the totalising framework to develop a theology of the kingdom where proton and eschaton are linearly linked in a kind of overall scheme (see Jonker 1994:16-19 and the dissertation by Theron 1984). In his view of the church Heyns therefore finds it very difficult to accept the ecclesial implications of the discontinuity of sin and new creation in Christ. Despite his worthy rejections of some arguments for the pluriformity (read: separateness) of the church, Heyns retains a cultural-ethnic motive linked to what he calls the psychic orientation (*psigiese gesteldheid*) of each *volk*. This motif is the basis for spiritual differences, he contends, which makes true communion very difficult if not impossible, and therefore constitutes a "legitimate pluriformity" of the church (1977:127 and repeated in 1978:379).

Although Heyns – with his strong ties to the Afrikaner establishment – played a significant role in the DRC's later decisions on church unity (as moderator of the general synod from 1986 to 1990), the theological impulse was carried by Jonker and his later colleague Flip Theron. Jonker's consistent ecclesial contribution from his dissertation in 1955 onward is evident from his many writings on the subject and has been outlined as the key feature of his theology (see especially Van Wyk 1989).

---

4   I understand the importance of both discontinuity and continuity between creation and recreation, but the focus here is on the difference in emphasis between Heyns and others.

In his own words: "My struggle has especially been against the DRC as *volkskerk*, which according to me threatened the identity of the church as the church of Christ. I thought that the best way to change this was simply by doing good Reformed theology" (Jonker 1991:121, my translation). *The church cannot be just another "samelewingsverband" like volk and state: its uniqueness lies in Christ* (Jonker 1977:4-13) and as the body of Christ it must be seen to be one church (Jonker 1986). "The church as *kaine ktisis* is through and through an eschatological qualification", writes Theron (1978:73). As such the church is a sign of the eschaton where incarnation and not nation, the Holy Spirit and not the spirit of culture, determine the new people of God (Theron 1988:170).

The important point is that these somewhat theoretical theological notions carried in them a transformative vision of society. As shown above, this was exactly the assumption. It would be very difficult to draw direct lines here, but one could conclude that the theological basis of apartheid theology – and therefore its moral legitimacy – was eroded from this view of the church. The visible unity stood in contrast to a spiritual or higher unity; the normativity in Christ stood in contrast to the norm of pluriformity-as- separateness; the new people of God stood in contrast to the volk as biologically determined collectivity.[5]

This was obviously not a unique theological position. Its significance, however, lies in the fact that a new generation of theologians and ministers from the DRC accepted this view, as is evident from the General Synod's decisions on an open church and church unity in 1986 and 1990. Those in power – and ordinary Christians – understood the societal impact and were therefore perhaps better equipped for the transformation which took on special significance as from 2 February 1990.

That the transformation in South Africa also took place despite the church (including the DRC) must obviously be said. The DRC family is still struggling (stumbling) to become one. The verdict of the Truth and Reconciliation Commission (1998) is clear: despite their principles, faith communities in South Africa generally mirror the image of a divided society in their very own constitution.

2.2. The struggle for the relevance of the church

A second question about the church lurked beneath the surface and came to the fore only in the mid-eighties. This relates not so much to the church's identity as to its relevance. Whereas the first question arose from a pre-critical consciousness, the second arose from a critical consciousness as the implications of the Enlightenment started to become evident in the practical situation of the DRC.

In a paper on South Africa's theological links with Europe Willie Jonker marks the Enlightenment of the 18th century in Europe as the hour of birth of the modern European person. This had traumatic consequences for church and theology (1988:148-149). The destruction of "Christian Europe" as *corpus Christianum* and the radical questioning of all forms of tradition led to a cultural situation where the church and faith became increasingly irrelevant. Because of the basic European

---

5 I follow Kinghorn's three core elements of an apartheid theology (1986:139-143). The specific role of DRC theologians in requesting the government to withdraw the Immorality Act in 1982 is a sign that theological views had real social consequences.

orientation of DRC theology, the questions of the *Aufklärung* were unavoidable in South Africa.

It is interesting to note that Dirkie Smit in a later article about theological education sums modernity up in the notions of rationalism (flight from authority), historicism (flight from tradition) and individualism (flight from community). Specifically the last issue is important, as people are alienated from the church by a radical emphasis on individual freedom, including the freedom of choice and association, "resulting in extreme pluralism and the functional differentiation of important subsystems of society" (Smit 1999: 5). This weakens people's sense of belonging – including their "belonging" to the church of a specific tradition.

The phrase used by DRC theologians to describe this intricate phenomenon was "secularisation" and its (negative) corollary "secularism". Three articles by Snyman, Potgieter and Van der Watt respectively, illustrate this

S.D. Snyman writes about the role of the DRC family in the future of South Africa and starts his article as follows: "In the formulation of the topic for this contribution there are at least two points of departure. The first is that the DRC family does indeed have a role to play in the future of South Africa. This is a point of departure which is probably still in force in 1987, but which need not be in force indefinitely". He then gives two reasons why he doubts this: "The inner conflict that weakens the family of the DRC, and the fact that church's relevance will be questioned critically in a community which is becoming increasingly secularised" (Snyman 1987:53, my translation). P.C. Potgieter echoes this a year later in the same journal. References are made to the post-Christian era in Europe and the impression that, for many people, religiosity functions without the church community. This pattern is emerging in South Africa and the church is becoming more and more irrelevant. J.G. van der Watt refers to the same issue of secularisation in his analysis of corresponding developments in Germany and South Africa, and is in the light of this compelled to make certain suggestions "regarding *the relevance* of the Dutch Reformed Church in such a changing society" (1992:200, my translation).

The question of relevance (not restricted to the DRC) is the paradoxical outcome of the churches' own struggle for a political dispensation in which the ideas of the Enlightenment would later receive constitutional and legal protection. This raises the difficult theological question of how to be church in a new situation without giving up the encompassing message of the gospel.

An attempt to address the issue of relevance "toward the inside" of the DRC saw the rise of a new theological discipline, namely congregational studies (*gemeentebou*) with its own practical theological paradigm.

An attempt to address the issue of relevance "toward the outside" of the DRC saw the rise of social ethics as more autonomous theological discipline with its own themes and topical agenda.

Let us deal with each of these in turn.

2.2.1. Congregational Studies (Gemeentebou)

"In the DRC gemeentebou (Gemeindeaufbau) has become a household word ... One cannot speak about the contemporary theology of the DRC without reference to

gemeentebouteologie" (Britz and Erasmus 1994:374, my emphasis). Our topic does not allow full analysis here, but one could say that *gemeentebou* in both its phases of individual "equipment" (1970-1977) and full-blown congregational studies (since 1978[6]) became the depository for the long evangelical tradition in the DRC. This may be argued both historically and theologically.

Historically the focus on the role of individual members grew from the American evangelism-in-depth idea, and the focus on small group ministry from Campus Crusade for Christ, with McGavern's Church Growth movement a strong influence on a new "strategic" orientation to mainline churches. Theologically *gemeentebou* focused sharply on the spiritual renewal and building up of the individual congregant, who then reaches out to others in a "person-to-person action" in the context of a neo-evangelical functional ecclesiology (see Breytenbach and Pieterse 1992). As more serious academic work was completed, the initial personalistic views were slowly transformed and superseded by a broader theological outlook and the establishment of an autonomous discipline (Nel 1986; 1987). It is especially Daniel Louw (1992) and Coenie Burger (1991) who attempted to link biblical and systematic considerations to practical theological considerations, thus ensuring that this discipline does not merely become a pragmatic action-theoretical discourse which could be construed as alien to a Reformed way of doing theology.

It is even now too early to judge the impact of *gemeentebou* on the DRC in a time of transition. What is clear, however, is that its success on congregational level and ascendance in theological faculties stem from the fact that it grew from a desire to respond to cultural and political shifts – not unrelated to the Enlightenment legacy – which directly affected the DRC.[7] Suffice it to say that it surely engendered wide and enthusiastic support for the gospel in its individual and faith community dimensions. The issue from where the new missionary awakening in the DRC originates will be addressed later in this conference. I believe it might be an extension of the evangelical tradition, which culminated in faith communities accepting responsibility for sending missionaries to "unreached peoples".

On the whole, *gemeentebou* has succeeded to stem – at least temporarily – the impact of certain Enlightenment trends and provided a sense of belonging in a time of radical societal change.

It is not easy to judge whether its effect was much wider than the members and congregations of the DRC itself. A cynical view could reconstruct *gemeentebou* as a neo-evangelical act of self-preservation – even as an inward flight to a last safe haven for Afrikaners, who had to face a radical loss of power in almost every other social sphere. Before a final verdict can be given, such a view should at least keep the second response to the question of relevance in mind.

The issue of relevance[8] "toward the outside" of the DRC can be linked to the rise of (social) ethics as a more autonomous discipline in theology.

---

6   I am discerning a third phase where the focus is on synodical structures and their functioning – analysed and transformed in terms of the ground rules of management practices by church consultants.
7   See Burger (1991:14) and the introduction to Hendricks (1992).
8   It remains a pity that Jonker's study on the relevance of the church which he completed for the HSRC in 1987 was never published – perhaps as part of the Du Rand-Jonker

2.2.2. Social ethics as a distinct "discipline"

In his article on the DRC's orientation toward Europe, Jonker makes the important observation that the DRC never fully understood the combined effect of the Second World War and the second Enlightenment as expressed in the critical theories of philosophers such as Horkheimer, Adorno, Habermas and Marcuse. The abhorrence of nationalism and racism, with a radical focus on the social-ethical implications of the Christian faith, exactly at a time when apartheid theology was in the making, and a reliance on earlier, pre-critical European theology at a time when ideology critique became an indispensable part of any theoretical construct, delayed the DRC's full confrontation with new European theological trends and led to its almost total ecumenical isolation. "From the view of the outside world as a whole, the theology of the Afrikaans churches is too uncritical, too naive with regard to the ideological presuppositions of our thoughts, too much orientated to period in the *Geistesgeshichte* that has passed, and shows too little willingness to accept the implications of the Enlightenment" (Jonker 1988:154, my translation).

With regard to ethically orientated work, the two giants of DRC theology in the 1970s and 1980s, Heyns and Jonker, laid the foundation. Heyns published his reflections on the Decalogue in 1970 already, followed by his more elaborate theology of obedience (1972), philosophical reflections on the essence of the ethical (1979), and popularised *Etiek van liefde* (1981). Then followed his theological ethics in three parts published in 1982, 1986 and 1989 (social ethics), which in sheer volume and scope are unsurpassed to this day.

Jonker wrote about the importance of social ethics as early as 1973 in the *Festschrift* for inter alia BB Keet (Jonker 1973a). He also published an article on Calvin's social ethics in the same year (Jonker 1973b), but despite contributions on issues such as human rights and medical ethics, he never saw himself as making a specific ethical contribution in the technical sense of the word.

The doctoral promotion in ethics on the distinctiveness of Christian morality under Kuitert in the Netherlands (1978) saw Etienne de Villiers return to South Africa to make a sustained contribution during the period under discussion. His co-operation with Danie du Toit, who became known for his original work in medical ethics and human rights (Du Toit 1984), and with Johann Kinghorn, Bernard Lategan and others on the Mixed Marriages/Immorality Acts and values for inclusive democracy (see Kinghorn 1990), and since 1994 with Dirkie Smit on pluralism in ethics, ensured theologically that the DRC retained a public face and therefore at least some social relevance in a changing and changed South African context.

What is particularly significant about De Villiers's work is that he combined his ethical reflection with a definitive focus on the DRC's ecumenical position (De Villiers 1986, 1989). He consequently placed ethics on the "edges" of the church and by implication in the midst of its ecclesial and social relevance.

That DRC ethicists were indeed sensitive to their changing context can easily be established by a chronological ordering of topical issues: conscientious objection and freedom of conscience in the militarised South Africa of the early eighties (De

---

dogmatic series? (Editor's note: This work was published by *Bybel-Media* in 2008 as *Die relevansie van die kerk*).

Villiers 1983); mixed marriages (De Villiers and Kinghorn 1984); issues in medical ethics such as abortion and genetic engineering (1982-1985 and after); human rights (Du Toit 1984); disinvestment (De Villiers 1985); the theology of apartheid and democracy (Kinghorn 1986); the question of peace in South Africa (De Villiers 1988); the church's pastoral responsibility in the growing AIDS crisis (Louw 1988); civil disobedience (Taute and Du Toit 1990); the ethics of distributive economic justice (1991-1993) and a growing understanding of the radical pluralistic nature of moral language as the new South Africa is seen to undergo a moral collapse (1994 and further, see De Villiers and Smit 1996).

One could perhaps draw the conclusion that (social) ethics at least attempted to steer the naive, uncritical theology of the DRC towards a more critical consciousness and simultaneously towards a church with a public face despite its ecumenical isolation. One could therefore also mark ethicists' contribution to the transition as theologically and socially significant as – at least academically – certain shifts of opinion on topical issues were fostered.

There are two further "critical" lines within DRC theology which are less obvious but theologically of great significance. The first is the reception of Karl Barth and the second – of much wider scope – is the major developments in hermeneutics and biblical scholarship.

3. THE RECEPTION OF KARL BARTH

There is no room to fully develop the intriguing and complex reception of (the equally complex) Karl Barth within DRC theology. One could refer to the extended encounters with Barth[9] in the dogmatic series written by Du Rand and Jonker, in Johan Heyns' dogmatics, and in Adrio Konig's attempts (inter alia) to develop a Reformed view of the covenant. For the sake of this paper, the fundamental issue in Barth's relation to DRC theology is not so much differences on views of revelation, Scripture, election and universalism, but on the critical element introduced against all forms of natural theology in its religionistic, anthropocentric and humanistic formation.

Jaap du Rand's well known view in this regard is worth repeating. He argues that Afrikaner civil religion was formed and sustained by both Scottish evangelicalism and Kuyperian neo-Calvinism. Kuyper's cosmology and emphasis on the orders of creation – though not as crude as German *Ordnungstheologie* – "combined with orthodox Reformed Christology in such a way that any effort to subject theology to a Christological criticism was defused from the start. As a result the dominant natural theology was never recognised for what it was. One of the great tragedies in the development of Afrikaner Reformed theology in the three decisive decades of its evolvement (1930-1960) was that Karl Barth's criticism of religion and natural theology was never really heard or given the opportunity to be heard in those

---

9 Despite their academic merit, I would not judge the philosophical-theological encounters with Barth by e.g. Van Huyssteen (1986:23-36) and Van Niekerk (1984) and Potgieter's discussion of personal faith in the theology of Barth (1987) as being of specific transformational significance as understood in this paper.

Kuyperian circles that needed it most" (Du Rand 1985:40, my emphasis; Du Rand 1988:121-123).[10]

Because of the elements of natural theology and nationalism in his theology, Heyns could not really set forth and appreciate the critical element in Barth's theology.[11] Contrary to some other churches (see Villa-Vicencio 1988), there was also not a DRC reception of the "socialist" and "political" Barth introduced by Marquardt and Gollwitzer (see few comments in Verster 1991). The "public" and "social" value of Barth for the DRC lies in his ability to (on the one hand) dismantle the natural theological elements in Neo-Calvinism which provided the theological basis for apartheid and (on the other hand) expose the anthropocentric tendencies of pietism in its Gestalt as inner-focused religion.[12]

Jonker – in his Barth centenary lecture – sums it up as follows: "The complacency of the church, the self-satisfaction of some forms of Neo-Calvinist theology with which we were acquainted, the shallow moralism of Christianity as a whole, the self-deception of pietistic, Arminian and Methodist preoccupation with personal holiness and perfection with which we were perpetually confronted within our circles – these were the things to which Barth opened our eyes" (Jonker 1988:30-31, my translation).[13]

In an indirect way, one could conclude, Barth's theology looms over the erosion of apartheid's theological basis (negative) and provided the thrust for a confessing church (positive) exemplified in the status confessionis (1982) and Belhar confession (1986). As far as the latter was concerned, mainstream DRC thinking was (and is) not ready. The "confessing" Barth has since then been carried with great impact by the DRMC/URCSA, destroying the last shreds of theological respectability of the apartheid system and enriching the Reformed tradition with a dynamic confession in the South African context with definite universal significance.

4. THE CONTRIBUTION OF BIBLICAL SCHOLARSHIP

Any South African theologian will feel justifiably proud about the international quality of biblical scholarship from this country. This is also true of the DRC, whose Old and New Testament scholars played a magnificent role in establishing and maintaining several academic associations and journals of international repute. No justice can be done to the varied contributions over such a wide field in the

---

10 See Bennie Keet's overview of theology at the centenary of the Stellenbosch seminary in 1955, where he specifically pleads for greater attention to Karl Barth than was seen as acceptable at that stage.
11 See Heyns (1977:126-127; 1978:379; 1991:47-49) and Jonker's comments in Jonker (1994; 1998:133-134).
12 One should not bundle pietism or evangelicalism together as purely inner-focused Christianity. A case could be made that someone like Beyers Naudé came from an evangelical background and translated the passion for mission into a social vision for South Africa (see Du Rand 1985:48).
13 The value of Jonker's contribution lies in his argument – following D. Schellong, *Karl Barth und die Neuzeit* (1973) – for an interpretation of Barth as *modern* theologian who responded to the Enlightenment challenge in a unique manner.

space of this paper. Suffice it to say: the heart of the battle for ecclesial and social transformation in the period 1980-1994 lay in the interpretation of the Bible.

The relevance of the Bible for socio-political matters was a *sine qua non* of both the defence (e.g. E.P. Groenewald, J.D. du Toit, W.J. Snyman) and rejection (e.g. B. Marias, B.B. Keet, A. Geyser) of apartheid in the years between 1947 and 1960. This assumption of the link between "the Bible" and "the current situation" surfaced again in the late 1980s with the publication of J.A. Loubser's *The apartheid Bible* (1987) and two volumes edited by C. Breytenbach: *Eenheid en konflik* (1987) and *Church in context* (1988), as well as the establishment at Stellenbosch of a Centre for Contextual Hermeneutics (by 1987).

Because of its strong international orientation and sensitivity to developments in the North, South African biblical scholarship, however, suffered the same fate so well expounded by Elizabeth Schussler-Fiorenza in her 1987 SBL presidential address (published 1988) and subsequently echoed by Francis Schussler-Fiorenza in an article on Scriptural authority in *Interpretation* (1990).

In its struggle to free itself from dogmatic and ecclesiastical control, biblical scholarship increasingly adopted the nineteenth-century positivist view of history. "For the sake of exactitude the historical method excludes seeking the meaning of the text for our contemporary situation or for our faith. As critical, this method seeks to investigate in a historicist fashion what the text meant in its original context by excluding consideration of any ecclesial or confessional tradition" (F. Schussler-Fiorenza 1990:356). Biblical scholarship also became increasingly specialised to the point of sharing in the pathology of modernity (Habermas), where a technocratic or means-end rationality associated with "objectivity" and "value neutrality" led to a total separation of the expert and the everyday reader of the Bible.

In summary: by the late 1980s, and reflecting over a period of 40 years, the president of the SBL and others find biblical scholarship wanting in a number of respects: an assumed value neutrality oblivious to the political context of interpretation; an inability to translate meaning beyond the historical investigation of the text; little or no consideration of ecclesial or confessional traditions; and the creation of a closed world of expert scholarly inquiry which denies the interests and values underlying their communicative practice (E. Schussler-Fiorenza 1988:4).

She then calls for an ethics of interpretation which encompasses both the historical reading and an accountability for the ethical consequences of the text's meaning in contemporary socio-political settings.

South African biblical scholars were confronted with this ethical imperative and a call for a responsible hermeneutics from outside their professional ranks. It was systematician and ethicist Dirkie Smit who challenged the New Testament scholars (see Smit 1988, 1990) and heavily criticised their attempt to write an ethics of New Testament books in *Geloof en Opdrag* (1992:303-325). Two years later he poses the same challenge to Old Testament colleagues (Smit 1994): he closes his address with a series of rhetorical-critical questions which ends with: "In short, what are those who are seen as Old Testament scholars doing with their enormous 'power to read'. Now *that* is an ethical question" (Smit 1994:292, his emphasis).

In a rough overview such as this generalisations are unavoidable, and I probably owe an apology to the exceptions to what is described here. But this "scientist ethos" – where the true interlocutors are other biblical scholars (Smit 1992:322), where a kind of in-house discourse is created (Botha 1993) and the medieval notion of a tropological sense of the Bible is lost – explains the relative silence of expert biblical scholars on the great issues facing South African society in the crucial period between 1970 and 1985. It was mostly left to others "to let the Bible speak" on issues ranging from the ordination of women, conscientious objection and inclusive democratic values to the enormous disaster created by HIV/AIDS.

The rhetoric of scientific correctness in pursuing historicist and structuralist modes of reading[14] created a twofold paradox.

First. Despite their immensely "critical" approaches, biblical scholars were ideologically naive/uncritical and (like most other disciplines) blind to both the underlying and consequential ethical implications of their communicative strategies. The admission (confession?) by J. Botha (1992:179) tells its own story: "During the seventies and eighties a scientist ethos of scholarship dominated in the guild of South African New Testament scholars. Many of us tended to 'hide behind' our literary and structural analyses, *hiding from the pressing social realities of our country* – even if it was not a conscious choice to do so and even if it was not consciously perceived as such by members of the guild" (my emphasis).

Second. Despite their *de jure* appointment by the church and outspoken desire to do theology in and for the church,[15] biblical scholars found it very difficult to engage in the 'wirkungsgeschichtliche' reality of the church and its confessions – except perhaps for the issue of church unity.[16]

Three examples illustrate this:

- It was mostly left to systematicians[17] to try and sort out the radical questioning of Scriptural authority after the Dutch report *God met ons* was accepted by the Synod of Delft in 1979. Unless I have missed other contributions, W.S. Prinsloo's defence of the Old Testament authority[18] (1985) and an article each by New

---

14   I am aware of the shift toward reception-type readings of the Bible and specifically Bernard Lategan's contributions in this regard (Lategan and Vorster 1985; Lategan 1987). They do promote a much more acute awareness of the world in front of the text – specifically the role of the reader/receptor – in constituting meaning. See also Schussler-Fiorenza's positive development of a reception hermeneutic (1990:365ff) because "(i)ts challenge to positivist historical reading of the text requires that diverse receptions of the text, *including present popular understanding of the text as concretisation of its meaning*, be included in the problem of the interpretation of the meaning of the text" (my emphasis).
15   See the foreword to the first issue of *Skrif en Kerk* (1980) to motivate the title of the new journal!
16   See Schussler-Fiorenza's reference above to the exclusion of ecclesial of confessional traditions.
17   I refer inter alia to J.W.V. van Huyssteen and B.J. du Toit's controversial *Geloof en Skrifgesag* (1982).
18   It is interesting to note how Prinsloo approaches the problem: "As biblical scholar it is almost impossible for me to speak theoretically about the authority of the Old Testament. I leave it to my colleagues in Dogmatics to speak about the theoretical foundation and dogmatic aspects. When I speak about the authority of the OT, I cannot do so otherwise than in alignment with a concrete text" (1985:410-411) – in this case Joel 2. One cannot but

Testament scholars H.J.B. Combrink and A.B. du Toit in 1990 on the crisis and future of Scriptural authority are the only substantial attempts from biblical scholars to assist us in understanding the meaning of *sola Scriptura* to prevent a pre-critical fundamentalist confessionalism in the midst of a bewildering barrage of reading strategies.[19]

- The professionalisation and radical differentiation of biblical scholarship made it very difficult to read the First and Second Testaments *as testaments* and the Scriptures as *one Scripture*, i.e. as canon of the Christian church (and therefore in itself a valid reception to be reckoned with in an intertextual reading of the empirical text as communication event). Despite being Reformed scholars, expert biblical exegetes would find the notion of *theology* as *sacra pagina* in practice very difficult to uphold. "Jesus loves me, this I know, for the Bible tells me so", will probably elicit the response: "Who is (the historical) Jesus? Whose Bible are you referring to? To which meaning of love do you refer? And – most importantly: How do you know?" This is not to ridicule academic discourse, but to lament the almost narcissistic problematisation of Scripture in disregard of the public of the church (Tracy) and the *de facto* significant authority however critical or uncritical – ordinary church members accord the Bible.

- Whereas the first example refers to the "principle" of authority and the second to the canon itself, one can (following Schussler-Fiorenza) also ask the question about the confessional tradition. In their collective struggle not to be seen as unscientific confessionalists (my interpretation of Schussler-Fiorenza 1988:10-11), one would not expect biblical scholars to naturally do academic work on the confessional tradition of the church – not even in a conservative Reformed church. But our overview period is different. Confronted by a confessional event – unique in the DRC's own history since the Canons of Dordt in 1618-19 – the question arises: Where were the exegetical studies *from the DRC* on the role of credos in both Israel and the New Testament church? Or on the Belhar confession's use of Scripture in the decisive kairos period of eight years between the *status confessionis* of 1982 and the first DRC synodical response in 1990? Or where are the reception-theoretical analyses of Belhar's non-reception *as confession* after 1982?

Nevertheless, the debate of the early 1990s was not in vain and is still continuing. I also do not think for a moment that other theological disciplines can exempt themselves from the criticism above. Biblical scholarship itself has no doubt been affected and a much greater contextual responsibility is emerging.[20] In the earlier part of the period under discussion, however, DRC-aligned biblical scholars mostly

---

gain the impression that a flight into the safe world of the text – however critically read – is actually a naive (read: uncritical) attempt to avoid discussing the difficult theoretical presuppositions underlying the credo-like statement directly preceding Prinsloo's comment: "It is my basic presupposition that the Old testament is the authoritative Word of God".

19 Ferdinand Deist's 3-volume unpublished HRSC report *Wetenskapsteorie en Vakmetodologie in Bybelwetenskaplike Navorsing* (1994) does not deal directly with the question of authority, but remains extremely helpful in "plotting" hermeneutical developments – also in the DRC – over the last century.

20 See Botha 1992 note 5 and e.g. the *NGTT* issues since 1994.

avoided the uncomfortable questions of both the "ethics of interpretation" and the development of a "biblical ethic" or "public ethos" which takes the canon as canon seriously in an attempt to overcome the pathological impoverishment of their (and our) communicative action (Habermas).

What were they – and all of us from the DRC – doing with our enormous 'power to read' the most powerful Book in South Africa? (Now *that* is an ethical question!)

5. REFLECTION ON THE DIACONAL TASK OF THE CHURCH

Let us turn our attention briefly to academic reflection on the *diakonia* task of the church in the world. In this limited overview a comparison is drawn between M.M. Nieuwoudt's article in 1982 and the large volume on the DRC and its diaconal ministry by A.J. Smuts, J.J. de Klerk, P.B. van der Watt and M. Nieuwoudt in 1990. Despite the admirable theological reflection on a base theory for the diacony and its integration with mission in an encompassing sense, the move from "mercy" to "justice", from "diaconal relief" to "political diacony" has been an uncomfortable one.

Nieuwoudt, a respected figure in the DRC's diacony over many years, specifically refers to the diaconal aspect of "social justice" (1982:249), which means *inter alia* to stand in for the oppressed and those who suffer injustices. He then notes that many criticise the DRC not only for its silence on political injustices, but even complicity in establishing a system of social injustice. In defence of the DRC he "categorically rejects" such allegations: "We want to state it categorically that the DRC also on this level only applied the norm of Scripture within the specific political dispensation and always negotiated the best Christian relief for each with his God-given identity … specifically for minority groups". He admits that there might have been errors of judgement, but that the DRC gave of her best talent according to the light that she saw and to her conscience before God, and not with a view to impress people (1982:249, my translation).

Nieuwoudt clearly understands that not everything is *kosher*, but was at that stage not able to penetrate the very ideological basis of the comprehensive relief work of the DRC in its own ranks and in co-operation with the "daughter churches". The close relation between church and state had great financial benefits for the DRC's diacony (see figures provided in Nieuwoudt 1982:248) and it was therefore very difficult to question "the specific political dispensation" or to give up the privileged position of negotiating on behalf of itself and others – *nogal* called "minority groups", each with a "God-given identity"! Rhetorically Nieuwoudt covers his uneasiness with references to Scripture, conscience and possible errors of judgement.

That this was not only a DRC problem emerges from Paul Schrotenboer's article in the same *NGTT*, "The RES and world relief" (Schrotenboer 1982: 292): "We have all, with few exceptions, stopped short of involving ourselves in *political* structural changes in those areas where poverty and hunger are endemic. … we (must) squarely face the issue whether, and if so, how and to what extent, we should become active in effecting *political* changes both in our own nations and in other lands so that there may be greater sharing of the benefits of the earth".

Eight years later – in his review of the volume by Smuts et al. – Daniel Louw (1993) laments the fact that the church-state relations in the specific South African context is not addressed adequately (see Smuts et al. 1990:65ff) and that the view of black people on the DRC's work over the last fifty years is omitted. Louw refers to the absence in the volume of constructive critical thinking on the complexities of human relations in a pluralistic society and notes that there is no attempt to address the issue of diacony with regards to violence and conflict in South Africa (103). The reason for this is stated by the authors themselves toward the very end of their work: the DRC fears political diacony as it does death! (362).

The issue of diacony and social justice has therefore been noted, but the DRC was up to the early 1990s not able to penetrate the very socio-political power base of its own thinking and action. Reasons are plentiful: the identity formation of the DRC diacony through its extensive involvement with the "poor white" problem in the thirties and forties (First Carnegie Report), which created a primary inward-looking focus over many years; an absolute disdain for the Reformed Churches in the Netherland's Programme to Combat Racism in the seventies; the growing ecumenical isolation of the DRC specifically because of its theology of apartheid; the fact that it remained a middle-class church where poverty remained with "others" to whom we gave "from afar" via commissions; the social location of upper-class theological faculties weakly positioned to [verb missing?] a theology of the poor (see below); the uncritical nature of its theology in general – showing specific difficulty to integrate insights from critical theory and the sociology of knowledge.

It was toward the end of the apartheid era – and in reaction to the Second Carnegie Report[21] – that the issue of poverty and diacony was put in a different perspective. During a conference by SEVTO (University of Pretoria) in May 1993, Piet Meiring (*Poverty – The road ahead. A theological perspective*) unequivocally links poverty to an unjust society. He pleads for a community-based strategy (over against structural and institutional approaches) which requires that the church first listens to those in need before reacting in its own wisdom.[22]

Notwithstanding the criticism above, much was done at great personal and collective cost, and many people in and outside the DRC benefited from its multifaceted relief work. But it is clear that with regards to diacony –potentially one of the most powerful changing forces at the church's disposal – the DRC primarily mirrored the society in which it lived and missed the opportunity to make a socially transformative contribution in the decade preceding 1994.

Time and space are running out. The project has become bigger than I expected. I have not yet said anything about missiology[23] or other dimensions of practical

---

21 The findings were popularised in *Uprooting Poverty. The South African challenge*, a book with a fundamental impact on my own views of poverty and the "real people" behind statistics.
22 The work of KAN and NOVA are creative examples of such community-based diacony. See Vosloo (1994) for an overview of the conference in Pretoria.
23 See the contribution from Prof. Kritzinger later at this conference. Suffice it to refer to the notorious exclusion of David Bosch from the Stellenbosch faculty, and the great impact of Dionne Crafford and Piet Meiring to make the DRC see the African realities in which we live. See discussion in closing paragraphs.

theology such as pastoral theology[24] or homiletics.[25] Neither do we have the time to talk about church historical work[26] or the crucial decisions implicit in rewriting the orders of the church.[27]

Allow me, nevertheless, to devote our last few paragraphs to the general orientation of DRC theology in the overview period.

6. THE GENERAL ORIENTATION OF DRC THEOLOGY.

There can be no doubt: in the period under discussion DRC theology was fundamentally orientated toward Europe (and to a lesser extent the USA). Jonker's statement in response to my criticism (see Naudé 1991:117) that he missed opportunities to translate his theological insights for an African continent is worth quoting at length:

> We all have our limitations and no theologian can jump across his own shadow. My own theological position was to a great extent determined by my formation and situation. ... This means that I was from the outset oriented towards European theology. *To tell the truth, until recently many of us did not even notice that it was European theology. For us it was simply 'theology'*... The realisation that the theology from Europe has a contextual character itself only recently dawned upon us. The task to think through the full implications of this for our theological reflection in South Africa I gladly leave to the younger generation (Jonker 1991:120, my translation and emphasis).

That Jonker clearly understood the issue is evident from his earlier speech before the *Akademie*: "The challenge before which we stand is to work with others toward an understanding and interpretation of the Bible in our situation as *people who are steeped in the European tradition but who, in the meantime, became people of Africa*. Here

---

24 One is struck by the theological quality and contextual awareness of Daniel Louw's work. One should be aware of the limitation of this paper, which focuses on the macro level without regard for the fact that individual people went through enormous change and needed some form of spiritual and theological reorientation normally provided by pastoral theological frameworks.

25 One can refer to Bethel Muller's attempts to understand the role of public religion in the period just before 1990; Johan Cilliers's analytical work on sermons from contrasting contexts, and the liturgical work by A.C. Barnard, C. Vos and J. Muller.

26 A revisionist attempt with regard to our perceptions of history (and our role in it) is a crucial part of "transformation". That church historians (and not only "secular" ones) have a special responsibility arises from the fact that apartheid itself was built on an idealised conflation of Afrikaner and Israelite histories (Kinghorn 1986:139). Hanneke du Preez from Unisa published a study in 1990 on the master symbols of history text books for schools. She concludes that one of these "symbols" is that whites are superior to blacks and that the Afrikaner enjoys a privileged relationship with God and that the country rightfully belongs to the Afrikaner (*Sunday Times* 8 July 1990:18). The sensitivity about such "revision" was illustrated by the Floors van Jaarsveld incident on the theme of the day of the vow. Van Jaarsveld's critical stance on Afrikaners as a "verspätete Nation" is of great significance. *I have my doubts whether DRC historians understood their task then and now – as revising our symbolic universe toward the reconstruction of our narrative identity.*

27 The proof of the pudding will be in the "eating" of a church order for an expanding URCSA.

we live and work, we think and pray. ... We are called to do theology on the edge ("*breuklyn*") between the First and the Third World" (Jonker 1988:156, my translation and emphasis).

I am not suggesting that mainstream DRC theology did not address the issues of contextuality and Africa. I am also not adhering to a static, romantic or exclusively "black" view of what "Africa" means. The problem is that the issue of contextuality – specifically in New Testament science[28] – became more of a methodological issue than one of material significance in constructing theology. And the many articles about Africa and its realities emerged mainly from missiological reflections[29] without an "orientation" effect on DRC theology as such.

Why is this so important? Because your intellectual orientation determines your reflective agenda. One should not underestimate the importance of wrestling with South Africa's radical *Absturz* into modernity (Smit 1994:15) and the immense problems created for theology and the church in South Africa by the *simultaneous impact* of pre-modernity, modernity and post-modernity. The DRC owed it to herself, her congregants and the church at large to continue the intellectual struggle with issues such as authority and tradition, church-state relations in a secularised framework as well as the rule of law based on the sovereignty of God and the law of nature. These issues have – through globalisation and the effects of colonialism – become African issues as well.

But the DRC has nowhere – to this day – really confronted the material effect of our African context for theology. (We can obviously not jump over our own shadow, but we can change our position relative to the sun!)

This has had at least two effects on DRC theology.

First. The very question of cultural thought forms and expressions in a discipline so deeply Western was not adequately addressed[30] from the rich variety of alternative perspectives. We only belatedly saw the preliminary and local nature of our own thought and did not know how to deal with this. Neither do we know better today.

Second. The link between theology and sub-modernity[31] was never really forged. One can only speculate about the effect on DRC theological faculties if, during the overview period, women and others from the non-powerful world could have influenced academic work. I am reminded by Frederick Herzog's critique of David Kelsey's book on theological education (*To understand God truly*). By focusing

---

28 One may refer to the work of H.J.B. Combrink (see especially his very informative *Die Bybel lewe in Afrika* written after a visit to Kenya in April 1991). Also the very substantial contributions on contextual hermeneutics by B.C. Lategan, e.g. his "The challenge of contextuality" (1991) and "Aspects of a contextual hermeneutics for South Africa" (1994).
29 The works by Dionne Crafford and Piet Meiring over many years – too many to list here – are a pillar of hope in this regard. Although not academically influential, Nico Smith's views and his trek from Stellenbosch to Mamelodi served a great symbolic purpose.
30 My work on orality and the very notion of theology/literacy as well as a Zionist christology may be noted, although it represents very preliminary ideas. See Naudé (1993, 1996).
31 I am quite aware that "sub-modernity" represents another variety of modernity as a fundamental Western phenomenon not applicable to all spheres of South African society. But it does help to express the "social location" of reality "below" the powers of modernity.

exclusively on the *Wissenchaft* of Berlin and the *paideia* of Athens, the poverty of Lima was forgotten. "Lima reminds us that 'seeing' God is never direct, always indirect. *Paideia* (Athens) and *Wissenschaft* (Berlin) have to be brought under the scrutiny of the vast encampment of the poor who are banging, as it were, at the doors of our theological schools". He adds: "What's theological about the theologian? It is understanding what intellect can and cannot do in the face of poverty. It is something for which the theologian's eyes need to be opened time and again – in an ever new Emmaus experience. The problem, of course, is that God is often the theologian's favorite toy" (Herzog1994:276, 275, my emphasis).

If the relation between Stellenbosch and Crossroads, Pretoria and Mamelodi, Bloemfontein and Botshebelo were ecclesially and socially established, the theological orientation would no doubt have been different. And swept forward by the hermeneutical spiral between theory and practice, the DRC could have become herself a greater transformative force in South Africa and not a church which in most cases mirrored[32] the (changing) realities of her own situation.

The reservoir of intellectual potential in the DRC is immense and probably unsurpassed on the African continent. Some shifts not reported here did indeed occur in the post 1994 period. But new challenges are facing us. The question is whether the DRC will be self-critical enough about her past to assume her theological responsibility for the future.

What are we going to do with our power-to-reflect? What will be theological about our theology?

BIBLIOGRAPHY

Albert, L. & F. Chikane, F. (eds.) 1991. *The Road to Rustenburg: the church looking forward to a new South Africa*. Cape Town: Struik Christian Books.

Bax, D. 1979. *A different gospel. A critique of the theology behind apartheid*. Johannesburg: The Presbyterian Church of South Africa.

Boesak, A.A. 1979. *Die vinger van God*. Johannesburg: Ravan Press

Boesak, A.A. 1979. "Tensy 'n wonder gebeur...". In Meiring en Lederle (red.), pp. 147-158.

Botha, J. 1992. "The ethics of New Testament interpretation". *Neotestamentica* Vol. 26, No. 1, pp. 169-194.

Botha, J. 1993. "Aspects of the rhetoric of South African New Testament scholarship anno 1992". *Scriptura* Vol. 46, pp. 80-99.

Breytenbach C. & Lategan, B. (red.) 1992. "Geloof en opdrag. Perspektiewe op die etiek van die Nuwe Testament". *Scriptura* S9, pp. 303–325.

---

32 It is utterly ironical that Afrikaans Reformed churches in South Africa as well as the DRC family were by the middle 1990s about the only non-unified structures in the new South Africa. That destroyed their witness and obviously their ability to provide experiential exposure to diversity. They share in the worldwide phenomenon of denominationalism, where separateness becomes constitutive of identity.

Breytenbach, H.S. & Pieterse H.J.C. 1992. "Doelwitte vir gemeentebou in die lig van 'n prakties-teologiese ekklesiologie". *Praktiese Teologie in Suid-Afrika* Vol. 7, No. 2, pp. 87-100.

Britz, R.M. & Erasmus L.M. 1994. "'n Oorsig van die ontwikkeling van 'n gemeentebouteologie in die Nederduitse Gereformeerde Kerk 1970-1994". *NGTT* Vol. 35, pp. 374-388

Burger, C.W. 1991. *Die dinamika van 'n Christelike geloofsgemeenskap*. Kaapstad: Lux Verbi.

Combrink, H.J.B. 1990. "Die krisis van Skrifgesag in die gereformeerde eksegese as geleentheid". *NGTT* Vol. 31, No. 3, pp. 325-335.

Combrink, H.J.B. 1991. "Die Bybel lewe in Afrika". *Acta Theologica* Vol. 11, No. 2, pp. 81-90.

De Gruchy, J.W. 1979. *The church struggle in South Africa*. Cape Town: David Philip.

De Villiers, E. 1983. "Putting the recent debate on conscientious objection into perspective". *Scriptura* Vol. 6, pp. 65-80.

De Villiers, D.E. and Kinghorn, J. (eds.) 1984. *Op die skaal: Gemengde huwelike en ontug*. Kaapstad: Tafelberg.

De Villiers, E. 1986. "Kritiek uit die ekumene". In J. Kinghorn (red.), pp. 144-164

De Villiers, E. 1989. "Tussen simpatie en veroordeling". In: P.F. Theron & J. Kinghorn (red.), pp. 144-163.

De Villiers, E. 1989. "Peace conceptions in South Africa in the light of the Biblical concept of peace". *Scriptura* Vol. 28, pp. 24-40.

De Villiers, E. & Smit, D.J. 1996. "Waarom verskil ons so oor wat die wil van God is?" *Skrif en Kerk* Vol. 17, No. 1, pp. 31-47.

De Villiers, P. (ed.) 1985. *Disinvestment and human suffering*. Roodepoort: CUM.

Du Rand, J. 1985. "Afrikaner piety and dissent". In C. Villa-Vicencio & J. De Gruchy (eds.), pp. 39-51.

Du Rand, J. 1988. "Church and state in South Africa. Karl Barth vs Abraham Kuyper". In C. Villa-Vicencio (ed.), pp. 121-138.

Du Toit, A.B. 1990. "Die toekoms van die Skrifgesag in die moderne eksegese. 'n Hoofsaaklik Nuwe Testamentiese perspektief". *NGTT* Vol. 31, No. 4, pp. 509ff.

Du Toit, D.A. (red.) 1984. *Menseregte*. Kaapstad: Tafelberg.

Hendriks, H.J. 1992. *Strategiese beplanning in die gemeente*. Wellington: Hugenote Uitgewers.

Herzog, F. 1994. "Athens, Berlin and Lima". *Theology Today*, pp. 270-276.

Heyns, J. 1970. *Die nuwe mens onder weg: Oor die tien gebooie*. Kaapstad: Tafelberg.

Heyns, J. 1977. *Die kerk*. Pretoria: NG Kerkboekhandel.

Heyns, J. 1978. *Dogmatiek*. Pretoria: NG Kerkboekhandel.

Heyns, J. 1979. "Wese van die etiese". In P.C. Potgieter (red.), pp. 1-14

Heyns, J. 1981. *Etiek van die liefde*. Pretoria: Daan Retief.

Heyns, J. 1982. *Teologiese etiek*. Deel 1. Pretoria: NG Kerkboekhandel.

Heyns, J. 1986. *Teologiese etiek*. Deel 2/1. Pretoria: NG Kerkboekhandel.

Heyns, J. 1989 *Teologiese etiek*. Deel 2/2. Pretoria: NG Kerkboekhandel.

Heyns, J. 1991. "Burgerlike ongehoorsaamheid". *Skrif en kerk*. Vol. 12, No. 1, pp. 36-53.

Jonker, W.D. 1973a. "Die aktualiteit van die sosiale etiek". In P.A. Verhoef (ed.), pp. 78-107.

Jonker, W.D. 1973b. "Heilige Skrif en sosiale etiek by Calvyn". *Bulletin van die Suid-Afrikaanse vereniging vir die bevordering van Christelike wetenskap* Vol. 39, pp. 31-37.

Jonker, W.D. 1977. "Die unieke karakter van die kerk". *In die Skriflig* Vol. 11, pp. 4-13.

Jonker, W.D. 1986. "Afsonderlike kerke vir afsonderlike bevolkingsgroepe?" *Scriptura* Vol. 17, pp. 1-14.

Jonker, W.D. 1988a. "Some remarks on the interpretation of Karl Barth". *NGTT* Vol. 29, pp. 29-40.

Jonker, W.D. 1988. "Suid-Afrika se verbondenheid met Europa: Die teologie". *Tydskrif vir Geesteswetenskappe* Vol. 28, pp. 146-157.

Jonker, W.D. 1991. "Reaksie op Naude en Furstenburg se bespreking van Uit vrye guns alleen". *NGTT* Vol. 32, No. 1, pp. 119-123.

Jonker, W.D. 1991b. "Understanding the Church Situation and Obstacles to Christian Witness in South Africa". In L. Albert & F. Chikane (eds.), pp. 87-98.

Jonker, W.D. 1994. "In gesprek met Johan Heyns". *Skrif en Kerk* Vol. 15, No. 1, pp. 13-26.

Jonker, W.D. 1998. *Selfs die kerk kan verander*. Kaapstad: Tafelberg.

Jonker, W.D. & Theron, P.F. 1979. *Vreemde gemeenskap. Preke rondom die tema: die kerk in die wereld*. Pretoria: NGKB.

Jonker, W.D. 2008. *Die relevansie van die kerk: Teologiese reaksies op die betekenis van die kerk in die wêreld*. Wellington: Bybel-Media.

Kinghorn, J. & Borchardt, C.F.A. (red.) 1986. *Die NG Kerk en apartheid*. Johannesburg: Macmillan.

Kinghorn, J. 1990. *'n Tuiste vir almal.'n Sosiaal-teologiese studie oor 'n gesamentlike demokrasie in Suid-Afrika*. Stellenbosch: Sentrum vir Kontekstuele Hermeneutiek.

Lategan, B.C. and W.S. Vorster, W.S. 1985. *Text and Reality: Aspects of Reference in Biblical Texts*. Philadelphia: Fortress.

Lategan, B.C. 1987. "Inleidende opmerkigs oor resepsieteorie en die uitleg van Bybelse materiaal". *NGTT* Vol. 28, No. 2, pp. 112-118.

Lategan, B.C. 1991. The challenge of contextuality. *Scriptura* S9, pp. 1-6.

Lategan, B.C. 1994. "Aspects of a contextual hermeneutics for South Africa". In J. Mouton & B. Lategan (eds.), pp. 17-30.

Loubser, J.A. 1987. *The apartheid Bible*. Cape Town: Maskew Miller Longman.

Louw, D.J. 1988. "Vigs, die radikale siekte met die radikale uitdaging aan die pastorale bediening". *NGTT* Vol. 29, No. 1, pp. 66.

Louw, D.J. 1992. "Die ontwerp van 'n prakties-teologiese ekklesiologie vir gemeentebou". *Praktiese Teologie in Suid-Afrika* Vol. 7, No. 2, pp. 119-136.

Louw, D.J. 1993. "Resensie van Smuts, AJ (et al.) 1990". *NGTT*, pp. 102.

Meiring, P. 1979. *Die kerk in die nuwe Afrika*. Kaapstad: Tafelberg.

Meiring, P. 1993. "Poverty – The road ahead. A theological perspective". *Skrif en Kerk* Vol. 14, pp. 263-276.

Meiring, P. & H.I. Lederle (red.) 1979. *Die eenheid van die kerk*. Kaapstad: Tafelberg.

Mouton, J. & Lategan, B. (eds.) 1994. *The relevance of theology for the nineties*. Pretoria: HSRC.

Naudé, Piet 1991. *Uit vrye guns alleen*: grondlyne vir 'n pastorale dogmatiek. NGTT 32/1, 110-118

Naudé, P.J. 1993. "Toward a local Zionist theology? The role of the outsider theologian". *Scriptura* Vol. 45, pp. 29-46.

Naudé, P.J. 1996. "Theology with a new voice? The case for an oral theology in the context of South Africa". *JTSA* Vol. 94, pp. 18-31.

Ned Geref Kerk. 1975. *Ras, volk en nasie en volkereverhoudinge in die lig van die Skrif*.

Nel, M. 1986. *Teologiese perpsektiewe op gemeentebou*. Pretoria: NG Kerkboekhandel.

Nel, M. 1987. "Die verhouding van gemeentebou tot ander dissiplines van die vak Praktiese Teologie en ander teologiese vakke". *Praktiese Teologie in Suid-Afrika* Vol. 2, pp. 26-37.

Nieuwoudt, M. 1982. "Die historiese beoefening van die diens van barmhartigheid deur die Ned Geref Kerk met verwysing na die evangeliese, missiologiese en sosiale geregtigheidsaspekte daarvan". *NGTT* Vol. 3, pp. 235-250.

Potgieter, P.C. (red.) 1979. *Etiese probleme in bybelse perpektief*. Pretoria: NG Kerkboekhandel.

Potgieter, P.C. 1988. "Die kerk in 'n bestaanskrisis?" *Fax Theologica* Vol. 1, pp. 60-64.

Potgieter, P.C. 1987. "Personal faith in the theology of Karl Barth". *NGTT* Vol. 28, pp. 153-159.

Prinsloo, W.S. 1985. "Die gesag van die Ou Testament: 'n praktiese illustrasie uit Joel 2:12-17". *NGTT* Vol. 26, No. 4, pp. 410-416.

Schrotenboer, P.G. 1982. "The RES and world relief". *NGTT* Vol. 3, pp. 286-297.

Schussler-Fiorenza, E. 1988. "The ethics of interpretation: De-centering biblical scholarship". *JBL* Vol. 107, pp. 3-17.

Schussler-Fiorenza, F. 1990. "The crisis of Scriptural authority. Interpretation and reception". *Interpretation* Vol. XLIV, No. 4, pp. 353-368.

Smit, D.J. 1981. "Resente Suid-Afrikaanse literatuur oor die kerk". *Scriptura* Vol. 1, pp. 61-68.

Smit, D.J. 1988. "Responsible hermeneutics: A systematic theologian's response to readings and readers of Luke 12:35-48". *Neotestamentica* Vol. 22, pp. 441-484.

Smit, D.J. 1992. "Oor 'Nuwe Testament etiek', die christelike lewe en Suid-Afrika vandag". In Breytenbach & B. Lategan (reds.), pp. 303-325.

Smit, D.J. 1994. "The future of Old Testament studies in South Africa: An ethicist's perspective". *Old Testament Essays* Vol. 7, No. 4, pp. 286-292.

Smit, D.J. 1999. "Modernity and theological education – crises at 'Western Cape' and 'Stellenbosch'?" *Journal of African Christian Thought* Vol. 2, No. 1, pp. 34-44.

Smuts, A.J. (et al.) 1990. *Die diens van barmhartigheid en die Ned Geref Kerk*. Pretoria: NG Kerkuitgewers.

Snyman, S.D. 1987. "Gedagtes oor die rol van die Ned Geref Kerk-familie in die toekoms van Suid-Afrika". *Fax Theologica* Vol. 1, pp. 53-57.

Taute, J.H.F. & Du Toit D.A. 1990. "Die etiek van burgerlike ongehoorsaamheid". *NGTT* Vol. 31, No. 2, pp. 191.

Theron, P.F. 1984. *Die koninkryk van God in die teologie van JA Heyns*. Unpublished DTh dissertation. Pretoria: Unisa.

Theron, P.F. 1978. *Die ekklesia as kosmies-eskatologiese teken*. Pretoria: NG Kerkboekhandel.

Theron, P.F. 1988. "Natuur en genade, kerk en volk". In C.J. Wethmar & C.J.A.Vos (eds.), pp. 157-172.

Theron, P.F. & Kinghorn, J (reds.) 1989. *Koninkryk, kerk en kosmos. Huldigingsbundel ter ere van Prof WD Jonker*. Bloemfontein: Pro Christo.

Truth and Reconciliation Commission Report. 1998. Cape Town: Juta.

Van der Watt, J.G. 1992. Aktualiteit? Die Ned Geref Kerk in Suid-Afrika in die lig van die situasie in Duitsland". *Verbum et Ecclesia; Skrif en Kerk* Vol 13, No 2, pp. 200-220. doi: 10.4102/ve.v13i2.1057

Van Huyssteen, J.W.V. 1986. *Teologie as kritiese geloofsverantwoording*. Pretoria: RGN.

Van Huyssteen, J.W.V. & Du Toit, B.J. 1982. *Geloof en skrifgesag*. Pretoria: NGKB.

Van Niekerk, A.A. 1984. "Analogia Fidei teenoor analogia entis: Karl Barth en die verstaanbaarheid van ons spreke oor God". *NGTT* Vol. 24, No. 4, pp. 410-420.

Van Wyk, J.H. 1989. "WD Jonker as ekklesioloog". In P.F. Theron & J. Kinghorn (reds.), pp. 74-86.

Verhoef, P.A. (ed.) 1973. *Sol Iustitiae. Festschrift for B.B. Keet*. Kaapstad: NG Kerk-uitgewers.

Verster, P. 1991. "Politiek en teologie: Oos-Europa 1990 – Barth agterhaal?" *NGTT* Vol. 32, pp. 614-621.

Villa-Vicencio, C. & J. De Gruchy, J. (eds.) 1985. *Resistance and Hope*. Cape Town: David Philip.

Villa-Vicencio, C. (ed.) 1988. *On reading Karl Barth in South Africa*. Grand Rapids: Eerdmans.

Vosloo, W. 1994. "Fokus op armoede". *NGTT* Vol. 35, pp. 55-64.

Weisse, W & Anthonissen, C. (eds). 2004. *Maintaining apartheid or promoting change? The role of the DRC in a phase of increasing conflict in South Africa*. Berlin: Waxmann, pp. 31-52

Wethmar, C.J. & Vos, C.J.A. (eds.) 1988. *'n Woord op sy tyd. Feesbundel aangebied aan Prof Johan Heyns*. Pretoria: NG Kerkboekhandel.

Wilson, F. & Ramphele, M. & Philip, D. 1989. *Uprooting poverty — The South African challenge*. New York: W. W. Norton & Company.

3.10 CONSTRUCTING A COHERENT THEOLOGICAL DISCOURSE

The main challenge facing the Dutch Reformed Church in South Africa[1]

INTRODUCTION

Instead of making a list of possible challenges[2] facing the DRC in South Africa today, I wish to argue in this paper that the DRC actually faces only one major challenge, namely to construct, and enact in its life and work, a coherent theological discourse.

Within the constraints of one paper only the main "mapping points" of such a discourse will be outlined, setting the agenda for open discussion and material construction later. To honour the fact that a church has not only an institutional face (the DRC as represented in its general and regional synods, official newspapers, theological faculties) but also a congregational face (actual churches in cities and towns, ordinary members who live as Christians in the world), each of the theological dimensions below will be translated into ecclesiological terms partially derived from the Nicene and Apostolic creeds. This determines the structure of the paper, as indicated below.

The challenge to reconstruct a coherent theological discourse[3] requires at least the following four interrelated tasks:

1. The reinterpretation and re-appropriation of our tradition rooted in Reformed theology: the church as a community of thought;

2. The enrichment of our tradition via an ecumenical theology: the church as one, catholic community;

3. The conscious effort to construct a critical, public theology: the church as holy community;

4. An honest engagement with our continent toward an African theology: The church as Christian community.

1　Paper read at a symposium hosted by the University of Hamburg (Germany) in Stellenbosch, South Africa, 12-14 March 2003. As a member of the DRC, I am writing this with the advantages and limitations of an insider perspective. My fervent hope is to write theology from within and for a broader Reformed and ecumenical church in the near future so as to transcend the current introspective phase of DRC theology.

2　See footnote 50 and its related paragraph below.

3　This challenge was outlined by Russel Botman at the previous conference organised by our Hamburg colleagues on the role of the DRC in the period of transition in South Africa. He relies on Trinstan Borer's argument that changes in a church occur as a result of three factors, of which an evolving religious context is related to what Botman calls a changing "universe of theological discourse". The rest of his article explains this in terms of the tension between Kuyperian and Barthian thought and the fruitful role that the confession of Belhar could play in reconstructing such a discourse. I might venture to say that the paper presented here is to try and fill – at least methodologically – the void left by what Botman calls disempowered Barthians and "wasted Kuyperians" (Botman 2001:39).

1. THE REINTERPRETATION AND RE-APPROPRIATION OF OUR TRADITION ROOTED IN REFORMED THEOLOGY: THE CHURCH AS A COMMUNITY OF THOUGHT.

In highly simplified terms, the dominant theological paradigm of the DRC until the mid-1980s was shaped by a combination of four forces stemming from 19th-century European thought. Each played an ambiguous role of positive identity formation whilst simultaneously contributing to a certain theological "deformation".[4]

1.1. The strength of Abraham Kuyper's (1837-1920) neo-Calvinism was its affirmation of God's rule over the whole of creation and the unity of humanity as created in the image of God. Its weakness, however, is an idealist analogy between God and creation via Kuyper's notion of general grace (*gemeene gratie*), which is the basis for an evolutionary development of *essentiae* toward *potentiae* according to a fundamental God-willed pluriformity (see Velema 1989). The anthropological implication is that each grouping of people has its own unique "law-stream" according to which it realises its potential in history (see Strauss 1995). Where this potential meets God's particular grace in Christ, the highest form of civilisation (as in Europe and America) is reached, whereas groups sharing only in general grace exhibit a lower form of civilisation (like some African tribes).[5] He is of the opinion that the Afrikaner people, because of their Calvinist origins, shared in the best that this tradition could offer and had the God-given obligation to rule over less civilised people until the latter reached the same level of development (see Kuyper 1943). The ecclesiological implication (see Jonker 1989) is a disregard of the institutional, visible unity of the church as this constitutes a form of "churchism" that restricts the freedom of people to form their own churches according to their conception of external forms of differentiation such as language and culture.

Kuyper's idea of a differentiation in creation, a hierarchical construction of civilisation, and subjectivist ecclesial pluriformity struck a powerful chord in the minds of Afrikaners suffering in the time after the British war (1899-1901), and the depression of the early 1930s compounded by severe droughts in an agriculture-based economy. It enabled leading Afrikaner intellectuals (such as S.J. du Toit, D.J. du Toit, F.J.M. Potgieter, A.B. du Preez, J.D. Vorster and A.P. Treurnicht) to turn Kuyper's specific brand of structured pluriformity into a theologically guided political ideology where separateness and *voogdyskap* could be presented as an ordinance of God, and the spiritual, invisible unity of the church could be viewed as adequate expression of the one body of Christ.

---

4   The discussion below is a summary of a paper entitled "From pluralism to ideology. The roots of apartheid theology in Abraham Kuyper, Gustav Warneck and theological pietism" (see Naudé 2002a). This paper contains the references to original and secondary sources assumed in the summary given here. *Die NG Kerk en apartheid*, with contributions by Johann Kinghorn (the editor) and others, published in 1986, remains one of the best theological overviews of apartheid as a theology and is a fruitful source of original references to what is stated here in broad and sweeping terms.

5   The idea of the racial superiority of the Caucasian race was supported by Social Darwinism, where evolutionary theories of human societies required some implicit hierarchy of lower and higher forms of civilization. See Paris 2000:265-266. See also the interesting note by Cornell West that the notion of black people as human beings "is a relatively new discovery in the modern west" (West 1982, as cited in Paris 2000:264).

1.2. The strength of missiological reflection by Gustav Warneck (1934-1919) was his insight and emphasis on the fact that mission needs to take the nature of its object – specifically its cultural forms – seriously if the gospel is to be mediated not as something foreign, but as linking to the structure of the own history and identity. His weakness was, however, to interpret *ta ethne* in the great commission (Matthew 28:19) in ethnological terms (instead of salvation-historical terms) and ultimately choosing for *Volkschristianisierung* (against *Einzelbekehrung* and the establishment of *ecclesiola*) as both object and method of mission.[6] In this way the establishment of ethnically-based independent churches was seen not only as the historical result of mission, but its ultimate aim.

Warneck's work provided the theological rationale for defending the establishment of separate churches for different race groups in the DRC family since 1881. If the *Volk* in its ethnological sense is the object of mission, it follows that *Volkskirchen* should be established. And this in turn implies that, as a result of different cultural expressions (e.g. language) and specific pastoral needs, these churches should be independent denominations. The move from the ecclesial practice of racial separation to a political design that enforces racial separation (presented as the only viable Christian solution to the race problem) is then an easy one to make and to defend, despite the fact that this was not the intention of Warneck's own design.

1.3. The strength of Romanticism, with its emphasis on "das Gefühlsmassige, Irrationale und Volkstümliche", was that it provided an effective cultural alternative to rationalism (*LThK* 8:1268-1269). Its weakness was, however, the inherent potential of a theological and political misuse of exactly this romantic *Volksbegriff*. "The word Volk is quite untranslatable", bemoaned the Oxford Missionary Conference of 1938, "because it designates both sentiment and a body of convictions to which there is no exact, or even approximate, parallel elsewhere" (see Hoekendijk 1948:99, note 9).

There is no doubt that both Kuyper and Warneck (and many others of the same period) were influenced by romantic ideas about the *Volk*. In Kuyper it resonates in his successful political ambitions, his romanticising of the glorious Dutch past, and his overt nationalism. In Warneck it underlies the idea of both the German people and their relation to other nationalities: "Den Deutschen eignet als besondere Charisma eine ... Respektierung fremder Nationalität, die sie befähight, seblstlos, unbefangen schonend auf den Eigenthümlichkeiten anderer Völker einzugehen" (*Evangelische Missionslehre* III:23).

The rise of Afrikaner nationalism in the early part of the twentieth century was a natural and fertile ground for the seeds of romantic ideas about the own culture and the *Volk*. The mission policy of the Cape DRC in 1932 stated that Christianity "does not want to rob the Bantu of his language and culture, but wants to permeate and cleanse his whole nationalism so that evangelisation can never imply de-nationalisation". Each *Volk* has to develop according to its own *volksaard* (*eigentümliche Volksart*) and in its own geographical and socially defined context insofar as this is practically possible (see Kinghorn 1986:87).

---

6   See Warneck (1897), the discussion by Bosch (1983) and the brilliant analysis of the relation between church and *volk* in German missiology of the nineteenth centry in Hoekendijk (1948).

1.4. The strength of Pietism was its emphasis on a holy lifestyle and full commitment to following Christ, a warmth of worship in new music, prayers and other liturgical forms, as well as a "passion for souls" leading to a strong missionary focus (see Bosch 1983:25, and see *LThK* 8: 291-293). Its weakness was strands of anti-theological and other-worldly attitudes, which resulted in literal and, in some cases, fundamentalist readings of Scripture, and a blind eye to the social construction of reality.

This tradition provided the warmth of evangelical preaching and sustained the long Pentecostal tradition (*Pinksterbidure* and the *Halleluja* hymnal book!) that uniquely shaped the DRC's spirituality (see Jonker 1988). It also, however, allowed for a privatisation of religion, and a mistrust of intellectuality and critical scholarship (to which I will turn in more detail below in point 3).

What has happened to this theological discourse with its inner tensions, but nevertheless moulded together under the specific cultural and political conditions of the apartheid era? Because each in a specific way supported apartheid as a theology, the demise of apartheid both as theology[7] and political structure by 1994 left us with a huge vacuum and loss of direction. In this vacuum – and in the absence of a critical or viable alternative – the theological canopy collapsed and a dramatic "pluralisation" of the DRC took place in the very short period between 1994 and 2000. The centrifugal cohesive force of an ecclesial-cultural-political universe turned itself outward in a dramatic and fractious process of identity de- and reconstruction amongst white Afrikaans-speaking South Africans in general and the DRC in particular.

The DRC is consequently today no longer one church that thinks or looks the same wherever it is found. There is a much stronger diversity of theological thought ranging from orthodox Reformed,[8] "Reformed"[9] (still the official view), evangelical/Pentecostal,[10] to liberal forms of modernist and post-modernist[11] thinking about

---

7   There is good reason to argue that the theological justification of apartheid started to crumble in the mainline thinking of the DRC in the early 1980s and found its first (albeit tentative) expression in the document *Kerk en Samelewing* (1986, and amended in 1990). When membership was declared "open" and based on faith in Jesus Christ alone, those who were of a different conviction knew the end of apartheid theology was in sight and formed the *Afrikaanse Protestantse Kerk* with about 40 000 former DRC members shortly after 1986.

8   I refer here to those theologians and pastors who struggle against the composite nature of the DRC's theological character and who would insist that the "evangelical" stream represents forms of Methodism and Pelagianism that are to be denounced by a theology in which God's pre-election of the faithful and the objectivity of grace are emphasised against perceived subjective, anthropological elements (like calls to those in the covenant to confess sins and accept God's grace).

9   I put Reformed in inverted commas to indicate that this is no unitary category. In terms of Hesselgrave and Rommen's typology (1989:144-157), the mainline theology in the DRC could be described as being between orthodox and neo-orthodox, whereas academic theology would tend in the direction of different shapes of liberalism.

10 Evangelical and Pentecostalist ideas rarely, if ever, appear in writing in DRC circles, but are alive and well in some of the liturgical renewals and associated preaching, as well as in aspects of a renewed missionary awareness in the DRC over the last decade.

11 Excellent examples in this regard are Ben du Toit (2000) and the volume *Die nuwe Hervorming* under editorship of Piet Muller (2002). See also the recent analysis of (post-)modernity in the Afrikaans churches by Jaap Durand (2002).

tradition, authority and truth. There is a similar congregational differentiation: examples are mega-city-churches, so-called community churches, traditional suburban and rural churches, and experiments in small alternative house or family churches.

The landscape of the DRC has changed irrevocably. And when I argue for a "theological coherence", it is not a plea to turn back to a situation of unitary or authoritarian theological constructs. What I do wish to argue for are forms of theological interconnectedness that provide a sufficient (though not exclusive) framework within which the DRC can renegotiate her own identity between two extremes: on the one hand, theological foundationalism and essentialism that does not allow for critical plurality and requires authoritarian, homogenous ecclesial forms; on the other hand lies deconstructive, chaotic differentiation sometimes linked to forms of epistemological nihilism that foster ecclesial independentism.[12] The concrete theological concepts that may determine this interconnectedness are in my view the list discussed in this paper: Reformed, ecumenical, public and African. They might form, I suggest, the boundary points or co-ordinates within which to map and reconstruct DRC theologies that are indeed pluralist, but nevertheless coherent enough to form the space of our future habitation – hopefully in a broader family of South African churches.

To explain the background to this notion of theological coherence, I take my cue from Clifford Geertz's redefinition of "culture"[13] in semiotic-symbolic terms (see especially Geertz 1973) and James Clifford's idea of culture as negotiation of meaning (see Clifford 1988). "Culture" is here not perceived as an organic whole that moves naturally through successive phases of maturation, but rather as a discrete human collective that shows an ambiguous character where metaphors of unity and dissolution are kept in tension in the process of identity seeking, identity revision and even identity subversion. "Culture is a long, relational struggle to maintain and recreate identities" (Clifford 1988: 338). In this negotiation of identity amidst chaos and order Clifford emphasises that, despite constant flirtation with fragmentation (and we might add: despite sometimes dramatic collapses of symbolic universes), the assumption of forms of symbolic human connectedness cannot simply be abandoned (Clifford 1988: 145), as without this life would be mere chaos. Delwin Brown, in his well-known book on traditions, argues that canon and ritual play an indispensable role in re-creating tradition as the boundaries of our habitation (Brown 1994).

And this Christian, and specifically Reformed, tradition – expressed in the ecumenical creeds, Reformed Formulae of Unity and the Belhar confession, and most vividly carried forth by the early church fathers, John Calvin and Karl Barth

---

12   The presbyterial system of church governance indeed allows for the relative autonomy of the local congregation, but there are growing examples that some ("successful"?) congregations build their profile increasingly independently of the church in broader circuit or synodical structures, and some congregations are even hostile to the institutional church in its broader sense. In its worst form, this easily leads to theological sectarianism based on us-them typologies.

13   For both Geertz and Clifford culture entails processes of human collectivities of which religion is a part. In the same way, I take theology as a part of what would constitute identity in the DRC.

– needs to be re-appropriated in a way that make sense for today. We shall have to deconstruct terms such as Calvinism[14] and Reformed,[15] and translate[16] the confessions into a language of and for today. We shall further have to forge a link between hermeneutically enabling theological scholarship and the realities of congregations where this theology is to be translated into sermons, liturgies, catechesis and a life *coram Dei*. The lure towards an uncontemplative actionism, where the church is called upon to assist in many of the crises of our country, but where she is unable to both root and shape this assistance in her own theological character, must be equally resisted as uninhibited doctrinal freedom where the church tries to be everything to everybody. This doctrinal freedom specifically relates to the Protestant roots of Reformed theology as a polemical theology in search of the truth as revealed in Scripture, and being able to posit the marks of the true church exactly in the gospel, the sacraments and church discipline.

It might sound elitist, but I remind you of the ground-breaking work by J.H. Oldham who – in preparing the second conference of Life and Work (Oxford 1937) – aptly described the church as a "community of thought", calling to its aid the best minds that it can command. If we nurture this "community of thought" as a "truth-seeking community" (Polkinghorne) it will prevent us from both anti-theological spirituality and a non-spiritual theology, enabling us to serve God and the world with the best Reformed theology we can construct under the constraints of our tradition and our time.

Will and should an overarching paradigm like the one mentioned above emerge? I think the answer is no. We will learn to live in a more fragile theological house, a bit more eclectic than systematic, deriving coherence from the inner thrust of Reformed theology itself: *semper reformanda*.

The task has only just begun.

---

14 The popular notion of Calvinism is that it relates to people who work (too) hard and are highly moralistic. For a worthy reclamation of Calvin and Reformed values, see the popular but well-informed publication *Ons weet aan wie ons behoort* by Coenie Burger (Burger 2002).

15 In the alternative Afrikaans music revival of the early 1990s one of the most popular bands named itself *Die Gereformeerde Blues Band* and one of the lead singers became known as Johannes Kerkorrel. A superficial reading of both the lyrics and the movement suggest that it became the vehicle for deconstructing the Afrikaner authoritarian past constituted by church (specifically the DRC as Gereformeerd) and political party (see the highly successful hit, *Sit dit af*). The first tour was aptly named the *Vrye Voëlvlug-toer* and was banned from at least two traditionally Afrikaans campuses at the time!

16 I use "translate" here in the double sense of actually rewriting our confessions in modern Afrikaans (see the success of *Die Boodskap* as a really dynamic equivalent Bible), but also as reappropriating them as speaking to the spiritual issues of today. A good example of work related to creeds and confessions is Dirkie Smit's trilogy of collected sermons on the Nicene Creed published by *Lux Verbi* (see Smit 2001, 2002, 2003), and *Op weg met Belhar*, a popular introduction to the Belhar confession by Johann Botha and Piet Naudé (1997).

2. THE ENRICHMENT OF OUR TRADITION TOWARD AN ECUMENICAL THEOLOGY: THE CHURCH AS ONE, CATHOLIC COMMUNITY.

In a current series of international conferences the Centre for Theological Inquiry (Princeton) is pursuing the theme of *Reformed identity and ecumenicity*. The results so far[17] confirm the basic tenet of Reformed theology to be nothing other than truly Christian and therefore ecumenical theology. The Reformation was not driven by schismatic notions of a sectarian church, and the Reformed confessions are at pains to emphasise their confirmation and continuation of the apostolic faith and ecumenical creeds (see Belgic confession article 9 and Wethmar 1991).

The DRC shared this ecumenical orientation and played an important role in Reformed and ecumenical bodies up to 1960. After the disastrous rejection of the Cottesloe consultation (7-14 December 1960) by the Cape and Transvaal Synods, the DRC was slowly but surely ecumenically isolated and became instead the object of witness for many church consultations in the ensuing years (see Naudé 2002a). This culminated in the dramatic events of Ottawa in 1982, when a *status confessio* was accepted by the World Alliance of Reformed Churches and membership of the DRC and Gereformeerde Kerk was suspended. In her own family the DRC became increasingly lonely. This position was intensified by her inability to hear the ecumenical voice that spoke through the Belhar confession in the period between 1982 and 1990.[18]

The history of increasing ecumenical isolation is told elsewhere.[19] The impact on us had been severe. It led to the DRC becoming a typically denominational church whose identity and self-understanding lay in her very separateness. There is enough evidence to support what Lukas Vischer has observed in the broader ecumenical movement: "Frequently, confessional positions are not defended by a concern for the purity of their teaching. The real motive is often simply preservation of one's identity which has developed over the course of history. ... These may be matters of language, ethnic identity, national pride, or other things" (Vischer 1984:232).[20]

---

17 Three conferences have been held so far. Proceedings of the first conference were published in 1998 as *Toward the future of Reformed theology*, edited by Welker and Willis (see German title in bibliography). I was fortunate to be part of the other two conferences held in Heidelberg, Germany (systematicians) and Stellenbosch, South Africa (biblical scholars) in 1999 and 2001 respectively.

18 For an analysis of how the Belhar confession grew from and exceeded ecumenical witnesses between 1948 and 1982 see Naudé (2002b).

19 See the overview of the DRC and ecumenics for the period 1948-1982 with good reference to primary literature in De Villiers (1986). An illuminating early reflection, open to ecumenical relations, is found in A.J. van Wijk (ed.) *Die Ekumene. 'n Besinning oor interkerklike verhoudinge* (1964) with contributions by *inter alia* W.A. Landman, J. Durand and B. Marais. On pages 21-23, see the very interesting – and at points contradictory – declaration on ecumenical relations and church unity by the Gefedereerde Ned Geref Kerk before the different synods joined together in 1962.

20 Although from a completely different perspective, Wesley Kort in his *Bound to differ* (1992:135, 139) is quite cynical about what is called "Christian identity" as it is a social demand expressed in the need to categorise and be categorised in order to control. The declaration of a Christian identity is, according to him, therefore not actually Christian pressure.

If we accept with Hauerwas (1981:1) that a faith community is a story-formed community, and with Ritschl (1984:45ff) that "Story" with its implicit axioms determines our identity, a narrative analysis seems an appropriate method to "uncover" the identity of faith communities in particular and denominations in general.[21] So the question is: What were the major factors which formed the self-understanding of the DRC?[22] It is obviously a very complex question that can only be addressed by a multiplicity of interdisciplinary studies including literary criticism, history, sociology and economics. Three South African (theological) studies – based on the concept of "myth" as a belief held to make sense of the world – are helpful in this regard.

First: in his analysis of sermons in the period 1960-1980 Cilliers (1994) found a decisive structure in the myth of the "volk", where the overriding urge for preservation is not only seen as a divine decree, but intensified by a process of clear delineation between the insiders and outsiders, "us" and "the enemy". Second: in their discussion of apartheid as neurotic myth and dominant social source of church formation in South Africa Adonis and Smit (1991) refer to mounting fear and an apocalyptic mind-set in the face of social change. Third: in his analysis of ten congregations from the DRC in the period up to 1990 Hendriks notes that the prescriptive power of myths (determining a view of the world) results in an astonishing lack of historical consciousness of the context in which the congregations operate and that they hold a romantic view of the past (Hendriks 1992:61ff).

As a (partial) "snapshot" of the DRC stemming from the period before 1994, the conclusions of studies from different angles nevertheless point in the same direction. We see an ecumenically isolated, denominational church, struggling to preserve her identity in a collapsing socio-political world which underpins her dominant myths, and which is in turn supported by the very same myths. This "narrative closure" points to a definite "hermeneutical closure" where alternative (ecumenical) – and specifically counter-myths – are excluded, or very difficult to "read".

Ecumenical isolation also inhibited the growth of a Reformed theology that deliberately seeks to be an ecumenical theology. I understand an ecumenical theology not as one confined to an overt engagement with discussions related to the modern ecumenical movement, nor as a kind of "supra-confessional" effort. Ecumenical theology is characterised by a spirit of constructing theology with an urgency and openness to engage with and learn from the broader Christian tradition and inter-faith dialogue, whilst declaring the basis or specific confessional tradition from which its views are derived.[23]

---

21 See Richard Niebuhr: *The social sources of denominationalism* published as early as 1929. A well-known example of this approach in the field of practical theology is James Hopewell: *Congregations Stories and structures* (1987).
22 The next few paragraphs are taken from Naudé 2001.
23 There are many examples of this form of ecumenical theology in recent times. A random list close to the ecumenical movement may include Edmund Schlink, Geoffrey Wainwright, Dietrich Ritschl, Konrad Raiser and many others. A recent example of how a Reformed scholar treats a specific systematic-theological question from an ecumenically enriching perspective is Michael Welker's *What happens in holy communion*, a translation of *Was geht vor bei dem Abendmahl?* (2000). Miroslav Volf's treatment of Trinitarian theology in his *After our likeness. The church as the image of the Trinity* (1997) is another example of how different traditions (in his case Catholic and Orthodox) are taken seriously in a critical

The DRC's isolation made it impossible for the church to follow ecumenical debates, share ecumenical concerns and participate in ecumenical projects. On the contrary, during the period 1960-1986 the DRC was overtly anti-ecumenical as it attempted to defend its own theological viewpoint and practices against growing criticism from churches inside and outside South Africa (see De Villiers 1986:164). (The most important counter-voice from within the DRC during this period was systematic theologian Willie Jonker,[24] who was able to develop and defend a biblical, Reformed theology whilst engaging with e.g. Catholic theology, Pentecostalism and creative but dissenting voices such as Bultmann and Barth. No wonder he himself has on occasions been called both liberal and Catholic!).

Where are we heading? The tide has turned. The DRC, as confirmed by its unconditional confession on apartheid in 1999 and decisions on ecumenicity at its recent General Synod (Oct 2002), is eager to re-join the ecumenical church in a variety of ways. The DRC commitment reads: "We commit ourselves to greater unity with other churches. We really want to re-unite with our church family, as we believe God wills it. We also want to confirm and extend our ecumenical relations and take hands with other Christians to build our country and relieve painful circumstances" (my translation). The DRC knows the first step is reunification in the DRC-family – a complex process, but with the promise of heal the rift that dates back to 1881, when the Mission Church was founded.

In this process the DRC will for the first time in many decades learn how much it needs others and the riches derived from ecclesial reciprocity. The opportunity now arises to both construct an ecumenical theology and realise in congregations the confessional unity of the church so forcefully witnessed to in the Nicene Creed and article 2 of the Belhar confession. This will also enable the DRC to move from a denominational self-understanding to confirm the richness of the church's catholicity. This catholicity implies that each local congregation represents the full church of Christ, but at the same time stands in communion with the universal church in both space (the whole world) and time (the church through the ages). It also expresses the promise of the church's future, because in the catholic church is represented the rule of Christ, a king who cannot be without subjects at any one point in history (see Heidelberg Catechism question and answer 54; Belgic Confession article 27).

I cannot think of a more solid basis for hope than this – especially for a church whose members are in dire need to see the opportunities of being Christians in Africa. But for this to be realised, two further tasks need to be undertaken.

3. THE CONSCIOUS EFFORT TO CONSTRUCT A CRITICAL, PUBLIC THEOLOGY: THE CHURCH AS HOLY COMMUNITY.

The notion of a "public theology" or "revisionist theology" has its origin and major representation in the USA and to a lesser degree in Germany.[25] Despite quite

---

but open ecumenical approach.
24   For a moving tribute to Jonker's ecumenicity, see Smit 1989. It remains a pity that Jonker's work did not find a wider readership in English or German in the period between 1960 and 1998.
25   South African Reformed theologians who give overt attention to this idea include the many works over many years by John de Gruchy, and in recent times by Ernst Conradie

substantial differences among different strands of public theologies, there are at least three shared common concerns.

First: Public theology is a reaction to the displacement of religion from the public sphere by philosophical and political developments inherent to modernity. It attempts to regain a foothold in the public square of society so as to combat the privatisation of religion and concomitant secularisation of public life. Second: Public theology addresses issues of public concern from a theological perspective so as to contribute to a better society. Third: Public theology puts a high premium on the "publicness" of its own arguments and develops forms of communication that are accessible and open to scrutiny beyond the closed circle of professional theologians.

The urgent need for a theology of this nature (whether it is called "public" or not) stems from the fact that the demise of apartheid and transition to a liberal democracy exposed South African society to the forces of modernity. One may refer to the emphasis on individual freedom of choice, the questioning and even rejection of traditional authority, and the introduction of a constitutional dispensation that shattered the *de facto* and implicit *corpus christianum* from which Christian churches had operated for decades in South Africa. No one will in principle question the valuable gains of a modernist democracy, but we slowly realise the completely different demands it puts on doing theology after 1994, and modernity's eroding effect on the historical mainline churches,[26] of which the DRC is one.

Although South African society is an interesting mix of all the stages of modernity and, despite its constitutional dispensation, it is definitely not a secularist society.[27] The rules for "being heard on the public square" have nevertheless changed irrevocably. They shifted from an assumed prophetic role for theology and the churches to one where "prophecy" – if not replaced by a more "priestly" mode – is tied up with the art of democratic processes and lobbying at all levels of government, often in the context of inter-religious rather than exclusively Christian negotiations. It includes the difficult requirement that theology and the church meet other societal spheres (business, NGO and CBO structures, forms of civil society) on their own turf whilst in some way retaining a distinctly theological voice. It is then further required that theology and the church communicate its stance on issues of public concern in a manner that reaches the hearts and minds of leaders and ordinary citizens alike. No wonder Keith Clements – writing from a British and Irish ecumenical perspective – argues that the church is in desperate need of "learning to speak" (see Clements 1995).

(see Conradie's work on David Tracy and discussion in Conradie 1993), Dirkie Smit (see recent paper, Smit 2002b), and Piet Naudé (see Bezuidenhout and Naudé 2002). References to major authors and different currents are found in these articles.

26 There are two groups of churches that maintain their growth despite modernist influences: the charismatic house churches and the African Independent Churches. Both show a remarkable ability to shelter their members from the debilitating forces of individualism and secularism. There is no room here to pursue the reasons for this, nor to evaluate the theological tenets underlying these church movements. For a very brief overview of the hermeneutics involved, see Chapters 24 and 25 in Maimela and Konig (1998).

27 See an analysis of the present government's ambiguous policy toward religion in public life by Lombaard (2001) as a reflection of how to deal skilfully(?)with the broad public's religious sensibilities despite a liberal constitution.

(For example: the link between the church and the mass media is more important than ever, but it requires a different skill to utilise the media in a situation where you are by assumption "newsworthy" to one where you have to "make news" in a way that supports and promotes the integrity of your public voice).

How prepared is the DRC to develop such a public theology? The will to make a difference in society has recently been confirmed in the General Synod commitment,[28] and is in line with the traditional Calvinist conviction of Christ's rule over the whole of creation (all spheres of society) that has always been part of the DRC's "make-up".

A public theology, however, implies a form of critical theology in a multiple sense of the word: a critical analysis of society and its modernisation; a critical judgement of core issues affecting society, and a critical mode of discourse enabling debate in the public realm, as well as self-critical forms of communication with a variety of publics. I am not sure whether the DRC can as yet meet these demands. Let me explain this with two remarks on critical scholarship[29] – one theological and the other hermeneutical.

In an interesting paper on the relation between South Africa and Europe, Willie Jonker observes that the DRC never fully understood the combined effect of World War Two and the second Enlightenment represented by the critical theories of Horkheimer, Adorno, Marcuse and Habermas. What happened, says Jonker, is that the DRC relied on an earlier, pre-critical European theology (in the form of romantic and self-satisfied neo-Calvinism) exactly at a time when ideology critique was accepted as an indispensable part of any theoretical construct. This delayed the DRC's full confrontation with new European theological trends and led to its almost total intellectual and ecumenical isolation: "From the view of the outside world as a whole, the theology of the Afrikaans churches is too uncritical, too naive with regard to the ideological presuppositions of our thoughts, too much oriented to a period in the *Geistesgeschichte* that has passed, and shows too little willingness to accept the implications of the Enlightenment" (Jonker 1988a:154).

It lies beyond the scope of this paper to show how many – Jaap du Rand (1985:40), Willie Jonker (1988:30-31), and recently Russel Botman (2001 and 2002:352), Dirkie Smit (2000) and Piet Naudé (2001:94-95) – have indicated that the theological roots of a critical theology could potentially be found in the thought of Karl Barth who was – until the mid-eighties – not appropriated in DRC theology because of perceived problems with his views on revelation, Scripture, baptism and election. One can now add: the invigorating theologies of liberation (black, African, feminist) that started to emerge in the early seventies with their overt ideological-critical[30] approach and

---

28 There is a renewed commitment to Africa and overt expression of the will "to make a difference" as salt of the earth and light of the world (NGK 2003).
29 The section on critical scholarship is derived from a paper on the future of Reformed scholarship delivered to the Ecumenical Institute, Heidelberg on 10 January 2003.
30 This type of thinking emerged in the circles of ABRECSA, whose charter and supplementary declaration (1981) are a brilliant reclamation of the Reformed tradition in answer to the crucial question of how it is possible to be black and Reformed (related to the title of Allan Boesak's well-known book). Although one could question the almost naive re-appropriation of Marxist ideology-critique by most forms of liberation theologians, it does not diminish their role in focusing theological attention on "the underside of history" (Gutierrez). Reformed liberation theologians were consequently

fresh insight in to the message of the Bible, could in principle not be heard in a church and society defending themselves exactly against such revolutionary forces that "mix religion and politics" in an "unacceptable" way.[31]

The hermeneutical remark stems from Bernard Lategan. He argues that Reformed hermeneutics in general suffered from a structural deficit in its inability to deal with the question of history as posed by the Enlightenment. Whereas the Lutheran tradition could accept critical historical ideas, utilising the *was Christum treibet* principle and practising internal *Sachkritik*, Reformed scholars developed a dogmatic resistance against *Geschichtlichkeit* in their understanding of Scriptural authority on the assumption of truth as historical truth (i.e. correspondence between historical events recorded in Scripture and their actual occurrence). "This necessitated the defence of biblical history as historically correct" and as precondition for its truthfulness. Except for textual criticism, "there was no natural uptake and exploiting of the historical family of hermeneutical methods – historical criticism, tradition criticism, redaction criticism, composition criticism and the like".[32]

I indicated earlier that biblical scholarship in South Africa – probably our most enlightened group of scholars with high international standing – limited the impact of their critical scholarship in a number of ways (Naudé 2001b). This was summarised by Elizabeth Schűssler-Fiorenza (1988:4) with regard to biblical scholarship in general: an assumed value-neutrality oblivious to the political context of interpretation; an inability to translate meaning beyond the historical investigation of the text; little or no consideration for ecclesial or confessional traditions; and the creation of a closed world of expertly scholarly inquiry which denies the interests and values underlying their communicative practice. I do not want to repeat the concrete examples here (Naudé 2001b:97), but the broader critical effect of our biblical scholars was neutralised in advance by their "scientist ethos" (Botha 1992:197) and the fact that, despite their good intentions (see the foreword to the very first edition of *Skrif en Kerk*), biblical scholars usually found themselves extremely uneasy to engage in the *wirkunsgeschichtliche* realities of the church and its confessions, avoiding the difficult question of what *sola Scriptura* could mean after the Enlightenment.

---

able to develop a credible alternative hermeneutical key to "justification by faith alone" in their insistence on the epistemological privilege of the marginalised and the poor. One of the Belhar confession's important achievements is that it was able to draw these two lines together in one confession – look at the inner consistency and "logic of grace" in the movement from the first to the highly contested fourth article. Up till now our mainline scholarship has not been able to take the second line seriously. For text and discussion, see Cloete and Smit (1984).

31 This is clearly illustrated in my analysis of why the DRC struggled to accept the confession of Belhar as confession: once it was popularly labelled as "liberation theology", its fate was sealed, despite even official denials from the DRC leadership. See Naudé (1997).
32 See Lategan 2001. He then – following Nash – reconstructs the well-known Du Plessis case in terms of its implications for critical theological scholarship which they believe shifted from the Stellenbosch Seminary to Philosophy (Kirsten, Rossouw) and Semitic Languages (Fensham, Deist).

Their only option was to combine a highly critical biblical scholarship with a fairly naive dogmatics, leaving the poor dogmaticians (in the view of biblical scholars) with both a naive theology and even more naive reading strategy.[33]

The chickens have now come home to roost in two forms: Ben du Toit's book on faith in a post-modern age entitled *God? Geloof in 'n postmoderne tyd* (2000), and the surge of a so-called "new reformation" driven by critical biblical and classical scholars in alliance with the Jesus seminar (see Muller 2002). Critical scholarship has hit the streets and the pages of *Beeld*, well-known and influential Afrikaans daily newspaper.

Du Toit's book is the first attempt in Afrikaans Reformed circles to take critical scholarship to the heart of our confessional tradition.[34] His own roots lie in the critical realist school set up in South Africa by Wentzel van Huyssteen (1986) and appropriated hermeneutically by Ferdinand Deist (1994). In Ben du Toit's own thought, the lines of a methodologically post-Barthian systematic theology and a critical hermeneutic[35] come together in a very interesting genre that is more confession than formal dogmatics. This convergence has not happened before in our theology. This explains the ambiguous reaction of both rejection as obviously unorthodox and acceptance as a liberative, post-modern account of faith. We need a lot more thinking in this regard.

A few remarks about the "new reformation": I am sure any reasonably informed theologian understands that the questions announced by our colleagues are indeed 19th-century type questions about which we were informed all along (although the details obviously differ). But because of the failed ecclesial and confessional integration of biblical scholarship, referred to by Schüssler-Fiorenza, it now appears to ordinary believers as a "surprise" or a new freedom from an authoritative church, "who kept these things secret". The reality is that DRC synodical reports on both Scripture and ethical issues since the debate about the ordination of women in the 1970s and around apartheid in the mid-1980s appear to deal with the issue of history in a very responsible and open manner and clearly broke with a fundamentalist reading to include a more historical-critical approach. We have perhaps failed our *dominees* and congregants by not supporting them in making this paradigm shift

---

33 See the very interesting remark by Bertie du Plessis, former NT scholar at Unisa, in his newspaper review of the *Festschrift* for Willie Jonker: "For the subject specialist the thoughts of Heyns (and Jonker) appear to be naive, because they do not reflect in any way the problems arising from the exegetical discipline". This is *inter alia* linked to a "*probleemlose beroep op die Skrif*" (my translation?, emphasis original). I know that some biblical scholars also said that about Adrio Konig's systematic work ("more sermons than exegesis").

34 When I saw the unpublished manuscript, I sensed this *novum*, and immediately agreed to write the recommendation on the back cover despite the ambiguities in the argument. We realised that it would be difficult to find a publisher. It is a bit ironic that the *Christelike Lektuurfonds* (CLF) – known for its printing and distribution of more pietist literature – had the courage to take the project on.

35 See his book written with Van Huyssteen on the authority of Scripture in reaction to the Synod of Delft (Netherlands) report *God met ons* in 1979: J.W.V. van Huyssteen and B.J. du Toit, *Geloof en skrifgesag* (1982). The basic shift was away from a correspondence theory of truth to a relational, constructivist view of truth with obviously radical implications for an interpretation of Scripture and its authority.

where "truth" and "history" are linked in a more complex, but much more satisfying and intellectually honest, manner.

The dualism between exegesis (critical biblical scholarship) and dogmatics (confessional tradition) is now as glaring as ever. The "new Reformation"[36] will help us to face the difficult reflective task of greater theological and ecclesial coherence – even if we have to admit to more pluralities of thought than we would feel comfortable with.

It is too early to make a judgment on whether the DRC's commitment to a public theology and public church will be more than project-driven, ad hoc engagements, or whether it will mark the very existence of the church as *communio sanctorum*. Will the DRC be able to overcome the false tension between the "evangelical" and "social" mission of the church? And will she be able to live our "logic" of the Christian religion, namely to give herself to God as holy and acceptable sacrifice (Rom 12:1-2)? There are indeed positive signs of remarkable involvement of ordinary Christians in the public sphere – represented by their daily task as a life *coram Dei*. On an institutional level, holiness is realised and "made public" in a threefold manner.

First, the act of God in Christ, who accord believers the status of holy priesthood despite and against their own inability to be holy (1 Cor 1:30, 1 Pet 2:9, see Barmen article II). This is the undeniable theological basis of a public church, as much as faith is the basis for works. Second, the act of simply being church and exemplifying holiness in God – like internal relations[37] – specifically the obligation and joy to serve one another with the gifts of the Spirit (Heidelberg Catechism: Question and Answer 55). Third, a public life in and before the world, according to the law as fulfilled in the gospel, that serves as witness to the character of the Holy God (Lev 11:44; 1 Pet 1:15), who calls the church to be salt and light so that by her good works the Father who is in heaven be honoured and glorified (Math 5:13-16).

Let us remind ourselves that the aim of a critical public theology and concomitant public church is not the self-promotion of the church in a public relations exercise, but exactly a pointing away[38] from the church to the Holy One to whom we are called to witness.

---

36 The book *Die nuwe Hervorming* is at times a moving account of (post-)modern believers and scholars attempting to "make sense" of their faith, and at times a gross oversimplification of "orthodox" faith. One has to see the pastoral as well as academic intent of this movement to understand its widespread support (and opposition to it). From the website I was struck by the fact that some of the leading academics in the new Reformation try to draw up a kind of "statement of faith" to clarify their position. This is exactly the point: they realise you cannot deconstruct at will, without reconstructing you presuppositions. And these statements confirm my insistence that Bultmann's notion of *Vorverständnis* always includes systematic theological convictions as well, and they lead [right? – not quite sure what "lead" – the convictions?] these thinkers into views directly contradicting long-held Christian convictions such as the Trinity and physical resurrection of Christ.

37 This is why sexism, racism and classism are such devastating counter-forces when they play such a determinant role in the churches' internal structures and reciprocal relations. They deny the gift of holiness and destroy the basis for publicness.

38 As members of the Year of Hope commission (2001), we had several discussions with civic leaders on the role of the DRC in the future of our country. Aggrey Klaaste – then still editor of the *Sowetan* – answered in one sentence: "Build a home for AIDS orphans

Let us now turn to the last task in the building of a coherent theological discourse.

4. AN HONEST ENGAGEMENT WITH OUR CONTINENT TOWARD AN AFRICAN THEOLOGY: THE CHURCH AS CHRISTIAN COMMUNITY.

One of the distinctive features of the Reformed tradition is its openness to new contexts. I earlier (see Naudé 2001) explained this from three perspectives. From a theological perspective, the Reformers of the 16th century rediscovered and vigorously defended the Bible as normative canon for the church over and against the papal magisterium and "the tyranny of human traditions which is haughtily obtruded upon us in the name of the Church".[39] In this way Calvin and other Reformers not only set the Scriptures free from what they perceived threatened its sovereignty, but they simultaneously also set it free for varied interpretations in varied contexts. "Charakterisch für die reformierte Theologie is die Grunderkenntnis, *dass die reformatorische und reformierende Aktivität in der Kirche und in ihren Umgebungen von Gottes Wort ausgheht*" (Welker and Willis 1998:10; original emphasis). That is why historical, social and cultural factors which question the power of God's Word in fact also bring the identity of Reformed theology into question (Welker and Willis 1998: 174-175). Moltmann's summary statement "Reformierte Theologie ist als reformierende Theologie – biblische Theologie ..." (1998:172) clarifies the fundamental hermeneutical nature of reformed theologians' endeavours.

From a historical perspective, it is interesting to note that as churches of the Reformation spread across Europe and later all over the world, a rich variety of churches identifying themselves as "Reformed" (not necessarily by name) were established with a concomitant rich variety of theologies.[40] From a confessional perspective, the Catholic faith community lives within the normative tradition of the Councils[41] as well as the definitive context of encyclicals as official papal teaching. The Lutheran faith community has in the *Confessio Augustana* (1530) a definitive shared confession[42] as well as a relative closure of interpretative activity in the *Konkordienbuch* (1580). This stands in contrast to the "open" Reformed confessional developments in response to various challenges in various contexts over the past

---

and do not say the DRC gave the money". This sounds very much like the Sermon on the Mount about left and right hands!

39 Calvin, *Institutes*: Book IV, 10.18. See Calvin's extensive exegesis specifically of the Old Testament – in his arguments against the Pope and Catholic Church in Book IV of his *Institutes*. The basic point remains: "Let us understand that the name of the Church is falsely pretended wherever men contend for that rash human licence *which cannot confine itself within the boundaries prescribed by the word of God*, but perpetually breaks out, and has recourse to its own invention" (IV, 10.17, my emphasis).

40 The South African journal *Acta Theologica* devoted its first number of 1992 to a special edition in which "leading Reformed theologians from various parts of the world" gave an account of theologies in their region. Unfortunately the contributors were restricted to first world countries (USA, Canada, The Netherlands, Scotland and Australia) and South Africa, excluding many exciting developments in Latin America, Korea and the then Eastern Europe, as well as "alternative" voices within these regions.

41 Obviously the Reformed tradition also sees itself as in congruence with the Ecumenical Councils between Nicea I (325) and Chalcedon (451).

42 This, according to Moltmann, is the reason why Barmen was never accepted as confession by the Lutheran churches in Germany (1998:159).

five centuries.⁴³ The very concept of Christian "confessions" and the church as "confessing church" is seen by some as a typical contribution of Reformed theologies to the broader Christian faith: "Das aktuelle Bekennen des Glaubens ist geradezu die Eigenart der reformierten Kirchen von ihren Anfänge an bis heute" (Moltmann 1998:159, my emphasis).

Cumulatively seen, these perspectives explain the fundamentally contextual sensitivity (and therewith vulnerability) of Reformed theology and churches. Looking back on 350 years in Africa, a vital question is whether the DRC became an African church with a concomitant African contextual theological orientation. This is quite a complex question since sub-Saharan "Africa" is in itself a differentiated concept, and there are obviously many forms of "contextual theologies" in Africa between the extremes of theologies of inculturation (e.g. Mbiti, Pobee, Setiloane) and liberation (e.g. Buthelezi, Mosala) with many differences in between. These depend on the "arrangement" and "interpretation" of the four main sources of African theologies, namely African indigenous religion, the Bible, the African life experience and relation to Western theology.⁴⁴

The answer to the question of an African church and theology with regard to the DRC is not a simple no, because the DRC mission churches indeed succeeded to gain their independence and enculturalised successfully in countries such as Malawi, Mozambique, Zimbabwe, Zambia and elsewhere. And the Afrikaner or Afrikaans-speaking community that forms the core of the DRC up to this day did form its own identity, culture and language that differ from their Dutch, French and German origins. Although rooted in Europe, one could say that the theology supporting apartheid prevalent in the DRC for much of the twentieth century was a uniquely African adaptation to the difficult questions of identity and differentiation, colonialism and the struggle for freedom, the question of minority rights, and the ambiguous social power of religion that can at once liberate and enslave. By its inward orientation and self-preserving identity formation, the DRC did indeed develop a contextual African theology, but in doing so the "other faces" of Africa – those outside the circle of exactly this theological ideology – were excluded.

At the previous conference on the DRC in transition I discussed this issue under the rubric of the general orientation of DRC theology as being fundamentally European and North American. I repeat a few points made then (see Naudé 2001b:100-102), starting with a comment of Willie Jonker in reaction to my criticism (see Naudé

---

43 This ranges from the need to teach (Heidelberg Catechism 1563), doctrinal struggles in the narrower sense of the word (Dordt 1518) to contemporary issues of church-state relations under National Socialism (Barmen 1934), weapons of mass destruction (Declaration of the Reformierte Bund in Germany, 1981), general renewal of the Christian faith (The Confession of 1967, Presbyterian Church, USA) and the witness for justice, unity and reconciliation (Belhar 1986). Sources which attempt to list all confessions are quickly outdated by the ongoing process. Authoritative attempts, though, were E.F.K. Müller: *Die Bekenntnisschriften der reformierten Kirche* (1903) and the more recent Lukas Vischer: *Collection of confessions and statements of faith issued by reformed churches* (1982).

44 See the emerging work on African theologies by Tinyiko Sam Maluleke, recently appointed professor of African theology at Unisa.

1991:117) that he missed opportunities to translate his theological insights on election and covenant for an African continent:

> We all have our limitations and no theologian can jump across his own shadow. My own theological position was to a great extent determined by my formation and situation. ... This means that I was from the outset oriented towards European theology. To tell the truth, many of us did not even notice until recently that it was European theology. For us it was simply 'theology'... The realisation that the theology from Europe has a contextual character itself only recently dawned upon us. The task to think through the full implications of this for our theological reflection in South Africa I gladly leave to the younger generation (Jonker 1991:120, my translation).

That Jonker clearly understood the issue is evident from his earlier speech before the *Akademie*: "The challenge before which we stand is to work with others toward an understanding and interpretation of the Bible in our situation as people who are steeped in the European tradition but who, in the meantime, became people of Africa. Here we live and work, we think and pray ... We are called to do theology on the faultline (*breuklyn*) between the First and the Third World" (Jonker 1988a:156, my translation).

I am not suggesting that mainstream DRC theology did not address the issues of contextuality and Africa. I am also not adhering to a static, romantic or exclusively "black" view of what "Africa" means. The problem is that the issue of contextuality – specifically in New Testament science[45] – became more of a methodological issue than one of material significance in constructing theology. And the many articles about Africa and its realities emerged mainly from missiological reflections[46] without an "orientation" effect on DRC theology as such.

Why is this so important? Because your intellectual orientation determines your reflective agenda. Therefore the DRC – to this day – has been unable to really confront the material effect for theology of the African context beyond the social world of white South Africa.

This had at least two effects on DRC theology.

First: The very question of cultural thought forms and expressions in a discipline so deeply Western was not adequately addressed[47] from the rich variety of alternative perspectives. We only belatedly saw the "locality" of Western thought and did not know how to deal with it. Neither do we know better today.

---

45 One may refer to exceptions such as the work of H.J.B. Combrink (see his very informative *Die Bybel lewe in Afrika* written after a visit to Kenya in April 1991. See also the very substantial contributions on contextual hermeneutics by B.C. Lategan, e.g. his "The challenge of contextuality" (1991) and "Aspects of a contextual hermeneutics for South Africa" (1994).
46 The work by David Bosch, Dionne Crafford and Piet Meiring over many years – too many to list here – is a pillar of hope in this regard. For a specific example, see Crafford (1994).
47 My work on orality and the very notion of theology/literacy as well as a Zionist Christology may be noted as an attempt to take our African context seriously, albeit it represents very preliminary ideas. See Naudé (1993, 1996).

Second: The link between theology and sub-modernity[48] was never really forged. One can only speculate about the effect on DRC theological faculties if women and others from the non-powerful spheres could have influenced academic work. Let us remind ourselves what Thomas Kuhn (1962!) taught us about scientific paradigms: they are community constructs that embody the commitment of a community of scientists "to see the world in a certain way" and from which the relevant questions are then generated as scientific puzzles. The best way to "interrupt" a "view of the world" and the "relevant questions posed" is to alter the composition of your community of inquirers. The new members bring with them a different social construction of reality that will most probably alter the very questions asked and the very problems addressed.[49]

If the relation between Stellenbosch and Crossroads, Pretoria and Mamelodi, Bloemontein and Botshebelo had been ecclesially and socially established earlier, the theological orientation would no doubt have been different. And swept forward by the hermeneutical spiral between theory and practice, the DRC could have become herself a greater transformative force in South Africa and not a church which in most cases mirrored the (changing) realities of her own situation (see Nicol 2001).

What is the potential for change in this regard? The joint theological education at Stellenbosch, the recent ecumenical efforts at all three faculties of theology traditionally related to the DRC, and reunification of the DRC family all provide huge opportunities for a renewed contextualisation of our theology. The Belhar confession is of enormous significance as the first Reformed confession speaking about the issues of unity, reconciliation and justice in our context, but at the same time making a unique contribution to the universal church's understanding of the gospel today (see Naudé 2003b). The growing sense of white congregants that this continent is our home, and the DRC's recent explicit commitment to Africa at its General Synod (see earlier quotation), bodes very well for our future.

From this extended community an extended agenda[50] will arise. This is already evident in the emerging theological perspectives on HIV/AIDS, the creative on-going reflection on truth, reconciliation and restorative justice; an analysis of a public ethos and moral regeneration; land redistribution and ecology; the debt trap of African countries in a global market economy in relation to a *processus confessionis*; and the crucial issue of identity and community that requires a restated theological anthropology. There is no doubt (and I repeat): our theological task has only just begun.

---

48 I am quite aware that "sub-modernity" represents another variety of modernity as a fundamental Western phenomenon not applicable to all spheres of South African society. I owe the notion to colleague Bert Olivier from Philosophy at UPE, who pointed out that exactly this situation represents South Africa as a post-modern reality! But "sub-modernity" does help to express the "social location" of reality "below" the powers of modernity.

49 This will not happen automatically: A specific ideology-critical intellectual disposition is required.

50 This agenda lists for me the most urgent material theological challenges before the DRC – and before the church in South Africa in general. If I have to rewrite a paper with a less methodological focus, these are the issues I would address. The "list" is obviously provisional and open to correction and extension. I am keenly aware of my own social location in "constructing" such challenges.

The ecclesial translation of contextuality is depicted in the church as Christian church. The incarnation of Christ is the most radical expression of God's contextuality and deep love for the world. Recent developments in Trinitarian theology[51] attempt to infer from the cycle of perfect self-donation of the immanent Trinity a sense of the church's being in the world. Miroslav Volf rightly points out that the self-donation of God in Christ and the Spirit (economic Trinity) is met with the resistance of non-love, deceit and injustice that led to the cross. For a Christ-like (i.e. Christian) church *imitatio crucis* implies that "we are called to imitate the earthly love of that same Trinity that led to the passion of the Cross, because it was from the start a passion for those caught in the snares of non-love" (Volf 1998: 415).

In a paraphrase of one of the earliest Christian hymns (see Phil 2:5-11) one could state: The same attitude must be in you that is in Christ. Do not cling to your social status and position of a powerful church, but rather humble yourselves to be equal with those who suffer in Africa. Humble yourselves by taking the nature of a servant – even if it means your death, yes your death, in imitating the cross. Through your attitude and service God will honour and lift the name of Christ on high, so that every knee shall bow and every tongue confess that Jesus is indeed the Lord, to the glory of God the Father.

5. CONCLUSION

This paper merely tries to set the framework for constructing a coherent theological discourse in the DRC and her broader family, and does not make a substantial contribution to the actual development of such a discourse. To what extent this framework might be useful for a broader post-apartheid theology, and for being the Christian church in (South) Africa in a new millennium, needs to be answered in the course of a wider debate. If our colleagues and friends from Hamburg could assist in this regard (as they have done to unravel our past and future), it will be highly appreciated.

If we needed good theology to lead us from apartheid to democracy, our current challenges – including the very sustenance of democracy – clearly require an equally vibrant church, and equally vigilant theologies that are mapped along Reformed, ecumenical, public-critical and African lines.

God bless Africa.

BIBLIOGRAPHY

Bezuidenhout, R. and Naudé, P. 2002. "Some thoughts on 'public theology' and its relevance for the South African context". *Scriptura* Vol. 79, pp. 3-13.

Bosch, D. 1983. "Nothing but a heresy". In J. de Gruchy and C. Villa-Vicencio (eds.), pp. 25-38.

---

51 The list is too long to include here, but recent work by Stackhouse, Hodgson, Zikmund, Lochman, Moltmann, Pannikar, Zizioula, Boff, Gunton and Volf springs to mind. The list already suggests the immensely fruitful exploration of Trinitarian thought for our understanding of personhood, identity and social relations.

Botha, J. 1992. "The ethics of New Testament interpretation". *Neotestamentica* Vol. 26, pp. 169-194.

Botha, J and Naudé, P. 1998. *Op weg met Belhar*. Pretoria: Van Schaik.

Botman, R. 2001. "Belhar and the white DRC: Changes in the DRC 1974-1990". *Scriptura* Vol. 76, pp. 33-42.

Botman, R. 2002. "Is blood thicker than justice?" In L.E. Lego (ed.), pp. 342-361.

Brown, D. 1994. *Boundaries of our habitations. Tradition and theological construction*. New York: State University of New York Press.

Burger, C. 2002. *Ons weet aan wie ons behoort. Nuut gedink oor ons Gereformeerde tradisie*. Wellington: Lux Verbi.BM.

Calvin, J. 1975. *Institutes of the Christian religion* (Vol. 2). Grand Rapids: Eerdmans.

Cilliers, J.H. 1994. "Die teologiese onderbou van die prediking". *Praktiese teologie in Suid-Afrika*, pp. 1-13.

Clements, K. 1995. *Learning to speak. The church's voice in public affairs*. Edinburgh: T & T Clark.

Clifford, J. 1988. *The predicament of culture: Twentieth-century ethnography, literature and art*. Cambridge: Harvard University Press.

Cloete, G.D. and Smit, D.J. 1984. *A moment of truth*. Grand Rapids: Eerdmans.

Combrink, H.J.B. 1991. "Die Bybel lewe in Afrika". *Acta Theologica* Vol. 11, pp. 81-90.

Conradie, E. 1993. "How should a public way of doing theology be approached?" *Scriptura* Vol. 46, pp. 24-49.

Crafford, D. 1994. "The church in Africa and the struggle for an African identity". *Skrif en Kerk* Vol. 14, No. 2, pp. 163-175.

Deist, F. 1994. *Ervaring, rede en metode in Skrifuitleg*. Pretoria: RGN.

De Villiers, E. 1986. "Kritiek uit die ekumene". In Kinghorn (ed.), pp. 144-164.

Du Toit, B. 2000. *God? Geloof in 'n postmoderne tyd*. Bloemfontein: CLF.

Durand, J. 1985. "Afrikaner piety and dissent". In C. Villa-Vicencio and J. de Gruchy (eds.), pp. 38-47.

Durand, J. 2002. *Ontluisterde wereld. Die Afrikaner en sy kerk in 'n veranderde Suid-Afrika*. Wellington: Lux Verbi.BM

Geertz, C. 1973. *The interpretation of cultures*. New York: Basic Books.

Hendriks, J.H. (red.) 1992. *Gemeentes vertel. Verandering in 'n christelike geloofsgemeenskap*. Kaapstad: Lux Verbi.

Hesselgrave D.J. and Rommen E. 1989. *Contextualisation: Meanings, methods and models*. Leicester: Apollos.

Hoekendijk, J.A. 1948. *Kerk en volk in de Duitse zendingswetenschap*. Amsterdam: Rodopi.

Jonker, W.D. 1988a. "Suid-Afrika se verbondenheid met Europa: die teologie". *Tydskrif vir Geesteswetenskappe* Vol. 28, pp. 146-157.

Jonker, W.D. 1988b. "Some remarks on the interpretation of Karl Barth". *NGTT* Vol. 29, pp. 29-40.

Jonker, W.D. 1989. "Die pluriformiteitsleer van Abraham Kuyper. Teologiese onderbou vir die konsep van aparte kerke vir aparte volksgroepe?" *In die Skriflig* Vol. 23, No. 3, pp. 12-23.

Kinghorn, J. (ed.) 1986. *Die NG Kerk en apartheid*. Johannesburg: Macmillan.

Kort, W. 1992. *Bound to Differ: The Dynamics of Theological Discourses*. Pennsylvania: Pennsylvania State University Press.

Kuyper, A. 1943. *Calvinism. Six Stone Foundation Lectures*. Grand Rapids: Eerdmans.

Lategan, B.C. 1991. "The challenge of contextuality". *Scriptura* S9, pp. 1-6.

Lategan, B.C. 1994. "Aspects of a contextual hermeneutics for South Africa". In J. Mouton and B. Lategan (eds.), pp. 17-30.

Lategan, B.C. 2000. History, historiography and Reformed theology at Stellenbosch. Unpublished paper at CTI Princeton conference on Reformed identity and ecumenicity held at the University of Stellenbosch, April.

Lego, L.E. (ed.) 2000. *Religion, pluralism and public life. Abraham Kuyper's legacy for the twenty first century*. Grand Rapids: Eerdmans.

Lombaard, C. 2001. "The left governing hand and the right governing hand". *JTSA* Vol. 109, pp. 17-24.

Maimela, S. and Konig, A. (eds). 1998. *Initiation into theology*. Pretoria: Van Schaik.

Moltmann, J 1998. "Theologia reformata et semper reformanda". In M. Welker and D. Willis (eds.), pp. 157-172.

Mouton, J. and Lategan, B. (eds.) 1994. *The relevance of theology for the nineties*. Pretoria: HSRC.

Muller, P. (red.) 2002. *Die nuwe Hervorming*. Pretoria: Protea Boekehuis.

Naudé, P. 1991. "Uit vrye guns alleen. Grondlyne vir 'n pastorale dogmatiek". *NGTT* Vol. 32, No. 1, pp. 110-118.

Naudé, P. 1993. "Toward a local Zionist theology? The role of the outsider theologian". *Scriptura* Vol. 45, pp. 29-46.

Naudé, P. 1996. "Theology with a new voice? The case for an oral theology in the context of South Africa". *JTSA* Vol. 94, pp. 18-31.

Naudé, P. 1997. "Die Belharstryd in ekumeniese perspektief". *NGTT* Vol. 38, No. 3. pp. 226-243.

Naudé, P. 2001a. "Reformed confessions as hermeneutical problem. A case study of the Belhar confession". Unpublished paper presented at the CTI Princeton conference on Reformed identity and ecumenicity at the University of Stellenbosch, April.

Naudé, P. 2001b. "The DRC's role in the context of transition in South Africa: Main streams of academic research". *Scriptura* Vol. 76, pp. 87-106.

Naudé P. 2002a. "From pluralism to ideology. The roots of apartheid theogloy in Abraham Kuyper, Gustav Warneck and Pietism". Unpublished paper, University of Heidelberg, 15 November 2002.

Naudé, P. 2002b. "The theological coherence between the Belhar confession and some antecendent church witnesses in the period 1948-1982". Unpublished paper, University of Heidelberg, Germany, 29 November 2002.

Naudé, P. 2003a. "Is there a future for scholarship? Reformed scholarship in a transforming higher education environment". Unpublished paper, University of Heidelberg, Germany, 10 January 2003.

Naudé, P. 2003b. "'It is a gift from heaven'. The ecumenical reception and significance of the Belhar confession". *NGTT* Vol. 44, No. 3 & 4, pp. 407-420.

Nederduits Gereformeerde Kerk. 1986. *Kerk en samelewing. 'n Getuienis van die Ned Geref Kerk.* Bloemfontein: Pro Christo.

Nederduitse Gereformeerde Kerk. 2003. Verklaring van die Algemene Sinode. *Die Kerkbode*, 1 November: 13

Nicol, W. 2001. "Accompanying the flock – the development of the DRC 1974-1990". *Scriptura* Vol. 76, pp. 133-138.

Paris, P. 2000. "The African and African-American understanding of our common humanity: A critique of Abraham Kuyper's anthropology". In L.E. Lego (ed.), pp. 263-280.

Ritschl, D. 1984. *Zur Logik der Theologie*. München: Kaiser.

Schussler-Fiorenza, E. 1988. "The ethics of interpretation: De-centering biblical scholarship". *JBL* Vol. 107, pp. 3-17.

Smit, D.J. 1989. "Om saam met al die heiliges Chrsitus te ken …". In P.F. Theron en J. Kinghorn (reds), pp. 11-32.

Smit, D.J. 2000. "Social transformation and confessing faith? Karl Barth's view on confession revisited". *Scriptura* Vol. 1, pp. 67-85.

Smit, D.J. 2001. *Wat Here is en lewend maak*. Kaapstad: Lux Verbi.

Smit, D.J. 2002a. *Lig uit lig*. Wellington: Lux Verbi.BM.

Smit, D.J. 2002b. "Openbare getuienis en publieke teologie vandag? Vrae oor verskeie vanselfsprekende vooronderstellings". Unpublished lecture at the opening of the Stellenbosch Theological Faculty, February.

Smit, D.J. 2003. *Vernuwe – na die beeld van ons Skepper*. Wellington: Lux Verbi.BM.

Strauss, P.J. 1995. "Abraham Kuyper, apartheid and the Reformed churches in South Africa in their support for apartheid". *Theological Forum* Vol. XIII, No. 1, pp. 4-27.

Theron, P.F. and J. Kinghorn, J. (reds) 1989. *Koninkryk, kerk en kosmos. Huldigingsbundel ter ere van Prof WD Jonker*. Bloemfontein: Pro Christo Publikasies.

Van Huyssteen, J.W.V. 1986. *Teologie as kritiese geloofsverantwoording*. Pretoria: RGN.

Van Huyssteen, J.W.V. and Du Toit, B.J. 1982. *Geloof en Skrifgesag*. Pretoria: NGBK.

Van Wijk, A.J. (red.) 1964. *Die ekumene. 'n Besinning oor interkerlike verhoudinge*. Stellenbosch: Kosmo Uitgewery.

Velema, W.H. 1989. "Kuyper als theoloog. Een persoonlike evaluatie na dertig jaar". *In die Skriflig* Vol. 23, No. 91, pp. 56-73.

Müller, E.F.K. (ed.) 1903. *Die Bekenntnisschriften der reformierten Kirche*. Leipzig: A. Deichert.

Villa-Vicencio, C. and de Gruchy, J. (eds.) 1983. *Apartheid is a heresy*. Cape Town: David Philip.

Villa-Vicencio, C. and J. de Gruchy, J. (eds.) 1985. *Resistance and hope*. Cape Town: David Philip.

Vischer, L. 1982. *Collection of confessions and statements of faith issued by reformed churches.* Bern: Evangelische Arbeitsstelle Oekumene Schweiz.

Vischer, L. 1984. "The process of "reception" in the ecumenical movement". *Mid-Stream* Vol. 23, pp. 221-233.

Volf, M. 1998. "'The Trinity is our social program': The doctrine of the Trinity and the shape of social engagement". *Modern Theology* Vol. 14, No. 3, pp. 403-423.

Miroslav Volf, M. 1997. *After our likeness. The church as the image of the Trinity.* Grand Rapids: Eerdmans.

Warneck, D.G. 1897. *Evangelische Missionslehre. Ein missionstheorethischer Versuch III.* Gotha: Berthes.

Welker, M. 2000. *What happens in Holy Communion?* Grand Rapids: Eerdmans.

Welker, M. and Willis, D. (eds.) 1998. *Zur Zukunft der Reformierten Theologie. Aufgaben – Themen – Traditionen.* Vluyn: Neukirchener.

Wethmar. C.J. 1991. "Die ekumeniese roeping van die kerk in die lig van die gereformerde belydenisskrfite". *NGTT* Vol. XXXII, No. 3, pp. 447-454.

INDEX

A

Academic disciplines 324
African Independent Churches 30, 58, 145, 354
African theology 45, 48-49, 52, 109, 135, 137, 145, 169, 238, 239, 345, 359, 360
AIDS 62, 113, 124, 233, 291, 330, 358
Apartheid 1, 67, 69-73, 86, 91, 93, 105, 123-124, 135, 141, 180, 225, 230-233, 248-249, 251, 253, 254, 257-258, 274, 284, 285, 287, 295, 296, 298, 301-303, 305, 317, 319, 323, 324, 326, 329-332, 336-337, 346, 348, 352-354, 357, 360, 363
Apostles' Creed 9
Assmann, Jan 26, 28-30, 33

B

Baptism, Eucharist and Ministry 13-14, 57, 60, 85
Barmen declaration 111-112, 301
Barth, Karl 81, 87, 97, 104, 114, 122, 136, 187, 188, 192, 195, 227, 256, 267, 270, 272-277, 279, 298, 300, 315, 330-331, 349, 355
Belgic confession 351
Belhar confession x, 24, 60, 74, 103, 136, 185, 228, 247, 255-257, 274, 277, 285, 301-303, 311-313, 320, 323, 331, 334, 349-351, 353, 356, 362
Black theology 48, 200, 270-271
Body of Christ 106, 262, 266, 326, 346
Boesak, Allan 136, 228, 247, 254, 270, 296, 304, 313, 325, 355
Boff, Leonardo 133, 190, 202, 216
Bonhoeffer, Dietrich 121, 136, 192, 256, 265, 279, 282, 319
Botman, Russel 103, 227, 254, 345, 355

C

Calvinism 67, 71-72, 76, 227, 232, 249-255, 274, 276, 325, 330-331, 346, 350, 355
Canons of Dordt 248, 334
Capitalism 48, 124, 135, 247, 288-289, 317
Catholicism 269
Charismatic movement 82, 104, 305
Christian ethics 287
Christian humanist 223
Christology 140, 146, 149-150, 162, 192, 195, 267, 270, 280, 282, 330, 361
Church and Society 106, 178-179, 225, 228, 249, 275, 297, 318, 356
Confessing the One Faith 11, 26, 57, 61-63, 83, 86, 87-88, 180
Confession 12-13, 24, 37, 38, 51, 57-60, 74, 81-92, 96-97, 103,-107, 115-117, 120, 136, 154, 169, 179-185, 191, 195, 228-229, 247, 248, 254-256, 257, 262, 265, 272, 274, 277, 285, 289, 300-303, 311-316, 318-320, 323, 331-334, 345, 349-353, 356, 357, 359, 362
Contextual theology 146, 168, 249
Creedal formation 151, 153, 154, 162
Creeds 2, 9, 27, 32-33, 38, 58-62, 103-104, 153, 155-156, 177, 179, 185, 282, 345, 349-351
Croatto, Severino 207, 211-216

D

De Gruchy, John 52, 72, 136-138, 141, 223, 230-231, 247, 251-256, 313, 325, 353
Democracy 1, 58, 105, 223, 232-233, 258, 286-287, 295, 304-305, 324, 329-330, 354, 363
Denominationalism 25, 96, 339, 352
Diacony 335, 336
Dogma/Dogmatic 36-39, 50-54, 69-70, 74-77, 94, 107, 114-120, 147, 151, 157, 188-191, 195, 201, 228, 249, 317, 329-333, 356
Doxology 32, 38, 45, 51, 119, 161
Dutch Reformed Church 2, 24, 67, 70-71, 74, 103, 105, 107, 223, 227, 232, 248, 323, 327, 345
Dutch Reformed Mission Church 86, 88-92, 107, 124, 248, 254, 256, 274, 296, 302, 311, 315, 316, 319, 331

E

Ecclesiology 9, 14, 118, 149-150, 203, 232, 249, 252, 256, 279-280, 284, 287, 296, 312, 325, 328
Ecology 362
Ecumenical Movement 9, 12-14, 23-24, 27, 32-33, 38-40, 50, 58-61, 67-68, 73, 81-85, 91, 94, 96, 112-113, 118, 287, 302, 351-352
Ecumenism 7, 24, 60-62, 81-82, 85, 88, 90-94, 97, 114
Education 82, 225
Enlightenment 13, 45-49, 133, 192, 227-229, 238, 258, 268, 273-276, 280, 298, 326-331, 355-356
Ethics 74, 287

F

Faith and Order 9, 10, 14, 23-28, 31-37, 40, 57, 60-61, 67, 71, 73-74, 82-86, 90-93, 113-114
Feminism 177-179
Feminist theology 135, 178
Fundamentalism 122, 299, 305

G

Gassmann, Günther 67-68, 83, 90, 93

Gender 63, 72, 177, 180, 182, 183, 184, 185, 258, 284, 285, 286, 291
Globalisation 284, 288, 289, 291, 338
Gutierrez, Gustavo 133, 187, 189-194, 200-202, 206, 208, 211-216, 228, 238, 279, 355

H

Heidelberg Catechism 9, 70, 103-104, 248, 353, 358, 360
Heresy 71, 147, 182, 189, 191, 247-248, 254-258, 296, 315
Hermeneutics 7, 23-26, 33, 73, 89-92, 114, 129-130, 134-135, 140, 173, 177, 179, 185, 199-209, 211-216, 228-229, 233, 241-242, 258, 273, 316, 330, 332-333, 338, 354, 356-357, 361
Heyns, Johan 231, 304, 324-325, 329-331
Holy Communion 113, 257, 266
Holy Spirit 38, 58, 77, 89, 91, 97, 118, 121, 138, 152, 153-154, 182, 255, 264, 268-269, 282-283, 326
Hope 30, 35, 45, 55, 60, 114, 120, 280, 281, 353, 358
Huber, Wolfgang 61-62, 73, 95
Human dignity 124, 282, 316
Hymns 31, 33, 137-140, 145-149, 150-152, 154-156, 158, 161-165, 167-168, 363

I

Identity 39, 67, 228, 249, 263, 281-282, 284-285, 318-319, 324-326, 335-336, 346-349
Ideology 53, 89, 184, 193, 202, 227-228, 253, 257, 264-265, 289, 315-317, 329, 346, 355, 360, 362
Inclusivity 181
Injustice 50, 184, 192, 254, 257-258, 265, 271, 276, 291, 313-314, 317, 335, 363
Inspiration 173, 268-269, 275
Inter-confessional 10, 83, 113
Interdisciplinary 67, 352

J

Jesus Christ 31, 51, 57, 62, 76, 82, 103, 107, 112, 118, 120, 124, 147, 154, 173, 181, 194, 203, 208, 254, 258, 261, 264, 266-267, 270-271, 275-276, 282, 291, 300, 348
Jonker, Willie 2, 227, 229, 231, 247, 251, 255, 273-276, 295-298, 303-304, 313, 325, 326, 353, 355, 357, 360
Justice 27, 52, 54, 62, 77, 91-92, 103, 105-106, 132, 137-138, 180, 183-185, 226, 233, 247, 253-258, 262, 264-268, 275-277, 284, 286, 302-306, 313, 316, 318-319, 330-331, 335-336, 360, 362

K

Kinghorn, Johann 93, 136, 232, 325, 329-330, 346
Kuhn, Thomas 53, 81, 237, 240-241, 272, 316, 362
Kuyper, Abraham 232, 247, 249, 269, 346

L

Lategan, Bernard 24, 228-329, 333, 356
Liberation theology 48, 90, 136, 145, 187-196, 200-201, 205, 211-217, 228, 238-239, 242, 276, 313, 356
Literacy 26-29, 130-132, 137, 158, 162, 317, 338, 361
Liturgy 1, 12, 23, 26, 31-36, 40, 51, 57-58, 74, 90, 105, 117, 119, 121, 151, 263, 266, 287, 305
Local theology 134, 140, 145-149, 152, 153-155, 157
Luther 29, 71, 110, 112, 120, 132, 136, 241-242, 262, 281, 283, 297-298
Lutheran 11, 12, 33, 57, 67-68, 87, 92-93, 110-115, 118, 122-123, 162, 228, 248, 263, 296, 319, 356, 359

M

Marxism 48, 178, 189-190, 203, 215, 228, 313, 316, 355
Methodology 155, 178-179, 187, 193-195, 199,-204, 211-212, 214, 270-273
Metz, Johann Baptist 2
Míquez-Bonino, José 187, 190, 206-207, 212, 214
Mission 82, 83, 91, 93, 105, 107, 135, 248, 254-256, 296, 300, 311, 316, 353
Modernity 13, 30, 273-276, 288, 296, 327, 332, 338, 348, 354, 362
Mofokeng, Takatso 267, 270-271, 276
Moltmann, Jürgen 2, 241, 279-280, 282-286, 288
Moral/Morality 14, 46, 47, 62, 67, 95, 124, 135, 188, 191, 225-226, 249, 253, 275, 286-288, 291, 298, 302, 326, 329-330, 362

N

Nanga 140, 149, 152, 156, 157, 161, 163, 164, 168, 169
Narrative theology 36, 72, 109, 122, 140, 178, 270, 287, 289, 337, 352
Natural sciences 53, 241, 271, 276
Natural theology 195, 267, 273, 302, 315, 318, 330-331
Naudé, Beyers 247, 254, 295, 304, 314, 319, 331
Neo-Calvinism 71, 227, 232, 251-252, 274, 276, 325, 330-331, 346, 355

O

Objectivity 37, 51, 81, 178, 217, 272-273, 332, 348
Oppression 48, 93, 136-137, 141, 171, 173, 177, 179, 183-184, 189, 192-193, 200,-203, 205, 216, 270
Oral theology 1, 26, 129-137, 139-141, 145
Oral theory 26, 129, 140

P

Paradigm 30, 48, 54, 61-62, 81, 119, 132-134, 150, 153, 177, 195, 230-233, 237-243, 273, 316, 320, 327, 346, 350, 357
Peace 27, 32, 62, 152, 184, 256, 261, 264, 266, 282, 313-314, 330
Pentecostalism/Pentecostal theology 123, 232, 305-306, 353

Pietism 1, 46, 71, 91, 232, 250, 274, 285, 298, 305, 319, 331, 346, 348

Pneumatology (see also Holy Spirit) 14, 85, 150, 282

Potgieter, FJM 253, 267-269, 275

Poverty 62, 124, 136, 201, 253, 282, 284, 288, 290, 335-336, 339

Power 39, 40, 70-71, 73, 75-76, 85, 93, 106, 111, 162-166, 168, 178, 184-185, 208-209, 231, 233, 250, 257, 264, 274, 279-283, 287, 289-290, 300, 303, 305, 316-317, 320, 324-326, 328, 332, 335-336, 339, 352, 359-360

Praxis 45, 52, 54, 61-63, 133, 139, 154-155, 173, 187, 188-195, 200-216, 242, 270-271

Preaching 51, 75, 105, 114, 120, 161, 166, 211-217, 262, 264, 299-300, 348

Problem-solving 53-54, 191, 224, 230-231, 240-243

Protestantism 33, 46, 68-72, 83, 85-86, 94, 110-113, 123, 179, 231, 248, 275, 297, 350

Public theology 62-64, 295-300, 303-306, 345, 353-355, 358

R

Racism 95, 105, 107, 200, 248, 254, 313, 329, 336, 358

Ras, volk en nasie 92, 295, 314, 325

Reception 1, 7-15, 23-40, 68, 74, 81-82, 84-92, 94, 97, 103, 119, 180, 247, 252-254, 267, 268, 277, 298, 311, 330-331, 333-334

Reconciliation 62- 63, 70, 72-74, 91-95, 103, 105,-106, 177, 180, 183-185, 209, 226, 256-258, 270, 271, 275, 284, 302-304, 312-313, 316, 318, 319, 326, 360, 362

Reformed Church in America 82, 86, 103, 104, 105, 106, 107

Reformed theology 1, 67-71, 75, 91-92, 123, 221, 226, 233, 255, 267, 326, 330, 345-346, 350-353, 359-360

Reformed tradition 2, 33, 71-72, 76, 83, 89, 228, 250, 269, 273, 276, 295-298, 300, 314-319, 331, 355, 359

Religion 35-36, 46-49, 64, 71, 76, 95, 106, 110, 129, 138, 141, 146, 147, 150, 156, 164, 171-172, 184, 189, 223, 225, 228, 230-232, 254, 265, 267, 275, 280, 287, 300, 316-317, 330, 331, 337, 348-349, 354, 356, 358, 360

Religious experience 1, 36, 38, 45, 47-50, 54, 55, 110, 149, 155, 172

Righteousness 76, 118, 123, 124, 184

Rite/Ritual vii, 23, 26, 28, 29, 30, 33, 36, 39, 74, 349

Ritschl, Dietrich 1, 40, 41, 72, 73, 74, 90, 295, 352

Roman Catholic 9, 11, 12, 24, 30, 82, 83, 113, 153, 252, 269, 276, 295, 297, 314, 318

S

Sacrament 31, 90, 93, 114, 118, 261, 287, 350

Schleiermacher, Friedrich 36, 45, 52, 54, 241-242, 272-273, 295-297

Schlink, Edmund 1, 33, 36,-38, 45, 50-52, 90, 93, 109-125, 352

Schreiter, Robert 1, 53, 134, 146, 147, 148, 149, 153, 154, 155, 157, 167, 168

Secularism 13, 95, 327, 354

Sexism 107, 171, 178, 179, 182, 183, 200, 358

Smit, Dirkie x, 7, 14, 15, 31, 33, 34, 40, 67, 69, 70, 71, 76, 82, 88, 90, 91, 92, 93, 94, 95, 123, 136, 180, 228, 247, 248, 254, 256, 268, 274, 275, 276, 279, 287, 288, 296, 298, 304, 311, 313, 315, 319, 324, 327, 329, 330, 332, 333, 338, 350, 352, 353, 354, 355, 356

Sobrino, Jon 133, 187, 203, 204, 215, 238, 270, 279

Status confessionis x, 70, 86, 90, 91, 180, 247, 248, 253, 255, 262, 274, 314, 315, 316, 318, 323, 331, 334

Symbol/Symbolic 61, 147, 149, 150, 151, 156, 157, 168, 169, 265

Systematic theology 2, 37, 49, 51, 54, 112, 145, 147, 161, 162, 190, 191, 195, 229, 233, 237, 238, 239, 241, 357

T

Textuality vii, 23, 24, 26, 29, 130, 133, 140, 191

Theological method 187, 193

Trinity/Triune God 55, 63, 120, 130, 158, 180, 185, 208, 279, 280, 284, 291, 312, 352, 358, 363

Truth and Reconciliation Committee 123, 177, 303

U

Uniting Reformed Church of South Africa 81, 82, 83, 84, 86, 95, 97, 105, 107, 331, 337

V

Van Huyssteen, Wentzel 2, 191, 229, 237-240, 244, 271-273, 276, 330, 357

Villa-Vicencio, Charles 136,-137, 139, 141, 231, 248, 267, 274, 314, 331

Vischer, Lukas 34, 35, 36, 68, 70-71, 84-86, 94, 96, 114, 351, 360

W

Wainwright, Geoffrey 32, 51, 67, 90, 161, 352

Welker, Michael 3, 13, 67, 75, 76, 279, 352, 359

Womanist theology xi, 2, 172, 174, 177, 178, 231

World Alliance of Reformed Churches 67, 71, 91, 124, 180, 247, 248, 254, 296, 319, 324, 351

World Council of Churches 1, 9, 10, 24, 25, 27, 28, 31, 57, 60, 61, 63, 74, 82, 113, 120, 180, 247

Worship vii, 10, 23, 28, 31, 32, 33, 34, 35, 36, 37, 38, 39, 40, 51, 52, 57, 67, 75, 82, 90, 91, 107, 109, 121, 147, 155, 161, 262, 304, 305, 306, 348

Z

Zion Christian Church 1, 134, 145, 151, 154, 156, 158, 162, 168

Zionist theology v, 26, 145, 153

www.ingramcontent.com/pod-product-compliance
Lightning Source LLC
Chambersburg PA
CBHW080633230426

43663CB00016B/2850